OECD
ECONOMIC
OUTLOOK

88

NOVEMBER 2010

The *OECD Economic Outlook* is published on the responsibility of the Secretary-General of the OECD. The assessments given of countries' prospects do not necessarily correspond to those of the national authorities concerned. The OECD is the source of statistical material contained in tables and figures, except where other sources are explicitly cited.

Please cite this publication as:
OECD (2010), *OECD Economic Outlook*, Vol. 2010/2, OECD Publishing.
http://dx.doi.org/10.1787/eco_outlook-v2010-2-en

ISBN 978-92-64-08524-4 (print)
ISBN 978-92-64-09014-9 (PDF)

Series: OECD Economic Outlook
ISSN 0474-5574 (print)
ISSN 1609-7408 (online)

The statistical data for Israel are supplied by and under the responsibility of the relevant Israeli authorities. The use of such data by the OECD is without prejudice to the status of the Golan Heights, East Jerusalem and Israeli settlements in the West Bank under the terms of international law.

Photo credits: Cover © Radius Images/Inmagine.

Corrigenda to OECD publications may be found on line at: *www.oecd.org/publishing/corrigenda*.

TABLE OF CONTENTS

Boxes

Tables

Figures

This book has…

StatLinks

A service that delivers Excel® files from the printed page!

Look for the *StatLinks* at the bottom right-hand corner of the tables or graphs in this book. To download the matching Excel® spreadsheet, just type the link into your Internet browser, starting with the *http://dx.doi.org* prefix.
If you're reading the PDF e-book edition, and your PC is connected to the Internet, simply click on the link. You'll find *StatLinks* appearing in more OECD books.

Conventional signs

$	US dollar	.	Decimal point
¥	Japanese yen	I, II	Calendar half-years
£	Pound sterling	Q1, Q4	Calendar quarters
€	Euro	Billion	Thousand million
mb/d	Million barrels per day	Trillion	Thousand billion
. .	Data not available	s.a.a.r.	Seasonally adjusted at annual rates
0	Nil or negligible	n.s.a.	Not seasonally adjusted
–	Irrelevant		

Summary of projections

	2010	2011	2012	2010 Q3	2010 Q4	2011 Q1	2011 Q2	2011 Q3	2011 Q4	2012 Q1	2012 Q2	2012 Q3	2012 Q4	Q4/Q4 2010	Q4/Q4 2011	Q4/Q4 2012
									Per cent							
Real GDP growth																
United States	2.7	2.2	3.1	2.0	1.9	2.1	2.5	2.8	2.9	3.2	3.3	3.5	3.7	2.3	2.6	3.4
Japan	3.7	1.7	1.3	3.9	1.0	2.7	0.6	0.8	1.2	1.3	1.5	1.7	1.8	3.3	1.3	1.6
Euro area	1.7	1.7	2.0	1.5	1.3	1.3	1.7	1.8	1.9	2.0	2.1	2.2	2.2	2.1	1.7	2.1
Total OECD	2.8	2.3	2.8	2.2	1.7	2.2	2.4	2.5	2.6	2.8	2.9	3.1	3.2	2.7	2.4	3.0
Inflation[1]									year-on-year							
United States	1.7	0.9	0.9	1.4	1.0	0.7	0.9	0.9	0.9	0.9	0.9	0.8	0.8			
Japan	-0.9	-0.8	-0.5	-0.8	-0.6	-1.0	-0.9	-0.7	-0.7	-0.6	-0.5	-0.5	-0.4			
Euro area	1.5	1.3	1.2	1.7	1.5	1.4	1.3	1.3	1.2	1.2	1.2	1.2	1.3			
Total OECD	1.8	1.5	1.4	1.7	1.7	1.4	1.5	1.5	1.4	1.3	1.3	1.4	1.4			
Unemployment rate[2]																
United States	9.7	9.5	8.7	9.6	9.7	9.7	9.6	9.4	9.2	9.0	8.8	8.5	8.3			
Japan	5.1	4.9	4.5	5.1	5.0	4.9	4.9	4.8	4.8	4.6	4.5	4.4	4.3			
Euro area	9.9	9.6	9.2	9.9	9.8	9.8	9.7	9.6	9.5	9.4	9.3	9.2	9.0			
Total OECD	8.3	8.1	7.5	8.3	8.3	8.2	8.1	8.0	7.9	7.7	7.6	7.5	7.3			
World trade growth	12.3	8.3	8.1	9.4	7.3	7.5	7.7	8.0	8.0	8.1	8.2	8.3	8.4	11.9	7.8	8.3
Current account balance[3]																
United States	-3.4	-3.7	-3.7													
Japan	3.4	3.7	3.7													
Euro area	-0.2	0.3	0.9													
Total OECD	-0.7	-0.7	-0.5													
Fiscal balance[3]																
United States	-10.5	-8.8	-6.8													
Japan	-7.7	-7.5	-7.3													
Euro area	-6.3	-4.6	-3.5													
Total OECD	-7.6	-6.1	-4.7													
Short-term interest rate																
United States	0.5	0.7	1.8	0.6	0.3	0.3	0.4	0.9	1.1	1.2	1.5	2.0	2.5			
Japan	0.2	0.2	0.2	0.4	0.3	0.2	0.2	0.2	0.2	0.2	0.2	0.2	0.2			
Euro area	0.8	1.1	1.8	0.9	1.0	1.0	1.1	1.1	1.2	1.4	1.7	1.9	2.1			

Note: Real GDP growth, inflation (measured by the increase in the consumer price index or private consumption deflator for total OECD) and world trade growth (the arithmetic average of world merchandise import and export volumes) are seasonally and working-day (except inflation) adjusted annual rates. The "fourth quarter" columns are expressed in year-on-year growth rates where appropriate and in levels otherwise. Interest rates are for the United States: 3-month eurodollar deposit; Japan: 3-month certificate of deposits; euro area: 3-month interbank rate.

The cut-off date for information used in the compilation of the projections is 12 November 2010.

1. USA; price index for personal consumption expenditure, Japan; consumer price index and the euro area; harmonised index of consumer prices.
2. Per cent of the labour force.
3. Per cent of GDP.

Source: OECD Economic Outlook 88 database.

StatLink http://dx.doi.org/10.1787/888932346591

EDITORIAL
REBALANCING POLICY

The global recovery has been underway for some time now, although unemployment remains persistently high in many countries. Growth has been much stronger in emerging market economies, but remains weak and uneven in much of the OECD, and has faltered recently. As financial markets continue to normalise, and households and firms reduce their indebtedness, growth is projected to gradually strengthen in the OECD area in 2011-12. Against such background, the challenge will be to guide the transition from a policy-driven recovery to self-sustained growth. As stimulus is withdrawn, policy will have to provide a credible medium-term framework, including for the financial sector, to stabilise expectations and strengthen confidence. To this effect, international collaboration, notably within the G20 process, will be essential.

Enhanced confidence could result in a faster-than-projected recovery, especially given the much improved position of corporations and the strengthening position of households. However, there are significant risks on the downside, notably those stemming from renewed declines in house prices in the United States and the United Kingdom, high sovereign debt in some countries, and possible abrupt reversals in government bond yields. Were some of them to materialise and threaten to derail the recovery, additional policy responses would be warranted in countries that still have room for manoeuvre.

Global imbalances remain wide, and in some cases have started widening again, and there are rising concerns that they may threaten the recovery. Abundant liquidity, associated with protracted monetary accommodation, has spurred large capital flows towards emerging market economies, attracted by higher interest rates and growth expectations. This has contributed to significant exchange rate appreciation, where there is flexibility, or further reserve accumulation, where this is lacking. In some cases, exchange rates are moving in a direction consistent with a rebalancing of current accounts, in other cases less so. Some countries have been reacting to capital inflows through unilateral measures to stem the consequences on their domestic economies. Protracted unilateral action of this sort is likely to have little – or even counterproductive – effects and risks triggering protectionist moves.

However, such unilateral actions also signal dissatisfaction with the progress that has been achieved because of the lack of a cooperative response. As discussed in *Economic Outlook 87*, a combination of coordinated macroeconomic, exchange rate and structural policies would yield superior results over the medium term in terms of higher growth, stronger fiscal consolidation and smaller external imbalances.

In a rebalanced policy regime, fiscal consolidation is necessary both to achieve debt sustainability and to regain room for manoeuvre on fiscal policy; structural reforms are needed to boost growth, while contributing to budget consolidation and external rebalancing; and monetary policy must gradually return to a more normal stance.

Fiscal consolidation requirements are substantial. Merely stabilising debt-to-GDP ratios by 2025 from current positions may require strengthening the underlying primary balance by more than 8% of GDP in the United States and Japan, and by 5-6 percentage points in the United Kingdom, Portugal, the Slovak Republic, Poland and Ireland.

Given the current and projected levels of deficit and debt in most OECD countries, consolidation should start in the course of 2011, unless significant downside risks to the projection materialise. In most countries, the automatic stabilisers should be allowed to work, even as underlying budget positions are strengthened. In some countries, implementation should be frontloaded taking specific circumstances into consideration. These include: a weaker state of public finances, higher funding costs, a stronger economy, weaker short-term multiplier effects, greater scope for monetary policy to offset adverse effects on growth, and larger negative longer-term effects from delaying consolidation. In a few countries, global capital markets have already forced sharp fiscal corrections.

The benefits from fiscal consolidation are fully realised over the medium term, although in the short term aggregate demand growth is reduced. In the longer term, growth would benefit from lower interest rates associated with lower debt-to-GDP ratios. OECD analysis shows that the negative impact of debt on growth is accentuated by high indebtedness. Indeed, beyond some critical debt-to-GDP ratio, a rise in indebtedness may be increasingly costly. Implementing decisive and credible fiscal consolidation would avoid the risk of a vicious circle linking higher debt ratios to higher risk premia and lower growth, and would instead promote higher growth and a virtuous circle.

In many countries, monetary policy, given the very low level of interest rates, is not in a position to compensate the short-term drag on growth from fiscal restraint, although quantitative easing can in some cases provide additional stimulus. In the medium term, as growth strengthens and output gaps close, interest rates should begin to return to neutral levels, not least to mitigate the undesirable effects of protracted easing.

The current policy environment is unique in that fiscal consolidation is needed in several countries simultaneously, with supposedly adverse short-term consequences on growth. International spillovers are important and the negative effects on demand would be amplified. However, our judgement, as reflected in the projections presented in this *Economic Outlook*, is that, given consolidations now planned, such adverse consequences would be limited. In the medium term, spillovers would act in the opposite direction, reinforcing the positive growth effects of consolidation.

A rebalanced policy regime must provide substance to the notion of "growth-friendly" fiscal consolidation, by looking more closely at the composition of public finance both on the spending and the revenue sides, and facilitating new sources of growth. Measures should include improving public sector efficiency, while preserving outputs, in growth-enhancing areas, such as education and innovation. The tax structure should move away from corporate and labour income taxes towards higher taxes on consumption, property and externalities such as greenhouse gasses.

Robust growth will also require a decisive acceleration of structural reform, which has slowed during the global recession. Progress is being made in financial sector reform, thanks to effective international collaboration, but more will be needed. Structural reforms are urgent in labour markets to increase employment, facilitate reallocation of jobs and workers and help ensure that the unemployed and vulnerable groups remain attached to the labour market. Implementing this labour-market agenda is urgent, since otherwise the large and growing number of long-term unemployed may become permanently and structurally unemployed. Product market reform is also needed. Reduction of barriers to competition, especially in service sectors, and of restrictive housing policies would increase flexibility and set the stage for renewed sustainable growth.

Structural reforms would also help fiscal consolidation by raising growth potential and by lowering government expenditure and, in the medium term, by raising employment and tax revenues. OECD estimates indicate that a 1 percentage point reduction in unemployment may improve government balances by up to 0.8% of GDP.

Structural reforms can also contribute to a rebalancing of global growth through a number of channels and help address a fundamental asymmetry in international relations by offering both surplus and deficit countries a broader menu of policy tools. For example, strengthening welfare systems in surplus countries where they are currently weak would reduce precautionary saving in the former, and removal of burdensome product market regulations could spur investment in the latter. Structural policies can likewise contribute to addressing imbalances within the euro area both in surplus countries, by spurring investment through liberalisation, and in deficit countries, by increasing wage flexibility.

Fiscal consolidation and structural policies can work together to reduce global imbalances. OECD analysis indicates that the fiscal tightening required to stabilise debt-to-GDP ratios by 2025 could reduce the size of imbalances by almost one sixth. If, in addition, Japan, Germany and China were to align product market regulation to OECD best practice and China were to raise public health spending by 2 percentage points of GDP and liberalise financial markets, global imbalances could decline by twice as much.

Rebalancing policy can deliver substantial benefits as we recover from the deepest recession in many decades. Rebalancing needs to be implemented gradually but decisively, leaving no doubt as to the direction the global economy is taking. Resolute and collaborative policy action to restore macroeconomic balance and a renewed commitment to structural reforms will boost confidence, hasten the exit from the recession and revitalise sustained growth in living standards worldwide.

18 November 2010

Pier Carlo Padoan
Deputy Secretary-General and Chief Economist

OECD Economic Outlook
Volume 2010/2
© OECD 2010

Chapter 1

GENERAL ASSESSMENT
OF THE MACROECONOMIC SITUATION

Overview

The recovery continues, albeit at a slower pace in the near term

The global economy is continuing to recover, but progress has become more hesitant. Output and trade growth have softened since the early part of the year, as temporary growth drivers, including the boost from fiscal support measures, have faded and not yet been fully replaced by self-sustaining growth dynamics. With monetary policies remaining accommodative even as fiscal consolidation becomes widespread, the present soft patch in output growth is not projected to persist for long. Even so, in the OECD economies at least, near-term growth appears unlikely to gain the momentum seen in earlier cyclical upturns. With emerging economies also growing at a slightly lower, and more sustainable, pace than earlier in the recovery, global output growth is expected to be around 4¼ per cent in 2011 and 4½ per cent in 2012 (Table 1.1). On this basis, OECD unemployment would decline moderately, to around 7¼ per cent by the end of 2012, compared with the pre-crisis trough of just over 5½ per cent. Inflation should stabilise gradually at a low rate. Outside the OECD area, domestic demand is expected to be strong, with spare capacity diminishing and policy normalisation continuing.

Table 1.1. **The global recovery will remain moderate**

OECD area, unless noted otherwise

	Average 1998-2007	2008	2009	2010	2011	2012	2010 Q4 / Q4	2011 Q4 / Q4	2012 Q4 / Q4
				Per cent					
Real GDP growth[1]	2.7	0.3	-3.4	2.8	2.3	2.8	2.7	2.4	3.0
United States	3.0	0.0	-2.6	2.7	2.2	3.1	2.3	2.6	3.4
Euro area	2.3	0.3	-4.1	1.7	1.7	2.0	2.1	1.7	2.1
Japan	1.2	-1.2	-5.2	3.7	1.7	1.3	3.3	1.3	1.6
Output gap[2]	0.3	0.0	-4.7	-3.5	-2.9	-2.1			
Unemployment rate[3]	6.4	6.0	8.1	8.3	8.1	7.5	8.3	7.9	7.3
Inflation[4]	2.8	3.2	0.6	1.8	1.5	1.4	1.7	1.4	1.4
Fiscal balance[5]	-2.0	-3.3	-7.9	-7.6	-6.1	-4.7			
Memorandum Items									
World real trade growth	6.8	3.1	-11.1	12.3	8.3	8.1	11.9	7.8	8.3
World real GDP growth[6]	3.8	2.6	-1.0	4.6	4.2	4.6	4.5	4.4	4.8

1. Year-on-year increase; last three columns show the increase over a year earlier.
2. Per cent of potential GDP.
3. Per cent of labour force.
4. Private consumption deflator. Year-on-year increase; last 3 columns show the increase over a year earlier.
5. Per cent of GDP.
6. Moving nominal GDP weights, using purchasing power parities.
Source: OECD Economic Outlook 88 database.

StatLink ᘓᗗᘓ http://dx.doi.org/10.1787/888932346610

But risks remain substantial...

The risks around the forecast remain substantial, and are deeper on the downside than on the upside. Downside risks are to a large extent associated with particular events that could trigger renewed weakness in activity against the background of vulnerabilities related to continued fragile financial markets, ongoing household balance sheet deleveraging, sovereign debt problems and tensions in foreign exchange markets. Most of the risks are inter-related, and if they were to materialise, could generate feedback loops between asset prices, private sector balance sheets and demand and financial sector outcomes. A corollary is that more favourable outcomes in one area should also serve to diminish risks in others. Specific risks on the downside and upside are as follows:

... on the downside...

- A particular downside risk is that renewed declines in house prices in the United States and the United Kingdom would have a negative effect on household balance sheets, thereby slowing consumption and raising saving rates. Clear risks also remain from ongoing concerns about public debt sustainability in some OECD countries; if these were to strengthen, they could disrupt financial markets and confidence. Other areas of downside risk in financial markets relate to the possibilities of an abrupt reversal in government bond yields, lingering uncertainties about banks and the availability of credit during the recovery, the adverse effects of large capital inflows into many emerging economies and the tensions created by recently widespread currency interventions which could spill over into protectionist policy action.

... and the upside

- On the upside, there is the possibility of higher business investment on the back of elevated corporate profits and a stronger recovery in equity markets, with shares being priced at multiples of earnings below historical norms in some countries. An additional upside risk is that already-normalised aggregate financial conditions could provide greater delayed stimulus to the economy than projected, or even improve further.

Policy considerations remain closely interlinked

With the normalisation of monetary, fiscal, financial and crisis-related structural measures expected to gain momentum over the next two years, and take place in an increasingly large number of countries simultaneously, domestic policies in one domain will need to take into account policy settings in others and in other countries. International cooperation, including through the G20, will be essential to boost the credibility of this policy effort. In countries that have a choice, the extent and speed of fiscal consolidation will depend in part on the scope for monetary policy to offset the adverse near-term effects on demand from fiscal tightening by reducing or delaying increases in policy interest rates. Equally, the pace of reforms to financial regulations will affect monetary and fiscal policy settings. Structural policies, in addition to strengthening the economy in the longer term, can contribute to fiscal consolidation, create room for monetary policy to extend the period of accommodation by raising potential output and also help strengthen demand in the short term. In addition, certain structural reforms that are desirable on domestic grounds alone can also contribute to narrowing international imbalances, both at the global level and inside the euro area.

Economic policy requirements are: ...

Against this background, the policy requirements at present and in the longer term are as follows:

... to actively pursue fiscal consolidation...

● Budget consolidation to bring public finances onto a sound footing should be pursued actively from 2011 onwards in almost all OECD countries. The pace of withdrawal of fiscal stimulus should be commensurate with the state of the public finances, the ease at which government debt can be financed, the strength of the recovery and already-announced consolidation commitments. The automatic stabilisers should be allowed to operate around the planned consolidation path to offset any temporary weakness in activity, except in countries at acute risk of losing credibility. In countries with more comfortable fiscal positions, the underlying pace of consolidation could be softened if growth were to turn out weaker than projected. Overall, based on the current set of projections, the planned consolidation in most OECD countries is appropriate in both 2011 and 2012.

... to normalise policy rates at a pace contingent on the recovery....

● The challenge for most monetary authorities will be to exit from exceptional stimulus in a way consistent with macroeconomic developments, without exacerbating fragilities in financial markets. With still-wide output gaps and sizeable fiscal consolidation in prospect, the normalisation of policy interest rates in the United States and the euro area should begin in earnest only from the first half of 2012, with monetary policy remaining accommodative beyond the projection horizon. In Japan, against the backdrop of persistent deflation, policy rates should remain at their current low levels throughout 2011 and 2012, and significant quantitative easing should be implemented to give stimulus to the economy. If output growth were to turn out weaker than projected in the major OECD economies, the normalisation of policy interest rates should be delayed further, and, depending on the duration and extent of economic weakness, firmer actions might be needed to lower real interest rates further out in the maturity spectrum *via* additional quantitative easing and communications policies. In OECD and non-OECD countries alike, it remains important that exchange rate changes consistent with necessary international rebalancing are not resisted.

... to maintain momentum towards financial reforms...

● The momentum toward financial reform needs to be maintained to strengthen the stability of the global financial system. The implementation of the recently agreed global reform package for the banking sector will contribute to this end. The prolonged phasing-in of the reforms will help to achieve the transition in a way that does not imperil the recovery. Additional reforms, including steps to address distorted incentives for systemically-important financial institutions and tighten regulations on non-bank financial institutions, remain to be tackled.

... and implement structural reforms to overcome the legacy of the crisis and narrow global imbalances

- Structural reforms need to be implemented to raise potential output in the long term, thus facilitating fiscal consolidation, and to help tackle some of the specific legacies of the recession, not least weakness in labour markets that threatens to have durable negative consequences. Reforms to improve public-sector productivity, remove barriers to job creation, change the tax structure and implement pollution-pricing mechanisms would all help to protect growth and employment and facilitate fiscal consolidation. Structural reforms will also be instrumental in addressing the underlying determinants of global imbalances through their impact on saving and investment. A well-designed package of structural reforms to reduce product market regulations in sheltered sectors and improve social welfare systems in non-OECD countries, in conjunction with fiscal consolidation, would do much to narrow global imbalances in the years ahead.

Forces acting on the OECD economies

The forces acting on the OECD economies remain favourable

Global economic activity has softened more than previously expected since the early part of the year with the handover from temporary to self-sustaining growth drivers proving uneven. However, surveys of business confidence and order levels, which had eased in the summer, have now begun to turn up once again. On balance, the forces acting on OECD economies remain favourable, with the softening of growth likely to prove only temporary rather than a reflection of a stronger underlying weakness of private spending. Global developments and financial conditions remain supportive and good progress is being made in tackling pre-recession imbalances, although there are clear areas of weakness, most notably labour markets, where adjustments remain far from complete.

Global trade growth remains solid...

Global trade growth is now moderating; the annualised rate of trade growth in the third quarter is estimated to have been around 9%, compared to growth above 15% in both the first and second quarters of the year. The slowdown in trade growth reflects in part the normalisation that would be expected after a period in which trade and industrial production have rebounded rapidly from the trough of the recession. Recent monthly trade and global indicators suggest that trade growth could soften a little further to an annualised rate of 7¼ per cent by the year end. Even so, global trade volumes will have risen past their pre-crisis peak in the course of the second half of 2010. The gap between the rate of trade growth in the OECD and non-OECD economies has narrowed during 2010, reflecting some moderation in domestic demand and import growth in the non-OECD area, and a rise in the trade intensity of growth in the OECD countries, associated in part with a pick-up in fixed investment, a component of demand which is particularly trade intensive. After the near-term slowdown, global trade growth is expected to generally remain buoyant through 2011-12, continuing to grow at close to the pre-crisis (2004-2008) rate of 1.7 times world output growth (Figure 1.1).

Figure 1.1. **World trade growth remains solid**
Percentage change

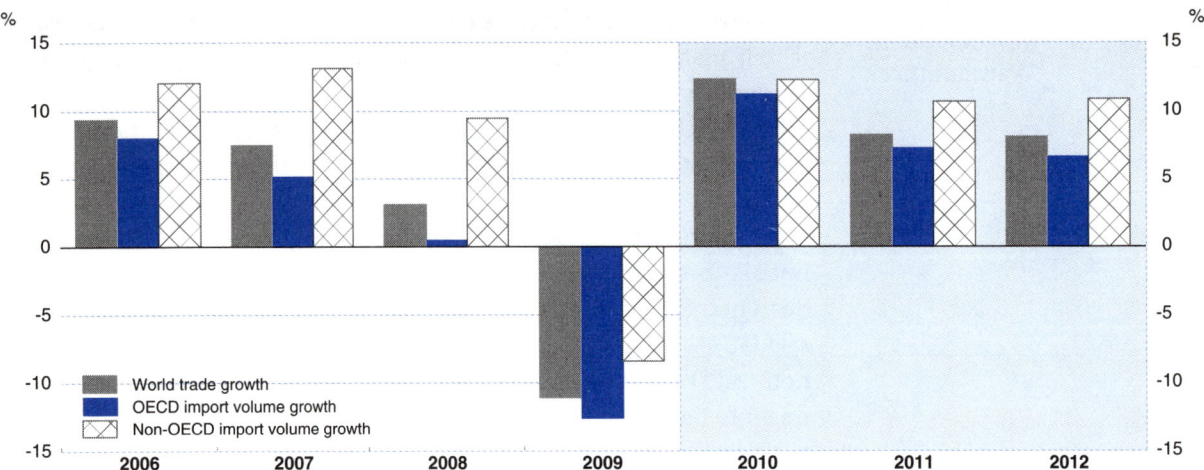

Note: The import volume figures include intra-region trade. Based on a trade in goods and services volume matrix in 2005, just over a half of global trade is within OECD countries, about a third between OECD and non-OECD countries and the rest between non-OECD countries.
Source: OECD Economic Outlook 88 database.

StatLink ⬛⬛⬛ http://dx.doi.org/10.1787/888932344976

... as does domestic demand in the non-OECD economies

The upturn in activity in the non-OECD economies has moderated since the spring, especially in industrial sectors closely integrated into global supply chains. Even so, final domestic demand remains robust, helping to support external demand in the OECD economies. In China, the economy lost some momentum earlier this year as policy normalisation got underway and excessive stock levels were reduced, although GDP growth picked up again in the third quarter, to an annualised rate estimated to be around 9½ per cent. Retail sales growth remains solid, and business sentiment, as reflected in the PMI, has now turned up once again. Output growth has also moderated a little this year in India, although domestic demand remains strong and business sentiment remains solid. Active steps towards monetary policy normalisation have begun amidst inflationary pressures. In Brazil, the output gap has closed rapidly in the aftermath of the recession, with robust domestic demand growth over the past year. Net trade has been a drag on growth, in part because of a sizable appreciation of the effective exchange rate due to heavy capital inflows. Macroeconomic policy normalisation has begun and signs of a slowing in activity growth have now emerged. Growth remains more sluggish in Russia and South Africa and comparatively dependent on external demand and higher international commodity prices.

Aggregate financial conditions remain supportive of growth...

Financial conditions, as summarised by the OECD financial conditions indices (FCIs), have remained broadly stable since early in the year, at close-to-normal levels in the main OECD areas (Figure 1.2). Given the lags involved, the earlier improvements in aggregate financial conditions will continue to support activity for some time. The recent

Figure 1.2. **Financial conditions indices have improved markedly**

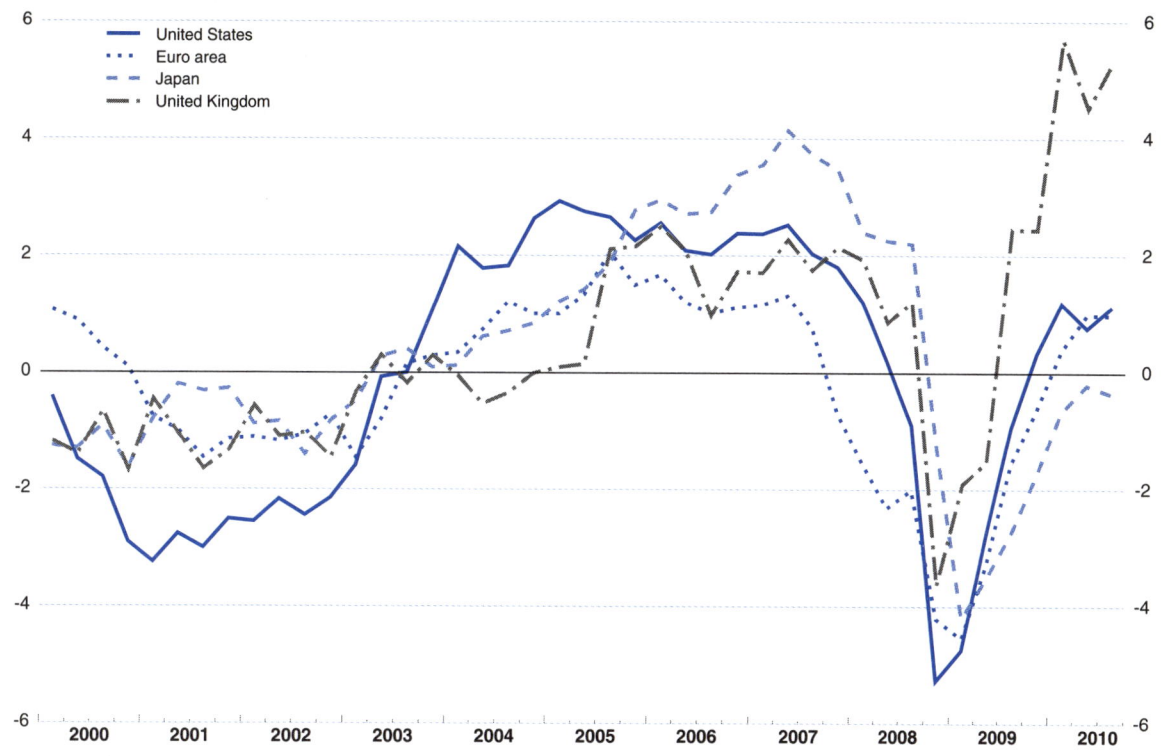

Note: A unit decline in the index implies a tightening in financial conditions sufficient to produce an average reduction in the level of GDP by 1/2 to 1% after four to six quarters. See details in Guichard *et al.* (2009).

Source: Datastream; OECD Economic Outlook 88 database; and OECD calculations.

StatLink ᴍ📊 http://dx.doi.org/10.1787/888932344995

stability of the aggregate FCIs masks disparate developments in their components – real interest rates, bond spreads, credit conditions, real exchange rates and household net wealth. In the United States, lower real interest rates, especially at the long end of the curve, and looser credit conditions have offset continued weakness in household net wealth. In the euro area, lending standards have tightened a little and the offset coming previously from a weaker exchange rate has faded. In Japan, the improvement in credit conditions and spreads has broadly offset the impact of the yen appreciation and equity price declines. Key factors helping to support financial conditions include:

... money market rates and benchmark bond yields have eased...

- Low money market rates and government bond yields provide support to financial conditions at present, despite the renewed strains in financial markets from the concerns about public-debt sustainability in several euro area countries (discussed further below). The stress tests on the EU banking sector have helped to alleviate immediate market concerns, although lingering worries about counterparty risk remain visible in the cost of insuring bank bonds against default, which has remained high, especially in some smaller euro area economies.[1] Long-term benchmark government bond yields have fallen to exceptionally low levels in the United States and Germany, and also declined in Japan and many other European countries (see Box 1.4 below). In the emerging economies, financial conditions have also been buoyed by lower sovereign bond yields. Strong capital inflows have boosted asset prices in many of these countries, but have also put upward pressure on exchange rates.

... corporate bond markets have remained resilient...

- Corporate bond markets have remained resilient, despite the European sovereign debt turmoil, providing companies, especially larger ones, with cheap financing prospects. Yields for investment-grade borrowers have eased to very low levels and also fallen back for riskier borrowers, after rising markedly at the height of concerns in sovereign debt markets earlier this year. Bond issuance by non-financial companies this year is below the 2009 record level, but remains above long-term averages, especially in the euro area, and private securitisation markets have begun to revive, albeit gently.[2]

... equity prices have risen...

- Equity markets have experienced significant volatility in recent months, but are above their levels at the start of the year in most developed countries, although Japan is a notable exception. Prices appear moderate relative to estimates of trend earnings in some countries (Figure 1.3), suggesting that there is only a limited risk of further large declines in prices, with adverse effects on household net wealth. Stock markets in many emerging economies have been a little more buoyant than in the OECD during 2010, but generally remain closely linked to developments in the global economy.

... and conditions for banks have stopped deteriorating...

- Helped by very low funding costs, banks remained highly profitable in the first half of 2010. Bank lending surveys for the third quarter showed a continued gentle relaxation in lending standards in the United States, but a very small net tightening of credit standards in the euro area. With declining benchmark long-term interest rates, bank lending rates have generally eased for mortgages and consumer credit. Possibly as a reflection, signs of a modest pick-up in bank lending volumes to the private sector have emerged in the euro area through not yet in the United States (Figure 1.4). As the recovery matures, lending conditions may be relaxed, spurring a pick-up in lending to the private sector. However, as discussed further below, there remains some longer-term

---

1. The stress tests showed that the short-term risks, including from sovereign default, were much lower than many had feared. The tests did not consider losses on sovereign debt on banks' banking books (where most of it is held) and, thus, did not assess associated longer-term risks but nonetheless provided information about these exposures (Blundell-Wignall and Slovik, 2010).
2. Examples of new deals include collateralised debt obligations (CDOs) of mortgage-backed securities and collateralised loan obligations (CLOs) of leveraged loans.

Figure 1.3. **Price-earnings ratios remain below long-run averages**

Last observation: November 2010

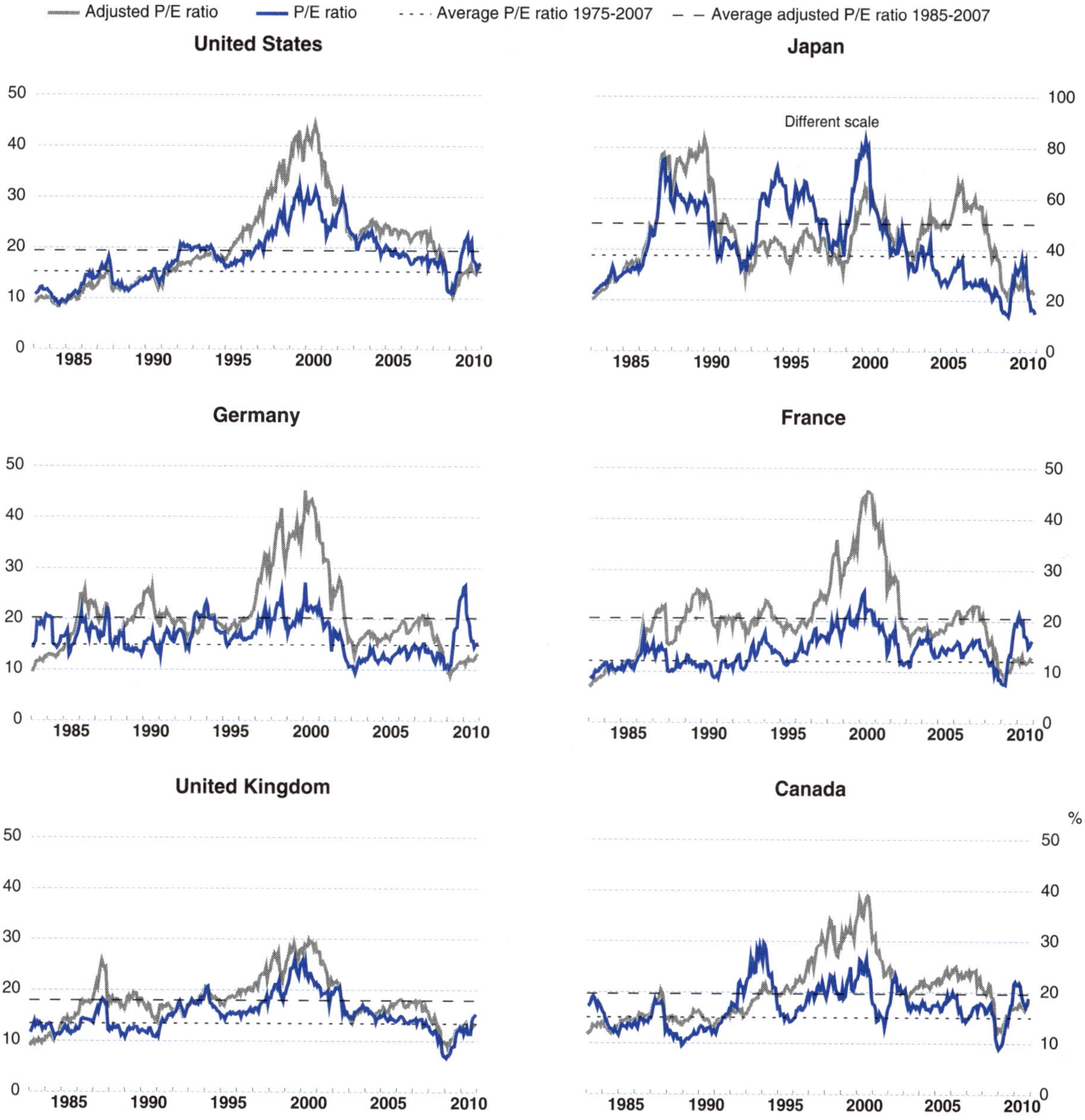

——— Adjusted P/E ratio   ——— P/E ratio   - - - Average P/E ratio 1975-2007   — — Average adjusted P/E ratio 1985-2007

Note: Adjusted P/E ratios are calculated as the ratio of stock prices to the moving average of the previous 10 years' earnings, adjusted for nominal trend growth. Averages shown exclude the period 1998-2000 to remove the asset bubble effects. Last observations refer to 12 November 2010.

Source: Datastream; and OECD calculations.

StatLink ⟪🔗⟫ http://dx.doi.org/10.1787/888932345014

uncertainty about the impact of new regulatory requirements on banks' balance sheets and on lending growth.

Going forward, aggregate financial conditions are likely to remain supportive, although moderating gently towards normal levels as the gradual move towards normalisation of policy rates begins and bond yields rise.

Figure 1.4. **Bank lending may be bottoming**
Year-on-year growth rate

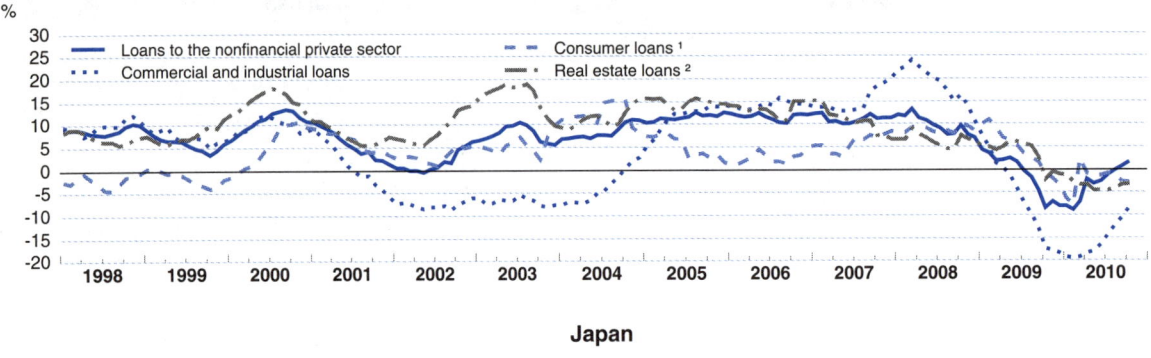

United States

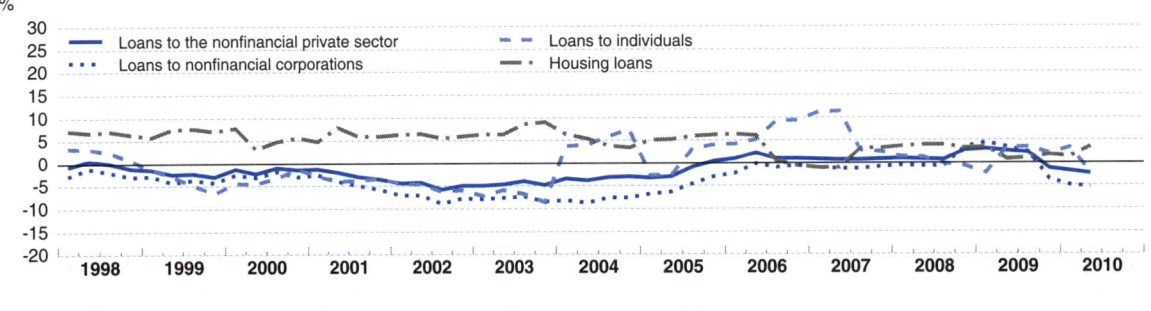

Japan

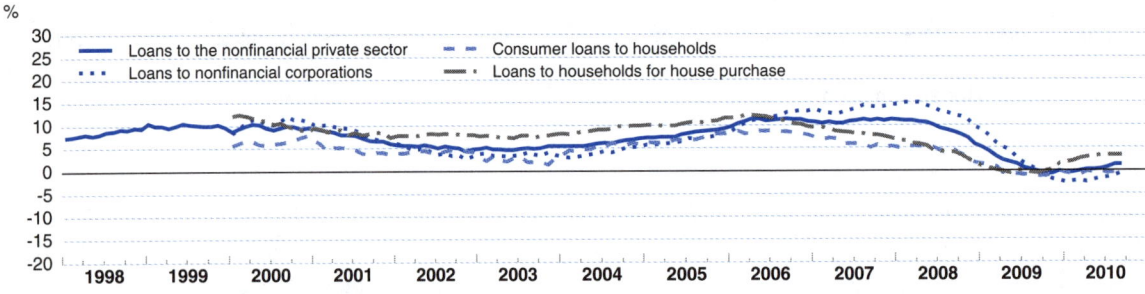

Euro area

Note: Data refer to all commercial banks for the United States; to monetary financial institutions (MFIs) for the euro area; to all banks for Japan. Year-on-year growth rates are calculated from end-of-period stocks. For the euro area, these are adjusted for reclassifications, exchange rates variations and any other changes which do not arise from transactions.

1. United States data from April 2010 concerning consumer loans have been modified to take into account a change of concept.
2. The definition of real estate loans for the United States is broader than housing loans as it includes also loans related to commercial real estate. Moreover, both for the United States and for Japan real estate / housing loans can include loans to the corporate sector.

Source: Thomson Financial.

StatLink ⟨⟨⟨ http://dx.doi.org/10.1787/888932345033

... helping business investment to rebound this year

OECD-wide business investment remains well below the average intensity of the previous three decades, despite the upturn in investment volumes since the start of the year (Figure 1.5). This should limit the risk of any further downside adjustment in investment levels and provides ample scope for business investment to gain additional momentum as the recovery proceeds, especially in new equipment and software. Improvements in capital markets and in corporate profitability (Figure 1.6)

Figure 1.5. **Business investment has started to pick up**

Percentage of nominal GDP

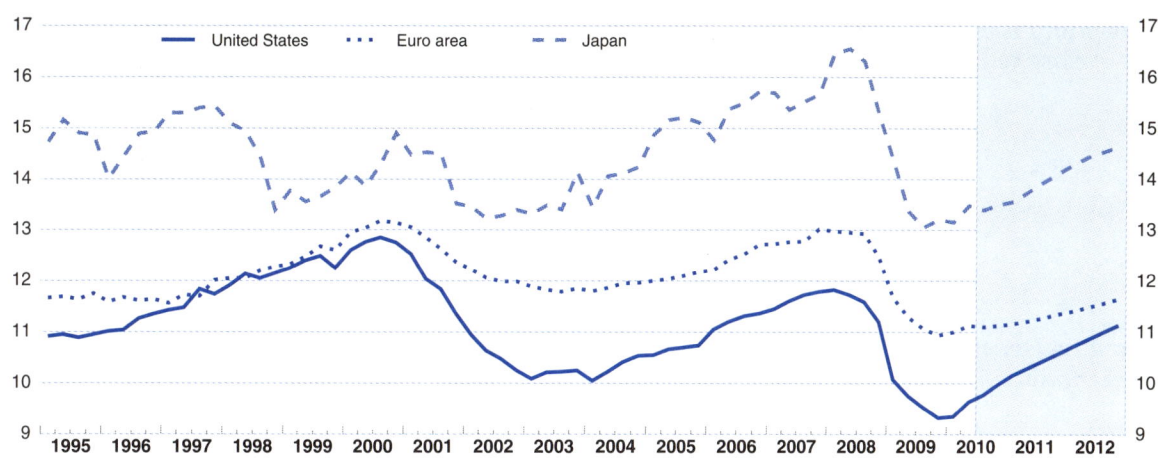

Source: OECD Economic Outlook 88 database.

StatLink ᠍᠍᠍ http://dx.doi.org/10.1787/888932345052

have eased financing conditions for businesses this year, even though bank borrowing remains subdued, and non-financial corporate balance sheets are in a healthy state in several countries. Capital-goods shipments and orders have continued to expand in the major OECD economies, although they have softened somewhat since mid-year, especially in the United States, suggesting that equipment investment growth in the latter part of this year may be a little weaker than earlier in the year. Further

Figure 1.6. **The profitability of non-financial corporations has improved**

Index 2007=100

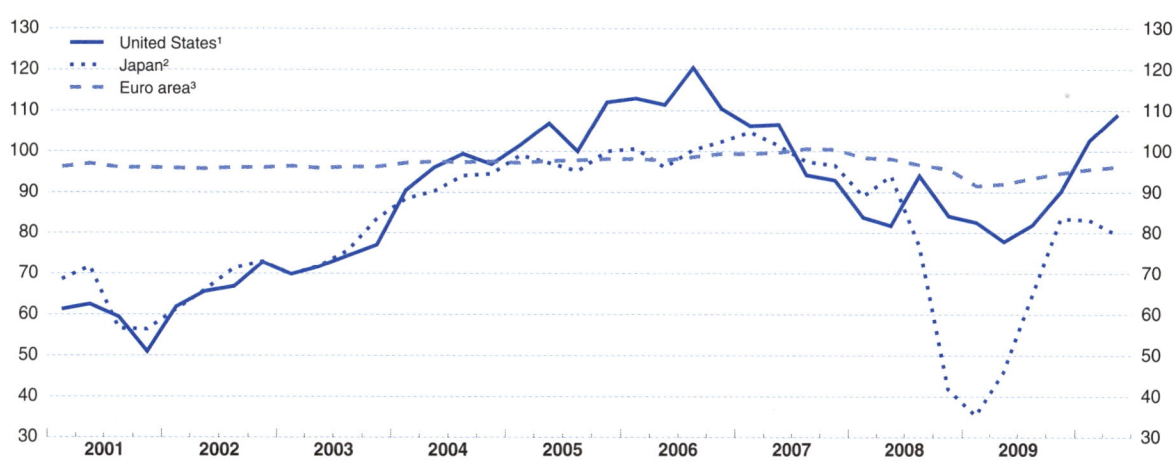

1. Ratio of pre-tax profits to gross value-added of nonfinancial corporations.
2. Ratio of ordinary profits to sales reported by all incorporated businesses.
3. Ratio of gross operating surplus to gross value-added of nonfinancial corporations.

Source: BEA; Eurostat; and Datastream.

StatLink ᠍᠍᠍ http://dx.doi.org/10.1787/888932345071

ahead, normal cyclical forces and healthier financial conditions should lift investment levels over the projection period.

Inventory levels are now close to longer-term norms...

The upturn in the inventory cycle since mid-2009 is now moderating in several OECD economies. With few signs that inventories are presently at an excessive level in the major OECD economies, the likelihood both of temporary weakness in final demand being reinforced by a significant contraction in inventory levels, and of marked further growth in inventory levels appears limited. The contribution of inventories to quarterly output growth is assumed to be zero from the second quarter of 2011 onwards in the projections.

... and household balance-sheet adjustment is well underway

Household saving rates have remained elevated this year in most OECD countries relative to pre-crisis norms. Thus private consumption growth has remained comparatively subdued, held back by the need to repair household balance sheets and still fragile, but gradually easing, credit and labour-market conditions. The improvement in asset prices together with higher saving have helped to rebuild household balance sheets since the recovery began (Box 1.1). Wealth-to-income ratios remain

---

Box 1.1. **Household balance sheets and the saving rate**

Private consumption will play a crucial role for the overall recovery in OECD economies as temporary cyclical factors and fiscal support measures are fading. The ongoing repair in household balance sheets has pushed up household saving rates and depressed private consumption in all major OECD economies. An important question is how far balance-sheet adjustments have advanced and thus whether saving rates have already peaked or are expected to increase further over the projection period. This box looks at some key household balance sheet developments in major OECD areas (see Figure) and outlines possible implications for the saving rate.

Household balance sheets have recovered over the past year in the OECD area on the back of stabilising housing markets, gains in stock markets and continued deleveraging. However, household net wealth remains below immediate pre-crisis peaks[1] in most countries and risks remain of a renewed weakening of housing markets in some OECD countries.

- In the United States, the ratio of net worth to disposable income in the second quarter of 2010 stood at around three quarters of its immediate pre-crisis peak and was still below its 5 and 10 year pre-crisis averages. The ratio of net financial assets to disposable income also stood 25% below its pre-crisis peak and remained below its 5 and 10 year pre-crisis average, despite stock market gains and a 10 percentage points decrease in the liabilities-to-income ratio since the onset of the crisis. While net financial assets are expected to have recovered in the third quarter from the temporary stock market weakness in the second quarter, the state of the housing market continues to be a drag on household balance sheets and represents a significant risk: a 10% fall in house prices would cancel more than a third of the increase in net worth from the trough in first quarter of 2009 to the first quarter of 2010.

- In Japan, the ratio of net financial assets to disposable income now stands at about 10% below its immediate pre-crisis peak but is above its 5 and 10 year pre-crisis averages. Little debt deleveraging has occurred since the onset of the crisis and housing wealth is likely to have further weakened as house prices continued to fall over the year to the second quarter of 2010.

Box 1.1. **Household balance sheets and the saving rate** (*cont.*)

- In the euro area, the ratio of net worth to disposable income in the second quarter of 2010 was around 5% below its immediate pre-crisis peak but above its 5 and 10 year pre-crisis averages. The ratio of net financial assets to disposable income has rebounded to the pre-crisis average, despite upward trending financial liabilities, but is still about 10% below the pre-crisis peak. Housing wealth, which is larger than financial assets in the euro area, started to increase moderately over the year to the second quarter of 2010.

- In the United Kingdom, the ratio of net worth to disposable income has also rebounded markedly and is now above the 5 and 10 year pre-crisis averages. However, it remains about 10% below its pre-crisis peak. Continuous deleveraging and stock market gains have been supporting forces behind the rebound in net financial assets. The ratio of net financial assets to disposable income is close to the 5 and 10 year pre-crisis averages.

Wealth and saving
% of disposable income

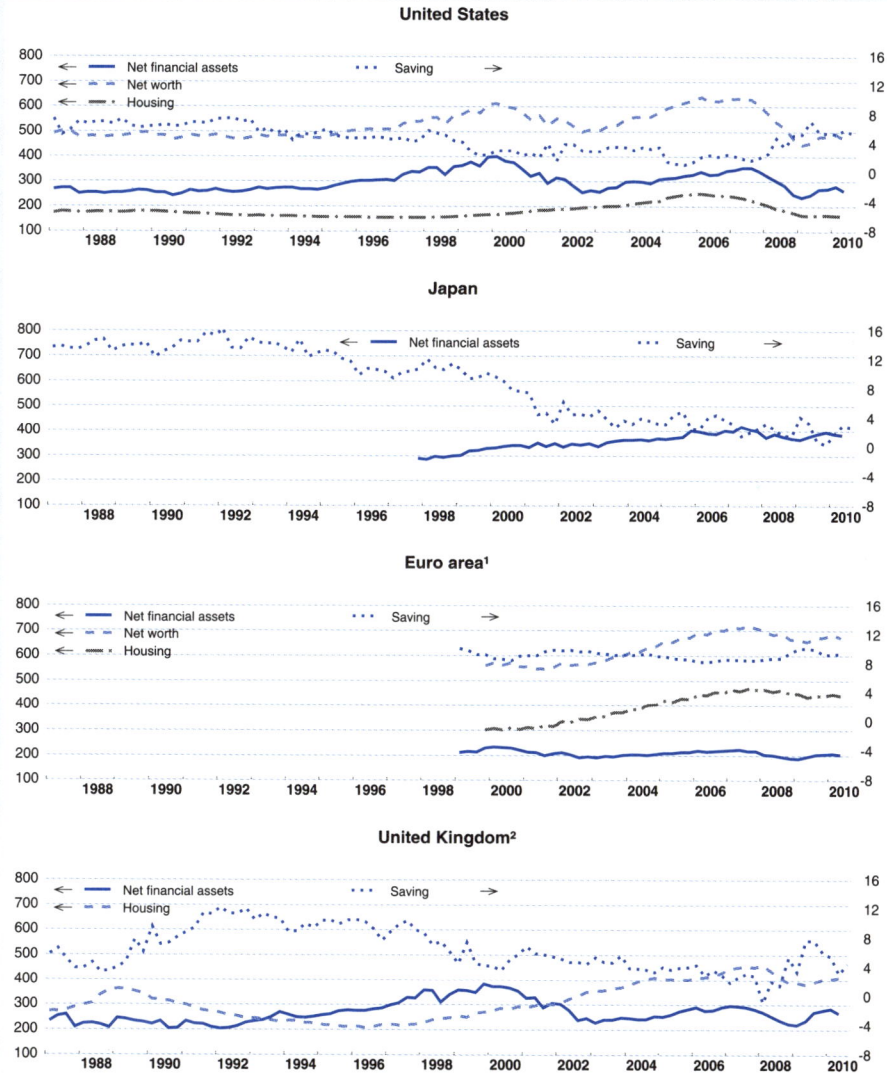

1. Uses data for all euro area member states for the level of financial assets and data for the EA-14 member states otherwise.
2. Gross disposable income and gross saving ratios.

Source: OECD Economic Outlook 88 database; Federal Reserve; Bank of Japan; and ECB.

StatLink 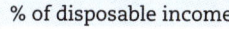 http://dx.doi.org/10.1787/888932345090

Box 1.1. **Household balance sheets and the saving rate** (*cont.*)

Analysis relating saving rates to longer-term fundamentals suggests that prior to the onset of the crisis in 2007 the saving rate in the United Kingdom was about 1 percentage point below its long-run equilibrium, conditional on household wealth (Hüfner and Koske, 2010). The saving rate was closer to the suggested long-run equilibrium values in the United States and the euro area. The losses in household net wealth since the beginning of the crisis have put pressure on the equilibrium saving rates. Simple back-of-the-envelope calculations based on long-run elasticities of consumption to net wealth can help shed some light on the magnitude of these necessary additional long-term adjustments in saving rates. Given the observed falls in net financial assets from mid-2007 to the second quarter of 2010, all else equal, it would be reasonable to expect saving rates to be roughly 2½ percentage points higher in the United States, 1 percentage point in Japan and ½ percentage points in the euro area and in the United Kingdom, than the level seen prior to the onset of the crisis.[2] If allowance is made for separate housing wealth effects, which are found to be especially important in the United States and the United Kingdom and more moderate in the euro area (*e.g.* ECB 2009), the saving adjustment would be about 1 percentage point higher in the United States and ½ a percentage point higher in the United Kingdom.[3] These adjustments appear to have already taken place, with the saving rate having risen 4 percentage points since the beginning of the crisis in the United States and the United Kingdom and 1 percentage point in the euro area. Indeed, saving rates in the euro area and the United Kingdom may well have peaked in the middle of 2009.

Several near term risks exist, however, which might keep saving rates elevated for some time or even push them up further temporarily. The first risk relates to credit conditions, which play an important role for the future saving path, both directly and in interaction with house prices. First, favourable credit conditions limit the need for precautionary saving and thus should reduce the saving rate, all else being equal. Second, recent research suggests that credit conditions may also affect the impact of housing wealth on household consumption and saving by affecting the extent to which housing wealth can be used as collateral for household borrowing (Aron *et al.*, 2010; Kerdrain, 2010). In the near term, both of these factors imply that the impact of further declines in house prices on household consumption might be exacerbated if credit conditions tighten again, pushing the saving rate up further. A second risk to saving rates stems from ongoing deleveraging. Debt-to-income ratios have fallen substantially since the onset of the crisis in the United States and United Kingdom, and estimates of debt service ratios in the United States are back to longer-term historical averages (Deutsche Bank, 2010). However, the process of deleveraging is not yet finished: debt-to-income ratios remain well above longer-term historical averages in the United States and the United Kingdom; households may wish to hold debt-to-income ratios well below those seen immediately prior to the crisis for precautionary reasons; and tighter lending standards of banks may also require lower debt-to-income ratios. If households decide to reduce debt-to-income ratios as Japanese households did in the 1990s, saving rates might rise further (Glick and Lansing, 2009). Finally, unemployment rates are likely to remain elevated in many major OECD economies, suggesting that saving rates might remain at current high levels for some time. Similarly, government debt levels have risen sharply and are expected to rise even further in the near future. This may induce households to save more in anticipation of future tax increases, though, arguably, such adjustments might also have already taken place.

1. In what follows, the pre-crisis peak refers to the second quarter of 2007 for all countries and regions.
2. These calculations assume a representative long-run elasticity of consumption with respect to net financial wealth of 0.09 (with the elasticity of consumption with respect to income being 0.91). This implies $\ln(c/y)=0.09\ln(w/y)$ where c, w and y are consumption, net financial wealth and income (omitting any constant). This is consistent with estimates presented for the euro area in OECD (2009), which were consistent with a marginal propensity to consume out of wealth of roughly 0.04. Similar figures have been estimated for a number of countries including those outside of the euro area, though there is substantial variability in these estimates (see for example Altissimo *et al.* 2005 and Mishkin 2007). With this specification and using the approximation that changes in the saving rate are equal to the opposite of changes in the log of the consumption to income ratio, $\Delta S=-0.09\Delta\ln(w/y)$ where S is the saving rate. Dale (2009) has noted that an approach like this may exaggerate the extent of the necessary adjustment. For example, it ignores that wealth including human capital (which depends on future labour earnings) is likely to have fallen less dramatically than financial wealth.
3. This calculation is based on assuming that $\ln(c/y)=0.04\ln(hw/y)+0.08\ln(fw/y)$ where hw and fw are net housing and net financial (net of home mortgages) wealth. The coefficients are based on estimates of the elasticities of consumption with respect of housing and stock prices for OECD countries in Ludwig and Slok (2002).

below their immediate pre-crisis levels in the major economies, but are now close to 5-10 year pre-crisis norms in the euro area, Japan and the United Kingdom, which suggests that the saving ratio may have either passed, or be close to, its peak, provided there is not renewed weakness in asset prices and labour markets. In the United States, comparatively more adjustment remains to be done, reflecting the ongoing weakness in the housing market and in household net worth, suggesting that the saving rate could remain at its current high level for a while and even rise further if credit conditions were to deteriorate. An updated comparison of actual and trend car sales, with the latter derived using information on income per capita, population growth and scrapping rates (Haugh *et al.*, 2010), provides an additional indication of an underlying robustness in consumer demand at present. Car sales in the euro area, Japan, the United Kingdom and the United States all appear to be below trend in recent months (Figure 1.7). On this basis, in all of these economies, and the United States in particular, future downside risks for sales appear to be limited.

But the recovery in housing and commercial property markets remains hesitant...

The recovery in housing markets broadened in the first half of 2010, but these markets remain fragile in some countries. Both investment volumes and real house prices were rising in a majority of countries in the second quarter (Figure 1.8). The ratio of housing investment to GDP is now close to, or even below, the level seen in past troughs in the majority of OECD economies, suggesting that the likelihood of any further sizable deterioration is small in most countries, and limiting the aggregate impact on GDP even if such an adjustment were to occur.

... and recovery is likely to be slow

Going forward, OECD-wide housing investment is expected to rise gently relative to GDP from the fourth quarter of 2010 onwards, although its contribution to the overall recovery is likely to be much smaller than in the past (Box 1.2). However, house prices remain elevated relative to incomes and rents in many economies, with the exception of the largest three (Table 1.2), in part because of the present low interest rate environment. Thus, some downside risks remain for house prices, and hence housing investment and household balance sheets as monetary policy begins to normalise and bond yields increase. Housing markets remain comparatively weak in the United States (where a marked downturn has occurred since the expiration of the homebuyer tax credit at the end of April), the United Kingdom, Spain and Ireland. Non-residential construction spending now appears to be close to bottoming out in the United States, although commercial property prices continued to weaken through to August. Considerable excess capacity remains in this sector, which should damp business investment in structures. Worldwide, many countries also continue to report rising distressed commercial property sales.

Labour-market conditions have begun to improve...

Labour market conditions have begun to improve this year in most OECD countries. The OECD-wide unemployment rate, which peaked at 8½ per cent at the end of 2009, declined to an estimated 8¼ per cent by the

Figure 1.7. **Car sales are generally below trend levels**
Actual and trend car sales 1995-2012; number of cars, Millions

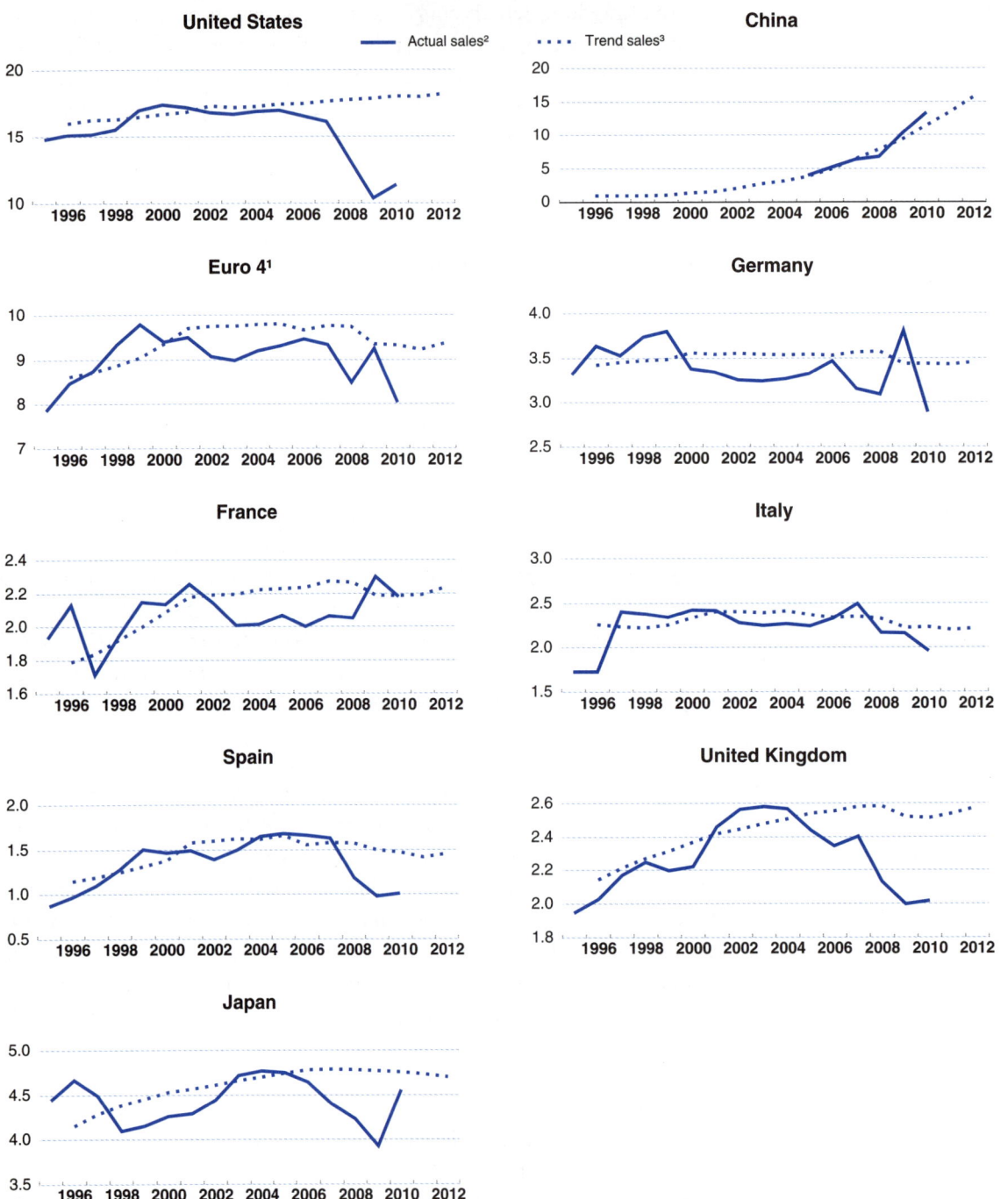

1. Euro 4 includes Germany, France, Italy and Spain.
2. For 2010 based on annualised sales in first nine months for Japan, and in first ten months for the United States, China, Germany, France, Italy, Spain and the United Kingdom.
3. Trend car sales are derived using a non-linear relationship between income per capita and car ownership, population growth and scrapping rates.

Source: Haugh *et al.* (2010); Datastream; China Association of Automobile Manufacturers; and OECD calculations.

StatLink ⤥ http://dx.doi.org/10.1787/888932345109

Figure 1.8. **Housing markets continue to recover**

Proportion of OECD countries with rising real house prices[1]
Based on quarter-on-quarter change

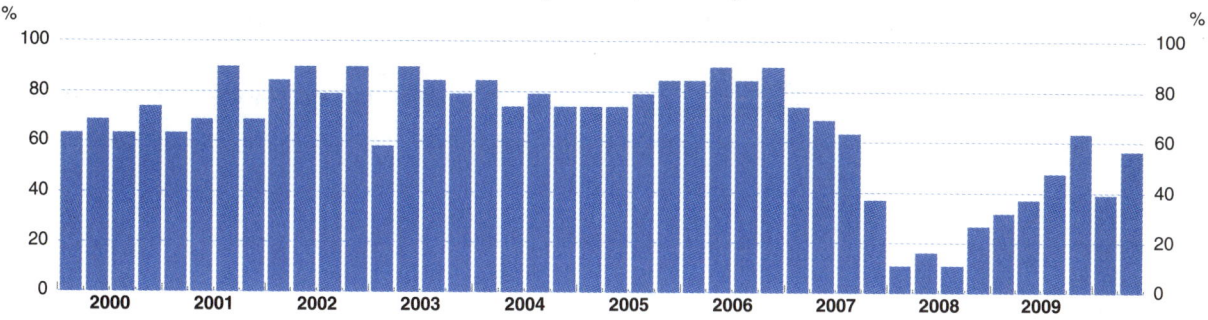

Proportion of OECD countries with rising real housing investment
Based on quarter-on-quarter change

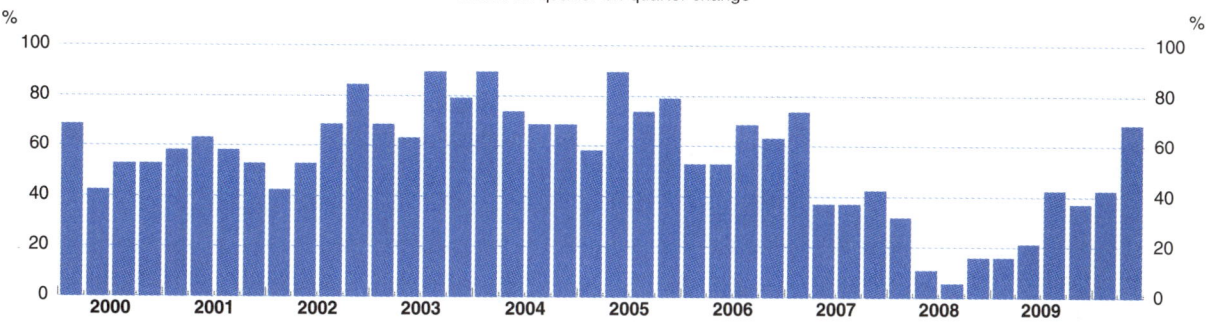

1. House prices deflated by the private consumption deflator. Calculation based on 19 countries (18 available in 2010q1 and 16 available in 2010q2).

Source: OECD Economic Outlook 88 database; and various national sources, see table A.1 in Girouard *et al.* (2006).

StatLink http://dx.doi.org/10.1787/888932345128

Box 1.2. **Housing market developments**

In most previous recessions, housing markets have supported the recovery process. In the United States, for example, housing investment contributed 0.6 percentage points to GDP growth in the year following the trough in GDP on average in previous recessions (see table), and house prices have on average increased by 4%, modestly supporting private consumption *via* wealth effects. In contrast, the growth contribution from residential investment in the latest recovery has been significantly smaller at 0.1 percentage point, reflecting both lower growth in investment as well as a smaller share of investment in GDP after the collapse in housing investment. House prices even continued to fall, which has likely contributed to weak private consumption growth.[1] While housing markets continued to recover in the majority of OECD countries in the first half of 2010 (see main text), some countries show continued or renewed weakness. Among them are, most notably, the United States, Spain, Ireland and, more recently, the United Kingdom.

● In the United States, home-builders' business confidence remains low, and prices have edged down on some measures, with sales having plunged and permits having stalled after the expiration of the homebuyer tax credit earlier this year. Moreover the stock of unsold houses has edged up again since the spring, and the number of foreclosures started has remained elevated. These recent indicators, together with a slow recovery and a stubbornly high unemployment rate, suggest that the US housing market might remain weak for a prolonged period. A complicating factor, which however seems unlikely to change this conclusion, is the range of procedural problems at banks that may hold up foreclosures for some period.

Box 1.2. **Housing market developments** *(cont.)*

Housing investment and house prices in previous recessions

Trough in GDP	House price increase in the year following the trough in GDP in %	Contribution of housing investment to real GDP growth in the year following the trough in GDP in percentage points
Mar-58		1.5
Dec-60		0.5
Mar-70	6.4	0.6
Mar-75	5.1	0.9
Sep-80	4.7	-0.2
Mar-82	2.4	0.7
Mar-91	2.8	0.5
Average of previous recessions	*4.3*	*0.6*
Jun-09	-5.0	0.1

Source: OECD calculation.

StatLink ᴍᴸ *http://dx.doi.org/10.1787/888932346724*

- In the United Kingdom, while real house prices increased in the year up to the second quarter of 2010, several recent signs point to renewed weaknesses in the housing market. Survey indicators of price expectations from the Royal Institute of Chartered Surveyors have slipped markedly in recent months, signs of increasing instructions to sell have emerged and several recent monthly house price indices point to falling house prices. Possibly underlying these renewed signs of weakness are expectations of slowing economic activity and income and thus housing demand.

- Ireland and Spain were among the countries experiencing the most pronounced housing boom-and-bust cycle and are still in the process of downward corrections. Real house prices, as well as ratios of house prices to rents and income continue to fall from historically high levels. Strong fiscal consolidation measures are likely to put a further drag on already weak income growth and thus housing demand. In Spain, housing permits continue to decline, and housing investment remains elevated relative to GDP compared to previous troughs, suggesting further likely downward adjustments. In Ireland, renewed financial market stress due to ongoing concerns about the health of the banking system may lead to a renewed tightening of credit conditions. In addition, recent signs of increased net outward migration from Ireland may weaken housing demand further.

One approach to gauge the eventual magnitude of the impact of possible further negative demand shocks on housing prices and new housing supply is to use estimated long-run supply and demand (semi-) elasticities.[2] On the basis of the country-specific elasticities reported by Caldera Sànchez and Johansson (2010), holding all other factors constant (including housing supply), a negative income shock of about 1% would eventually decrease house prices by 3.5% in the United Kingdom. The impact would also be more than proportional in Spain (1.6%). In the United States and Ireland, prices would decrease slightly less than proportionally by 0.8% and 0.6% respectively. In contrast, a tightening of financial conditions would hit the Irish housing market particularly hard: a 2 percentage point increase in interest rates would eventually, all else equal, reduce prices by about 3% in Ireland, while the effect would be smaller in the United States (2%), Spain (1%) and the United Kingdom (0.5%).

Box 1.2. **Housing market developments** (*cont.*)

However, such price responses to demand shocks would trigger supply responses that would vary widely across countries (see figure). For example, a 6% decrease in real house prices (which roughly corresponds to the magnitude of price declines in the United States and Spain over the year to the second quarter of 2010), would, if long-lasting, be expected to translate into a 12% decline in housing investment in the United States. The same price decrease would trigger smaller investment declines of about 4%, 2.7% and 2.4% in Ireland, Spain and the United Kingdom, respectively. These calibrated effects suggest that if a further, long-lasting, negative demand shock in the housing market occurred, much of the adjustment required to bring demand and supply back into line could come from the supply side in the United States. In contrast, in the other countries discussed here, adjustments would have to come through larger price decreases stimulating housing demand, although this would be likely to have a negative impact on private consumption *via* adverse balance-sheet effects. It should be underlined, however, that the calibrations are based on observed past behaviour which may not be fully replicated in current housing market conditions with unusually low levels of housing investment.

Price responsiveness of housing supply: selected countries

Estimates of the long-run price-elasticity of new housing supply[1]

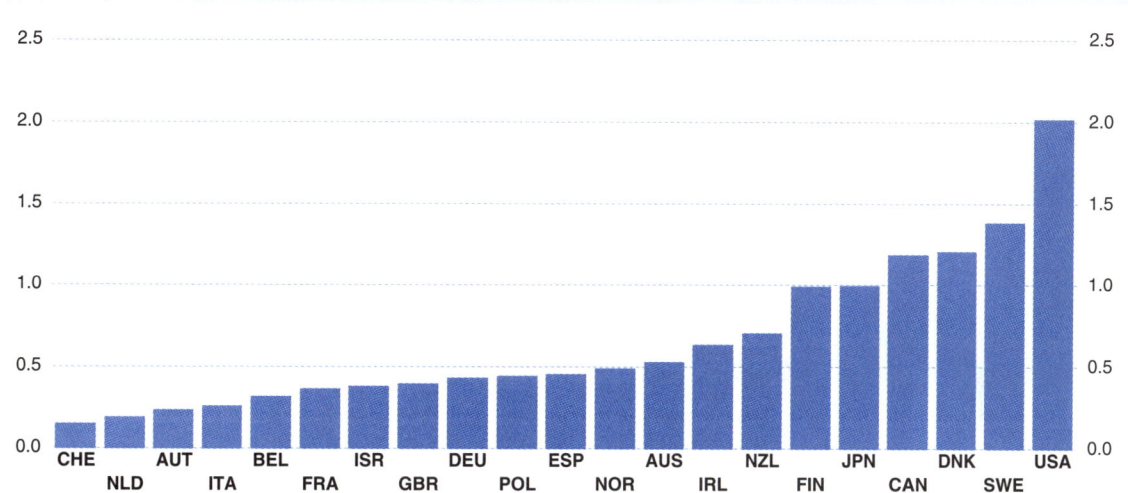

1. Estimates of the long-run price elasticity of new housing supply where new supply is measured by residential investments (*i.e.* the coefficient on lagged prices in a long-run investment equation). All elasticities are significant at least at the 10% level. In the case of Spain, restricting the sample to the period 1995-2007, which would reflect recent developments in housing markets (such as the large stock of unsold houses resulting from the construction boom starting in 2000 and peaking in 2007-09), only slightly increases the estimate of the elasticity of housing supply from 0.45 to 0.58. Estimation period early 1980s to early/mid-2000s. See Caldera Sánchez and Johansson (2010) for details.

Source: OECD estimates.

StatLink ⟶ http://dx.doi.org/10.1787/888932345147

1. A similar picture emerges for the aggregate of G7 countries with respect to housing investment and house prices when previous recessions are compared with the latest one.
2. Some evidence suggests that house prices may have not yet completely adjusted to values justified by longer-term fundamental house price determinants in Spain, the United States, the United Kingdom (see EC, 2010) and the euro area (Gattini and Hiebert, 2010). This would imply that prices would have to fall further than suggested by the simple simulations conducted here.

Table 1.2. **Real house prices remain fragile in some countries**

	Per cent annual rate of change				Level relative to long-term average [1]		
	2001-2007	2008	2009 [2]	Latest quarter [3]	Price-to-rent ratio	Price-to-income ratio	Latest available quarter
United States	4.5	-6.2	-4.1	-6.7	109	93	Q2 2010
Japan	-3.4	-2.0	-1.7	-2.0	64	66	Q1 2010
Germany	-2.5	-0.7	-1.0	-1.9	74	72	Q4 2009
France	9.5	-1.6	-6.7	4.7	138	131	Q2 2010
Italy	5.4	-1.4	-3.5	-3.9	108	126	Q1 2010
United Kingdom	8.6	-3.9	-9.0	4.7	144	137	Q2 2010
Canada	8.4	-2.8	4.0	7.9	156	131	Q2 2010
Australia	7.8	0.7	0.3	13.2	163	150	Q2 2010
Belgium	6.8	1.6	0.1	3.1	163	153	Q2 2010
Denmark	7.9	-7.4	-13.2	0.6	128	133	Q2 2010
Finland	5.6	-2.8	-0.8	9.1	139	109	Q2 2010
Ireland	5.4	-11.6	-10.0	-14.8	120	93	Q2 2010
Korea	4.4	-0.5	-2.3	0.8	110	67	Q2 2010
Netherlands	2.4	1.5	-2.7	-3.6	139	148	Q2 2010
Norway	6.8	-4.5	-0.6	7.7	157	131	Q2 2010
New Zealand	11.6	-7.7	-4.0	2.3	156	159	Q2 2010
Spain	10.5	-3.2	-7.7	-5.6	138	126	Q2 2010
Sweden	7.6	0.4	-0.3	7.7	144	133	Q2 2010
Switzerland	1.7	0.0	5.5	4.0	90	93	Q2 2010
Euro area [4,5]	4.5	-1.4	-3.9	-1.3	114	112	
Total of above countries [5]	3.9	-3.6	-3.4	-2.3	107	98	

Note: House prices deflated by the private consumption deflator.
1. Average from 1980 (or earliest available date) on = 100, latest quarter available.
2. Average of available quarters where full year is not yet complete.
3. Increase over a year earlier to the latest available quarter.
4. Germany, France, Italy, Spain, Finland, Ireland and the Netherlands.
5. Using 2005 GDP weights, calculated using latest country data available.
Source: Girouard *et al.* (2006); and OECD.

StatLink ᴍᴤᴘ *http://dx.doi.org/10.1787/888932346629*

third quarter of 2010, and total employment has started to edge up. Labour market developments in Germany continue to be stronger than in most other countries, with unemployment continuing to decline, alongside job growth, thanks to labour market reforms over the past decade. Nonetheless, considerable slack remains in OECD-wide labour markets, with the unemployment rate in the third quarter over 2½ percentage points higher than at the onset of the crisis (Figure 1.9) and comparatively weak hiring intentions in business surveys.

... but employment growth is unlikely to be strong

With economic growth picking up only modestly, prospects for strong employment growth appear limited (Table 1.3), especially given the scope in many economies, notably Japan and some European economies, to meet increases in output by raising cyclically-low working hours and productivity. The OECD-wide unemployment rate is projected to decline

Figure 1.9. **Unemployment rates remain high**
Percentage of labour force

Unemployment and estimated NAIRU in the OECD area

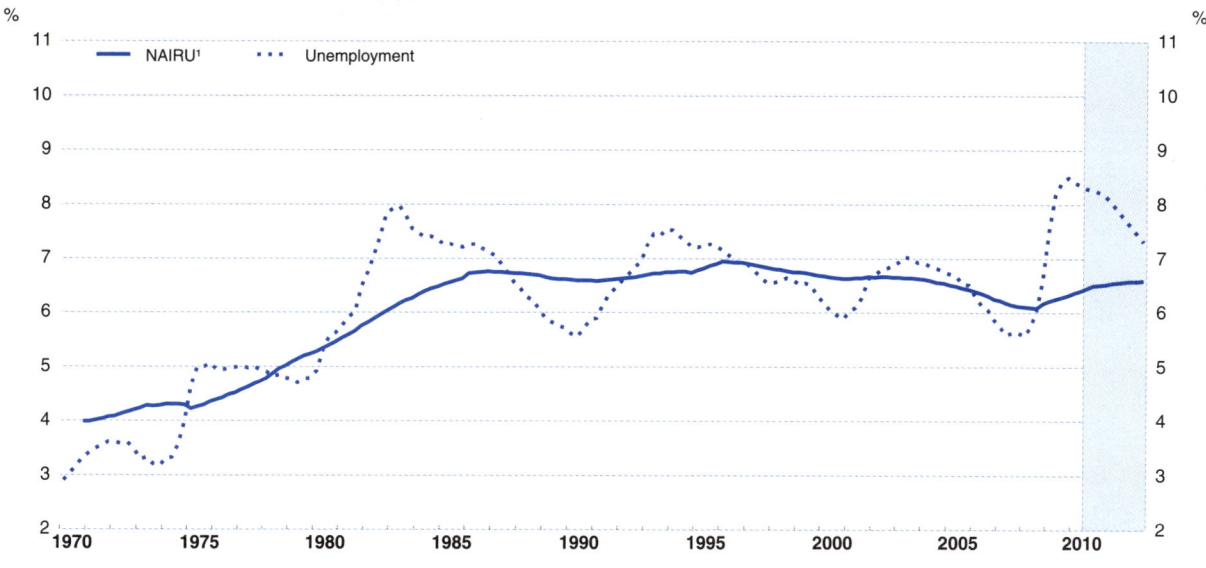

Unemployment in the three main regions

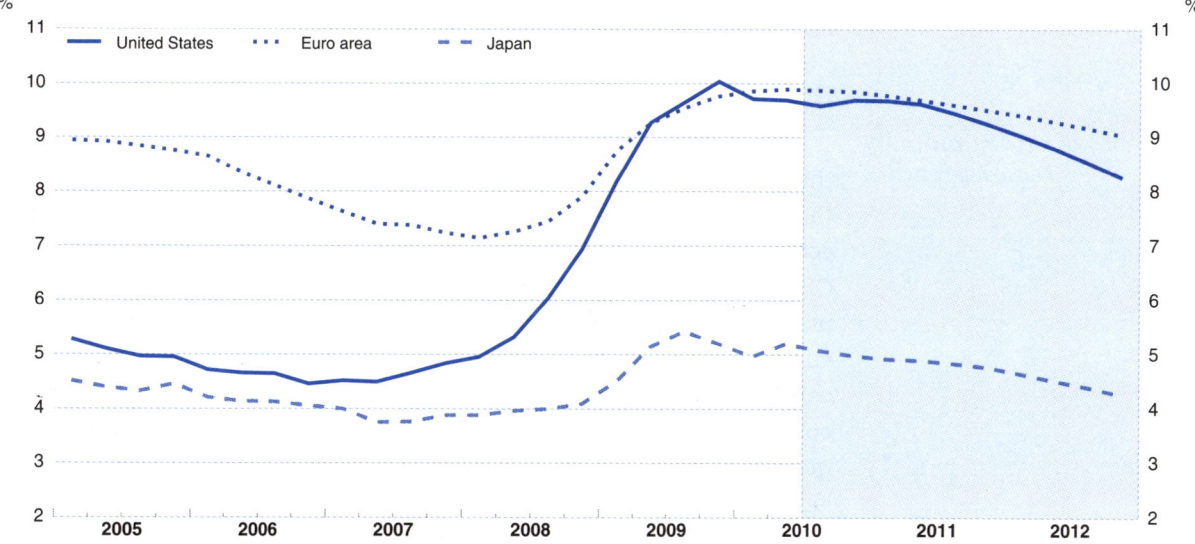

1. NAIRU is based on OECD Secretariat estimates.
Source: OECD Economic Outlook 88 database.

StatLink ⟨ᵃᵐˢᴸ⟩ *http://dx.doi.org/10.1787/888932345166*

to just above 7¼ per cent by the end of 2012, a rate which would still leave considerable labour market slack, damping wage pressures. A key policy challenge will be to minimise the transformation of cyclical into structural unemployment, especially in countries, such as the United States, where there has been an exceptionally large rise in unemployment in a context of a long-run downward trend in the outflow rate from unemployment

Table 1.3. **Labour market conditions will improve slowly**

	2007	2008	2009	2010	2011	2012
	Percentage change from previous period					
Employment						
United States	1.1	-0.5	-3.8	-0.5	1.2	1.6
Japan	0.5	-0.4	-1.6	-0.4	0.1	-0.3
Euro area	1.8	1.0	-1.8	-0.5	0.3	0.6
OECD	1.5	0.6	-1.8	0.3	1.0	1.1
Labour force						
United States	1.1	0.8	-0.1	-0.1	1.0	0.6
Japan	0.2	-0.3	-0.5	-0.4	-0.2	-0.8
Euro area	0.9	1.0	0.3	0.1	0.1	0.1
OECD	1.0	1.0	0.5	0.5	0.7	0.5
Unemployment rate	Per cent of labour force					
United States	4.6	5.8	9.3	9.7	9.5	8.7
Japan	3.8	4.0	5.1	5.1	4.9	4.5
Euro area	7.4	7.4	9.3	9.9	9.6	9.2
OECD	5.7	6.0	8.1	8.3	8.1	7.5

Source: OECD Economic Outlook 88 database.

StatLink ꜛ http://dx.doi.org/10.1787/888932346648

(Elsby *et al.*, 2010). Structural labour market policies will have an important role to play in this regard, as discussed further below.

Growth prospects

Growth is set to gradually gather pace...

Output growth was relatively subdued in the OECD economies in the third quarter, and growth was also weaker in the non-OECD economies than earlier in the recovery. Looking ahead, the soft patch in the global economy is expected to prove only temporary, with growth in the non-OECD economies and, more hesitantly, in the OECD economies gradually picking up from the start of next year (Figure 1.10), provided that policy stimulus is withdrawn in a gradual manner (Box 1.3), and that financial conditions remain favourable. Accommodative monetary policies should continue to support growth throughout the projection period but necessary fiscal consolidation and continued headwinds from the legacies of the recession, including ongoing balance-sheet adjustment and weak labour markets, will allow only a moderate upturn.

The key features of the economic outlook for major economies and world trade are as follows:

... in the United States...

● Growth in the United States is expected to remain subdued until the end of 2010 before slowly gaining momentum through 2011-12, despite being damped by substantial fiscal consolidation over this period. Strong corporate profits, lagged effects from past improvements in aggregate financial conditions, and normal cyclical forces will all help equipment investment to remain robust, with housing and commercial property investment picking up more gradually once excess supply diminishes in property markets. Ongoing balance-sheet adjustment is

Figure 1.10. **Global growth continues be led by the non-OECD economies**

Contribution to annualised quarterly world real GDP growth

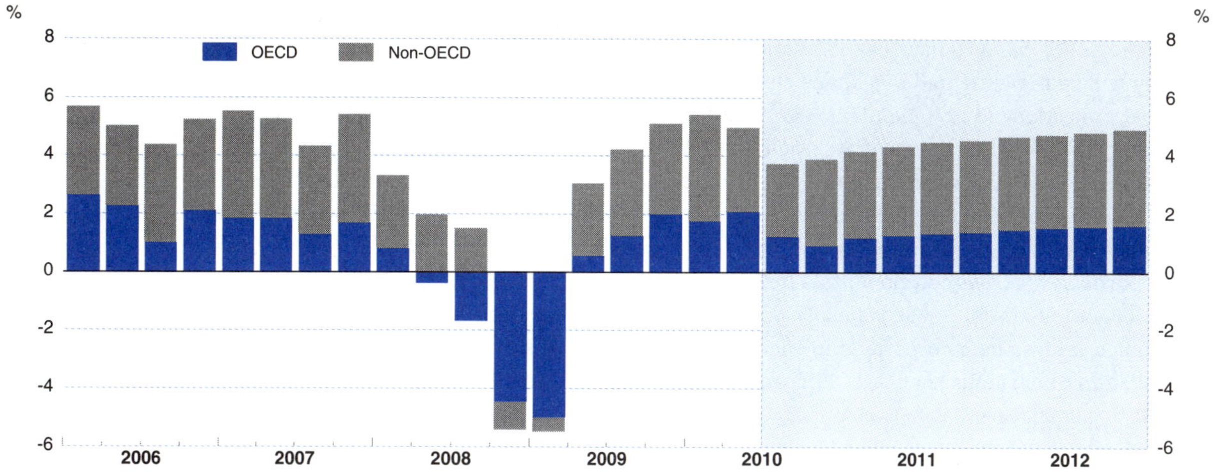

Note: Calculated using moving nominal GDP weights, based on national GDP at purchasing power parities.
Source: OECD Economic Outlook 88 database.

StatLink ⬛⬛⬛ http://dx.doi.org/10.1787/888932345185

likely to keep the household saving rate at or just above its current level, but private consumption growth should be helped by gradual improvements in labour market conditions. Despite a pick-up in employment growth, the unemployment rate is projected to remain elevated, declining only to around 8¼ per cent by the end of 2012, implying that marked economic slack will persist for some time.

... Japan... ● Growth picked up in the third quarter in Japan, with private consumption brought forward to benefit from time-limited tax incentives. This will likely weaken consumption in the coming months. But the new fiscal packages announced in the autumn should help to support activity through to the first quarter of 2011. Thereafter, output growth is projected to be more modest, reflecting *inter alia* softer external demand, in part due to the appreciation of the real exchange rate. Continued improvements in labour market conditions and strong corporate profitability should help to support domestic demand, although public spending is likely to decline from mid-2011. The unemployment rate is expected to decline gently over the projection period, but will remain above its pre-crisis level.

... and the euro area ● In the euro area, domestic demand is expected to strengthen gradually over the projection period, helped by accommodative monetary policy, strong corporate profits and past improvements in financial conditions, but the pace of the upturn will be damped by fiscal consolidation and ongoing balance-sheet adjustments in the private sector. Area-wide government demand is expected to decline consistently from the start of 2011 onwards. Labour market conditions are likely to improve slowly, with ongoing employment growth and the unemployment rate edging

Box 1.3. **Policy and other assumptions underlying the projections**

Fiscal policy assumptions for 2011 are based as closely as possible on legislated tax and spending provisions. Where policy changes have been announced but not legislated, they are incorporated if it is deemed clear that they will be implemented in a shape close to that announced. Where government plans are available for 2012, fiscal projections follow the plans. Otherwise, in countries with impaired public finances, a tightening of the underlying primary balance of at least 1% of GDP in 2012 has been built into the projections. The tightening is assumed to be larger for countries in serious fiscal problems and facing market pressure, and smaller for countries in more comfortable positions. Where there is insufficient information to determine the allocation of budget cuts, the presumption is that they apply equally to the spending and revenue sides, and are spread proportionally across components. These conventions, which differ from the practice in previous OECD fiscal projections, allow for needed consolidation in countries where plans have not been announced at a sufficiently detailed level to be incorporated in the projections. Along this line, the following assumptions were adopted (with additional adjustments if OECD and government projections for economic activity differ):

- For the United States, fiscal policy follows the Administration's proposed budget in the August 2010 Mid-Session Review.

- For Japan, the projections include the stimulus packages announced in September and October, with half of the outlays in the latter being spent in fiscal year 2010. Government expenditure in 2011-12 is limited in line with the Fiscal Management Plan announced in June 2010.

- For Germany, the government's medium-term consolidation programme, announced in September 2010, as well as the phasing out of the temporary components of the fiscal stimulus packages has been built into the projections. For France, the projections incorporate the government's medium-term consolidation programme. For Italy, the projections incorporate the measures announced in the 2011 budget legislation. For the United Kingdom, the projections are based on tax measures and spending paths set in the June 2010 budget.

Policy-controlled interest rates are set in line with the stated objectives of the relevant monetary authorities, conditional upon the OECD projections of activity and inflation, which may differ from those of the monetary authorities. The interest rate profile is not to be interpreted as a projection of central bank intentions or market expectations thereof.

- In the United States, the target federal funds rate is assumed to remain constant at ¼ per cent until mid-2011, as the economic recovery is relatively weak and inflationary pressure is likely to remain subdued. The programme of quantitative easing is assumed to be implemented as announced. Subsequently, and in order to re-establish the normal functioning of money markets and limit adverse effects of near-zero rates, the Federal Funds rate is raised, reaching 1% by the end of 2011. Once the recovery is projected to be more firmly established, around the middle of 2012, the policy rate is assumed to rise again so as to reach just over 2% by the fourth quarter of 2012.

- In the euro area, against the background of well anchored inflation expectations, the refinancing rate is assumed to remain at the current level until the first quarter of 2012, after which it rises to 2% by the end of the projection period.

- In Japan, the short-term policy interest rate is assumed to remain at 10 basis points for the entire projection horizon, as consumer prices continue to fall.

The projections assume unchanged exchange rates from those prevailing on 26 October 2010: $ 1 equals ¥ 81.39, € 0.72 (or equivalently, € 1 equals $ 1.39) and CNY 6.66.

Over the projection period, the price of a barrel of Brent crude oil is assumed to be at a level close to $ 80. Non-oil commodity prices are assumed to stabilise around current levels.

The cut-off date for information used in the projections is 12 November 2010. Details of assumptions for individual countries are provided in Chapter 2 and Chapter 3.

down over 2011-12 by just under 1 percentage point. This should help to support private consumption, which is likely to be further boosted by a moderation in the saving rate. The recovery is expected to remain uneven, with growth being more robust in the core economies than in those at the periphery, where sizable fiscal consolidation is needed, and, in some cases, is combined with a need for strong private-sector balance sheet repair.

And remain robust in the non-OECD area...

- In China, output growth is projected to remain robust, averaging 9¾ per cent over 2011-12. Domestic demand is expected to remain strong, with private consumption growth supported by tightening labour markets and a reorientation of public spending to meet social objectives, but net trade should be a drag on growth. In India, the recent moderation in activity is expected to prove only temporary. Helped both by strong investment and consumption, output growth is projected to reach its trend growth rate of around 8½ per cent from mid-2011. In Brazil, domestic demand is set to rebound by year-end. Solid economic growth is projected over the next couple of years, helped by large public infrastructure and energy development programmes, despite some modest drag from declines in net exports and ongoing policy normalisation. In Russia, activity growth is projected to rebound from the weather-affected third quarter this year, and remain at a pace slightly above potential through 2011 and 2012, even as policy normalisation gets underway.

... with solid global trade growth

- The moderation in trade volume growth in the latter half of this year has taken the rate down towards historical norms. With global activity projected to pick up from the start of 2011, trade growth is expected to remain solid, averaging just over 8% over 2011-12, remaining especially strong in many Asian economies and Brazil (Table 1.4).

Core inflation is continuing to moderate...

In recent months the annual rate of headline inflation has picked up somewhat in most major OECD economies, reflecting the firming in global commodity prices and, in some countries, price-level adjustment following indirect tax increases (Figure 1.11). Although oil prices remained broadly constant in the six months to late October, non-oil commodity prices rose by close to 20% during this period. But core inflation rates, abstracting from the direct effects of food and energy price inflation, and statistical measures of underlying inflation have generally continued to moderate, albeit relatively gently considering the considerable economic slack that remains in labour and product markets. The annual rate of core (private consumers' expenditure, PCE) inflation has dropped to around 1¼ per cent in the United States this year, and, in the euro area the core inflation rate has been at or below 1% since the start of the year. In Japan, the annual rate of deflation continues to be close to an underlying rate of 1%. Higher-frequency estimates of core or underlying inflation point to continued

Table 1.4. **World trade remains robust and imbalances will widen gradually**

	2008	2009	2010	2011	2012
Goods and services trade volume	Percentage change from previous period				
World trade[1]	3.1	-11.1	12.3	8.3	8.1
of which: OECD	1.2	-12.2	11.4	7.3	7.0
OECD America	0.7	-12.8	13.5	8.5	8.5
OECD Asia-Pacific	3.4	-13.0	16.0	8.9	9.0
OECD Europe	1.0	-11.8	9.5	6.4	5.8
China	6.5	-4.0	25.8	13.5	13.3
Other industrialised Asia[2]	6.7	-10.3	18.0	10.2	9.9
Russia	7.0	-17.1	8.9	8.3	7.0
Brazil	8.4	-11.0	21.3	8.0	12.0
Other oil producers	8.2	-6.4	2.9	8.0	8.4
Rest of the world	7.4	-10.9	0.7	7.3	7.4
OECD exports	2.0	-11.8	11.3	7.2	7.2
OECD imports	0.5	-12.6	11.2	7.3	6.6
Trade prices[3]					
OECD exports	9.1	-9.0	3.0	4.7	1.0
OECD imports	11.1	-11.1	3.9	4.3	1.2
Non-OECD exports	14.9	-13.7	10.4	3.8	1.7
Non-OECD imports	11.8	-9.7	8.0	3.6	1.6
Current account balances	Per cent of GDP				
United States	-4.7	-2.7	-3.4	-3.7	-3.7
Japan	3.3	2.8	3.4	3.7	3.7
Euro area	-0.8	-0.4	-0.2	0.3	0.9
OECD	-1.5	-0.5	-0.7	-0.7	-0.5
China	9.6	6.0	5.8	5.9	5.5
	$ billion				
United States	-669	-378	-496	-559	-587
Japan	157	142	191	219	221
Euro area	-100	-43	-26	42	121
OECD	-671	-220	-316	-304	-257
China	436	297	340	396	421
Other industrialised Asia[2]	95	135	69	65	60
Russia	102	49	84	59	49
Brazil	-28	-24	-53	-76	-107
Other oil producers	497	92	313	358	384
Rest of the world	-194	-85	-3	-1	-6
Non-OECD	907	464	750	801	801
World	237	244	434	497	544

Note: Regional aggregates include intra-regional trade.
1. Growth rates of the arithmetic average of import volumes and export volumes.
2. Chinese Taipei; Hong Kong, China; Malaysia; Philippines; Singapore; Vietnam; Thailand; India and Indonesia.
3. Average unit values in dollars.
Source: OECD Economic Outlook 88 database.

StatLink ⟪ *http://dx.doi.org/10.1787/888932346667*

disinflationary pressures in the United States and Japan, with the annualised rate of inflation over three and six-month periods being below annual rates. Labour-cost pressures presently remain minimal. Unit labour costs have fallen especially sharply in the United States and, more recently, in Japan and the euro area, helped by higher labour productivity growth and continued wage moderation. A moderate pick-

Figure 1.11. **Underlying inflation is set to remain subdued**

12-month percentage change

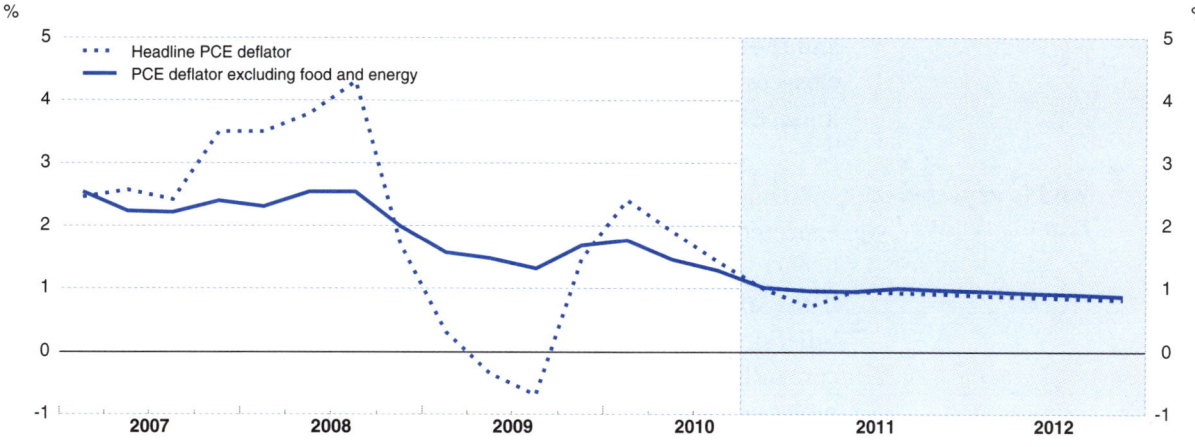

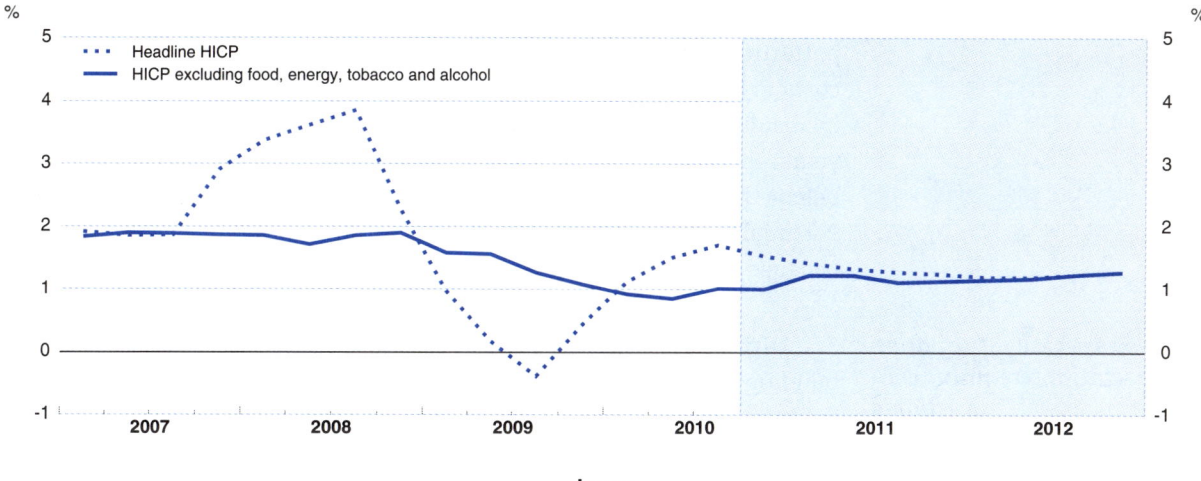

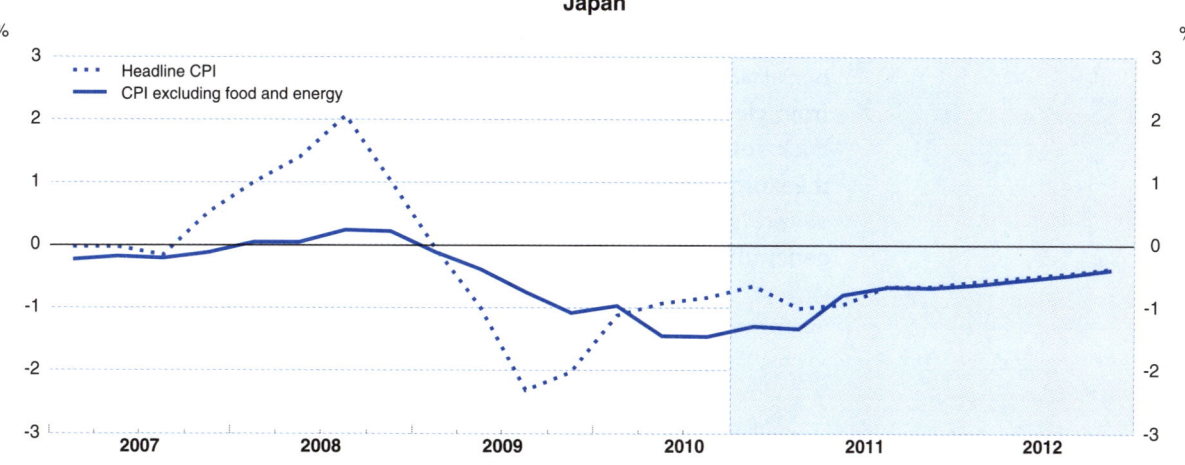

Note: PCE deflator refers to the deflator of personal consumption expenditures, HICP to the harmonised index of consumer prices and CPI to the consumer price index.

Source: OECD Economic Outlook 88 database.

StatLink ⟨⟨⟨ http://dx.doi.org/10.1787/888932345204

up in private sector wage inflation in the euro area is projected to occur from 2011, but with ongoing productivity growth and public sector wage restraint in several countries, economy-wide unit labour cost growth should be minimal. Outside the OECD area, rising food prices, and the increasing extent to which many economies are now operating close to full capacity, have generated some inflationary pressures in India, China and Brazil.

... and is expected to remain subdued...

Ongoing economic slack, although difficult to measure precisely, is expected to diminish only slowly through the projection period and is likely to continue to bear down on inflation for some time to come, even if the effect of persistent large output gaps appears to diminish as inflation eases (Meier, 2010).[3] In the United States, the annual rate of core inflation is projected to drift down to average just below 1% over the projection period. Deflation is expected to persist in Japan, although at a slowly diminishing pace over the projection period. In the euro area, core inflation is expected to edge up towards 1¼ per cent in 2011-12, due largely to higher profit margins. A gradual reversal of past cost inflation patterns is expected within the euro area; economy-wide unit labour costs in Ireland, Spain, Portugal and Greece are projected to decline, both in absolute terms and relative to the euro area average over the next two years. Price inflation in Spain and Ireland is also projected to be at or below the euro area average over 2011-12. In contrast, in Greece and Portugal, price inflation is expected to remain more elevated, in part because of higher indirect taxes.

... especially if inflation expectations remain well-anchored

Ultimately, the likelihood of widespread deflationary pressures building up throughout the OECD area should be contained if longer-term inflation expectations remain well anchored. At present, inflation expectations remain relatively close to explicit or implicit inflation objectives of monetary authorities in most economies, suggesting that weak, but positive, inflation remains the most likely outcome over the next two years. Measures of longer-term inflation expectations derived from yield differences between nominal and indexed bonds have slipped back somewhat in recent months, but that could partly reflect a mis-measurement due to a flight to more liquid nominal bonds during the sovereign debt turmoil. Survey-based expectations measures have generally been somewhat more stable.

3. Recent estimates for the United States suggest that the projected gap between the unemployment rate and its minimum value over the previous three years might reduce core inflation by at least 0.5 percentage point, and possibly up to 1 percentage point between mid-2010 and mid-2011 (Stock and Watson, 2010), which would result in an extremely low, but still positive, inflation rate.

External imbalances have started to widen in some economies

The early stages of the recovery have seen measured global imbalances begin to widen once more, with an increase in underlying deficits and surpluses.[4] Imbalances are projected to remain wide and in some cases increase through the course of 2011 and 2012 (Figure 1.12). The US current account deficit rose by ½ percentage point of GDP over the year to mid-2010 and could increase by a ¼ percentage point over the next two years. Whilst the sizable current account surplus of Japan is projected to remain stable in 2011 and 2012, that of Germany is projected to rise, helped by the relative exposure of domestic exporters to fast-growing Asian markets. Most traditional euro-area deficit countries are set to experience improvements in their external account that exceed those in traditional surplus countries. External surpluses of the major non-OECD oil-producing economies, already bolstered by the firmness of oil prices in 2010, are also set to increase in the coming years. By contrast, the Chinese current account surplus, which was already lower in the first half of 2010 than in 2009, is expected to show a further slight decline over the next two years, helped by buoyant domestic demand growth.

Figure 1.12. **Global imbalances will remain pronounced**

Current account balance, in per cent of GDP

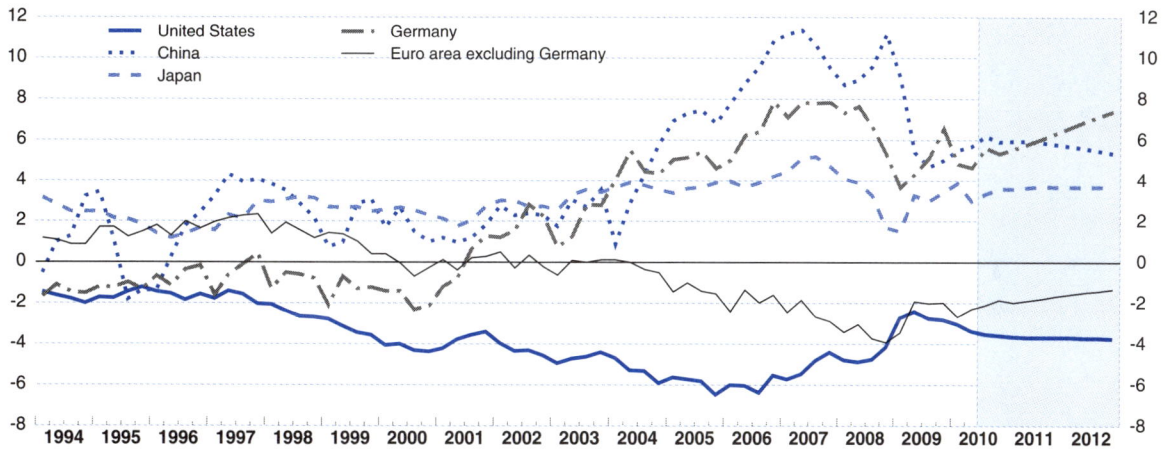

Source: OECD Economic Outlook 88 database.

StatLink http://dx.doi.org/10.1787/888932345223

Risks are deeper on the downside and include...

The short-term risks around the projection remain considerable. It remains possible that the underlying momentum of the recovery in the OECD economy could pick up more markedly than thought after the current soft patch, but the risks are deeper on the downside. Such risks are largely associated with the possibility of interactions between particular events and existing fragilities that could prompt a new period of sustained weakness in private-sector activity. Many of the fragilities that

4. Underlying (cyclically-adjusted) trade balances in the major OECD economies (Cheung et al., 2010) are estimated to have widened somewhat this year, with an increase in the surplus in Japan and the euro area and a slight rise in the US structural deficit.

remain stem from the continued legacies of the recession and the boom that preceded it. At present, key risks include:

... intensified concerns about sovereign debt...

- An adverse feedback loop between the government and financial sectors could materialise if intensified concerns about sovereign debt in fiscally weak countries led to new losses for banks. Even if the European sovereign debt turmoil abated with the establishment of temporary support facilities, interest rate spreads have widened more recently in Greece, Ireland and Portugal, though without unsettling interbank and foreign exchange markets. However, a risk remains of sovereign-debt stress becoming more widespread and having more systemic consequences. More generally, a loss of confidence in the ability of governments to arrest unsustainable fiscal positions would give rise to corresponding losses in financial institutions as bond yields increase. Such a development could have further international ramifications and could destabilise the global financial system if a large country was involved and its banks reacted by repatriating funds from their foreign subsidiaries.

... an abrupt reversal in bond yields...

- A broader risk relates to the very low levels of long-term interest rates in major OECD economies. The current levels of long-term rates are difficult to reconcile with the projection of a mild but sustained recovery (see Box 1.4). The present set of projections reflects an assumption that long-term interest rates revert gradually to historical norms over the medium term. However, historical experience suggests that the adjustment could occur more abruptly. A rapid unanticipated increase in long-term interest rates could weaken the recovery through its direct effects on investment. As a possible order of magnitude, simulations on the OECD Global Model (Hervé *et al.*, 2010) indicate that the impact of a simultaneous 100 basis points increase in bond yields in all countries could be to reduce output growth by around ½ percentage point in both the first and second years of the increase. An abrupt backup in yields could also threaten the recovery indirectly, *via* its effects on the financial sector, because the associated declines in bond prices would confront banks and other investors with a new wave of losses.

... continued pressures on banks...

- Specific risks continue to emanate from banks. A number of fiscally weak euro area countries have banking sectors that are still highly dependent on liquidity support from the ECB (Figure 1.13). If these banks cannot regain market confidence in the coming quarters, they may experience funding difficulties when, as expected, the ECB stops its exceptional liquidity facilities because they become inappropriate for the needs of the euro area financial sector as a whole. Another risk coming from the banking sector is the possibility that, instead of adapting gradually to the new capital standards with few adverse effects on economic growth (see below and Box 1.6), banks engage in a race to reach the new standards by either compressing balance sheets, and thereby credit, or by issuing shares, pushing up the cost of equity for the broader economy.

Box 1.4. **Risks associated with current low bond yields**

Government bond yields have fallen to very low levels in major OECD economies, stoking fears of a bubble that could burst with serious consequences for financial stability, government finances and the economy more generally (see first figure). In Germany, long-term interest rates have fallen to their lowest level in more than fifty years. In the United States, they are very close to their historical lows of December 2008-January 2009. This fall has occurred even for the euro area benchmark bond, where the decrease in German, French and Dutch long-term interest rates since the beginning of the year has more than offset the increase in credit spreads in fiscally-weaker members of the currency union.

Yields on long-term government bonds
Last observation: 12 November 2010

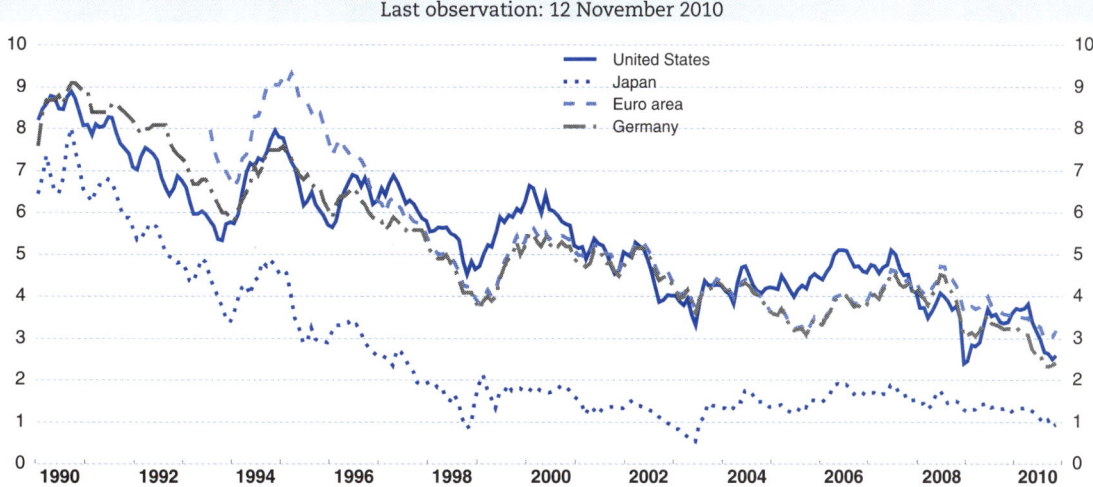

Source: Datastream.

StatLink 🔗 http://dx.doi.org/10.1787/888932345242

Yields on long-term government bonds issued by the major OECD economies are well below the average assumed level of short-term interest rates over the next ten years underpinning the OECD projection and its long-term extension (see Chapter 4 and second figure).[1] Prima facie, this configuration goes against the normal pricing of long-term bonds, which should remunerate investors above expected average short-term rates so as to compensate them for their exposure to interest rate risk. Indeed, the outlook for public debt could be expected to raise bond yields given the need to fund very large government deficits and the increase in the credit risk of sovereign issuers.

One factor behind the discrepancy might be that markets anticipate a lower path of short-term interest rates over the next ten years than that assumed in the projections. Interest rate swaps, which value market expectations of average money-market rates, point in this direction, as they lie well below the average of assumed short-term rates underpinning the projections (see second figure).[2] This difference could reflect expectations in financial markets of much weaker inherent growth dynamics than in the OECD short and longer-term projections, thus justifying persistent low policy interest rates to achieve convergence of output to potential and return inflation to objectives. However, it is also conceivable that market expectations reflect anticipation that pre-crisis interest-rate setting behaviour will continue, including the severe downward deviation in the past decade by some major OECD central banks from the levels of interest rates prescribed by simple rules. In contrast, the present projection is based on the assumption that past deviations, which contributed to the credit bubble, will not be repeated.[3]

Box 1.4. **Risks associated with current low bond yields** (*cont.*)

Government bond yields *vs.* future short rates

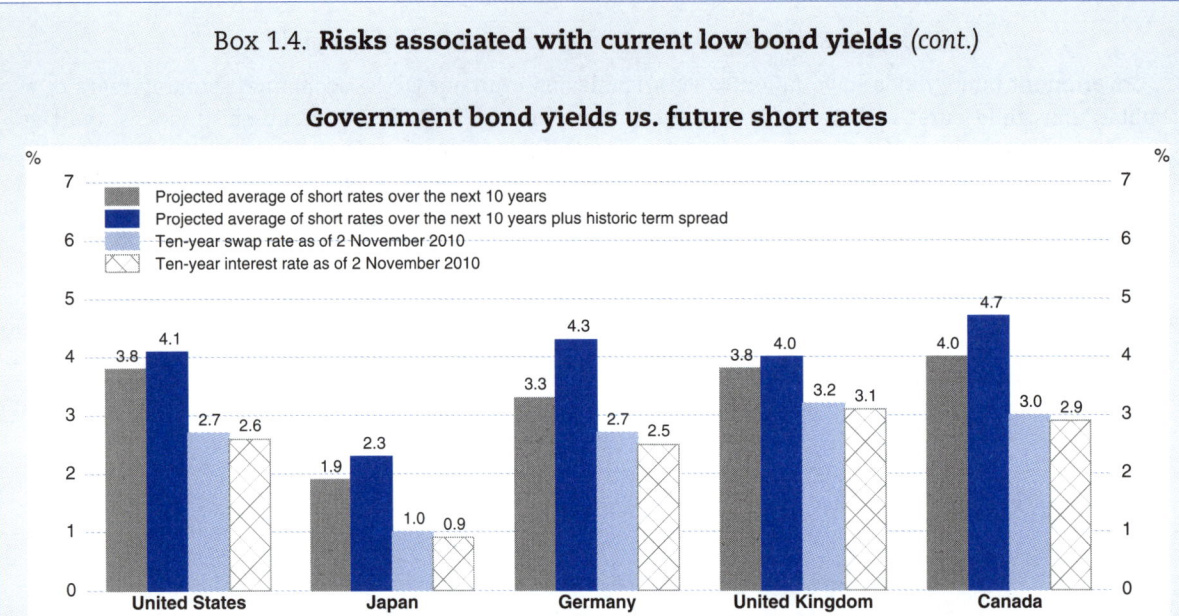

Source: Datastream, OECD Economic Outlook 88 database and OECD calculations.

StatLink http://dx.doi.org/10.1787/888932345261

The sovereign debt crisis that has hit a number of euro area countries is also likely to have contributed to the reduction of interest rates in the main countries as investors sought to rebalance their portfolio in favour of government bonds seen as having lower credit and liquidity risk. Resolution of sovereign-debt problems, or just anticipation thereof, should lead to a diminution of this effect.

Quantitative easing is another possible driving force behind the current low levels of interest rates. The Federal Reserve and the Bank of England have purchased large amounts of bonds issued or guaranteed by the government with the aim of reducing yields and easing financial conditions. There are large differences in the estimated effect of these policies. Work conducted at the US Federal Reserve and the Bank of England suggests that the impact has been large, in the 30-100bp range in the United States and close to 100bp in the United Kingdom (Doh, 2010; Gagnon *et al.*, 2010; Joyce *et al.*, 2010). Academic research, on the other hand, has found insignificant or small effects (Hamilton and Wu, 2010; Stroebel and Taylor, 2010).

Overall, it appears likely that the current levels of long-term interest rates are largely the result of expectations, in part shaped by quantitative easing, that the major central banks will keep short-term rates very low for an exceptionally long period of time. The present set of projections assumes that, as the recovery takes hold, these expectations will gradually adjust to reflect the likely subsequent normalisation of policy-controlled interest rates so that long-term interest rates will progressively become closer to the projected average of future short-term rates. The possibility of an abrupt adjustment, however, cannot be entirely excluded and represents a downside risk to the projection.

1. Beyond the projection period, short-term interest rates are assumed to converge gradually to their equilibrium level.
2. Even if interest rate swap rates are by design very tightly linked to expected future money market rates, they are also connected to government bond yields as any significant deviation between the two opens arbitrage opportunities.
3. See for instance Ahrend *et al.* (2009) and Taylor (2009) for a discussion of the link between market excess and downward deviations of policy-controlled interest rates from simple rules.

... net capital inflows to emerging markets and associated exchange rate tensions...

- Capital flows have risen sharply this year from countries with weak activity and accommodating monetary policies towards countries with more buoyant activity and less accommodating monetary policy, including emerging markets, especially in Asia and Latin America.

Figure 1.13. **Banks in some euro area countries have become dependent on central bank facilities**

Liquidity provided by the central banks as per cent of total assets of monetary and financial institutions

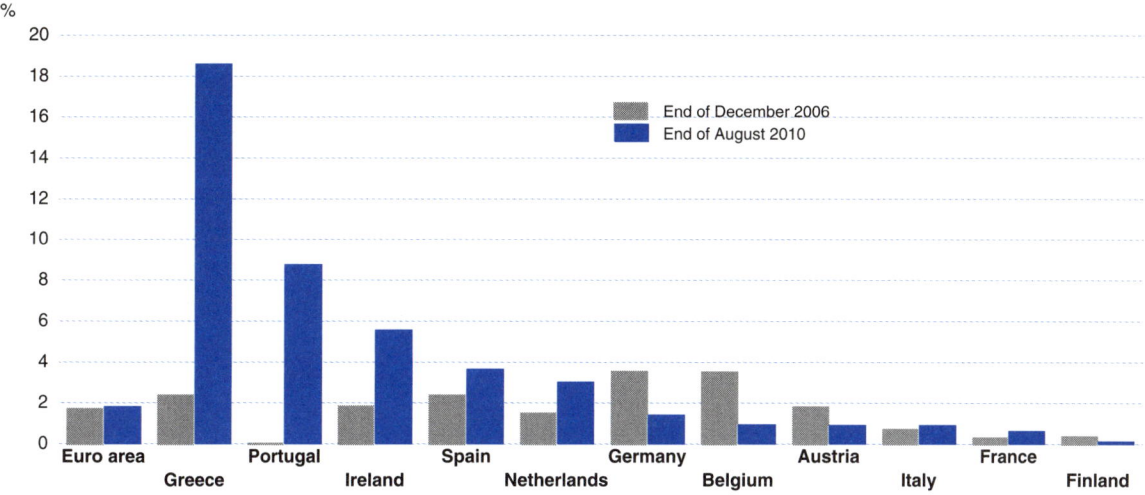

Source: ECB and respective national central banks.

StatLink http://dx.doi.org/10.1787/888932345280

Associated changes in real exchange rates or attempts to resist them may, however, trigger political tension. Given the potentially adverse growth effects from exchange rate movements in trading partners (Table 1.5), currency intervention, if seen to be motivated largely by aims of maintaining or strengthening competitiveness, may trigger retaliatory actions, including protectionist measures, with serious consequences for the world economy.

Table 1.5. **The activity effects of exchange rate depreciations**

Difference from baseline, percentage points

	US dollar depreciation[1]		Euro depreciation[2]		Yen depreciation[3]	
	Year		Year		Year	
	1	2	1	2	1	2
United States						
GDP growth	0.5	0.5	-0.1	-0.1	0.0	-0.1
Japan						
GDP growth	0.0	-0.2	0.0	-0.1	0.4	0.4
Euro area						
GDP growth	-0.2	-0.2	0.7	0.6	-0.1	-0.1

1. The US dollar falls by 10% against all currencies.
2. The euro falls by 10% against all currencies.
3. The yen falls by 10% against all currencies.
Source: Hervé *et al.,* (2010).

StatLink http://dx.doi.org/10.1787/888932346686

... and renewed house-price declines

- As mentioned above, renewed declines in nominal and real house prices cannot be excluded in some countries and have become a more acute risk in the United States and the United Kingdom due to weak sales and high inventories. Lower house prices would have a negative effect on household wealth and result in private consumption slowing further. Simulations on the OECD Global Model suggest that a 10% decline in US house prices would reduce US output growth by about 0.2% in 2011 and 0.4% in 2012, under the assumption of unchanged macroeconomic policies, with negative, though small, spillover effects onto other countries. An OECD-wide decline of 10% in house prices would have larger effects, reducing OECD GDP by 0.8% after two years, and consumer price inflation by around ¼ percentage point in both 2011 and 2012. The risk of stronger negative feedback loops between house prices, private-sector demand and financial sector weakness cannot be excluded, although they are not considered in the model simulations.

But there are also upside risks from business investment...

- On the upside, business investment could recover more strongly than projected from its current depressed level if high profits and improved cash-flow were to have the same impact on capital spending as in the past (Martinez-Carrascal and Ferrando, 2008). And, given its exceptional compression in the downturn, residential construction might also be stronger than anticipated, provided house prices do not weaken, though this would have only modest effects on GDP, given the historically low share of residential investment in most OECD economies.

... and from financial markets

- The financial sector is also a source of upside risk. For example, shares are priced at multiples of earnings that are below historical averages in some countries, implying a possibility of upward adjustment. Such a development would facilitate the balance-sheet adjustment of the private sector, possibly leading to a lower saving rate than in the current set of projections.

Policy responses and requirements

Crisis-related policies need to be normalised and structural reforms pursued

With the present soft patch in growth projected to be only temporary, policy decisions over the next years need to reflect two main challenges – the need for widespread normalisation of crisis-related policies and the need for reforms to strengthen future growth and employment prospects and the durability of the recovery. At the same time, policy needs to stand ready to react if risks such as those discussed above materialise. This comprises action on fiscal and monetary policies as well as financial and other structural reform.

Fiscal Policy

Fiscal deficits are falling but are set to remain high

Following record highs in 2009, the OECD area-wide fiscal deficit is expected to fall to around 6% of GDP in 2011 (Table 1.6), with reductions in almost all OECD countries. Announced consolidation measures are the

Table 1.6. **Fiscal positions will improve in coming years**

Per cent of GDP / Potential GDP

	2008	2009	2010	2011	2012
United States					
Actual balance	-6.3	-11.3	-10.5	-8.8	-6.8
Underlying balance[2]	-5.9	-8.8	-8.6	-7.6	-6.0
Underlying primary balance[2]	-4.2	-7.4	-7.0	-5.8	-3.9
Gross financial liabilities	71.1	84.4	92.8	98.5	101.4
Japan					
Actual balance	-2.1	-7.1	-7.7	-7.5	-7.3
Underlying balance[2]	-3.5	-5.7	-6.7	-6.4	-6.3
Underlying primary balance[2]	-2.6	-4.7	-5.5	-5.3	-4.7
Gross financial liabilities	173.9	192.8	198.4	204.2	210.2
Euro area					
Actual balance	-2.0	-6.2	-6.3	-4.6	-3.5
Underlying balance[2]	-2.1	-4.1	-3.9	-2.8	-2.2
Underlying primary balance[2]	0.6	-1.7	-1.4	-0.3	0.5
Gross financial liabilities	76.0	86.3	91.6	94.8	96.3
OECD[1]					
Actual balance	-3.3	-7.9	-7.6	-6.1	-4.7
Underlying balance[2]	-3.7	-6.2	-6.1	-5.2	-4.2
Underlying primary balance[2]	-2.0	-4.7	-4.4	-3.3	-2.1
Gross financial liabilities	79.1	90.6	96.9	100.7	102.8

Note: Actual balances and liabilities are in per cent of nominal GDP. Underlying balances are in per cent of potential GDP. The underlying primary balance is the underlying balance excluding the impact of the net debt interest payments.
1. Total OECD excludes Mexico and Turkey.
2. Fiscal balances adjusted for the cycle and for one-offs.
Source: OECD Economic Outlook 88 database.

StatLink http://dx.doi.org/10.1787/888932346705

main driver of deficit reductions, but cyclical factors are also projected to contribute, more than offsetting rising interest payments.[5] Public finances will continue to improve in 2012 on the basis of government announced plans and OECD assumptions about consolidation in that year (see below and Box 1.3) and the strengthening of cyclical positions. Nonetheless, though estimates are subject to considerable uncertainty, more than three-quarters of deficits are likely to be structural in 2012. The emergence of these large structural deficits reflects mainly the disappearance of the extraordinary revenue buoyancy prior to the crisis, the remaining parts of crisis-related stimulus measures, the impact of the crisis-induced reduction in the level of potential output, and the run-up in debt service payments. In the OECD as a whole, the ratio of gross government debt to GDP is set to continue rising, exceeding 100% by 2011 (Figure 1.14).

5. The decomposition of fiscal balances into underlying and cyclical components is based on potential output and output gap estimates along the lines described in *OECD Economic Outlook*, No. 85. Given the uncertainties about the impact of the crisis on potential output levels and growth in the recent past and the near future, estimates of structural and cyclical components of budget balances are particularly uncertain at present.

Figure 1.14. **Accumulated debt and evolution of underlying deficits**
% of GDP

Decomposition of the debt in 2012

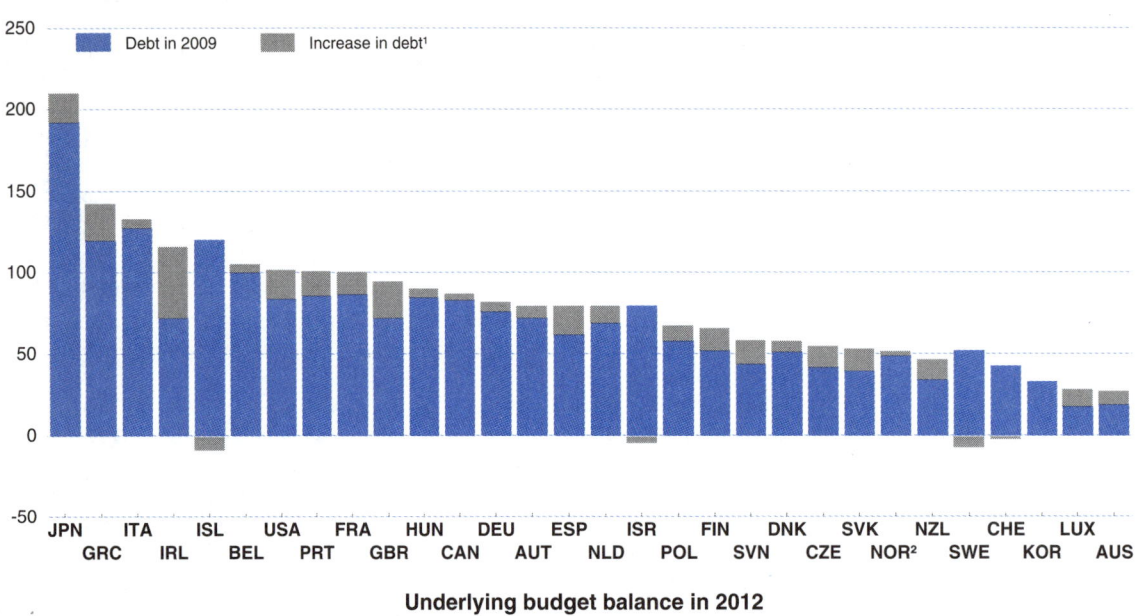

Underlying budget balance in 2012

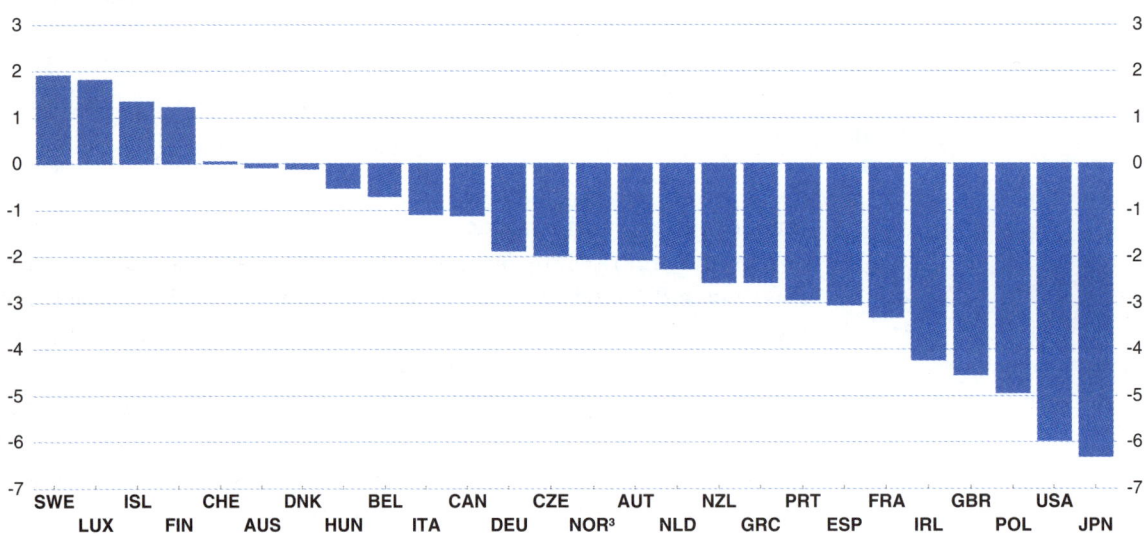

1. This includes cumulated deficit for 2010-12, debt-increasing equity participations in companies and the impact of GDP growth.
2. Cumulated deficits correspond to mainland only.
3. As a percentage of mainland potential GDP.

Source: OECD Economic Outlook 88 database.

StatLink 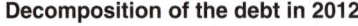 http://dx.doi.org/10.1787/888932345299

Consolidation needs are large in most countries

Calculations by the OECD indicate that, based on plausible assumptions about medium-term growth and interest rates, the mere stabilisation of the debt-to-GDP ratio before 2025 would call for a tightening of underlying primary balances after 2010 of over 8% of GDP in Japan and the United States, which belong to the countries with the largest primary deficits (see Chapter 4). Moreover, for many countries stabilisation of the debt ratio would occur at high levels. This would raise the vulnerability of government finances to financial market volatility and reduce the scope and effectiveness of fiscal policy measures to counteract future economic downturns. Bringing debt ratios back to pre-crisis levels or to more comfortable levels of some 60% of GDP would require substantially greater consolidation than for debt stabilisation (see Chapter 4).

International cooperation will enhance the credibility of consolidation

Fiscal consolidation will have short-term negative effects on demand, particularly so with a large number of countries pursuing consolidation simultaneously. Such effects will, however, be minimised when consolidation is embedded in credible long-term consolidation programmes that may help reinforce confidence and accelerate the recovery of self-sustained growth. Although country-specific aspects can influence the consolidation path, the credibility of consolidation can be enhanced further if sustained by stronger international cooperation, including through the G20 framework for strong, sustainable and balanced growth. As shown in OECD *Economic Outlook* No. 87, a coordinated implementation of macroeconomic, exchange rate and structural policies would strengthen growth, accelerate fiscal consolidation and narrow global imbalances.

The speed of consolidation should depend on…

The pace at which countries should consolidate in the short term depends on a number of factors:

… the state of the public finances…

● The state of public finances. The greater the overall consolidation required to stabilise debt at reasonable levels, the more intensive consolidation will need to be in the short term.

… the ease of funding public debt…

● The ease at which government debt can be funded. Fiscal consolidation should be more rapid if government debt has become increasingly difficult to finance and if delays of consolidation policies would excessively undermine future GDP through higher long-term interest rates. The fact that spreads between benchmark sovereign bond yields in Germany and the countries affected by the European debt crisis still stand at record levels is witness to the difficulties of restoring market confidence in sound government finances once it has been lost (Figure 1.15).

… the strength of the recovery…

● The strength of the recovery. Countries enjoying a robust recovery can afford to reduce budget deficits faster than countries with more fragile recoveries. Also, if growth were to turn out markedly weaker than projected, the pace of consolidation could be moderated in those countries with reasonably sound public finances and credible medium-term consolidation strategies. More generally, in such circumstances, the automatic stabilisers could also be allowed to operate around the planned consolidation path in countries that have not lost the confidence of financial markets. Countries in poor fiscal shape and

Figure 1.15. **Sovereign bond spreads in the euro area remain elevated**
Spread with German yield (percentage points)

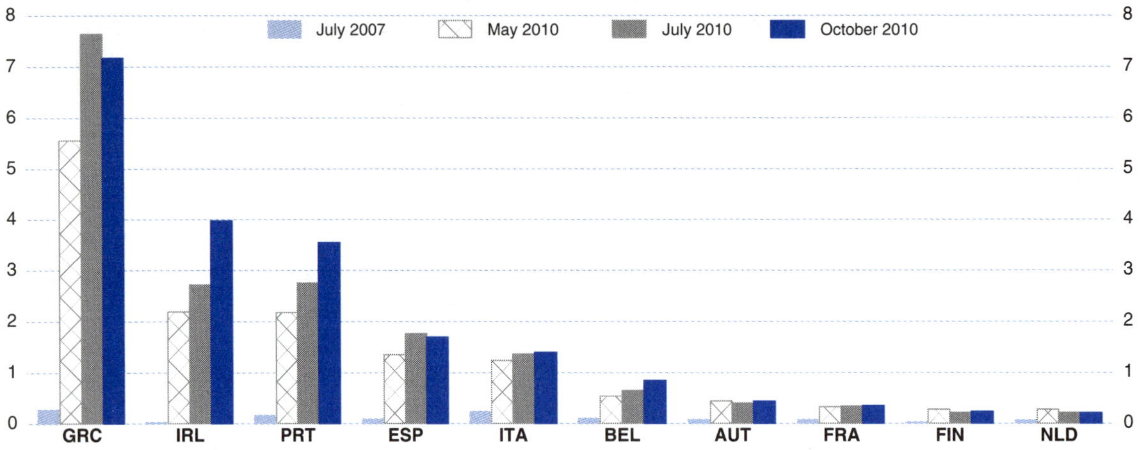

Source: Datastream.

StatLink ⍥ http://dx.doi.org/10.1787/888932345318

with little credibility could, however, be forced to react procyclically to weaker activity – which illustrates the importance of preserving credibility.

... the scope for monetary policy to provide stimulus...

- The scope for monetary policy to offset demand-restraining effects of fiscal contraction. At present, with policy interest rates close to zero in most OECD areas, monetary authorities are constrained in providing additional stimulus. However, if needed, the future pace of the normalisation of interest rates could be adjusted to offset economic weakness as a result of budget improvements. Hence, future consolidation should be more rapid where there is scope to delay interest-rate normalisation and moderate its pace.

... and existing commitments

- Existing commitments. Governments need to honour existing commitments for consolidation or risk undermining their credibility.

Planned consolidation in 2011 is appropriate in most countries...

Against the background of these criteria, the planned strengthening of structural budget positions in 2011 in most OECD countries appears to be appropriate:

- In the United States, taking into account projected state-level consolidation, the Administration's budget proposal implies general government consolidation of around 1¼ percentage points of GDP, striking a balance between the need to arrest unsustainable debt dynamics and the need to avoid withdrawing stimulus too quickly. The underlying deficit nonetheless remains very high by historical standards, with the gross debt-to-GDP ratio increasing further to 98½ per cent.

- In Japan, consolidation measures to be implemented in 2011 are likely to improve the underlying budget balance by around ¼ percentage point of GDP, after taking into account stimulus measures contained in the recent supplementary budget for the current fiscal year. While this limited consolidation would be consistent with the government's medium-term strategy, its implementation is subject to unusually high political uncertainty. The debt ratio is expected to increase to nearly 205%. In the light of the extraordinarily high debt levels, stronger consolidation than currently planned would be warranted.

- In the euro area, unwinding of stimulus measures and fiscal restraint are likely to improve underlying balances by 1 percentage point of GDP on average. Forceful consolidation is projected for most countries that are or have been exposed to market pressure, notably Greece, Ireland, Portugal and Spain, with improvements in underlying balances projected to total between 2 and 4¾ percentage points of GDP. In Ireland, extraordinary budgetary costs, related to the recapitalisation of the banking system, led to a steep increase in the headline fiscal balance in 2010, but such measures should not affect public finances in 2011. In France, the reduction in the underlying deficit by 1% of GDP is needed in view of the high debt and deficit levels. By contrast, in several other euro area countries, including Germany and Italy, consolidation gains are likely to be more modest, in the order of ½-1 percentage points of GDP, which is appropriate given their comparatively low underlying budget deficits and economic slack. In a few European countries, near-term improvements in structural budget balances are to be achieved partly by one-off measures and accounting changes (such as extraordinary receipts in exchange for assuming pension liabilities of private companies and the recording of contributions to second-pillar pensions as government revenues) that will not durably strengthen public finances. Box 1.5 reviews recent initiatives to strengthen the coordination and surveillance of fiscal policy in the euro area.

- In the United Kingdom, the authorities' consolidation plan is expected to improve the underlying balance by 1¼ per cent of GDP in 2011, as a further stage in the process to avoid unsustainable debt accumulation.

... and needs to be followed by significant further steps in 2012

Further significant steps towards sustainable fiscal positions are necessary in 2012. Where government plans are available for 2012, the fiscal projections in this *Economic Outlook* follow those plans. Where this is not the case, consolidation has been assumed to proceed along the lines set out in Box 1.3.

- In the United States, with the upswing projected to gain strength, a high underlying deficit and rising debt call for significant consolidation efforts. The projected reduction in the underlying deficit by about 1 percentage point of GDP, consistent with the Administration's aim as reported in the August Mid-Session Review, appears to be appropriate.

Box 1.5. **Fiscal rules and arrangements in the euro area**

High levels of debt and large fiscal deficits in some euro area countries have led to concerns about fiscal sustainability, which has created turbulence for the area as a whole in recent months. This has drawn attention to weaknesses in the performance and design of euro area fiscal arrangements. In consequence, the fiscal governance of the euro area needs to be strengthened. This can be pursued through a combination of stronger institutions and more intense market discipline.

Strengthening the institutional framework

To achieve the necessary fiscal discipline, the European Commission announced in September 2010 a package of legislative proposals that seek to strengthen coordination and surveillance of fiscal policies in individual member countries and to ensure adherence to the Stability and Growth Pact. Many of these proposals were included in the report of the EU Taskforce, published on 21 October and endorsed by the European Council on 29 October. Major elements of the overall package are:

- Better *ex ante* coordination of national budgets through a "European Semester" in the early part of the year, with the ECOFIN issuing country-specific recommendations that can be taken into account in setting national budgets. The establishment of this mechanism had already been agreed before the presentation of the legislative package.

- Earlier and wider ranging enforcement of the Stability and Growth Pact (SGP). In case of non-compliance with the preventive arm, an interest-bearing deposit could be levied. Under the Pact's "corrective arm", a non-interest-bearing deposit would be levied as soon as an Excessive Deficit Procedure is engaged, which could be converted into a fine if a country did not follow through on its commitment to rectify its deficit.

- Increased focus on public debt and fiscal sustainability in the implementation of the Stability and Growth Pact, with clear debt-reduction benchmarks set for each member country with debt ratios above the SGP reference value of 60% of GDP.

- Stronger national fiscal frameworks by establishing minimum quality standards, such as legally-enshrined national fiscal rules reflecting EU obligations, multi-annual budgetary plans and better forecasting systems.

Overall, these proposals aim to enforce fiscal discipline by moving towards more *ex ante* sanctions that can influence behaviour before a country gets into a very weak fiscal position. To counter the unwillingness of the ECOFIN Council to sanction its own members in some cases, it is envisaged that the new sanctions would be adopted on a recommendation from the Commission by default, unless the Council decides against it by qualified majority within ten days. The quasi-automatic nature of sanctions could help to improve compliance, as in the current setting an explicit majority decision needs to be taken to apply disciplinary procedures. However, these proposals are still being discussed by member countries.

In addition to reducing the risk of crises, it is well recognised that an institutional framework is required to resolve crises that may occur.[1] Towards this end and consistent with an approach based on *ex ante* surveillance, an arrangement along the lines of the three-year European Financial Stability Facility (EFSF) could be made a permanent feature of the euro area financial architecture thereby filling an important gap in terms of providing short-term liquidity insurance for countries facing difficulties in raising finance. However, such mechanisms create the risk of moral hazard and undermine efforts to improve fiscal discipline if they are viewed as providing bailouts for countries that pursue poor policies without strict conditionality. Countries with solvency problems should not have access to the EFSF and this practice could be extended to those with a record of non-compliance with the SGP. More generally, providing individual euro member countries with financial rewards for sound public finances could strengthen fiscal governance in the area as a whole. One option would be to entitle countries with a track record of fiscal soundness, based on clear objective criteria, but facing problems due to contagion to borrow from a common facility (like the EFSF) without conditionality (as in the IMF Flexible Credit Line (FCL) facility) or with minimal conditions attached. This would encourage countries to pursue policies to qualify for the insurance associated with such arrangements.

> ### Box 1.5. **Fiscal rules and arrangements in the euro area** (*cont.*)
>
> At the same time, well defined procedures of how to deal with sovereign solvency issues are required to make conditionality credible and minimise the risk of serious turbulence in financial markets that could emerge from denying access to the EFSF. If introduced in the near term, such procedures could destabilise financial markets, given the weak state of public finances in some countries in the euro area. However, they would nonetheless seem to be an important part of a medium-term framework.
>
> **Increasing reliance on market-based mechanisms**
>
> In the longer term, allowing for the possibility of restructuring of sovereign debt of countries based on voluntary agreements, supported by appropriate legal frameworks, could strengthen incentives to follow sound budgetary policies. Such incentives would arise both from the penalty in the form of higher borrowing costs likely to be imposed by markets on a country pursuing unsound policies and from the fact that, if invoked, debt restructuring would have serious consequences for the country in question. Such a country would most likely be shut out from raising funds in international markets in the short term and might have to pay a substantial premium for some time after it returned to the markets.
>
> To be effective, market discipline has to be based on belief that countries with unsustainable fiscal positions would not be bailed out and that the private sector would take losses in the event of debt restructuring. This would encourage financial markets to enhance their monitoring of fiscal developments so that unsustainable positions would be reflected in higher yields. However, a necessary condition for markets to adequately price restructuring risk is that it be seen as credible.
>
> Establishing restructuring as a credible option in the longer term would be helped by rules and institutions to facilitate the orderly and voluntary restructuring of sovereign debt. The priority of claims would have to be clearly established, in particular whether claims held by governments of other member states have priority over private claims. While the priority order of claims and the minimum share of creditors required to accept restructuring of debt that is binding for all creditors can be decided by national law, common standards for all euro area countries could contribute to orderly debt workouts and minimise conflicts among creditors.
>
> Debt restructuring could have serious consequences for other members of the monetary union if their financial institutions were heavily exposed to public or private debtors in the country in question, particularly if financial institutions were already in a fragile state with limited capacity to absorb losses. This creates the risk of forbearance with respect to countries which get into solvency problems. With banking systems set to become more solid in coming years, reducing the risk of financial contagion, and with the current phase of sovereign turbulence behind, financial regulations within the euro area should take into account the possibility of sovereign default both in terms of capital requirements and in requiring appropriate diversification of risk. The existence of differentiated sovereign risk might also need to be taken into account in the context of collateral for central bank liquidity.
>
> 1. The European Council has asked for a report by December 2010 on how to achieve this, based on a limited change to the EU Treaty. The role of the private sector and the IMF will be considered.

As market pressures are unlikely to be an imminent concern, automatic stabilisers should be allowed to operate around the projected consolidation path and some temporary support could be provided if activity were to be much weaker than anticipated.

● Based on the government's medium-term spending plan, and with no allowance for changes in tax policy, the Japanese underlying balance is projected to remain unchanged. With the upswing projected to strengthen and given the serious persistent fiscal imbalance in Japan, more ambitious consolidation would seem to be required.

- Also, there is no alternative to continued implementation of stringent consolidation policies in European countries whose public finances were particularly hard hit by the financial crisis or the subsequent sovereign debt crisis. The deficit reductions in Greece, Portugal and Spain embedded in government programmes of between ½ and 1 percentage point of GDP will be less than in the initial phase of their consolidation process, while in Iceland the underlying balance is projected to continue to improve at a rapid pace, by 2½ percentage points of GDP. For Ireland, the projected reduction in the underlying balance is 1½ percentage points of GDP, assuming that the government will implement its plan announced in early November 2010.

- In France and Italy, underlying balances are projected to tighten by 1 and ½ percentage points of GDP, respectively, assuming that sufficient measures are introduced to meet the governments' consolidation targets. In both countries it is important that measures be implemented to meet the plans, given the substantial consolidation effort required to bring public debt to the 60% of GDP reference value stipulated in the EU Stability and Growth Pact (see Chapter 4), though automatic stabilisers should be allowed to operate were activity to turn out different from projections.

- In the United Kingdom, a high underlying deficit and unsustainable debt dynamics warrant a continued consolidation of just above 1 percentage point of GDP, as implied by the government's programme. The automatic stabilisers should be allowed to operate to provide support for the economy if necessary. Even if the economy showed signs of turning out weaker than projected, planned structural fiscal adjustments should continue, though some temporary support could be provided in the event of a significant slowdown.

- For most other countries, with relatively low debt and less impaired fiscal positions, consolidation is projected to proceed on a more moderate path. In particular, for the Nordic countries, Austria, Germany and Switzerland underlying balances are projected to improve by around ½ per cent of GDP. Automatic stabilisers should be allowed to operate in these countries and the pace of consolidation could be further moderated if needed.

Outside the OECD area consolidation needs are less pressing

Consolidation needs vary widely across emerging markets and in some countries are much less pressing than within the OECD area. Indeed, in the case of China borrowing levels should be maintained with government spending continuing to be reoriented to meet social objectives. In contrast, in India, where government deficit and debt levels are comparatively high, a steadfast commitment to timely fiscal consolidation will be important for ensuring balanced growth ahead. In several emerging markets, including Russia, fiscal consolidation should be pursued *via* reducing subsidies, some of which were extended in the context of anti-crisis measures.

Medium-term consolidation plans need to be developed further

Looking further ahead, most OECD countries have announced medium-term consolidation programmes. However, in some cases, these may not suffice to halt adverse debt dynamics (Figure 1.16). Also, several programmes provide little specific information on what spending and revenue measures are to be used to meet consolidation targets and on how action should be phased.

Figure 1.16. **Gross debt ratios under announced government consolidation plans**

Percentage of GDP

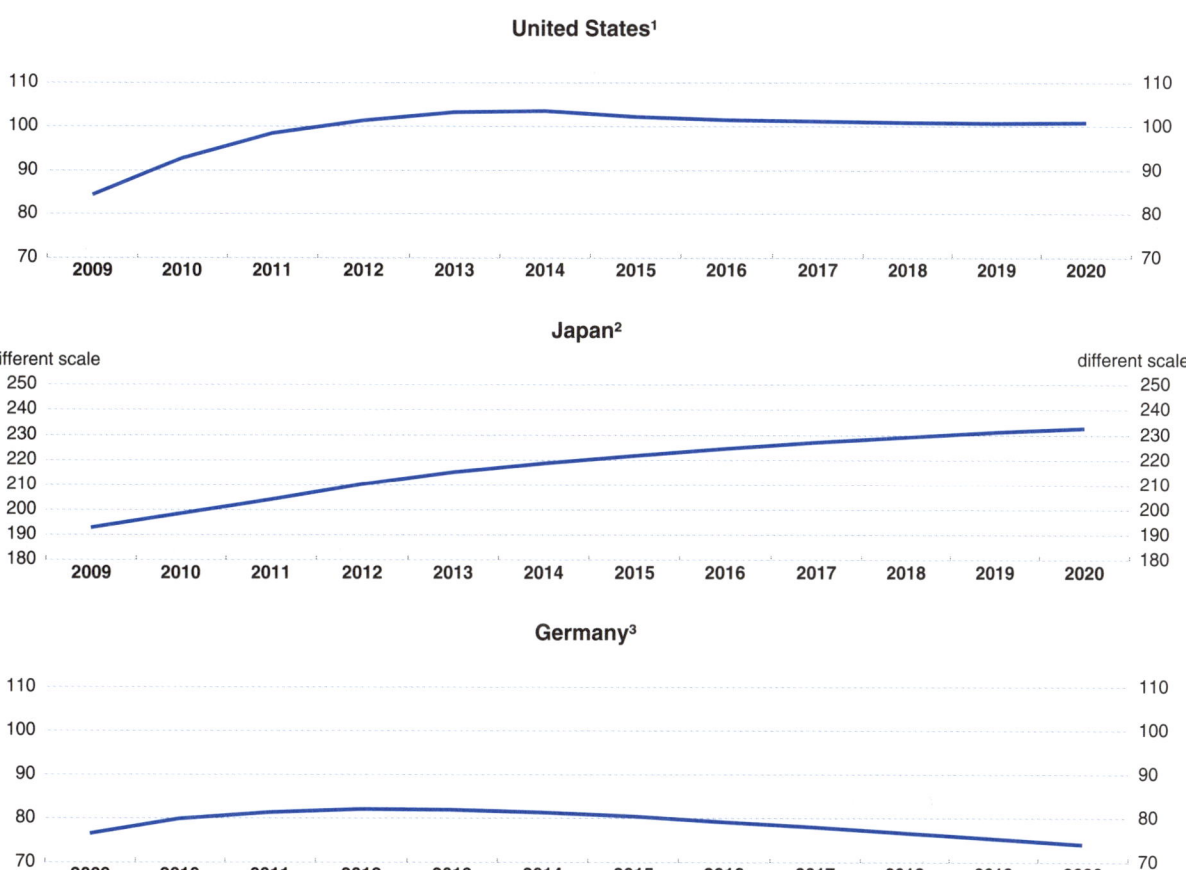

Note: Up to 2012, growth, interest rate and fiscal projections are taken from Economic Outlook No. 88. Thereafter, growth rates and gross asset ratios are based on the long-term scenario, while fiscal projections are derived using the assumptions explained below.

1. The debt path is consistent with the intention to balance the primary balance of the federal government by fiscal year 2015. After 2015, the primary balance is assumed to be constant. The general government balance is assumed to evolve in line with the federal government balance.

2. The debt path is consistent with the intention to halve the primary balance of the central and local governments between 2010 and 2015 and then to balance it by 2020.

3. The debt path is consistent with the constitutional fiscal rule requiring that the cyclically adjusted budget deficit of the federal government must not exceed 0.35% of GDP by 2016 and that the cyclically adjusted budgets for the Länder must be balanced by 2020.

Source: OECD Economic Outlook 88 database; and OECD calculations.

StatLink http://dx.doi.org/10.1787/888932345337

- In the United States, the Administration aims to eliminate the federal primary fiscal deficit by 2015. If GDP growth and interest rates evolve as assumed in the long-run scenario presented in this *Economic Outlook*, this would stabilise the general government debt-to-GDP ratio in the second half of the decade. However, concrete measures are yet to be specified. Also, in view of future spending pressures, it would be desirable for the United States to introduce consolidation objectives, such as declining debt-to-GDP ratios, for the period after 2015.

- The Japanese government, not withstanding recent stimulus measures, aims to halve the primary deficit of the central and local governments from fiscal year (FY) 2010 to FY 2015 and achieve a primary surplus by FY 2020. To meet these targets government spending, net of interest payments, over the period FY 2011-2013 will not be allowed to increase from the FY 2010 level. Under the growth and interest rate assumptions of the *Economic Outlook*, this plan would not stabilise the debt-to-GDP ratio within this decade. As achieving medium-term consolidation targets will likely be challenging due to ageing-related fiscal pressures, credible consolidation measures, possibly involving tax increases, to meet the targets need to be announced.

- In Germany, the constitutional deficit targets are likely to put the debt ratio on a downward trend, following further increases over the next three years. The government has presented a medium-term consolidation programme, providing targets for major revenue and spending items while leaving a significant part of envisaged budgetary improvements unspecified.

More detail on what measures can be used to fulfil current consolidation requirements in OECD countries, taking into account the scope for each instrument to generate budget improvements and its impact on growth and equity, is given in Chapter 4.

Monetary Policy

There has been a partial reversal in the normalisation process...

Against the backdrop of generally-resilient financial markets and the gradual global economic recovery, exceptional crisis-related measures have begun to be withdrawn in some countries. However, central banks in other countries have paused or even taken further steps to boost activity, reflecting continued disinflationary pressures and indications of subdued growth.

... in the United States...

- The Federal Reserve closed down access to all its special liquidity provision facilities by the end of June and terminated net purchases of securities. However, the subsequent decision in August to keep the size of the securities portfolio constant (instead of allowing it to fall with the maturing and prepayment of agency debt and mortgage-backed securities) put on hold the exit from extraordinary long-term asset holdings. More recently, in view of the weak recovery and low inflation, the Federal Reserve has announced an additional quantitative easing programme worth $600 billion. This is to take the form of regular small purchases of longer-term Treasury securities up to mid-2011, expanding the Federal Reserve balance sheet by a further one-quarter. The pace and eventual size of additional asset purchases are to be adjusted according to economic developments. Much of the impact of the announcement seems likely to have been priced into financial markets beforehand, but if markets expect further significant asset purchases above those already announced, real bond yields could fall further. However, given the exceptionally low yields at present (Box 1.4), there are limits to how much further nominal yields can fall, though other asset prices may be affected. Separately, the Federal Reserve has also engaged in discussion of greater acceptance of future inflation overshooting. To the extent this increases inflation expectations, it could be seen as helpful in current circumstances. However, the risk would seem to be non-negligible that such an approach could un-anchor long-term inflation expectations, with adverse consequences for the credibility of the monetary authorities. By contrast, the recent clarification of the medium-term goal for inflation may be useful to strengthen the credibility of the authorities' price stability objective.

... Japan... ● After closing most of the temporary facilities and asset-purchase programmes that were introduced at the height of the crisis, the Bank of Japan has in recent months introduced new measures to respond to the deterioration of the economic outlook, expanding its credit facilities for financial institutions in August,[6] and, acting as an agent for the Treasury, intervening in foreign exchange markets to curb the appreciation of the yen. In October, the Bank of Japan reduced its target for the main policy rate from 0.1% to a 0-0.1% band, committed to maintain this policy until the medium-to-long-term inflation outlook becomes positive and created a new facility (worth 1% of GDP) to purchase government and corporate bonds as well as commercial paper and real-estate investment trusts.

... and the euro area... ● While the European Central Bank has completed, as planned, the purchase of covered bonds, tensions in financial markets in Europe in May led the Bank to reschedule its exit from emergency liquidity measures. This involved extending the application of full-allotment procedures for some time, as well as enacting a new programme of outright purchases of government and private securities (the Securities Markets Programme).

... and a pause in the United Kingdom... ● The Bank of England has committed for now to keep the stock of securities unchanged at £200 billion, after the already completed implementation of its asset purchase programme.

---

6. The three-month credit line to financial institutions (up to 20 trillion yen) introduced last December was expanded in August by adding a six-month facility, up to 10 trillion yen.

... while other countries have started to tighten policy...

- In OECD countries where the economic recovery has been more solid, such as Australia, Canada, Israel, Korea, Norway and Sweden, central banks have gone further and have already started to increase policy interest rates.

... especially outside the OECD area

- The move to normalise monetary policy stances is even more evident in non-OECD economies, where economic recovery generally has gained momentum and raised concerns about inflation and asset price increases, with Brazil having increased policy rates, India continuing to increase policy rates and China also having taken a number of tightening steps, including increases in bank reserve requirements and interest rates.

Monetary policy should remain supportive...

The current and future stance of monetary policy should reflect the prospects for inflation and economic activity, including the effects from fiscal consolidation. With recent announcements suggesting more significant fiscal consolidation than previously expected in coming years, and given the sluggish nature of the recovery in many OECD countries, inflationary pressures are likely to be well contained into the foreseeable future and there is even a non-negligible risk of deflationary tendencies. In principle, the aim of monetary authorities should be to bring policy rates to their neutral levels by the time economic slack is eliminated. However, assessing the level of slack is fraught with difficulties following the deep recession. This has reduced the level of potential output to an extent that is difficult to pin down with normal margins of error. Exceptional uncertainty about the degree of slack renders it preferable for policy to rely on more directly observable gauges of where demand is situated relative to capacity (Pain and Koske, 2008). Hence, central banks may need to give more weight to survey measures of resource utilisation and inflation expectations and to whether price inflation is accelerating or declining.[7] Acting only when there is a clear acceleration in underlying inflation would be a risky strategy in normal conditions because core inflation is a delayed indicator and monetary policy acts with long and variable lags. But in the current environment, with still low resource utilisation in many countries, low inflation and inflationary expectations close to the objectives of the monetary authorities, there are limited risks from monetary policy remaining supportive and moving decisively towards neutral rates only once underlying inflation seems set to turn up.

... but financial stability would benefit from small, yet positive interest rates

However, abundant liquidity provision at near-zero funding costs could keep alive insolvent banks, allowing them to roll over the debt of unviable businesses. In addition, extremely low interest rates may discourage activities in money markets, which could hinder the

---

7. To the extent that there is greater confidence in estimates of the growth rate of potential output, as compared with its level, there would also be useful information from the difference between actual and potential growth rates.

normalisation process in the future. Also, prolonged near-zero interest rates could lead to intensified search for yield, compressing spreads and distorting the pricing of risk, ultimately resulting in investment going to the wrong projects, or a build-up of financial fragilities, or more likely a combination of both. Zero rates in larger advanced countries could spill over into asset price inflation in emerging countries, triggering further distortive policy responses in these countries. Thus, conditional on the recovery being solid, and deflation risks having evaporated, there is a case for central banks to move policy-controlled interest rates to levels that are still very low, to support sluggish demand, but are clearly above zero so as to reduce the risks associated with free money.

Central banks should follow a two-step approach... Against that background, central banks should move away from close-to-zero rates relatively early, once recovery looks firm and deflation risks fade, but then wait until signs of incipient inflation increases begin to emerge before starting to normalise in earnest:

... in the United States... ● In the United States, the economic recovery has softened more than expected, and, as a result, inflationary pressure is likely to remain very subdued in the foreseeable future, even with the new round of additional quantitative easing. As a result, the creation of a buffer above zero rates should wait until mid-2011. Once the recovery is more firmly established, around the middle of 2012, the Federal Reserve should start to raise interest rates so as to make policy gradually less accommodative, although the pace of tightening should be moderated by the marked fiscal consolidation planned in 2012 and the following years.

... in the euro area... ● In the euro area, the ECB should keep its main refinancing rate steady at 1% and maintain its policy of full allotment for a while. As the functioning of the money market improves,[8] the overnight rate should stay close to the main refinancing rates. Once the recovery gathers momentum, the normalisation of the policy rate can commence in 2012, though at a measured pace, particularly because, in the area as a whole, large fiscal consolidation is planned in the years ahead, weighing on economic activity.

... and the United Kingdom ● In the United Kingdom, against the backdrop of the recent slowdown in the global economy and stronger fiscal consolidation, the Bank of England should keep the current policy stance until the middle of 2011. It could then increase the buffer above the zero bound from ½ to 1 per cent

8.   In the current situation, as a precaution, stressed banks are borrowing more liquidity than the required minimum from the Eurosystem, at 1%, and then parking it at the deposit facility at ¼ per cent or lending it in the overnight market at rates that have been averaging below ½ per cent until recently. As funding conditions have improved, banks have become increasingly reluctant to pay a ½ to ¾ per cent spread on their excess reserves. The resulting shrinkage of excess reserves has led the overnight rate to converge towards the ECB main refinancing rate.

in the second half of 2011. Further moves toward normalisation should not begin before the economic recovery is judged to be further advanced, which is projected to be around the second quarter of 2012.

Rates can be raised earlier in Canada...

- In Canada, normalisation should continue as the recovery gains momentum, with the pace of policy rate increases strengthening in the second half of 2011.

... but much later in Japan

- In Japan, persistent deflation suggests that interest rate hikes should wait until inflation is firmly positive, likely beyond 2012. The priority for the monetary authority is to counteract entrenched deflationary tendencies. Recent decisions by the Bank of Japan to expand its provision of credit and offer banks opportunities to refinance their lending in growth-enhancing areas are aimed at achieving this end. However, the authorities need to continue exploring further means to boost the economy. Purchasing long-term government bonds on a far larger scale than currently planned would be particularly urgent if the recent appreciation of the yen and muted domestic spending threaten the economic recovery and add to deflationary pressure.

In China the current stance can be maintained for some time

- In China, past policy actions appear to have been effective in slowing credit and money growth and in taming increases in real estate prices. The recent moderation in the economic expansion and a weaker near-term global economic outlook suggest that there is no need for the monetary authorities to further tighten policy settings, at least for some time, despite some recent increase in inflation. In the medium term, the decision in June to allow exchange rates to fluctuate within a wider band should be accompanied by a greater focus on achieving an appreciation against a basket of currencies.

Further tightening should occur in Brazil and India

- In Brazil, monetary tightening has paused in recent months, in part due to marked exchange rate appreciation and the recent moderation in headline inflation. But with labour markets being tight, and capacity utilisation above long-run average levels, further moves to normalise monetary policy settings should resume soon. In India, monetary policy normalisation has continued in recent months, even though the upward pressures on headline inflation from rising food prices have moderated. With domestic demand continuing to grow strongly, and only limited spare capacity, additional policy tightening remains warranted.

A new downturn would require additional stimulus

While concerns about a double-dip have abated since summer, monetary authorities need to pay due attention to risks that the current soft patch turns out to be more protracted and deeper than appears likely at present and should be ready to provide further stimulus to the economy, if needed. Given that room for further reduction of policy rates is now very limited, even if mildly negative interest rates are considered a possibility, further stimulus could also come from additional quantitative easing (over and above that already announced) *via* the purchase of government bonds. Decisions about extensive further quantitative easing need to take into account the risk that large holdings of private and public assets may keep the cost of finance artificially low, leading to a misallocation of resources and a reduction in potential output. Finally, central banks can also strengthen their commitments to keep policy rates close to zero for an extended period.

Foreign exchange market interventions should be limited

Strong capital inflows and upward pressure on currencies have recently prompted several countries (including Japan, Israel, Korea, Switzerland, Brazil and South Africa) to intervene in currency markets or change regulations on capital movements. In the case of emerging market countries, large inflows and currency appreciation are consistent with their relatively good economic prospects and will help global balancing. However, the pressures on some of these countries with relatively open capital accounts and floating exchange rates have arguably been exacerbated by other large emerging countries restraining capital and currency movements. Moreover, weaknesses in domestic financial regulation can lead to concerns about the robustness of financial institutions should capital flows reverse, which in some cases may constitute an argument for measures to restrict volatile inflows, though the efficiency of such measures is open to doubt. Instead, first-best approaches may focus on micro and macro-prudential policies. In general, countries should refrain from interventions in foreign exchange markets for the purpose of competitive devaluation of currencies. Foreign exchange interventions are effective mainly when not sterilised, so that they change the stance of monetary policy. Moreover, as discussed above, they raise a strong risk of mutually offsetting interventions that could ultimately result in protectionist measures with adverse consequences for not only the recovery but also long-term prosperity.

Financial and macro-prudential policy

Financial reform is essential and affordable

Individual countries and jurisdictions have taken initiatives to reform financial regulation to tackle the failures that led to the financial crisis. Measures to strengthen framework conditions in financial markets have nevertheless proceeded at different speeds across countries, advancing especially rapidly in the United States. In particular:

The United States has implemented wide-ranging reforms

● In the United States, the financial reform legislation enacted in July establishes a consumer financial protection entity, creates a systemic risk regulator (the Financial Stability Oversight Council), gives regulatory bodies the authority to determine which derivatives should be cleared through centralised clearing houses, creates a banking liquidation authority and establishes a size-related levy on banks (to accumulate in a liquidation fund). It also bans banks from using regulatory capital to finance some categories of risky investments (*Volcker rule*), and, in particular, requests that banks spin off part of their proprietary trading desks. Most provisions are expected to be implemented within the next two years.

The European Union is putting in place several oversight bodies

- At the level of the European Union, the authorities have decided to establish a macro-prudential oversight body (the European Systemic Risk Board) and new European supervisory authorities to regulate banking, securities and insurance. The new bodies will set common technical standards that are binding, though only in some areas, and should make some progress in the direction of harmonising financial supervision across national borders within the union.[9] The authorities have also made advances towards harmonising and simplifying deposit guarantee schemes (increasing the overall level of protection), as their heterogeneity proved disruptive for financial stability during the crisis. They also intend to put in place a banking crisis management mechanism to deal effectively with the failure of European banks, which could include a levy to pre-fund resolution costs. As well, the European Commission has launched a consultation document to harmonise rules and tools relating to short selling across member states.

Some EU countries have taken specific national measures

- At the national level, some EU countries have taken, or are planning, measures on their own. In the United Kingdom, the authorities intend to give responsibility for oversight of prudential regulation to the Bank of England. The new UK regulatory system is not expected to be completed before 2012, to give time for the financial sector to adjust. Moreover, an independent commission has been given one year to report to the UK authorities on the issue of separating retail and investment banking and the need to break up large banks. Sweden and the United Kingdom have introduced a levy on banks to ensure fair burden sharing and to discourage risky funding.[10] Germany imposed a ban on *naked* short-selling of some kinds of securities.[11]

Regulators have agreed on new bank capital requirements

An international effort to achieve financial reforms, led by the Financial Stability Board, is also being taken under the auspices of the G20. Regulators have recently agreed on key elements of a global reform package for the banking sector, namely the definition and the minimum required levels of bank capital (see Box 1.6). Experimentation mechanisms

9. The intention is that the European Systemic Risk Board and the three new supervisory bodies be operational from January 2011. The new supervisory bodies will oversee mandatory supervisory colleges for cross-border institutions.

10. The proposed levy in the United Kingdom will be set at 0.07 per cent of total liabilities excluding Tier 1 capital and deposits and will apply to financial institutions with £20 billion or more in assets. The rate will be lower (0.04 per cent) for 2011, and there will be also a reduced rate for longer-maturity funding.

11. In addition, a bank-restructuring measure is currently being discussed in parliament in Germany and should be implemented by end-year. It envisages setting up a fund for troubled banks (paid for by a bank levy), with the intention of simplifying bank restructuring.

Box 1.6. **Estimating the macroeconomic impact of Basel III capital requirements**

The higher standards decided by the Basel Committee on Banking Supervision (BCBS) in September 2010 raise banks' minimum capital ratios for common equity and aggregate Tier I capital between 2011 and 2015 (see first table). Gradually, over the course of the following four years, these two ratios as well as the total capital ratio will be augmented by a further 2½ percentage point "conservation" buffer, within which banks will not be considered insolvent but will face restrictions on dividend payments and share buybacks. The Basel III framework also involves liquidity and other requirements, which are not examined in this box.

Bank capital: current and future requirements
Per cent of risk-weighted assets

	Current requirement	Requirement in 2015	Requirement in 2019 (incl. conservation buffer)
Common equity Tier I capital	2	4.5	7
Tier I capital	4	6	8.5
Total capital	8	8	10.5

Source : BCBS (2010).

StatLink http://dx.doi.org/10.1787/888932346743

The degree of effort that will be required to meet Basel III capital standards can be gauged by comparing bank capitalisation in 2006 and 2009. It appears likely that in 2006, at the top of the credit boom, banks held as little discretionary capital as possible above the regulatory minimum. After the crisis broke out, however, market pressure and the anticipation of reform led them to build up precautionary buffers. The Tier 1 ratio rose by close to 1½ percentage points in the United States, the euro area and Japan between 2006 and the end of 2009 (see second table). The tangible common equity ratio (TCE ratio), a more restrictive definition of capital which is comparable to common equity Tier I, also increased during the same period, although to a lesser extent in Japan. Insofar as the accumulation of capital between 2006 and 2009 occurred in anticipation of the new standard, banks can be expected to use this part of their discretionary buffers to meet the requirements up to 2019. It seems unlikely that they would go beyond that and reduce their discretionary capital buffers below their 2006 levels in the aftermath of what has been a major banking crisis. Against this background, it is assumed here that banks will increase their capital ratios by an amount equal to the increase in capital requirements between 2010 and 2019 minus the buffers they built up between 2006 and 2009 (see third table). Consistent with the objective of improving the quality of capital, it appears that the binding requirement will be the one concerning common equity (rather than full Tier I) and that it will be greatest in Japan where banks currently have comparatively low amounts of core capital.

Pre-crisis and current levels of bank capital

	Percentage of risk-weighted assets				Percentage points
	2006	2007	2008	2009	2006 – 2009
United States					
Tier 1	9.8	9.4	9.7	11.4	1.6
TCE	8.6	8.6	8.4	10.5	1.9
Euro area					
Tier 1	8.0	7.7	8.6	9.4	1.4
TCE	6.8	6.6	7.3	8.0	1.2
Japan					
Tier 1	5.4	5.6	5.6	6.9	1.5
TCE	3.3	3.3	3.3	4.1	0.8

Source : IIF (2010) and OECD calculations.

StatLink http://dx.doi.org/10.1787/888932346762

Box 1.6. **Estimating the macroeconomic impact of Basel III capital requirements** (*cont.*)

Required increase in bank capital ratios to attain Basel III standards

Percentage points

	Required	Achieved in 2006-09	Remaining
United States			
Tier 1	4.5	1.6	2.9
TCE	5.0	1.9	3.1
Euro area			
Tier 1	4.5	1.4	3.1
TCE	5.0	1.2	3.8
Japan			
Tier 1	4.5	1.5	3.0
TCE	5.0	0.8	4.2

Source: OECD calculations.

StatLink ⟊⟊ http://dx.doi.org/10.1787/888932346781

If, despite the higher capital requirements, banks maintain the same return on equity as before the crisis by hiking their lending rates, more expensive bank credit will have a damping impact on activity. The magnitude of the effect can be gauged using results from a wide range of models developed under the aegis of the Macroeconomic Assessment Group (MAG) of the Financial Stability Board (FSB) and the BCBS. Using the headline estimate in the MAG report and the evaluation of the remaining effort shown in the third table, the Basel III requirements could have the effect of reducing annual output growth by 0.07 percentage points in the United States and 0.1 percentage point in Japan through 2011-2018 (see the fourth table).[1] If quantitative credit-supply constraints become binding in addition to higher lending spreads, based on the main results for this situation in the MAG study, the effects would be larger, from 0.12 percentage points per annum through 2011-2018 in the United States to 0.17 percentage points in Japan. All the effects mentioned assume no response from monetary policy but, to the extent that it becomes free from the zero lower bound, it could be used to reduce the size of the impact. It should be noted that the main results from the MAG study are surrounded by substantial uncertainty. Looking for instance at the case of Japan, if the headline results reported in the MAG report are replaced with model simulations prepared by the Bank of Japan and also reported in the MAG report, the corresponding impact estimate on GDP growth rises from 0.17 to almost 0.6 percentage points per annum in models with quantitative credit constraints. Although quantitative restrictions are a possibility in Japan, where low bank profitability reduces the scope for meeting the requirements by accumulating retained earnings, the long phase-in period for the new requirements greatly reduces the risk that they may become binding.

Impact estimates on average annual GDP growth rates in 2011–2018

Percentage points

United States	-0.07 - -0.12
Euro area	-0.09 - -0.15
Japan	-0.10 - -0.17

Source : MAG (2010) and OECD calculations

StatLink ⟊⟊ http://dx.doi.org/10.1787/888932346800

Box 1.6. **Estimating the macroeconomic impact of Basel III capital requirements** *(cont.)*

Nevertheless, if banks decide to attain the new capital levels in advance, the costs will tend to come up front rather than in the longer term and in a period when monetary policy has very little room to offset the impact. Moreover, as the bank regulatory reform proposals include a change in the definition of capital, differences in capital composition across countries might result in additional cross-country variation in macroeconomic impacts. In countries where tangible common equity as a share of Tier 1 is currently relatively high, like in the United States and the euro area, the impact can be expected to be comparatively mild. By contrast, the impact on GDP is likely to be higher in Japan, where the banking sector might need to raise substantial amounts of common equity, and where low bank profitability makes it difficult to increase the capital base through retained earnings.

If the new regulations lead to permanent change in the financial sector, they can have an effect on the equilibrium level of output in the long-term. Indeed, the new regulations can result in permanently higher lending spreads if banks prove capable of maintaining their return on equity at pre-crisis levels. MAG results suggest that a one percentage point increase in core capital requirements can raise banking lending spreads by 16 basis points. If higher spreads translate one-for-one into higher lending rates which in turn raise capital costs in proportion with the share of bank lending in the external financing of non-financial businesses, estimates in Cournède (2010) suggest an impact on potential output of the order of 0.2% in the United States and 0.6% in the euro area. These calculations, however, omit the reasons behind the new capital framework, which are to reduce the likelihood and cost of financial crises and to improve the quality of capital allocation in the economy. These effects have been estimated to more than offset any gross costs of the new regulations, by a wide margin (BCBS, 2010).

Overall, the gross economic costs of Basel III capital requirements are likely to be small. Although in theory credit-supply effects could result in a more noticeable impact, in practice the very long phase-in period means that such effects are unlikely to materialise, especially in countries where banks have already accumulated large discretionary capital buffers above regulatory minima. In the long term, higher capital requirements could be associated with some widening of lending spreads and a small reduction in the equilibrium capital stock. However, this negative effect is likely to be far more than offset by the benefits of sounder banking in terms of reducing the frequency and cost of future financial crises.

1. Alternative estimates using the OECD Global Model and OECD financial conditions indices yield very similar results (Slovik and Cournède, 2010).

have been decided for the introduction of a leverage ratio and liquidity standards. Consultations are on-going on forward-looking provisioning, contingent capital and capital surcharges for systemically important financial institutions. Regulators have agreed that counter-cyclical buffers will be set at the national level in the range of 0 to 2½ per cent of risk-weighted assets.

The cost of reform is likely to be limited

The agreed reform of capital and liquidity requirements should reduce the frequency and economic costs of future financial crises.[12] Although the proposed regulatory changes have prompted an intense debate about their impact on lending rates, credit dynamics and economic activity, estimates by the Macroeconomic Assessment Group

12. Research has found that banking-sector capital adequacy and liquidity, alongside real house price growth, are the most important banking crisis determinants in a group of 14 OECD economies over the period 1980-2006, see Barrell *et al.* (2010). Recently, the BCBS has also presented an evaluation of the benefits of stronger capital and liquidity requirements, see BCBS (2010).

(MAG) of the Financial Stability Board and the Basel Committee on Banking Supervision suggest that the impact on GDP of higher capital standards would be relatively moderate and distributed through time though, as noted above, effects could be larger were banks to rush to attain the new standards ahead of the deadline. Furthermore, because it removes the previous uncertainty regarding the new capital framework, the fact that agreement has been reached should in itself work in the direction of supporting lending activity.

Problems with too-big-to-fail institutions must be addressed...

A key issue that regulatory reform yet has to address is the presence of banks that are so big or so interconnected that they become systemically important and therefore cannot be allowed to fail. Because these systemically important financial institutions enjoy a *de facto* government backstop, they have an incentive to take excessive risk and benefit from a competitive edge in terms of funding costs and collateralisation requirements over smaller competitors that do not enjoy such a guarantee. One manifestation of their advantage is that the largest banks are significantly less capitalised than their smaller competitors, which enables them to offer investors a higher return on equity (Table 1.7). Although such institutions existed before the crisis, and contributed to the excesses that led to the financial collapse, the crisis has exacerbated the problem: government support has become explicit and concentration has increased considerably.

Table 1.7. **The largest banks hold less capital to generate a higher return on equity**

2006

	United States		Europe	
	Tier 1 capital	Pre-tax profit	Tier 1 capital	Pre-tax profit
	per cent of risk-weighted assets	*per cent of Tier 1 capital*	*per cent of risk-weighted assets*	*per cent of Tier 1 capital*
Top 10 banks	8.8	29	9	29
11th to 50th largest banks	10	27	8.1	19
51st to 100th largest banks	13	24	9.3	15
101st to 150th banks	12	20	13	19
151st to 200th banks	15	18	12	12

Source: The Banker Database and OECD calculations.

StatLink ⟶ http://dx.doi.org/10.1787/888932346819

... with restructuring or through other means

The too-big-to-fail problem can be addressed in different ways. The most direct way is to break up systemically important institutions.[13] Where political economy considerations make this option unrealistic, an

13. The gross welfare cost of the measure could be benign, as empirical research indicates that banking involves no significant economies of scope or scale beyond a relatively small size (Amel *et al*, 2004). Practical options are available to ensure that the transition cost is limited as well: one of them is to group the key central support services of the former megabank in a separate entity that would serve the individual banks resulting from the break-up.

alternative possibility is to impose higher capital requirements, including in the form of contingent capital notes, as has been proposed recently in Switzerland.[14] In addition, systemically important financial institutions could be mandated to prepare "living wills" detailing how they should be unwound, including how losses would be distributed across creditors and counterparties, in case of failure. A difficulty in applying specific regulations to a particular set of firms is that this implies implicit regulatory recognition of the too-big-to-fail status, which works in the direction of compounding the problem they try to address. This difficulty may, however, be overcome in the case of requirements to hold more capital in equity or contingent notes if, instead of applying to a designated set of institutions, the surcharge is universal but specified as an increasing function of bank size and interconnectedness.

Reforms are needed to maximum leverage, accounting standards and non-bank financial institutions

Successful financial reform requires further progress along other dimensions. A key component of the reformed capital requirement framework will be the imposition of a maximum leverage ratio, applicable to all assets. This will guard against the inevitable regulatory arbitrage inherent to the risk-weighting approach that underpins the already agreed minimum capital ratios. Progress on a binding standard for the leverage ratio has been hindered by a lack of international convergence in accounting standards on whether or not to allow the netting of derivative positions. In addition to facilitating the adoption of a common leverage ratio, ending the netting of derivative positions in financial statements would help to reduce the possibility that investors may underestimate exposure to counterparty risk in jurisdictions where derivatives are currently still reported on a net basis. Finally, financial reform cannot be confined to banking. Other things being equal, the tightening of bank regulation will encourage the shifting of risk to other parts of the financial sector. In this respect, it is particularly important to ensure that insurance and pension fund regulations are capable of avoiding the build-up of systemic risk in these activities.

Structural Policies

Structural reforms remain essential...

The risk of lower potential output post-crisis and the need to strengthen public finances mean that growth-enhancing structural reforms are needed now more than ever before. Indeed, the medium-term effects from implementing such reforms could facilitate the fiscal consolidation that is needed over a similar timeframe (see Chapter 4), as well as providing a boost to longer-term growth and helping to narrow global imbalances. A range of possible interactions between structural reforms, saving and investment balances and fiscal consolidation

---

14. Contingent capital notes are hybrid debt instruments that convert into equity when a certain threshold is crossed. A potential issue is that the fear of conversion may create or amplify a panic when the issuer approaches the threshold. See Penacchi *et al.* (2010) for ways to implement contingent capital notes without generating undesirable amplification effects at times of stress.

Table 1.8. **Growth-enhancing structural reforms can also help to reduce fiscal and external imbalances**

Particularly suitable for external surplus countries with :

High or moderate need for fiscal consolidation

Ease product market regulation

Reduce state control of potentially competitive activities

Reduce support to agriculture

Enhance efficiency of public spending in health, education and pensions

Increase retirement age

Reduce tax wedge on labor and change tax structure

Reduce corporate Income tax and change tax structure

Relax FDI restrictions

Low need for fiscal consolidation

Increase growth-enhancing public spending (education, innovation, infrastructure)

Increase ALMP spending

Reduce tariffs on international trade

Particularly suitable for external deficit countries with :

High or moderate need for fiscal consolidation

Reform of employment protection

Reforms to unemployment and disability/sickness benefits

Low need for fiscal consolidation

Measures to enhance price and non-price external competitiveness (increased public support for innovation; reduced employers' labour costs).

Note: Reforms reported could either reduce or be neutral for current account imbalances in all economies. Reforms reported as suitable for countries with high or moderate need for fiscal consolidation are either positive or neutral for fiscal positions.

Countries with low fiscal consolidation needs are ones where sufficient fiscal space exists to implement the suggested reforms.

The table does not report reforms that would enhance growth prospects but further increase current account and/or – for countries with high or moderate fiscal consolidation needs – fiscal imbalances. Only the direct fiscal effects of reforms are considered here: in the medium to longer run, many reforms contribute indirectly to fiscal consolidation through their positive impact on labour utilisation and/or productivity.

Source: OECD classification, Going for Growth 2011, forthcoming.

StatLink ⟡ *http://dx.doi.org/10.1787/888932346838*

requirements suggested by past and ongoing OECD work is summarised in Table 1.8.[15]

... and can help fiscal consolidation directly...

As discussed in Chapter 4, several structural reforms can facilitate fiscal consolidation:

... by increasing public-sector productivity...

● Reforms to increase productivity in the public sector would improve fiscal positions markedly in many countries. Particular measures include the scope for improving public-sector efficiency by moving to national or international best practice in the provision of health and education services.

15. Such interactions arise over and above the indirect effects of reforms on budgetary and external balances via their impact on macroeconomic conditions.

... and raising employment...

- Employment-friendly reforms, discussed further below, could have immediate effects on fiscal positions by lowering government expenditure, and medium-term effects by raising employment and tax revenues. OECD estimates suggest that a 1 percentage point improvement in potential employment may improve government balances by between 0.3-0.8 per cent of GDP.

... and indirectly from changes in the tax structure...

- The implementation of revenue-neutral changes in the tax structure, away from taxes on corporate and labour income to higher taxes on consumption and property, would have indirect benefits for fiscal positions by enhancing incentives and medium-term growth.

... reform of tax expenditures and subsidies...

- Reform of tax expenditures and subsidies could bolster government budgets directly and also, in many cases indirectly, through increased activity.

... and additional pollution-pricing mechanisms

- Additional pollution-pricing mechanisms, such as green taxes and the auctioning of emission permits, could not only aid fiscal consolidation but also enhance welfare.

Structural reforms can also help rebalance global growth...

Structural reforms that are already desirable on efficiency, and/or welfare and equity grounds, can also contribute to a rebalancing of global growth, in part through their impact on fiscal outcomes (Table 1.8).[16] In particular:

... including improved social welfare systems in high-saving non-OECD countries...

- Improvements in the coverage and quality of social welfare systems, which are desirable in their own right, would reduce precautionary saving in external surplus countries outside the OECD. In a context of adequate regulation, liberalisation of financial markets in the emerging economies could reduce credit constraints for the private sector, and thereby enhance welfare by reducing forced saving.

... reforms to extend working lives in OECD countries...

- Reforms to improve the sustainability of public pension schemes by extending working lives may also help to reduce saving in OECD countries with an external surplus.[17]

... and removing anti-competitive product market regulations...

- Removal of anti-competitive product market regulations, especially in comparatively sheltered service sectors could encourage higher capital spending, narrowing the current account balance of surplus countries.

---

16. See also OECD *Economic Outlook* No. 87, Paris, 2010.
17. Such reforms would also aid fiscal consolidation efforts in all OECD countries.

... thus narrowing global imbalances

Simulation and scenario analyses suggest that a comprehensive package of reforms could help to narrow global imbalances by up to one-third in the medium term.[18] Many of these reforms are also desirable in countries that do not have large fiscal or external imbalances. If implemented more broadly, this could weaken the overall impact of reforms on global imbalances. It would, however, enhance welfare, by providing a stronger boost to economic growth in the medium-term.

Structural reforms might also have short-term benefits...

In the near term, the effects of growth-friendly structural policies could also facilitate the recovery from the crisis, with the future beneficial effects of new reforms being incorporated into forward-looking asset prices, helping to strengthen balance sheets and support demand. Equally, some reforms can also unleash pent-up demand and supply, as was the case in the past with telecoms reform. Tackling some of the legacies of the recession, especially the marked slack in labour markets, would also smooth the recovery. More generally, by raising the output capacity of the economy, growth-enhancing structural reforms would also allow monetary accommodation to continue for a longer period, contributing to a more vigorous recovery. However, the picture is more complicated in some instances; some reforms that are advisable on the basis of their strong long-term benefits, such as certain reforms to improve product market competition, can have negative side-effects in the near term if they hasten job losses in declining industries, although such side-effects will be small if competition-friendly reforms are implemented in sectors in which there is a strong potential for new job growth, such as retail trade and professional services.

... especially in labour markets...

Structural reforms are especially urgent in labour markets to help countries make greater use of their available labour resources more quickly. In the absence of such reforms, there is a substantial risk that high unemployment will prove persistent. In particular, reforms can help to make the recovery more job-rich; facilitate the reallocation of jobs and workers across sectors and regions; and help ensure that job losers and vulnerable groups remain attached to the labour market. This is particularly the case in many continental EU countries where labour-market institutions remain less employment-friendly despite the reforms of recent years.

... where a broad mix of reforms would be beneficial

Particular actions that should be undertaken (see *OECD Economic Outlook* 87) include: maintaining spending on active labour market

18. A scenario analysis indicates that the necessary fiscal tightening required to stabilise debt-to-GDP ratios in OECD countries by 2025 could reduce the size of global imbalances – measured as the GDP-weighted sum of countries' ratios of absolute saving-investment gaps to GDP – by almost one-sixth. If, in addition, Japan, Germany and China were to deregulate their product markets, aligning the level of economy-wide product market regulation with OECD best practice, and China were to raise public health spending by 2 percentage points of GDP (in a fiscally neutral way) and liberalise its financial markets, global imbalances could decline by twice as much (Kerdrain *et al.*, 2010).

policies, with priority being given to ensuring strong activation measures for job seekers; rebalancing employment protection towards less-strict protection for regular workers, but more protection for temporary workers; scaling back crisis-related improvements in benefit generosity; and tightening eligibility criteria for benefit measures that might otherwise be used as pathways out of the labour force. Hiring subsidies and additional expenditure on training, though not structural measures, could also be considered in the current environment, although in a context of tight fiscal constraints, they would need to be only temporary and well targeted. Such measures may be particularly useful in the United States, where the experience rating of unemployment insurance, alongside uncertainty about the durability of the recovery, may be contributing to employers' reluctance to hire new workers. Reductions in anti-competitive product market regulations could also help to make the recovery more job-rich, especially if undertaken in relatively labour-intensive service sectors, such as retail trade and professional services.

Housing market reforms can also improve labour outcomes

Restrictive housing policies, alongside negative housing equity, can limit residential mobility across regions and thus hamper the smooth functioning of labour markets by affecting the job-matching process. This is particularly important at present, given the need for reallocation of labour across sectors and regions in many OECD countries. New OECD estimates suggest that residential mobility tends to be markedly lower in countries with stricter rent regulation and high transactions costs of moving.[19] Mobility is also typically lower in areas in which new housing supply is fairly unresponsive to improvements in the profitability of house building. This suggests that structural reforms, such as redesigning rent regulations that go beyond correcting market failures, reconsidering land-use and planning policies, and addressing barriers that raise transactions costs, could improve residential mobility, with associated labour market benefits.

---

19. Estimates in Andrews *et al.* (2010) suggest that reducing rent control from the strictest level to the average level across OECD countries (equivalent to a change of 2 standard deviations) would increase average household mobility by around 4 percentage points. Reducing the transaction costs of moving from the highest to the average level across countries (equivalent to a 2 standard deviation change) would raise the probability of moving (which is 12% over a two-year period) by 1½ percentage points.

Bibliography

Ahrend, R., B. Cournède and R. Price (2009), "Monetary Policy, Market Excesses and Financial Turmoil", *OECD Economics Department Working Papers, No. 597*.

Altissimo, F., E. Georgiou, T. Sastre, M.T. Valderrama, G. Sterne, M. Stoker, M. Weth, K. Whelan and A. Willman (2005), "Wealth and Asset Price Effects on Economic Activity", *ECB Occasional Paper, No. 29*.

Amel, D., C. Barnes, F. Pancetta and C. Salleo (2004), "Consolidation and Efficiency in the Financial Sector: A Review of the International Evidence", *Journal of Banking and Finance*, Vol. 28.

Andrews, D., A. Caldera Sánchez A. and Å. Johansson (2010), "Housing Markets and Structural Policies in OECD countries", *OECD Economics Department Working Papers*, forthcoming.

Anil, K. Kayshap, and David Weinstein (eds.), *Japan's Bubble, Deflation and Long-term Stagnation*, Cambridge: MIT Press.

Aron, J., J., Duca, J., Muellbauer, K., Murata and A. Murphy (2010), "Credit, Housing Collateral and Consumption: Evidence from the UK, Japan and the US", *University of Oxford Discussion Paper, No. 487*.

Barrell, R., E.P. Davis and T. Fic (2009), "Optimal Regulation of Bank Capital and Liquidity: how to Calibrate New International Standards", *Financial Services Authority Occasional Paper Series*, No. 38, London.

Barrell, R., E.P. Davis, D. Karim and I. Liadze (2010), "Bank regulation, property prices and early warning systems for banking crises", *Journal of Banking and Finance*, forthcoming.

Basel Committee on Banking Supervision (2010), *An assessment of the long-term economic impact of stronger capital and liquidity requirements*, BIS, August.

Blundell-Wignall, A. and P. Slovik (2010) The EU Stress Test and Sovereign Debt Exposures," *OECD Working Papers on Finance, Insurance and Private Pensions*, No. 4, OECD Financial Affairs Division.

Caldera Sánchez, A. and Å. Johansson (2010). "The Price Responsiveness of Housing Supply in OECD Countries", *OECD Economics Department Working Papers*, forthcoming.

Cheung, C., D. Furceri and E. Rusticelli (2010), "Structural and Cyclical Factors behind Current Account Balances", *OECD Economics Department Working Papers*, No. 775.

Cournède, B. (2010), "Gauging the Impact of Higher Capital and Oil Costs on Potential Output", *OECD Economics Department Working Papers, No. 789*.

Cournède, B. and D. Moccero (2010), "Is There a Case for Price-Level Targeting?", *OECD Economics Department Working Papers*, No. 721, OECD.

Dale, S. (2009), "Separating fact from fiction – household balance sheets and the economic outlook", *BIS Review*, No. 114.

De Mello, L. and P.C. Padoan (2010), "Are Global Imbalances Sustainable? Post-Crisis Scenarios", *OECD Economics Department Working Papers*, No. 795.

Deutsche Bank (2010), Global Economics Perspective, 8, September 2010.

Doh, D. (2010), "The Efficacy of Large-Scale Asset Purchases at the Zero Lower Bound,"*Federal Reserve Bank of Kansas City Economic Review*, Second Quarter.

EC (European Commission) (2010), *Quarterly Report on the Euro Area*, Vol. 9, No. 3.

ECB (European Central bank) (2009), "Housing Wealth and Private Consumption in the Euro Area", *Monthly Bulletin*, January.

Elsby, M., B. Hobijn and A. Sahin (2010), "The Labor Market in the Great Recession", *Federal Reserve Bank of San Francisco Working Paper*, No. 2010-07.

Gagnon, J., M. Raskin, J. Remache and B. Sack (2010), "Large-Scale Asset Purchases by the Federal Reserve: Did They Work?", *Federal Reserve Bank of New York Staff Reports*, No. 441.

Gattini, I. and P. Hiebert (2010), "Forecasting and Assessing Euro Area House Prices Through the Lens of Key Fundamentals", *ECB Working Paper*, No. 1249.

Girouard, N., M. Kennedy, P. van den Noord and C. André (2006), "Recent House Price Developments: the Role of Fundamentals", *OECD Economic Department Working Papers*, No. 475.

Glick, R. and K.J. Lansing (2009), "US Household Deleveraging and Consumption Growth", *FRBSF Economic Letter*, No. 16.

Hamilton, J. and C. Wu (2010), "The Effectiveness of Alternative Monetary Policy Tools in a Zero Lower Bound Environment," mimeo, 25 August.

Haugh, D., A. Mourougane and O. Chantal (2010), "The Automobile Industry In and Beyond the Crisis", *OECD Economics Department Working Papers*, No. 745.

Hervé, K., Pain, N., Richardson, P., Sédillot, F. and P.O. Beffy (2010), "The OECD's New Global Model", *Economic Modelling*, forthcoming.

Hüfner, F. and I. Koske (2010), "Explaining Household Saving rates in G7 Countries: Implications for Germany", *OECD Economics Department Working Papers*, No. 754.

Institute of International Finance (2010), *Interim Report on the Cumulative Impact on the Global Economy of Proposed Changes in the Banking Regulatory Framework*, Washington, DC.

Joyce, M., A. Lasaosa, I. Stevens and M. Tong (2010), "The Financial Market Impact of Quantitative Easing", *Bank of England Working Papers*, No. 393.

Kerdrain, C. (2010), "How Important is Wealth for Explaining Household Consumption over the Recent Crisis? An Empirical Study for the United States, Japan and the Euro Area", *OECD Economics Department Working Papers*, forthcoming.

Kerdrain, C., I. Koske and I. Wanner (2010), "The Impact of Structural Policies on Saving, Investment and Current Accounts", *OECD Economics Department Working papers*, forthcoming.

Ludwig, A. and T. Slok (2002), "The Impact of Changes in Stock Prices and House Prices on Consumption in OECD Countries", *IMF Working Paper*, Vol. 02/1.

Macroeconomic Assessment Group (2010), *Assessing the macroeconomic impact of the transition to stronger capital and liquidity requirements*, Interim Report, Financial Stability Board and Basel Committee on Banking Supervision, August, Basel.

Martinez-Carrascal, C. and A. Ferrando, (2008), "The impact of financial position on investment: an analysis for non-financial corporations in the euro area", *ECB Working Paper* No. 943.

Meier, A. (2010), "Still Minding the Gap: Inflation Dynamics during Episodes of Persistent Large Output Gaps", *IMF Working Paper*, No. WP/10/189.

Mishkin, F. (2007), "Housing and the Monetary Transmission Mechanism", *Finance and Economics Discussion Paper*, No. 40.

OECD (2009), *Economic Survey of the Euro Area*, Paris.

OECD (2010), *OECD Economic Surveys*: China 2010, Paris.

Pain, N. and I. Koske (2008), "The Usefulness of Output Gaps for Policy Analysis", *OECD Economics Department Working Papers* No. 621.

Pennacchi, G. G., Vermaelen, T. and Wolff, C., "Contingent Capital: The Case for COERCs", *INSEAD Working Paper* No. 2010/89/FIN.

Slovik, P. and B. Cournède (2010), "Estimating the impact of Basle III", *OECD Economics Department Working Papers*, forthcoming.

Stock, J. and M. Watson (2010), "Modelling Inflation After the Crisis", paper presented at Federal Bank of Kansas City Symposium, Jackson Hole, August.

Stroebel, J. and J. B. Taylor (2009), "Estimated Impact of the Fed's Mortage-Backed Securities Purchase Program", *NBER Working Papers*, No. 15626.

Taylor, J. B. (2009), "The Financial Crisis and the Policy Responses: An Empirical Analysis of What Went Wrong", *NBER Working Papers*, No. 14631.

OECD Economic Outlook
Volume 2010/2
© OECD 2010

Chapter 2

DEVELOPMENT IN INDIVIDUAL OECD COUNTRIES

UNITED STATES

After turning around briskly in the second half of 2009 and into the early part of this year, US economic growth slowed in the second and third quarters of 2010. Fiscal support continues to be substantial, but the effect of the stimulus on growth is diminishing and is assumed to turn negative in future quarters. The pace of the recovery is projected to remain moderate through 2011-2012 as households continue to rebuild net worth and the unemployment rate declines slowly.

The Federal Reserve should continue to support growth, as inflation remains well contained and the economy continues to run well below capacity. In addition to keeping policy interest rates broadly unchanged in 2011, the Federal Reserve could also reaffirm its commitment to price stability by adopting an explicit medium-term inflation target. If growth turns out to be significantly weaker than projected, action to lower real long-term rates *via* further quantitative easing would be justified, notwithstanding uncertainties associated with the use of such unconventional policy tools. With high budget imbalances and a fast-rising federal debt, however, fiscal authorities need to reduce the deficit, although only gradually to avoid harming the recovery. The Administration should follow through on its plan to stabilise the debt-to-GDP ratio by 2015, which will entail further consolidation measures than have currently been laid out, such as implementing the upcoming recommendations of the President's Fiscal Commission in the challenging areas of tax policy and entitlement spending.

The economic recovery has slowed considerably...

After growing briskly late 2009 and early 2010, the recovery slowed considerably to around a 2% annual pace in the second and third quarters of 2010, with a broadly similar pace expected for the remainder of the year. Recent output growth, while positive, has been too weak to bring about a significant reduction in the unemployment rate. Government support for the economy continues to be substantial, but the effect of the stimulus on economic growth is winding down and, on current plans, will turn negative in future quarters.

United States

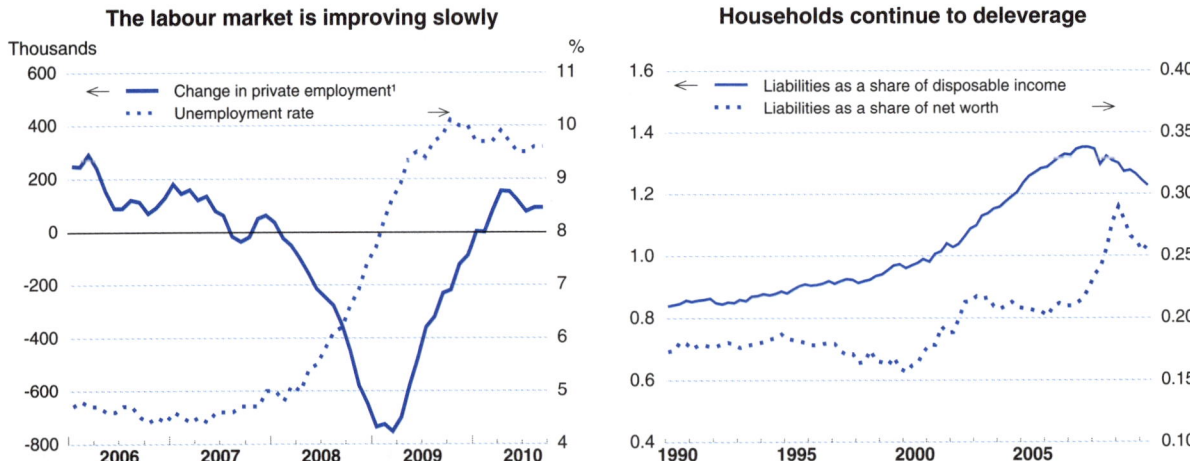

1. Three-month moving average of one-month actual change of total private employment.
Source: OECD Economic Outlook 88 database; Bureau of Economic Analysis and Federal Reserve.

StatLink ᴍᵴᴾ http://dx.doi.org/10.1787/888932345356

United States: **Employment, income and inflation**
Percentage changes

	2008	2009	2010	2011	2012
Employment[1]	-0.7	-4.2	-0.5	0.9	1.7
Unemployment rate[2]	5.8	9.3	9.7	9.5	8.7
Employment cost index	2.9	1.5	1.8	1.3	1.1
Compensation per employee[3]	2.9	0.5	2.2	2.5	2.6
Labour productivity	0.7	1.6	3.3	1.3	1.4
Unit labour cost	2.6	-0.6	-0.9	1.3	1.3
GDP deflator	2.2	0.9	1.0	1.2	0.9
Consumer price index	3.8	-0.3	1.6	1.1	1.1
Core PCE deflator[4]	2.3	1.5	1.4	1.0	0.9
PCE deflator[5]	3.3	0.2	1.7	0.9	0.9
Real household disposable income	1.7	0.6	1.2	2.6	2.7

1. Based on the Bureau of Labor Statistics (BLS) Establishment Survey.
2. As a percentage of labour force, based on the BLS Household Survey.
3. In the private sector.
4. Deflator for private consumption excluding food and energy.
5. Private consumption deflator. PCE stands for personal consumption expenditures.
Source: OECD Economic Outlook 88 database.

StatLink http://dx.doi.org/10.1787/888932346857

... and the economy continues to run far below capacity

The slowing of the recovery has left the economy operating well below its potential, with high unemployment and a substantial output gap. Both capacity utilisation and average hours worked for those currently employed have recovered only about half of their decline during the recession.

Nonetheless, a double dip is unlikely

The burst of growth late last year and early in 2010 sprung from significant contributions of inventories and, to a much lesser extent, net

United States

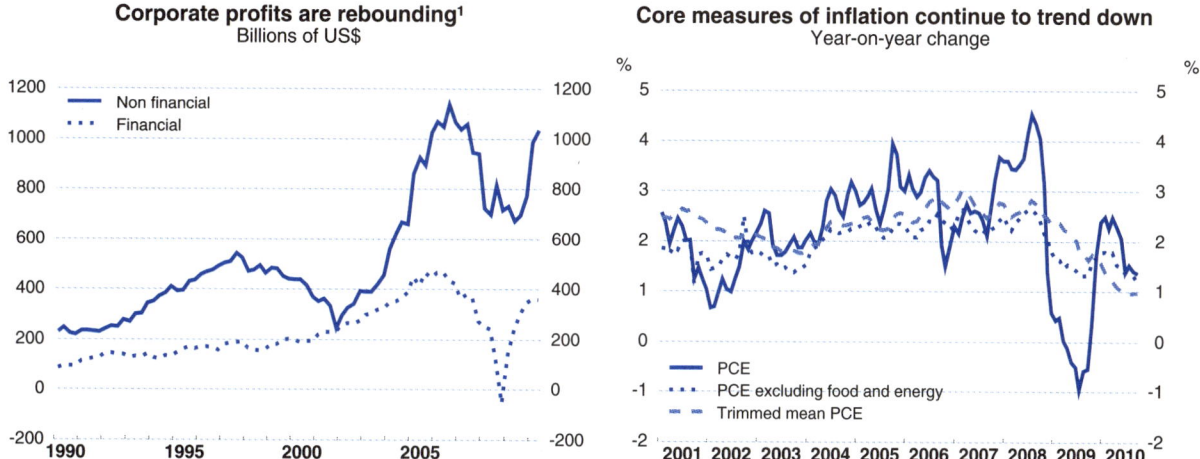

Corporate profits are rebounding[1]
Billions of US$

Core measures of inflation continue to trend down
Year-on-year change

1. Corporate profits before tax with inventory valuation adjustment.
Source: OECD Economic Outlook 88 database; Federal Reserve; United States Department of Commerce; Bureau of Economic Analysis and Datastream.

StatLink http://dx.doi.org/10.1787/888932345375

United States: **Financial indicators**

	2008	2009	2010	2011	2012
Household saving ratio[1]	4.1	5.9	5.7	6.0	6.1
General government financial balance[2]	-6.3	-11.3	-10.5	-8.8	-6.8
Current account balance[2]	-4.7	-2.7	-3.4	-3.7	-3.7
Short-term interest rate[3]	3.2	0.9	0.5	0.7	1.8
Long-term interest rate[4]	3.7	3.3	3.1	3.3	4.5

1. As a percentage of disposable income.
2. As a percentage of GDP.
3. 3-month rate on euro-dollar deposits.
4. 10-year government bonds.
Source: OECD Economic Outlook 88 database.

StatLink ⟨⟩ http://dx.doi.org/10.1787/888932346876

exports. Both have since moderated as the inventory cycle waned and as US demand growth outpaced that of its trading partners. Outside of these categories, growth appears to be more durable, but also much slower. Over the past five quarters personal consumption expenditures, accounting for about two-thirds of GDP, have grown at an annual rate of around 2%, a slow pace for a recovery, which has allowed households to increase savings. The pace of consumption growth is likely to increase gradually as households continue to deleverage and employment rises slowly.

United States: **Demand and output**

	2009	2010	2011	2012	Fourth quarter		
					2010	2011	2012
	Current prices $ billion	Percentage changes from previous year, volume (2005 prices)					
Private consumption	10 001.3	1.7	2.4	2.7	2.3	2.3	3.1
Government consumption	2 411.5	1.1	1.0	0.6	1.5	0.6	0.7
Gross fixed investment	2 219.8	3.4	7.2	6.8	7.1	6.6	7.1
Public	503.4	0.9	2.0	0.8	2.3	0.7	0.9
Residential	352.1	-2.6	2.8	6.4	-2.6	5.0	7.5
Non-residential	1 364.4	5.9	10.1	9.0	11.5	9.0	9.1
Final domestic demand	14 632.6	1.8	2.8	3.0	2.8	2.7	3.3
Stockbuilding[1]	- 127.2	1.6	-0.1	0.0			
Total domestic demand	14 505.5	3.4	2.7	3.0	3.8	2.5	3.3
Exports of goods and services	1 578.4	11.4	8.1	9.9	8.3	9.0	10.0
Imports of goods and services	1 964.8	14.3	9.9	7.7	17.1	7.2	7.9
Net exports[1]	- 386.4	-0.7	-0.6	0.0			
GDP at market prices	14 119.1	2.7	2.2	3.1	2.3	2.6	3.4

Note: National accounts are based on official chain-linked data. This introduces a discrepancy in the identity between real demand components and GDP. For further details see *OECD Economic Outlook* Sources and Methods *(http://www.oecd.org/eco/sources-and-methods)*.
Detailed quarterly projections are reported for the major seven countries, the euro area and the total OECD in the Statistical Annex.
1. Contributions to changes in real GDP (percentage of real GDP in previous year), actual amount in the first column.
Source: OECD Economic Outlook 88 database.

StatLink ⟨⟩ http://dx.doi.org/10.1787/888932346895

United States: **External indicators**

	2008	2009	2010	2011	2012
	\$ billion				
Goods and services exports	1 843.4	1 578.4	1 826.3	2 006	2 238
Goods and services imports	2 553.8	1 964.8	2 365.1	2 604	2 859
Foreign balance	- 710.5	- 386.4	- 538.9	- 597	- 622
Invisibles, net	41.6	8.0	43.2	39	35
Current account balance	- 668.9	- 378.4	- 495.7	- 559	- 587
	Percentage changes				
Goods and services export volumes	6.0	- 9.5	11.4	8.1	9.9
Goods and services import volumes	- 2.6	- 13.8	14.3	9.9	7.7
Export performance[1]	2.0	2.6	- 1.6	0.0	1.5
Terms of trade	- 5.2	6.0	- 1.5	1.5	- 0.5

1. Ratio between export volume and export market of total goods and services.
Source: OECD Economic Outlook 88 database.

StatLink http://dx.doi.org/10.1787/888932346914

Investment should continue to increase

High interest margins and improving market conditions have boosted financial industry current-period profits since late 2008, but markdowns and writeoffs, which are not included in such profits, continue to weigh heavily on financial industry balance sheets. Non-financial corporate profits are also increasing strongly and they have now returned to nearly pre-recession levels. Strong profit growth, combined with corporate bond yields that have fallen below their pre-crisis levels, has spurred vigorous increases in business fixed investment since the beginning of 2010, and should continue to support elevated business investment growth in future quarters despite capacity utilisation rates that remain well below pre-recession levels.

Unemployment will remain high for some time

Employment continues to expand, but at a pace that is too slow to increase the employment-population ratio and recover the ground lost during the recession. Nevertheless, the unemployment rate has fallen by ½ a percentage point since peaking in late-2009, largely from declining labour force participation. Despite a projected gradual pick-up in employment growth over the next couple of years, the unemployment rate is likely to come down only slowly and still be far above its pre-recession levels by the end of 2012. Productivity growth should ease from the rapid pace in 2009 when it surged as employment contracted.

Real estate is slowly improving

Except for a spurt prior to the expiration of the homebuyers' tax credit in the second quarter of 2010, residential investment remains weak and will likely continue so for some time. The rate of new home construction remains low and the significant backlog of delinquencies and foreclosures which have yet to be put on the market will be an impediment to residential construction, house price increases and financial industry balance sheets over the next couple of years. Related troubles also weigh down the commercial real estate market, though there are signs that the contraction in that market has ended.

Fiscal imbalances are large

Budget positions at all levels of government remain severely affected by the recession and the relatively poor positions prior to it. The present projection assumes that budgetary measures are implemented in line with the government's goal of stabilising the federal debt-to-GDP ratio by 2015. General government net lending is thus projected to fall from above 10½ per cent of GDP in 2010 to around 6¾ per cent in 2012. This improvement largely reflects the fiscal stimulus winding down and economic growth gradually lowering unemployment and raising tax revenue. Further progress to unwind fiscal imbalances beyond 2012 would require ambitious reforms of the tax system and entitlement spending, perhaps along the lines to be recommended by the President's Fiscal Commission in late 2010.

Expansionary monetary policy should continue for some time

With substantial slack in the economy, low levels of inflation and subdued bank lending, monetary policy should remain very accommodative for the next few years and be withdrawn only as the economy recovers. Such support will help the banking system adjust to the stricter capital standards expected following the adoption of Basel III rules. The second round of quantitative easing seeks to provide additional support to growth. At present, there is little sign that continued extraordinarily loose macroeconomic policy settings are leading to an unanchoring of inflation expectations or another asset price bubble (outside of certain commodities), though the risk of such outcomes will rise the longer the normalisation of monetary conditions is delayed.

The current account deficit will deteriorate somewhat

The recession led to a considerable improvement in the foreign trade balance as domestic demand collapsed. The current account deficit fell from 6% of GDP in 2006 to 2¾ per cent in 2009. However, it is widening again as the government deficit has increased and private investment has outpaced saving. Some additional deterioration is likely, but the current balance should remain significantly smaller than its pre-recession levels.

Despite a projection of slow growth, significant downside risks exist

The turnaround in the economy over the past year has largely been driven by the extraordinary macroeconomic policy support, and it is unclear if output growth is yet self-sustaining. House prices might yet fall further which would depress household wealth and consumption growth. On the other hand, the significant deleveraging of household balance sheets may slow, leading to more robust consumption growth, and business investment may prove stronger than anticipated.

JAPAN

Japan has responded to slowing growth with two fiscal packages in late 2010, which will support activity in 2011, with annual growth projected to reach 1¾ per cent. As the impact of the fiscal stimulus fades, stronger private domestic demand, underpinned by improving labour market conditions and high corporate profitability, will support the expansion through 2012. Nevertheless, deflation is projected to continue, with unemployment remaining above its pre-crisis level.

With gross public debt projected to top 200% of GDP in 2011, more ambitious consolidation than currently planned for 2011 and 2012 would be warranted. At a minimum, it is necessary to avoid additional fiscal stimulus and contain government spending in 2011-12 in line with the Fiscal Management Strategy. Additional tax revenue is necessary to achieve the target of halving the primary budget deficit from its FY 2010 level by FY 2015. The Bank of Japan should implement more ambitious quantitative easing measures to relax monetary conditions in the face of entrenched deflation and maintain such policies until underlying inflation is significantly positive. The New Growth Strategy announced by the government in June 2010 should focus on policies to boost productivity growth, especially in non-manufacturing.

Although the recovery from the crisis paused in mid-2010...

Exports, the main driver of Japan's recovery from its worst recession of the post-war era, stalled in mid-2010, reflecting weaker shipments to Asia, particularly China. In addition, the 13% appreciation of the yen in trade-weighted terms since April 2010 has reduced Japan's share of global markets. Weaker external demand was accompanied by slowing domestic demand, as the impact of the 2008-09 fiscal stimulus waned. Private consumption was flat in the second quarter, although it rebounded strongly in the third quarter thanks in part to a jump in car sales before the expiration of incentives for the purchase of energy-efficient vehicles in

Japan

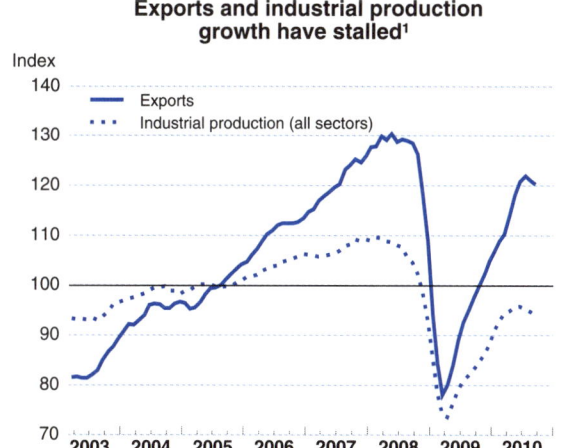

Exports and industrial production growth have stalled[1]

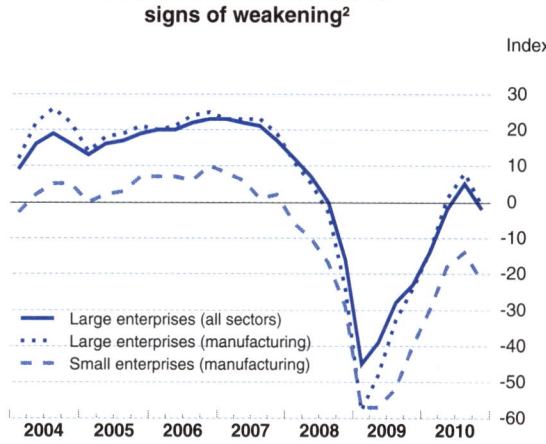

Business confidence shows signs of weakening[2]

1. Data are three-month moving averages of seasonally-adjusted volume indices (2005=100).
2. Diffusion index of "favourable" minus "unfavourable" business conditions in the Tankan Survey. The numbers for December 2010 are companies' projections in September 2010.

Source: Ministry of Economy, Trade and Industry; Bank of Japan.

StatLink ⬛ http://dx.doi.org/10.1787/888932345394

Japan: **Employment, income and inflation**
Percentage changes

	2008	2009	2010	2011	2012
Employment	-0.4	-1.6	-0.4	0.1	-0.3
Unemployment rate[1]	4.0	5.1	5.1	4.9	4.5
Compensation of employees	0.7	-4.0	1.4	1.2	0.7
Unit labour cost	1.9	1.3	-2.2	-0.6	-0.6
Household disposable income	-0.2	-2.0	1.0	0.3	1.0
GDP deflator	-0.8	-0.9	-1.8	-0.8	-0.8
Consumer price index[2]	1.4	-1.4	-0.9	-0.8	-0.5
Core consumer price index[3]	0.1	-0.6	-1.3	-0.9	-0.5
Private consumption deflator	0.4	-2.2	-1.7	-0.7	-0.8

1. As a percentage of labour force.
2. Calculated as the sum of the seasonally adjusted quarterly indices for each year.
3. Consumer price index excluding food and energy.
Source: OECD Economic Outlook 88 database.

StatLink http://dx.doi.org/10.1787/888932346933

September 2010. Sluggish exports and domestic demand halted the recovery in industrial production, which remains about 14% below its pre-crisis peak. The marked improvement in confidence is ending, as companies expect a deterioration in business conditions in the final quarter of 2010 and consumer confidence has started to weaken.

... new fiscal stimulus and private demand are supporting growth

However, a number of factors should prevent a double-dip recession in Japan. First, the government introduced fiscal stimulus packages in September and October 2010, amounting to 0.2% and 1.1% of GDP, respectively. The packages increase public works spending, subsidies to

Japan

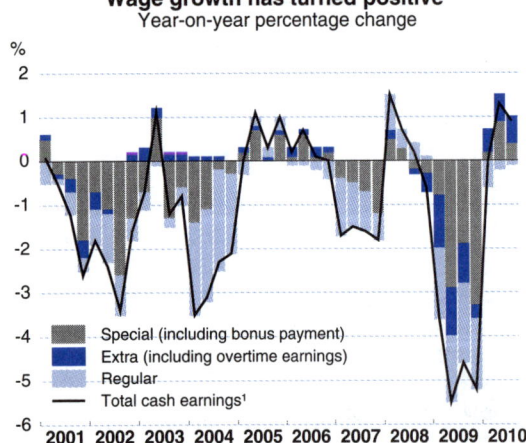

Wage growth has turned positive
Year-on-year percentage change

Special (including bonus payment)
Extra (including overtime earnings)
Regular
Total cash earnings[1]

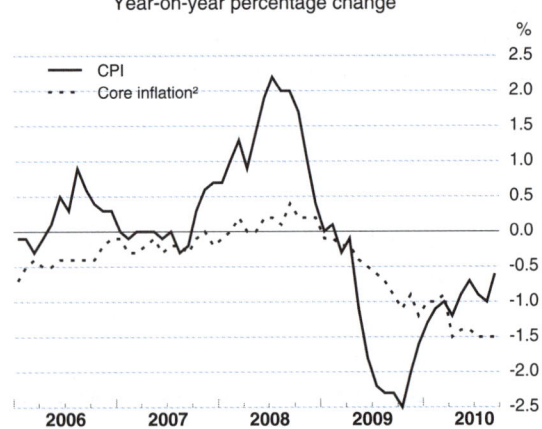

Deflation has become entrenched
Year-on-year percentage change

CPI
Core inflation[2]

1. Total cash earnings of all workers, including bonuses.
2. Corresponds to the OECD measure of core inflation.
Source: Ministry of Health, Labour and Welfare; Ministry of Internal Affairs and Communications.

StatLink http://dx.doi.org/10.1787/888932345413

Japan: **Financial indicators**

	2008	2009	2010	2011	2012
Household saving ratio[1]	2.3	2.2	2.7	2.8	3.1
General government financial balance[2]	-2.1	-7.1	-7.7	-7.5	-7.3
Current account balance[2]	3.3	2.8	3.4	3.7	3.7
Short-term interest rate[3]	0.7	0.3	0.2	0.2	0.2
Long-term interest rate[4]	1.5	1.3	1.1	1.2	1.7

1. As a percentage of disposable income.
2. As a percentage of GDP.
3. 3-month CDs.
4. 10-year government bonds.
Source: OECD Economic Outlook 88 database.

StatLink 🔗 *http://dx.doi.org/10.1787/888932346952*

encourage investment in low-carbon activities, child-care support and labour market outlays and extend subsidies for purchases of energy-efficient homes and appliances. As for private demand, corporate profitability is high, helping to sustain business investment. In addition, nominal wage growth turned positive in the second quarter of 2010 for the first time in two years, as large profits boosted bonus payments and firms increased overtime work. However, employment in the first half of 2010 was down almost 1% from a year earlier, keeping the unemployment rate

Japan: **Demand and output**

	2009	2010	2011	2012	Fourth quarter		
					2010	2011	2012
	Current prices ¥ trillion	Percentage changes from previous year, volume (2000 prices)					
Private consumption	282.7	2.4	1.0	1.4	1.7	1.1	1.5
Government consumption	93.6	1.6	1.7	0.3	1.7	1.2	0.1
Gross fixed investment	98.0	-0.1	3.2	2.3	3.4	1.9	3.7
Public[1]	20.3	-1.5	-1.9	-10.9	0.4	-11.6	-3.3
Residential	13.6	-7.3	4.5	6.1	3.8	5.0	7.1
Non-residential	64.0	1.8	4.6	5.5	4.3	5.5	4.8
Final domestic demand	474.2	1.7	1.6	1.4	2.0	1.3	1.7
Stockbuilding[2]	- 1.4	0.0	0.0	0.0			
Total domestic demand	472.9	1.7	1.6	1.4	2.4	1.3	1.7
Exports of goods and services	59.5	25.4	6.7	5.8	17.0	5.5	5.9
Imports of goods and services	58.1	10.5	6.6	6.5	11.7	5.4	7.0
Net exports[2]	1.4	1.9	0.1	0.0			
GDP at market prices	474.3	3.7	1.7	1.3	3.3	1.3	1.6

Note: National accounts are based on official chain-linked data. This introduces a discrepancy in the identity between real demand components and GDP. For further details see *OECD Economic Outlook* Sources and Methods *(http://www.oecd.org/eco/sources-and-methods).*
Detailed quarterly projections are reported for the major seven countries, the euro area and the total OECD in the Statistical Annex.
1. Including public corporations.
2. Contributions to changes in real GDP (percentage of real GDP in previous year), actual amount in the first column.
Source: OECD Economic Outlook 88 database.

StatLink 🔗 *http://dx.doi.org/10.1787/888932346971*

Japan: **External indicators**

	2008	2009	2010	2011	2012
	\$ billion				
Goods and services exports	853.7	637.6	843.9	941	989
Goods and services imports	847.6	621.9	774.6	865	922
Foreign balance	6.1	15.7	69.3	77	67
Invisibles, net	151.3	126.5	121.4	142	154
Current account balance	157.4	142.2	190.8	219	221
	Percentage changes				
Goods and services export volumes	1.6	- 23.9	25.4	6.7	5.8
Goods and services import volumes	1.2	- 16.7	10.5	6.6	6.5
Export performance[1]	- 2.4	- 16.6	8.5	- 3.5	- 4.0
Terms of trade	- 9.1	11.2	- 6.3	- 0.1	- 0.8

1. Ratio between export volume and export market of total goods and services.
Source: OECD Economic Outlook 88 database.

StatLink http://dx.doi.org/10.1787/888932346990

high at around 5%, while the job-offer-to-applicant ratio is still low at around 0.5. With large slack remaining in the economy, the rate of core deflation has worsened to about 1.5% (year-on-year) since April, although ½ percentage point is due to the elimination of tuition fees for upper-secondary schooling. In addition, asset prices are falling; the average residential land price fell 3.4% in the year to July 2010, the 19th straight year of decline, while the stock price index has dropped 15% since April, reflecting, at least in part, concern about the strong yen.

While fiscal stimulus is to be followed by a spending freeze in 2011-12...

The June 2010 Fiscal Management Strategy aims at stabilising and eventually reducing the public-debt ratio, which is projected to reach 211% of GDP by 2012. The medium-term target is to halve the primary budget deficit of central and local governments relative to GDP between FY 2010 and FY 2015. Projections attached to the Strategy – which do not take account of the two most recent fiscal packages – estimate the FY 2010 primary deficit at 6.4% of GDP, implying an improvement of 3.2% of GDP over the next five years. To meet the target, central and local government spending (excluding debt repayment and interest payments) over FY 2011-13 is not to exceed the level in the initial budget for FY 2010.

... an increase in tax revenues is needed to meet fiscal objectives...

Given that one-half of the October stimulus package is to be spent during FY 2011, the OECD projection assumes that spending (on a general government basis) in FY 2011 will slightly exceed the FY 2010 level, before falling below it in FY 2012. Based on these assumptions, the general government primary deficit is projected to fall from about 7½ per cent of GDP in 2010 to 6¼ per cent in 2012 (on a calendar-year basis, excluding one-off factors), roughly in line with the Strategy's deficit reduction target. However, given population ageing and the broad consensus to improve the quality of health care, achieving such spending restraint will require significant cuts in outlays in other areas. Moreover, it will be difficult to further extend the spending ceiling to FY 2014 and beyond, making tax increases necessary to meet the FY 2015 target. Indeed, the Strategy calls for multi-year revenue measures based on a comprehensive tax reform, including the consumption tax. The Strategy's long-term objective is a primary budget surplus for central and local governments by FY 2020, putting the public-debt ratio on a downward trend during the 2020s.

... while the central bank has introduced new initiatives to support growth

The Bank of Japan reduced the policy interest rate from the 0.1% set in December 2008 to between zero and 0.1% in October 2010. In addition, it has launched a number of schemes to provide extra liquidity: i) in June 2010, it decided to supply up to 3 trillion yen (0.6% of GDP) in one-year loans at the policy rate to financial institutions for lending to companies in "growth areas"; ii) in August 2010, it created a second fixed-rate, funds-supplying operation that will lend money to financial institutions at the policy rate for six months, up to an aggregate amount of 10 trillion yen (2% of GDP); and iii) in October 2010, it announced a 5 trillion yen (1% of GDP) fund to purchase risk assets, including corporate debt and commercial paper. However, the scale of quantitative easing since 2008 remains well below that implemented by some other major central banks. Moreover, the Bank of Japan is committed to maintain these policies only until it forecasts price stability, rather than when price stability is actually achieved. Finally, the authorities intervened in foreign exchange markets on 15 September 2010 in the amount of 2.1 trillion yen (0.4% of GDP) for the first time in six years. This intervention immediately reduced the currency's value relative to the dollar by almost 4% and prompted a rally in equity prices. By early October, though, the exchange rate had surpassed its pre-intervention level.

The expansion is projected to continue through 2012

Output growth is projected to slow in 2011 as the impact of the fiscal stimulus fades. However, private domestic demand is expected to sustain the recovery, with output growth reaching 1¾ per cent by the end of 2012. Continued wage gains and a fall in unemployment to around 4½ per cent are likely to support private consumption. Business investment, whose share in GDP has fallen by nearly 3 percentage points since the 2008 crisis, should be a second source of growth. Relatively buoyant private domestic demand will be partially offset by declines in public spending under the Fiscal Management Strategy, while Japan is likely to lose export market share in the context of the strong yen. The pace of recovery will not be rapid enough to eliminate the output gap by 2012, thus keeping Japan in deflation.

Risks are largely related to fiscal policy, external demand and the yen

There is uncertainty about how the government spending limits will be divided by category and their impact on growth in 2011-12. Nevertheless, such restraint will slow the run-up in the gross public-debt ratio, which is already the highest ever recorded in the OECD area, thus limiting Japan's vulnerability to a rise in long-term interest rates. On the external side, growth is particularly sensitive to exchange rate developments. Continued yen appreciation could further restrain export growth and prompt firms to shift investment and hiring overseas.

EURO AREA

A gradual recovery is underway, driven by strong exports and a rise in consumption and investment. Confidence has rebounded and financial conditions have improved. However, the pace of recovery is likely to be muted, due to on-going private sector balance sheet adjustments, necessary fiscal consolidation and prolonged adjustment to large imbalances in some peripheral countries. Unemployment has stabilised at a high level. Considerable slack will keep inflation low.

More credible and detailed plans for fiscal consolidation need to be set out for the coming years. Prolonged consolidation is required in countries with large debt burdens to reduce the debt-to-GDP ratio to a more prudent level. Provided the recovery stays on track, monetary policy stimulus should be gradually withdrawn as the recovery progresses and non-standard measures continue to be wound down as conditions allow. Cross-cutting and fundamental reforms of fiscal and macroprudential policies are required, alongside structural reforms, to make the economy more resilient.

A gradual but uneven recovery is underway

GDP in the second quarter of 2010 was 1.9% higher than a year earlier. Export growth was strong, especially in countries that specialise in capital goods, although it was broadly matched by rising imports. While strong growth in the second quarter partly reflected a bounce back from weakness earlier in the year, underlying private domestic demand has also been stronger. Private consumption and business investment expanded throughout the first half of the year, supported by rising confidence and low interest rates. Within the overall recovery, the turnaround in demand in some peripheral euro area countries that need to unwind large current account deficits has remained limited.

Euro area

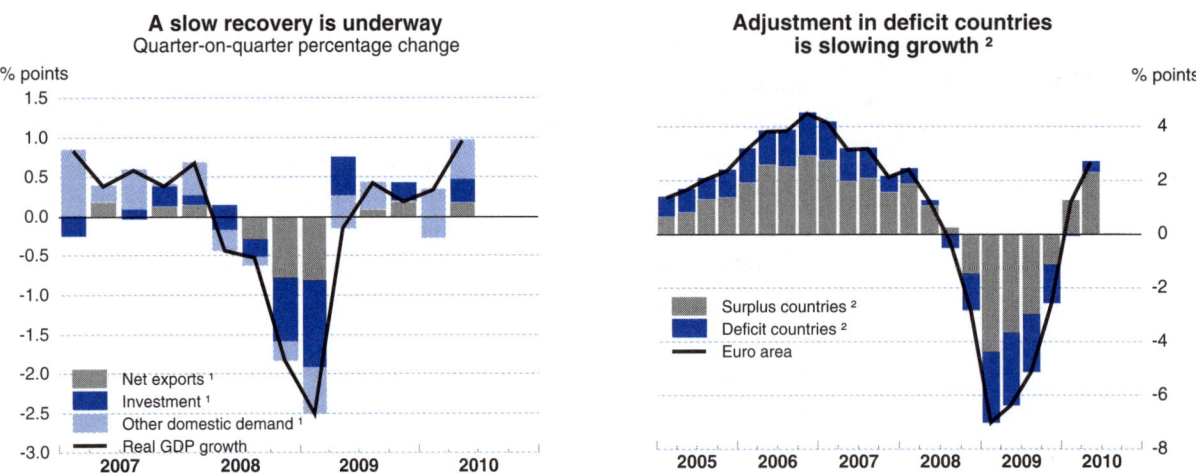

1. Contribution to the quarterly percentage change of the euro area GDP.
2. Contributions to year-on-year percentage change of the euro area GDP. The deficit and surplus countries are defined by their average current account balance as a share of GDP between 2002-07.

Source: OECD, OECD Economic Outlook 88 database.

StatLink ⟶ http://dx.doi.org/10.1787/888932345622

Euro area: **Employment, income and inflation**
Percentage changes

	2008	2009	2010	2011	2012
Employment	1.0	-1.8	-0.5	0.3	0.6
Unemployment rate[1]	7.4	9.3	9.9	9.6	9.2
Compensation per employee[2]	3.1	1.2	1.7	2.1	2.0
Labour productivity	-0.3	-2.2	2.2	1.3	1.4
Unit labour cost	3.8	4.0	-0.7	0.3	0.2
Household disposable income	3.5	-0.1	1.7	2.1	2.4
GDP deflator	2.0	1.0	0.8	1.0	1.1
Harmonised index of consumer prices	3.3	0.3	1.5	1.3	1.2
Core harmonised index of consumer prices[3]	1.8	1.4	0.9	1.2	1.2
Private consumption deflator	2.7	-0.2	1.7	1.4	1.2

Note: Covers the euro area countries that are members of the OECD.
1. As a percentage of labour force.
2. In the private sector.
3. Harmonised index of consumer prices excluding energy, food, drink and tobacco.
Source: OECD Economic Outlook 88 database.

StatLink 〰🖳 *http://dx.doi.org/10.1787/888932347332*

Financial conditions continue to improve

Financial conditions have improved overall under extensive policy support and due to growing confidence, despite successive rounds of market volatility regarding sovereign debt risks. Credit to the non-financial sector, notably households, is increasing and equity prices have risen. Despite the publication of the second EU-wide stress tests, the strength of the banking system and its ability to provide credit as demand picks ups remain concerns. Moreover, certain sovereign spreads have returned to the peaks of the fiscal crisis in May 2010, despite the EU support facilities now in place.

Euro area

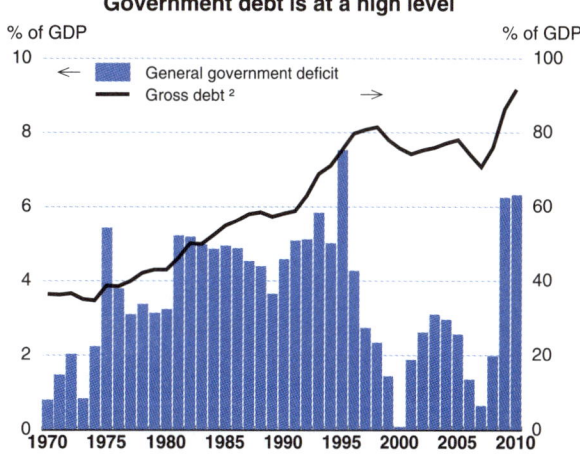

The labour market has stabilised
← Employment growth [1]
Unemployment rate →

Government debt is at a high level
← General government deficit
Gross debt [2] →

1. Quarter-on-quarter percentage change.
2. National accounts basis.
Source: Eurostat and OECD, OECD Economic Outlook 88 database.

StatLink 〰🖳 *http://dx.doi.org/10.1787/888932345641*

Euro area: **Financial indicators**

	2008	2009	2010	2011	2012
Household saving ratio[1]	8.9	9.9	9.4	9.1	8.8
General government financial balance[2]	-2.0	-6.2	-6.3	-4.6	-3.5
Current account balance[2]	-0.8	-0.4	-0.2	0.3	0.9
Short-term interest rate[3]	4.6	1.2	0.8	1.1	1.8
Long-term interest rate[4]	4.3	3.8	3.4	3.6	4.3

Note: Covers the euro area countries that are members of the OECD.
1. As a percentage of disposable income.
2. As a percentage of GDP.
3. 3-month interbank rate.
4. 10-year government bonds.
Source: OECD Economic Outlook 88 database.

StatLink ᴍᴤᴸ http://dx.doi.org/10.1787/888932347351

The labour market is stabilising

The unemployment rate has been broadly stable at around 10% over the year to September. However, there are large differences in performance among euro area countries. Employment has expanded somewhat since early 2010, the first increase in almost two years.

Inflationary pressures remain subdued

Headline annual inflation has risen modestly, boosted by higher energy prices and increases in administered prices. Core annual inflation has also risen but remains subdued at around 1%, reflecting the substantial economic slack. The growth of nominal hourly labour costs slowed further to reach 1.6% in annual terms in August. Inflation is likely

Euro area: **Demand and output**

	2009	2010	2011	2012	Fourth quarter 2010	Fourth quarter 2011	Fourth quarter 2012
	Current prices € billion	Percentage changes from previous year, volume (2009 prices)					
Private consumption	5 151.1	0.6	1.0	1.7	0.7	1.4	1.7
Government consumption	1 974.4	1.0	0.0	-0.1	0.9	-0.2	-0.1
Gross fixed investment	1 753.6	-1.0	1.6	2.8	1.6	1.9	3.2
Public	253.9	-3.4	-5.2	-4.4	-5.8	-6.0	-2.7
Residential	471.7	-3.6	0.4	1.7	-0.4	1.0	1.9
Non-residential	970.8	0.7	3.7	4.7	4.5	3.9	5.0
Final domestic demand	8 879.1	0.3	0.9	1.5	0.9	1.1	1.6
Stockbuilding[1]	- 67.9	0.6	0.1	0.0			
Total domestic demand	8 811.2	0.9	1.0	1.5	1.7	1.1	1.6
Net exports[1]	119.3	0.8	0.7	0.6			
GDP at market prices	8 930.5	1.7	1.7	2.0	2.1	1.7	2.1

Note: Detailed quarterly projections are reported for the major seven countries, the euro area and the total OECD in the Statistical Annex.
Covers the euro area countries that are members of the OECD.
1. Contributions to changes in real GDP (percentage of real GDP in previous year), actual amount in the first column.
Source: OECD Economic Outlook 88 database.

StatLink ᴍᴤᴸ http://dx.doi.org/10.1787/888932347370

Euro area: **External indicators**

	2008	2009	2010	2011	2012
			$ billion		
Foreign balance	150.9	168.9	174.5	264	340
Invisibles, net	- 250.6	- 212.2	- 200.8	- 222	- 219
Current account balance	- 99.7	- 43.2	- 26.3	42	121

Note: Covers the euro area countries that are members of the OECD.
Source: OECD Economic Outlook 88 database.

StatLink ⫘⫙ http://dx.doi.org/10.1787/888932347389

to remain subdued in view of the remaining slack, and inflation expectations are well anchored.

Monetary conditions have remained supportive

Monetary conditions have continued to support activity over recent months. The ECB's main refinancing rate has remained at 1%, while short-term interbank rates have tended to rise towards this level as abundant liquidity support in the interbank market is scaled back. Further large long-term refinancing operations are due to expire in the coming months, although the ECB has committed to continuing refinancing operations on a full allotment basis at least until the end of 2010. Provided that the recovery remains on track, and given the weakness of inflation pressures and the expected fiscal consolidation, monetary policy stimulus should largely remain in place during 2011 and non-standard measures should continue to be wound down as conditions allow. The main refinancing rate should gradually be increased from the early part of 2012, unless higher than expected inflationary pressures emerge.

Fiscal consolidation is the immediate priority

The public finances are in poor shape. Deficits are large and debt is rising to high levels in many economies. Fiscal consolidation is already underway in some countries that have large debt burdens and are facing intense market pressures, but should begin in all euro area economies in 2011. Prolonged consolidation and tight public finances will be required in many countries to reduce the debt-to-GDP ratio to prudent levels and meet the 60% ceiling set out in the Stability and Growth Pact. Detailed medium-term consolidation plans should be set out in all euro area countries to increase the credibility of the consolidation process. The commitment to consolidation would be further enhanced by reforms to strengthen market discipline, the Stability and Growth Pact, and national fiscal institutions.

The recovery will gather strength going forward

The recovery is projected to continue, although growth is expected to have moderated during the second half of the year compared with the exceptionally strong pace in the second quarter. In 2011, consumption is projected to accelerate due to low interest rates, the recovery in household incomes and financial wealth, and as confidence recovers. Private non-residential investment will increase as growth prospects improve, although the high level of excess capacity will constrain the pace of the recovery. The necessary fiscal consolidation will be a drag on the recovery. With the fading support from the weaker effective exchange rate, contribution of exports to growth will be largely determined by the strength of world demand. The overall pace of recovery will be held back by continued rebalancing needs, the near-term weakness of potential output and underlying structural growth trends. The recovery will also be uneven, as large imbalances and lost competitiveness are gradually repaired in the countries with large debt overhangs and current account deficits.

The risks are broadly balanced

Substantial risks remain around the strength and pace of the recovery, although they are broadly balanced. Domestic demand may strengthen more rapidly than anticipated, as business investment may recover more strongly than projected. However, the euro area remains sensitive to financial market conditions and the strength of world trade. Markets remain sensitive to the weakness in the fiscal position in some countries and this may lead to wider financial tensions, although the creation of the European Financial Stability Facility (EFSF) provides an important near-term crisis management mechanism. The quality of bank balance sheets and its impact on credit growth is another risk for growth and public finances.

GERMANY

The economy is recovering strongly on the back of the improvement in world trade. Private consumption, investment and government spending on infrastructure have also been strong. The labour market continues to remain surprisingly resilient and unemployment has now fallen to its lowest level since reunification. Although annual growth is expected to slow somewhat over the projection horizon, the pre-crisis real GDP level will be reached in the course of 2011.

Government finances are benefitting from the strong cyclical recovery, although fiscal stimulus measures will lead to an increase of the general government deficit this year. From 2011 onwards the government is planning ambitious consolidation measures in order to fulfil the structural deficit target set by the new fiscal rule. These consolidation policies should be coupled with structural policies to raise the potential growth rate.

Real GDP has rebounded sharply...

Economic activity continued to rebound in the first half of 2010 with the growth of real GDP in the second quarter being the strongest since reunification. This reflected buoyant export growth as well as solid domestic demand with both private consumption and investment spending rising markedly. To some extent this was related to a rebound in construction after the impact of severe winter weather and to public infrastructure projects which are part of the fiscal stimulus package implemented since 2009. Growth slowed in the third quarter but the underlying dynamics remain intact, helped by continued increases in employment which support consumer confidence. Headline consumer price inflation has increased since the beginning of the year due to rising energy costs. By contrast, annual core inflation continued to remain at levels below 1%.

... and growth momentum is expected to remain

Going forward, domestic demand components are expected to strengthen and demand from the main trading partners is likely to remain solid, underpinning a continued recovery. Labour input is

Germany

Source: Ifo Institut für Wirtschaftsforschung; OECD, National Accounts database.

StatLink http://dx.doi.org/10.1787/888932345432

Germany: **Employment, income and inflation**
Percentage changes

	2008	2009	2010	2011	2012
Employment	1.4	0.0	0.2	0.4	0.1
Unemployment rate[1]	7.3	7.4	6.9	6.3	6.2
Compensation of employees	3.6	0.3	2.0	2.8	2.1
Unit labour cost	2.8	5.2	-1.5	0.3	-0.1
Household disposable income	3.2	-1.0	2.0	2.6	2.6
GDP deflator	1.0	1.4	0.8	1.0	1.2
Harmonised index of consumer prices	2.8	0.2	1.0	1.2	1.4
Core harmonised index of consumer prices[2]	1.3	1.3	0.6	1.1	1.3
Private consumption deflator	1.7	0.0	1.9	1.4	1.4

1. As a percentage of labour force, based on national accounts.
2. Harmonised index of consumer prices excluding food, energy, alcohol and tobacco.
Source: OECD Economic Outlook 88 database.

StatLink http://dx.doi.org/10.1787/888932347009

expected to continue increasing, both through an extension of working hours and new hiring, thus supporting wage income. Some investment spending is likely to be shifted into 2010 in anticipation of the phasing out of favourable depreciation allowances at the end of 2010. Firms continue to benefit from favourable financial conditions. The consolidation measures announced by the government are envisaged to have only moderate adverse growth effects in 2011. However, the phasing out of the government's infrastructure spending will weigh on construction activity.

Labour market performance is robust

The labour market has remained exceptionally robust during the crisis with unemployment barely rising. Employment has started to increase this year and unemployment has fallen below its pre-crisis

Germany

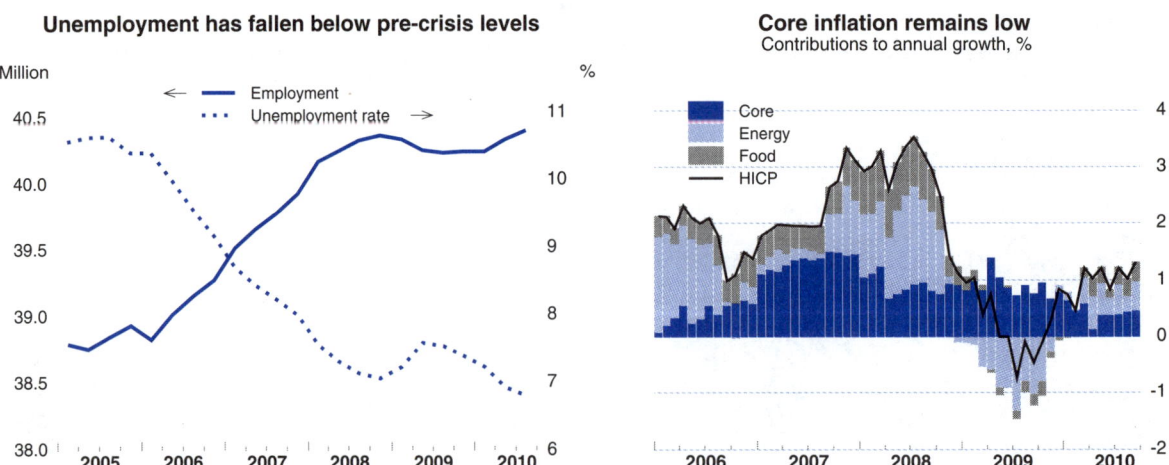

Unemployment has fallen below pre-crisis levels

Core inflation remains low
Contributions to annual growth, %

Note: Core refers to the harmonised index of consumer prices (HICP) excluding food, energy, alcohol and tobacco.
Source: Eurostat; OECD, National Accounts database.

StatLink http://dx.doi.org/10.1787/888932345451

Germany: **Financial indicators**

	2008	2009	2010	2011	2012
Household saving ratio[1]	11.7	11.1	11.5	11.6	11.4
General government financial balance[2]	0.1	-3.0	-4.0	-2.9	-2.1
Current account balance[2]	6.7	4.9	5.1	6.0	7.0
Short-term interest rate[3]	4.6	1.2	0.8	1.1	1.8
Long-term interest rate[4]	4.0	3.2	2.7	3.0	3.8

1. As a percentage of disposable income.
2. As a percentage of GDP.
3. 3-month interbank rate.
4. 10-year government bonds.
Source: OECD Economic Outlook 88 database.

StatLink ⧉ http://dx.doi.org/10.1787/888932347028

levels. The stability of employment during the recession is reflecting to a large extent the significant adjustment in hours worked (and equivalent in compensation) per employee. Though the government's short-time work scheme supported this adjustment, most of it was due to increased working time flexibility at the firm level as agreed between the social

Germany: **Demand and output**

	2009	2010	2011	2012	Fourth quarter		
					2010	2011	2012
	Current prices € billion	Percentage changes from previous year, volume (2000 prices)					
Private consumption	1 411.4	-0.1	1.3	1.6	0.9	1.5	1.5
Government consumption	472.1	2.6	0.7	0.6	2.3	0.8	0.6
Gross fixed investment	421.7	4.9	2.7	1.2	7.6	1.0	1.6
Public	39.3	3.1	0.5	-15.9	0.8	-9.6	-13.3
Residential	134.2	3.5	1.6	2.0	4.4	1.5	2.0
Non-residential	248.2	6.0	3.7	3.6	10.6	2.5	3.7
Final domestic demand	2 305.2	1.4	1.4	1.3	2.4	1.2	1.3
Stockbuilding[1]	- 27.8	0.8	0.0	0.0			
Total domestic demand	2 277.4	2.3	1.5	1.3	3.9	1.2	1.3
Exports of goods and services	976.7	15.2	9.0	5.6	16.9	6.3	5.5
Imports of goods and services	859.2	13.6	7.4	4.1	18.6	4.9	3.9
Net exports[1]	117.6	1.4	1.1	1.0			
GDP at market prices	2 395.0	3.5	2.5	2.2	4.1	2.1	2.3
Memorandum items							
GDP without working day adjustments	2 397.2	3.6	2.5	2.0			
Investment in machinery and equipment	182.2	7.1	3.0	1.7	10.2	1.4	1.6
Construction investment	239.6	3.3	2.5	0.8	5.7	0.7	1.6

Note: National accounts are based on official chain-linked data. This introduces a discrepancy in the identity between real demand components and GDP. For further details see *OECD Economic Outlook* Sources and Methods *(http://www.oecd.org/eco/sources-and-methods)*.
Detailed quarterly projections are reported for the major seven countries, the euro area and the total OECD in the Statistical Annex.
1. Contributions to changes in real GDP (percentage of real GDP in previous year), actual amount in the first column.
Source: OECD Economic Outlook 88 database.

StatLink ⧉ http://dx.doi.org/10.1787/888932347047

partners. In addition, structural unemployment has probably continued to fall owing to past labour market reforms. Furthermore, skilled labour shortages in some sectors have induced companies to hold on to their employees, thereby limiting the decline in manufacturing employment during the crisis. A further supporting factor for the labour market was the trend rise in service sector employment, for example in the education sector, which continued throughout the crisis. With jobs now being added again in manufacturing, overall employment is set to continue growing. As the unemployment rate will fall further below its estimated structural level and working hours continue to normalise, wages per employee are likely to rise substantially over the projection horizon. As inflationary pressures are projected to remain moderate, real disposable incomes are set to increase markedly, supporting private consumption spending.

Government finances are set to improve in 2011

The high growth in real GDP and the decrease in unemployment translate into higher tax revenues and lower social security benefit payments, thus limiting the increase in the budget deficit in 2010 that is induced by the fiscal stimulus measures implemented since 2009. From 2011 onwards, the government is assumed to implement its ambitious consolidation programme, amounting to around 3% of GDP until 2014, in addition to phasing out the temporary fiscal stimulus measures. Around two-fifths of overall consolidation is set for the expenditure side, notably higher public sector efficiency and streamlined social benefit payments. Revenues are to be raised by phasing out some tax exemptions and by introducing some new levies, such as a tax on air travel. While the overall focus of the package is welcome, some of its elements still have to be specified in more detail, such as the planned financial transactions tax from 2012 onwards. The discretionary consolidation in 2011 and 2012 will amount to around ½ per cent of GDP in each year which is in line with the requirements set by the fiscal rule and appropriate given the state of the economy and government finances. While in 2011, the decrease in discretionary spending primarily reflects the impact of the consolidation package, the lowering of the structural deficit in 2012 is also due to the phasing out of the government's spending on infrastructure. On current projections, the headline deficit may fall below 3% of GDP in 2011.

The recovery is likely to continue into 2012

The outlook over the projection horizon is fairly bright. Growth is likely to remain dynamic during 2011 with world trade projected to remain on an upward trend. In addition, private consumption growth is envisaged to be stronger than usual at this stage of the upswing, owing to continued employment gains and solid wage increases. The improved financial situation of households and favourable financing conditions should contribute to growth in residential investment. Increased capacity utilisation will underpin investment growth going forward. Real GDP is expected to grow by 3½ per cent in 2010 and 2½ per cent in 2011, implying that the pre-crisis real GDP level will be reached in the course of 2011. In 2012, economic activity is envisaged to grow at around 2¼ per cent, and thus above its trend growth rate. Nevertheless, the output gap is set to remain in negative territory over the whole projection horizon, thereby damping inflationary pressures. Notwithstanding the growth of domestic demand, the current account surplus is set to rise to around 7% of GDP. A more balanced growth outcome could be achieved by implementing structural reforms that would raise domestic investment spending. In view of the ageing of the population and the low share of tertiary graduates by OECD standards, reforms of the education system and increased high-skilled immigration should have priority. In addition, reducing the degree of regulation of some segments of the services sector would be beneficial.

Risks are broadly balanced

The risks surrounding these projections are broadly balanced. Developments in world trade pose risks in both directions. Domestically, private households may choose to lower their saving rate, boosting private consumption further. Also, business investment may turn out to be stronger than projected. On the negative side, financial conditions, notably the situation in the banking sector, may deteriorate with adverse consequences for investment spending.

FRANCE

Following a mild slowing of activity in recent months, real GDP growth is projected to pick up slowly towards an annualised pace of 2% by 2012, led by business investment and exports. The unemployment rate has peaked but is set to decline only slightly, while price pressures will remain subdued, with underlying inflation at about 1% per year.

The fiscal stance will need to be tight in 2011. Thereafter, further consolidation should aim to stabilise the debt-to-GDP ratio by 2013 (before it hits 95%) by curbing spending and broadening the tax base. With the pension reform now passed, cutting spending in a sustainable way while raising long-term potential output could be achieved through reforms of health care and public administration. If needed, revenue increases should focus on raising environmental and property taxes. The fiscal policy framework should also be reinforced to boost credibility.

The pace of the recovery has moderated since the spring

Real GDP growth reached a peak of 2.8% at an annualised rate in the spring, and high-frequency indicators suggest a subsequent relatively modest slowdown. After a pause, in part due to the progressive phasing out of the "cash-for-clunkers" scheme, private consumption has resumed its uptrend, while both business and residential investment growth have turned positive for the first time since the end of 2007. House prices have recovered most of their 2008/09 losses, and transactions have also rebounded sharply. Exports have been robust, and stockbuilding has also contributed substantially to growth. Although industrial production has been erratic, business confidence has been steadily improving.

Labour productivity fell sharply in 2008-09 but has bounced back in 2010 in line with past recoveries. The unemployment rate has started to decrease slowly from a peak of 10%, but long-term unemployment has

France

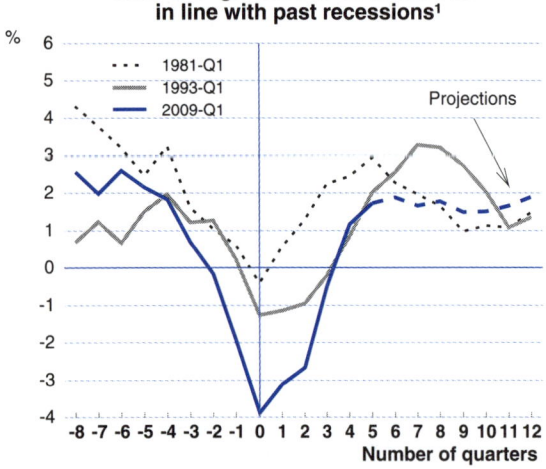

Real GDP growth has bounced back in line with past recessions[1]

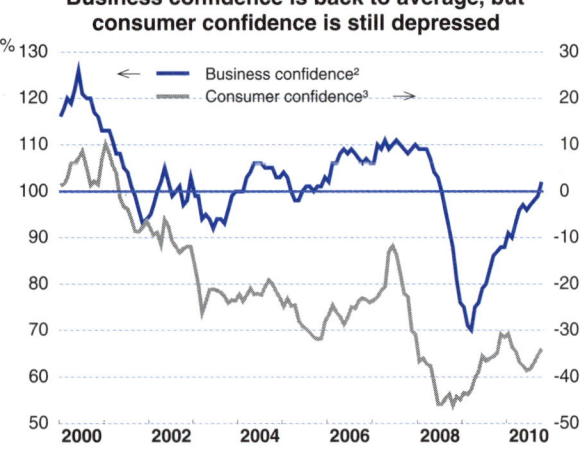

Business confidence is back to average, but consumer confidence is still depressed

1. 0 corresponds to the quarter in which the troughs of the series have occurred; year-on-year growth rates.
2. Balance of responses, per cent; the indicator is normalised in order to have its long-term average equal to 100.
3. Balance of responses, in points.

Source: INSEE; OECD, Economic Outlook 88 database.

StatLink ⟶ http://dx.doi.org/10.1787/888932345470

France: **Employment, income and inflation**
Percentage changes

	2008	2009	2010	2011	2012
Employment	1.4	-0.9	0.3	0.7	0.7
Unemployment rate[1]	7.4	9.1	9.3	9.1	8.8
Compensation of employees	3.1	0.1	2.4	2.5	2.8
Unit labour cost	3.0	2.7	0.8	0.9	0.7
Household disposable income	3.0	1.1	2.2	2.0	2.5
GDP deflator	2.6	0.5	0.4	1.0	1.1
Harmonised index of consumer prices	3.2	0.1	1.6	1.1	1.1
Core harmonised index of consumer prices[2]	1.8	1.4	1.0	1.0	1.1
Private consumption deflator	2.9	-0.4	1.1	0.9	1.0
Memorandum item					
Unemployment rate[3]	7.8	9.5	9.7	9.5	9.3

1. As a percentage of labour force, metropolitan France.
2. Harmonised index of consumer prices excluding food, energy, alcohol and tobacco.
3. As a percentage of labour force, national unemployment rate, includes overseas departments and territories.
Source: OECD Economic Outlook 88 database.

StatLink ᴍ𝑠🔗 http://dx.doi.org/10.1787/888932347066

kept increasing rapidly. While younger workers had been particularly affected by the rise in unemployment in the first phase of the crisis, older workers have been experiencing a more difficult time since the beginning of 2010. Consumer confidence remains at a depressed level and underlying inflation seems to have stabilised but at a low level.

Financial conditions have been supportive...

Declining long-term interest rates and, until recently, a weak euro have given support to the economy, although this will fade away. The four French banks stress-tested by the Committee of European Banking

France

Inflation pressures are subdued

The public deficit has stabilised but at a high level[2]

1. Year-on-year growth rates.
2. As a percentage of GDP; 0 corresponds to the quarter in which the troughs in the GDP series have occurred.
Source: OECD, Economic Outlook 88 database.

StatLink ᴍ𝑠🔗 http://dx.doi.org/10.1787/888932345489

France: **Financial indicators**

	2008	2009	2010	2011	2012
Household saving ratio[1]	15.4	16.2	15.9	15.5	14.9
General government financial balance[2]	-3.3	-7.6	-7.4	-6.1	-4.8
Current account balance[2]	-1.9	-1.9	-2.2	-2.3	-2.4
Short-term interest rate[3]	4.6	1.2	0.8	1.1	1.8
Long-term interest rate[4]	4.2	3.6	3.0	3.3	4.1

1. As a percentage of disposable income (gross saving).
2. As a percentage of GDP.
3. 3-month interbank rate.
4. 10-year benchmark government bonds.
Source: OECD Economic Outlook 88 database.

StatLink http://dx.doi.org/10.1787/888932347085

Supervisors showed slightly greater resistance than the European Union average: the stress scenario generated only a small drop, from 9.9% to 9.3%, in their average tier-one capital ratio. Credit to the private sector has expanded at 3% over the past year thanks to residential mortgage lending in a context of favourable credit supply conditions.

... and labour market policies have contributed to smooth the shocks

Although the increase in long-term unemployment is worrying due to possible hysteresis effect that might raise structural unemployment, policymakers have avoided past mistakes during this recession by

France: **Demand and output**

	2009	2010	2011	2012	Fourth quarter		
					2010	2011	2012
	Current prices € billion	Percentage changes from previous year, volume (2000 prices)					
Private consumption	1 112.6	1.5	1.6	2.2	1.1	1.9	2.4
Government consumption	469.7	1.6	0.6	0.0	1.0	0.2	-0.1
Gross fixed investment	392.1	-1.8	2.8	4.3	0.8	3.6	4.4
Public	63.9	-0.7	0.9	0.4	-0.4	0.8	0.1
Residential	110.2	-2.5	1.3	2.4	0.1	1.9	2.5
Non-residential	218.0	-1.8	4.1	6.3	1.4	5.3	6.6
Final domestic demand	1 974.4	0.9	1.6	2.1	1.0	1.8	2.2
Stockbuilding[1]	- 30.0	0.6	0.4	0.0			
Total domestic demand	1 944.3	1.5	2.0	2.1	1.9	1.8	2.2
Exports of goods and services	439.6	9.9	6.4	6.3	11.7	5.5	6.7
Imports of goods and services	476.7	8.8	7.5	6.2	11.8	5.5	6.5
Net exports[1]	- 37.1	0.1	-0.5	-0.1			
GDP at market prices	1 907.2	1.6	1.6	2.0	1.7	1.7	2.1

Note: National accounts are based on official chain-linked data. This introduces a discrepancy in the identity between real demand components and GDP. For further details see *OECD Economic Outlook* Sources and Methods (http://www.oecd.org/eco/sources-and-methods).
Detailed quarterly projections are reported for the major seven countries, the euro area and the total OECD in the Statistical Annex.
1. Contributions to changes in real GDP (percentage of real GDP in previous year), actual amount in the first column.
Source: OECD Economic Outlook 88 database.

StatLink http://dx.doi.org/10.1787/888932347104

resisting the promotion of early-retirement schemes and, more generally, have sought to maintain the attachment of displaced workers to the labour market. Access to unemployment benefits for those on short-term contracts has been eased. Temporary measures have been adopted to facilitate part-time unemployment, expand subsidised jobs and provide funding facilities for small firms. It is important that these measures be withdrawn as the recovery progresses. Moreover, the pension reform that has just been passed is expected to boost long-term potential output *via* increased labour force participation of older workers, while contributing to a structural improvement in public finances.

The fiscal stance will be appropriately tightened in 2011

After being broadly neutral in 2010, fiscal policy will turn restrictive from 2011. With relatively strong tax revenues and lower interest paid on debt, the general government deficit is expected to narrow slightly to 7.4% of GDP in 2010. The government is committed to reducing it to 6% of GDP in 2011 and progressively to 2% in 2014, which would then start to curb the debt-to-GDP ratio. Given the debt level reached before the crisis and its subsequent evolution, the pace of consolidation implied by this plan is needed for public finances not to threaten macroeconomic stability.

A number of measures will contribute to consolidation

For 2011, the cyclically-adjusted primary balance is expected to improve by about 1% of GDP thanks to almost equal contributions from self-reversing measures included in the anti-crisis package; removal of accompanying measures taken to help implement the withdrawal of the local business tax that penalised investment; cuts in tax expenditures; and cuts in current spending. The latter two measures are both to be deepened in 2012. Other announced measures that have a smaller impact include a pay freeze, the non-replacement of half of all retiring workers in central government and a new tax on banks. The projection implies a reduction in the total deficit by 1.3% of GDP in 2012, which differs from the government's objective only due to disparate output growth assumptions.

Reforms are needed to stay the course of consolidation

Further action will eventually be needed. The increasing trend in health-care costs needs to be reined in, in part by reducing administrative costs. Savings can also be achieved by deepening the reform of the state, *via* reducing the large number of sub-national levels of government and extending the General Public Policy Review to all feasible levels of public administration. As tax increases might also be needed to meet the fiscal targets, tax bases should be widened by cutting back further on the least efficient tax expenditures. Consideration should also be given to heavier taxation of environmental externalities such as carbon emissions and raising other taxes in the least distortive manner – in particular, on property and the VAT, especially on low-rated items.

Credibility needs to be reinforced

As for long-term credibility, France's poor track record in meeting the objectives of its successive stability programmes suggests that the fiscal framework should be strengthened. This could be done by making the commitments in the Stability and Growth Pact concomitant with multiannual legislation voted by the parliament; limiting spending deviations from budget in the course of the year; and creating an independent fiscal council to forecast macroeconomic developments, monitor budgetary execution and provide *ex post* evaluations.

Activity will pick up slowly

Real GDP growth is projected to increase gradually from 1.6% in 2010 to 2.0% in 2012. Private investment and exports should be buoyant, helped by dynamic world activity and stronger German domestic demand. However, the unemployment rate is likely to decline only moderately, leaving price pressures subdued, with underlying inflation at about 1%. Private consumption should accelerate steadily, helped by a drop in the saving rate towards pre-crisis levels as consumer confidence improves in view of lower joblessness and the declining government deficit. The current account deficit should edge up to around 2½ per cent of GDP.

Substantial risks remain

The risks to the economy have not been substantially reduced. Considerable uncertainty surrounds both economic activity abroad and exchange-rate developments. Difficulties associated with financing needs of EU peripheral countries might re-emerge in 2011, generating volatility in government bond markets, thereby harming business confidence. On the other hand, efforts to restore the health of public finance across the board might be rewarded by a lessening of precautionary behaviour.

ITALY

After one of the deepest recessions in the OECD area, Italy's economy has begun a moderate recovery which will strengthen somewhat over the next two years. Investment and exports lead the upturn in demand. Unemployment may be near its peak, but as use of the *Cassa Integrazione* wage support schemes unwinds it may not fall very fast. Household income growth will remain sluggish and depend on a recovery in self-employment income, which dropped severely during the downturn. Consumer price inflation has picked up during the year but will remain subdued through 2012.

These projections assume that sufficient measures are introduced to meet the government's target for the underlying deficit over the next two years, though weaker growth than in the official projections may prevent the actual deficit falling below 3% of GDP. It will be a challenge to hold the line on these measures, though the benefit of past action has been seen in the relative stability of the interest rate on Italian government debt. To ensure credibility, structural (as opposed to one-off) budget measures need to be put in place. In addition, supply-side reforms should be promoted to improve the long-term potential of the Italian economy.

The modest recovery continues   The economy has been recovering from the strong decline in 2009 and picked up through the first half of 2010, led by a strong bounceback in both exports and investment. To a considerable extent this was due to greater confidence in credit markets, which reduced the need for companies to economise on working capital and investment. The increase in machinery and equipment investment was partly due to temporary tax breaks whose withdrawal may lead to a pause in the second half of 2010. By contrast, private and public consumption have both remained sluggish. Key reasons are the significant fall of household

Italy

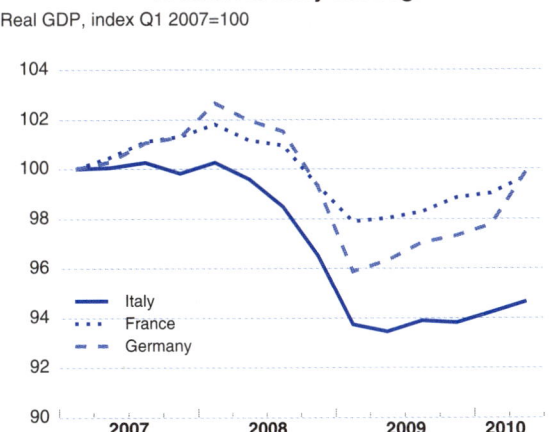

A weak recovery has begun

Real GDP, index Q1 2007=100

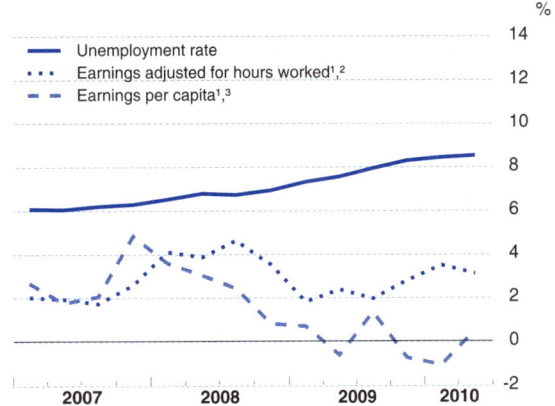

Earnings are affected by reduced hours

1. Percentage change from corresponding quarter of previous year.
2. Gross earnings per full-time equivalent.
3. Compensation per employee in the private sector.
Source: Institute National of Statistics (ISTAT) and OECD Economic outlook 88 database.

StatLink   http://dx.doi.org/10.1787/888932345508

Italy: **Employment, income and inflation**
Percentage changes

	2008	2009	2010	2011	2012
Employment[1]	0.3	-1.7	-0.4	0.5	0.8
Unemployment rate[1,2]	6.7	7.8	8.6	8.5	8.3
Compensation of employees	3.7	-0.6	0.6	2.7	2.1
Unit labour cost	5.1	4.7	-0.4	1.3	0.5
Household disposable income	2.2	-3.0	-0.1	2.8	2.6
GDP deflator	2.8	2.1	0.7	1.2	1.1
Harmonised index of consumer prices	3.5	0.8	1.5	1.4	1.4
Core harmonised index of consumer prices[3]	2.2	1.6	1.5	1.3	1.4
Private consumption deflator	3.2	-0.1	1.6	1.5	1.4

1. Data for whole economy employment are from the national accounts. These data include an estimate made by Istat for employment in the underground economy. Total employment according to the national accounts is approximately 2 million, about 10%, higher than employment according to the labour force survey. The unemployment rate is calculated relative to labour force survey data.
2. As a percentage of labour force.
3. Harmonised index of consumer prices excluding food, energy, alcohol and tobacco.
Source: OECD Economic Outlook 88 database.

StatLink http://dx.doi.org/10.1787/888932347123

income in the wake of the recession and restrained fiscal policy in view of the high level of public debt.

But there is a long way to go   Despite the recovery, GDP in mid-2010 remained more than 5% below its peak at the beginning of 2008. This is a larger fall than in the majority of OECD and EU countries, and the recovery so far appears to confirm the weak trend of growth of the last decade. While there has been a strong upturn in investment, it remains well below its long-run average share of GDP, as in other countries, cutting prospects for future growth.

Italy

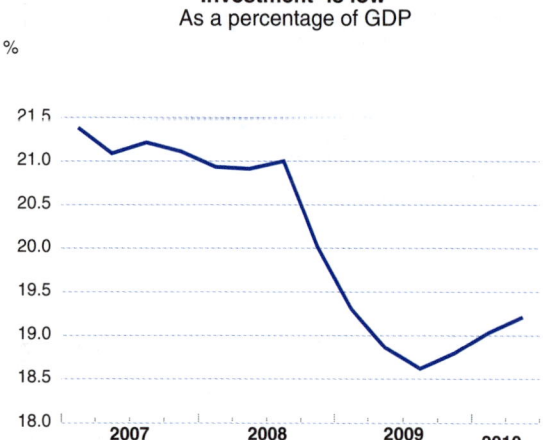

Investment[1] is low
As a percentage of GDP

Trade is recovering
Billion euros, 2000 prices

— Exports of goods and services,volume
··· Imports of goods and services,volume

1. Gross fixed capital formation.
Source: OECD Economic Outlook 88 database.

StatLink http://dx.doi.org/10.1787/888932345527

Italy: **Financial indicators**

	2008	2009	2010	2011	2012
Household saving ratio[1]	8.2	7.1	5.1	5.8	5.9
General government financial balance[2]	-2.7	-5.2	-5.0	-3.9	-3.1
Current account balance[2]	-3.6	-3.2	-3.3	-2.8	-2.3
Short-term interest rate[3]	4.6	1.2	0.8	1.1	1.8
Long-term interest rate[4]	4.7	4.3	3.8	3.7	4.5

1. Net saving as a percentage of net disposable income. Includes "famiglie produttrici".
2. As a percentage of GDP.
3. 3-month interbank rate.
4. 10-year government bonds.
Source: OECD Economic Outlook 88 database.

StatLink ⧉ http://dx.doi.org/10.1787/888932347142

Unemployment may soon peak, but self-employment income is very weak

The *Cassa Integrazione* wage support scheme has expanded considerably, providing earnings support to up to 350 000 effectively laid-off, but still formally employed, workers at its peak in 2009 (down to around 250 000 in mid-2010). The support is paid by the government through employers, causing data to show falls in per capita wages even as *hourly* earnings were affected only very modestly by the recession. This protection of employment has muted the increase in open unemployment, which has probably neared its peak – though it is difficult

Italy: **Demand and output**

	2009	2010	2011	2012	Fourth quarter		
					2010	2011	2012
	Current prices € billion	Percentage changes from previous year, volume (2000 prices)					
Private consumption	911.6	0.4	0.6	1.0	0.2	0.8	1.1
Government consumption	327.8	-0.3	0.1	0.0	-0.1	0.0	0.1
Gross fixed investment	287.3	2.0	1.5	3.1	2.5	2.3	3.4
Machinery and equipment	131.7	8.0	3.3	4.4	7.9	3.5	4.9
Construction	155.7	-3.1	-0.3	1.8	-2.2	1.1	1.9
Residential	71.7	-3.4	0.5	1.8	-0.4	1.1	1.9
Non-residential	84.0	-2.9	-0.9	1.8	-3.7	1.1	1.9
Final domestic demand	1 526.8	0.5	0.7	1.2	0.6	0.9	1.3
Stockbuilding[1]	- 0.4	0.2	-0.1	0.0			
Total domestic demand	1 526.4	0.7	0.6	1.2	0.3	0.9	1.3
Exports of goods and services	363.9	7.9	6.7	5.3	10.2	5.7	5.3
Imports of goods and services	369.9	6.6	3.7	3.9	5.7	3.6	4.1
Net exports[1]	- 6.0	0.3	0.8	0.4			
GDP at market prices	1 520.3	1.0	1.3	1.6	1.3	1.5	1.7

Note: National accounts are based on official chain-linked data. This introduces a discrepancy in the identity between real demand components and GDP. For further details see *OECD Economic Outlook* Sources and Methods *(http://www.oecd.org/eco/sources-and-methods).*
Detailed quarterly projections are reported for the major seven countries, the euro area and the total OECD in the Statistical Annex.
1. Contributions to changes in real GDP (percentage of real GDP in previous year), actual amount in the first column.
Source: OECD Economic Outlook 88 database.

StatLink ⧉ http://dx.doi.org/10.1787/888932347161

to predict what will happen as workers begin to emerge from the maximum two-year eligibility for the short-time working schemes. Overall, household income was more strongly affected by non-wage income than earnings from employment: net income from self-employment and property fell over 10% in 2009 and saving fell despite reduced consumption.

Inflation has picked up

Consumer price inflation has picked up in recent months reaching 1.8% year-on-year in the third quarter, up from 1.3% in January. This is partly the result of higher energy prices.

Budgetary discipline has been rewarded and...

Italian government debt has performed relatively well on the bond markets compared with that of other southern European countries. The government is concerned to maintain this performance and to start the process of getting the very high level of public debt on a downward path. It further tightened fiscal policy in the budget legislation for 2011-13 and aims at reducing the general government deficit to 2.7% of GDP in 2012 and 2.2% in 2013.

... the announced further tightening is feasible but challenging

The OECD projections assume that measures to achieve these objectives will be fully implemented in the remaining two years of the 2011-13 budget period. The measures include a three-year freeze on pay in the public sector and significant cuts in finance for sub-national government expenditure. It is also assumed that measures to reduce tax evasion will improve revenues by about 0.4% of GDP. Such measures are necessary, but will require consistent application to ensure continuing increases in the tax take above the modest increases in income that can be expected. Despite the difficult situation, the government has appropriately refrained from significant further "one-off" measures. The OECD projection for borrowing in 2012 is slightly above official projections which are based on stronger output growth; the ratio of debt to GDP should peak in 2012 at around 120%.

The shape of the projected recovery reflects confidence indicators

September surveys indicated that consumer confidence has not yet recovered from its decline earlier in 2010, whereas the confidence climate among manufacturing and extractive firms has continuously improved over the past 18 months. Reflecting this, the continuation of the modest recovery in demand is concentrated on investment and exports rather than household spending. Private consumption will nevertheless grow somewhat as incomes recover and employment stabilises and begins to grow again. Public consumption growth will be limited by fiscal restraint. Construction investment, both housing and non-housing, may not pick up until 2012.

Growth in trade will continue

Exports will continue to respond to growth in world demand, though the labour market shows no sign of helping to reverse the decline in Italy's competitiveness position; to achieve this, more will need to be done in structural policy to improve the ability of the economy to respond to demand. Further losses of market share can therefore be expected, but exports will nevertheless grow significantly more than imports over the next couple of years.

A segmented labour market contributes to above-average inflation

National wage agreements reached during this year seem to have been largely insensitive to the weakness of the economy. This is projected to continue, resulting in some acceleration in per capita earnings in 2010-11 as hours worked recover somewhat. On the other hand, flexibility in the large informal sector is no doubt reflected in the falls in self-employment income in 2009. Despite the large output gap, consumer price inflation is therefore also projected to be persistent, stabilising under 2% but likely slightly above the level in other large euro area members.

A key uncertainty is over investment

While external risk is always present, the main domestic risk to the growth projections is on business investment. If the surge in the first half of 2010 is due more to government incentives than improved prospects and financial conditions then it may fade, but there is also a possibility that it could grow considerably faster if businesses are willing and able to finance more normal levels of investment.

UNITED KINGDOM

The economy is recovering from the recession, supported by both growing domestic demand and rising exports. The substantial but necessary fiscal tightening and weak real income growth create headwinds and growth is projected to remain subdued in 2011. The recovery will gain a bit more momentum in 2012 when exports are expected to increase further and business investment to grow more robustly. Unemployment is set to fall gradually. Inflation will remain above the 2% target through 2011 due to an initial boost from the rise in VAT, but is projected to fall below the target in 2012 when the effects of the increase in the VAT rate wane. Underlying inflation, excluding effects from changes in VAT, remains low due to significant economic slack.

Fiscal consolidation is underway with detailed plans set out in the Spending Review. The government's ambitious medium-term plan has significantly reduced fiscal risks and could, in combination with efficiency improvements in health spending and structural reforms, support growth in the longer term. While monetary policy will need to remain expansionary over the forecast period against the background of a significantly tighter fiscal stance, the process of normalisation of interest rates will have to start in earnest during 2012 as underlying inflation starts to increase.

The pace of growth is robust but is set to slow

The economy is recovering from the deepest recession since the 1930s. GDP growth in the first three quarters of 2010 was robust, reflecting broad-based growth in domestic demand, including from a needed rebuilding of inventories. The pace is set to slow, however, as contributions from stockbuilding fade and fiscal consolidation creates increasing headwinds. Although deleveraging pressures on households have eased as house prices and overall wealth positions have picked up and saving rates risen, the modest rise in real incomes will contain household consumption going forward. Exports have risen significantly but continue to underperform relative to other OECD countries as

United Kingdom

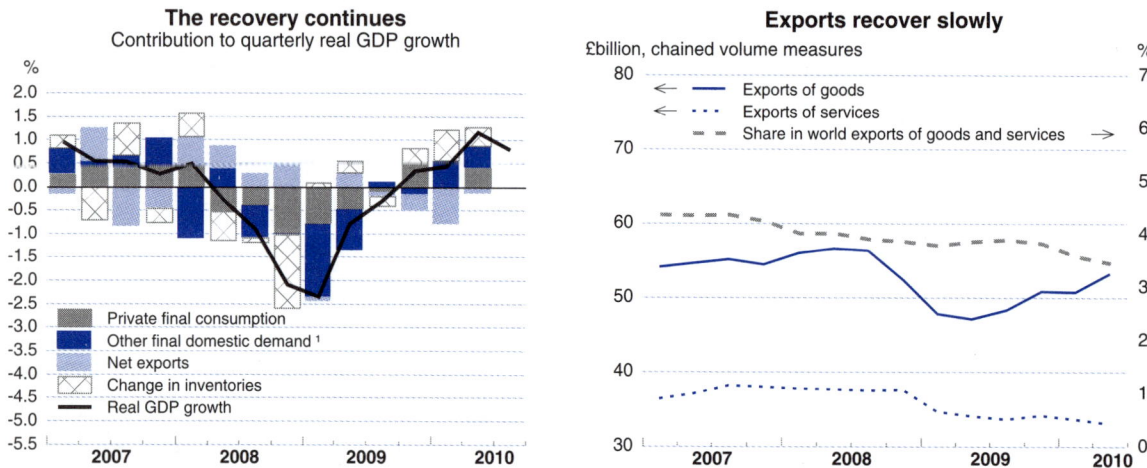

1. Consists of gross fixed capital investment, government consumption and statistical discrepancy.

Source: OECD Economic Outlook 88 database, Office for National Statistics.

StatLink ⟶ http://dx.doi.org/10.1787/888932345546

United Kingdom: **Employment, income and inflation**
Percentage changes

	2008	2009	2010	2011	2012
Employment	0.7	-1.6	0.0	0.3	0.5
Unemployment rate[1]	5.7	7.6	7.9	7.8	7.6
Compensation of employees	2.3	0.2	2.8	2.5	3.3
Unit labour cost	2.3	5.5	1.0	0.8	1.4
Household disposable income	5.4	2.6	3.5	3.4	3.8
GDP deflator	3.0	1.4	3.3	2.0	1.3
Harmonised index of consumer prices[2]	3.6	2.2	3.1	2.6	1.6
Core harmonised index of consumer prices[3]	1.6	1.7	2.6	2.6	1.6
Private consumption deflator	3.1	1.3	4.4	3.0	1.8

1. As a percentage of labour force.
2. The HICP is known as the Consumer Price Index in the United Kingdom.
3. Harmonised index of consumer prices excluding food, energy, alcohol and tobacco.
Source: OECD Economic Outlook 88 database.

StatLink http://dx.doi.org/10.1787/888932347180

financial service exports have not started to recover from the sharp fall in 2009.

Financial conditions are improving slowly. However, lending is subdued, reflecting both weak demand and continued deleveraging in the banking sector, which constrains credit supply to small firms and households. Large firms are cash rich and able to access sources of non-bank financing. The unemployment rate has remained stable since mid–2009, while employment has started to recover. Wage growth remains subdued. Headline inflation has fallen gradually in 2010 but remains

United Kingdom

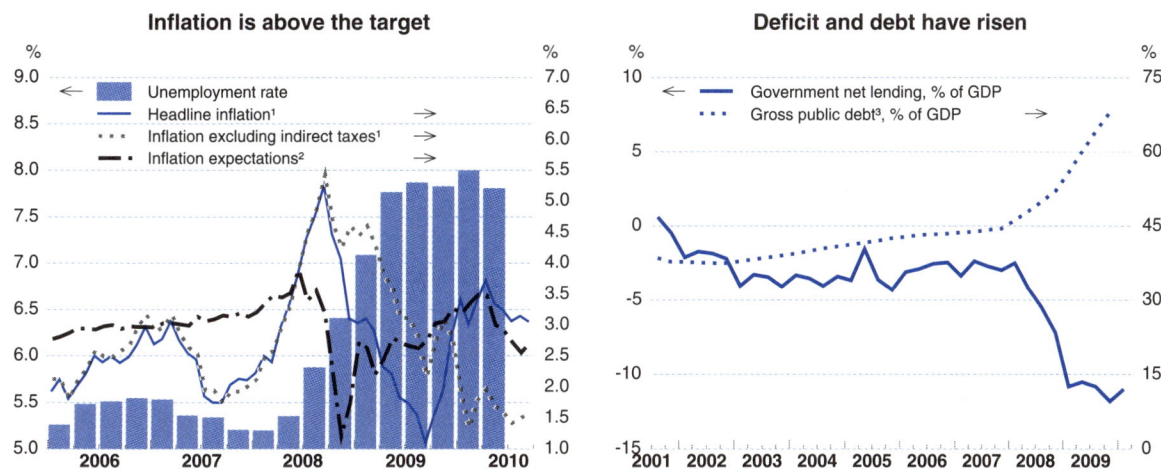

1. Year-on-year percentage change.
2. Implied by yield differentials between 10-year government benchmark bonds and inflation-indexed bonds.
3. Maastricht definition.
Source: OECD Economic Outlook 88 database, Bank of England and Office for National Statistics.

StatLink http://dx.doi.org/10.1787/888932345565

United Kingdom: **Financial indicators**

	2008	2009	2010	2011	2012
Household saving ratio[1]	2.0	6.3	4.4	3.5	3.4
General government financial balance[2]	-4.8	-11.0	-9.6	-8.1	-6.5
Current account balance[2]	-1.6	-1.3	-2.2	-1.6	-1.2
Short-term interest rate[3]	5.5	1.2	0.7	0.9	1.8
Long-term interest rate[4]	4.6	3.6	3.5	3.6	4.5

1. As a percentage of disposable income.
2. As a percentage of GDP.
3. 3-month interbank rate.
4. 10-year government bonds.
Source: OECD Economic Outlook 88 database.

StatLink http://dx.doi.org/10.1787/888932347199

above 3%, largely reflecting the end of the temporary cut in the VAT rate in January. However, stripped of tax adjustments, inflation has remained stable and significantly below the 2% target. Bond yields and inflation expectations have edged down, influenced by falling headline inflation and the improving fiscal outlook.

Fiscal austerity is here to stay

The government has stepped up the pace of consolidation and has set out plans to achieve a cyclically-adjusted current balance by the end of the budget year 2015-16. As a result, fiscal headwinds are set to strengthen, as the projection assumes that the fiscal consolidation

United Kingdom: **Demand and output**

	2009	2010	2011	2012	Fourth quarter		
					2010	2011	2012
	Current prices £ billion	Percentage changes from previous year, volume (2006 prices)					
Private consumption	908.5	1.2	1.7	1.8	1.8	1.3	1.9
Government consumption	327.4	1.9	-1.1	-1.7	1.8	-2.1	-1.5
Gross fixed investment	204.3	2.0	2.3	4.3	5.1	2.7	5.1
Public[1]	41.6	-4.9	-17.0	-5.2	-20.2	-11.0	-1.7
Residential	41.3	7.9	8.6	3.3	12.6	3.3	3.4
Non-residential	121.4	2.3	6.1	7.0	12.3	6.4	7.4
Final domestic demand	1 440.2	1.5	1.2	1.4	2.3	0.8	1.7
Stockbuilding[2]	- 14.5	1.2	0.1	0.0			
Total domestic demand	1 425.7	2.7	1.3	1.4	3.4	0.8	1.7
Exports of goods and services	386.2	4.4	5.0	6.4	3.2	5.6	6.6
Imports of goods and services	419.3	7.5	3.1	4.0	5.1	3.5	4.1
Net exports[2]	- 33.1	-1.0	0.4	0.5			
GDP at market prices	1 392.6	1.8	1.7	2.0	2.9	1.3	2.3

Note: Detailed quarterly projections are reported for the major seven countries, the euro area and the total OECD in the Statistical Annex.
1. Including nationalised industries and public corporations.
2. Contributions to changes in real GDP (percentage of real GDP in previous year), actual amount in the first column.
Source: OECD Economic Outlook 88 database.

StatLink http://dx.doi.org/10.1787/888932347218

United Kingdom: **External indicators**

	2008	2009	2010	2011	2012
	$ billion				
Goods and services exports	781.8	604.1	649.8	706	761
Goods and services imports	853.2	655.8	721.3	779	827
Foreign balance	- 71.3	- 51.7	- 71.4	- 72	- 66
Invisibles, net	28.3	24.6	22.1	34	35
Current account balance	- 43.1	- 27.1	- 49.4	- 38	- 30
	Percentage changes				
Goods and services export volumes	1.0	- 11.1	4.4	5.0	6.4
Goods and services import volumes	- 1.2	- 12.3	7.5	3.1	4.0
Export performance[1]	- 1.3	0.3	- 5.5	- 2.5	- 0.8
Terms of trade	0.0	- 1.0	0.7	- 1.1	- 0.8

1. Ratio between export volume and export market of total goods and services.
Source: OECD Economic Outlook 88 database.

StatLink ⌨📈 http://dx.doi.org/10.1787/888932347237

announced in the June budget and the Spending Review will be fully implemented. The implied fiscal deficit is projected to fall to 6.5% of GDP, and gross public debt to reach almost 95% of GDP, in 2012. Altogether, the fiscal contraction, measured in terms of the cyclically-adjusted primary balance, amounts annually to roughly 1.7% of GDP between 2009 and 2012 and will hamper growth. Tax increases, including higher social security contributions and a hike in the VAT rate in 2011, contribute significantly. However, expenditure cuts and restraints will appropriately account for the major part of consolidation. The Spending Review set out how the expenditure cuts will be delivered, supporting the credibility of the government's fiscal plans. Most spending areas, with exceptions for ring-fenced health spending and overseas aid, will be affected and significant falls in government investment, consumption and transfers are envisaged over the next few years.

Monetary policy needs to remain highly expansionary

With the Bank of England's policy rate close to zero and quantitative easing amounting to £200 billion (14% of GDP), monetary policy remains highly expansionary. This is appropriate as the large output gap and sluggish unit labour costs are expected to reduce inflation to below the 2% target during 2012, once the effect of the VAT increase fades. If the recovery proceeds as projected, first steps towards more normal settings of monetary policy should be taken during the second part of 2011 and withdrawal of stimulus should proceed in 2012 as the recovery gathers pace.

The recovery remains modest and gains strength only in 2012

Growth is projected to remain modest during 2011 as public consumption and public investment are set to fall significantly, while household consumption is expected to remain subdued, reflecting slow real income growth and stagnant asset prices. Further increases in exports, supported by rising global demand, the weak exchange rate and the fading drag from financial services exports, will eventually underpin a somewhat stronger recovery in 2012. Business investment has fallen to low levels and is also expected to gather pace in 2012 in response to rising exports. With weak domestic demand, imports will grow slowly and the current account position is expected to improve slightly, though remaining negative through 2012.

The labour market is slowly recovering

Employment has started to pick up, but will be sluggish as public employment is set to fall and firms can initially meet rising demand through productivity gains and increases in average working hours. As activity picks up during 2012, more substantial improvements in the labour market are expected and unemployment should start to fall gradually. Wage increases will remain subdued, reflecting significant economic slack.

Risks are tilted towards the downside

Substantial risks surround these projections and are more to the downside. The squeeze on households' disposable incomes from fiscal consolidation may bear down more than projected on household consumption, especially if access to credit remains constrained and the housing market weakens again. Similarly, renewed price falls on commercial property could trigger further losses in the banking sector. On the other hand, diminished uncertainty and improved confidence could encourage companies to deploy their strong cash positions to increase investment more than expected. Risks to the export outlook are significant on both sides. Whilst the weak performance of service exports, especially in financial services, remains a downside risk, a swifter recovery in exports in response to the weak pound cannot be ruled out.

Health sector reforms could lessen the impact of consolidation

By stepping up the speed of consolidation the government has significantly damped fiscal risks, contributing to lower bond yield spreads and diminished uncertainty. While fiscal adjustment will be challenging, such measures are necessary to rein in deficits and slow the build-up of debt. Further enhancing the medium-term fiscal framework would support the consolidation process. The setting up of the Office for Budget Responsibility is an important development and its credibility will depend crucially on its ability to make independent judgements. Given the scale of the fiscal effort, structural reforms to improve the efficiency of public service provision and overall productivity are more critical than ever. For example, further productivity-enhancing reforms in the health sector would leave room for significant spending cuts in this area while maintaining service delivery, thus allowing greater protection of infrastructure spending which is under pressure. Moving swiftly on financial sector reforms, by setting up a functional macroprudential framework and dealing with issues related to "too big to fail" banks, would improve financial stability.

CANADA

The economic recovery has slowed sharply as a result of waning expansion of external demand and a retrenchment in household spending growth. Activity is nevertheless projected to progress at a moderate pace through 2011-12 as employment prospects and external demand gradually pick up again. Business investment is expected to remain robust, bolstered by firms' healthy profitability and financial positions and low funding costs. Substantial economic slack should gradually diminish but keep inflation pressures subdued.

Barring a further deterioration in labour market conditions, governments should begin to withdraw stimulus and reduce structural deficits as planned over the course of 2011-12 to maintain investor confidence in the path towards public debt sustainability. While monetary policy currently remains accommodative, the Bank of Canada should delay further rate hikes until early 2011 when a recovery in private demand is expected to gain firmer traction, after which a gradual pace of tightening would be appropriate.

The recovery has lost momentum

Real GDP growth has slowed markedly, reflecting weaker external markets and diminishing fiscal impetus. Moderating demand from the United States and ongoing strength of the Canadian dollar have restrained export growth. Both consumption and housing activity have also decelerated following the expiry of the federal home renovation tax credit in January. Meanwhile, business investment increased vigorously, helped by strong corporate profits and financial positions, and low interest rates. With capital equipment purchased largely from abroad and thus made cheaper by a strong exchange rate, imports have surged, causing the current account deficit to widen to 2.7% of GDP. After strong job creation brought employment back to pre-recession levels by the first half of 2010,

Canada

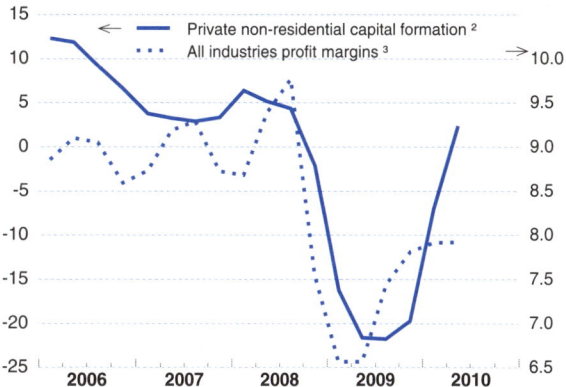

The strong exchange rate continues to weaken export performance

Business investment conditions are healthy
Percentage

1. Year-on-year percentage change in the ratio of export volume to export market (defined as the trade weighted average of trading partners' imports).
2. Year-on-year percentage change.
3. All industries operating profit as a share of operating revenue.

Source: Thomson Datastream; OECD Economic Outlook 88 database.

StatLink http://dx.doi.org/10.1787/888932345584

Canada: **Employment, income and inflation**
Percentage changes

	2008	2009	2010	2011	2012
Employment	1.5	-1.6	1.7	1.6	1.5
Unemployment rate[1]	6.2	8.3	8.1	7.8	7.4
Compensation of employees	4.3	0.1	3.8	4.0	5.0
Unit labour cost	3.8	2.6	0.9	1.6	2.0
Household disposable income	5.3	1.7	4.4	3.0	4.1
GDP deflator	4.0	-2.1	2.8	1.6	1.6
Consumer price index	2.4	0.3	1.6	1.7	1.5
Core consumer price index[2]	1.7	1.8	1.8	1.5	1.5
Private consumption deflator	1.6	0.5	1.2	1.5	1.3

1. As a percentage of labour force.
2. Consumer price index excluding the eight more volatile items.
Source: OECD Economic Outlook 88 database.

StatLink http://dx.doi.org/10.1787/888932347256

labour market improvements appear to have stalled, with the unemployment rate hovering close to 8% since then. Some household spending was likely brought forward into the first half of the year ahead of the July introduction of harmonised sales taxes in Ontario and British Columbia. Implementation of these taxes added to headline inflation in July, but year-on-year core inflation (which excludes such effects) has been edging lower, reaching 1.5% in September.

The economy continues to face headwinds...

Earlier labour market improvement and fiscal stimulus have bolstered household spending to date but are expected to subside going forward. Wage growth has moderated and household balance sheets are stretched, with debt levels having expanded to about 145% of personal

Canada

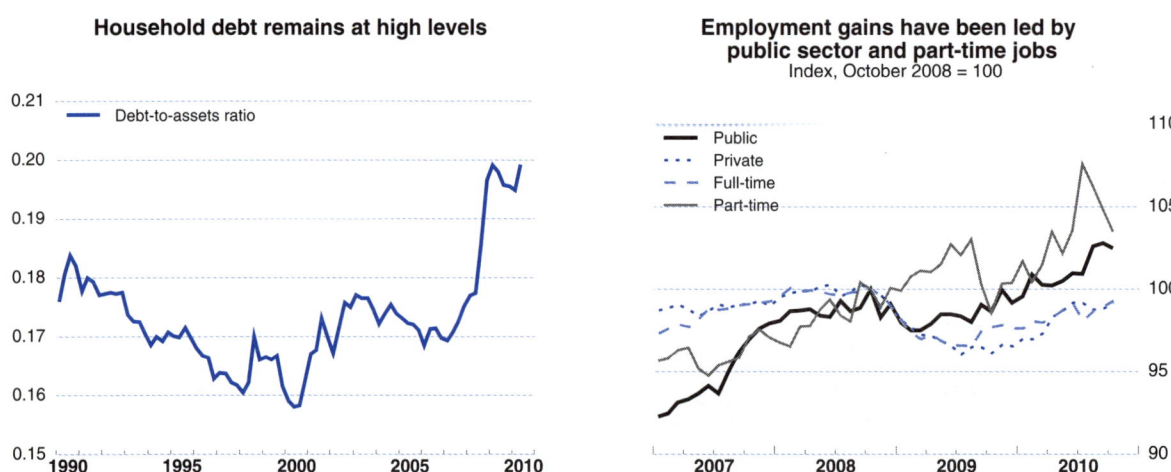

Household debt remains at high levels

Employment gains have been led by public sector and part-time jobs
Index, October 2008 = 100

Source: Statistics Canada; Thomson Datastream; OECD Economic Outlook 88 database.

StatLink http://dx.doi.org/10.1787/888932345603

Canada: **Financial indicators**

	2008	2009	2010	2011	2012
Household saving ratio[1]	3.6	4.6	4.6	4.0	3.9
General government financial balance[2]	0.0	-5.5	-4.9	-3.4	-2.1
Current account balance[2]	0.4	-2.8	-2.7	-2.8	-2.1
Short-term interest rate[3]	3.5	0.8	0.8	1.6	2.8
Long-term interest rate[4]	3.6	3.2	3.2	3.3	4.0

1. As a percentage of disposable income.
2. As a percentage of GDP.
3. 3-month deposit rate.
4. 10-year government bonds.
Source: OECD Economic Outlook 88 database.

StatLink http://dx.doi.org/10.1787/888932347275

disposable income. More subdued house price growth should further curtail the wealth effects that had earlier propelled household spending. With the construction and public sectors accounting for over half of the jobs created since the trough, employment gains are expected to ease. Sustained strength in the exchange rate continues to pose challenges for the manufacturing sector, which is in the process of restructuring. The sectoral shift of resources that has accompanied this restructuring has

Canada: **Demand and output**

	2009	2010	2011	2012	Fourth quarter		
					2010	2011	2012
	Current prices CAD billion	Percentage changes from previous year, volume (2002 prices)					
Private consumption	898.7	3.2	2.1	3.0	2.5	2.4	3.2
Government consumption	333.9	3.3	0.8	-0.3	1.8	0.1	-0.4
Gross fixed investment	328.5	6.6	4.8	2.6	7.2	4.0	2.1
Public[1]	58.2	11.7	-0.1	-8.8	4.5	-4.5	-9.0
Residential	99.0	10.3	0.4	3.2	3.0	3.0	2.7
Non-residential	171.2	2.7	9.5	6.3	11.0	7.7	5.4
Final domestic demand	1 561.1	3.9	2.4	2.2	3.3	2.3	2.2
Stockbuilding[2]	- 7.7	0.9	0.1	0.0			
Total domestic demand	1 553.4	4.8	2.5	2.2	4.1	2.3	2.2
Exports of goods and services	438.6	6.8	5.3	9.4	5.6	7.0	10.7
Imports of goods and services	464.7	12.7	5.7	6.6	9.7	5.6	7.2
Net exports[2]	- 26.2	-1.9	-0.2	0.8			
GDP at market prices	1 527.3	3.0	2.3	3.0	2.8	2.6	3.2

Note: National accounts are based on official chain-linked data. This introduces a discrepancy in the identity between real demand components and GDP. For further details see *OECD Economic Outlook* Sources and Methods *(http://www.oecd.org/eco/sources-and-methods).*
Detailed quarterly projections are reported for the major seven countries, the euro area and the total OECD in the Statistical Annex.
1. Excluding nationalised industries and public corporations.
2. Contributions to changes in real GDP (percentage of real GDP in previous year), actual amount in the first column.
Source: OECD Economic Outlook 88 database.

StatLink http://dx.doi.org/10.1787/888932347294

Canada: **External indicators**

	2008	2009	2010	2011	2012
	\$ billion				
Goods and services exports	532.2	385.7	465.2	502	558
Goods and services imports	507.4	408.8	489.6	529	573
Foreign balance	24.8	- 23.1	- 24.4	- 27	- 16
Invisibles, net	- 16.8	- 15.5	- 17.7	- 19	- 21
Current account balance	8.0	- 38.6	- 42.1	- 46	- 36
	Percentage changes				
Goods and services export volumes	- 4.6	- 14.2	6.8	5.3	9.4
Goods and services import volumes	1.2	- 13.9	12.7	5.7	6.6
Export performance[1]	- 3.4	- 1.2	- 6.1	- 3.9	1.4
Terms of trade	4.8	- 9.5	6.3	0.3	- 0.1

1. Ratio between export volume and export market of total goods and services.
Source: OECD Economic Outlook 88 database.

StatLink 🔢📈 http://dx.doi.org/10.1787/888932347313

created greater skills mismatch and retraining needs that may slow the adjustment in labour markets, thus restraining income growth.

... but investment conditions are improving

The fundamentals for business investment have picked up alongside higher corporate profitability, strong financial positions and improved access to credit. Recent fiscal policy initiatives, including introduction of the harmonised sales tax, capital tax cuts and corporate income tax reductions, should lower the cost of capital and buttress investment intentions. These advances in capital formation rates should eventually drive productivity gains and enhance employment prospects.

Fiscal stimulus should be withdrawn as the recovery solidifies

Further stimulus, including public infrastructure investments, tax relief and support for the unemployed, is continuing to sustain growth in 2010. With a weaker US outlook curbing the expected speed of economic recovery, the federal government announced plans in September to scale back the planned increase in employment insurance premiums, resulting in a somewhat slower pace of stimulus withdrawal. Barring a further deterioration in labour market conditions, governments should begin to withdraw stimulus and reduce structural deficits over the course of 2011-12 as planned so as to maintain investor confidence in the path towards public debt sustainability. As the economy recovers, consolidation plans will help return the total government budget close to balance in five years, in large part through restraining expenditure growth and trimming public sector employment and wage increases. Additionally, a small portion of deficit reduction will take the form of increases in taxes and user fees at the provincial level. The projection assumes fiscal consolidation is implemented as planned, with the total government deficit falling from 4.9% of GDP in 2010 to 2.1% of GDP in 2012.

Further monetary tightening should be delayed into early 2011

Despite narrowing for the past four quarters, the level of excess capacity remains sizable, and price pressures correspondingly weak. Monetary policy remains very accommodative, although the Bank of Canada began to withdraw monetary stimulus, raising its policy interest rate three times since June to 1% before pausing in October. Further rate hikes should be delayed into early 2011 when a recovery in private demand is expected to gain a firmer footing, after which a gradual pace of tightening should resume.

The outlook is for a resumption of moderate growth

Real GDP growth is expected to strengthen progressively over the projection period. Gradual improvements in full-time employment should continue to support consumption increases. Business investment should remain robust, although greater uncertainty over the US recovery and excess capacity in commercial real estate markets are expected to rein back gains from recent heights. Most of the inventory correction has likely occurred, as stock-to-sales ratios are now back to more normal levels. The strong exchange rate will continue to depress export performance, but external demand and employment prospects should begin to pick up from mid-2011. While narrowing steadily over the projection period, the large output gap is likely to exert downward pressure on prices, so that underlying inflation should remain stable.

Uncertainties around the outlook remain wide

There are both upside and downside risks to the outlook. On the downside, a deeper slowdown in the global and particularly the US economy or a further appreciation of the Canadian dollar could damage business confidence, discourage investment, and weaken exports. Housing affordability has deteriorated significantly in certain regions, and a downward correction in house prices could undermine domestic demand. On the upside, the recovery could be faster if external demand proves stronger than projected, or if commodity prices rise beyond their assumed flat path.

AUSTRALIA

The Australian economy, fuelled by the mining boom, should grow robustly in 2011 and 2012 at a rate of between 3½ and 4%. Strong growth, driven by terms of trade gains and dynamic investment, will reduce unemployment.

The projected increase in demand is likely to require a further tightening of monetary conditions to ensure that a non-inflationary recovery remains on track. The current fiscal consolidation plan must be pursued, as assumed in the projections, to rebuild the margins for manoeuvre used during the crisis. Reforms are needed to strengthen supply capacities in the housing and infrastructure sectors to reduce bottlenecks, which the mining boom is likely to exacerbate.

The recovery has strengthened

Growth, which is becoming more broad-based, reached 3% in the first half of 2010, year on year. Private consumption and housing investment have strengthened, exports have benefited from continued demand from Asian countries and public spending has remained solid despite a slowdown in the second quarter. This dynamism of activity, despite being slowed by the fall in inventories and growth in imports, should continue during the rest of the year. Business and household confidence remains high. Firms have increased their profits and stepped up already ambitious investment projects. The outlook is particularly favourable in the mining sector due to high commodity prices as a result of strong demand from the Chinese market. Demand for full-time labour, which fell during the crisis, has strengthened and labour supply remains buoyed by growth in immigration. The unemployment rate fell to 5.1% in September 2010. However, wage increases have remained moderate so far. Underlying inflation, which fell to 2½ per cent in the third quarter of 2010, has returned within the middle of Reserve Bank of Australia's (RBA) target

Australia

The basis of the recovery has broadened
Contribution to real GDP growth [1]

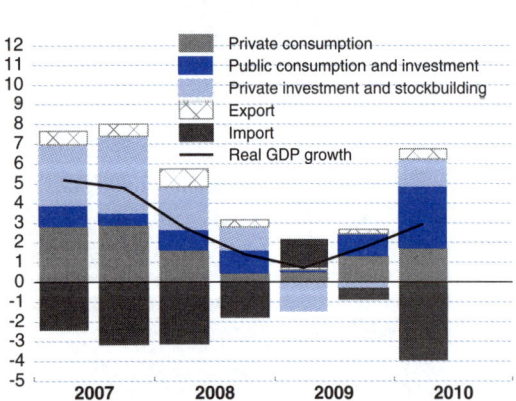

Commodity prices and the terms of trade have picked up again
Index year 2000=100

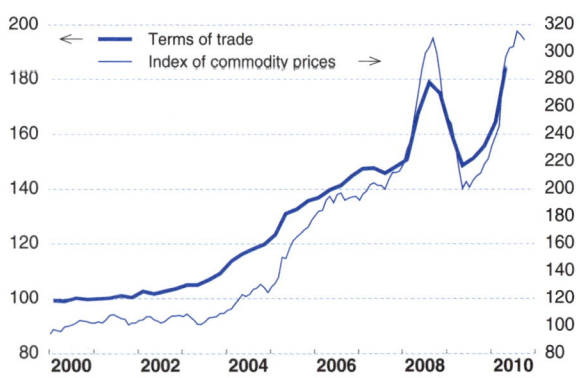

1. Year-on-year percentage change.

Source: OECD, Economic Outlook 88 database and Reserve Bank of Australia.

StatLink http://dx.doi.org/10.1787/888932345660

Australia: **Demand, output and prices**

	2007	2008	2009	2010	2011	2012
	Current prices AUD billion	Percentage changes, volume (2007/2008 prices)				
Private consumption	635.9	1.9	1.7	3.3	3.2	3.2
Government consumption	192.9	3.3	2.8	5.2	2.1	1.7
Gross fixed capital formation	323.5	9.0	-1.1	7.0	6.6	8.5
Final domestic demand	1 152.4	4.1	1.1	4.7	4.0	4.5
Stockbuilding[1]	6.5	-0.4	-0.5	0.4	0.0	0.0
Total domestic demand	1 158.9	3.7	0.5	5.1	4.0	4.5
Exports of goods and services	217.6	3.1	1.0	4.7	6.1	6.5
Imports of goods and services	239.0	11.1	-8.3	13.3	8.1	8.4
Net exports[1]	- 21.4	-1.7	2.0	-1.8	-0.6	-0.6
GDP at market prices	1 137.5	2.1	1.2	3.3	3.6	4.0
GDP deflator	_	6.4	0.3	5.9	3.5	2.5
Memorandum items						
Consumer price index	_	4.4	1.8	2.9	2.8	2.9
Private consumption deflator	_	3.7	3.1	2.6	2.7	2.9
Unemployment rate	_	4.2	5.6	5.2	4.9	4.7
Household saving ratio[2]	_	1.9	5.1	2.2	2.5	2.9
General government financial balance[3]	_	0.4	-4.0	-3.3	-1.7	-0.4
Current account balance[3]	_	-4.5	-4.4	-2.3	-1.9	-2.6

1. Contributions to changes in real GDP (percentage of real GDP in previous year), actual amount in the first column.
2. As a percentage of disposable income.
3. As a percentage of GDP.
Source: OECD Economic Outlook 88 database.

StatLink 🔗 http://dx.doi.org/10.1787/888932347408

range of 2-3%. Headline inflation, driven by increases in tobacco and housing costs, rose to 2.8% in the third quarter

Further tightening of monetary conditions will be necessary

Monetary policy, which was tightened earlier than in other OECD countries, has maintained a neutral stance between May and October 2010, with the RBA's cash rate being held at 4.5%. In November 2010, the RBA raised its policy rates again by 25 basis points to 4.75%. Growth in lending is recovering only gradually, reflecting a cautious approach to debt by both households and firms. The stock market has made practically no gains over the past year. The effective exchange rate, which had remained stable at its pre-crisis level in the year through August 2010, has appreciated by about 5% since then. OECD projections include further tightening of monetary policy to moderate demand pressures and rein in the level of inflation, which is relatively high at the beginning of this cycle.

The budgetary situation is well under control

Public debt is low and the deficit, at around 4% of GDP in 2009, is expected to decline as a result of stronger growth and the fiscal consolidation plan currently being pursued. The plan limits the increase in real federal expenditure to less than 2% a year until the return to a budgetary surplus of 1% of GDP. The pursuit of this strategy, which the projection assumes will be implemented, will have a restrictive effect on economic activity and should ensure a return to surplus by as early as 2013.

Growth, driven by investment, should be robust

Increased business investment should be the main engine of growth, which is expected to exceed its trend rate over the projection period. The strength of demand from the major Asian countries and the terms of trade will favour the mining sector, whose expansion should have a knock-on effect on the rest of the economy. These developments will probably compensate for weaker public demand and stimulate job creation, which should support household incomes and consumption. Unemployment could fall to below 5% after mid-2011. The maintenance of a negative output gap over the projection period should allow inflation to stabilise between 2¾ and 3 per cent.

The risks associated with this scenario are broadly balanced

The positive medium-term outlook associated with the development of China could boost confidence and produce stronger than expected growth in domestic demand. However, this scenario might also be adversely affected by renewed financial turbulence in the OECD area or by an unexpected slowdown in the Chinese economy.

AUSTRIA

The export-led recovery strengthened in 2010. However, the projected pick-up in private sector consumption and investment demand will be tempered by fiscal consolidation, leaving growth at around 2% in both 2011 and 2012. The unemployment rate will fall slightly, while core inflation picks up somewhat.

The excessive fiscal deficit calls for consolidation to begin immediately as the economy is projected to grow above potential. The government has announced a medium-term consolidation plan tilted towards revenue measures. Austria could reap a double dividend, in terms of medium-term growth and fiscal stability, by making the tax structure more growth friendly and reducing distorting subsidies and tax expenditures.

The recovery has gained momentum

The recovery gained momentum in the second quarter of 2010, driven by the increase in world trade and strong economic growth in Germany, Austria's largest trading partner. Capacity utilisation rose towards its long-term average level and investment picked up. Business sentiment has risen and other recent indicators also point to a continuation of the recovery, although at a somewhat slower pace. Private consumption expenditure continued to show moderate growth, reflecting low income growth and some decline in the household savings ratio, indicating that the recovery has not yet become broad-based.

Labour market performance is improving

Recent labour market developments have been favourable, with a drop in the unemployment rate to 4.5% in the second quarter of 2010. Employment growth has now spread to the manufacturing sector, but most newly created jobs are still in lower-productivity service-related activities and often on a part-time basis. Core inflation remained stable at

Austria

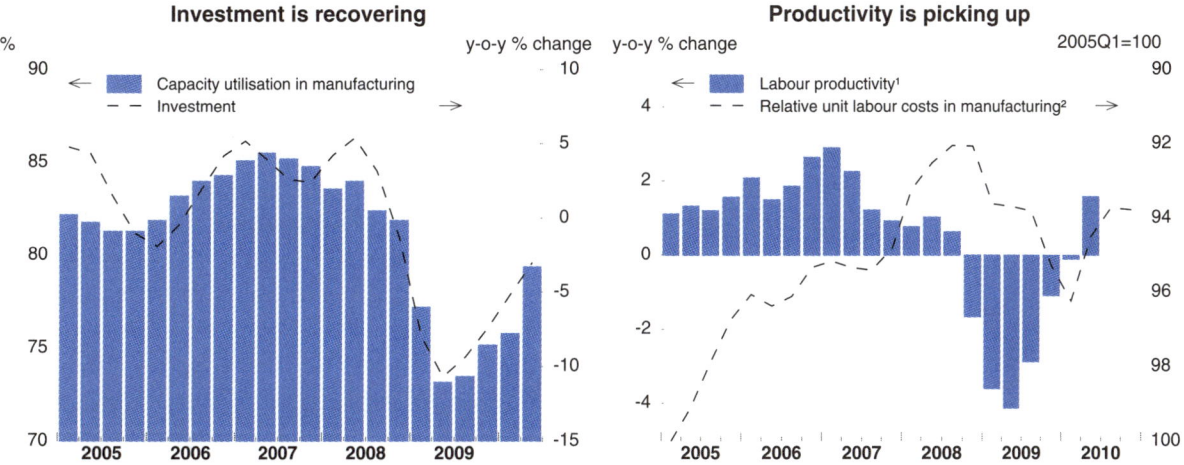

1. Total economy measure.
2. Scale inverted.

Source: OECD Economic Outlook 88 database and OECD Main Economic Indicators Database.

StatLink ᓂᕆᔅ *http://dx.doi.org/10.1787/888932345679*

Austria: Demand, output and prices

	2007	2008	2009	2010	2011	2012
	Current prices € billion	Percentage changes, volume (2005 prices)				
Private consumption	143.7	0.7	1.1	0.9	1.1	1.5
Government consumption	49.2	3.7	0.5	0.8	-0.2	-0.5
Gross fixed capital formation	58.3	2.8	-8.9	-2.4	2.5	3.2
Final domestic demand	251.2	1.7	-1.4	0.2	1.1	1.5
Stockbuilding[1]	5.0	-0.6	-0.9	0.5	0.0	0.0
Total domestic demand	256.1	1.1	-1.5	0.3	1.1	1.5
Exports of goods and services	160.6	-0.4	-13.9	8.1	7.6	5.8
Imports of goods and services	145.0	-1.7	-11.9	5.5	6.6	5.3
Net exports[1]	15.5	0.7	-1.8	1.6	0.9	0.6
GDP at market prices	271.7	1.9	-3.8	2.0	2.0	2.0
GDP deflator	_	1.5	1.0	1.5	1.1	1.2
Memorandum items						
GDP without working day adjustments	272.0	2.2	-3.9	1.9	2.0	2.0
Harmonised index of consumer prices	_	3.2	0.4	1.6	1.8	1.9
Private consumption deflator	_	2.5	-0.7	1.8	1.8	1.9
Unemployment rate[2]	_	3.8	4.8	4.5	4.4	4.3
Household saving ratio[3]	_	11.8	11.1	10.0	9.7	9.5
General government financial balance[4]	_	-0.5	-3.5	-4.4	-3.4	-3.0
Current account balance[4]	_	3.3	2.7	2.6	3.1	3.8

Note: National accounts are based on official chain-linked data. This introduces a discrepancy in the identity between real demand components and GDP. For further details see _OECD Economic Outlook_ Sources and Methods _(http://www.oecd.org/eco/sources-and-methods)._
1. Contributions to changes in real GDP (percentage of real GDP in previous year), actual amount in the first column.
2. Based on Labour Force Survey data.
3. As a percentage of disposable income.
4. As a percentage of GDP.
Source: OECD Economic Outlook 88 database.

StatLink ᵐᵍ⊐ http://dx.doi.org/10.1787/888932347427

around 1.3% in the first half of the year, whereas headline inflation picked up to 1.8%, a lagged response to previous oil price increases.

Stronger foreign demand is driving the recovery

Strong growth in foreign demand is expected to continue into 2011 and 2012 despite the outlook for weaker domestic demand in surrounding countries with high fiscal consolidation needs. The recovery has led to greater use of labour hoarded during the recession and cost-competitiveness is improving. A lift in productivity back towards trend should help to underpin future competitiveness gains. Sustained export growth will reduce spare capacity and support the recent turnaround in investment. An accommodative monetary policy environment will provide further support. Core inflation will remain moderate although it will pick up a little in 2011 and 2012 as spare capacity continues to decline. Tax increases will put some upward pressure on headline inflation in 2011.

Unemployment will decline mildly

Growth in GDP will help to reduce the unemployment rate. The reversal of labour hoarding and cuts in average hours during the recession, as well as government restriction of public sector employment growth, will moderate both employment increases and declines in the unemployment rate. Modest wage gains and improved household confidence arising from the improving labour market, along with low real interest rates, will contribute to somewhat stronger household consumption growth, which is however held back by increasing mortgage debt servicing costs.

A fiscal consolidation strategy has been announced

Latest economic and financial developments suggest a better-than-expected budgetary outturn. Nevertheless, the general government deficit is projected to widen to about 4.4% of GDP this year. A consolidation strategy in accordance with the requirements under the EU Stability and Growth Pact has been announced by the government, relying mainly on revenue measures, including a bank levy and an increase in fuel taxation. The projection builds in a degree of fiscal consolidation in line with this announcement, which should bring down the headline deficit to 3.4% by 2011 and 3% by 2012. The increase in fuel excise and other environmental taxes will have a double dividend for the fiscal position and the environment. Cuts in wasteful social expenditure should increase labour market incentives and potential growth. The consolidation plan should focus more on additional expenditure savings and also on making the tax structure more growth friendly by shifting the tax burden from labour income to property taxes, and reducing distorting subsidies.

External headwinds could strike but domestic demand may be stronger

The overall risks to the projection are balanced. The current projection assumes that the rate of decline in export market share observed since mid-2005 is arrested by recent and ongoing gains in cost-competitiveness. If this fails to materialise, exports and the recovery are likely to be weaker. By contrast, as confidence returns, extremely low interest rates may eventually spark a larger increase in interest rate sensitive expenditure than the moderate response currently built in. Weak competition in the non-tradeables sector could lead to higher core inflation pressures than are currently projected. Recent increases in the price of basic food commodities may put upward pressure on headline inflation, further undermining purchasing power.

BELGIUM

Following the growth spurt in the first half of 2010, the pace of economic expansion appears to be moderating but is likely to pick up again into 2012. Over the projection horizon, the recovery will be driven by world trade as fiscal policy becomes restrictive. High unemployment, if it persists, may translate into higher levels of structural unemployment.

To secure fiscal sustainability, fiscal consolidation in the form of expenditure restraint at all levels of government should be vigourous and have a special emphasis on limiting growth in ageing-related costs. This should be complemented by labour market reforms to boost employment levels, particularly through more flexible wage formation and stronger job search incentives.

The economy is on a slow recovery path

After an unusually strong growth in exports and stockbuilding in early 2010, the economy slowed despite supportive fiscal and monetary policies. Retail sales recovered strongly, particularly reflecting higher car sales that were boosted by an environmental bonus with incentives to forward purchases. Industrial production increased sufficiently to bring the historically low capacity utilisation back towards its long-term average. These trends are likely to continue on the back of marked improvements in consumer confidence, which returned to its pre-crisis levels, and to a lesser extent in business sentiment, reflecting a sluggish recovery in export orders. Employment started to increase towards the end of 2009 in response to higher labour demand in the services sector. Nevertheless, the unemployment rate increased by around ¾ percentage points during 2010 to around 8¾ per cent owing to the scaling back of the reduced-working-time scheme and – considering the still weak growth prospects – a surprisingly strong expansion of the labour supply.

Wage indexation is pushing up inflation

Higher energy prices led to an acceleration of inflation during spring 2010, bringing it to about 2½ per cent by mid-year. Thereafter

Belgium

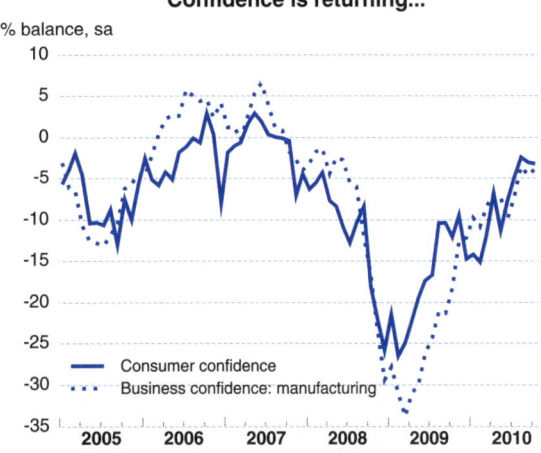

Confidence is returning...

% balance, sa

Legend:
— Consumer confidence
···· Business confidence: manufacturing

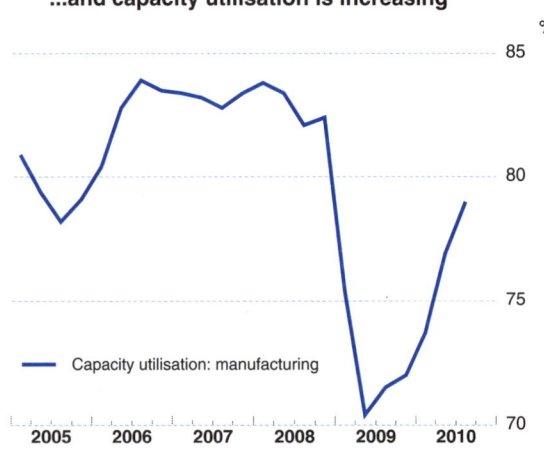

...and capacity utilisation is increasing

%

Legend:
— Capacity utilisation: manufacturing

Source: OECD, Main Economic Indicators database.

StatLink ⏷ http://dx.doi.org/10.1787/888932345698

Belgium: **Demand, output and prices**

	2007	2008	2009	2010	2011	2012
	Current prices € billion	Percentage changes, volume (2008 prices)				
Private consumption	170.9	1.4	-0.2	1.5	1.7	1.8
Government consumption	74.8	2.5	0.4	1.1	1.3	0.4
Gross fixed capital formation	72.8	2.4	-4.9	-1.7	2.8	3.7
Final domestic demand	318.6	1.9	-1.1	0.7	1.8	1.9
Stockbuilding[1]	3.5	0.0	-1.0	0.8	0.1	0.0
Total domestic demand	322.1	1.9	-2.1	1.5	1.9	1.8
Exports of goods and services	279.4	1.4	-11.4	10.1	5.2	4.8
Imports of goods and services	266.5	2.8	-10.9	9.1	5.3	5.0
Net exports[1]	13.0	-1.0	-0.5	1.0	0.0	0.0
GDP at market prices	335.1	0.8	-2.7	2.1	1.8	1.8
GDP deflator	_	1.9	1.1	1.5	1.5	1.7
Memorandum items						
Harmonised index of consumer prices	_	4.5	0.0	2.1	1.6	1.8
Private consumption deflator	_	3.2	-0.5	2.3	1.7	1.8
Unemployment rate	_	7.0	7.9	8.6	8.8	8.7
Household saving ratio[2]	_	11.9	13.4	12.2	12.0	11.6
General government financial balance[3]	_	-1.4	-6.1	-4.9	-4.5	-3.6
Current account balance[3]	_	-1.9	0.8	1.0	1.0	1.1

Note: National accounts are based on official chain-linked data. This introduces a discrepancy in the identity between real demand components and GDP. For further details see *OECD Economic Outlook* Sources and Methods *(http://www.oecd.org/eco/sources-and-methods)*.
1. Contributions to changes in real GDP (percentage of real GDP in previous year), actual amount in the first column.
2. As a percentage of disposable income.
3. As a percentage of GDP.
Source: OECD Economic Outlook 88 database.

StatLink 🔗 *http://dx.doi.org/10.1787/888932347446*

inflation pressures increased further as the automatic wage indexation mechanism was triggered, leading to an upwards adjustment of social security benefits in September, public sector salaries in October and most private sector salaries subsequently. As a consequence, core inflation started to increase in mid-year after having remained stable at around 1¼ per cent in the first half the year. The yet-to-be-concluded 2011-12 wage agreements are expected to yield negotiated wage growth that is broadly within the wage norm of developments in Belgium's three main trading partners. Nevertheless, external competitiveness is expected to continue its erosion because of relatively sluggish productivity developments.

Fiscal sustainability needs to be vigorously pursued

The 2010 general government deficit should narrow by nearly 1¼ percentage points of GDP to just below 5% of GDP, reflecting some budget consolidation, higher growth and the non-repetition of some negative one-off revenue measures. At the time of writing, the coalition negotiations had failed to produce a new government. Thus, the fiscal assumption in 2011 is that Belgium will achieve about three-quarters of the planned 1% of GDP consolidation laid down in the medium-term consolidation programme. In 2012, it is assumed that consolidation will amount to 1% of GDP with an even split between revenue raising measures and spending cuts. Combined with faster growth, this should secure deficits of about 4½ and 3½ per cent of GDP in 2011 and 2012, respectively. Thus, the medium-term objective of balancing the budget in 2015 (as part of the efforts to put public finances on a path towards sustainability) could be achieved through similar sized consolidation efforts in the following years. According to inter-governmental agreements, the federal government and the social security system is responsible for two-thirds of the short-term consolidation, and the communities and the regions for the rest, irrespective of the new fiscal federalism arrangements that are being discussed in the coalition negotiations.

Growth prospects are improving

The pace of economic recovery should pick up again as world trade strengthens, although activity will be restrained by the tightening of fiscal policy. Thus, employment growth will remain relatively lacklustre in 2011 and unemployment will only start to fall towards the end of the year. The main downside risk is a negative impact of lasting political uncertainties on business sentiments and consumer confidence. On the upside, faster-than-projected world trade growth would improve the export outlook.

CHILE

The Chilean economy has embarked on a strong recovery. Supported by high copper prices and strong domestic demand after the February earthquakes, the pace of growth is projected to remain high in 2011 and 2012. Inflation is likely to temporarily exceed the central bank's inflation target of 3% in the second half of 2010 and early 2011, but then fall back gradually as policy tightening takes effect.

Monetary policy should continue moving toward a neutral stance to keep inflation expectations well anchored. Similarly, the government is right to aim for a reduction in the structural budget deficit to 1% of GDP by 2014, to preserve hard-won fiscal credibility and reduce the risk of overheating. If the recovery unfolds as projected, there would even be room for a somewhat faster fiscal adjustment than currently envisaged.

Activity is expanding vigorously

Though the natural disasters of February 2010 had tragic effects, activity was depressed only temporarily and strong output growth resumed soon after. Domestic demand is the main engine of the upswing, supported by high copper prices, normalising financial conditions and rapidly falling unemployment. Investment is expanding particularly strongly, with gross fixed capital formation in the second quarter up almost 30% from one year before. Because capital goods are largely imported, the current account is rapidly moving into deficit. Despite the surge in activity, inflation has so far remained well contained, in part reflecting downward pressure on prices of tradable goods due to the recent appreciation of the Chilean peso.

The central bank should continue withdrawing monetary stimulus

The policy rate has been raised from 0.5% in July to 2.75% in October. According to a central bank survey, inflation expectations one year ahead have increased somewhat after the February natural disasters, partly

Chile

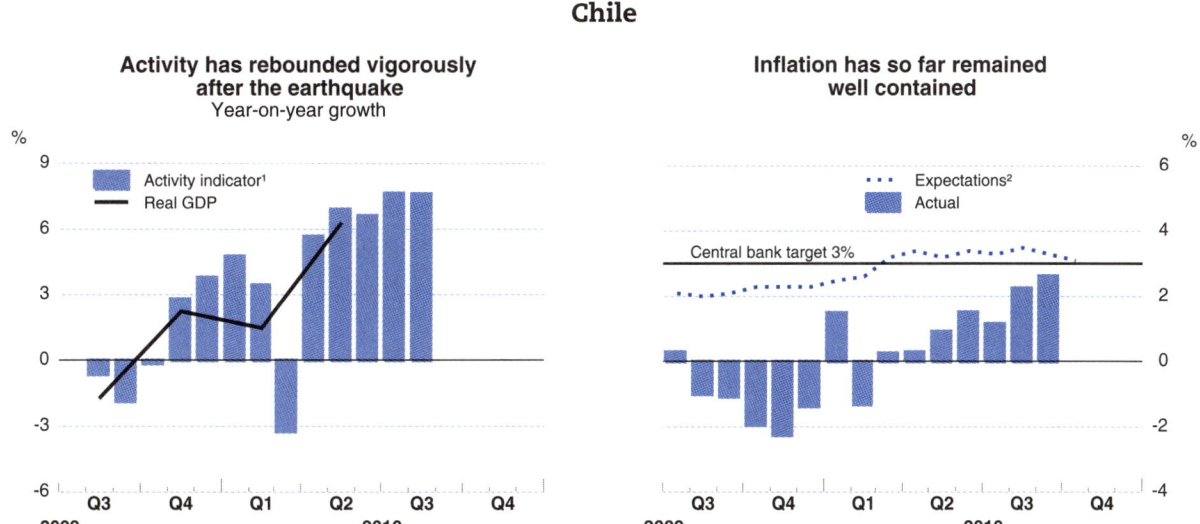

1. Indicator Mensual de Actividad Económica (IMACEC), monthly indicator of economic activity.
2. One year ahead, Monthly Survey of Economic Expectations.
Source: Central Bank of Chile.

StatLink ᵃᵍᵉᵖ *http://dx.doi.org/10.1787/888932345717*

Chile: **Demand, output and prices**

	2007	2008	2009	2010	2011	2012
	Current prices CLP billion	Percentage changes, volume (2003 prices)				
Private consumption	46 870.2	4.6	0.9	9.4	6.3	5.2
Government consumption	9 371.7	0.5	6.8	2.9	4.2	3.1
Gross fixed capital formation	16 983.4	18.6	-15.3	24.2	14.2	10.5
Final domestic demand	73 225.3	7.5	-2.8	12.0	8.1	6.4
Stockbuilding[1]	602.7	0.0	-3.4	4.8	0.4	0.0
Total domestic demand	73 828.0	7.4	-5.8	16.8	8.3	6.3
Exports of goods and services	40 561.3	3.1	-5.6	-0.5	9.9	8.5
Imports of goods and services	28 539.5	12.2	-14.3	28.3	13.2	9.4
Net exports[1]	12 021.8	-2.6	3.3	-8.8	-0.6	0.2
GDP at market prices	85 849.8	3.4	-1.4	5.2	6.2	5.4
GDP deflator	_	0.5	4.1	9.6	6.6	4.3
Memorandum items						
Index of consumer prices	_	8.7	0.4	1.6	3.8	3.1
Private consumption deflator	_	7.7	2.9	1.2	3.7	3.1
Unemployment rate	_	7.8	10.8	8.1	7.3	7.2
Cenral government financial balance[2]	_	4.8	-4.4	-1.0	-0.8	-0.7
Current account balance[2]	_	-1.8	2.5	-1.3	-1.3	-1.1

1. Contributions to changes in real GDP (percentage of real GDP in previous year), actual amount in the first column.
2. As a percentage of GDP.
Source: OECD Economic Outlook 88 database.

StatLink ⬛ *http://dx.doi.org/10.1787/888932347465*

reflecting rapidly diminishing excess capacity, but remain close to the central bank's inflation target of 3%. If the recovery proceeds as expected, monetary policy should continue gradually raising the policy rate to its neutral level to keep inflation expectations well anchored.

The government's financial assets should be rebuilt

As the result of a large fiscal stimulus in support of domestic demand in the 2008-09 recession and earthquake reconstruction spending, the structural fiscal balance moved from surplus to a deficit of around 3% of GDP in 2009 and 2% in 2010. By financing the reconstruction partly through temporary tax increases and by limiting real expenditure growth, the government plans to gradually move toward a structural budget deficit of 1% of GDP by 2014. A good part of the reduction in the structural deficit will come about automatically, as the fiscal stimulus is withdrawn and reconstruction spending is completed. The government is right to implement a fiscal tightening, as this will help to rebuild financial safety buffers in the sovereign stabilisation fund, which has demonstrated its usefulness during the adverse events of the past two years. Indeed, if the recovery unfolds as projected, there would be room to reduce the structural deficit somewhat more rapidly than currently planned by the government and assumed in the projections by firmly limiting expenditure growth, which has been exceptionally high over the past two years.

GDP is projected to grow above potential in 2011 and 2012

GDP growth is expected to exceed 5% in 2010 and 6% in 2011, supported by strong domestic demand. Falling unemployment and the start of major reconstruction projects in the second half of 2010 will result in strong private consumption and investment in the near term. As the reconstruction effort tapers off, GDP growth will gradually normalise, reaching around 5½ per cent on average in 2012. The current account will remain in deficit throughout the projection period as strong domestic demand fuels import growth. Annual CPI inflation is expected to be somewhat above the central bank's target of 3% at the end of 2010, but should then gradually come down as the effects of higher interest rates kick in and well anchored inflation expectations contain nominal wage increases.

Downside risks from external economic developments, upside risks from reconstruction

The major downside risk to the projections stems from the uncertainties surrounding the global economic recovery. As a small and very open economy, Chile is heavily exposed to developments in the world economy and a slowdown in global growth would have a significant impact on domestic economic developments. By contrast, growth and inflation may come in higher if the start of major reconstruction projects in the second half of 2010 exerts a stronger impulse on domestic demand than expected.

CZECH REPUBLIC

Exports continue to drive the recovery in real GDP, which is set to grow by 2.4% in 2010 and 2.8% in 2011, with domestic demand more subdued because of the weak labour market and fiscal consolidation. By 2012 the economy is likely to be growing by 3.2%. Temporary inflationary pressures are coming from energy prices and housing costs, but the inflation target of 2% should be achieved.

The new government has proposed fiscal consolidation for 2011, focusing primarily on cuts in operational expenditures. The opportunity offered by the economic recovery should be seized to address structural issues to improve the underlying balance of the public finances and enhance economic potential.

The recovery is underpinned by improving exports and strengthening orders

The economy has been growing in tandem with Germany since the second half of last year. Recovery continues to be driven by exports but private consumption has also shown some resilience. Industrial production, in particular the important automotive sector, is recovering strongly from last year's slump while new orders remain strong. Private consumption held up fairly well during the downturn and it started to grow again at the beginning of this year. However, construction still remains weak and below the levels of last year. Also, the recovery in confidence indicators has slowed somewhat.

Domestic inflationary pressures have emerged

The main monetary policy rate remains at the historically low level of 0.75%. The headline inflation rate has picked up somewhat to 2% year-on-year in October. There are further inflationary pressures on the horizon but monetary policy can remain accommodative for some time due to ongoing fiscal consolidation. Continuing deregulation of rents is increasing housing costs. Moreover, electricity prices are expected to rise in 2011. This is due to over-subsidisation of solar-energy production that

Czech Republic

Trade growth has resumed

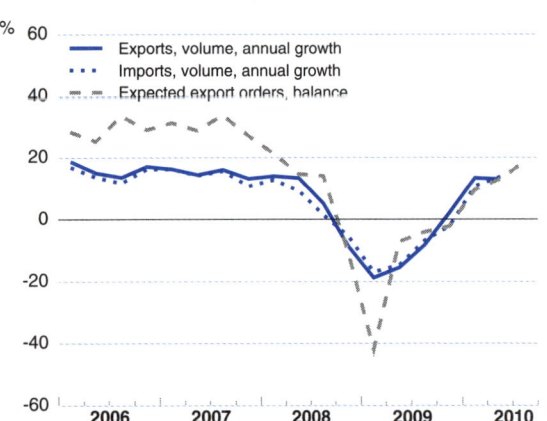

Domestic demand is also recovering
Contributions to quarterly real GDP growth, %

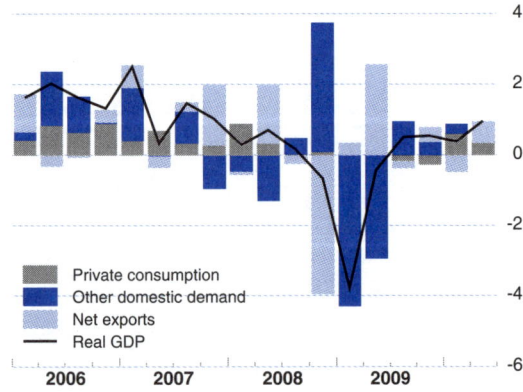

Source: European Commission; OECD, National Accounts database.

StatLink ᵍᵐˢ⋿ http://dx.doi.org/10.1787/888932345736

Czech Republic: **Demand, output and prices**

	2007	2008	2009	2010	2011	2012
	Current prices CZK billion	Percentage changes, volume (2000 prices)				
Private consumption	1 688.0	3.5	-0.1	1.5	1.5	2.4
Government consumption	718.2	1.0	4.2	1.1	0.6	1.1
Gross fixed capital formation	890.3	-1.5	-9.2	-3.6	5.8	6.2
Final domestic demand	3 296.4	1.6	-1.5	0.2	2.3	3.0
Stockbuilding[1]	66.9	-0.5	-2.0	1.3	0.0	0.0
Total domestic demand	3 363.4	1.1	-3.6	1.6	2.2	2.9
Exports of goods and services	2 836.0	5.7	-10.5	11.4	7.7	6.0
Imports of goods and services	2 660.3	4.3	-10.4	11.0	7.2	5.8
Net exports[1]	175.7	1.3	-0.6	0.9	0.7	0.5
GDP at market prices	3 539.1	2.3	-4.0	2.4	2.8	3.2
GDP deflator	_	1.8	2.6	0.0	2.2	1.4
Memorandum items						
Consumer price index	_	6.3	1.0	1.6	1.9	1.7
Private consumption deflator	_	4.9	0.3	0.8	1.8	1.7
Unemployment rate	_	4.4	6.7	7.5	7.1	6.8
General government financial balance[2]	_	-2.7	-5.8	-5.2	-4.2	-3.4
Current account balance[2]	_	-0.6	-1.0	-1.9	-0.8	-0.7

Note: National accounts are based on official chain-linked data. This introduces a discrepancy in the identity between real demand components and GDP. For further details see *OECD Economic Outlook* Sources and Methods *(http://www.oecd.org/eco/sources-and-methods).*
1. Contributions to changes in real GDP (percentage of real GDP in previous year), actual amount in the first column.
2. As a percentage of GDP.
Source: OECD Economic Outlook 88 database.

StatLink ⬛ *http://dx.doi.org/10.1787/888932347484*

led to rapid expansion in producing capacities and whose generous feed-in tariffs translate into increases in the regulated component of the energy price.

Restrictive fiscal policy is needed to achieve targets

Fiscal retrenchment is already under way in 2010 and the proposed budget for 2011 continues the consolidation. In contrast to this year's budget, in which the improvement in the balance was based mainly on VAT and excise tax increases, the draft for 2011 puts emphasis on cuts in recurrent expenditures and central government wage restraint. The projection takes account of the proposed 2011 consolidation, which aims for a deficit target of 4.6% GDP. Furthermore, it assumes a continued prudent fiscal policy for 2012. Broad fiscal targets have been set in the framework of medium-term expenditure ceilings. These aim at a general government deficit of 3% in 2013 and a balanced budget by 2016. Specific steps on how to get to these targets have yet to be decided. At a time when much of the improvement in headline budget numbers can occur from increased economic growth, the recovery phase of the cycle needs to be used for addressing structural issues, including efficiency gains in public sector operations. The current coalition government, given its majority in the parliament, is in a position to seize the opportunity to implement a number of reform proposals such as in tertiary education or pensions.

Prospects have improved with the recovery in world trade and domestic demand

Growth has accelerated in 2010 as the main export markets picked up strongly in the first half of the year. Growth is likely to ease somewhat during 2011 with both private and government consumption subdued, but then will rise again in 2012 as investment is expected to recover quickly. Adjustment in the labour market will be gradual but the unemployment rate is expected to have peaked this year. Together with fiscal restraint, the weak labour market situation will weigh on private consumption, which is nonetheless expected to pick up in 2012. Foreign trade will continue to perform strongly. Inflationary pressures at the beginning of next year will be temporary and as the economy will be below potential, the 2% inflation target should be reached.

Risks relate mainly to external developments

There are balanced risks, primarily based on developments in major export markets, in particular the euro area. On the downside, households' response to the governmental spending restraint and announced increases in housing and electricity prices could result in weaker domestic demand.

DENMARK

The recovery is expected to gain strength gradually as world trade expands, and to become broad-based as private domestic demand improves. With still substantial slack in the economy, inflation is set to remain subdued.

The implementation of the fiscal consolidation plan would allow the fiscal position to be brought back to a path consistent with long-term targets. However, this requires that the government's plans to lower public consumption growth are implemented without the drift that has been a feature in the past, especially at the local government level. To limit labour supply distortions, the envisaged income tax hikes could be partly replaced by measures to raise the efficiency of public spending.

The recovery has gained strength

The economy has now been recovering for over a year, with strong growth in the second quarter of 2010. The upturn had initially been driven mainly by government demand and private consumption, which picked up on the back of strong fiscal and monetary stimulus. More recently, the stockbuilding cycle turned around and exports and private investment surged in the second quarter. Short-term supply-side indicators point to weaker growth for the remainder of the year in most sectors, except manufacturing. Consumer confidence has declined slightly but is above its long-term average.

The labour market shows signs of improvement

Employment has been growing since the start of 2010, driven by public-sector and, more recently, private demand. With relatively high participation rates, however, unemployment continued to rise, as did long-term unemployment, albeit from a low level. As wages have decelerated only modestly, employment is set to recover slowly and unemployment is unlikely to start decreasing before 2011.

Denmark

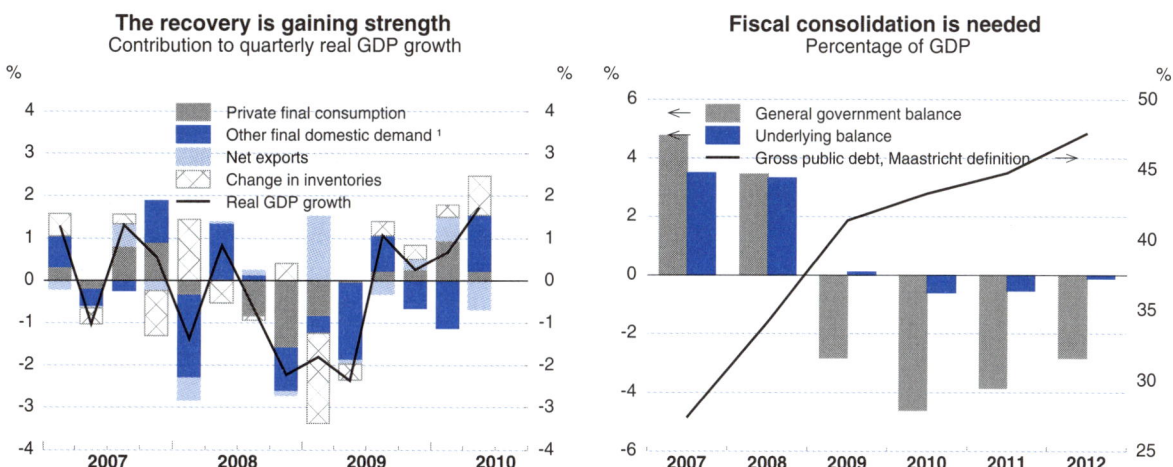

The recovery is gaining strength
Contribution to quarterly real GDP growth

- Private final consumption
- Other final domestic demand [1]
- Net exports
- Change in inventories
- Real GDP growth

Fiscal consolidation is needed
Percentage of GDP

- General government balance
- Underlying balance
- Gross public debt, Maastricht definition

1. Consists of gross fixed capital investment, government consumption and statistical discrepancy.
Source: OECD, Economic Outlook 88 database.

StatLink http://dx.doi.org/10.1787/888932345755

Denmark: **Demand, output and prices**

	2007	2008	2009	2010	2011	2012
	Current prices DKK billion	Percentage changes, volume (2000 prices)				
Private consumption	821.7	-0.2	-4.6	3.0	1.6	2.2
Government consumption	439.1	1.6	3.4	2.0	-0.3	0.3
Gross fixed capital formation	376.6	-4.8	-13.0	-3.9	4.4	6.2
Final domestic demand	1 637.3	-0.8	-4.2	1.4	1.5	2.3
Stockbuilding[1]	12.9	0.3	-2.0	1.2	0.0	0.0
Total domestic demand	1 650.2	-0.5	-6.2	2.2	1.5	2.3
Exports of goods and services	886.4	2.4	-10.2	3.7	4.5	5.1
Imports of goods and services	845.1	3.3	-13.2	4.1	5.5	6.0
Net exports[1]	41.3	-0.4	1.3	-0.1	-0.2	-0.1
GDP at market prices	1 691.5	-0.9	-4.7	2.2	1.6	2.1
GDP deflator	_	3.6	0.4	2.9	1.0	2.0
Memorandum items						
Consumer price index	_	3.4	1.3	2.3	1.4	1.5
Private consumption deflator	_	3.2	1.4	2.4	1.4	1.5
Unemployment rate[2]	_	3.2	5.9	7.2	7.2	6.5
Household saving ratio[3]	_	-2.8	0.1	-1.2	-2.3	-2.5
General government financial balance[4]	_	3.4	-2.8	-4.6	-3.9	-2.8
Current account balance[4]	_	2.7	3.6	4.4	4.4	4.8

Note: National accounts are based on official chain-linked data. This introduces a discrepancy in the identity between real demand components and GDP. For further details see _OECD Economic Outlook_ Sources and Methods (http://www.oecd.org/eco/sources-and-methods).
1. Contributions to changes in real GDP (percentage of real GDP in previous year), actual amount in the first column.
2. The unemployment rate is based on the Labour Force Survey and differs from the registered unemployment rate.
3. As a percentage of disposable income, net of household consumption of fixed capital.
4. As a percentage of GDP.
Source: OECD Economic Outlook 88 database.

StatLink ⟨⟩ http://dx.doi.org/10.1787/888932347503

Financial conditions are normalising

Bank lending to households and companies remained broadly flat during the first half of the year. The housing market shows signs that it has bottomed out, with house prices stabilising. Equity prices have continued to rise.

Policies will be less supportive

The government adopted a Fiscal Consolidation Agreement in May 2010 to consolidate general government finances, with an overall fiscal effort of 1.5% of GDP over 2011-13. The Agreement includes a freeze in public consumption growth in real terms. The projection assumes that the Agreement will be fully implemented. However, for fiscal consolidation to succeed, the government will have to slow public consumption growth markedly, which may be hard to achieve in 2010. The government expects its plan to boost labour market incentives and employment. The cut in duration of unemployment benefits would enhance incentives for the unemployed to find a job. This would be only partly offset by the decision to freeze the nominal tax thresholds, which increases marginal effective tax rates. In 2011, monetary conditions will be very stimulative but they will be somewhat less so in 2012.

The recovery will be driven by both external and private demand

After some temporary slowing in the second half of 2010, the recovery is expected to regain strength gradually. Public demand is set to contribute less to growth while private demand takes the lead. Exports will benefit from expanding world trade and business investment is projected to gain momentum, with the investment-to-GDP ratio approaching pre-crisis levels by end-2012. Private consumption growth is expected to be subdued in 2011, but to pick up in 2012 on the back of improving labour market conditions. With growth mainly driven by private demand, imports are also projected to grow strongly. Inflation is set to remain subdued as economic slack will remain substantial.

Risks relate mainly to the implementation of the fiscal consolidation plan

The recovery could be weaker if the government fails to reduce public consumption and decides to raise taxes further, which could adversely affect labour supply. It could also be stronger, especially beyond the near term, if the plan is used as an opportunity to undertake structural reforms to raise productivity growth. There are risks that the housing market will not stabilise soon despite low interest rates, and that exports benefit less from the buoyancy in world trade should competitiveness improve less than expected.

FINLAND

The economy has rebounded strongly on the back of sharply recovering exports, and unemployment has started to recede. Activity will continue to benefit from firm world trade growth, while renewed confidence and lower unemployment will support domestic demand, leading to robust investment and output growth in the years ahead. Remaining slack will nevertheless hold inflation down.

The resumption of growth and fiscal consolidation will improve public finances markedly. The fiscal deficit is expected to exceed 3% of GDP this year, but to shrink rapidly thereafter. Nevertheless, structural reforms to contain public spending and increase labour force participation, which remains low compared to Nordic peers, remain essential to support medium-term growth and fiscal sustainability.

The economy is gathering strength

Output growth rebounded in the second quarter of 2010, boosted by rapidly expanding exports. Domestic demand is recovering at a slower pace, but is gaining momentum with booming residential investment and rebuilding of inventories underway. Private consumption is also accelerating, supported by improving consumer confidence, steady income growth and increasing wealth with the recovery of asset prices. Private business investment has yet to strengthen, but rising business confidence may well be signalling a turnaround.

Unemployment has started to recede

Unemployment peaked around the turn of the year and has declined substantially since then, despite fairly high labour force participation compared to past recessions. In addition, hours worked per employee are back to their trend level, suggesting that further rises in output could rapidly translate into higher employment and productivity. As the output gap remains large, consumer prices have been increasing only moderately, notwithstanding a hike in value added tax.

Finland

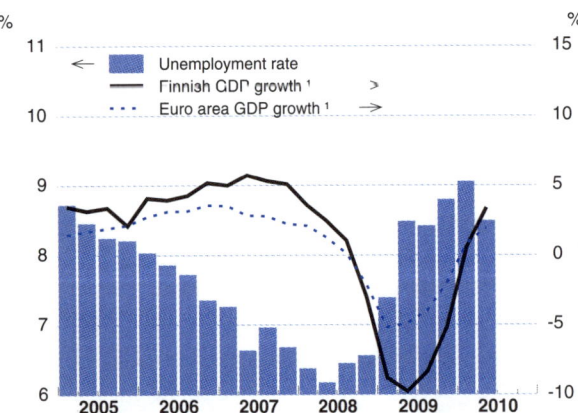

Activity is gathering strength

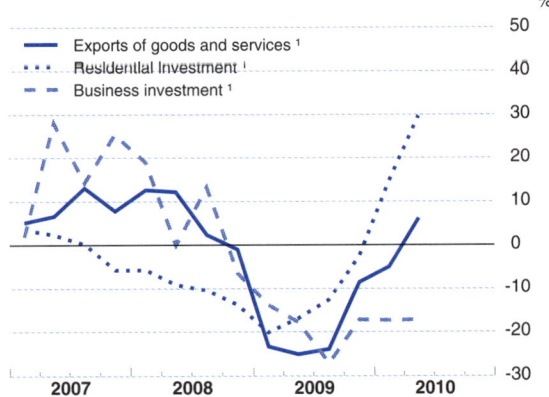

Exports and residential investment are booming

1. In volume, year-on-year percentage change.

Source: OECD, OECD Economic Outlook 88 databases.

StatLink http://dx.doi.org/10.1787/888932345774

Finland: Demand, output and prices

	2007	2008	2009	2010	2011	2012
	Current prices € billion	Percentage changes, volume (2000 prices)				
Private consumption	90.7	1.6	-1.9	2.2	2.5	2.7
Government consumption	38.6	2.6	1.2	0.4	0.6	0.6
Gross fixed capital formation	38.2	0.0	-14.5	1.1	5.3	4.5
Final domestic demand	167.5	1.5	-4.0	1.5	2.5	2.5
Stockbuilding[1,2]	3.1	-0.8	-1.4	0.3	0.3	0.0
Total domestic demand	170.6	0.6	-5.5	1.9	2.9	2.6
Exports of goods and services	82.2	6.4	-20.5	4.6	9.0	5.7
Imports of goods and services	73.2	6.5	-18.1	3.5	8.4	4.8
Net exports[1]	9.1	0.3	-1.9	0.5	0.5	0.5
GDP at market prices	179.7	1.0	-8.1	2.7	3.0	3.0
GDP deflator	_	1.8	1.0	1.8	1.7	1.7
Memorandum items						
GDP without working day adjustments	_	0.9	-8.0	..	..	..
Harmonised index of consumer prices	_	3.9	1.6	1.4	1.8	2.0
Private consumption deflator	_	3.5	0.6	1.4	2.3	2.0
Unemployment rate	_	6.4	8.3	8.6	8.2	8.0
General government financial balance[3]	_	4.2	-2.7	-3.3	-1.7	-0.7
Current account balance[3]	_	2.9	2.7	1.5	1.7	2.0

Note: National accounts are based on official chain-linked data. This introduces a discrepancy in the identity between real demand components and GDP. For further details see *OECD Economic Outlook* Sources and Methods *(http://www.oecd.org/eco/sources-and-methods).*
1. Contributions to changes in real GDP (percentage of real GDP in previous year), actual amount in the first column.
2. Including statistical discrepancy.
3. As a percentage of GDP.
Source: OECD Economic Outlook 88 database.

StatLink ⬛⬛ *http://dx.doi.org/10.1787/888932347522*

Growth will be boosted by strong external and domestic demand

Sustained increases in foreign demand are driving the recovery and export order books point to a further expansion ahead. Imports are also expected to grow rapidly, as they constitute a sizeable input for exports and will be boosted by accelerating domestic demand. As economic prospects continue to brighten, restocking will contribute significantly to output during the second half of 2010. Rising household real income, and wealth from a rebound in housing prices, coupled with growing confidence bode well for private consumption, which should continue to accelerate. These factors have also contributed to the strong rebound in residential investment, though this might lose steam as interest rates increase and worries about the sustainability of past house price increases mount. Robust demand and strong business confidence should lead to a revival of business investment as spare capacity shrinks. From 2011 onwards, fiscal policy will be turning from an expansionary to a tighter stance. This is unlikely to put the recovery at risk since private demand is projected to take over. Overall, the economy should expand at a rate of around 3% in the coming years, without generating significant inflationary pressures as the output gap remains substantial despite the projected decline in unemployment. However, inflation will be pushed up slightly by increases in indirect taxes.

Fiscal consolidation is underway

The fiscal position of Finland is fairly solid in comparison to most other OECD countries. The deficit is expected to slightly exceed 3% this year as a result of delayed effects from the recession and fiscal stimulus. Strong growth will boost revenues, but the government has also taken steps to consolidate public finances, which are incorporated in the current projections. Increases in indirect taxes – mainly VAT and energy taxes – and social contributions will bring additional revenues. Spending needs to be kept under control as ageing-related pressures are building up. Structural reforms to raise labour force participation, improve the sustainability of the pension system and enhance public sector efficiency would reinforce medium-term growth prospects and the fiscal outlook.

A less supportive international environment is a risk

A supportive international environment would ensure a durable recovery. However, a significant weakening of growth in Finland's main trading partners could cast a shadow on the rebound. An overheating housing market, boosted by exceptionally low mortgage rates and over-optimistic expectations over future house prices, could carry risks for medium-term economic and financial stability.

GREECE

Economic activity is contracting, in large part reflecting the sizeable fiscal consolidation underway. The economy is expected to return to positive growth by 2012 as the impact of structural reforms takes hold and external demand strengthens. Headline inflation has edged up, largely due to tax hikes, but should trend downwards given economic slack and rising unemployment.

The rigorous implementation of the Economic Policy Programme agreed in May with the European Commission (EC), European Central Bank (ECB) and the International Monetary Fund (IMF) will stabilise the level of public debt and boost competitiveness. Success hinges upon strict expenditure control and improvements in tax compliance, coupled with decisive reforms to reduce deep-rooted rigidities in labour and product markets. A strong commitment to longer-term fiscal consolidation and continued structural reforms is essential to secure sustainable finances and to restore confidence and growth.

The economy remains in recession

Real GDP contracted by 3¾ per cent (year-on-year) in the first three quarters of 2010, driven by a sharp cut in public consumption and investment. Private investment also plunged, with the housing sector registering a fall of around 20%. Private consumption growth remained positive in the first quarter of the year as households dug into their savings, but contracted in the second quarter in view of the worsening labour market, fiscal retrenchment and a further slowdown in credit. The unemployment rate rose to over 12% at mid-year. Activity indicators, such as industrial production and new car sales, point to further weakness in the coming months, although the recent upturn in new orders and tourism provide positive signals. Headline inflation was 5.2% in October 2010, reflecting indirect tax hikes under the austerity programme. Core inflation has also edged up since the beginning of the year to 3¼ per cent in September, widening the differential *vis-à-vis* the euro-area average to 2¼ percentage points.

Greece

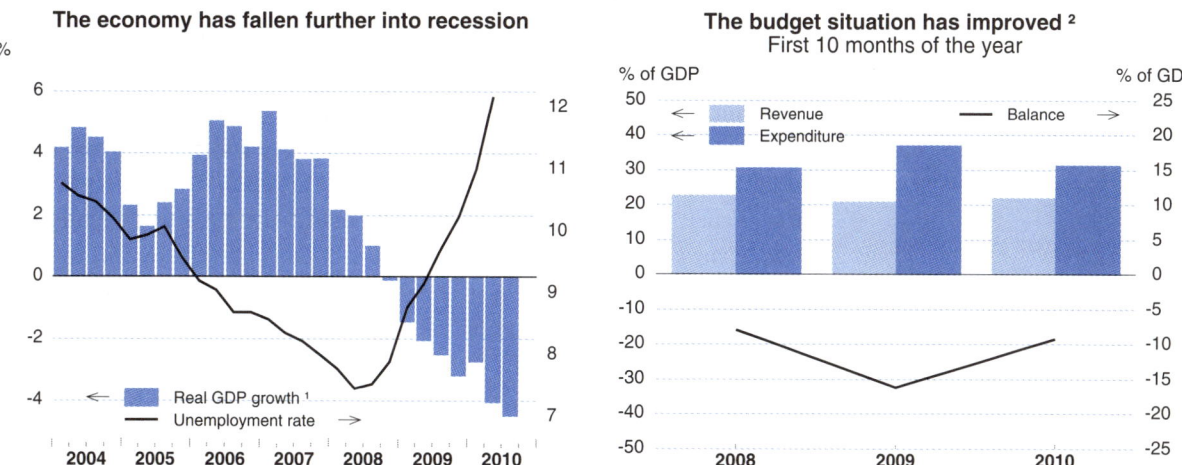

1. Year-on-year percentage change.
2. The central government budget as per cent of GDP, OECD calculations.

Source: OECD Economic Outlook 88 database and General accounting office, Greece.

StatLink http://dx.doi.org/10.1787/888932345793

Greece: **Demand, output and prices**

	2007	2008	2009	2010	2011	2012
	Current prices € billion	Percentage changes, volume (2000 prices)				
Private consumption	162.7	2.3	-1.8	-3.9	-4.3	-0.3
Government consumption	38.5	0.6	9.6	-8.9	-6.9	-5.8
Gross fixed capital formation	48.4	-7.4	-13.9	-18.2	-10.6	-2.2
Final domestic demand	249.6	0.1	-2.5	-7.2	-5.7	-1.4
Stockbuilding[1,2]	2.0	1.1	-0.1	1.3	-0.3	0.0
Total domestic demand	251.6	1.0	-2.5	-5.9	-5.8	-1.4
Exports of goods and services	51.4	4.0	-18.1	-3.5	3.9	8.2
Imports of goods and services	76.6	0.2	-14.1	-11.7	-10.0	-0.5
Net exports[1]	- 25.1	0.9	0.7	3.0	3.7	1.9
GDP at market prices	226.4	1.3	-2.3	-3.9	-2.7	0.5
GDP deflator	_	3.5	1.3	3.3	2.4	1.0
Memorandum items						
Harmonised index of consumer prices	_	4.2	1.3	4.7	2.5	0.7
Private consumption deflator	_	4.1	1.3	4.0	2.5	0.7
Unemployment rate	_	7.7	9.5	12.2	14.5	15.2
General government financial balance[3]	_	-7.8	-13.7	-8.3	-7.6	-6.5
Current account balance[4]	_	-14.7	-11.4	-10.5	-7.5	-5.9

Note: The fiscal projections, which were finalised on the 12th November, do not take into account subsequent upward revisions in the 2009 deficit and debt.
1. Contributions to changes in real GDP (percentage of real GDP in previous year), actual amount in the first column.
2. Including statistical discrepancy.
3. National Accounts basis, as a percentage of GDP.
4. On settlement basis, as a percentage of GDP.
Source: OECD Economic Outlook 88 database.

StatLink ⚙⬛ http://dx.doi.org/10.1787/888932347541

Continued fiscal consolidation is critical for restoring confidence

The implementation of the sizable fiscal adjustment aiming to bring the deficit below 3% of GDP in 2014 is broadly on track. However, the projections, which were finalised on the 12th November, do not take into account subsequent upward revisions in the 2009 deficit and debt. Based on the performance over the first 10 months of the year, the expected reduction of the 2010 deficit may fall slightly short of the targeted adjustment. Primary expenditure has been under better control than targeted, but revenues remained subdued despite indirect tax hikes and efforts to reduce tax evasion. For 2011, the preliminary draft budget aimed to lower the deficit to 7% of GDP, slightly below the 7.6% of GDP target in the Economic Policy Programme, with a mix of expenditure and revenue measures. A further decline in the deficit to around 6½ per cent of GDP is assumed in the projection for 2012 in line with the Economic Policy Programme. However, in view of lower projected growth by the OECD, this would require additional measures compared to the Programme. Revisions to the 2009 deficit put also at risk the government fiscal target, unless additional measures are adopted. Lowering the deficit to below 3% by 2014, as set by the Programme, is essential to correct the unsustainable fiscal imbalances, even if this would require further austerity measures. Moreover, consolidation efforts need to continue beyond the Programme horizon to reduce the very high debt burden. Curbing widespread tax evasion and reforming loss-making public enterprises are critical for sustainable public finances and restoring market confidence.

The economy should gradually exit from the recession

The economy is projected to continue contracting in 2011 by 2¾ per cent under the weight of fiscal retrenchment, tight credit conditions and weak sentiment. The rate of decline is expected to slow, however, from the third quarter of 2010 as structural reforms aimed at boosting investment and competitiveness get underway and stronger international demand boosts shipping and tourism. Growth is projected to turn positive in 2012 as the reforms take hold, and European Union structural funds are absorbed. Unemployment looks set to rise to over 15% in 2012, and large economic slack should lower inflation. Wage growth in the private sector may remain moderately positive as the new collective agreement, signed in July 2010, grants increases equal to euro area inflation for 2011 (mid-year) and 2012. Boosting productivity will therefore be key to restoring competitiveness, which requires further deep structural reforms. The current account deficit is likely to narrow to around 6% of GDP in 2012 as the economy contracts and rebalances and competitiveness improves.

Downside risks surround the recovery

Successful pursuit of the Programme would minimise the risks to the projected recovery, but it could be slowed by social opposition. The external environment poses additional uncertainties, especially as regards the growth of main trading partners.

HUNGARY

Economic growth resumed in 2010 and was mainly fuelled by robust external demand, while private consumption and investment continued to fall. Growth is projected to gain momentum as domestic demand gradually recovers. Headline inflation is expected to stabilise around the medium-term target of 3%.

After a slippage in the general government deficit for 2009 and a further deterioration in the first half of 2010, temporary measures have been imposed to meet the deficit targets. Further tax cuts will take place from 2011 but offsetting expenditure cuts have yet to be spelled out. A renewed commitment to credible and sustainable fiscal consolidation is required to reduce financing costs and instil private sector confidence, which will support growth prospects.

The recession has just come to an end

Growth rebounded in early 2010, before settling at a sufficient pace to stabilise the labour market. Supported by favourable external demand conditions, surveys of manufacturing sentiment suggest that growth is set to continue. The volume of retail trade has also been edging up, but construction activity remains sluggish.

The labour market is slowly recovering

The employment rate has improved somewhat and, despite a slight rebound in the participation rate, the unemployment rate has declined moderately from a peak reached in the first quarter of 2010. Further support for private sector job creation is expected from a significant drop in labour taxes between 2009 and 2011, and the absence of wage pressures, despite the rise in VAT last year. On the other hand, a further contraction in public sector employment is expected as fiscal consolidation progresses.

Hungary

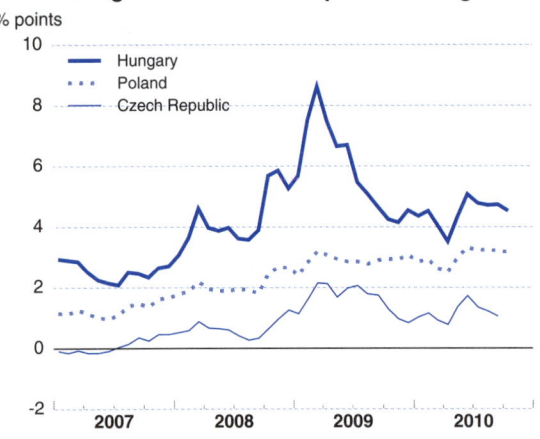

Long-term interest rate spreads are high[1]

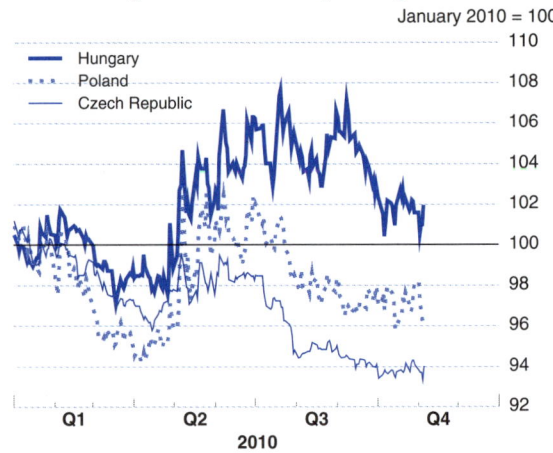

The exchange rate has recently strengthened[2]

1. Ten year government bond spreads relative to the German rate.
2. Daily exchange rates against the euro. An increase in the index indicates a depreciation of the currency.

Source: OECD Main Economic Indicators database and Datastream

StatLink http://dx.doi.org/10.1787/888932345812

Hungary: **Demand, output and prices**

	2007	2008	2009	2010	2011	2012
	Current prices HUF billion	Percentage changes, volume (2000 prices)				
Private consumption	13 695.3	0.4	-7.9	-3.9	2.0	3.0
Government consumption	5 390.1	1.0	-0.1	0.3	-4.3	0.0
Gross fixed capital formation	5 408.3	3.2	-9.2	-4.3	3.2	4.3
Final domestic demand	24 493.7	1.1	-6.4	-3.0	0.7	2.6
Stockbuilding[1]	538.7	-0.3	-4.4	1.9	0.4	0.0
Total domestic demand	25 032.4	0.7	-11.5	-0.6	0.9	2.6
Exports of goods and services	20 459.6	5.7	-9.6	13.3	8.1	8.4
Imports of goods and services	20 170.5	5.8	-14.6	11.5	6.6	8.1
Net exports[1]	289.1	0.0	4.0	2.0	1.6	0.7
GDP at market prices	25 321.5	0.8	-6.7	1.1	2.5	3.1
GDP deflator	_	4.8	4.4	1.6	1.9	3.1
Memorandum items						
Consumer price index	_	6.0	4.2	4.9	2.9	3.1
Private consumption deflator	_	5.4	4.1	4.5	2.7	2.9
Unemployment rate	_	7.9	10.1	11.3	11.7	11.0
General government financial balance[2]	_	-3.7	-4.4	-4.2	-3.1	-2.9
Current account balance[2]	_	-7.0	0.3	-0.3	-1.1	-1.3

Note: National accounts are based on official chain-linked data. This introduces a discrepancy in the identity between real demand components and GDP. For further details see *OECD Economic Outlook* Sources and Methods *(http://www.oecd.org/eco/sources-and-methods)*.
1. Contributions to changes in real GDP (percentage of real GDP in previous year), actual amount in the first column.
2. As a percentage of GDP.
Source: OECD Economic Outlook 88 database.

StatLink ᴍ᠍ᔍ *http://dx.doi.org/10.1787/888932347560*

A sustainable fiscal consolidation is needed

While the authorities have made significant efforts to reduce the deficit during the recession, the fiscal outlook has worsened more recently as a significant fiscal slippage occurred in the first half of 2010. This was mainly driven by increases in investment on the spending side and lower income taxes and social contributions on the revenue side. Further tax cuts also became effective in July 2010. To meet deficit targets of 3.8% of GDP in 2010 and 2.9% in 2011 a heavy temporary surtax on financial institutions and additional exceptional taxes on telecommunication, energy and retail distribution sectors have been imposed. Moreover, the authorities have decided to redirect pension contributions from the second (funded) to the first (pay-as-you-go) pillar for fourteen months starting November 2010. While this measure is expected to bring additional revenues of 1.5% of GDP, it is only a one-off and it may undermine confidence in the pension system, pushing household savings up further. Plans to introduce a flat-rate personal income tax as from 2011 will widen the structural deficit, and offsetting measures on the expenditure side are yet to be spelled out. Renewed effort is urgently needed to put public finances on a sustainable path through credible fiscal consolidation and to comply with the new framework of domestic fiscal rules (which is assumed to be the case in these projections in 2012). A strong political mandate and the freeing up of the domestic election calendar over the next three and a half years should create favourable conditions to reach such a target.

Monetary policy has been supportive

Despite jittery markets marked by currency depreciation and a renewed widening in bond spreads, the central bank has appropriately kept interest rates on hold at 5.25% since April. Headline inflation should converge to the central bank target of 3% as economic slack constrains wages and firms pricing power.

Growth should pick up

Growth is projected to gradually gather pace over the next two years. Private consumption is likely to be held back in the near term by ongoing weaknesses in the labour market and the need for households to repair their balance sheets, partly offset by tax cuts. Private investment should eventually pick up on the back of the strength in external demand and the gradual improvement of credit conditions. With the outlook for the traded goods sector still favourable, export growth is likely to moderate from the recent double digit rates but remain just above 8% over the projection period. With domestic demand picking up through 2011-2012, the economy should be growing close to 3% by 2012.

Downside risks are on the fiscal side

Downside risks could arise in the absence of credible fiscal consolidation and would be compounded if no precautionary agreement is reached with multilateral organisations. A loss in foreign investor confidence could trigger a depreciation of the currency and a rise in borrowing costs. On the positive side, a stronger recovery in Germany and other trading partners could boost business investment.

ICELAND

After the deep recession of the past two years, Iceland is making progress towards unwinding its economic imbalances and laying the foundations for durable economic growth. The recovery is projected to get underway in the second half of 2011, led by planned privately-driven investment in large energy projects and strengthening private consumption expenditure. Inflation is projected to fall below the 2½ per cent target of monetary policy.

The authorities are implementing tight adjustment policies in line with the programme supported by the IMF Stand-By Arrangement. The government should continue to implement measures sufficient to achieve its fiscal consolidation goals and strengthen the budget framework, as planned. Monetary policy should continue to target low inflation and currency stability, and capital controls should be further liberalised as soon as conditions permit.

The recession persists

The deep recession continued through mid-2010, with the decline in GDP from a year earlier reaching almost 9% by the second quarter. Business investment continued to shrink owing to depressed economic activity, deleveraging and the ending of large energy-intensive projects. Private consumption expenditure continued to fall through to the second quarter of 2010 in response to declining disposable incomes and the need to rebuild wealth. Economic activity was also temporarily depressed by the spring volcanic eruption, which reduced tourism. Foreign trade in goods and services nevertheless remained in substantial surplus, although the current account recorded a small deficit owing to high debt-interest payments. Employment (seasonally adjusted) fell in the third quarter of 2010 and average hours worked were lower than a year earlier (and significantly lower than before the recession). But the unemployment rate (seasonally adjusted) remained broadly stable at 7.4%. Nominal wage increases have picked up slightly, to 4.6% in the year

Iceland

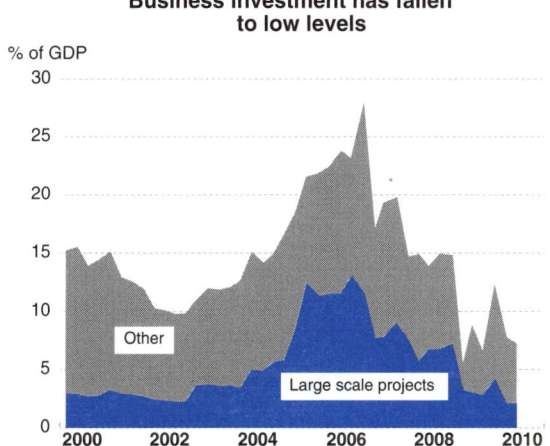

Business investment has fallen to low levels

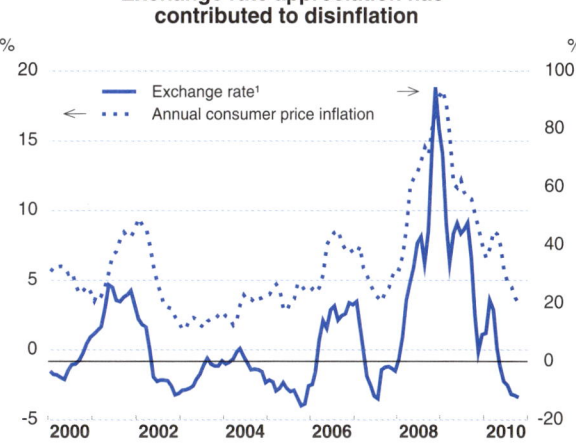

Exchange rate appreciation has contributed to disinflation

1. Year-on-year percentage change in price of foreign exchange (narrow trade index).

Source: Central Bank of Iceland and Statistics Iceland.

StatLink ᓂᔑᐧ http://dx.doi.org/10.1787/888932345831

Iceland: **Demand, output and prices**

	2007	2008	2009	2010	2011	2012
	Current prices ISK billion	Percentage changes, volume (2000 prices)				
Private consumption	751.6	-7.9	-16.0	-0.8	2.2	2.8
Government consumption	316.8	4.6	-1.7	-2.0	-2.5	-2.0
Gross fixed capital formation	373.0	-20.9	-50.9	-14.7	8.4	17.1
Final domestic demand	1 441.5	-8.5	-20.8	-3.3	1.7	3.4
Stockbuilding[1]	6.6	-0.4	-0.1	-0.1	0.0	0.1
Total domestic demand	1 448.1	-8.8	-20.9	-3.7	1.5	3.5
Exports of goods and services	453.3	7.1	7.4	-0.1	1.6	2.0
Imports of goods and services	592.9	-18.2	-24.1	0.4	1.7	3.5
Net exports[1]	- 139.6	10.7	14.7	-0.2	0.1	-0.5
GDP at market prices	1 308.5	1.0	-6.8	-3.6	1.5	2.6
GDP deflator	_	11.9	8.9	6.0	3.5	1.8
Memorandum items						
Consumer price index	_	12.7	12.0	5.3	1.8	1.6
Private consumption deflator	_	14.0	15.3	5.7	2.3	1.6
Unemployment rate	_	3.0	7.3	7.5	8.1	7.5
General government financial balance[2]	_	-13.5	-9.9	-6.3	-2.7	0.6
Current account balance[2]	_	-22.1	-2.2	-0.9	2.2	2.4

Note: National accounts are based on official chain-linked data. This introduces a discrepancy in the identity between real demand components and GDP. For further details see *OECD Economic Outlook* Sources and Methods *(http://www.oecd.org/eco/sources-and-methods)*.
1. Contributions to changes in real GDP (percentage of real GDP in previous year), actual amount in the first column.
2. As a percentage of GDP.
Source: OECD Economic Outlook 88 database.

StatLink ⟨⟩ *http://dx.doi.org/10.1787/888932347579*

to the second quarter, with public sector increases lagging those in the private sector. The annual inflation rate fell further, to 3.3% in October

A large fiscal consolidation programme is being implemented

A large fiscal adjustment was implemented in 2010, reducing the general government primary budget deficit by 4¼ percentage points of GDP to 2¾ per cent in 2010. The projection assumes that the government will implement its plans to achieve a primary surplus of ½ per cent of GDP in 2011 and 4% of GDP in the following year. Spending restraint accounts for about one half of the planned consolidation. If these plans are realised, general government debt should peak in 2010 at 125% of GDP in gross terms. Net debt will peak at 46% of GDP in 2011.

Monetary policy remains disinflationary

Monetary policy continues to be aimed at preserving currency stability and reducing inflation. In view of the recent króna strength and continued balance of payments inflows, the Central Bank of Iceland (CBI) has been purchasing foreign exchange since August to strengthen reserves ahead of the eventual easing of capital controls. The CBI lowered its policy rates by a further 0.75 percentage point in September, to 6.25% for loans against collateral, leaving real rates at still-high levels given the large amount of slack in the economy. Further cuts in policy rates are assumed in the projection, but real rates remain high to support the currency. The next step in liberalising capital controls, which will involve lifting them on long-term assets, is conditional on banks having enough liquidity to handle possible outflows and sufficient capital to buffer against any losses.

A recent Supreme Court ruling will cause losses to banks

A recent Iceland Supreme Court ruling that foreign exchange indexation clauses in domestic currency loans are illegal will cause large losses to Iceland's banks. The authorities will require the owners of the three new commercial banks to recapitalise them. If any of the banks does not meet capital adequacy requirements within the designated time frame, the government will inject Tier 1 capital using an instrument structured to isolate it from potential future losses.

Economic recovery should get underway in late 2011

The economy is projected to begin to recover in the second half of 2011, led by private domestic demand. Investment in energy-related projects is scheduled to expand significantly from late 2011. The unemployment rate is projected to continue rising until late 2011 but to fall back to 7% by the end of 2012. Inflation should continue to decline to 1.6% by 2012. The current account balance is projected to rise to a surplus of 2½ per cent of GDP by 2012 reflecting increases in the terms of trade and a declining factor income deficit.

Delays in debt restructuring and associated debt deleveraging could slow the recovery

The Supreme Court decision on foreign exchange indexed loans could delay private sector debt restructuring and discourage FDI in Iceland, which would depress growth prospects. Administrative delays and financing difficulties could also hamper energy-intensive projects in 2011, although this could represent an upside risk for 2012 if such investment is simply delayed by one year. There is also a risk that deleveraging could be greater than projected, reducing private consumption and investment expenditure. On the other hand, if a final agreement with the British and Dutch governments concerning Icesave deposits were to be reached, this would facilitate Iceland's reintegration into global capital markets and increase FDI in Iceland.

IRELAND

The economy is undergoing massive adjustment. Past imbalances are unwinding in banking, the housing market, the government budget and the labour market, leaving a large impact on public debt and unemployment. After two years of deep recession, activity seems to have reached a bottom in the first half of 2010. A mild recovery is projected to be driven by exports, while domestic demand is likely to remain sluggish. The government intends to continue policies to bring the fiscal accounts closer to balance and to restore competitiveness. If sustained, this should help bolster activity and support employment growth in the medium run.

The banking restructuring strategy aims at transferring risky land, development and associated loans to a government-backed asset management agency, and then injecting public funds into undercapitalised banks. While this approach has the merit of preserving banking stability, it comes at a high cost for the public finances and is creating stress in the Irish sovereign debt market. Specifying and then implementing the recently outlined 4-year consolidation plan will be essential to achieve the government's ambitious objective of reducing the deficit to 3% of GDP by 2014.

Signs of a fragile recovery

While the economy temporarily rebounded in the first quarter of 2010, real GDP unexpectedly contracted during the second quarter. Since the peak of the cycle at the end of 2007, activity has declined by 13.4%. Nevertheless, it seems to have reached a bottom and a few signs indicate a fragile recovery, essentially driven by exports, even though domestic demand remains weak.

The recession has severely reduced employment

The unemployment rate reached 13.2% in the second quarter of 2010 and the labour force has declined substantially. The overall fall in participation was 1.2 percentage points of the working-age population, while the fall for those aged 20-24 was 4.7 percentage points. Outward

Ireland

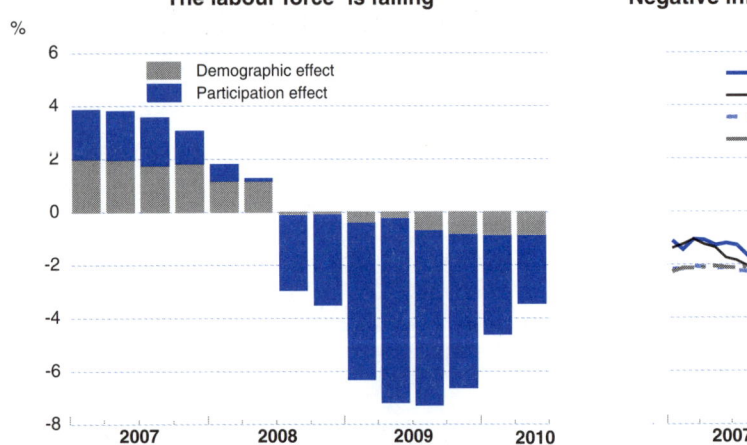

The labour force[1] is falling

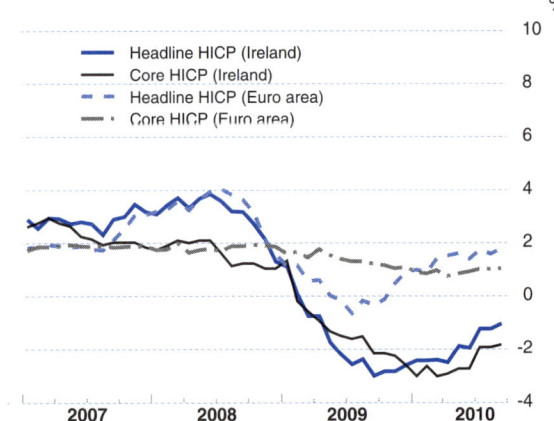

Negative inflation persists, although at a slower rate[2]

1. Change in total labour force. The demographic effect is a change in the size of total working-age population and the participation effect is a change in the participation rate (year-on-year % change).
2. Year-on-year % change.

Source: OECD Economic Outlook 88 database and Central Irish Statistics Office.

StatLink ⟨⟨⟩⟩ http://dx.doi.org/10.1787/888932345850

Ireland: Demand, output and prices

	2007	2008	2009	2010	2011	2012
	Current prices € billion	Percentage changes, volume (2008 prices)				
Private consumption	89.7	-1.8	-7.2	-1.2	-0.6	0.8
Government consumption	30.9	2.8	-4.2	-3.8	-2.7	-0.3
Gross fixed capital formation	50.1	-14.4	-30.9	-17.9	2.8	1.8
Final domestic demand	170.7	-4.7	-12.3	-4.8	-0.5	0.7
Stockbuilding[1]	1.4	-0.8	-1.4	0.7	0.2	0.0
Total domestic demand	172.2	-5.5	-13.8	-4.0	-0.3	0.7
Exports of goods and services	152.4	-0.8	-4.2	9.8	6.7	5.8
Imports of goods and services	135.3	-2.9	-9.8	7.5	6.2	5.0
Net exports[1]	17.1	1.4	3.8	3.2	1.8	1.9
GDP at market prices	189.3	-3.6	-7.6	-0.3	1.5	2.5
GDP deflator	_	-1.4	-4.0	-1.7	0.7	1.2
Memorandum items						
Harmonised index of consumer prices	_	3.1	-1.7	-1.6	0.9	1.2
Private consumption deflator	_	2.8	-4.1	-2.1	1.0	1.2
Unemployment rate	_	6.0	11.7	13.6	13.6	12.6
General government financial balance[2,3]	_	-7.3	-14.2	-32.3	-9.5	-7.4
Current account balance[2]	_	-5.6	-3.0	-0.3	0.7	3.2

Note: National accounts are based on official chain-linked data. This introduces a discrepancy in the identity between real demand components and GDP. For further details see _OECD Economic Outlook_ Sources and Methods (http://www.oecd.org/eco/sources-and-methods).
1. Contributions to changes in real GDP (percentage of real GDP in previous year), actual amount in the first column.
2. As a percentage of GDP.
3. Includes the one-off impact of recapitalisations in the banking sector.
Source: OECD Economic Outlook 88 database.

StatLink ⬛⬛ http://dx.doi.org/10.1787/888932347598

migration, estimated at close to 2.3% of the labour force in the year to the second quarter of 2010, is also continuing to play a role in the labour market adjustment. Long-term unemployment has also risen sharply, increasing the risk that cyclical unemployment becomes structural.

The housing market continues to contract

The housing market continued to contract in the first half of 2010. In the year ending August 2010, both total house completions and new house registrations fell by 48%. The decline in property prices seems to have moderated, although with differences across regions. The fall of house prices has accelerated in Dublin, while price falls outside Dublin have moderated. The values of commercial property continue to fall across all sectors, but at a modest pace.

Negative inflation persists, although at a lower pace

Though inflation remains negative, it is becoming less so. Harmonised inflation (HICP) was –0.8% in October 2010 (year-on-year), less negative than before, while the national CPI (which includes housing costs) increased by 0.7% during the same period. Core inflation is expected to rise only modestly in 2011, with the persistent margin of spare capacity likely to continue to bear down on consumer prices. Higher inflation is projected for 2012 though it is unlikely to rise much above 1%.

A modest resumption of domestic demand is expected

Growth is expected to resume in 2011, driven by non-residential investment and exports. Private consumption is forecast to still contract in 2011 and to grow sluggishly in 2012. Spending will remain weak, as unemployment is set to remain high and further fiscal austerity measures will restrain the growth of domestic demand. The unemployment rate is likely to decline only modestly from mid 2011 onwards, because the recovery of activity will be driven by exporting sectors, which are less employment-intensive than domestically-oriented sectors. The current account should display a surplus already in 2011.

The ongoing fiscal consolidation process is appropriate

The 2010 budget, which included a tightening effort equivalent to 2.5% of GDP, was an important contribution to the process of stabilising public finances, although the headline budget deficit will be pushed temporarily higher by the cost of rescuing the banking sector. Against the background of fast-rising public indebtedness and bond-market concerns about sovereign risks, the government has announced a 4-year budgetary plan, which aims at bringing the public deficit down to 3% of GDP in 2014, as required by the European Union. The current projections assume that this plan will be fully implemented, with a frontloading of the consolidation measures in 2011 (around 3.7% of GDP) followed by a further effort in 2012 (around 2%). On this basis, the long-term interest rate differential vis-à-vis Germany is projected to fall to around 2 percentage points by the end of 2012. Retaining policy credibility is key to minimising risks arising from episodes of market volatility and will require demonstrated political commitment and consensus.

Risks surround the recovery

Ireland's approach to address problems in the financial sector has the merit of being transparent and it may finally restore the restructured banking sector to health. But the challenge is to wean the banking sector off public support and stabilise public debt despite the weak recovery and market concerns about sovereign risks. As a small open economy, Ireland's fate will be sharply influenced by the strength of the worldwide recovery. On the positive side, the substantial ongoing improvement in price and cost competitiveness, if sustained, should help bolster exports and support a recovery in employment growth in the medium run.

ISRAEL*

Recovery from the relatively mild downturn has already tightened the labour market and growth may be running somewhat above potential by the end of 2012. Annual inflation is currently well within the 1-3% target band but is likely to trend towards the upper limit.

The Bank of Israel needs to continue raising its policy rate. The simultaneous use of foreign-currency purchases to shield the export sector from adverse exchange-rate movements is increasingly unwarranted.The achievement of deficit targets through to 2012 depends heavily on recovery in corporate-tax revenues and planned hikes in indirect taxation.

Economic recovery is rapidly soaking up labour reserves

Real GDP growth picked up significantly in the first half of 2010, with growth of 4.6% in the second quarter (seasonally adjusted annualised rate). However, monthly trade figures and tax receipts point to a slower pace of growth in the second half of the year. So far, the recovery has been job-rich. Indeed, in the second quarter the unemployment rate reached 6.2%, which is not far off the low reached in 2008.

Market expectations point to some inflationary pressure

Annual inflation has recently dropped to well within the official target band. However, bond market measures suggest expected annual inflation one year ahead of 2.7%. Rent increases have been the key driver of inflation in recent quarters. While property prices do not feed directly into the housing component of the CPI index, the continuing rapid rise is probably contributing to increases in rents. The latest data show a 20%

Israel

The economy is rapidly absorbing spare labour capacity

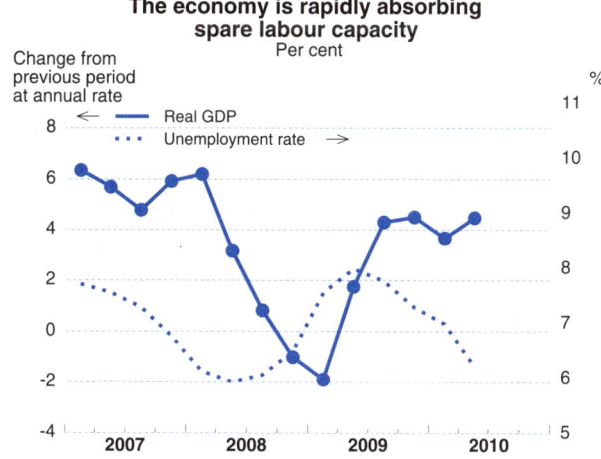

Rent increases have contributed to inflation

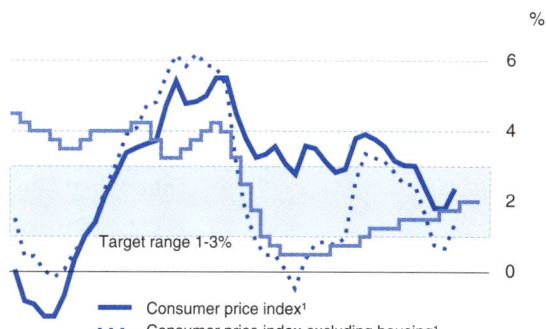

1. Year-on-year change.

Source: Bank of Israel; CBS; OECD Economic Outlook 88 database.

StatLink http://dx.doi.org/10.1787/888932345869

* The statistical data for Israel are supplied by and under the responsibility of the relevant Israeli authorities. The use of such data by the OECD is without prejudice to the status of the Golan Heights, East Jerusalem and Israeli settlements in the West Bank under the terms of international law.

Israel: **Demand, output and prices**

	2007	2008	2009	2010	2011	2012
	Current prices NIS billion	Percentage changes, volume (2005 prices)				
Private consumption	389.6	3.0	1.7	5.2	3.9	4.2
Government consumption	171.3	2.4	1.9	1.1	1.5	1.5
Gross fixed capital formation	130.5	4.1	-6.5	6.1	6.2	6.5
Final domestic demand	691.4	3.0	0.3	4.3	3.7	3.9
Stockbuilding[1]	7.7	-0.4	-0.6	-0.7	0.0	0.0
Total domestic demand	699.0	2.6	-0.4	3.6	3.7	4.0
Exports of goods and services	292.9	5.9	-11.7	16.3	8.9	8.8
Imports of goods and services	301.8	2.3	-14.1	14.3	8.4	8.3
Net exports[1]	- 8.9	1.5	1.1	1.0	0.4	0.4
GDP at market prices	690.1	4.2	0.8	3.9	4.0	4.3
GDP deflator	_	0.9	5.0	0.7	1.5	2.3
Memorandum items						
Harmonised index of consumer prices	_	4.6	3.3	2.6	2.5	2.7
Private consumption deflator	_	4.8	2.4	3.0	2.2	2.7
Unemployment rate	_	6.1	7.6	6.4	6.1	5.9
General government financial balance[2,3]	_	-3.1	-5.8	-4.8	-3.8	-2.7
Current account balance[2]	_	1.0	3.9	3.0	2.6	2.5

Note: National accounts are based on official chain-linked data. This introduces a discrepancy in the identity between real demand components and GDP. For further details see _OECD Economic Outlook_ Sources and Methods (http://www.oecd.org/eco/sources-and-methods).
1. Contributions to changes in real GDP (percentage of real GDP in previous year), actual amount in the first column.
2. As a percentage of GDP.
3. Excluding Bank of Israel profits and the implicit costs of CPI-indexed government bonds.
Source: OECD Economic Outlook 88 database.

StatLink 〰〰 http://dx.doi.org/10.1787/888932347617

annual increase in house prices, though it is possible that a peak has already been reached.

Foreign-currency purchases continue, alongside rate hikes

For monetary policy, the developments in house prices and inflationary expectations suggest a need to normalise the policy rate fairly quickly. Countering this are concerns for the tradeables sector, including that policy rate increases may cause a currency appreciation because such rates elsewhere have generally remained flat. Accordingly, the Bank of Israel has attempted to strike a balance with a moderate pace of normalisation; since September 2009 the rate has been raised by 150 basis points to 2%. In addition, it has tightened rules on mortgage lending. The Bank has also continued its policy of discretionary foreign-currency purchases, in an effort to partially shield the tradeables sector from appreciation. Given the economic recovery, however, the risks to this sector have diminished substantially. Also, the domestic rate hikes imply increasing conflict with intervention and a rising carrying cost of holding foreign currency reserves, which have reached 30% of GDP. In any case, the Bank can, at best, only temper trends; the real effective exchange rate has appreciated, albeit modestly, since discretionary intervention began in August 2009. Thus, an early return to conventional monetary policy should be made, perhaps compensated by a somewhat slower pace of normalisation in policy rates.

Fiscal policy is on track to meet targets

The mild downturn and prudent fiscal policy meant a comparatively small increase in the general government deficit (from 3.1% of GDP in 2008 to 5.7% in 2009, according to a standardised OECD definition). The government's second two-year budget (covering 2011 and 2012) adheres to its spending rule and implies annual deficit reductions of 1 percentage point of GDP, while maintaining a programme of personal and corporate income tax rate cuts. Increased indirect taxation, notably on retail gasoline and coal, is planned to meet this goal.

Growth is expected to increase moderately

Output is expected to grow by 3.9% in 2010 and 4% in 2011, roughly in line with estimated potential rates, and by 4.3% in 2012, which is somewhat above potential. The most robust spending aggregates should be exports and investment. Unemployment is expected to trend down, reaching just below 6% in 2012. Underlying consumer price inflation may edge up, reaching 2.8% by the end of 2012. It is assumed that the policy rate will rise by a further 150 basis points by the end of 2011 (to 3.5%) and by another 100 basis points in 2012. These increases may be smaller if the shekel appreciates further, which in turn partly depends on whether the Bank continues its interventions. The projection embodies deficit reductions equal to those foreseen in the budget (1 percentage point of GDP each year). Projected nominal spending increases reflect the spending rule plus some one-off factors. On the revenue side, the projection allows for the programmed cuts in personal and corporate tax rates and assumes indirect tax measures sufficient to achieve consolidation.

Risks from external demand and house prices remain

External risks to real GDP growth remain important. Further monetary tightening should temper house price increases but could be outweighed by the formation of a speculative bubble. Fiscally, there is uncertainty regarding the pace of recovery in business tax receipts and in the revenue impact of the indirect tax increases in the 2011-12 budget.

KOREA

Although Korea's strong recovery from the 2008 global recession slowed in the latter half of 2010, double-digit export growth and buoyant domestic demand are projected to boost growth to a 5% rate by late 2011. The decline in the unemployment rate to less than 3½ per cent in mid-2010 and high capacity utilisation are putting upward pressure on wages and inflation.

With the economy approaching capacity constraints, fiscal policy should continue to focus on achieving the deficit-reduction targets in the medium-term fiscal plan, while the central bank should normalise interest rates. An appreciation of the won would also help contain inflation pressures. Sustaining high growth over the medium term requires structural reforms to enhance productivity, particularly in services. Expanded assistance to small and medium-sized enterprises should be phased out, not least to avoid supporting non-viable firms.

Although growth has slowed to a more sustainable rate...

After reaching a 7.3% annual rate during the first half of 2010, the fastest in a decade, output growth has slowed, in line with trends in other Asian countries. Export growth moderated significantly in the third quarter, reflecting weaker demand from Asia, notably China. Slower export growth, in turn, has damped increases in business investment and industrial production. In addition, inventory rebuilding, which accounted for one-half of output growth in the first half of 2010, appears to be nearing an end. Construction investment has been weak, mainly due to the residential sector. Moreover, housing prices are falling slightly, given the large stock of unsold homes, despite government measures to revitalise the housing market. In particular, the debt-to-income regulation on mortgage lending, which had been tightened in October 2009, was abolished until March 2011 in most of the country and transaction taxes on housing have been reduced or waived.

Korea

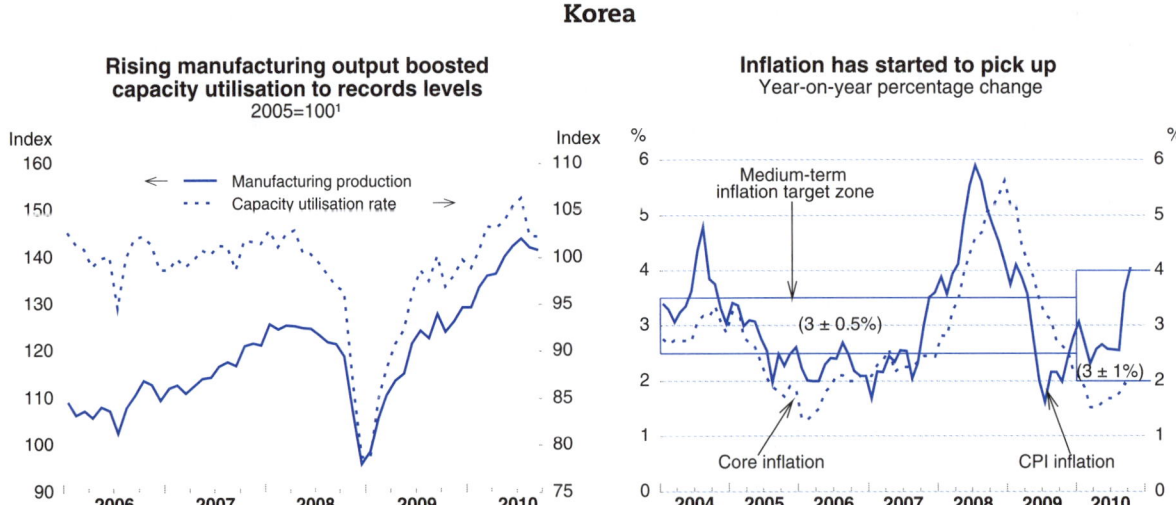

Rising manufacturing output boosted capacity utilisation to records levels
2005=100[1]

Inflation has started to pick up
Year-on-year percentage change

1. Seasonally-adjusted.

Source: Korea National Statistical Office, OECD Economic Outlook 88 Database and Bank of Korea.

StatLink ⟶ http://dx.doi.org/10.1787/888932345888

Korea: **Demand, output and prices**

	2007	2008	2009	2010	2011	2012
	Current prices KRW trillion	Percentage changes, volume (2005 prices)				
Private consumption	530.3	1.3	0.2	4.3	4.6	5.0
Government consumption	143.3	4.3	5.0	3.9	2.0	3.0
Gross fixed capital formation	278.2	-1.9	-0.2	7.9	5.7	5.3
Final domestic demand	951.7	0.8	0.8	5.3	4.5	4.8
Stockbuilding[1]	8.6	0.6	-4.6	2.3	-0.1	0.0
Total domestic demand	960.3	1.4	-3.8	7.9	4.4	4.8
Exports of goods and services	408.8	6.6	-0.8	14.3	12.8	13.5
Imports of goods and services	394.0	4.4	-8.2	18.3	13.3	13.5
Net exports[1]	14.7	1.0	4.0	-1.3	0.0	0.1
GDP at market prices	975.0	2.3	0.2	6.2	4.3	4.8
GDP deflator	_	2.9	3.4	3.2	1.8	2.6
Memorandum items						
Consumer price index	_	4.7	2.8	2.8	3.2	3.4
Private consumption deflator	_	4.5	2.6	2.4	3.1	3.4
Unemployment rate	_	3.2	3.6	3.7	3.4	3.3
Household saving ratio[2]	_	2.9	3.6	2.8	2.9	2.8
General government financial balance[3]	_	3.0	0.0	1.6	2.1	3.0
Current account balance[3]	_	-0.5	5.2	3.0	2.3	2.4

Note: National accounts are based on official chain-linked data. This introduces a discrepancy in the identity between real demand components and GDP. For further details see *OECD Economic Outlook* Sources and Methods *(http://www.oecd.org/eco/sources-and-methods)*.
1. Contributions to changes in real GDP (percentage of real GDP in previous year), actual amount in the first column.
2. As a percentage of disposable income.
3. As a percentage of GDP.
Source: OECD Economic Outlook 88 database.

StatLink ⃟ *http://dx.doi.org/10.1787/888932347636*

... the economy is facing capacity constraints

The growth slowdown coincides with signs that the economy is approaching capacity constraints. Rapid employment gains have reduced the unemployment rate to around 3½ per cent, close to its pre-crisis level, and the capacity utilisation rate in manufacturing reached a record high in July. Consumer price inflation, which had been steady at 2.6% (year-on-year) since April 2010, jumped to 4.1% in October, above the central bank's 2% to 4% inflation target, reflecting in part a jump in food prices. Monetary conditions are exceptionally relaxed, particularly given the stage of the business cycle. Although the Bank of Korea raised the policy interest rate by 25 basis points from a record-low 2% in July, it remains negative in real terms. In addition, the won has depreciated by about 5% since April in trade-weighted terms and by about 13% relative to the yen, significantly boosting Korea's export competitiveness. Significant fiscal consolidation is under way. Central government spending is set to slow to a 4.8% annual rate in nominal terms under the National Fiscal Management Plan for 2010-14, helping to reduce the consolidated central government deficit (excluding the social security surplus) from 4.1% of GDP in 2009 to 1.1% in 2012, despite cuts in personal and corporate income tax rates. The Plan projects a surplus by 2014.

Output growth is projected to pick up strongly...

Following the recent slowdown, output growth is projected to pick up to a 5% rate by late 2011, in spite of some drag from fiscal policy. Business and consumer confidence remains high, despite some decline in recent months. Competitiveness gains should help sustain double-digit export growth, thereby encouraging business investment. Construction investment is likely to turn positive as a result of the policies to promote the housing sector. Tighter labour market conditions are expected to lead to faster wage growth, underpinning buoyant private consumption. With growth picking up, a normalisation of the policy interest rate is needed to keep inflation within the central bank's target zone. Strong domestic demand growth will also reduce the current account surplus from 5.2% of GDP in 2009 to 3% in 2010.

... depending on developments in the world economy

Given that exports account for almost one-half of GDP in Korea, the worlds' eighth-largest exporter, the major risks relate mainly to the global economic environment. The outlook is particularly sensitive to demand from China, which accounts for one-third of Korean exports. In addition, a realignment of exchange rates could have a significant impact on Korean trade. On the domestic side, the major concern is the high level of household debt, which exceeds 150% of household income. As mortgage loans, primarily with floating interest rates, account for 94% of household debt, rising interest rates could have a larger-than-expected impact on private consumption. Another uncertainty is the pace of restructuring of SMEs, which received significant support in 2008-09 to cope with the crisis and recession.

LUXEMBOURG

A recovery is underway, led by private domestic demand. Exports of financial services should start to contribute more strongly to growth as financial market conditions improve. Activity is projected to grow faster than the euro area average, although uncertainties remain regarding the future of the dominant financial sector in the medium term.

Fiscal consolidation needs to be implemented as planned, with an emphasis on containing current expenditure, while pension reform remains a priority for sustainability. Labour market reforms are needed to ensure that employment recovery is reflected in lower unemployment rates among residents.

Volatile financial conditions have led to an uneven recovery

After strong recovery in the second half of 2009, the pace of activity slowed to an annualised rate of 1% over the first half of 2010. This reflects volatile and weak exports, as softness of international equity prices and renewed volatility in financial markets affected exports of financial services. However, higher equity prices and continued positive net inflows into mutual funds over recent months suggest that net exports are likely to recover in strength as international financial conditions improve.

Domestic private demand is gaining strength

Private domestic final demand is recovering at robust pace. Both private consumption and investment have expanded at high rates, reflecting improvements in confidence and low interest rates. In addition, activity has been recovering rapidly with significant increases in industrial production, construction and retail sales.

Employment is expanding

Employment growth has picked up, with year-on-year growth of 2.3% in August. Both domestic and cross-border employment has increased. While the unemployment rate remains broadly stable at around 6%, the

Luxembourg

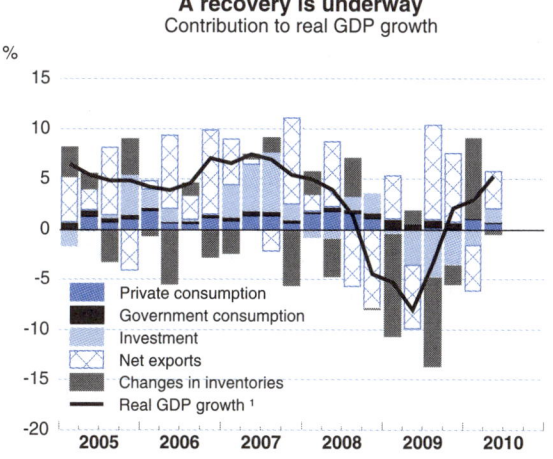

A recovery is underway
Contribution to real GDP growth

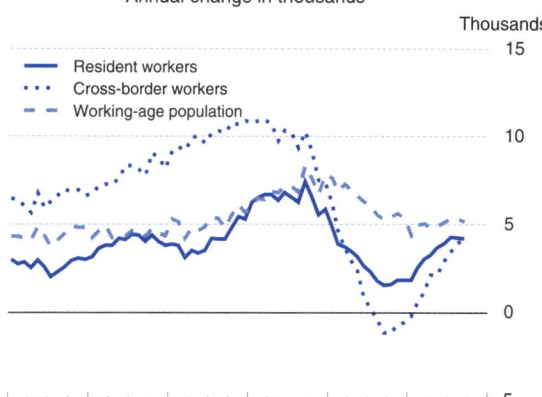

Employment is recovering
Annual change in thousands

1. Year-on-year percentage change.

Source: OECD, Economic Outlook 88 database and Statec.

StatLink 📊📈 http://dx.doi.org/10.1787/888932345907

Luxembourg: **Demand, output and prices**

	2007	2008	2009	2010	2011	2012
	Current prices € billion	Percentage changes, volume (2000 prices)				
Private consumption	12.0	4.8	0.3	2.7	3.2	3.3
Government consumption	5.5	2.7	4.5	1.0	0.3	0.9
Gross fixed capital formation	7.8	1.4	-19.2	3.5	3.6	2.6
Final domestic demand	25.3	3.3	-4.7	2.5	2.6	2.6
Stockbuilding[1]	0.1	-0.1	-0.8	1.6	-0.7	0.0
Total domestic demand	25.4	3.1	-5.9	5.0	1.6	2.6
Exports of goods and services	66.0	6.6	-8.2	8.8	4.8	3.4
Imports of goods and services	53.8	8.5	-10.3	10.0	4.3	3.2
Net exports[1]	12.1	-0.6	0.3	1.2	2.3	1.4
GDP at market prices	37.5	1.4	-3.7	3.3	3.3	3.2
GDP deflator	_	4.2	-0.4	1.5	0.1	1.9
Memorandum items						
Harmonised index of consumer prices	_	4.1	0.0	2.6	1.8	2.2
Private consumption deflator	_	2.0	0.8	1.1	1.9	2.2
Unemployment rate	_	4.4	5.7	6.0	5.9	5.8
General government financial balance[2]	_	3.0	-0.7	-2.2	-1.2	-0.3
Current account balance[2]	_	5.3	6.7	7.8	5.1	5.7

Note: National accounts are based on official chain-linked data. This introduces a discrepancy in the identity between real demand components and GDP. For further details see *OECD Economic Outlook* Sources and Methods *(http://www.oecd.org/eco/sources-and-methods)*.
1. Contributions to changes in real GDP (percentage of real GDP in previous year), actual amount in the first column.
2. As a percentage of GDP.
Source: OECD Economic Outlook 88 database.

StatLink ⟪⟫ *http://dx.doi.org/10.1787/888932347655*

number of vacancies has more than doubled in 2010 and use of the short-time working scheme continues to be phased out.

Core inflation has increased

Annual headline inflation stood at 2.2% in August. Core inflation increased from 1% in April to 1.6%, partly reflecting automatic wage and price indexation, and an increase in water charges. Inflation is expected to stabilise, and the next index-linked wage adjustment will not take place before at least October 2011.

The financial sector will take over as the driver of growth

The recovery is anticipated to continue over the coming quarters with growth above the euro area average. Stronger exports of financial and business services, linked to improved financial conditions, will drive the expansion. Domestic demand will maintain momentum from consumption as labour demand strengthens, and investment will continue to recover as spare capacity diminishes. Monetary conditions will remain accommodative, although fiscal consolidation will modestly damp activity. Overall employment will continue to increase but the unemployment rate of Luxembourg residents will remain high for some time, held up by structural policies that constrain demand for low-skilled workers..

Fiscal consolidation starts in 2011

The general government deficit has deteriorated from 0.7% of GDP in 2009 to a projected 2.2% in 2010. This is the result of a large stimulus package, together with lower revenues and higher social spending related to the crisis. The 2011 budget aims at bringing the deficit to 1.2% of GDP with restraint on expenditures, notably public investment and subsidies to enterprises, and tax increases, including a hike in the top income tax rate. The projection assumes that measures needed to meet the objective of balancing the budget by 2014 and keep gross debt below 30% of GDP will be implemented, with further consolidation amounting to 0.9% of GDP put in place in 2012. The large future pensions costs will only partly be covered by reserves, which adds to the immediate need to consolidate public finances. However, a fundamental reform will be needed to ensure long-term sustainability.

Risks are balanced but uncertainty is large

The main risks relate to uncertainty about international financial conditions and the improvement in world trade. Further ahead, there is great uncertainty around the medium-term potential of the economy in the aftermath of the crisis given the narrow specialisation in certain financial activities and changes in the international regulatory environment.

MEXICO

The Mexican economy has embarked on a vigorous recovery, which started in 2009 on the back of strong export growth. Activity is projected to grow by 5% in 2010, before slowing somewhat to a bit below 3½ per cent in 2011, as export dynamics normalise. The reliance on exports to the US market, where the recovery has weakened, is a source of risk.

A prudent fiscal stance is advisable in view of the decline in oil production, the source of a significant proportion of fiscal revenues. The projection thus assumes that the government implements its plan to return to a balanced budget excluding Pemex's investment. This will require some expenditure restraint over the next two years. The government should also consider further tax reform to reduce dependence on oil-related receipts and should scale back energy subsidies. With activity well below potential, inflation is projected to recede gradually. This gives monetary policy some leeway to remain accommodative and support the recovery.

Activity has rebounded thanks to strong exports

After a sharp recession, the economy is recovering strongly, although unemployment is coming down only slowly. Over the past 12 months GDP has increased at an annualised rate of close to 8%. It has accelerated further in the second quarter of 2010 on the back of booming demand for Mexican exports, in particular from the United States, where Mexico has gained market share. Private consumption and investment strengthened as well. Short-term indicators suggest that export growth is slowing, while domestic demand might also weaken somewhat in the short term. However, formal employment has now started to recover strongly and this should eventually support private consumption.

Mexico

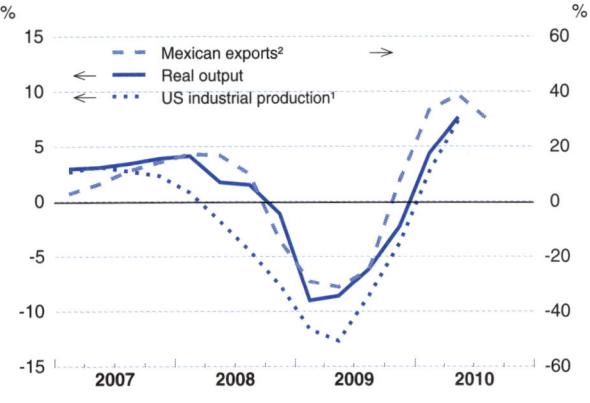

Exports have rebounded thanks to US demand
Year-on-year percentage change

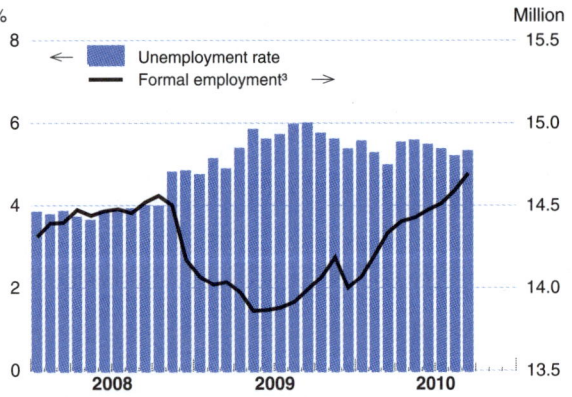

The decline in unemployment is slow despite recovering formal employment

1. Excluding construction.
2. Export data are expresssed in USD.
3. Workers affiliated with Instituto Mexicano del Seguro Social.

Source: OECD Economic Outlook 88 database; Bank of Mexico; INEGI.

StatLink http://dx.doi.org/10.1787/888932345926

Mexico: **Demand, output and prices**

	2007	2008	2009	2010	2011	2012
	Current prices MXN billion	Percentage changes, volume (2003 prices)				
Private consumption	7 313.5	1.9	-6.2	3.9	4.1	4.1
Government consumption	1 178.8	0.9	2.3	3.8	1.5	1.2
Gross fixed capital formation	2 392.6	4.4	-10.1	1.3	5.2	7.9
Final domestic demand	10 885.0	2.3	-6.2	3.3	4.0	4.6
Stockbuilding[1]	493.4	0.0	-1.9	1.0	0.3	0.0
Total domestic demand	11 378.3	2.3	-8.0	4.4	4.3	4.6
Exports of goods and services	3 158.7	0.7	-15.1	24.2	7.2	8.3
Imports of goods and services	3 336.8	3.1	-18.5	20.8	9.2	9.0
Net exports[1]	- 178.2	-0.8	1.7	0.5	-0.8	-0.4
GDP at market prices	11 200.1	1.5	-6.6	5.0	3.5	4.2
GDP deflator	_	6.6	4.3	4.0	3.9	4.0
Memorandum items						
Consumer price index	_	5.1	5.3	4.1	3.8	3.5
Private consumption deflator	_	5.1	8.4	3.4	4.0	3.5
Unemployment rate[2]	_	4.0	5.5	5.2	4.6	4.1
Public sector borrowing requirement[3,4]	_	-1.3	-5.5	-2.8	-2.7	-2.4
Current account balance[4]	_	-1.5	-0.7	-0.9	-1.4	-1.8

1. Contributions to changes in real GDP (percentage of real GDP in previous year), actual amount in the first column.
2. Based on National Employment Survey.
3. Central government and public enterprises.
4. As a percentage of GDP.
Source: OECD Economic Outlook 88 database.

StatLink http://dx.doi.org/10.1787/888932347674

Inflation has fallen within the target range of the central bank

After prolonged persistence, in part related to exchange rate and commodity price developments as well as tax increases, both headline and core inflation have recently fallen, undershooting expectations for several months in a row. They are now within the central bank's target range (3% +/- 1%). The peso/dollar exchange rate has appreciated by more than 20% compared to its post-crisis peak of March 2009, helping to restrain price increases.

Fiscal policy is tightening

Taxes were increased and expenditure was cut in 2010 to compensate for the trend decrease in oil-related revenues due to falling oil production, leading to a tighter fiscal stance. As a result, the public sector borrowing requirement, a measure of the combined deficit of the federal government and its public enterprises, is expected to fall sharply from around 5½ per cent of GDP in 2009 to less than 3% of GDP in 2010. The projection assumes that the government will implement some further expenditure restraint in 2011 and 2012, as foreseen in the budget. The public sector borrowing requirement is expected to fall further to around 2½ per cent in 2012, despite an expected decline in the share of public revenues in GDP, related to the development of oil production. This would translate into a closing of the deficit based on the government's definition, which excludes PEMEX investment while including a number of pure financing operations. These prudent fiscal policies are needed to avoid losing market confidence in the sustainability of Mexico's public finances. In the longer term, the budget needs to become more independent from oil revenues, for example through tax base broadening and a gradual removal of energy subsidies.

Monetary policy is still supportive

The policy interest rate is well below its neutral level, appropriately supporting the recovery of domestic demand. Mexico can afford to keep policy rates low for some time in view of declining inflation. Medium-term inflation expectations are reasonably well-anchored, according to the central bank's survey, with experts expecting inflation to remain within the upper half of the central bank's target range.

After 2010 growth should decelerate somewhat

Real GDP is projected to grow by 5% in 2010, although a normalisation of export and output growth is expected in the second half of the year. Domestic demand should strengthen throughout 2011 and 2012, but this will not fully compensate for lower export growth. GDP growth is thus expected to decline to 3½ per cent in 2011, before strengthening again to above 4% in 2012, as domestic demand takes off and export growth accelerates on the back of stronger world trade. The current account deficit is projected to widen mildly throughout the projection period, mainly due to swiftly growing imports as domestic demand recovers. Inflation should increase somewhat in the second half of 2010, due to administrative and food price increases, but then resume its downward trend in 2011, given still substantial unused capacity. It should remain within the central bank's target range in 2011 and 2012 on year average, although some inflationary pressures could arise in late 2012 as the output gap narrows.

Downward risks from the United States, upward risks from domestic demand

A slower than expected US recovery would weaken Mexican growth prospects through lower exports and remittances. On the other hand, the US economy could also grow faster than projected and the Mexican labour market could recover faster than expected, leading to stronger consumer confidence and a faster recovery in domestic demand.

NETHERLANDS

As the temporary growth spurt in the first half of 2010 fades, the economy is becoming more reliant on the recovery in world trade. Private consumption is likely to be subdued by fiscal tightening, a fragile housing market and pension funds' recovery measures. Low capacity utilisation will prevent more than a gradual pick-up in business investment.

The new government is assumed to pursue the spending cuts in the 2011 budget and the announced medium-term consolidation plans aimed at further savings of 3% of GDP over the following four years. Doing so would be a significant step towards assuring the sustainability of public finances. Nevertheless, additional measures are required to control ageing-related costs.

Growth slowed as the stock building cycle terminated

The boost to growth in the first half of 2010 reflected restocking and a turnaround in business investment, which had been contracting since mid-2008. Since then, business investment has been relatively moderate, reflecting capacity utilisation which has stabilised only slightly above historical lows. Retail sales remained stagnant, although the recovery in consumer confidence could have indicated a pick-up. On the other hand, the strong growth in export orders suggests that exports will remain relatively buoyant. The increase in the unemployment rate slowed, leaving it at above 4%, by the end of 2010, reflecting only modest increases in employment, mainly in the healthcare and education sectors.

Pension fund solvency problems put household incomes under pressure

The financial crisis created solvency problems for the quasi-mandatory pension funds, forcing them to hike contribution rates and decrease pension indexation. Falling interest rates in 2010 further reduced solvency rates, triggering additional measures, which for the first time included lower pension payments. Thus, the implemented measures have reduced disposable incomes and increased future income uncertainty.

Netherlands

Retail sales are lagging behind the improvements in consumer confidence

The housing market remains weak

Source: OECD, Main Economic Indicators database and CBS, Statistics Netherlands.

StatLink http://dx.doi.org/10.1787/888932345945

Netherlands: **Demand, output and prices**

	2007	2008	2009	2010	2011	2012
	Current prices € billion	Percentage changes, volume (2000 prices)				
Private consumption	264.1	1.1	-2.5	0.2	1.0	1.4
Government consumption	143.9	2.5	3.7	1.9	0.2	-0.4
Gross fixed capital formation	114.3	5.1	-12.7	-4.6	1.8	3.8
Final domestic demand	522.3	2.4	-3.0	-0.3	0.9	1.3
Stockbuilding[1]	2.5	-0.1	-0.9	1.2	-0.5	0.0
Total domestic demand	524.8	2.2	-4.0	1.0	0.3	1.3
Exports of goods and services	424.2	2.8	-7.9	10.4	6.0	6.0
Imports of goods and services	377.2	3.4	-8.5	10.5	4.6	5.9
Net exports[1]	47.0	-0.2	-0.2	0.6	1.5	0.7
GDP at market prices	571.8	1.9	-3.9	1.7	1.7	1.8
GDP deflator	_	2.4	-0.2	1.6	1.4	1.4
Memorandum items						
Harmonised index of consumer prices	_	2.2	1.0	0.8	1.4	1.4
Private consumption deflator	_	1.4	-0.6	1.3	1.4	1.4
Unemployment rate	_	2.7	3.4	4.1	4.4	4.3
Household saving ratio[2]	_	5.7	6.8	8.1	7.6	7.4
General government financial balance[3]	_	0.5	-5.4	-5.8	-4.0	-3.1
Current account balance[3]	_	4.3	4.6	5.3	6.2	6.7

Note: National accounts are based on official chain-linked data. This introduces a discrepancy in the identity between real demand components and GDP. For further details see _OECD Economic Outlook_ Sources and Methods _(http://www.oecd.org/eco/sources-and-methods)._
1. Contributions to changes in real GDP (percentage of real GDP in previous year), actual amount in the first column.
2. As a percentage of disposable income, including savings in life insurance and pension schemes.
3. As a percentage of GDP.
Source: OECD Economic Outlook 88 database.

StatLink ᵐˢᵖ http://dx.doi.org/10.1787/888932347693

Inflation should stabilise over 2011-12

Headline inflation increased in the second half of the year reflecting rising fuel prices. A further temporary hike is expected in early 2011 owing to the relatively slow adjustment of Dutch energy prices to the high 2010 oil prices. As these effects fade inflation should stabilise around 1½ per cent. Core inflation fell throughout most of 2010 to below 1%. This reflects the slow growth of wages, a development that is not expected to disappear over the projection period due to the weak labour market.

Fiscal consolidation will begin in 2011

The 2010 budget deficit will reach almost 6% of GDP in 2010, a ½ percentage point higher than the year before. The previous government budgeted for a consolidation of about 0.3% of GDP for 2011, mainly through public administration cuts, as part of the process of putting public finances on the path towards sustainability. Together with faster growth and a revival in corporate tax revenues as company profitability recovers, this should reduce the 2011 deficit to about 4% of GDP. The new minority government plans to implement cumulative savings of about 3% of GDP over 2012-15 (on average ¾ per cent per year) relying mainly on spending cuts, savings in the health care funds and some tax increases. In line with these plans, fiscal consolidation in 2012 is assumed to be ¾ per cent of GDP, mainly through cuts in public consumption and transfers, allowing the deficit to fall to just above 3% of GDP. The medium-term consolidation programme is steering public finances towards a sustainable path. Nevertheless, additional measures to control ageing-related costs are required to secure overall sustainability. These should include linking the legal retirement age to developments in life expectancy.

Domestic demand will be fragile in the medium term

Growth over the next two years will mostly be export driven, as the domestic economy only slowly gathers pace. The modest wage pressures and an expected recovery in productivity should help restore profitability, laying the ground for renewed growth in business investment. Private consumption will continue to be subdued as households' disposable income will remain under pressure from weak wage growth, a slow decline in unemployment, cuts to real pension income and increases in social security and pension contributions. Prospects could be more positive if private consumption is boosted by a stronger-than-expected recovery of pension funds, which could lead to a more rapid fall in the household savings rate. But growth could be weaker if low capacity utilisation holds companies back from increasing investment as much as projected.

NEW ZEALAND

Growth has slowed thus far in 2010, mainly as high indebtedness and economic uncertainty weigh on households and firms. The major earthquake last September has exacerbated near-term weakness, though providing a boost to activity as reconstruction gathers pace. The recovery will become self-sustaining as businesses hire and invest to meet reviving export and consumer demand.

Monetary and fiscal policies are providing ongoing stimulus and would best continue to do so until around mid-2011. Recent tax reforms will help to reinforce the structural shift, induced by balance-sheet deleveraging, from consumption toward savings and non-residential investment.

The recovery remains fragile...

The recovery appeared to stall in first half of 2010, mainly as sluggish private consumption resulted from still high debt and unemployment (most recently at 6.4%) and softening housing markets. Against this, business investment began to recover from extremely low levels in late 2009, though business sentiment subsequently worsened. Housing investment surged after muted growth following a long period of decline, but consents are falling. Exports have been a mainstay, notwithstanding competitiveness losses, thanks to robust demand in New Zealand's two main export markets, Australia and China. However, much of this demand has been met from inventory drawdown rather than increased output. The current account has improved, with stronger external than domestic demand and terms-of-trade gains from high dairy prices and currency appreciation.

... reflecting balance-sheet adjustment

A process of financial consolidation is underway in the aftermath of the global crisis. Households have curtailed their appetite for mortgage debt because of declining house prices and less favourable tax treatment

New Zealand

Interest margins have widened

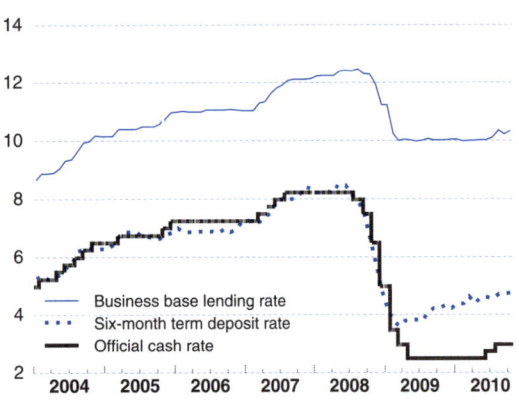

Household debt has peaked

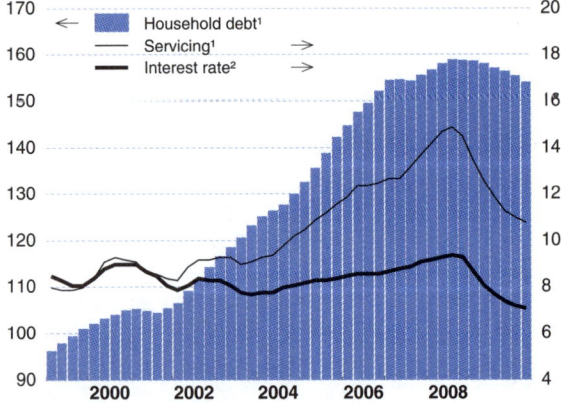

1. As a percentage of disposable income.
2. Weighted average interest rate on total household debt.

Source: Statistics New Zealand; Reserve Bank of New Zealand.

StatLink ⭲ http://dx.doi.org/10.1787/888932345964

New Zealand: **Demand, output and prices**

	2007	2008	2009	2010	2011	2012
	Current prices NZD billion	Percentage changes, volume (1995/1996 prices)				
Private consumption	104.6	-0.4	-0.6	1.7	2.0	2.2
Government consumption	33.1	5.0	1.4	2.9	0.6	0.5
Gross fixed capital formation	41.4	-3.5	-12.0	4.1	11.6	7.0
Final domestic demand	179.0	-0.1	-2.7	2.4	3.6	2.9
Stockbuilding[1]	0.0	0.0	-0.6	0.2	0.2	0.0
Total domestic demand	180.0	0.4	-5.1	2.9	3.6	2.9
Exports of goods and services	49.8	-1.1	0.4	3.4	4.0	6.0
Imports of goods and services	51.9	2.3	-14.8	7.2	7.7	7.4
Net exports[1]	- 2.1	-1.0	5.0	-1.0	-0.9	-0.3
GDP at market prices	178.0	-0.5	-0.4	2.2	2.7	2.5
GDP deflator	_	3.6	1.6	3.0	4.3	2.1
Memorandum items						
GDP (production)	_	-0.2	-1.7	1.7	2.6	2.5
Consumer price index	_	4.0	2.1	2.4	4.3	2.3
Core consumer price index[2]	_	2.0	2.2	2.0	3.8	2.3
Private consumption deflator	_	3.6	2.5	2.0	3.9	1.8
Unemployment rate	_	4.2	6.2	6.5	5.9	5.3
General government financial balance[3]	_	0.4	-3.7	-5.3	-4.5	-3.4
Current account balance[3]	_	-8.8	-2.9	-3.2	-5.3	-6.0

Note: National accounts are based on official chain-linked data. This introduces a discrepancy in the identity between real demand components and GDP. For further details see *OECD Economic Outlook* Sources and Methods (*http://www.oecd.org/eco/sources-and-methods*).
1. Contributions to changes in real GDP (percentage of real GDP in previous year), actual amount in the first column.
2. Consumer price index excluding food and energy.
3. As a percentage of GDP.
Source: OECD Economic Outlook 88 database.

StatLink ⬛🔗 http://dx.doi.org/10.1787/888932347712

of investment property. Farmers are paying down debt rather than increasing spending, as both they and their bank lenders are being cautious. Business borrowing is falling at a 7% annual rate. The cost of credit has declined much less than policy rates because of increased risk aversion and tighter bank wholesale funding regulations, while deposit rates have actually risen somewhat, contributing to a growing wedge between policy and retail rates.

The earthquake will have important effects

In September, a devastating earthquake struck Christchurch, the second largest city. The damage to homes, business capacity (mainly buildings) and local infrastructure (water and sewage systems) is estimated at around 2% of GDP. This disrupted economic activity in the third quarter but will subsequently boost activity as reconstruction gets underway. The destruction of capital stock and pressure on resources from rebuilding could add to near-term inflation, however. Businesses may face higher insurance premiums, and the public insurer of households (the Earthquake Commission) will need to be recapitalised once it sells assets in order to cover present losses.

Monetary tightening has been postponed...

After raising its policy rate by 25 basis points in both June and July, the Reserve Bank decided to pause at its September and October reviews, citing weaker economic data and increased uncertainty associated with global developments. Inflation has remained around or below the mid-point of the Bank's 1-3% target range but will spike in late 2010 due to policy measures, notably an increase of the Goods and Services Tax rate from 12.5 to 15%. A concurrent reduction in personal income tax rates should boost disposable incomes and thereby restrain any wage response, as will the still soft labour market. In accordance with its mandate, the Bank has said it will "look through" temporary inflation increases arising from one-off tax increases and natural disasters. The projections embody a resumption of policy tightening only in mid-2011.

... as has fiscal consolidation

According to the May 2010 Budget, fiscal policy will remain expansionary in 2010, turn roughly neutral in 2011, and then tighten by some 1.5% of GDP in 2012. This consolidation will take place through expenditure restraint. The "operating allowance" on new discretionary current spending is set at NZD 1.1 billion per year over the medium term (in effect, growing only 60% as fast as GDP), though taking into account excluded benefit, pension and finance costs, the cumulative spending increase is roughly twice as great. The projection assumes the government's fiscal plans are implemented and reduce the deficit to 3.4% of GDP in 2012, below its 2009 level. Reconstruction of earthquake-damaged public infrastructure will apparently now cost less than the initially estimated NZD 1 billion, and thus should be mostly covered within existing budgets.

The growth outlook is subdued

Although policy stimulus is about to be withdrawn, reconstruction should provide support to GDP over the next year or so. Private consumption should also be boosted by the rugby World Cup in 2011 though decelerating thereafter, even as job creation and optimism return, with ongoing deleveraging. Business confidence seems to be turning the corner, and investment should bounce back as diminishing slack in the labour market increases the cost of further substitution of capital by labour. Export growth should benefit from a waning of adverse exchange-rate appreciation effects while market growth moderates. A risk may stem from possible wage demands following the temporary spike in inflation, which would oblige the Bank to tighten more rapidly.

NORWAY

The economic recovery in mainland Norway, following a shallower recession than elsewhere, is projected to continue and gradually strengthen. For the first time in several years, public expenditure will not provide a strong boost to activity; private investment and consumption will be the main sources of demand growth. As from 2011, mainland GDP will be growing sufficiently rapidly to reduce excess capacity and by 2012 demand pressure will start to push inflation upwards again.

The central bank expects to have to continue to raise interest rates, though with subdued inflation and low interest rates in other countries it has made no move since May. While fiscal policy is assumed to avoid further expansion in 2011 and 2012, overall demand is growing faster than potential output and thus monetary policy will need to tighten through 2011 and 2012. Measures to improve labour supply and to improve competition and productivity in some sectors could help to alleviate long-term pressure on capacity.

The recovery continues

The recovery from Norway's relatively shallow recession is now quite well-established. Although monthly production data have been erratic and suggest that there was some short-term slowdown in the late summer, business confidence indicators suggest continuing strength. As for consumers, while retail sales figures have also been erratic, house prices continued their strong growth, at least up to the second quarter. The 12-month inflation rate had jumped to around 3½ per cent in March but, as electricity prices receded, has fallen back since then; both headline inflation (1.9%) and most measures of underlying inflation were below the central bank's target of 2½ per cent in September. While real wages continue to increase, they slowed substantially in 2010 as coordination among the social partners limited nominal earnings growth to a little over 3%. Employment fell by less than 1½ per cent in the recession and picked

Norway

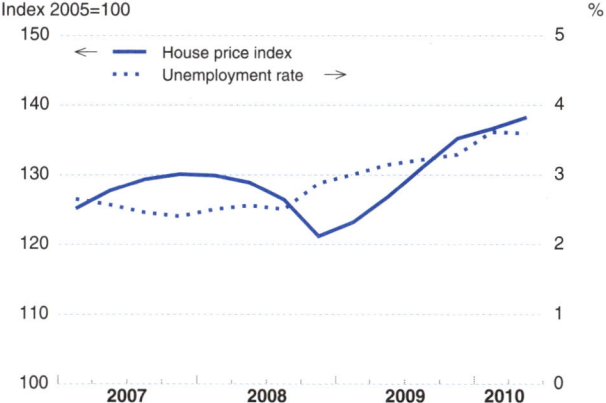

Unemployment has increased moderately, but house prices have recovered

Interest rates are low and inflation is contained for the moment

1. Percentage changes from corresponding quarter of previous year.
Source: Statistics Norway and OECD Economic Outlook 88 database .

StatLink ⟶ http://dx.doi.org/10.1787/888932345983

Norway: **Demand, output and prices**

	2007	2008	2009	2010	2011	2012
	Current prices NOK billion	Percentage changes, volume (2007 prices)				
Private consumption	940.1	1.6	0.2	2.5	2.8	3.5
Government consumption	446.5	4.1	4.7	2.9	2.0	2.0
Gross fixed capital formation	503.9	2.0	-9.1	-5.4	4.6	3.8
Final domestic demand	1 890.5	2.3	-1.2	0.7	3.0	3.2
Stockbuilding[1]	32.8	-0.3	-2.0	2.6	0.2	0.0
Total domestic demand	1 923.3	1.9	-3.7	3.8	3.2	3.1
Exports of goods and services	1 039.7	1.0	-4.0	-0.4	1.8	2.8
Imports of goods and services	691.4	4.3	-11.4	9.0	6.1	5.4
Net exports[1]	348.3	-0.8	1.4	-2.7	-0.9	-0.4
GDP at market prices	2 271.6	0.8	-1.4	0.5	1.8	2.3
GDP deflator	_	10.0	-4.0	4.2	2.7	2.3
Memorandum items						
Mainland GDP at market prices[2]	_	1.8	-1.4	1.4	2.5	3.3
Consumer price index	_	3.8	2.2	2.4	1.5	2.5
Private consumption deflator	_	3.6	2.5	2.0	1.9	2.5
Unemployment rate	_	2.6	3.2	3.6	3.9	3.5
Household saving ratio[3]	_	3.7	7.3	6.3	6.9	6.9
General government financial balance[4]	_	19.3	9.9	9.5	8.7	8.8
Current account balance[4]	_	17.7	13.0	13.8	13.4	13.1

Note: National accounts are based on official chain-linked data. This introduces a discrepancy in the identity between real demand components and GDP. For further details see *OECD Economic Outlook* Sources and Methods *(http://www.oecd.org/eco/sources-and-methods).*
1. Contributions to changes in real GDP (percentage of real GDP in previous year), actual amount in the first column.
2. GDP excluding oil and shipping.
3. As a percentage of disposable income.
4. As a percentage of GDP.
Source: OECD Economic Outlook 88 database.

StatLink ⃞ᵍ⃞ *http://dx.doi.org/10.1787/888932347731*

up at the same time as output, unlike in many other countries, so that labour productivity per worker has been flat or falling this year.

Monetary tightening has paused...

The Norwegian central bank was early in terminating special assistance to financial markets and beginning conventional monetary tightening in late 2009. The main policy rate has been fixed at 2% since May and expected further increases have not occurred as inflation came in lower than the Bank forecast, the recovery has been erratic and the fall in long-term interest rates abroad has increased potential upward pressure on the krone.

... and the "mainland" deficit has stopped rising

Although the implicit "mainland" fiscal deficit is large, at some 7% of mainland GDP, it is no longer expanding rapidly. Budget plans, which these projections assume will be fully implemented, call for public expenditure to grow much more slowly than in the past, so that with unchanged tax rates there will be some modest tightening. With strong growth in the Government Pension Fund Global (GPFG), the repository of net petroleum revenues, this should bring the structural non-oil government deficit near to or below 4% of assets in the GPFG in 2012, consistent with the fiscal guidelines. The overall budget surplus may decline slightly as a share of GDP, despite high oil prices, as petroleum production declines.

Projected growth will gradually put pressure on wages and prices

Easier financial conditions and demand from the offshore sector should encourage a continuing robust increase in investment after its substantial fall during the recession. Non-oil export volumes should continue to recover, but with petroleum export volumes declining and domestic demand rising, import growth will outstrip exports throughout the projection period. The current account surplus, including petroleum, will nevertheless remain very large. Having succeeded in limiting wage growth this year, the social partners are likely to agree to higher wage growth in 2011 and 2012 as the recovery establishes itself and the labour market stabilises and begins to tighten. This will support slowly increasing consumption growth. It will also generate some pressure on prices and, although inflation is projected to remain around the central bank's objective in 2012, the Bank will have to tighten at least as fast as its latest projections indicate to head off accelerating inflation thereafter.

The short-term durability of the recovery is still uncertain

Though the recovery seems assured, some signs of weaker investor and consumer confidence may indicate a risk of weaker demand growth than projected here; balancing this risk, investment and consumption could bounce back faster or imports grow more slowly if domestic supply responds more effectively to demand growth.

POLAND

A strong recovery is underway thanks to booming exports, a recovery in private and public consumption and stock rebuilding. Real GDP growth is projected to be sustained by infrastructure investments, partly financed by EU funds, and driven to some extent by the 2012 football championship.

After bottoming in summer 2010, inflation is projected to rise, pointing to the need for an early start to monetary tightening, given the long lags involved. The general government deficit is likely to reach nearly 8% of GDP in 2010, up from 6.8% in 2009. Announced measures will bring the budget deficit to below 7% of GDP in 2011. Capping public spending along with tax hikes should help to bring public finances a step closer to a sustainable path in 2012.

The economy has shifted up a gear

Real GDP growth has started to pick up, driven by exports, public and private consumption and stockbuilding. Industrial production has accelerated, and business confidence indicators suggest continued expansion. Weather-related losses in the construction sector have been largely recovered. Credit to the domestic economy seems to be slowly recovering. Inward direct investment may reach 3% of GDP in 2010. The standardised unemployment rate peaked at 9.9% in March and has fallen half a percentage point since then.

Fiscal consolidation is back-loaded

Despite robust growth, the government expects the budget deficit to rise to almost 8% of GDP in 2010, well above the 6.9% foreseen in Poland's EU convergence programme. Consolidation measures representing almost one percentage point of GDP coupled with strong growth are projected to bring down the budget shortfall only to 6.7% of GDP in 2011. The budget measures include capping the growth of discretionary central government

Poland

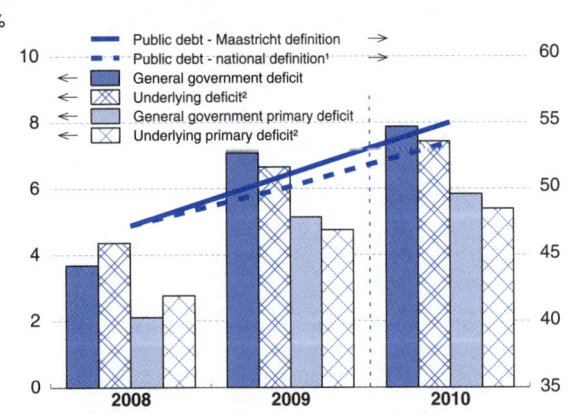

Rising general government deficit and public debt
As a percentage of GDP

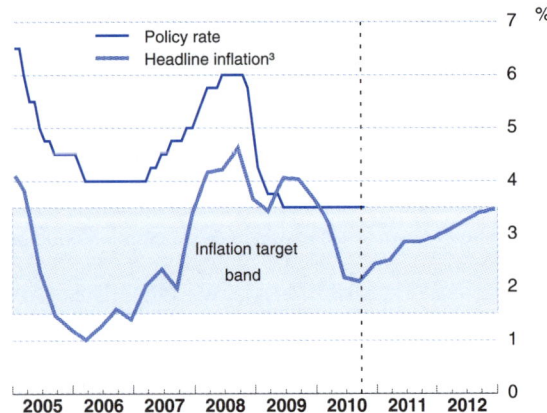

The monetary tightening cycle should start soon

1. Calculated as the projected Maastricht debt minus 1.5 percentage points for 2010.
2. As a percentage of potential GDP.
3. Year-on-year growth rates.

Source: NBP; OECD, Economic Outlook 88 database.

StatLink ⟲ http://dx.doi.org/10.1787/888932346002

Poland: **Demand, output and prices**

	2007	2008	2009	2010	2011	2012
	Current prices PLN billion	Percentage changes, volume (2000 prices)				
Private consumption	713.2	5.3	2.6	2.5	3.0	3.5
Government consumption	210.0	6.9	2.6	2.1	1.6	1.5
Gross fixed capital formation	251.5	9.7	-0.7	-0.6	17.8	12.5
Final domestic demand	1 174.7	6.5	1.9	1.8	5.7	5.1
Stockbuilding[1]	32.2	-1.1	-2.5	2.2	-0.3	0.0
Total domestic demand	1 206.9	5.3	-0.6	4.0	5.3	5.1
Exports of goods and services	481.8	5.8	-6.0	11.6	5.8	6.7
Imports of goods and services	512.1	6.2	-13.2	11.7	8.4	8.4
Net exports[1]	- 30.3	-0.3	3.4	-0.1	-1.1	-0.9
GDP at market prices	1 176.6	5.0	1.7	3.5	4.0	4.3
GDP deflator	_	3.1	3.6	2.0	3.0	3.2
Memorandum items						
Consumer price index	_	4.2	3.8	2.4	2.5	3.1
Private consumption deflator	_	4.5	2.0	2.5	2.5	3.0
Unemployment rate	_	7.1	8.2	9.6	8.9	7.8
General government financial balance[2,3]	_	-3.7	-6.8	-7.9	-6.7	-4.8
Current account balance[2]	_	-4.8	-2.2	-2.4	-3.2	-3.8

Note: National accounts are based on official chain-linked data. This introduces a discrepancy in the identity between real demand components and GDP. For further details see *OECD Economic Outlook* Sources and Methods *(http://www.oecd.org/eco/sources-and-methods).*
1. Contributions to changes in real GDP (percentage of real GDP in previous year), actual amount in the first column.
2. As a percentage of GDP.
3. With private pension funds (OFE) classified outside the general government sector.
Source: OECD Economic Outlook 88 database.

StatLink http://dx.doi.org/10.1787/888932347750

expenditures at one percentage point above inflation, freezing public payroll, cutting employment in central government by 10% by 2013 and increasing VAT

Fiscal consolidation should continue in 2012

It is assumed that the government will make continued efforts to keep public spending under control, and that a further rise in VAT and an increase in income taxes accompanied by solid growth will bring the budget deficit below 5% of GDP in 2012. Nevertheless, Poland, along with most new EU members, submitted a proposal to the European Commission to redefine its public debt and budget deficit by excluding spending related to public pension reform. This would reduce Poland's Maastricht debt by one third and would jeopardise fiscal consolidation.

Public debt will remain below 60% of GDP in 2012

The government intends to keep public debt below the intermediate constitutional threshold of 55% of GDP in 2010 and the ultimate ceiling of 60% in 2011 and 2012 using a variety of existing and new measures in addition to reducing the deficit: *a)* privatising state-owned companies; *b)* improving the public sector's liquidity management; *c)* shifting some public infrastructure spending to the National Road Fund, which is excluded from the domestic definition of public debt; *d)* transferring assets managed by the demographic reserve fund to the social insurance fund; and e) decreasing interest payments on public debt by borrowing from cheaper sources, such as the European Investment Bank, to finance large infrastructure projects.

Risk management in banking is improving

Stress tests of Polish banks carried out by the central bank indicate that most of them are well capitalised and that they could withstand a major economic slowdown. Nevertheless, in August the authorities implemented part of "Recommendation T" according to which individual households' debt repayments are capped at 50%-65% of actual salaries. Further regulations to limit foreign-currency lending are expected to become binding in the first half of 2011.

Growth may strengthen, unemployment decrease and inflation edge up

Growth is expected to pick up, driven mainly by fixed investment fuelled by EU funds, the preparations for the 2012 football championship and a revival of private consumption. Unemployment is projected to continue its gradual decline. Headline inflation is projected to rise as output begins to outstrip potential levels.

Risks are broadly balanced

A delay in starting the monetary tightening cycle is likely to strengthen domestic demand. A positive growth surprise in the euro area would boost Poland's exports and private investment via capital inflows. On the other hand, if a large negative foreign shock were to increase the debt-to-GDP ratio (national definition) above the constitutional thresholds of 55% and 60%, pro-cyclical fiscal action would be legally required. The large share of portfolio investment in total capital inflows that Poland receives may be destabilising if global risk appetites for emerging-market assets decrease.

PORTUGAL

The economy is expected to be very weak in the rest of 2010 and into 2011, due to strong fiscal consolidation and tight credit conditions. Growth is expected to resume in 2012 as external demand and wage moderation support exports and investment. Unemployment is set to rise further.

The government has recently announced a new fiscal tightening package, to shore up the credibility of its deficit-reduction targets. Strictly implementing consolidation measures, as is assumed in the projections, and promptly correcting any slippages in order to meet those targets are essential to reduce the cost of external financing, and thus stave off the major downside risk of a credit contraction. Reforming the budgetary framework is key to reinforcing the sustainability of consolidation. Reducing the duality of the labour market should help boost potential growth.

Consumption is running out of steam

In the first half of 2010, GDP growth was stronger than expected, largely driven by consumption, especially of durable goods, and to a lesser extent by net exports. With fiscal consolidation gathering pace to strengthen the authorities' credibility in international capital markets, and durables' consumption hampered by tighter credit conditions and the rise in the VAT by 1 percentage point in July 2010, domestic demand growth is likely to have become negative in the third quarter; exports, however, should have supported GDP growth. Consumption is expected to be a bit more dynamic in the last quarter of 2010, ahead of an additional rise in the standard VAT rate of 2 percentage points on 1 January 2011 (see below). After increasing to 10.6% in the first half of 2010, monthly data suggests that the unemployment rate has essentially stabilised. Headline inflation has accelerated and should stay high in early 2011 following the second increase in VAT, notwithstanding the downward pressures arising from the economic slowdown.

Portugal

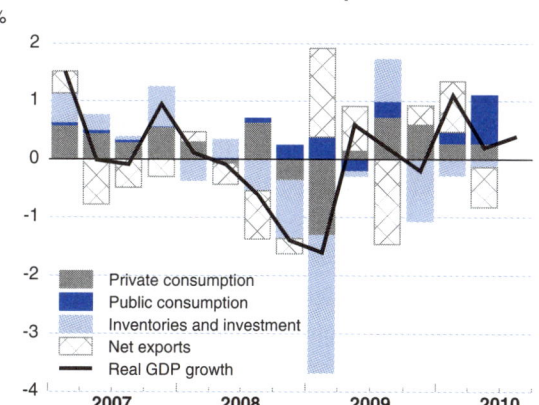

Recovery in the first half of 2010 relied on consumption[1]

Private consumption
Public consumption
Inventories and investment
Net exports
Real GDP growth

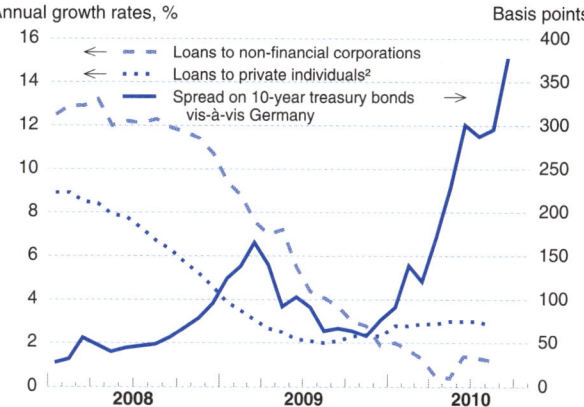

Credit conditions have deteriorated

Annual growth rates, % Basis points

Loans to non-financial corporations
Loans to private individuals[2]
Spread on 10-year treasury bonds vis-à-vis Germany

1. Contribution to real GDP growth.
2. Annual growth rate adjusted for securitisation operations.
Source: Banco de Portugal; OECD Economic Outlook 88 database.

StatLink http://dx.doi.org/10.1787/888932346021

Portugal: **Demand, output and prices**

	2007	2008	2009	2010	2011	2012
	Current prices € billion	Percentage changes, volume (2006 prices)				
Private consumption	110.6	1.8	-1.0	1.9	-0.7	0.6
Government consumption	33.0	0.8	2.9	2.1	-6.0	-1.3
Gross fixed capital formation	37.6	-1.8	-11.9	-4.1	-3.5	2.3
Final domestic demand	181.3	0.9	-2.5	0.8	-2.2	0.5
Stockbuilding[1]	1.0	0.3	-0.6	0.0	0.2	0.0
Total domestic demand	182.3	1.2	-3.0	0.9	-2.0	0.5
Exports of goods and services	54.5	-0.3	-11.8	8.4	6.3	7.6
Imports of goods and services	68.0	2.8	-10.9	5.1	0.0	3.2
Net exports[1]	- 13.5	-1.2	0.7	0.5	2.0	1.3
GDP at market prices	168.7	0.0	-2.5	1.5	-0.2	1.8
GDP deflator	_	2.0	0.2	1.1	1.3	1.1
Memorandum items						
Harmonised index of consumer prices	_	2.7	-0.9	1.4	2.3	1.3
Private consumption deflator	_	2.7	-2.3	1.5	2.3	1.3
Unemployment rate	_	7.6	9.5	10.7	11.4	11.1
Household saving ratio[2]	_	7.8	11.0	10.8	8.4	8.1
General government financial balance[3,4]	_	-3.0	-9.4	-7.3	-5.0	-4.4
Current account balance[3]	_	-12.6	-10.3	-10.3	-8.8	-8.0

1. Contributions to changes in real GDP (percentage of real GDP in previous year), actual amount in the first column.
2. As a percentage of disposable income.
3. As a percentage of GDP.
4. Based on national accounts definition.
Source: OECD Economic Outlook 88 database.

StatLink ⧉ http://dx.doi.org/10.1787/888932347769

Credit contraction risks are looming

Spreads on Portuguese public debt have been trending upwards since the end of May, reaching historic peaks. Persistent financial market stress has also severely restricted Portuguese banks' access to wholesale debt markets and made them more dependent on ECB liquidity provision, despite good results in the July EU-wide stress tests. Though credit growth for both companies and households has so far remained positive, it is widely expected to slow further, and could become negative.

Fiscal consolidation is set to accelerate

Fiscal consolidation had a slower start in Portugal than in other peripheral euro area countries. In the first half of 2010 there was virtually no deficit reduction relative to 2009, despite the good performance of fiscal revenues. Expenditure growth remained robust, due *inter alia* to rising social transfers and sizeable wage drift. Though progress is underway in the second half of the year, the 2010 deficit target (7.3% of GDP) will only be met by resorting to large one-off proceeds (notably 1.5% of GDP received from the main telecom company as compensation for the transfer of its pension liabilities to the state). New consolidation measures were presented in late September, mostly for 2011, including cuts in civil servants' wages (5% on average), a nominal freeze on pensions, a 2 percentage points increase in the standard VAT rate and further cuts in social and health care spending, public investment and tax expenditures.

These and previous measures are incorporated in the OECD projections, which in addition assume that both pensions and public wages are kept frozen in 2012. Though the new consolidation package is welcome, the size of the adjustment makes budget implementation particularly challenging, and reform of the budgeting process ever more pressing.

Prospects are bleak as imbalances are still unwinding

The economy is projected to contract in early 2011 and then start a mild, export-based recovery. Activity should gradually become more robust as Portugal's interest-rate spreads fall in response to fiscal consolidation. In annual terms, GDP is projected to fall slightly in 2011, but picking up significantly by end 2011 and growing by 1.8% in 2012. Unemployment is set to rise until the second half of 2011, and to decline somewhat afterwards as growth picks up. Inflation is likely to edge up to over 2% in 2011, largely as a result of the successive hikes in VAT rates, even though the economic slowdown will have a damping effect and underlying pressure from wages is absent.

A credit contraction is the main downside risk

The possibility of abrupt deleveraging due to a strong credit contraction remains a major downside risk in the short and medium term, making it all the more necessary that fiscal targets be strictly met. As any GDP growth will heavily depend on exports, developments in international trade and external demand will also be important sources of uncertainty and risk.

SLOVAK REPUBLIC

The economy is recovering at a strong pace driven by net exports, but domestic demand remains more subdued. In 2011, fiscal consolidation and somewhat slower demand from Slovakia's main trading partners are expected to slightly moderate growth to around 3.5%. Real GDP is envisaged to accelerate again in 2012 with a gradual improvement in the labour market.

The budget deficit turned out to be 8% of GDP in 2009 and is expected to deteriorate somewhat further in 2010, substantially worse than planned. The government rightly plans to implement fiscal consolidation measures, which are reflected in the projection, of around 2½ per cent of GDP next year, and to reduce the deficit to below 3% in 2013. The public pension system should be reformed to ensure the long-run sustainability of public finances.

The recovery continues at a fast pace...

After falling sharply until the beginning of 2009, economic activity has since been improving. The recovery has been primarily driven by exports, reflecting buoyant external demand, and stock building. By contrast, in the second quarter, fixed capital formation declined sharply and private consumption weakened further, despite some recovery in employment. Public consumption supported growth in the first quarter but decreased significantly afterwards. Headline inflation remained at low levels of around 1% and core inflation stabilised after a sharp decrease in 2009.

... but the short-term outlook is mixed

Monthly indicators are mixed and show signs of a slowing recovery. Industrial production has slackened in recent months and business confidence indicators stabilised after a sharp improvement. Retail sales are declining, but at a slower rate, as consumer confidence has deteriorated since the beginning of the year. The unemployment rate fell somewhat in the second quarter after rising by almost 5 percentage

Slovak Republic

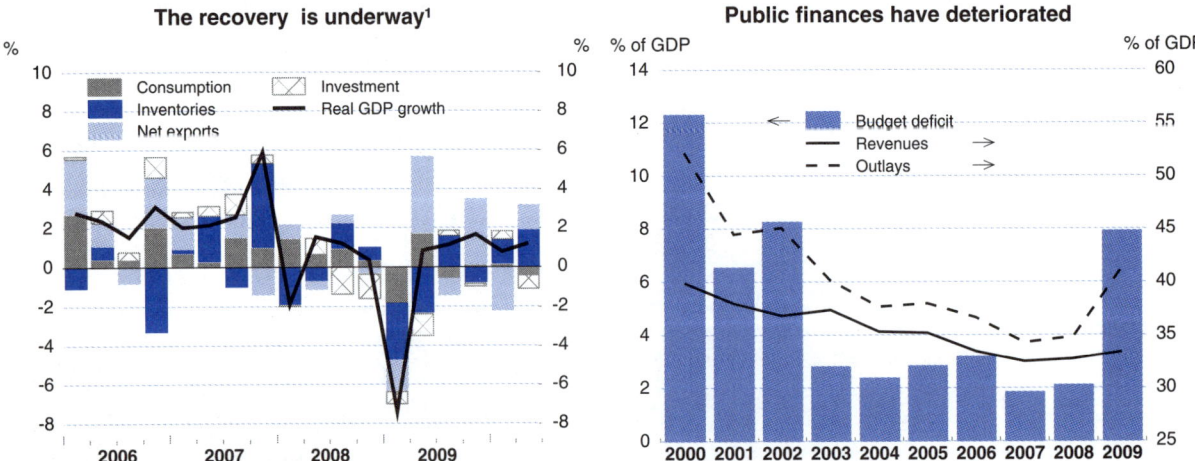

1. Contribution to real GDP growth.
Source: OECD Economic Outlook 88 database.

StatLink http://dx.doi.org/10.1787/888932346040

Slovak Republic: **Demand, output and prices**

	2007	2008	2009	2010	2011	2012
	Current prices € billion	Percentage changes, volume (2000 prices)				
Private consumption	34.5	6.0	-0.7	-0.1	0.4	3.3
Government consumption	10.6	5.3	2.8	1.6	-3.7	1.0
Gross fixed capital formation	16.1	1.8	-10.5	-0.7	6.1	6.9
Final domestic demand	61.2	4.8	-2.5	0.1	0.9	3.7
Stockbuilding[1]	1.0	1.3	-3.4	2.4	0.5	0.0
Total domestic demand	62.2	6.0	-5.8	2.6	1.3	3.7
Exports of goods and services	53.4	3.2	-16.5	14.1	9.9	6.9
Imports of goods and services	54.0	3.1	-17.6	11.6	7.0	6.1
Net exports[1]	- 0.6	0.1	1.3	1.7	2.4	0.8
GDP at market prices	61.5	6.2	-4.7	4.1	3.5	4.4
GDP deflator	_	2.9	-1.2	0.1	2.2	2.3
Memorandum items						
Harmonised index of consumer prices	_	3.9	0.9	0.8	3.4	2.9
Private consumption deflator	_	4.5	1.0	0.4	3.3	2.9
Unemployment rate	_	9.5	12.1	14.1	13.4	12.5
General government financial balance[2]	_	-2.1	-7.9	-8.0	-5.2	-4.0
Current account balance[2]	_	-6.5	-3.2	-3.1	-0.9	-0.3

Note: National accounts are based on official chain-linked data. This introduces a discrepancy in the identity between real demand components and GDP. For further details see *OECD Economic Outlook* Sources and Methods *(http://www.oecd.org/eco/sources-and-methods)*.
1. Contributions to changes in real GDP (percentage of real GDP in previous year), actual amount in the first column.
2. As a percentage of GDP.
Source: OECD Economic Outlook 88 database.

StatLink ⟐ *http://dx.doi.org/10.1787/888932347788*

points since the end of 2008. However, recent data suggest a stabilisation, rather than continued improvement, in the labour market. Moreover, the incidence of long-term unemployment may rise further due to hysteresis effects.

Fiscal consolidation measures will damp domestic demand

The general government budget deficit is set to increase to around 8% of GDP this year due to both revenue shortfalls and fiscal stimulus measures. The newly elected government plans an ambitious fiscal consolidation package to cut the deficit by 2½ percentage points of GDP in 2011 by reducing public expenditures and increasing revenues, including by raising the standard VAT rate. Regarding the following years, the government announced a less pronounced reduction in the deficit (1% of GDP in 2012) to reach gradually a deficit target of 2.9% of GDP in 2013. The projection assumes these fiscal consolidation efforts will be implemented and, as no specific measures have been announced for 2012, that cuts in public expenditures will be pursued further to reach the target set by the authorities. Doing so should bring down the fiscal deficit to around 5¼ per cent in 2011 and 4 per cent in 2012, but may also adversely affect domestic demand. In particular, the planned increase in indirect taxes may hamper growth of private consumption in 2011, especially if households chose to move purchases forward to this year. In addition, planned cuts in public consumption will directly reduce domestic demand.

The recovery will be initially driven by exports

Growth in 2010 may reach around 4%, mainly driven by very strong exports. Also, consumption may increase towards the end of the year as households anticipate the rise in indirect taxes in 2011. Notwithstanding stronger gross fixed investment due to construction of motorways and new foreign direct investments over the projection horizon, growth is projected to slow in 2011 as domestic and foreign demand growth weaken. GDP growth will remain heavily dependent on exports. Export market shares that were lost during the crisis are likely to be recovered. This is due to the absence of currency risk and the rise in financial integration linked to euro area membership, which underpins FDI inflows. In addition, moderate wage growth related to the high level of unemployment will also contribute. In 2012, GDP growth is projected to reach around 4.5%, as private consumption strengthens significantly, not least due to improvement in the labour market and a gradual reduction in the saving rate.

Risks are broadly balanced

Risks are broadly balanced and mainly relate to the future growth outlook in Slovakia's main trading partners and the effect of assumed fiscal consolidation measures on domestic demand.

SLOVENIA

The recovery has mainly been driven by rising exports so far. Growth should rebalance gradually towards private domestic demand through 2011 and 2012. The unemployment rate has yet to stabilise as government short-time work measures are being phased out and activity remains subdued. Considerable economic slack should keep inflation in check.

The government responded to fiscal slippages in early 2010 by additional consolidation measures but sustainable fiscal consolidation also requires a comprehensive pension reform and improvements in public sector efficiency. To enhance competitiveness and job creation, wage costs need to be contained, notably the minimum wage level following its steep increase in early 2010.

The external sector has sustained the recovery

The recovery in activity that commenced in the second half of 2009 paused in the first quarter of 2010, before rebounding strongly in the second quarter mainly supported by the resumption of export growth and restocking. By contrast, private consumption and investment continued to contract in the first half of the year. Recent short-term indicators show a slight improvement in business sentiment and in production, notably in manufacturing, but consumer confidence appears to have deteriorated in the third quarter, suggesting subdued final domestic demand growth. The capacity utilisation rate in manufacturing has risen significantly, but financing conditions are still tight and lending to the business sector remains weak. Inflation picked up in the first half of the year, largely on account of higher commodity and energy prices, a weak currency and increases in some excise taxes.

The labour market is still weak

Employment grew slightly in the first quarter but fell again in the second quarter, with the unemployment rate reaching its highest level

Slovenia

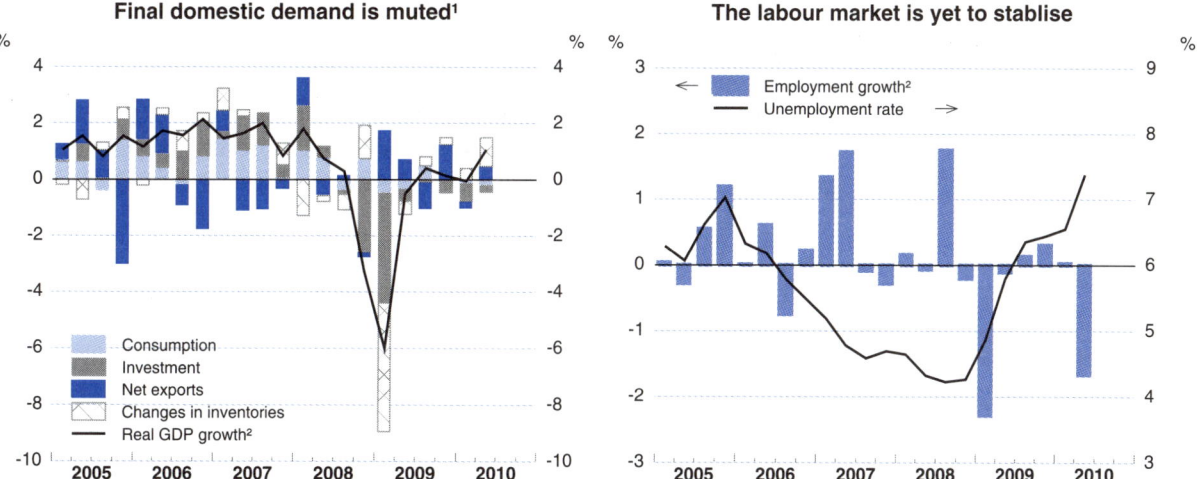

1. Contribution to real GDP growth over previous quarter.
2. Growth over previous quarter.

Source: OECD Economic Outlook 88 database.

StatLink ᴍ𝔰🔊 http://dx.doi.org/10.1787/888932346059

Slovenia: **Demand, output and prices**

	2007	2008	2009	2010	2011	2012
	Current prices € billion	Percentage changes, volume (2000 prices)				
Private consumption	18.2	2.9	-0.8	-0.6	1.0	2.5
Government consumption	6.0	6.2	3.0	0.3	-0.8	-0.3
Gross fixed capital formation	9.6	8.5	-21.6	-5.3	4.2	6.6
Final domestic demand	33.8	5.1	-6.1	-1.5	1.4	2.9
Stockbuilding[1]	1.4	-0.8	-4.0	1.7	0.7	0.0
Total domestic demand	35.2	4.2	-9.8	0.6	2.4	2.8
Exports of goods and services	24.0	3.3	-17.7	8.7	6.4	6.6
Imports of goods and services	24.6	3.8	-19.7	7.6	6.6	6.6
Net exports[1]	- 0.6	-0.4	2.0	0.7	-0.1	-0.1
GDP at market prices	34.6	3.7	-8.1	1.1	2.0	2.7
GDP deflator	_	4.0	3.2	0.5	1.0	1.9
Memorandum items						
Harmonised index of consumer prices	_	5.5	0.9	2.1	1.9	2.2
Private consumption deflator	_	5.4	0.0	2.4	1.7	2.1
Unemployment rate	_	4.4	5.9	7.2	7.6	7.4
General government financial balance[2]	_	-1.8	-5.8	-5.7	-4.7	-3.9
Current account balance[2]	_	-6.7	-1.5	-2.8	-3.9	-4.5

Note: National accounts are based on official chain-linked data. This introduces a discrepancy in the identity between real demand components and GDP. For further details see *OECD Economic Outlook* Sources and Methods *(http://www.oecd.org/eco/sources-and-methods).*
1. Contributions to changes in real GDP (percentage of real GDP in previous year), actual amount in the first column.
2. As a percentage of GDP.
Source: OECD Economic Outlook 88 database.

StatLink ⟶ *http://dx.doi.org/10.1787/888932347807*

since end–2005. Unemployment is expected to remain high over the next quarters to come as labour costs have started to rise due to the sizable minimum wage increase (23%) in 2010. Also, the short-time work measures, which facilitated labour hoarding, are coming to an end.

Fiscal consolidation is underway

The government has embarked on a fiscal consolidation path to bring down the budget deficit under 3% of GDP by 2013, as planned in the government consolidation strategy. In June 2010, in response to revenue shortfalls earlier in the year, the government adopted a supplementary budget for 2010 to maintain budgetary targets. Draft budgets for 2011 and 2012 are based on a slower consolidation path than previously planned, notably due to less optimistic revenue projections. In any case, a comprehensive pension reform is needed to put public finances on a sustainable footing in the long term and the government should consider whether its recent reform proposals are sufficient to address the daunting expected rise of pension costs by 2060.

Private investment and consumption should pick up gradually

Growth is projected to strengthen in 2011 and 2012 as private investment gathers momentum and wage increases support consumption. Unemployment will gradually diminish in 2012. Economic slack will ensure that price pressures remain moderate in 2011. Inflation is projected to edge up in 2012 as the economy gathers further momentum and the output gap narrows.

Risks are mainly to the down side

Softer global demand than projected could be compounded by weakened competitiveness to undermine growth. Headwinds in the financial sector with an over-leveraged corporate sector, a fragile housing market and potential hysteresis effects in the labour market constitute a risk as well. On the positive side, stronger-than-expected activity in the euro area would improve business and labour conditions.

SPAIN

Output is expected to remain flat in the second half of 2010 and to grow by 1% in 2011 and by 1¾ per cent in 2012. The unemployment rate is projected to decline to 16½ per cent by the end of 2012 while consumer price inflation may fall to below 0.5% once the effect of increased VAT rates drops out.

Budgetary consolidation at all levels of government is projected to result in a decline of the government deficit from 9% of GDP in 2010 to 6¼ per cent in 2011 and to 4½ per cent in 2012. Some planned spending reductions in 2012 still need to be specified and the government should stand ready to introduce further measures if needed to ensure its deficit targets are reached. Pension reform is necessary to put public finances on a sustainable basis. To reap the benefits of the recent labour market reform, the effectiveness of the public employment services needs to be raised.

Output is recovering slowly

Real GDP growth rose by 0.2% in the second quarter on the back of vigorous private consumption as disposable income was boosted by lower debt servicing costs and households brought forward spending ahead of the increase in VAT rates on 1 July. Lower interest rates also contributed to stabilising house prices, although the stock of empty new housing is being absorbed only gradually. Employment losses levelled off in seasonally adjusted terms, while the seasonally adjusted unemployment rate continued to edge up, rising above 20%. Headline inflation rose to 2.1% in September, reflecting past oil price increases as well as the higher VAT rates, which contributed about ½ a percentage point, whereas core inflation rose to 1%. Real GDP remained flat in the third quarter as private consumption weakened following the increase in VAT rates. The rise in export orders in manufacturing has flattened. Business confidence

Spain

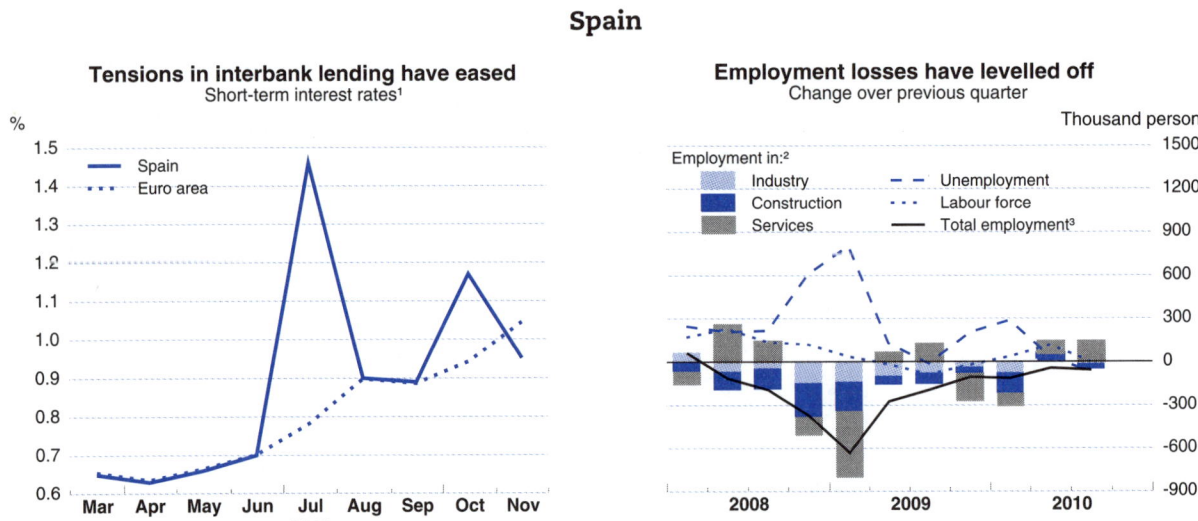

1. Three-month MIBOR (Madrid InterBank Offered Rate) and EURIBOR. November shows an average of daily data to 11th November.
2. Not seasonally adjusted data.
3. Seasonally adjusted.
Source: Datastream and Instituto Nacional de Estadística.

StatLink http://dx.doi.org/10.1787/888932346078

Spain: **Demand, output and prices**

	2007	2008	2009	2010	2011	2012
	Current prices € billion	Percentage changes, volume (2000 prices)				
Private consumption	604.4	-0.6	-4.2	1.5	1.7	2.3
Government consumption	193.5	5.8	3.2	0.3	-0.8	-1.3
Gross fixed capital formation	323.2	-4.8	-16.0	-6.8	-1.8	2.0
Final domestic demand	1 121.1	-0.7	-6.0	-0.7	0.4	1.5
Stockbuilding[1]	3.2	0.1	0.0	0.0	0.0	0.0
Total domestic demand	1 124.3	-0.6	-6.0	-0.7	0.4	1.5
Exports of goods and services	283.3	-1.1	-11.6	9.2	8.1	10.4
Imports of goods and services	354.1	-5.3	-17.8	6.4	5.8	8.7
Net exports[1]	- 70.8	1.5	2.7	0.5	0.4	0.3
GDP at market prices	1 053.5	0.9	-3.7	-0.2	0.9	1.8
GDP deflator	_	2.4	0.6	0.4	0.2	0.3
Memorandum items						
Harmonised index of consumer prices	_	4.1	-0.2	1.5	0.9	0.3
Private consumption deflator	_	3.5	0.1	2.3	1.0	0.3
Unemployment rate	_	11.3	18.0	19.8	19.1	17.4
Household saving ratio[2]	_	13.4	18.0	16.9	15.9	15.3
General government financial balance[3]	_	-4.2	-11.1	-9.2	-6.3	-4.4
Current account balance[3]	_	-9.7	-5.5	-5.5	-5.2	-4.9

Note: National accounts are based on official chain-linked data. This introduces a discrepancy in the identity between real demand components and GDP. For further details see *OECD Economic Outlook* Sources and Methods *(http://www.oecd.org/eco/sources-and-methods).*
1. Contributions to changes in real GDP (percentage of real GDP in previous year), actual amount in the first column.
2. As a percentage of disposable income.
3. As a percentage of GDP.
Source: OECD Economic Outlook 88 database.

StatLink ⬛🖳 *http://dx.doi.org/10.1787/888932347826*

declined following turbulence in euro area financial markets but has recently recovered in the services, notably in retailing.

Substantial budgetary consolidation is underway

Budgetary outcomes have improved in the course of 2010. The measures to stimulate the economy have mostly been withdrawn. In addition, the standard VAT rate was increased from 16% to 18% and the reduced rate from 7% to 8% on 1 July. Some regional governments also raised taxes, including on personal income. The tax increases are expected to generate revenues of 1.2% of GDP in 2010 and an additional 0.5% of GDP in 2011. Spending restraint measures include cutbacks in public investment and a pay cut of 5% for public sector workers in 2010. Governments at all levels are replacing only 1 out of 10 jobs falling vacant. In 2011, public sector wages and most pension payments will be frozen in nominal terms. Overall, spending cuts amount to 1.6% of GDP in 2010 and an additional 1.5% of GDP in 2011. The central government has announced further reductions of consumption and transfer spending in 2012 as well as its intention to cut infrastructure investment spending by as much as necessary to reach its deficit target of 4.4% of GDP. While the government will announce the specific measures only in future budgets, it is assumed in the projections that the general government budget deficit objective will be reached in 2012. Reformed labour market legislation, approved in September 2010, which includes steps to curb excessive dismissal costs as well as to better reflect individual firms' business conditions in wage setting, is expected to support job creation in 2012.

Financial market tensions linger

The turmoil in euro area financial markets raised funding costs for the government and in the inter-bank market in May and June, although liquidity provision by the European Central Bank limited the impact on businesses and households. Non-performing loan ratios have levelled off at 5%. The publication of wide-ranging stress test results for Spanish banks in July and improving budget outcomes contributed to stabilising investor confidence. Interest rates on government debt and banks' funding conditions eased significantly, although the interest rate spread on Spanish government debt vis-à-vis Germany has remained substantial.

A slow recovery will keep unemployment high

GDP growth is expected to resume in 2011, driven by external demand and, to some extent, private consumption. The unemployment rate is expected to fall to 19.2% at the end of 2011 and to 16.6% at the end of 2012. The government deficit is projected to fall from 9.2% of GDP in 2010 to 6.3% in 2011, somewhat above the government's target of 6%, and to 4.4% in 2012.

Investor confidence remains critical

A persistent interest rate spread on government debt could result in a deterioration of funding conditions in the private sector, especially when the European Central Bank withdraws extraordinary liquidity support. This risk underscores the need to achieve fiscal consolidation and press forward with structural reforms.

SWEDEN

The economy has recovered strongly from the recent recession. Solid, though more moderate, growth is expected to continue as external demand gains momentum. Unemployment is projected to decline, but rather slowly. Core inflation is expected to remain subdued, amid low wage pressures and still ample spare capacity.

Policy interest rates need to be gradually raised as planned as the expansion unfolds. The projection assumes that the government will exert the fiscal discipline needed to reach the medium-term surplus target.

The recovery continues

Real GDP grew very strongly in the second quarter of 2010, the fifth consecutive quarterly increase. The recovery is now broad-based, with private consumption, investment (including inventories) and net exports all contributing to growth. Business fixed investment has been supported by rising profits and more favourable financing terms, while housing prices and particularly investment have risen significantly over recent quarters. Consumer and business confidence are buoyant and industrial output has picked up, after having fallen particularly sharply during the recent crisis.

Financial conditions are mixed

Lending has remained weak. Growth in bank lending to households has eased over recent months, while lending to non-financial firms is still declining relative to a year ago, though at a more moderate pace. While long-term government bond rates have declined since the start of the year, interbank spreads have risen.

Unemployment is still high

The recession led to a marked deterioration of the labour market. Although the recovery has produced significant employment growth, the

Sweden

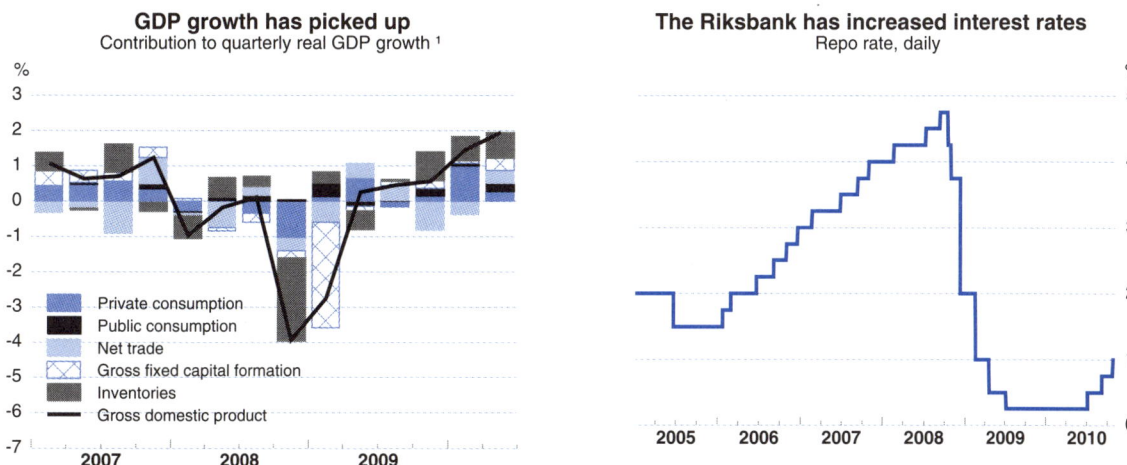

1. Contribution of inventories is calculated as a residual, assuming additivity.
Source: Datastream and Riksbank.

StatLink http://dx.doi.org/10.1787/888932346097

Sweden: **Demand, output and prices**

	2007	2008	2009	2010	2011	2012
	Current prices SEK billion	Percentage changes, volume (2009 prices)				
Private consumption	1 460.2	-0.2	-0.8	3.6	3.0	2.8
Government consumption	797.4	1.0	1.8	1.6	1.2	1.0
Gross fixed capital formation	612.0	1.3	-15.9	4.5	6.8	6.5
Final domestic demand	2 869.5	0.5	-3.3	3.2	3.2	3.0
Stockbuilding[1]	23.2	-0.4	-1.5	2.4	0.3	0.0
Total domestic demand	2 892.8	0.0	-5.0	5.7	3.4	3.0
Exports of goods and services	1 621.5	1.0	-12.3	10.6	8.0	6.6
Imports of goods and services	1 388.2	2.4	-12.9	13.3	8.7	6.2
Net exports[1]	233.2	-0.5	-0.6	-0.4	0.2	0.5
GDP at market prices	3 126.0	-0.6	-5.1	4.4	3.3	3.4
GDP deflator	_	3.4	1.9	1.1	1.2	1.5
Memorandum items						
Consumer price index[2]	_	3.4	-0.3	1.1	1.5	2.3
Private consumption deflator	_	2.9	1.9	0.8	0.9	1.7
Unemployment rate[3]	_	6.2	8.3	8.4	8.0	7.5
Household saving ratio[4]	_	11.2	12.9	10.3	10.1	8.6
General government financial balance[5]	_	2.2	-1.2	-1.2	-0.6	0.6
Current account balance[5]	_	9.3	7.4	6.8	6.8	7.3

Note: National accounts are based on official chain-linked data. This introduces a discrepancy in the identity between real demand components and GDP. For further details see _OECD Economic Outlook_ Sources and Methods (http://www.oecd.org/eco/sources-and-methods).
1. Contributions to changes in real GDP (percentage of real GDP in previous year), actual amount in the first column.
2. The consumer price index includes mortgage interest costs.
3. Historical data and projections are based on the definition of unemployment which covers 15 to 74 year olds and classifies job-seeking full-time students as unemployed.
4. As a percentage of disposable income.
5. As a percentage of GDP.
Source: OECD Economic Outlook 88 database.

StatLink ⟜⟊⟐ http://dx.doi.org/10.1787/888932347845

unemployment rate remains high. Changes in the sickness and disability benefit schemes will encourage labour force participation; while appropriate, this may hold back the decline in unemployment somewhat as the recovery continues.

Monetary and fiscal policies will become less stimulatory

Headline inflation (which includes mortgage interest payments) is expected to continue to rise, mainly reflecting increases in interest rates. However, core inflation (which keeps mortgage interest rates constant) is expected to be subdued, owing to ample spare capacity, moderate wage pressures (reflected in wage agreements earlier this year) and well-anchored long-term inflation expectations. The central bank has been unwinding unconventional monetary policy measures and began raising its policy interest rate in July. It expects and ought to continue doing so, although only gradually as real interest rates need to remain low to help entrench the recovery. On fiscal policy, the current projection assumes that the proposals of the recent budget are implemented, including new labour market measures, further pensioner tax cuts (which should help support consumption) and a new temporary local government grant to help provide welfare services. Overall fiscal policy is expected to be less stimulatory in 2011 than in 2010 and to tighten in 2012. The economic expansion and limits on public expenditure will help move the budget back to surplus.

The recovery should continue at a more moderate pace

The recovery is expected to continue, though its pace will ease into 2011 before regaining momentum towards the end of 2012. Low interest rates and less need for precautionary saving, as financial conditions normalise and unemployment falls, will encourage consumers to increase spending. Export growth is projected to pick up in 2012, broadly in line with export markets. Business investment is set to expand on the back of export growth.

Risks to growth are on both sides

A deterioration in global demand or a possible future appreciation of the krona, perhaps due to capital inflows associated with a flight to quality, could hurt the export sector. However, recent survey evidence may mean that in the short term growth is even stronger than projected and, with interest rates low and some signs of labour market bottlenecks, there is also a risk of greater inflationary pressures.

SWITZERLAND

Economic activity has gained significant momentum on the back of the global recovery, and then a strong pick-up in domestic demand growth from the middle of 2010. As the output gap closes, economic growth gradually slows to potential through the projection period. Unemployment will continue to decline slowly in 2011 and 2012 while inflation is projected to rise slightly above 1%.

Implementing the planned fiscal consolidation measures at the federal level for 2011 and 2012 is necessary to adhere to the debt-brake rule. Monetary policy rates will have to rise gradually from 2011 onwards to contain inflationary pressures that would otherwise gradually build up. The risks stemming from a potential large bank failure should be further reduced, including by tightening capital requirements for the two big banks as has been recommended recently by the Swiss expert commission "Too big to fail".

Economic activity has increased strongly

Real GDP expanded by 3.5% in the second quarter (year-on-year), driven by buoyant domestic demand, especially investment. Export growth has been weakening, however, reflecting the marked appreciation of the Swiss franc against the euro. Strong employment growth has allowed registered unemployment to continuously fall from its peak in January, while consumer price inflation was close to zero in the third quarter. Forward-looking business and consumer confidence suggest strong GDP growth in the coming months, supported by improved conditions in the financial services sector. Forward-looking labour market indicators, including a recent increase in vacancies, suggest that employment growth is also set to continue.

Switzerland

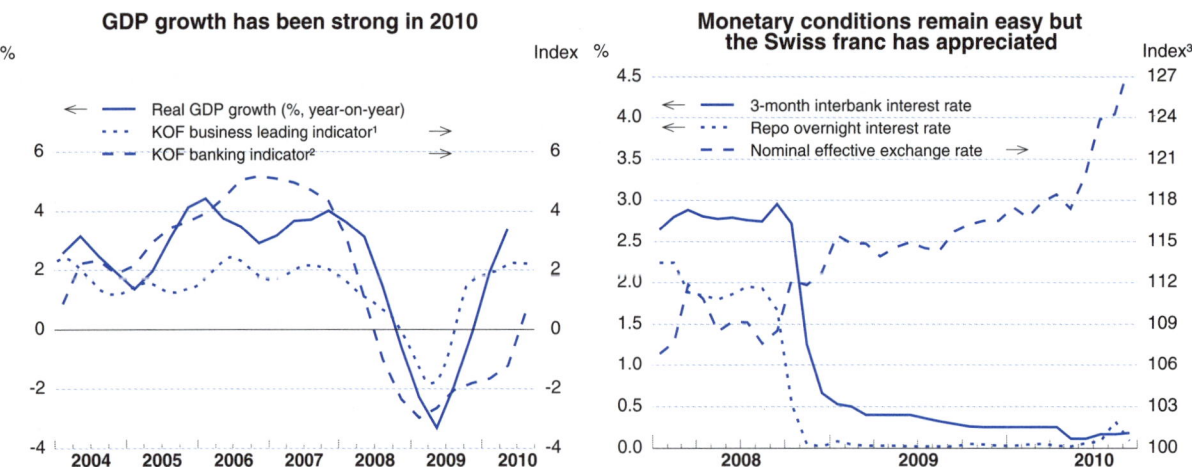

1. Composite leading indicator of business cycle trends in manufacturing, private consumption, financial services, construction and EU export markets.
2. Composite indicator of business confidence in the banking sector.
3. January 1999 = 100.

Source: KOF institute; OECD, Economic Outlook 88 database; SNB.

StatLink http://dx.doi.org/10.1787/888932346116

Switzerland: **Demand, output and prices**

	2007	2008	2009	2010	2011	2012
	Current prices CHF billion	Percentage changes, volume (2000 prices)				
Private consumption	296.8	1.3	1.0	1.7	2.0	2.4
Government consumption	56.4	1.7	1.6	0.2	0.4	0.9
Gross fixed capital formation	112.2	0.5	-4.9	3.7	4.2	2.8
Final domestic demand	465.4	1.2	-0.3	1.9	2.3	2.3
Stockbuilding[1]	2.2	-0.9	0.9	-1.2	0.2	0.0
Total domestic demand	467.6	0.2	0.6	0.7	2.6	2.3
Exports of goods and services	293.1	3.3	-8.7	10.6	4.8	5.5
Imports of goods and services	239.5	0.3	-5.4	8.3	6.4	6.2
Net exports[1]	53.5	1.7	-2.5	2.1	-0.1	0.4
GDP at market prices	521.1	1.9	-1.9	2.7	2.2	2.5
GDP deflator	_	2.5	0.3	0.1	0.7	0.7
Memorandum items						
Consumer price index	_	2.4	-0.5	0.5	0.1	1.1
Private consumption deflator	_	2.6	-0.4	0.5	0.7	0.8
Unemployment rate	_	3.5	4.4	4.4	4.3	4.1
General government financial balance[2]	_	2.3	1.2	-0.7	-0.4	0.0
Current account balance[2]	_	1.5	12.0	12.6	10.9	10.6

Note: National accounts are based on official chain-linked data. This introduces a discrepancy in the identity between real demand components and GDP. For further details see *OECD Economic Outlook* Sources and Methods *(http://www.oecd.org/eco/sources-and-methods)*.

1. Contributions to changes in real GDP (percentage of real GDP in previous year), actual amount in the first column.
2. As a percentage of GDP.

Source: OECD Economic Outlook 88 database.

StatLink http://dx.doi.org/10.1787/888932347864

Monetary policy remains expansionary

The appreciation of the Swiss Franc has tightened monetary conditions and, in view of lingering uncertainties concerning the global recovery, the Swiss National Bank (SNB) announced that it will keep the 3-month LIBOR (the policy rate for the SNB) close to 0.25% in the near future. Unlike earlier this year, the SNB no longer emphasises the need to intervene in the foreign exchange market in case of an excessive appreciation of the Swiss franc. At the same time, it has continued measures to absorb excess liquidity, including through issuing SNB bills.

Fiscal policy will turn slightly restrictive

The fiscal stance is likely to have been expansionary in 2010, as the lagged effects of the recession on personal income tax revenues result in a small deficit. From 2011 onwards, however, fiscal stimulus measures will be withdrawn and further consolidation measures are planned by the federal government. The consolidation programme, which is reflected in this projection, foresees expenditure cuts of about 0.3% of GDP in both 2011 and 2012. The programme is adequate to stabilise the annual expenditure growth over the near term future and hence to adhere to the budgetary rule which requires the structural federal government budget to be balanced.

GDP growth will lose some of its momentum

Real GDP growth is projected to be 2.7% in 2010, as investment growth continues and private consumption accelerates. However, growth will slow somewhat in 2011 and 2012, partly on account of the lagged impact of the strong appreciation of the Swiss franc, as the economy returns broadly to its potential. Due to the generally strong recovery, the unemployment rate will continue to decline with the closing of the output gap. The inflation rate is forecast to increase moderately to just above 1% (*i.e.* the mid-point of the SNB's target band for inflation) in 2012.

The main downside risk relates to the exchange rate

Uncertainties around the global economic recovery create both upside and downside risks for Switzerland. Further significant appreciation of the Swiss Franc would slow growth.

TURKEY

The recovery which started in the second quarter of 2009 has remained strong during 2010. GDP growth is projected to exceed 8% this year, and to remain above 5% in 2011 and 2012 as the post-crisis rebound of exports, consumption and investment tapers off.

The authorities have announced that both fiscal and monetary policy will be tightened gradually, and a prudent medium-term economic programme was published in October. Any additional gains from stronger-than-projected growth should be saved, to avoid pro-cyclical spending. Continuing with structural reforms to boost productivity and job creation in the formal sector would help anchor more balanced and sustainable growth.

The rebound has been vigorous

GDP growth was very strong in the first half of 2010, driven by both domestic and foreign demand. Fuelled by lower capital costs, business investment soared. Recent indicators of consumer and business confidence, white-good sales and housing sector activity confirm that domestic demand remained robust in the second half of the year. However, exports and industrial production have slowed, foreshadowing some deceleration of activity.

The gap between domestic and foreign demand has widened

Exporters have continued to improve non-price competitiveness and to diversify into new markets. The share of fast-growing Asian and Middle-Eastern economies in Turkey's total exports has increased markedly. However, nominal currency appreciation combined with high inflation is undermining exporters' profit margins and market shares. By contrast, the performance of domestic market-oriented services remains robust and aggregate employment rose by 6% between mid-2009 and mid-2010. The unemployment rate has declined despite strong labour force growth, but stays above 11%.

Turkey

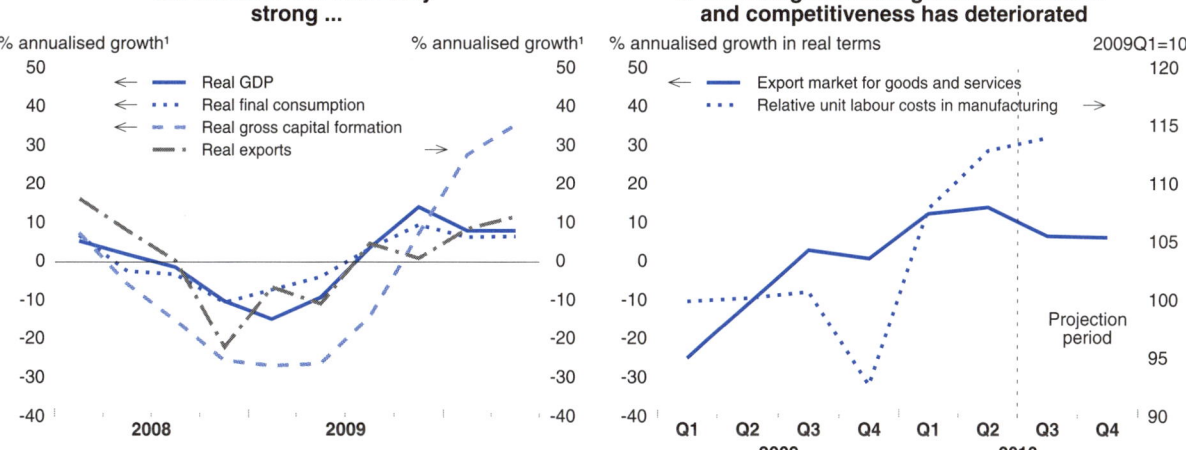

1. Annualised quarterly growth of 3-quarter moving average data.
Source: OECD Economic Outlook 88 Database.

StatLink ᔑᓵᔐ *http://dx.doi.org/10.1787/888932346135*

Turkey: **Demand, output and prices**

	2007	2008	2009	2010	2011	2012
	Current prices TRY billion	Percentage changes, volume (1998 prices)				
Private consumption	601.2	-0.3	-2.2	6.3	4.6	5.6
Government consumption	107.8	1.7	7.8	0.1	4.4	4.8
Gross fixed capital formation	180.6	-6.2	-19.1	25.3	13.4	12.2
Final domestic demand	889.7	-1.3	-4.3	8.6	6.2	6.8
Stockbuilding[1]	- 3.0	0.3	-2.3	0.5	0.4	0.0
Total domestic demand	886.7	-1.0	-6.4	9.2	6.6	6.8
Exports of goods and services	188.2	2.7	-5.3	7.1	5.8	8.2
Imports of goods and services	231.7	-4.1	-14.3	14.1	11.5	12.9
Net exports[1]	- 43.5	1.7	2.8	-1.8	-1.7	-1.7
GDP at market prices	843.2	0.5	-4.8	8.2	5.3	5.4
GDP deflator	_	12.1	5.3	7.1	6.2	5.7
Memorandum items						
Consumer price index	_	10.4	6.3	8.5	6.9	6.4
Private consumption deflator	_	10.8	5.0	8.5	6.7	6.4
Unemployment rate	_	10.7	13.7	12.0	11.7	11.0
Current account balance[2]	_	-5.6	-2.2	-5.1	-5.7	-6.3

Note: National accounts are based on official chain-linked data. This introduces a discrepancy in the identity between real demand components and GDP. For further details see *OECD Economic Outlook* Sources and Methods *(http://www.oecd.org/eco/sources-and-methods)*.
1. Contributions to changes in real GDP (percentage of real GDP in previous year), actual amount in the first column.
2. As a percentage of GDP.
Source: OECD Economic Outlook 88 database.

StatLink http://dx.doi.org/10.1787/888932347883

The current account deficit has increased...

The current account deficit has widened with the rebound in activity and is projected to be above 5% of GDP in 2010. It has been easily financed to date, though mostly by short-term capital such as portfolio debt and bank deposits. Total capital inflows approached 9% of the period's GDP in the first half of 2010.

... and disinflation is slow

Inflation has declined only slightly in 2010 as sizeable indirect tax increases and volatile food prices exerted upward pressure. However, all indicators of core inflation remain subdued and inflation expectations for year-end, at 7½ per cent, are inside the central bank's target band of 6½ ±2%.

The macroeconomic policy mix is changing

The macroeconomic policy response to the crisis combined supportive monetary conditions to underpin activity with a restrictive fiscal stance to preserve domestic and international confidence. In mid-2010 the central bank started to gradually roll back the liquidity facilities introduced during the crisis. Pointing to favourable developments in inflation and remaining international cyclical weaknesses, the central bank has indicated that the first policy interest rate hike could be in the last quarter of 2011. While this stance seems appropriate, care should be taken not to wait too long before withdrawing stimulus, as that could require abrupt and disruptive tightening later. The fast expansion of bank credit also calls for close prudential surveillance, and if necessary the use of new counter-cyclical measures.

The fiscal stance must be kept firm

The fiscal stance was kept tight in the first half of 2010, with a central government budget deficit of 3% of GDP, down from 5.5% in 2009 (consolidated general government accounts based on international standards are not yet published). A new medium-term economic programme announced in October aims for an annual deficit of about 4% of GDP in 2010 (excluding privatisation revenues), implying additional spending late in the year. This may be meant to offset the deceleration of exports and is taken into account in the OECD projection. However, the authorities should avoid amplifying the already widened gap between domestic and foreign demand in the remainder of the projection period. The goal of the programme to consistently tighten the fiscal stance is crucial in this regard. This also requires sticking to the absolute level of planned spending, and saving any revenue windfalls from stronger-than-projected growth. As Turkey enters an electoral period, a firm and unwavering fiscal policy is essential to preserve confidence.

Structural reforms should strengthen job creation and productivity in the formal sector

Additional real exchange rate appreciation is likely in the period ahead. New structural reforms to reduce employment costs in the formal sector would help contain this pressure. In particular, the regional differentiation of minimum wages would support job creation and the development of more productive and innovative formal businesses.

There are risks to growth on both sides

GDP is set to exceed 8% in 2010 before moderating to around 5% in 2011 and 2012 as the rebound of exports, consumption and investment tapers off. However, Turkey's business cycle is highly sensitive to the external environment and to export performance, and there are risks on both sides. If competitiveness and job creation improve, investment and growth may turn out even stronger. If, on the contrary, macroeconomic uncertainties arise in the electoral cycle, or if the international competitiveness of the business sector falters, the expansion may be weaker.

Chapter 3

DEVELOPMENTS IN SELECTED NON-MEMBER ECONOMIES

BRAZIL

The Brazilian economy has slowed markedly from the strong growth rates seen earlier in the year. It is expected to rebound, however, as income gains and resilient credit expansion sustain private consumption. Massive infrastructure projects should help lift growth rates anew in the coming years. Inflation is projected to hover above the target mid-point of 4.5% over the next two years, as labour markets remain tight and the price effects of the recent significant currency appreciation dissipate.

The central bank has stopped the monetary tightening cycle initiated in the spring and has intervened to prevent further strengthening of the real. The remaining monetary stimulus injected during the global crisis should now be rapidly withdrawn to damp rising inflationary pressures. Public consumption swelled ahead of the presidential election. Given the country's position in the business cycle, fiscal stimulus should be withdrawn as soon as possible. Improved predictability of fiscal arrangements would also be helpful.

Activity has temporarily slowed

Economic growth has been decelerating since the second quarter of the year, reflecting the withdrawal of some fiscal stimulus and monetary tightening. Domestic demand has been the main engine of growth, while export volumes have continued to grow at only a weak pace, partly due to the effective appreciation of the real. Short-term indicators are mixed. On the supply side, output and new orders in the manufacturing sector suggest further weakness in the second half of the year, despite robust growth in capital goods output. At the same time, formal employment has been growing rapidly, particularly in the construction sector, and the unemployment rate has continued to fall. Credit growth and confidence remain resilient, which, together with increases in job creation and real wages resulting in part from sizable gains in the terms of trade, should support consumption.

Brazil

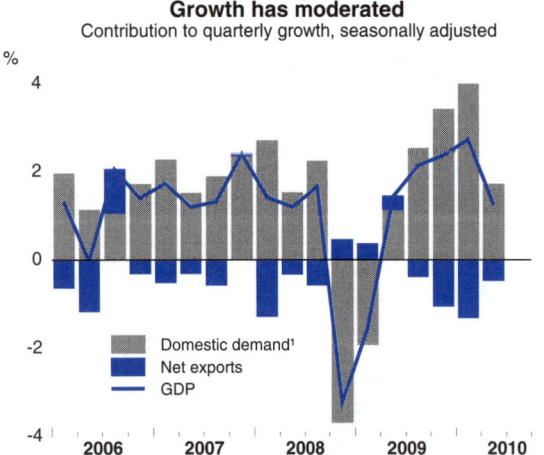

Growth has moderated
Contribution to quarterly growth, seasonally adjusted

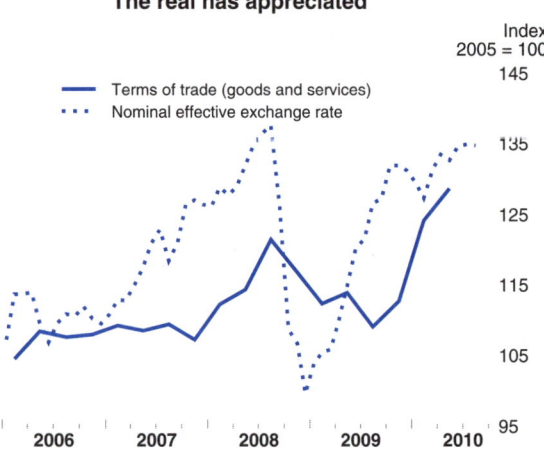

The real has appreciated

1. Includes stockbuilding and statistical discrepancy.
Source: Central Bank of Brazil, IBGE and FUNCEX.

StatLink http://dx.doi.org/10.1787/888932346192

Brazil: **Macroeconomic indicators**

	2008	2009	2010	2011	2012
Real GDP growth	5.1	-0.2	7.5	4.3	5.0
Inflation (CPI)	5.9	4.3	5.6	5.3	5.1
Fiscal balance (per cent of GDP)[1]	-1.9	-3.3	-0.9	-0.5	-0.4
Primary fiscal balance (per cent of GDP)[1]	3.5	2.1	3.3	3.1	2.7
Current account balance (per cent of GDP)	-1.7	-1.5	-2.6	-3.2	-4.0

Note: Real GDP growth and inflation are defined in percentage change from the previous period.
1. Takes into account a capital injection (0.5% of GDP) in the Brazilian Sovereign Wealth Fund in 2008, which
    was treated as expenditure, and excludes Petrobras from the government accounts.
Source: OECD Economic Outlook 88 database.

StatLink 🔗 *http://dx.doi.org/10.1787/888932347940*

***Massive capital inflows
have strengthened the real***

The recent capitalisation programme of the state-owned oil company, *Petrobras*, estimated at around USD 67 billion, attracted considerable foreign capital. This has put upward pressure on the exchange rate but also helped to finance the widening current account deficit, which has been driven by significantly stronger growth in Brazil than elsewhere. Looking ahead, capital inflows may increase the exposure of the economy to volatile short-term investments and to changes in global risk appetites. On the debt front, total external liabilities (at 11.9% of GDP in June) have remained broadly stable since the beginning of the year, but the share of short-term borrowing has increased significantly. The authorities have intervened several times since mid-September to remove the excess liquidity resulting from the *Petrobras* capitalisation programme and smooth its impact on the currency. Foreign-exchange reserves have therefore been rising, reaching USD 276 billion in September. The tax rate on foreign fixed-income investments has been raised twice to 6% to curb short-term capital inflows. Interventions and

Brazil

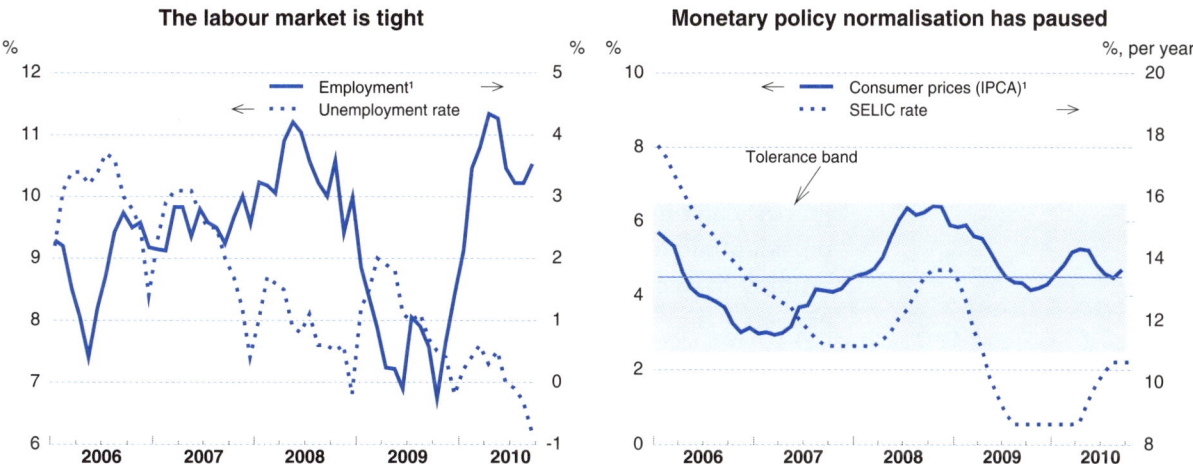

1. Year-on-year growth.
Source: Central Bank of Brazil and IBGE.

StatLink 🔗 *http://dx.doi.org/10.1787/888932346211*

Brazil: **External indicators**

	2008	2009	2010	2011	2012
	\$ billion				
Goods and services exports	227.1	178.2	236.7	291	332
Goods and services imports	224.1	180.2	258.7	329	398
Foreign balance	3.1	- 2.0	- 22.0	- 38	- 66
Invisibles, net	- 31.3	- 22.3	- 30.7	- 38	- 41
Current account balance	- 28.2	- 24.3	- 52.7	- 76	- 107
	Percentage changes				
Goods and services export volumes	- 0.8	- 10.3	7.2	3.1	8.0
Goods and services import volumes	18.0	- 11.5	33.7	11.5	14.7
Terms of trade	6.9	- 3.3	14.9	4.4	0.2

Source: OECD Economic Outlook 88 database.

StatLink http://dx.doi.org/10.1787/888932347959

taxing capital inflows to limit the currency appreciation may prove ineffective and costly in the context of a rise in the real equilibrium exchange rate due to the oil discoveries.

Monetary policy has been put on hold

The central bank has maintained its policy rate at 10.75% since June 2010, in a context of rising global uncertainties, its lower estimate of the neutral policy interest rate and a substantial rise in the real. The deceleration in economic activity, declines in food prices and the significant appreciation of the currency have helped to contain inflation. But these effects are expected to be short-lived, especially as rising food prices may push up headline inflation and the damping effect of the exchange-rate rise will dissipate. Inflation expectations have edged up above the central bank's target range mid-point. Capacity utilisation in the manufacturing industry has remained above its long-term average. Trend labour productivity growth has been declining, and the low unemployment rate has started to exert upward pressure on wages. Monetary tightening should resume as soon as possible to quell mounting inflationary pressures.

Budget targets have slipped

Despite stronger tax collection, the fiscal surplus was lower than initially envisaged for the first eight months of 2010, as public spending (in particular investment in infrastructure) surged ahead of the October presidential election. The central government cut the January-August primary-balance target by BRL 10 billion from 40 billion, and it is widely expected that the end-year target will be missed, unless accounting adjustments are made.

Fiscal stimulus should be entirely withdrawn

The projection assumes a somewhat slower pace of infrastructure investment spending than the BRL 960 billion (around 40% of GDP) announced by the government for the period 2011-14 during the second phase of the Growth Acceleration Programme (PAC). Although PAC disbursements have accelerated lately, bottlenecks confronting capital spending are still likely to slow programme execution. It is expected that the government will miss its BRL 125 billion target for the primary balance in 2011 and 2012, but some of the resources used to finance infrastructure programmes will be excluded from the primary balance, as is legislatively possible. In this regard, improving the predictability of the government's decisions with regard to adjustments to the primary balance would raise the credibility of the commitment to achieve fiscal targets. In addition, as recurrent spending is likely to weigh on public finances in the long run, the authorities need to withdraw discretionary stimulus introduced in response to the global downturn. Doing so would also ease inflationary pressures, which would otherwise require additional interest rate hikes.

Activity is expected to bounce back soon

The slowdown in activity is projected to be temporary. Domestic demand is set to rebound by year-end, as improving labour and credit-market conditions spur private consumption. A recovery in investment should be supported by improving growth prospects, sustained credit growth, increased capacity utilisation and large public infrastructure and energy development projects. Inflation could diminish slightly but is likely to remain above the mid-point of the target range. The current account deficit is expected to gradually widen due to the strength in domestic demand, and the deficit could reach almost 4% of GDP in 2012.

The main risks to the outlook are external

The Brazilian economy remains vulnerable to slower growth in China and in OECD countries and to shifts in global risk appetites. Inflation could also prove to be higher than expected, especially if the currency is prevented from appreciating and commodity prices continue to rise. In such a scenario tighter stabilisation policies would be required to ensure that inflation expectations remain anchored. Also putting pressure on inflation, while boosting demand, spending on infrastructure projects could be faster than envisaged. A continuous fall in the unemployment rate could boost labour income and offset the effect of monetary tightening on private consumption.

CHINA

With the impact of the stimulus plan fading, China's vigorous expansion slowed during the first half of 2010, but has picked up somewhat since then. This renewed buoyancy is projected to continue in 2011-12, as faster domestic demand offsets a renewed slowdown in exports, stabilising the current account surplus at around 5½ per cent of GDP. An acceleration in non-food prices is expected to be offset by an easing in food price inflation, resulting in a stabilisation of inflation at slightly above 3%.

Although the current account surplus is not projected to increase, further external adjustment will not be aided by the weakening of the effective exchange rate that has occurred despite a modest appreciation of the renminbi against the dollar in recent months. The stability of the domestic economy would be enhanced if exchange rate policy were more oriented to allowing an appreciation against a basket of currencies. In addition, government spending should continue to be reoriented to social objectives.

The impact of the stimulus has faded...

After a very strong expansion during 2009, GDP growth eased in the first half of 2010. Infrastructure spending under the government's stimulus plan levelled off and residential investment slowed as the impact of government measures designed to restrict the flow of credit to households became effective. In addition, the excessive level of stocks that had accumulated in early 2009 continued to be reduced, notably in the steel industry. In contrast, private business capital outlays remained buoyant and foreign enterprise investment recovered in tandem with exports. The total wage bill picked up markedly and household demand remained strong. Moreover, retail sales continued to grow faster than incomes.

... but growth may have bottomed out

Export growth slackened in the course of 2010, to around 18% by the third quarter – near the average of the previous decade. Import growth declined even more through the second quarter, particularly for a number of commodities, but gathered strength in the third quarter, driven by a

China

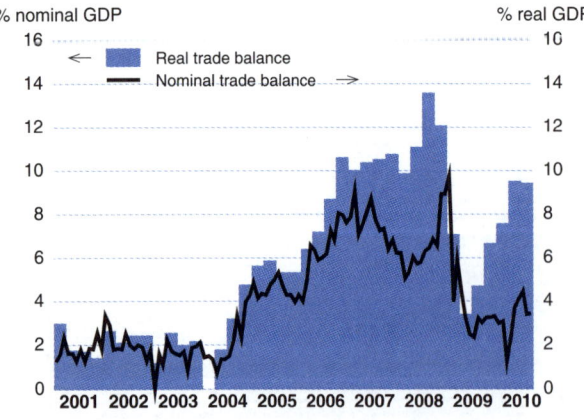

The trade surplus has been reduced by higher import prices

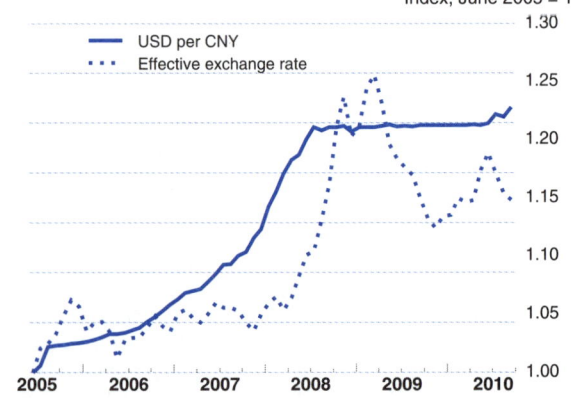

The effective exchange rate has weakened again

Source: CEIC.

StatLink http://dx.doi.org/10.1787/888932346154

China: **Macroeconomic indicators**

	2008	2009	2010	2011	2012
Real GDP growth	9.6	9.1	10.5	9.7	9.7
GDP deflator (per cent change)	7.8	-0.6	5.0	3.7	3.0
Consumer price index (per cent change)	5.9	-0.7	3.1	3.3	3.0
Fiscal balance (per cent of GDP)[1]	0.9	-1.2	-1.9	-2.2	-2.1
Current account balance (per cent of GDP)	9.6	6.0	5.8	5.9	5.5

Note: The figures given for GDP are percentage changes from the previous year.
1. Consolidated budget, social security and extra-budgetary accounts on a national accounts basis.
Source: OECD Economic Outlook 88 database.

StatLink ᵐˢᵖ *http://dx.doi.org/10.1787/888932347902*

pick-up in domestic demand. The current account surplus is estimated to have widened, but only marginally, to just over 6% of GDP in the third quarter, with two factors limiting its rise. One was a deterioration in the terms of trade, which remained below 2009 levels in the third quarter, as a result of higher prices for primary products, notably for metals and minerals. The other was the low growth of investment income, which was held back both by low global interest rates and a slowdown in the growth of China's foreign exchange reserves, which nonetheless reached $2.65 trillion by September 2010.

Government budget deficits remain low... The official national government budget continued to be managed conservatively during 2010. The deficit is set to reach around 3% of GDP

China

Retail sales continue to grow faster than the urban wage bill

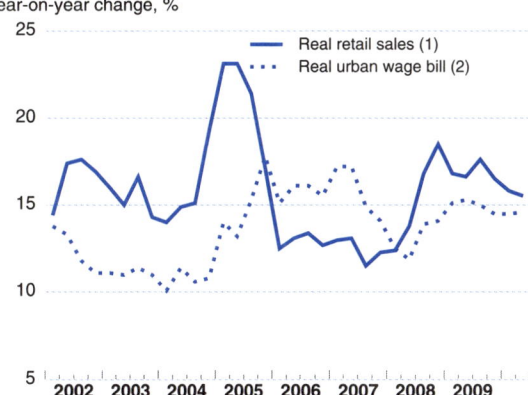

Off-budget infrastructure investment remains strong

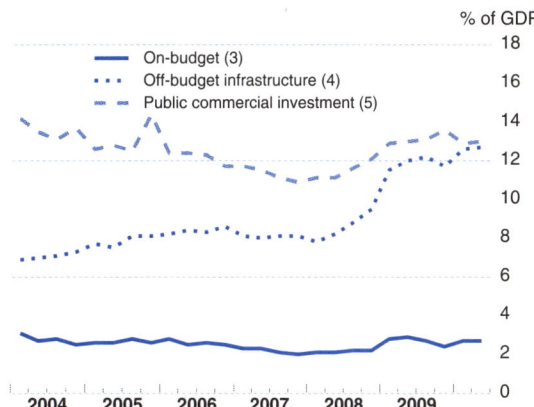

1. Retail sales have been deflated by the Retail Price Index. The data covers sales in urban areas from 2009 and sales in cities for prior years.
2. The urban wage bill has been deflated by the Consumer Price Index.
3. On-budget public investment is defined as investment in the education, health and public administration sectors.
4. Off-budget public infrastructure investment is defined as investment in public transport, highways and environmental services.
5. Public commercial investment is defined as total investment by state-held corporations less off-budget public investment.
Source: CEIC.

StatLink ᵐˢᵖ *http://dx.doi.org/10.1787/888932346173*

China: **External indicators**

	2008	2009	2010	2011	2012
	\$ billion				
Goods and services exports	1 581.7	1 333.3	1 767.9	2 087	2 388
Goods and services imports	1 232.8	1 113.2	1 518.4	1 789	2 073
Foreign balance	348.9	220.1	249.5	297	315
Net investment income and transfers	87.2	77.0	90.6	99	105
Current account balance	436.1	297.2	340.1	396	421
	Percentage changes				
Goods and services export volumes	8.5	- 10.2	30.2	13.2	12.0
Goods and services import volumes	3.9	4.6	20.6	13.9	14.9
Export performance[1]	4.9	2.7	15.8	4.0	3.5
Terms of trade	- 5.4	8.8	- 10.0	0.8	1.4

1. Ratio between export volume and export market of total goods and services.
Source: OECD Economic Outlook 88 database.

StatLink http://dx.doi.org/10.1787/888932347921

in 2010. National government expenditure rose by about two percentage points of GDP in the year to September, with some reorientation toward social outlays, notably on health care. The revenue share has risen somewhat less, though corporate tax intakes have been particularly buoyant due to the strong expansion of business profits. In addition, the social security system likely continued to run a surplus of 1% of GDP in 2010, as improved compliance of employers in paying contributions offset a further rise in medical insurance outlays due to expanding coverage in rural areas. Overall, the 2010 government deficit is therefore projected at about 2% of GDP. Given the relatively limited amount of liabilities issued by central and local governments, gross government debt is projected to stabilise at 19½ per cent of GDP. Continued accumulation of cash by the social security system will mean that the combined accounts of the national government and the social security system will show net financial assets of around 3½ per cent of GDP at the end of 2010.

... but some infrastructure outlays may eventually have to be budgetised

The official government spending figures belie the full extent of the increase in expenditure and debt engendered by the stimulus programme launched two years ago. Nearly all of it was undertaken either by public corporations, such as those that operate railways and mass transit systems, or by development corporations established by local governments but not consolidated into their financial accounts. In the two years since the launch of the stimulus in November 2008, public infrastructure spending has risen by nearly 4 percentage points of GDP. Borrowing by local development corporations has been even greater, bringing the debt of these vehicles to nearly 22% of GDP. Overall, the borrowing of local financing entities amounted to almost one-fifth of total outstanding bank loans in mid-2010. The bank regulator estimates that about one quarter of this amount may have served to finance projects of limited financial viability and consequently banks were asked to limit lending to such vehicles.

Monetary conditions are mixed but generally supportive

Since mid-year, monetary conditions broadly defined have been mixed but generally remain supportive. After three hikes in the banks' reserve ratio between January and May, monetary growth slackened markedly in the second quarter of the year, but this tendency was reversed in the third quarter with a marked surge in money growth and continued high growth of lending, which led to a temporary and selective hike in the reserve ratio in mid-October. This was followed by a 25 basis point hike in benchmark one-year lending and deposit rates. The effective exchange rate depreciated by 6% between the first week of June and mid-October, despite the decision of the authorities to allow the currency to appreciate against the US dollar and the subsequent 2½ per cent appreciation of the bilateral dollar exchange rate. After a weak spell in the first half of the year, equity prices rose 11% in the third quarter. In contrast, real estate prices have shown little movement since regulations concerning property lending were tightened in April.

The outlook is for continued strong growth

Growth is projected to pick up with the likely turn in the inventory cycle and to reach an annual rate of 10% in the fourth quarter, bringing the annual average to 10.5% for 2010. Further out, growth in public investment is projected to stabilise. Although the stimulus plan is coming to an end, other initiatives are taking the baton, notably a social housing programme, an effort to improve health care facilities and the launch of the new Five-Year Plan, which is likely to emphasise rapid urbanisation. Private consumption demand is set to remain strong, with buoyant real incomes as labour markets tighten. Overall, domestic demand should accelerate in the projection period, while export growth moderates as the expansion of world trade eases back to trend. As a result, GDP growth in 2011-12 is projected to average 9¾ per cent. With strong import prices, core inflation may pick up, offsetting a likely decline in food price inflation, resulting in inflation stabilising slightly above 3%. Stronger domestic demand may lead to a slight decline in the current account surplus.

Risks are balanced

Two major downside risks are present. First, the quality of bank balance sheets may deteriorate if property prices fall further, thereby straining property developers and worsening the prospects for timely repayment of some local authority debt. Second, continued weakness of the currency and strength of commodity prices could generate higher inflation. On the other hand, the continued move of industry inland could boost private investment more than expected and higher world commodity prices could also indicate that domestic investment demand is increasing faster than expected.

INDIA

The Indian economy expanded very strongly in early 2010. The agricultural sector enjoyed a sharp rebound, following a return of normal rainfall patterns, while the recovery in the non-agricultural sector continued to strengthen. More recently, activity has eased from its unusually strong pace and there are now signs that the economy is shifting from the recovery phase to one of sustained high growth. As fiscal stimulus continues to be withdrawn, a pick-up in consumption spending, aided by a recovery in farm incomes, and robust business investment are expected to be the mainstays of growth.

The recovery in the agricultural sector has helped to damp inflation, which appears to have peaked and is expected to continue to moderate in the near term. Nevertheless, with domestic demand strong and the current account deficit widening, a steadfast commitment to timely fiscal consolidation and further moves to normalise the stance of monetary policy will be important for ensuring balanced growth ahead.

Growth has strengthened and become more broad-based

Growth in the non-agricultural sector continued to strengthen into early 2010, buoyed by strong business sentiment and supported by an accommodative monetary policy stance and ongoing fiscal stimulus. At the same time, good winter rains underpinned a sharp recovery in agriculture, providing an additional boost to aggregate growth. More recently, growth has eased as agricultural production has returned to a more normal pattern of expansion and some unwinding of very rapid growth in business investment has occurred. With domestic demand strong in the first half of the year, the trade deficit widened. So did the current account deficit, which was financed by strong inflows of loans as well as direct and portfolio investment.

Inflation may have peaked

High inflation, caused largely by soaring food prices, has been a major source of concern, but is showing signs of moderation, aided by the recovery in the agricultural sector. In September, inflation measured by

India

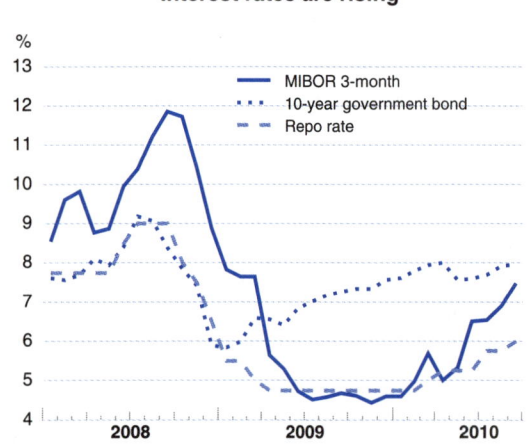

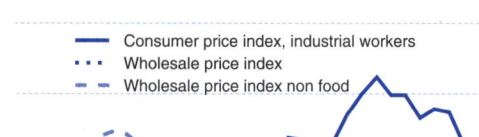

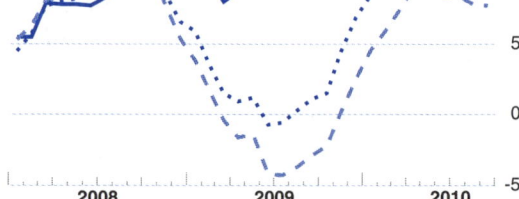

Source: CEIC.

StatLink http://dx.doi.org/10.1787/888932346268

India: **Macroeconomic indicators**

	2008	2009	2010	2011	2012
Real GDP growth[1]	5.1	7.7	9.1	8.2	8.5
Inflation[2]	7.2	3.7	11.3	5.8	5.1
Consumer price index[3]	9.1	12.4	9.1	5.8	5.2
Wholesale price index (WPI)[4]	8.0	3.6	8.1	5.7	5.5
Short-term interest rate[5]	9.6	4.9	6.7	7.6	7.6
Long-term interest rate[6]	7.6	7.3	7.8	7.9	7.9
Fiscal balance (per cent of GDP)[7]	-8.5	-9.6	-8.3	-7.4	-6.7
Current account balance (per cent of GDP)	-2.4	-2.8	-3.2	-3.0	-2.9
Memorandum: calendar year basis					
Real GDP growth	6.3	5.8	9.9	8.0	8.5
Fiscal balance (per cent of GDP)[7]	-7.0	-10.2	-8.3	-7.6	-6.8

Note: Data refer to fiscal years starting in April.
1. GDP measured at market prices.
2. Percentage change in GDP deflator.
3. Percentage change in the industrial workers index.
4. Percentage change in the all commodities index.
5. Mumbai three-month offered rate.
6. 10-year government bond.
7. Gross fiscal balance for central and state governments.
Source: OECD Economic Outlook 88 database.

StatLink 🔗 *http://dx.doi.org/10.1787/888932348016*

the newly weighted wholesale price index was 8.6% year-on-year, down from a peak of 11% in May. Consumer price inflation has also fallen in recent months, to 9.8% year-on-year in September from a peak of over 16% earlier in the year. Recently, food prices have generally shown little month-to-month variation, despite disruptions to food supply chains caused by heavy rainfall and flooding in some states. Some moderation in food prices is likely through the remainder of the year, damping headline

India

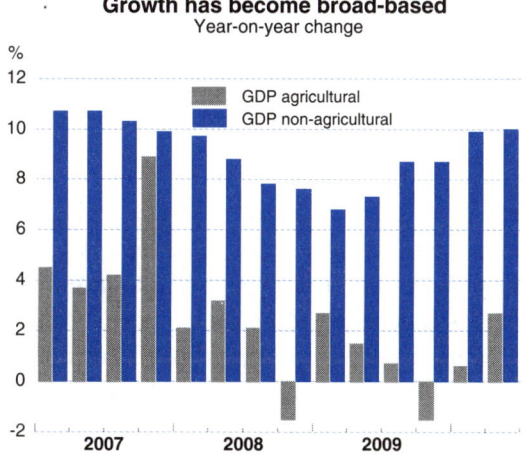

Growth has become broad-based
Year-on-year change

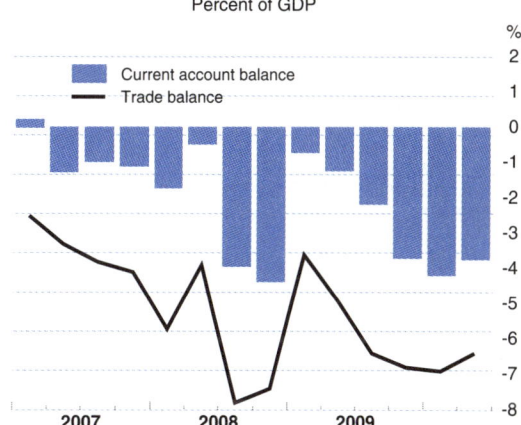

The current account deficit has widened
Percent of GDP

Source: CEIC.

StatLink 🔗 *http://dx.doi.org/10.1787/888932346287*

India: **External indicators**

	2008	2009	2010	2011	2012
	\$ billion				
Goods and services exports	289.1	275.5	341.2	413	491
Goods and services imports	365.3	336.0	435.4	523	620
Foreign balance	- 76.1	- 60.5	- 94.2	- 110	- 129
Net investment income and transfers	47.4	22.1	41.9	54	66
Current account balance	- 28.7	- 38.4	- 52.2	- 56	- 63
	Percentage changes				
Goods and services export volumes	18.0	- 5.6	3.3	14.8	13.6
Goods and services import volumes	22.9	- 9.0	9.1	13.9	13.0
Export performance[1]	22.0	- 3.2	- 9.0	5.2	3.5

Note: Data refer to fiscal years starting in April.
1. Ratio between export volume and export market of total goods and services.
Source: OECD Economic Outlook 88 database.

StatLink http://dx.doi.org/10.1787/888932348035

inflation. However, non-food inflation remains somewhat elevated, in part reflecting higher fuel prices.

Near-term fiscal consolidation remains on track

The budget passed earlier in the year planned for a decline in the central government deficit to around 5.5% of GDP in the current fiscal year, with some state governments also forecasting modest fiscal consolidation. Tax revenues have been buoyant so far this year and this target is on course to be met. The central government successfully completed planned auctions of mobile and broadband spectrum to private telecommunications companies, raising close to three times the projected receipts, but parliament approved government requests for extra-budgetary spending approximately equal to the revenue surprise. Beyond this year, the government has agreed to abide by the main recommendations of the Thirteenth Finance Commission, which provide a sound roadmap for medium-term fiscal consolidation. With strong, broad-based growth set to continue to underpin buoyant revenue intakes, the OECD projection assumes a total reduction in the deficit in the order of 1½ per cent of GDP over 2011 and 2012. Ideally, savings should focus on a greater rationalisation of expenditures, especially fertilizer and fuel subsidies.

Interbank interest rates have risen sharply

The process of monetary policy normalisation has continued in recent months with the Reserve Bank of India lifting the repo rate in 25-basis-point steps to 6.25% by November, bringing the total cumulative increase since emergency measures began to be unwound in March to 150 basis points. Market rates have risen even more briskly, with the 3-month interbank rate rising above 7%, close to its long-term average. This spread between official and market rates is likely to reflect tighter liquidity conditions due to strong credit demand from the public and private sectors. Given the strong growth momentum and the likely negligible spare capacity in the economy, additional incremental tightening seems to be warranted.

Growth should converge to trend soon

Normal monsoon rainfall this year will consolidate the recovery in the agricultural sector. With the non-agricultural sector now having expanded strongly for the past year, the economy is set to shift out of the recovery phase with growth expected to converge to a trend rate of around 8½ per cent in the coming quarters. Growth will continue to be supported by strong investment and consumption spending which, in the near term and in rural areas in particular, will be bolstered by the recovery in agricultural production and farm incomes.

The current account deficit is expected to narrow

As domestic demand growth eases and exports continue to benefit from an improved external environment, the trade deficit is expected to narrow. Strengthening economic conditions in OECD countries in particular are expected to support continued solid growth in net capital transfers and factor income receipts. Together, these factors will lead to a gradual narrowing of the current account deficit over the projection period. Nevertheless, the near-term deficit will remain relatively high by historical standards, but smooth financing should be ensured by strong capital inflows supported by high interest rates, improving conditions in global capital markets and good medium-term prospects for the Indian economy.

Sound macroeconomic policy settings will be key to balanced growth

The recovery in the agriculture sector and recent signs of a sharp moderation in inflation have all but eliminated the risk of an immediate inflation spiral, which would have demanded a strong monetary policy response. Nevertheless, managing the upswing in the cycle will present a challenge and it will be important to ensure that medium-term fiscal consolidation plans are implemented in order to reduce pressure in credit markets and promote balanced growth. This is particularly so given that the deficit will still be relatively high even if the target for the current fiscal year is met. The possibility of sharply higher international commodity prices, especially for energy-related products, presents a risk to stability. So too does the prospect of disproportionately large and volatile short-term capital flows attracted by relatively favourable economic and financial conditions.

RUSSIAN FEDERATION

The post-crisis economic recovery has been solid but unspectacular, and growth over the projection horizon of 4-4½ per cent is expected to reduce the degree of slack in the economy, with the output gap closing in 2012. Inflation has been pushed higher by a food price shock, but underlying pressures are likely to remain contained. The current account surplus is projected to roughly halve between 2010 and 2012 as import volume growth outstrips that of exports by a large margin. Public expenditure restraint is expected to shrink the budget deficit to near zero by 2012, with public debt levels remaining low.

The planned cut in real public spending will restrain domestic demand growth but is appropriate. As long as the food price spike, resulting from the effects of extreme weather in the summer, does not give rise to second-round effects, monetary policy can remain accommodative until the output gap has narrowed further. As the recession fades into the past and as economic slack dissipates, structural policy reforms to raise potential growth rates should be given renewed prominence. To that end, fiscal consolidation should focus on eliminating subsidies extended in the context of anti-crisis measures.

The recovery stuttered in the third quarter

Since output growth resumed in the third quarter of 2009, the recovery has been reasonably strong, albeit slowing, with annualised output growth easing from an average of 6.9% in the last two quarters of 2009 to 3.8% in the first two quarters of 2010. The recovery was initially export-led, consumption followed and investment made a sizable positive contribution to growth for the first time in the second quarter of 2010. The heat wave and wildfires which struck in July-August dented the momentum of real GDP growth *via* lost agricultural output and shutdowns of firms in areas affected by the heat and smog. Most leading and coincident indicators point to stagnation or worse in the third quarter. Despite the slowdown, however, sentiment indicators generally show continued improvement since the crisis, and credit growth has been

Russian Federation

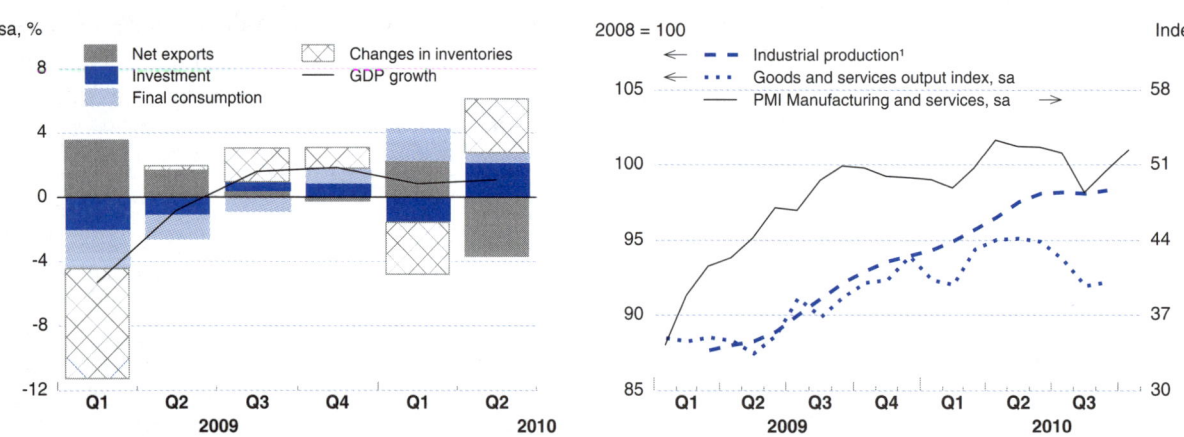

Domestic demand is increasingly driving the recovery
Contributions to growth over previous period

The recovery slowed in the third quarter

1. Seasonally and working-day adjusted, 3-month moving average.

Source: OECD calculations based on OECD Quarterly National Accounts database and Markit.

StatLink http://dx.doi.org/10.1787/888932346230

Russian Federation: **Macroeconomic indicators**

	2008	2009	2010	2011	2012
Real GDP growth	5.2	-7.9	3.7	4.2	4.5
Inflation (CPI), period average	14.1	11.7	6.8	7.7	6.0
Fiscal balance (per cent of GDP)[1]	5.7	-5.3	-2.7	-2.0	-0.9
Current account balance (per cent of GDP)	6.1	3.9	5.7	3.6	2.7

1. Consolidated budget.
Source: OECD Economic Outlook 88 database.

StatLink http://dx.doi.org/10.1787/888932347978

picking up markedly, spurred by a large and sustained reduction in interest rates.

Slack in the economy helped to bring down inflation

The 11% fall in output during the recession of 2008-09 opened a negative output gap that remains sizeable, notwithstanding the recovery to date. Employment in August 2010 was still nearly 2% below its pre-crisis level and the unemployment rate stood at 7%, up from 5.8% in August 2008. The output gap, combined with a strong rouble, helped to produce a large decline in consumer price inflation from early 2009 through mid-2010. Inflation reached a post-Soviet-era low of 5.5% in July, but the damage to Russian grain harvests from the summer heat wave and fires has led to an upsurge in food prices, which have a high weight in the consumer price index.

Russian Federation

Lower interest rates have revived bank lending growth

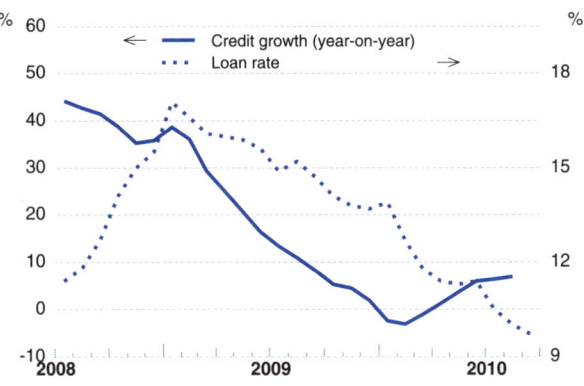

A surge in food prices has reversed the decline in inflation
Contributions to CPI growth over same period previous year

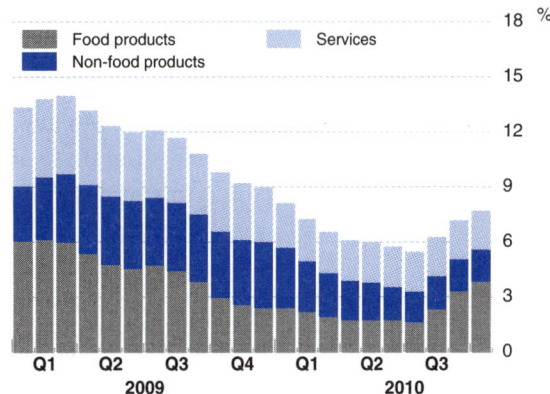

Source: OECD calculations based on Russian Federal Service For State Statistics and Central Bank of Russia.

StatLink http://dx.doi.org/10.1787/888932346249

Russian Federation: **External indicators**

	2008	2009	2010	2011	2012
	\$ billion				
Goods and services exports	522.9	343.7	445.4	477	504
Goods and services imports	367.7	251.4	312.7	366	402
Foreign balance	155.1	92.4	132.7	111	103
Invisibles, net	- 52.8	- 43.4	- 48.7	- 52	- 54
Current account balance	102.4	49.0	84.0	59	49
	Percentage changes				
Goods and services export volumes	0.6	- 4.7	5.1	4.0	5.4
Goods and services import volumes	14.8	- 30.4	14.5	13.9	9.0
Terms of trade	15.6	- 29.9	13.9	0.3	- 0.3

Source: OECD Economic Outlook 88 database.

StatLink ⟨⟨ *http://dx.doi.org/10.1787/888932347997*

Positive growth momentum is likely to reassert itself

Despite the slowdown in growth in the first half of 2010 and the negative shock from the summer heat wave, underlying growth momentum appears to be robust, sustained by easier credit conditions, high oil and gas prices, improving confidence, rising real wages and falling unemployment. Also, from the onset of the recession in the third quarter of 2008 through the second quarter of 2010 inventories had declined by more than 3 percentage points of GDP, leaving scope for a near-term boost to growth from restocking.

Monetary policy will be the key to maintaining macroeconomic balance

After a major expansion of public expenditure in 2009 to support domestic demand, the government is planning to cut spending in real terms in both 2011 and 2012, on top of a small real decline in 2010. This fiscal consolidation is intended to safeguard fiscal sustainability and reduce the vulnerability of the public finances to swings in oil prices by providing a stronger starting position in the event of a negative oil price shock. Monetary policy will therefore be the main instrument for steering economic activity towards its potential level. With a still-substantial output gap and growth having been only around potential on average in the first three quarters of 2010, there appears to be scope for interest rates to stay low well into 2011, so long as the food-price-induced pick-up in consumer price inflation resulting from the heat and fire damage to grain harvests fades as expected. As the recovery continues and the output gap narrows, monetary policy can be progressively tightened. Among the many structural policy measures that could improve potential output growth over the longer term, scaling back the subsidies extended as an anti-crisis measure is among the most pressing. Completion of the long process of WTO accession would also bring significant long-term growth benefits.

Growth should be sufficient to eliminate the output gap in 2012

Output growth is projected to rebound after the weather-affected third quarter, remaining at a pace slightly above the potential growth rate from the final quarter of 2010 through 2012, with domestic demand leading the way. The output gap is projected to disappear towards the end of the projection horizon. Import volume growth is projected to remain brisk in 2011 and 2012, reflecting Russia's high income elasticity of imports, the real appreciation of the rouble since early 2009 and the scope for a continued rebound from the huge decline during the crisis: the volume of imports of goods and services in the second quarter of 2010 was still some 25% below its pre-crisis highs. Export volumes are constrained by capacity in oil and gas (which account for about two thirds of total exports), and should therefore grow at a more moderate pace, close to that of real GDP. As a result, the current account surplus will shrink in 2011 and 2012 unless export prices rise strongly – the projections are based on unchanged oil prices.

The recent upturn in inflation is expected to prove to be temporary

Notwithstanding the food-price-driven upturn in inflation that began in August 2010, price pressures are expected to be moderate over the next two years. Annual average inflation is likely to be below 7% in 2010, the lowest rate recorded in the post-Soviet era, although the year-on-year rate is projected to rise from the July low of 5.5% to about 8% by December. Once the effect of the food price shock has fallen out of the year-on-year comparisons, inflation is projected to settle back to around 6% in the second half of 2011 and 2012.

The Russian economy is sensitive to changes in the external environment

A stronger-than-expected global economic recovery that raised commodity prices would fuel stronger domestic demand in Russia, particularly as it would be likely to be accompanied by private capital inflows. In such an event the output gap would close more quickly and inflation and interest rates would be higher, while there would be a revenue windfall for the budget, narrowing the budget deficit more quickly. The government estimates that each 10 dollar-per-barrel move in oil prices affects annual real GDP growth in the short term by about half a percentage point, which suggests that a return to oil prices in excess of $100 a barrel would be associated with growth of over 5%. Of course the vulnerability of growth to a large decline in oil prices, for example associated with a weaker-than-expected global recovery, remains considerable.

ESTONIA

Rebalancing of the economy continues in 2010, with consumption still weak while exports grow strongly. This pattern will also shape the recovery in 2011, while 2012 should see a return of robust growth in consumer spending. GDP growth is projected at 3.4% in 2011 and about 4% in 2012. Headline inflation accelerated in the second half of 2010, driven by food and energy prices and recovering mark-ups, and is expected to be about 3.4% in 2011. Constrained by high unemployment and ongoing slack in the economy, core inflation will pick up only gradually.

Fiscal policy remains under tight control and the general government deficit is assumed to stay below the 3% of GDP threshold. In order to prevent fiscal policy becoming pro-cyclical in the upswing, multi-year expenditure ceilings that take into account the cyclical position of the economy should be introduced.

Exports turned the economy around

Following a severe recession, real GDP recorded four consecutive quarters of positive growth to the third quarter of 2010, driven by exports. Manufacturing production has picked up strongly. Retail trade has recently bottomed out, but deleveraging of households and high unemployment will weigh on consumption for some time.

Unemployment has peaked but is very high

Recent labour market developments reveal some signs of improvement. Employment started to grow again in the second quarter of 2010 and the unemployment rate has fallen from its record high level near 20%. Wages have stopped falling and companies have improved profitability. Participation in active labour market programmes (ALMPs) and retraining have recently risen. However the risk of an increase in structural unemployment is high, especially because construction activity and employment opportunities will remain depressed for some time

Estonia

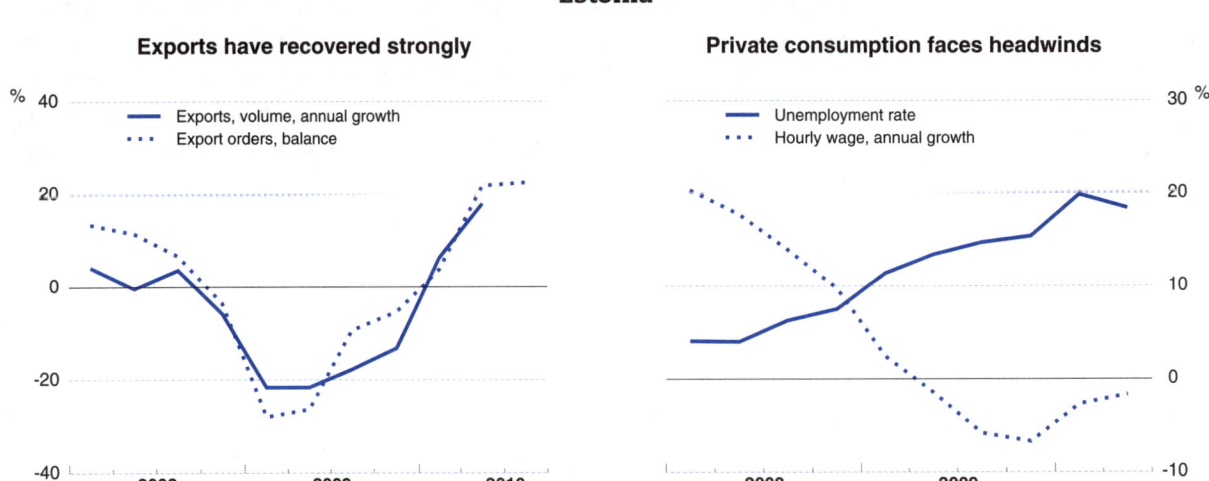

Note: Wages are average hourly gross nominal wages of full-time employees.

Source: European Commission; OECD Economic Outlook 88 database; OECD, National Accounts database; Statistics Estonia.

StatLink ⟨⟩ *http://dx.doi.org/10.1787/888932346306*

Estonia: **Demand, output and prices**

	2007	2008	2009	2010	2011	2012
	Current prices EEK billion	Percentage changes, volume (2000 prices)				
Private consumption	135.4	-5.4	-18.4	-1.6	1.8	4.3
Government consumption	41.4	3.8	0.0	-1.7	1.3	1.5
Gross fixed capital formation	85.3	-15.0	-32.9	-12.7	6.1	11.2
Final domestic demand	262.1	-7.1	-19.0	-4.1	2.5	5.1
Stockbuilding[1]	11.7	-4.1	-3.4	3.8	0.0	-0.1
Total domestic demand	273.8	-10.5	-22.1	-0.1	2.5	4.9
Exports of goods and services	167.3	0.4	-18.7	16.2	10.0	8.1
Imports of goods and services	193.5	-7.0	-32.6	17.5	10.1	9.4
Net exports[1]	- 26.1	5.7	11.3	0.2	0.6	-0.5
GDP at market prices	247.6	-5.1	-13.9	2.4	3.4	4.1
GDP deflator	_	7.2	-0.1	-0.7	1.8	2.0
Memorandum items						
Index of consumer prices	_	10.4	-0.1	3.0	3.4	2.5
Private consumption deflator	_	8.7	-0.9	2.9	3.3	2.5
General government financial balance[2]	_	-2.9	-1.8	-1.2	-1.9	-2.4

Note: National accounts are based on official chain-linked data. This introduces a discrepancy in the identity between real demand components and GDP. For further details see *OECD Economic Outlook* Sources and Methods (*http://www.oecd.org/eco/sources-and-methods*).
1. Contributions to changes in real GDP (percentage of real GDP in previous year), actual amount in the first column.
2. As a percentage of GDP.
Source: OECD Economic Outlook 88 database.

StatLink ⬛ *http://dx.doi.org/10.1787/888932348054*

Recent inflation developments are worrying

Inflation rose to 4% year-on-year in September 2010, despite significant slack in the economy. Some of this unwelcome hit to already weak purchasing power is due to past increases in indirect taxes and regulated prices and a more recent pick-up in food and energy prices. However, a considerable part remains unexplained and points to a lack of competition. Preparations for introducing the euro on 1 January 2011 are under way. Nevertheless, the recent inflation surprise should be a warning signal that extra vigilance may be required to prevent unwarranted price increases during the changeover.

Fiscal policy has contributed to confidence

Estonia had to make a remarkable consolidation effort in 2009 to meet the conditions for euro entry. Fiscal measures of around 9% of GDP were implemented, comprising expenditure cuts (including wage cuts in the public sector), tax increases, one-off dividend receipts from the state-owned companies and a diversion of contributions from the second pension pillar to the general government budget. Some further one-off receipts will temporarily reduce the deficit to about 1¼ per cent in 2010. No further consolidation is assumed in 2011 and 2012.

Export-led growth will shape the recovery

Strong growth in demand from neighbouring trading partners is expected to continue in 2011 and 2012. Weak domestic demand and increased cost-competitiveness will lead to a shift of resources into the traded goods sector, supporting market share gains and export growth.

Accommodating monetary conditions in the euro area and a reduction in spare capacity should eventually spark an investment recovery, mainly in the traded goods sector. Consumption will start to pick up significantly only in 2012, once there are clear signs of labour market improvement. GDP is projected to grow by 3.4% in 2011 and around 4% in 2012. Higher growth is feasible in the medium term, but will require structural reforms to increase innovation and internationalisation of the economy.

Unemployment will remain high for some time

Growth in GDP above potential will help to reduce the unemployment rate. However, the extraordinary restructuring from domestic to export-oriented sectors mean that unemployment will be in double digits for some years, posing a serious risk of an increase in structural unemployment and labour force withdrawal. In this context, it will be extremely important to ensure the effectiveness of ALMPs.

Risks are manifold but balanced

The risks to the projection are balanced. Estonia could be more or less successful than projected in rebalancing its economy, maintaining cost-competitiveness and winning export market share. The necessary deleveraging of over-indebted households may also proceed in a more or less orderly fashion than assumed.

INDONESIA

Robust domestic consumption and investment continue to drive the economy forward. External surpluses are narrowing as a result of weak foreign demand and buoyant import growth. Strong domestic demand is also putting upward pressure on inflation. Activity is projected to maintain momentum in 2011, buttressed by resilient private consumption and resurgent investment, and ease marginally in 2012.

Bank Indonesia (BI) has started to normalise monetary policy, raising primary reserve requirements by 300 basis points to 8%, but mounting inflationary pressures will require hiking interest rates before the end of the year if the end-2011 inflation target is to be met. The 2011 draft state budget envisages cuts in energy subsidies, making it less vulnerable to swings in international energy prices and freeing resources for growth-enhancing programmes, but government spending bottlenecks might thwart these ambitions and result in under-spending.

The pace of expansion is reaching pre-crisis peaks

In the first three quarters of 2010, real GDP growth accelerated, underpinned by strong domestic demand. Private consumption and investment picked up, supported by rising credit extension. Public consumption contracted significantly because of long-standing problems hampering budget disbursements. While imports surged in response to the strength of spending, exports rose more modestly. Economic activity is being driven by construction and services sectors, especially trade, hotels and restaurants, but it has yet to broaden to manufacturing industries. Unemployment is trending downward. Foreign exchange reserves have risen by 28% since March to $92 billion in September 2010 (around seven months of imports and servicing of official external debt), concomitant with robust direct and portfolio investment inflows. BI's expectations surveys point to continued robust economic activity, supported by rising household disposable income and retail sales.

Indonesia

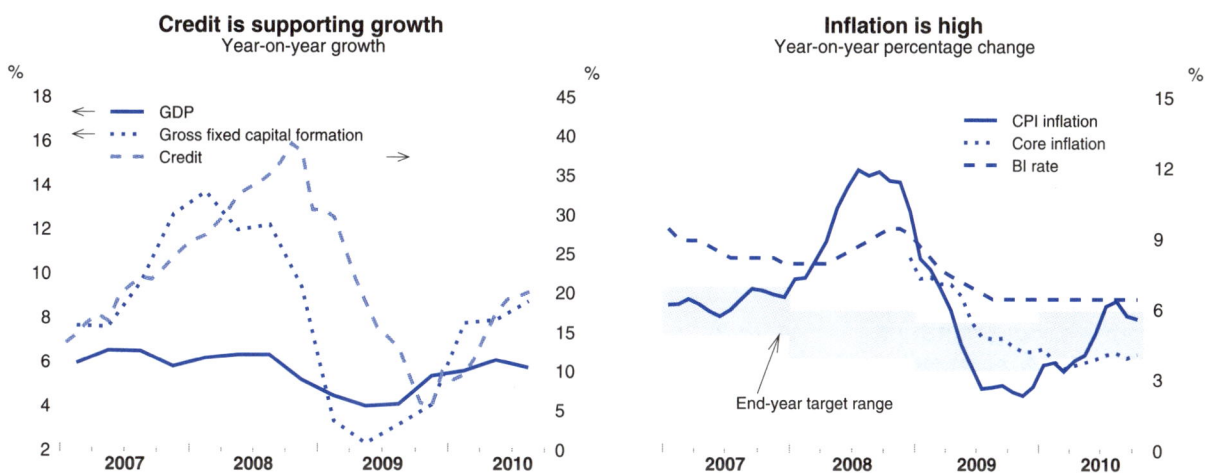

Source: OECD Main Economic Indicators, Statistics Indonesia (BPS), Bank Indonesia.

StatLink 🔗 http://dx.doi.org/10.1787/888932346325

Indonesia: **Macroeconomic indicators**

	2008	2009	2010	2011	2012
Real GDP growth	6.1	4.6	6.1	6.3	6.0
Inflation	10.2	4.4	5.1	6.4	5.3
Fiscal balance (per cent of GDP)	-0.1	-1.6	-1.4	-1.3	-1.3
Current account balance ($ billion)	0.1	10.7	2.5	-0.2	-3.8
Current account balance (per cent of GDP)	0.0	1.9	0.4	0.0	-0.4

Note: Real GDP growth and inflation are defined in percentage change from the previous period.
Source: OECD Economic Outlook 88 database.

StatLink http://dx.doi.org/10.1787/888932348073

Monetary policy normalisation has started

BI raised the primary reserve requirement from 5 to 8%, effective from November 2010, whilst keeping the policy rate at 6.5% since August 2009. This move will withdraw part of the exceptional liquidity support provided in response to the financial crisis and help to remove chronic excess liquidity in the banking system. Separately, in an attempt to encourage banks to lend rather than merely purchase low-risk securities, BI has also set a loan-to-deposit ratio target for lending institutions of between 78 and 100% as from March 2011. Banks not meeting the target will have to deposit additional reserves with BI.

Rising inflationary pressures require higher interest rates soon

Headline inflation has risen to the ceiling of the 4-6% end-year target on the back of mounting food prices and July's electricity tariff hike. Strong domestic demand is putting upward pressures on core inflation, whose annualised three-month moving average rate has increased steadily to 6.1% in October from the 2.4% trough in May. Survey-based expectations point to softening inflationary pressures in the near future, but favourable economic prospects and fading currency-appreciation effects are likely to exert further pressure on inflation in 2011. Interest rate increases will need to get underway by the end of 2010 for the authorities to be sure to achieve the 2011 inflation target.

Cuts in energy subsidies will free resources for pro-growth programmes

The 2011 central government budget aims for a deficit of 1.8% of GDP. Total spending will remain broadly stable in terms of GDP (at around 18%), but energy subsidies will be lowered by 5.6% to 11% of total spending, freeing resources for growth-enhancing programmes, especially capital outlays. Because of a well-known inability to implement all authorised spending, the deficit is likely to be smaller than planned.

Growth should maintain momentum

Activity is projected to pick up slightly in 2011, buoyed by private consumption and investment. Imports are expected to grow faster than exports, reversing the current account surplus. Unemployment should keep declining. Growth is likely to ease somewhat in 2012 as the effects of interest rate hikes feed through into activity.

Risks are mainly on the downside

Implementation bottlenecks with public capital spending may hinder the recovery prospects in investment growth, while the balance of payments might be vulnerable to pull-backs in international risk appetite, causing portfolio investment outflows and weaker FDI inflows. At the same time, social and political opposition to rising domestic energy prices could postpone or soften the energy subsidies reform, resulting in a higher budget deficit than projected. On the upside, a faster-than-anticipated recovery in global demand would provide an additional boost to exports. In 2012, growth could be higher than projected, provided that the government implements its pro-growth reform agenda, especially with regards infrastructure projects.

SOUTH AFRICA

Economic growth is expected to gain traction, led by domestic demand, while fast import growth is likely to widen the current account deficit. Inflation should remain within the target range in the context of a lingering negative output gap. Already programmed expenditure restraint combined with a projected cyclical recovery in revenues will shrink the budget deficit.

With inflation in line with objectives, monetary policy should remain accommodative in the short term to support growth, while fiscal policy could be further tightened to accelerate consolidation and ease upward pressure on the real exchange rate. Structural policies to increase employment are urgently needed, as the rates of economic growth foreseen through 2012 imply only a gradual decline in the very high rate of unemployment.

The recovery has been tepid so far, especially as regards employment

Despite the boost to economic activity from the World Cup in June-July, output growth slowed from an annualised rate of 4.6% in the first quarter of 2010 to 3.2% in the second and appears to have remained sluggish in the third quarter. In part reflecting the winding down of infrastructure projects related to the World Cup, fixed investment has been particularly weak, remaining lower in the second quarter than at the end of the recession a year earlier. Industrial unrest has intensified, with a transport strike affecting activity in the second quarter and major civil service and automotive strikes taking place in August-September. Employment fell sharply in the crisis and is only now bottoming out; the unemployment rate has risen to above 25%. Trade volumes have partially recovered from their slump during the global crisis, but volumes of exports of goods and services in the second quarter remained some 20% below pre-crisis levels, notwithstanding the substantial boost to services exports from the World Cup

South Africa

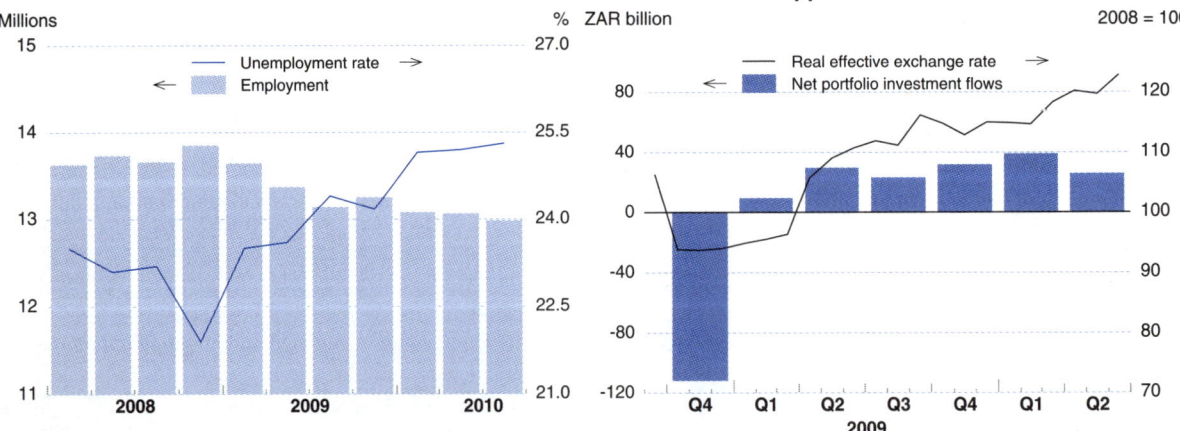

Employment was hard-hit and has yet to rebound

Portfolio inflows have driven a large real appreciation of the rand

Source: Statistics South Africa and South Africa Reserve Bank.

StatLink http://dx.doi.org/10.1787/888932346344

South Africa: **Macroeconomic indicators**

	2008	2009	2010	2011	2012
Real GDP growth	3.7	-1.8	3.0	4.2	4.5
Inflation	11.0	7.1	4.2	4.5	4.8
Fiscal balance (per cent of GDP)	-1.1	-7.6	-5.0	-3.9	-2.0
Current account balance ($ billion)	-20.1	-11.2	-12.4	-20.3	-26.0
Current account balance (per cent of GDP)	-7.1	-4.0	-3.4	-4.9	-5.8

Source: OECD Economic Outlook 88 database.

StatLink ⧉ http://dx.doi.org/10.1787/888932348092

The currency has been strong, helping to bring down inflation

Strong net private capital inflows have driven a very large appreciation of the rand in both nominal and real terms since the low point reached during the global crisis, when appetite for emerging market assets shrank sharply. Rand strength has helped reduce inflation, which fell to 3.2% in September, near the bottom of the 3-6% target range. Inflation expectations, as measured by surveys and break-even prices on inflation-linked bonds, have followed the realised inflation rate downward. Wage settlements have remained surprisingly high, given the amount of labour market slack.

Capital inflows pose policy challenges

South Africa risks being negatively affected the strength of the rand, which has appreciated strongly against both the major advanced country currencies, where interest rates have been kept extremely low, and the currencies of emerging-market countries that have forcefully resisted appreciation against the dollar and the euro. An overvalued rand does not necessarily mean below-potential growth in the near term, as consumption and non-tradables investment may boom, but it is likely to skew the structure of the economy, creating imbalances and hindering the sorely needed growth of low-skilled employment. With inflation falling well within the target zone, helped by appreciation, the central bank has adopted a more dovish monetary policy stance, while also stepping up foreign exchange intervention to resist nominal appreciation of the currency. However, such intervention on its own is unlikely to be effective in resisting appreciation driven by abundant liquidity in advanced economies and fixed or quasi-fixed exchange rates in some other emerging market countries. The government can help by tightening fiscal policy beyond its existing plan and removing the remaining controls on capital outflows, and the October 2010 Medium Term Budget Policy Statement goes in this direction. Communication by the government and the central bank to clarify policy objectives and reaction functions could help guide the market. In addition, the economy could better cope with the strong currency if labour market outsiders had a greater influence on wage settlements, which would make real wages more responsive to labour market conditions.

The output gap will close gradually, with inflation remaining contained

Annual growth is projected to exceed 4% in 2011, slightly ahead of potential, with strong increases in consumption and rising fixed investment growth but with imports rising substantially faster than exports. Faster investment growth should push the growth rate somewhat higher in 2012, allowing the output gap to be virtually eliminated. Unemployment is expected to fall only gradually over 2010-12, as some discouraged workers return to the labour force. The lagged effects of recent rand strength, combined with the initially sizeable negative output gap, suggest that inflation in 2011-12 will remain moderate (and low in historical terms for South Africa), although continuing wage pressures are expected to push inflation back up into the upper half of the target band.

Private capital flows are the main short-term swing factor

The central scenario of rising growth rates and moderate inflation is based on unchanged exchange rates and commodity prices. Swings in investor sentiment towards emerging markets in general and South Africa in particular, as well as large moves in commodity prices, would give materially different results. A reversal of private capital inflows, whether precipitated by external shocks or domestic factors such as political tensions and policy debates within the ruling coalition, would be expected to result in weaker domestic demand and some upward pressure on prices from currency weakness. Probably the more likely scenario at present, however, is a continuation of strong net inflows maintaining pressure for rand appreciation. That would allow even faster domestic demand to be reconciled with low inflation for a time, but would harm the tradeables sectors.

OECD Economic Outlook
Volume 2010/2
© OECD 2010

Chapter 4

FISCAL CONSOLIDATION: REQUIREMENTS, TIMING, INSTRUMENTS AND INSTITUTIONAL ARRANGEMENTS

Introduction

Major fiscal consolidation is needed in many OECD countries...

Most OECD countries face severe fiscal consolidation requirements. At a time when the recovery is still fragile and monetary policy already extended, difficult trade-offs arise between short-term growth and consolidation. Trade-offs also exist with other policy objectives, such as equity and long-term growth. Ultimately, difficult choices will have to be made and will depend on the economic and budget situations of individual countries. However, the choice of instruments used to improve public finances may help alleviate these trade-offs, with some measures potentially strengthening growth in the longer run, while also influencing the consequences of consolidation on equity and its political acceptance.

... raising issues of timing, instruments and institutions

This chapter discusses the size of current consolidation requirements and the pace at which budget positions should be strengthened in the context of a set of macroeconomic projections to 2025. It analyses what spending and revenue changes can be used to achieve consolidation, taking into account the scope for each instrument to generate budget improvements, its impact on growth and equity, and its likely political acceptance. The final section reviews the potential role of fiscal frameworks, rules and institutions.

Main findings are:...

The main findings are:

... consolidation needs are substantial...

- Consolidation requirements are substantial; merely to stabilise debt-to-GDP ratios by no later than 2025 requires strengthening the underlying primary balance from the current position by more than 5% of GDP in the OECD area on average. Tightening by more than 8% of GDP is called for in the United States and Japan, with the United Kingdom, Portugal, Slovak Republic, Poland and Ireland all requiring consolidation of 5 to 7 percentage points of GDP. Consolidation requirements would be much more demanding if the aim were to return debt-to-GDP ratios to their pre-crisis levels. In addition, for a typical OECD country, offsets of 3% of GDP will have to be found over the coming 15 years to meet spending pressures due to ageing, representing additional cumulative consolidation requirements of about ¼ per cent of GDP per year.

... the appropriate speed of consolidation depends on a range of factors...

- For countries with credibility and therefore choice as regards timing, the consolidation should be more frontloaded the weaker the state of public finances, the stronger the economy, the weaker the short-term multiplier effects, the greater the scope for monetary policy to offset growth-restraining effects or the larger the adverse long-term growth effects from delaying consolidation.

... and may imply a trade-off between temporary output losses and long-term gains...

- Typical estimates of short-run fiscal multipliers, representing the effects of a 1 percentage point of GDP consolidation on economic activity, are of the order of ½ to 1, depending on a range of factors including the policy instrument used and the openness of the economy. Hence, the short-run impact of consolidation on GDP growth is likely to be negative, but this may only last two to three years (depending on the degree to which monetary policy can provide offsetting support) and, if consolidation leads to reduced risk premia and lower interest rates, there may be permanent gains in the level of output beyond four to five years. Over and above this, reduction in debt levels may be a pre-requisite for fiscal policy to be able to cushion future downturns.

... spending cuts should be considered as a priority...

- There are arguments to spread the consolidation on both the revenue and the expenditure side of the budget, especially given the required scale of consolidation. However, past experience suggests that budget consolidation concentrated on spending cuts rather than revenue increases is more likely to result in durable retrenchment. Given the size of consolidation needs in many countries, cuts should be considered in most major components of spending. Priority should be given to pension reform, which may have important signalling effects and limited impacts on near-term demand; to expenditure categories where there is scope to increase efficiency, such as education and health care in many countries; and to reducing distortions, such as those created by many subsidies and tax expenditures. Some countries may also have scope to revise social spending with a view to limiting the long-term effects of the crisis on employment and to increase participation in the labour market, while limiting the costs to the budget.

... tax hikes should focus on property, consumption and pollution...

- Beyond eliminating distortive tax expenditures, tax hikes may be necessary to meet the consolidation requirements. They should concentrate on the tax components that have the least harmful impact on growth, such as taxes on immovable property and broad taxes on consumption. Environmental revenues, be it through taxation or through the auction of emission permits, would also bolster both budgets and welfare.

... structural reform can bolster consolidation and growth...

- Structural reforms, especially those that increase employment, would contribute to growth and consolidation. A durable drop in the unemployment rate of 1 percentage point could boost budget balances by ¼-¾ per cent of GDP. Some privatisation proceeds could also be used to reduce gross debt while contributing to higher growth, but should only be considered where and when market conditions are favourable.

... and fiscal rules and institutions can improve the chances of success

- Historical evidence suggests that fiscal rules and institutions can play an important role in consolidation. In current circumstances, specifying a debt objective including the path to stabilising and subsequently reducing the debt-to-GDP ratio would be useful. It could be supplemented by a spending and/or deficit rule, with a combination of such rules seemingly giving the best results. An independent fiscal watchdog can play an important role in assessing fiscal conditions in general and compliance with rules, with the implied greater discipline on policy helping to boost credibility.

Fiscal consolidation requirements in a stylised long-term scenario

Fiscal imbalances cannot be resolved in the short run

As observed in previous financial crises (Box 4.1), the recent crisis has led to a substantial build-up in government debt. Moreover, fiscal balances in most countries will remain far below levels that would be consistent with stable government debt at the end of the short-term projections described in Chapter 1. A stylised baseline scenario to 2025 has been constructed in order to consider how these fiscal imbalances might be resolved.

Projections are underpinned by potential output estimates

For OECD countries, the long-term growth projections are underpinned by projections of potential output (Box 4.2), while for non-OECD economies the scenario is constructed using a growth convergence framework (Duval and de la Maisonneuve, 2009).[1] Most of the

---

Box 4.1. The consequences of previous banking crises for public debt

Financial crises are not only typically associated with sharp economic downturns, but also with a substantial deterioration of fiscal positions. Declining revenues due to weaker economic conditions and higher expenditures associated with bailout costs and fiscal stimulus measures have historically led to a rapid deterioration of fiscal balances and a substantial increase in public debt.[1]

Analysing a panel of developed and developing economies, Reinhart and Rogoff (2009) estimate that in the three years after the occurrence of a banking crisis the real value of government debt rises on average by 86%. Furceri and Zdzienicka (2010) instead focus on the absolute change in the government gross debt-to-GDP ratio and, using an unbalanced panel of 154 countries from 1980 to 2006, find that severe banking crises (defined as those among the episodes identified by Laeven and Valencia (2008) in which the deviation of the annual GDP growth rate from the trend exceeds 4 percentage points) are associated with a significant and long-lasting increase of about 37 percentage points.[2] Analysis based on both severe and non-severe crises, suggests that the effect of banking crises on public debt is not statistically different between OECD and non-OECD countries.

In addition, the increase in public debt in the aftermath of a banking crisis is greater for countries that have a higher initial debt-to-GDP ratio. This can be partly explained by the fact that a higher initial level of debt means that a country may both be more likely to experience, and more vulnerable to, higher risk premia and an increased debt service burden. The empirical evidence suggests that those countries with a higher initial debt-to-GDP ratio (corresponding to the upper quartile of the distribution, *i.e.* above 76% of GDP) experience an increase in the debt-to-GDP ratio that is about 15 percentage points of GDP higher than in countries with a lower initial debt ratio (the first quartile, *i.e.* below 20% of GDP).

---

1. Duval and de la Maisonneuve (2009) develop and apply a simple "conditional growth" framework to make long-term GDP projections for the world economy. GDP per capita in each country depends on technology, investment in physical and human capital and the employment rate. As these vary across countries, conditional convergence implies that, in the very long run, differences will remain in per capita income levels, but not in growth rates.

Box 4.1. **The consequences of previous banking crises for public debt** *(cont.)*

Finally, the magnitude of the increase in public debt in the aftermath of banking crises is found to be sensitive to the amount of public foreign debt (foreign currency debt issued in foreign countries and under the jurisdiction of a foreign court). In particular, in countries with a higher initial foreign public debt-to-GDP ratio (corresponding to the upper quartile of the distribution, *i.e.* above 57% of GDP) the increase in the total public debt-to-GDP ratio in the medium term is about 23 percentage points higher than in countries with a lower initial foreign debt ratio (the first quartile, *i.e.* below 13% of GDP). Several factors can explain this result. First, countries with a high share of foreign public debt may face higher interest payments on debt coming due as capital markets become unwilling to continue rolling debt over. Second, when foreign exposure is heavy, expectations that debt service and repayment may be made difficult by currency depreciation may lead to a self-fulfilling public debt default. Third, in countries with a high foreign public debt ratio currency depreciation may lead to a substantial increase in the debt burden.

1. See, for example, Caprio and Klingebiel (1997), Honohan and Klingebiel (2000), Laeven and Valencia (2008), Reinhart and Rogoff (2008).
2. Based on this definition, during the period 1980-2006 only two OECD countries (Finland and Hungary in 1991) experienced a "severe" crisis; however, during the recent episode virtually all OECD countries experienced a "severe" crisis.

Box 4.2. **Assumptions underlying the baseline scenario**

The baseline represents a stylised scenario that is conditional on the following assumptions for the period beyond the short-term projection horizon from 2013 onwards:

- The gap between actual and potential output is eliminated by 2015 in all OECD countries. Thereafter GDP grows in line with potential output.

- Unemployment returns to its estimated structural rate in all OECD countries by 2015. Historical estimates of the structural unemployment rate are based on Gianella *et al.* (2008), on which is imposed a post-crisis hysteresis effect. The structural unemployment rate is assumed to eventually return to pre-crisis levels but at a speed which differs across countries based on previous historical experience (Guichard and Rusticelli, 2010); for those countries with more flexible labour markets structural unemployment returns to pre-crisis levels by 2015 and for other countries by 2025.

- Non-oil commodity prices remain unchanged in real terms, while oil prices rise by 1% per annum in real terms after 2012.

- Exchange rates remain unchanged in nominal terms in OECD countries; real exchange rates for non-OECD countries appreciate in line with growth differentials (through the so-called Balassa-Samuelson effect) from 2012.

- Policy interest rates remain low and are directed at avoiding deflation and, towards 2015, are normalised in order to bring inflation in line with medium-term objectives. For Japan it is assumed that once the output gap has closed and inflation returns to 1% in 2015, the target rate of inflation for monetary policy will be fixed at 2%.

- The adverse effects on the level of potential output resulting from the crisis (through adjustments to capital intensity, structural unemployment and labour force participation) have reached their peak by about 2013.

- After 2012, non-OECD economies show a slow convergence to US growth rates in per capita income (measured in purchasing power parity) (Duval and de la Maisonneuve, 2009).

- For the period 2015 to 2025, OECD countries experience a slow convergence to annual labour productivity growth of 1¾ per cent.

assumptions underlying the scenario tend to err on the optimistic side, including that: the crisis itself only reduces the level of potential output but has no permanent adverse effect on the rate of growth of total factor productivity or potential output; output gaps are closed by 2015 as a result of sustained above-trend growth with output growing in line with potential thereafter; and, with the exception of Japan, countries do not experience deflation despite continued negative output gaps over this period, and eventually return to targeted inflation by 2015.[2]

Demographics imply slowing potential growth

The scenario builds in a reduction in the level of potential output due to the effect of the crisis so that compared with OECD medium-term projections made prior to the crisis, the level of area-wide potential output is lowered by about 3%, with most of this reduction having already taken place by 2012. From 2013 onwards, the growth rate of OECD-wide potential output recovers to average about 2.0% per annum (Table 4.1), but this is still below the average growth rate of 2.3% per annum achieved over the seven years preceding the crisis. Most of this latter difference is due to slower growth both in participation rates and in the working-age population, mainly reflecting demographic trends rather than additional effects from the crisis.

Output is assumed to return to potential by 2015

Given the assumption that negative output gaps close by 2015, and despite slower potential growth, area-wide GDP growth averages 2¾ per cent per annum over the period 2010-15 (Table 4.2), compared with 2 per cent per annum over the period 2000-08. Unemployment is falling in all countries, with the area-wide unemployment rate down from 8¼ per cent in 2010 to a rate of just over 6% by 2015 and 5¾ per cent in 2025, reflecting both the recovery and the assumed eventual reversal of post-crisis hysteresis effects.

Fiscal consolidation requirements

Fiscal consolidation is essential to prevent unstable debt dynamics

In 2012, fiscal deficits and debt in many countries are large, and while there is more-than-usual uncertainty about the size of output gaps and thus about cyclically adjusted fiscal indicators, it is clear that in many countries there is a substantial component of the fiscal balance which is not explained by the cycle (Table 4.3, Box 4.3). In these circumstances, fiscal consolidation is inevitable for many countries, as is already recognised by many OECD governments which have announced plans for moving back towards more sustainable fiscal positions already in 2011 and 2012 (see Chapter 1).

As a stylised assumption, future fiscal consolidation sufficient to stabilise the ratio of government debt to GDP before 2025 has been incorporated in the baseline scenario (Box 4.4). However, the relatively modest pace of consolidation assumed (½ per cent of GDP per annum

2. This is consistent with inflation expectations remaining fairly well anchored (both upwards and downwards) and with the operation of "speed-limit" effects.

Table 4.1. **Potential output in the baseline scenario**

Annual averages, percentage change

	Output Gap	Potential GDP growth			Potential labour productivity growth (output per employee)		Potential employment growth		Components of potential employment[1]					
									Trend participation rate		Working age population		Structural Unemployment	
	2012	2000-2007	2010-2015	2016-2025	2010-2015	2016-2025	2010-2015	2016-2025	2010-2015	2016-2025	2010-2015	2016-2025	2010-2015	2016-2025
Australia	-1.6	3.3	3.2	2.5	1.6	1.4	1.5	1.1	0.1	-0.2	1.4	1.2	0.0	0.0
Austria	-2.1	2.2	1.8	2.1	1.2	1.7	0.6	0.4	0.4	0.5	0.2	0.0	0.0	0.0
Belgium	-5.8	2.2	1.7	1.6	1.3	1.6	0.4	0.0	0.0	-0.1	0.5	0.0	-0.1	0.1
Canada	-2.5	2.9	1.8	1.6	1.1	1.5	0.8	0.1	0.0	0.0	0.8	0.1	0.0	0.0
Chile	2.1	3.8	3.6	2.3	1.6	1.8	2.0	0.5	1.0	0.1	1.1	0.4	0.0	0.0
Czech Republic	-2.6	3.8	2.7	2.3	3.3	2.7	-0.5	-0.4	0.1	0.0	-0.5	-0.4	-0.1	0.1
Denmark	-4.7	1.7	1.3	1.1	1.5	1.5	-0.2	-0.4	-0.1	-0.3	-0.1	-0.1	0.0	0.1
Finland	-4.4	3.3	1.4	1.7	1.6	2.0	-0.2	-0.3	0.2	0.0	-0.4	-0.5	0.0	0.0
France	-2.9	2.1	1.4	1.7	1.3	1.5	0.0	0.2	-0.2	0.1	0.2	0.0	0.0	0.1
Germany	-1.2	1.3	1.4	1.2	1.4	1.7	0.0	-0.5	0.2	0.1	-0.2	-0.6	0.0	0.0
Greece	-8.3	3.7	0.5	1.4	0.9	1.5	-0.4	-0.1	0.0	0.0	-0.1	-0.3	-0.3	0.2
Hungary	-5.1	3.6	1.3	1.6	1.8	2.0	-0.5	-0.4	-0.1	0.1	-0.4	-0.6	-0.1	0.2
Iceland	-4.7	4.1	1.0	2.1	1.5	1.7	-0.4	0.5	-0.3	0.0	0.0	0.4	-0.1	0.1
Ireland	-6.7	5.8	1.4	2.7	1.7	1.8	-0.3	0.9	-0.5	-0.4	0.5	1.0	-0.3	0.4
Israel	0.5	3.6	3.6	3.4	1.2	1.5	2.3	1.8	0.5	0.5	1.6	1.3	0.2	0.0
Italy	-3.0	1.1	0.7	1.5	0.9	1.5	-0.2	0.0	-0.1	-0.1	0.0	-0.1	-0.1	0.1
Japan	-0.7	1.0	0.7	1.0	1.7	1.8	-1.0	-0.8	0.0	-0.1	-1.0	-0.7	0.0	0.0
Korea	0.3	4.6	3.7	1.8	3.2	2.6	0.4	-0.7	0.1	0.0	0.4	-0.7	0.0	0.0
Luxembourg	-3.9	4.2	2.8	2.5	1.5	1.7	1.3	0.8	0.1	0.0	1.1	0.8	0.0	0.0
Mexico	-0.9	2.6	2.9	2.6	1.2	1.6	1.7	1.0	0.2	0.2	1.5	0.8	0.0	0.0
Netherlands	-1.5	2.3	1.1	1.4	1.1	1.5	-0.1	-0.1	0.1	0.1	-0.1	-0.3	0.0	0.0
New Zealand	-1.9	3.1	1.8	2.4	0.7	1.5	1.1	0.9	0.0	0.0	1.1	0.9	0.0	0.0
Norway[2]	-1.1	3.4	2.0	2.6	1.5	2.3	0.5	0.3	0.0	0.0	0.6	0.3	0.0	0.0
Poland	0.3	3.9	2.9	1.4	3.0	2.3	-0.1	-0.9	0.0	0.0	-0.2	-0.9	0.1	0.0
Portugal	-2.1	1.7	1.2	2.1	1.3	1.9	-0.1	0.2	-0.1	0.0	0.1	0.0	-0.1	0.2
Slovak Republic	-1.7	5.1	3.3	2.0	3.6	2.8	-0.3	-0.7	-0.2	-0.1	-0.2	-0.7	0.1	0.0
Slovenia	-0.9	3.8	1.5	1.4	1.7	1.7	-0.1	-0.3	0.2	0.4	-0.1	-0.7	-0.1	0.0
Spain	-3.7	3.6	1.0	2.3	1.7	1.5	-0.7	0.8	-0.5	0.1	0.1	0.3	-0.3	0.4
Sweden	-2.5	2.8	2.0	2.0	1.7	1.9	0.3	0.1	0.0	0.0	0.3	0.1	0.0	0.0
Switzerland	-0.4	1.9	1.7	1.6	0.9	1.4	0.8	0.2	0.0	-0.1	0.6	0.1	0.0	0.0
United Kingdom	-3.4	2.5	1.4	1.9	1.3	1.7	0.1	0.2	-0.3	-0.1	0.4	0.3	0.0	0.0
United States	-2.0	2.6	2.0	2.4	1.6	1.7	0.4	0.7	-0.4	-0.2	1.0	0.9	0.0	0.1
Euro area	-2.7	2.0	1.2	1.6	1.4	1.6	-0.1	0.0	-0.1	0.1	0.0	-0.1	-0.1	0.1
OECD	-2.1	2.3	1.6	2.0	1.3	1.5	0.3	0.5	-0.1	0.1	0.5	0.3	0.0	0.0

1. Percentage point contributions to potential employment growth.
2. As a % of mainland potential GDP.
Source: OECD Economic Outlook 88 database.

StatLink 🔗 http://dx.doi.org/10.1787/888932348111

reduction in the underlying primary balance as of 2013 and for as long as it takes to stabilise debt) means that in many cases there is a further build-up in the government debt-to-GDP ratio before it does stabilise. The scale of consolidation required to stabilise debt-to GDP-ratios both in relation to 2010 and, following the projected consolidation, from 2012 is summarised in Table 4.4. For around one-half of OECD countries, given the efforts announced already for the short term, little or no further consolidation is required to stabilise debt beyond 2012. Some countries,

Table 4.2. **A macroeconomic summary of the baseline scenario**

	Real GDP growth		Inflation rate[1]		Unemployment rate		
	2010-15	2016-25	2010	2015-25	2010	2015	2025
Australia	3.6	2.5	2.6	2.5	5.2	5.1	5.1
Austria	2.3	2.1	1.8	2.0	4.5	4.3	4.3
Belgium	2.6	1.6	2.3	2.0	8.6	8.5	8.0
Canada	2.7	1.6	1.2	2.1	8.1	6.6	6.5
Chile	4.3	2.3	1.2	1.9	8.1	8.5	8.5
Czech Republic	3.2	2.3	0.8	2.1	7.5	6.3	5.8
Denmark	2.4	1.2	2.4	2.0	7.2	4.9	4.4
Finland	2.9	1.7	1.4	2.0	8.6	7.7	7.4
France	2.0	1.7	1.1	2.0	9.3	8.7	8.2
Germany	2.3	1.2	1.9	2.0	6.9	8.1	8.1
Greece	0.7	1.5	4.0	2.0	12.2	10.7	8.9
Hungary	2.6	1.6	4.5	2.1	11.3	8.0	6.6
Iceland	1.9	2.2	5.7	2.0	7.5	3.5	2.8
Ireland	2.9	2.8	-2.1	2.1	13.6	8.3	4.8
Israel	3.6	3.4	3.0	2.0	6.4	6.5	6.5
Italy	1.6	1.5	1.6	2.0	8.6	7.2	6.3
Japan	1.6	1.0	-1.7	2.1	5.1	4.1	4.1
Korea	4.3	1.8	2.4	2.0	3.7	3.5	3.5
Luxembourg	3.6	2.6	1.1	2.0	6.0	4.1	4.0
Mexico	4.0	2.6	3.4	3.2	5.2	3.2	3.2
Netherlands	1.7	1.4	1.3	2.0	4.1	3.8	3.5
New Zealand	2.6	2.4	2.0	2.1	6.5	4.2	4.0
Norway[2]	2.6	2.6	2.0	2.1	3.6	3.5	3.3
Poland	3.2	1.4	2.5	2.1	9.6	10.0	10.0
Portugal	1.7	2.1	1.5	2.0	10.7	8.4	6.9
Slovak Republic	3.8	2.0	0.4	2.1	14.1	11.0	11.0
Slovenia	1.9	1.5	2.4	1.9	7.2	6.4	6.0
Spain	1.8	2.3	2.3	2.0	19.8	12.7	9.1
Sweden	3.1	2.0	0.8	2.0	8.4	7.0	7.0
Switzerland	2.1	1.7	0.5	2.1	4.4	3.8	3.7
United Kingdom	2.2	1.9	4.4	2.1	7.9	5.7	5.3
United States	2.8	2.4	1.7	2.0	9.7	5.4	4.9
Euro Area	2.0	1.6	1.7	2.0	9.9	8.5	7.6
OECD	2.7	2.1	1.8	2.2	8.3	5.9	5.5

1. For OECD countries, percentage change from the previous period in the private consumption deflator.
2. As a % of mainland GDP.
Source: OECD Economic Outlook 88 database.

StatLink ▆▆▆ *http://dx.doi.org/10.1787/888932348130*

such as Iceland, Italy and Belgium for which the debt ratios are initially very high belong to this category, as they are already on a debt-reducing path. Japan and the United States require the most consolidation beyond 2012 to stabilise debt, with an adjustment in the underlying primary balance of around 8 and 5 percentage points of GDP beyond the short term, respectively, (i.e. a decade or more of consolidation at the assumed pace), whereas New Zealand, Poland, the Slovak Republic and the United Kingdom require 3 to 4 percentage points of consolidation beyond 2012.[3]

3. For Japan the required amount of consolidation (over 8% of GDP in 2012) is not achieved by 2025 given the assumed pace of consolidation of ½ percentage point of GDP per annum.

Table 4.3. **Fiscal trends in the baseline assuming a stylised fiscal rule**

As percentage of nominal GDP (unless otherwise specified)

	Underlying fiscal balance	Number of years of consoli-dation[1]	Financial balances[2]			Net financial liabilities[3]			Gross financial liabilities[4]			Long term interest rate[5] (%)		
	2012		2007	2010	2025	2007	2010	2025	2007	2010	2025	2007	2010	2025
Australia	-0.1	0	1.7	-3.3	0.0	-7	0	3	14	24	26	6.0	5.3	6.6
Austria	-2.1	1	-0.6	-4.4	-1.7	31	42	44	63	76	78	4.3	3.2	4.7
Belgium	-0.7	0	-0.4	-4.9	0.0	73	82	54	88	103	75	4.3	3.3	4.8
Canada	-1.1	1	1.4	-4.9	-0.8	23	31	26	67	84	79	4.3	3.2	5.0
Czech Republic	-2.0	3	-0.7	-5.2	-1.8	-14	3	20	34	49	65	4.3	3.9	5.1
Denmark	-0.1	0	4.8	-4.6	1.0	-4	0	-2	34	54	49	4.3	2.9	5.3
Finland	1.2	0	5.2	-3.3	0.6	-73	-57	-40	41	58	75	4.3	3.0	4.7
France	-3.3	5	-2.7	-7.4	-2.7	34	57	65	70	92	101	4.3	3.0	5.3
Germany	-1.9	1	0.3	-4.0	-2.0	42	50	50	65	80	80	4.2	2.7	4.7
Greece	-2.6	2	-5.4	-8.3	-3.9	73	97	105	105	129	137	4.5	9.1	6.8
Hungary	-0.5	0	-5.0	-4.2	-0.8	53	62	57	72	89	85	6.7	7.2	6.1
Iceland	1.3	0	5.4	-6.3	2.6	-1	45	9	53	125	77	9.8	5.1	7.2
Ireland	-4.2	2	0.0	-32.3	-4.2	0	61	79	29	105	121	4.3	5.5	6.3
Italy	-1.1	0	-1.5	-5.0	-1.9	87	103	85	113	131	113	4.5	3.8	6.1
Japan[6]	-6.3	13	-2.4	-7.7	-4.7	81	114	154	167	198	237	1.7	1.1	4.7
Korea	2.9	0	4.7	1.6	3.6	-40	-37	-63	28	33	5	5.4	4.9	5.0
Luxembourg	1.8	0	3.7	-2.2	0.6	-44	-42	-26	12	21	38	4.4	3.1	4.6
Netherlands	-2.3	2	0.2	-5.8	-1.6	28	35	40	52	75	80	4.3	2.9	4.7
New Zealand	-2.6	6	4.0	-5.3	0.1	-13	-4	7	26	39	49	6.3	5.5	5.8
Poland	-4.9	9	-1.9	-7.9	-2.2	17	29	52	52	64	83	5.5	5.8	6.2
Portugal	-2.9	0	-2.8	-7.3	-4.0	43	63	77	69	93	108	4.4	5.2	5.6
Slovak Republic	-3.0	6	-1.8	-8.1	-0.9	7	24	33	33	47	56	4.5	3.8	4.7
Spain	-3.0	3	1.9	-9.2	-2.6	19	43	54	42	72	81	4.3	4.1	4.8
Sweden	1.9	0	3.5	-1.2	2.8	-25	-21	-36	47	51	28	4.2	2.9	4.8
Switzerland	0.0	0	1.7	-0.7	0.0	9	6	3	46	42	38	2.9	1.6	3.1
United Kingdom	-4.6	7	-2.8	-9.6	-3.2	28	51	71	47	81	103	5.0	3.5	5.6
United States	-6.0	11	-2.9	-10.5	-2.4	42	68	83	62	93	106	4.6	3.1	6.0
Euro Area	-2.2	2	-0.6	-6.3	-2.1	42	59	59	71	92	92	4.3	3.4	5.2
OECD	-4.2	7	-1.3	-7.6	-2.0	38	58	79	73	97	112	4.8	3.5	6.1

Note: These fiscal projections are the consequence of applying a stylised fiscal consolidation rule and should not be interpreted as a forecast.
1. The number of years of fiscal consolidation beyond 2012 is determined so as to stabilise the ratio of government debt to GDP, assuming that each year of consolidation amounts to ½ percent of GDP (see Box 4.4).
2. General government fiscal surplus (+) or deficit (-) as a percentage of GDP.
3. Includes all financial liabilities minus financial assets as defined by the system of national accounts (where data availability permits) and covers the general government sector, which is a consolidation of central, state and local governments and the social security sector.
4. Includes all financial liabilities as defined by the system of national accounts (where data availability permits) and covers the general government sector, which is a consolidation of central, state and local governments and the social security sector. The definition of gross debt differs from the Maastricht definition used to assess EU fiscal positions.
5. Interest rate on 10-year government bonds.
6. Japan is the only country for which the required consolidation to stabilise debt is so large that it is not achieved in the baseline scenario by 2025 given the assumed pace of consolidation.
Source: OECD Economic Outlook 88 database.

StatLink http://dx.doi.org/10.1787/888932348149

Fiscal challenges are exacerbated by...

In addition to current high deficits and debt, a number of factors add to fiscal challenges going forward:

... rising interest rates...

● Interest rates are likely to increase across the maturity spectrum once the recovery becomes firmer. Over most of the past decade, long-term interest rates in the major OECD countries have been unusually low. While this may have partly resulted from global factors including lower

Box 4.3. **Uncertainty around output gap estimates and fiscal consolidation**

The size of current output gaps influences consolidation needs going forward. The more negative the output gap, the more cyclical recovery is likely to improve the fiscal balance, and the smaller the discretionary tightening required to achieve medium-term fiscal sustainability. While estimates of potential output and of output gaps are always uncertain, they are particularly uncertain now because the impact of the crisis on potential output remains unclear. Current OECD estimates suggest a peak OECD-wide reduction in potential output of about 3%. However, estimates of the nature and scale of the adverse effects on potential output vary across OECD countries, in part because the crisis had varying effects across countries but also because countries have different institutional and policy settings that influence the response of potential output to the downturn, particularly in the labour market (see OECD, 2010d, for details). Consequently, OECD estimates of output gaps for the United States, the euro area and Japan in 2009 currently differ significantly from those of the IMF and national sources (Table).

Output gap estimates for 2009
As a percentage of potential GDP

	OECD	IMF	National Sources[1]
United States	-4.6	-6.0	-6.4
Euro area	-4.8	-3.7	-3.1
Japan	-5.3	-7.1	-6.7

1. CBO (2010), *Budget and Economic Outlook - An Update - Detailed Economic Projections* and *Key Assumptions in Projecting Potential Output* for the US, European Commission (2010), "European Economic Forecast - Spring 2010", *European Economy*, Vol. 2/2010 for the euro area, and Cabinet Office estimate (unpublished) for Japan.
Source: OECD calculations.

StatLink ᴍᴨ http://dx.doi.org/10.1787/888932348320

Hence, an important issue in the current context is the sensitivity of projected consolidation needs to this uncertainty. OECD estimates suggest that the cyclical component of budget balances as a percentage of GDP are between 0.3 and 0.6 times the output gap, being lower in those economies (such as the United States and Japan) where tax revenues and expenditure are a smaller share of GDP. Against this background, estimates of the cyclical component of budget positions corresponding to the different output gap estimates fall within a fairly narrow range. Thus, the estimates in the table imply that in the United States and Japan, deficits could close by roughly 1½ to 2 percentage points of GDP as their output gaps are eliminated. The sensitivity of cyclical fiscal balances to output gaps is higher in European countries because of the greater importance of automatic stabilisers. Hence, changes in the euro area fiscal deficit as the area's output gap is eliminated would also range from 1½ to just over 2 percentage points of GDP despite the generally smaller output gap estimates shown above. The overall conclusion of this analysis is that despite some uncertainty around current output gap estimates, the implied uncertainty around the cyclical components of current deficits is relatively small in relation to the size of these deficits.

Another source of uncertainty in measures of cyclically-adjusted balances relates to the large asset and commodity price movements observed over the recent decade and their differences across countries. Buoyant asset and commodity prices just before the crisis may have led cyclically-adjusted budget balances to give an overly rosy picture of the underlying budget situation because no adjustment is made for these prices. Conversely, positive fiscal surprises might be forthcoming as the cycle recovers and asset and commodity prices go up. However, there are reasons to believe that the last cycle was exceptional and that the sustained increases in asset prices, corporate profits and government revenue during the great moderation is unlikely to come back. In any case, it would be imprudent to assume otherwise.

Box 4.4. **Fiscal policy assumptions used in the stylised scenario**

The fiscal consolidation path

The fiscal path that has been assumed in the baseline scenario from 2013 onwards is one in which there is gradual and sustained increase in the underlying fiscal primary balance sufficient to ensure that the ratio of government-debt-to-GDP is stable over the medium term given long-term trend growth and current long-term interest rates. It should be noted that in many cases this assumption implies a degree of fiscal consolidation which is less ambitious than incorporated in current government plans.[1] In addition, the stylised fiscal rule applied here is not necessarily consistent with national or supra-national fiscal objectives, targets or rules.

The basis for the fiscal rule can be derived from the government budget identity, whereby the change in the net government debt-to-GDP ratio (d) is explained by the primary deficit ratio ($-pb$) plus net interest rates payments on the previous period's debt, where is the effective interest rate paid on net government debt, so that approximately:

$$\Delta d_t = -pb_t + (i_t - g_t)\, d_{t-1},$$

where g is the nominal GDP growth rate. Then to avoid an ever-increasing debt-to-GDP ratio (so that $\Delta d_t \leq 0$), and if the effective interest rate on debt exceeds the nominal growth rate, the required primary balance (pb^*) must be in surplus and by a magnitude which is approximately given by:

$$pb^*_t \geq (i_t - g_t)\, d_{t-1}$$

To operationalise this rule the rate of growth g is taken to be the nominal growth rate of potential output over the medium term and i is the long-term interest rate on government debt (towards which it is assumed the effective interest rate on debt will tend). In practice a slightly more elaborate version of this rule is used to distinguish between the rate of interest on government liabilities and that earned on government assets (the latter has historically been typically lower than the former). Then for each year, starting with 2012, if the underlying primary balance (adjusted for cyclical effects) satisfies this condition it is held stable as a share of GDP. Otherwise, for each year that the underlying primary balance does not satisfy this condition the fiscal stance is tightened by raising the underlying primary balance by ½ per cent of GDP per annum, through a combination of a reduction in government spending and higher taxes, until the condition is satisfied. In practice, achieving the target primary balance does not immediately stabilise debt because dynamics in the model have to fully unwind. For example, the implicit interest rate paid on existing government debt will be different from the current long-term bond rate used in the rule, but the former is assumed to converge on the latter.

The implied pattern of fiscal consolidation varies greatly across countries according to this rule: for over one-third of countries which are already running a primary surplus or which are running a primary deficit which is explained by cyclical factors, the rule does not require any consolidation; other countries which in 2012 start out with large underlying deficits require more than a decade of continuous consolidation (the United States and Japan); but most OECD countries lie somewhere in between these extremes. Japan is the only country for which the required consolidation to stabilise debt (over 8% of GDP in 2012)) is not achieved by 2025 given the assumed pace of consolidation of ½ percentage point of GDP per annum. It is also noteworthy that a number of highly indebted countries require little further consolidation to stabilise debt, in part reflecting the arithmetic that for such countries the overall fiscal balance consistent with stable debt will be a substantial deficit. Of course, a higher level of debt also implies a greater risk from a range of shocks.

Other fiscal assumptions

There are no further losses to government balance sheets as a result of asset purchases or guarantees made in dealing with the financial crisis.

Effects on public budgets from population ageing and continued upward pressures on health spending are not explicitly included or, put differently, implicitly assumed to be offset by other budgetary measures.

1. For example, in Ireland the plan is to bring the deficit down to below 3% of GDP by 2014 and in the United Kingdom the announced pace of consolidation to 2015/16 would be roughly three times as fast.

Table 4.4. **Consolidation requirements to stabilise debt over the long-term**

As per cent of potential GDP

	Underlying primary balance in 2010	Underlying primary balance required to stabilise debt[1]	Required change in underlying primary balance	Projected Change in underlying primary balance in 2012-10	Requirement beyond 2012
	(A)	(B)	(C) = (B) - (A)	(D)	(C) - (D)
Australia	-1.6	0.0	1.6	2.8	-1.2
Austria	-1.2	0.5	1.7	1.4	0.2
Belgium	1.3	0.6	-0.7	1.4	-2.1
Canada	-2.8	-0.5	2.3	1.8	0.5
Czech Republic	-2.9	0.5	3.4	2.2	1.2
Denmark	-0.1	0.0	0.1	0.5	-0.3
Finland	-0.6	-0.5	0.1	1.2	-1.1
France	-3.2	1.0	4.3	2.2	2.1
Germany	-0.7	0.8	1.6	1.1	0.5
Greece	-0.3	3.5	3.8	2.9	0.9
Hungary	2.4	2.7	0.3	1.3	-1.0
Iceland	-1.2	0.6	1.9	5.7	-3.8
Ireland	-5.5	1.7	7.2	6.6	0.6
Italy	2.0	2.3	0.3	1.7	-1.4
Japan	-5.5	3.7	9.2	0.8	8.4
Korea	1.0	-3.3	-4.3	1.2	-5.5
Luxembourg	0.6	0.1	-0.4	1.6	-2.0
Netherlands	-2.0	0.3	2.3	1.5	0.8
New Zealand	-4.0	0.1	4.0	1.2	2.9
Norway	-4.1	-2.3	1.8	-1.1	2.9
Poland	-5.3	2.0	7.3	2.8	4.4
Portugal	-4.3	1.0	5.3	5.2	0.1
Slovak Republic	-5.3	1.2	6.2	3.8	2.4
Spain	-4.7	0.0	4.7	3.4	1.3
Sweden	1.9	-0.3	-2.2	1.1	-3.3
Switzerland	0.0	-0.1	-0.1	0.3	-0.3
United Kingdom	-5.0	1.2	6.2	3.0	3.2
United States	-7.0	1.4	8.5	3.1	5.3
Euro Area	-1.4	1.0	2.5	2.0	0.5
OECD	-4.1	1.3	5.3	2.2	3.2

1. Underlying primary balance required in 2025, based on gradual but steady consolidation paths, to stabilise debt-to-GDP ratios in the long-term baseline scenario. Debt stabilisation may take place at undesirably high levels.

Source: OECD calculations.

StatLink ᴍᴮ⬝ http://dx.doi.org/10.1787/888932348168

inflation pressures (Bernanke, 2005; Corden, 2009), policy rates have also been very low for much of this period, and in retrospect possibly even too low in some cases (Ahrend, Catte and Price, 2006a), at a time when risk was under-priced and both asset prices and credit grew unusually fast. The eventual normalisation of financial conditions and policy rates is thus likely to involve a general increase in long-term interest rates. High and rising government debt may add upward pressure on long-term government bond yields and depress growth (Box 4.5). For the purpose of the current exercise it is assumed that when gross government indebtedness passes a threshold of 75% of GDP then long-term interest rates increase (decrease) by 4 basis points for

Box 4.5. **Evidence on the effects of fiscal imbalances on interest rates and economic growth**

Though there is a very large empirical literature on the determinants of growth, there is only a small literature that explores the impact of public debt accumulation on medium and long-term growth in advanced economies (Reinhart and Rogoff, 2010; Caner, Grennes and Koehler-Geib, 2010; Checherita and Rother, 2010; Kumar and Woo, 2010). This literature suggests an inverse relationship between initial debt and subsequent growth. In Kumar and Woo (2010), a 10 percentage point increase in the initial debt-to-GDP ratio is associated with a slowdown in annual real per capita GDP growth of about 0.2 percentage points per year, with the impact being somewhat smaller in advanced economies. There is some evidence of non-linearity, with higher levels of initial debt having a proportionately larger negative effect on subsequent growth, particularly when debt reaches a threshold of roughly 75% of GDP. The adverse growth effect stems largely from a slowdown in labour productivity growth following lower investment and slower growth of the capital stock in response to higher interest rates.

An important transmission mechanism for the macroeconomic effects of fiscal imbalances works through higher interest rates. There is a large empirical literature that examines the impact of public deficits and debt on long-term government bond yields. Among studies that analyse fiscal deficits across countries, the estimated impact of a sustained increase in the actual or projected fiscal deficit by 1% of GDP on long-term government bond yields ranges from 10 to 60 basis points, whereas studies that examine the impact of actual or projected public debt on yields typically find that an increase in public debt of 1% of GDP raises yields by at most 10 basis points.[1] The relative magnitudes of the deficit and debt effects are broadly reconcilable through the government intertemporal budget constraint. Laubach (2009) has typical estimates for the United States: long-term yields increase about 25 basis points per percentage point sustained increase in the projected deficit-to-GDP ratio, and 3 to 4 basis points per percentage point increase in the debt-to-GDP ratio.

Evidence is also accumulating that interest rate effects may be non-linear and may tend to be greater at higher levels of indebtedness (*e.g.,* Faini, 2006; Ardagna, Caselli and Lane, 2004; Bayoumi, Goldstein and Woglom, 1995; Conway and Orr, 2002 and O'Donovan, Orr and Rae, 1996). For instance, Égert (2010) finds that the difference between short-term and long-term interest rates appear to be a non-linear function of public debt for the G7 countries (excluding Japan) in recent years. The estimation results indicate a 4 basis point increase in long-term rates relative to short-term rates for each percentage point of GDP in public debt above 76%.

There is also reason to believe that interest rates may now be more responsive to fiscal imbalances and other country-specific factors than suggested by some older empirical literature. Firstly, non-linearities in the response of long-term interest rates to public debt would mean that the responsiveness of interest rates may be greater at the higher post-crisis levels of indebtedness. In addition, one consequence of the crisis may be a permanent increase in risk aversion and hence risk premia as well as a greater focus on the country-specific factors that determine these risk premia. Recent studies of euro area sovereign spreads show that early in the crisis the surge in global risk aversion was a dominant influence on sovereign spreads, while recently country-specific factors such as short-term refinancing risks and long-term fiscal sustainability have started playing a more important role (Haugh, Ollivaud and Turner, 2009; Baldacci and Kumar, 2010; Hagen, Schuknecht and Wolswijk, 2010; Sgherri and Zoli, 2009; Caceres, Guzzo and Segoviano, 2010 and Dötz and Fisher, 2010). Country-specific factors that are found in these studies to influence government bond yields include financial-sector soundness, price competitiveness, fiscal track records, tax-to-GDP ratios, short-term refinancing needs, expected future deficits, bond market liquidity as well as a range of other institutional and structural factors.

Box 4.5. **Evidence on the effects of fiscal imbalances on interest rates and economic growth** (*cont.*)

In light of this empirical evidence, large fiscal deficits and rising public debt are likely to put significant upward pressures on sovereign bond yields in many advanced economies over the medium term. Countries with a high share of government debt held domestically, notably Japan, might find it easier to issue new government bonds. However, real government bond yields in Japan, which undercut those in the United States and the euro area by a large margin in the 1990s and most of the present decade, have been rising since the end of 2008 and are now roughly in line with real yields in the United States and the euro area. In some countries, notably the United States and Germany, deteriorations in fiscal positions do not yet seem to have put upward pressure on long-term interest rates, a situation partly explained by investors' perception of these countries as safe havens in times of great uncertainty. It is impossible to predict how long flight-to-safety effects will dominate investors' concerns on fiscal sustainability, but history suggests that expectations can shift suddenly (see Reinhart and Rogoff, 2009).

1. See OECD (2009a) for a partial survey. Other recent work on the impact of fiscal imbalances on long-term interest rates includes Kinoshita (2006), Baldacci, Gupta and Mati (2010), Hauner and Kumar (2006), Ardagna, Caselli, and Lane (2004), Baldacci and Kumar (2010), Schuknecht, Hagen and Wolswijk (2009), Hagen, Schuknecht and Wolswijk (2010), Dötz and Fisher (2010), Checherita and Rother (2010), Sgherri and Zoli (2009) and Caceres, Guzzo and Segoviano (2010).

---

every additional percentage point increase (decrease) in the government debt-to-GDP ratio – an assumption consistent with the work summarised in Box 4.5. An important exception is Japan which has seen a substantial increase in indebtedness over the last two decades with little effect so far on interest rates, probably because of the high proportion of debt which is financed domestically given the large pool of domestic savings and the stable domestic institutional investor base. To take this into account, and again erring on the optimistic side, the responsiveness of interest rates to debt in Japan is assumed to be only one-quarter that for other countries. On this basis, the increase in government debt compared to pre-crisis levels could eventually add over 100 basis points to OECD long-term interest rates.

... spending pressures from ageing populations...

- On the spending side of general government budgets, additional pressures arise from ageing populations. On unchanged policies, and generally conservative assumptions, increases in spending on health care, long-term care and pensions over the next 15 years are estimated to amount to between 1% and 5½ per cent of GDP in the OECD area, largely as a result of ageing (Table 4.5). In the typical OECD country, preventing or offsetting these pressures requires measures amounting to ¼ per cent of GDP every year over the coming 15 years, just to keep the underlying primary deficit unchanged, although it might be slightly less on average for the larger OECD countries. Such measures have been assumed but not specified in the baseline and have been assumed not to affect potential output estimates. By contrast, adverse demographic trends are taken into account in estimates of potential output growth.

Table 4.5. **Projected changes in ageing-related public spending for selected OECD countries**

Change 2010-25, in percentage points of GDP

	Health care	Long-term care	Pensions	Total
Australia	0.5	0.4	0.3	1.2
Austria	1.2	0.4	0.7	2.3
Belgium	1.0	0.4	2.7	4.1
Canada	1.4	0.5	0.6	2.5
Finland	1.3	0.6	2.7	4.6
France	1.1	0.3	0.4	1.8
Germany	1.1	0.6	0.8	2.5
Greece	1.2	1.0	3.2	5.4
Ireland	1.2	1.1	1.5	3.9
Italy	1.2	1.0	0.3	2.5
Japan	1.5	1.2	0.2	2.9
Luxembourg	1.0	0.9	3.5	5.5
Netherlands	1.3	0.5	1.9	3.7
New Zealand	1.4	0.5	2.4	4.2
Portugal	1.2	0.5	0.7	2.4
Spain	1.2	0.8	1.2	3.2
Sweden	1.1	0.2	-0.2	1.1
United Kingdom	1.1	0.5	0.5	2.0
United States	1.2	0.3	0.7	2.1

Note: OECD projections for increases in the costs of health and long-term care have been derived assuming unchanged policies and structural trends. The corresponding hypotheses are detailed in OECD (2006) under the heading "cost-pressure scenario". Projections of public pension spending are taken from the CBO (2010) Long-term Budget Outlook and Visco (2005) for the United states, from the Office of the Parliamentary Budget Officer (2010) and Visco (2005) for Canada, from the European Commission (2009) for EU countries, from Fukawa and Sato (2009) for Japan, from Commonwealth of Australia (2010) for Australia, from New Zealand Treasury (2009) for New Zealand, from Visco (2005) for Switzerland and from Dang *et al*. (2001) for Korea. In some cases this has required linear interpolation to derive the effects over the period 2010-25.

Sources: See bibliography.

StatLink ⟐ http://dx.doi.org/10.1787/888932348187

... and guarantees provided to financial institutions

- Future fiscal outcomes may be influenced by guarantees on assets of financial institutions provided by governments during the crisis. Such contingent government liabilities are particularly high in the United Kingdom at around 40% of GDP; they exceed 15% of GDP in France and Germany (IMF 2010a). Implicit guarantees for systemically important financial institutions also make public budgets more vulnerable to any future financial crises. The scenario assumes that these guarantees will not have to come into action over the period and will not translate into actual government additional debt and deficit.

Slow fiscal consolidation implies a further increase in debt

OECD general government net and gross debt is projected to increase by about 30 percentage points of GDP by 2012 relative to pre-crisis levels and, under the assumptions set out above, by about a further 13 percentage points of GDP before it stabilises thereafter. The number of OECD countries with gross debt levels that exceed 100% of GDP would rise from three prior to the crisis to eight by the next decade. The change in net debt levels, as a percentage of GDP, is similar to that for gross debt, although the level of net debt is lower, particularly for Japan, Canada and the Nordic countries.[4] The magnitude of the area-wide increase in debt is partly a reflection of the magnitude of the increase in some of the largest countries; in particular the increase in debt by 2025 compared to pre-crisis levels for the United States and Japan is around 40 and 70 percentage points of GDP, respectively, whereas the median increase across all OECD countries is around 25 percentage points of GDP.

Reducing debt levels would require much greater consolidation

The slow pace of consolidation and the high levels of debt reached may in practice not be sustainable in some countries. The extent of fiscal consolidation needs to be much larger if the aim is to significantly reduce debt-to-GDP ratios rather than merely stabilise them. Such a reduction would avoid high debt levels and associated high interest rates undermining economic growth and provide a safety margin for public finances to meet future crises. The total increase in the underlying primary balance from 2010 which is required to reduce debt either to pre-crisis (2007) levels or to 60% of GDP by 2025 is 9½ and 11½ percentage points of GDP, respectively, for the OECD as a whole (Figure 4.1).[5] This compares to the total consolidation of 5¼ percentage points of GDP projected in the baseline which would be just sufficient to stabilise OECD gross government debt by 2025, but at the much higher levels of over 110% of GDP.

The timing of consolidation

The timing of consolidation needs to balance short and long-term considerations

Fiscal consolidation needs to be conducted in a way that does not unduly reduce economic growth in the short or long term. Indeed, the time profile and strength of consolidation should be determined by the strength of the recovery, the magnitude of short-term fiscal multipliers, the scope for monetary policy to offset the demand constraining effects and also on the cost of delaying consolidation in terms of risks to credibility, long-term interest rates and economic growth in the medium and long run.

Typical multipliers imply that consolidation slows growth

Estimates of standard short-run fiscal multipliers suggest that rapid consolidation produces short-term headwinds that may weigh on activity and the recovery. A recent review of fiscal multipliers showed these to be

4. Net debt is in many respects the superior concept and underpins the fiscal rule described in Box 4.4. However, gross debt is more comparable across countries and represents what has to be rolled over and financed through government debt issuance. Moreover, valuation of government assets may in many cases be subject to considerable uncertainty.

5. To achieve the pre-crisis and 60% debt targets, these calculations assume a constant annual improvement in the primary balance over the period 2013-25, on top of the projected improvement over the period 2010-12 shown in column (D) of Table 4.4. These alternative calculations do allow for the effect that lower debt might have in lowering interest rates by 4 basis points for each percentage point reduction in the debt-to-GDP ratio while the ratio remains above 75% of GDP.

Figure 4.1. **Total consolidation required from 2010 to achieve alternative debt targets**

Total increase in the underlying primary balance, as a percentage of GDP

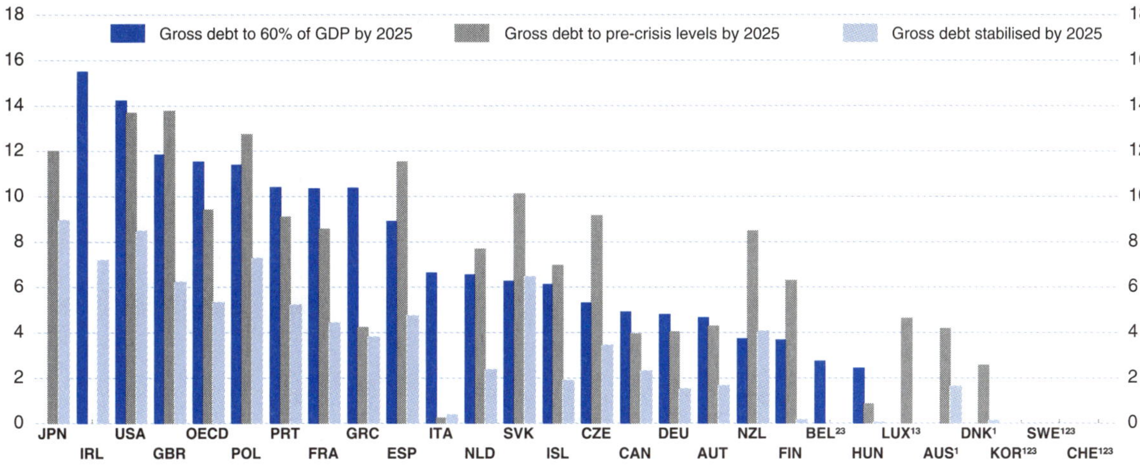

1. No consolidation is needed to achieve the 60% debt-to-GDP ratio by 2025.
2. No consolidation is needed to achieve the pre-crisis debt-to-GDP ratio.
3. No consolidation is needed to stabilise the debt-to-GDP ratio.

Note: The chart shows the total consolidation required to achieve a gross general government debt-to-GDP ratio equal to 60% of GDP and the pre-crisis (2007) ratio by 2025, assuming the projected improvement in the underlying primary balance between 2010-12 is as shown in column (D) of Table 4.4 with an additional constant improvement in the underlying primary balance each year between 2013 and 2025 calculated so as to achieve the debt target in 2025. These consolidation requirements are then compared with that required to stabilise the debt-to-GDP ratio by 2025 (at higher levels), as described in the baseline scenario summarised in Tables 4.3 and 4.4. The required consolidation for Japan to achieve a debt ratio of 60% of GDP and for Ireland to achieve the pre-crisis debt ratio are not shown, because in both cases it would call for a very large degree of tightening if this were to be achieved by 2025.

Source: OECD calculations.

StatLink ⫘ *http://dx.doi.org/10.1787/888932346382*

varying with trade openness and with the size of public sectors and suggested magnitudes of around ½ to 1 for government spending and tax multipliers that are significantly lower (Table 4.6).[6]

Multipliers are sensitive to constraints on monetary policy...

Multiplier effects will also be influenced by the macroeconomic environment including the scope to cut policy interest rates, the extent of initial fiscal imbalances, the credibility of consolidation plans and the international environment including whether many countries are undertaking consolidation at the same time. This can be illustrated by simulations on the OECD's Global Model (Hervé *et al.*, 2010) of a fiscal consolidation which is equally composed of spending cuts and direct tax increases (Table 4.7). The simulations suggest that the contractionary effects of consolidation could be up to one-third greater by the second year without a monetary policy offset. Thus, multiplier effects will be smaller and so fiscal consolidation could be more rapid if there is scope for monetary policy to provide an offset to fiscal tightening. At present, with policy interest rates close to zero in most OECD areas, monetary

6. For a review of fiscal multiplier estimates from a selection of macroeconomic models, see OECD (2009a).

Table 4.6. **Short-term fiscal multipliers**

	Expenditure			Revenue	
	Government consumption	Transfers to households	Investment	Indirect tax	Personal income tax
United States	0.90	0.70	1.10	-0.40	-0.70
Japan	0.90	0.70	1.10	-0.40	-0.70
Germany	0.60	0.50	1.00	-0.30	-0.50
France	0.80	0.60	1.00	-0.30	-0.60
Italy	0.80	0.60	1.00	-0.30	-0.60
United Kingdom	0.70	0.60	1.00	-0.30	-0.60
Canada	0.70	0.55	1.00	-0.30	-0.55
Belgium	0.50	0.40	0.90	-0.20	-0.40
Switzerland	0.60	0.45	0.90	-0.30	-0.45
Netherlands	0.50	0.40	0.90	-0.20	-0.40
Sweden	0.60	0.45	0.90	-0.30	-0.45

Note: Percentage effect on GDP, averaged over the first and second year, of a 1% of GDP change in the relevant budget component. Estimates are based on the survey of results described in Box 3.1 of the OECD Economic Outlook Interim Report of March 2009, adjusted for openness as measured by the ratio of imports to the sum of GDP and imports.

Source: OECD Economic Outlook, Interim Report (March 2009), Appendix 3.2.

StatLink ⬛🖙 *http://dx.doi.org/10.1787/888932348206*

Table 4.7. **The effect of fiscal consolidation on GDP**

	Multiplier		No. of years before positive effect on		Long-run rise in level of GDP[1] (%)
	Year 1	Year 2	GDP Growth	Level of GDP	
United States					
(A) With policy rate response	0.72	0.94	2	5	0.1
(B) With zero policy rate bound	0.81	1.26	3	6	0.0
(C) With fall in risk premia	0.61	0.76	2	4	0.3
(D) With OECD-wide consolidation	0.70	0.90	2	4	0.3
Euro area					
(A) With policy rate response	0.88	1.07	2	5	0.1
(B) With zero policy rate bound	0.90	1.26	3	6	0.1
(C) With fall in risk premia	0.81	0.89	2	4	0.3
(D) With OECD-wide consolidation	0.88	1.04	2	5	0.3
Japan					
(A) With policy rate response	0.56	0.85	4	7	0.0
(B) With zero policy rate bound	0.56	0.85	4	7	0.0
(C) With fall in risk premia	0.55	0.70	4	6	0.1
(D) With OECD-wide consolidation	0.73	0.92	4	6	0.2

Notes: Results based on simulations of the OECD's Global Model.

(A) Fiscal consolidation in one OECD region to generate an improvement in the primary balance equal to about 1 percent of GDP, and an eventual reduction in the government debt-to-GDP ratio of 10 percentage points. Tax rates are adjusted over the medium term to acheive the debt target. Consolidation measures are initially equally distributed between spending cuts and tax increases. A Taylor rule determines short-term policy interest rates, although in the case of Japan the zero bound prevents any cut in policy rates over the first 3 years.

(B) As per (A), but with unchanged policy rates over the first 3 years.

(C) As per (A), but with interest rates on long-term government bonds falling by 4 basis points for each percentage point reduction in the government debt ratio.

(D) As per (C) but with all OECD countries simultanously undertaking fiscal consolidation. The multiplier is calculated in respect of the consolidation taking place in the home country.

1. The long-run rise in the the level of GDP is based on the average increase in potential output after 10-15 years.

Source: OECD calculations.

StatLink ⬛🖙 *http://dx.doi.org/10.1787/888932348225*

authorities are constrained in providing additional stimulus.[7] If the recovery proceeds at the projected pace, the constraints on monetary policy should be less of a concern for fiscal consolidation from 2012 onwards for most countries and the pace of normalisation of interest rates could then be adjusted to partially offset any economic weakness resulting from budget improvements.

... as well as to the scale of initial fiscal imbalances

The contractionary effects of fiscal consolidation could also be partially offset to the extent that credible consolidation programmes reduce the risk of sovereign debt default, reducing risk premia on government securities, which, in turn, can lower interest rates (or raise them less than without consolidation) more generally. The responsiveness of long-term interest rates to substantial consolidation is likely to be stronger at high debt levels. In the simulations on the OECD's Global Model, long-term interest rates fall as a consequence of credible debt reduction by 10% of GDP which is achieved over the medium term, damping short-run contractionary multipliers by up to one-fifth. While fiscal consolidation remains contractionary in the short run, lower long-term interest rates can permanently boost output in the longer run by raising investment and productivity. The Global Model simulations reported in row (C) of Table 4.7 suggest that for the United States and the euro area, for each 10 percentage point reduction in the debt-to-GDP ratio the level of long-run potential output is raised by 0.3%.[8] Moreover, it should be emphasised that whereas the short-term losses in output are temporary, the long-term gains are likely to be permanent.

Spillover effects will boost both short-term losses and long-term gains in output

With most OECD countries consolidating their budget positions at the same time over the coming years, fiscal retrenchment in one country should take the spill-over effects from similar measures in other countries into account so as not to withdraw overall demand too rapidly. According to the OECD's Global Model, the spill-over effects between the major OECD areas, in terms of the impact on GDP of similar consolidation efforts in all key OECD regions simultaneously, would amount to between one-quarter and one-third of the size of the own-country fiscal multiplier (comparing rows (C) and (D) in Table 4.7).[9] However, within regions, such as the euro area, strong trade linkages are likely to magnify the spill-over effects, underlining the importance of implicit or explicit coordination at the regional level. At the same time, while simultaneous fiscal consolidation

7. In practice, this constraint may be less binding to the extent that central bank quantitative easing measures can influence asset prices and longer-term interest rates.
8. The long-run boost to GDP from a lower debt-to-GDP ratio is smaller for Japan because long-term interest rates are assumed to be less sensitive to government debt (see the earlier discussion).
9. Fiscal consolidation in the OECD area would likely result in a depreciation of OECD currencies *vis-à-vis* non-OECD currencies which, in turn, would tend to increase external demand for OECD products and provide some offset to the reduction in domestic demand caused by the fiscal retrenchment.

will tend to increase the short-run temporary losses in output, it will also tend to boost the permanent longer-run gains in GDP.

In some circumstances fiscal consolidation may raise output in the short run

The OECD Global Model simulations suggest that fiscal consolidation is typically contractionary in the short run and expansionary only after two to four years, a finding that aligns with the bulk of empirical evidence on this matter.[10] Several studies have, however, found evidence that fiscal contractions can be expansionary even in the short run (Giavazzi and Pagano, 1990, 1996; Alesina and Perotti, 1995, 1997 and Alesina and Ardagna, 1998, 2009). Though the direct demand effect of fiscal retrenchment is clearly always negative, an indirect positive effect on aggregate demand can occur through an induced change in expectations if the measures taken are understood to be part of a credible medium-term fiscal programme designed to prevent a larger, more disruptive consolidation effort in the future (Hellwig and Neumann, 1987). The expectations effect may work through a reduction in uncertainty, lowering precautionary savings and lowering the option value of waiting by consumers to buy durables and by firms to make investment decisions (Blanchard, 1990). Expectations can also work through the government intertemporal budget constraint: a cut in the deficit today means government debt will grow more slowly, so that a given level of future government spending is consistent with lower future taxes. This may raise private demand immediately, especially if it is distortionary taxes that are expected to be lower in the future. Expectations can also work through interest-rate effects: a fiscal adjustment believed to be credible and to reduce the probability of sovereign default may lower the risk premium on government bonds and pull down other interest rates, stimulating private demand components (Alesina, 2010).

Current conditions make positive expectational effects more likely

Positive expectational effects from consolidation are more likely, the closer a country is to a critical debt level beyond which output is thought to be negatively affected. Recent OECD work assessing "Ricardian equivalence" suggests that the private-public saving offset becomes larger with increasing government debt levels (Röhn, 2010). These considerations suggest non-linearities in the output response to a fiscal contraction, with positive effects more likely from higher debt levels and more permanent changes. Given that many OECD countries have high public debt levels and require significant and permanent deficit reductions, it seems more likely that fiscal consolidation may now have less contractionary effects than what has been observed in more normal times.

10. The latest evidence is from the IMF (2010b), which finds that fiscal consolidation typically lowers output and raises unemployment in the short term.

Faster consolidation could imply short-term output losses for long-term gains

Overall, the consolidation planned by countries in the OECD area appears to be appropriate for 2011, and going beyond the assumed consolidation for 2012 would appear to put the continued closing of output gaps at risk in many countries. Beyond 2012, in many countries there should be greater scope for consolidation to proceed more rapidly than the modest pace assumed in the stylised baseline. An alternative scenario of more rapid fiscal consolidation has been generated on the OECD Global Model by assuming that the pace of consolidation doubles to an *ex ante* improvement in the primary balance of 1 percentage point of GDP per annum from 2013; this is maintained for four years for the euro area, and six years for the United States and Japan (although in the case of Japan faster consolidation is delayed until 2015, when short-term interest rates are less constrained by the zero bound, so that monetary policy can be supportive). In all cases, the consolidation is split equally between spending cuts and direct tax increases and it is assumed that consolidation plans are credible so that risk premia immediately fall by 4 basis points for each percentage point reduction in debt that is eventually achieved by 2025. Faster fiscal consolidation does imply initially a weaker recovery, but beyond 2017 for the United States and euro area (and 2019 for Japan) growth is boosted (Figure 4.2) and there are permanent gains in the level of potential output. In addition, the government debt-to-GDP ratio is brought back close to pre-crisis levels in the United States and euro area and put on a clear downward trend in the case of Japan (Figure 4.3).

Instruments of consolidation

While effective consolidation appears to favour spending restraint...

For most countries, present consolidation plans envisage some mix of spending restraint and revenue-raising measures. If current spending and revenue collection arrangements reflect optimal public choice, with the marginal benefit of additional spending equal to the marginal costs of a corresponding tax hike, a case could be made to share consolidation efforts equally between spending cuts and tax hikes. Also, with unsustainable revenue buoyancy prior to the crisis having resulted in spending increases in some countries and tax cuts in others, it might be appropriate to revert back to earlier spending and revenue norms. On the other hand, OECD work has highlighted a number of arguments and empirical findings suggesting that consolidation driven by cuts in primary current expenditures, such as government consumption and social transfers, is likely to be more successful in reducing deficits than consolidation based on tax increases (Box 4.6). In particular, the likelihood of sustaining consolidation efforts until debt sustainability is reached is higher when governments tackle politically sensitive areas, such as social transfers (Guichard *et al.*, 2007). Given the large consolidation needs at present, these practical consolidations favour spending-based budget retrenchment over measures to increase revenue.

Figure 4.2. **The effect of more rapid consolidation on growth**

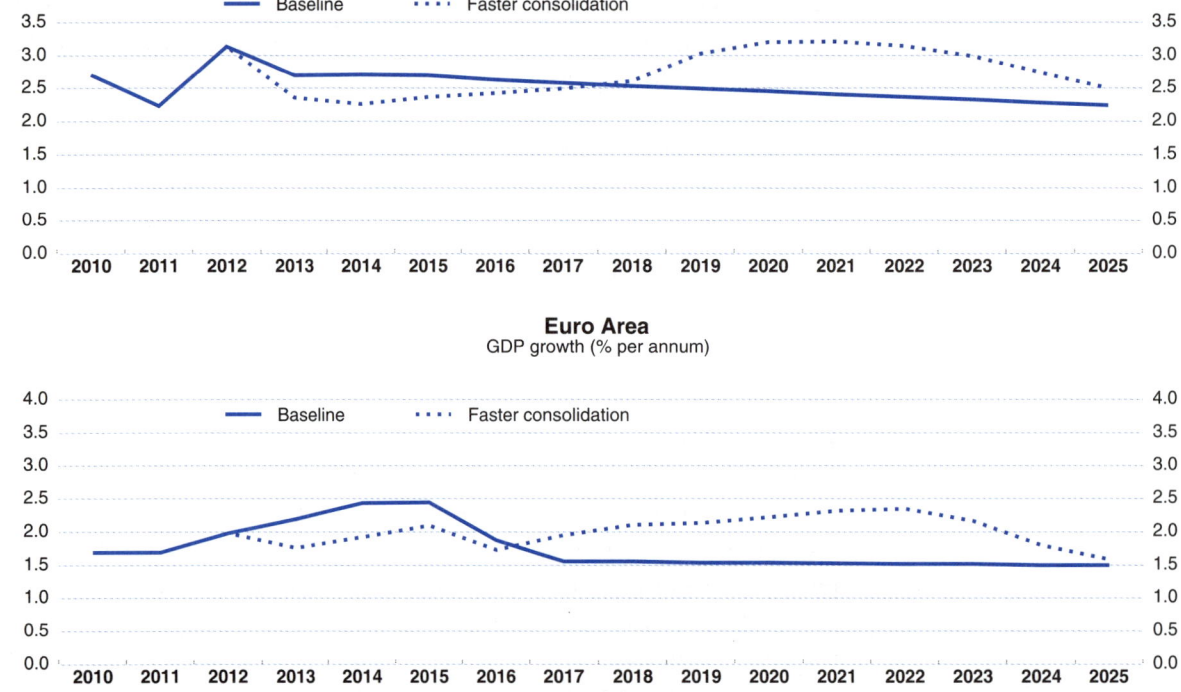

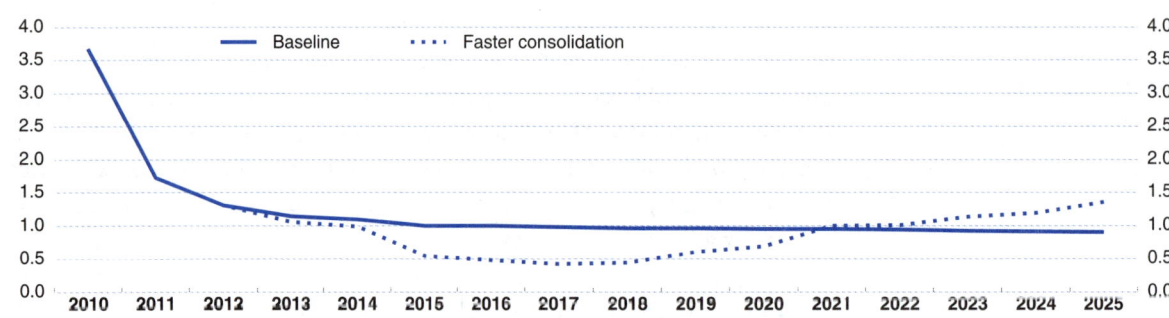

Note: The faster consolidation scenario is generated on the OECD Global Model.
Source: OECD calculations.

StatLink 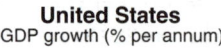 http://dx.doi.org/10.1787/888932346401

... various policy objectives matter for the choice of consolidation instruments

The choice of consolidation instruments needs to take into consideration their impact on a number of policy objectives beyond budget consolidation, including short-term aggregate demand, economy-wide efficiency and equity, as well as their political acceptance. Tables 4.8 and 4.9 give a tentative assessment of the impact of different consolidation instruments on key government objectives and a summary of their potential budgetary effects, respectively. While the discussion below highlights the relative advantages and disadvantages of different

Figure 4.3. **The effect of more rapid consolidation on government debt**

Gross government debt-to-GDP ratio (%)

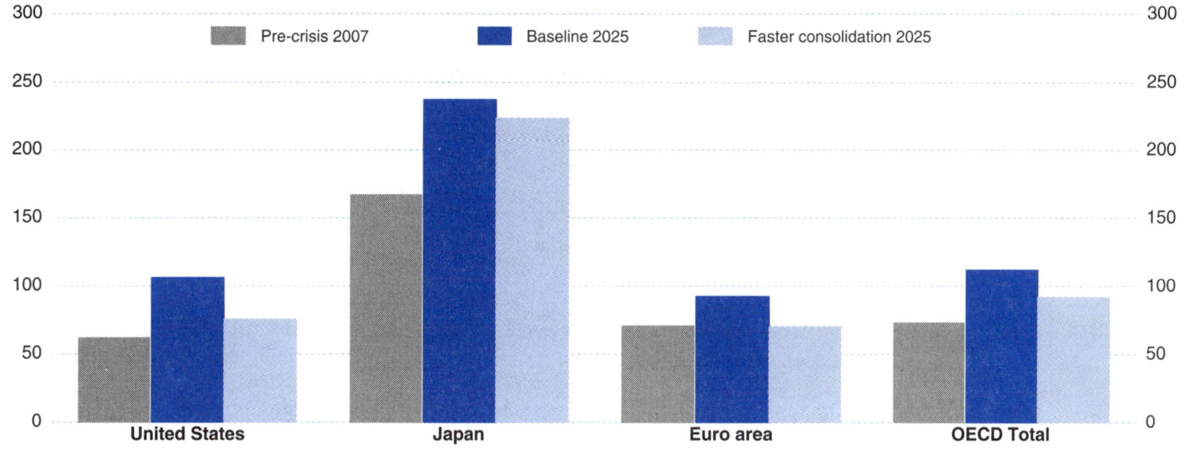

Note: Fiscal consolidation including exchange rate response.

Source: OECD calculations.

StatLink ⟡ http://dx.doi.org/10.1787/888932346420

Box 4.6. **What factors drive consolidation? Experience in the OECD**

Previous OECD empirical work (Ahrend, Catte and Price, 2006b; Guichard *et al.*, 2007) has studied a large number of historical consolidation episodes and indicates that there are a number of policy and other factors that are associated with fiscal consolidation efforts and influence their outcome:

● *Starting consolidation episodes:* Large initial deficits and high interest rates helped to prompt fiscal consolidation. More generally, signs of macroeconomic stress, including high inflation, currency depreciation and being at the trough of the cycle, raised the chance of consolidation starting. The interest rate effect is again confirmed by recent experience in the OECD area, where higher interest rates (actual or threatened) have helped to catalyse a spate of consolidation announcements.

● *Size of consolidation:* Large initial deficits and high interest rates are also associated with a larger overall size of consolidation achieved over a consolidation period. A larger weight on current expenditure, such as social transfers, was associated with a significantly larger size of the fiscal adjustment. However, the empirical association between current spending cuts and the size of consolidation could also just reflect that governments more determined to consolidate are more willing to cut spending.

● *Reaching debt sustainability:* Consolidation episodes that began under weak economic activity had a higher probability of success in the sense of stabilising the debt-to-GDP ratio. A greater weight on cuts in social spending also tended to increase the probability of success. Rather than direct causality, however, a reason for this could be that governments more committed to achieving fiscal sustainability may also be more likely to reform politically sensitive areas.

● *Institutions:* Budget balance rules combined with expenditure targets were found to encourage longer and larger consolidations than a budget balance rule alone. Using a spending rule on top of the budget rule also helped achieving and maintaining a primary balance that was sufficient to stabilise the debt-to-GDP ratio. However, it is uncertain whether this is because well-designed rules are effective or because prudent governments and/or electorates are more likely to institute a rule.

● *Monetary policy:* An accommodating monetary policy stance in the initial stages of the consolidation phase was found to encourage longer consolidation episodes and larger consolidation achievements. It should be noted, however, that the causality might run in the other direction as well, as central banks find it easier to adopt a more accommodative monetary policy stance if strong commitment to serious fiscal consolidation contributes to underpinning price stability.

Table 4.8. **Consolidation instruments and objectives**

	Fiscal effect	Equity	Short-run Demand	Medium-term growth	Policy acceptance
Public sector consumption and investment					
Wage Rates	+++	?	- -	+	-
Employment	++	?	-	+	- -
with efficiency gains	++	0	-	++	-
with no efficiency gains	++	-	-	0	- -
Competitive tendering of procurement	+	?	-	+	-
Subsidies and tax expenditures	++	?	-	++	- -
Pension reform					
Increase in retirement age	++	+	+	+	- -
Lower pension replacement rate	++	-	-	+	- -
Social Transfers					
Targeted cuts	++	+	-	?	-
Across the board cuts[1]	+++	- -	- -	?	- -
Income Taxes					
Across the board increases[1]	+++	-	- -	-	- -
Increase Progressivity	+	+	-	- -	-
Indirect Taxes					
Remove exemptions	++	-	-	+	-
Across the board increases	+++	-	- -	-	-
Environmental taxes / emission permits	++	?	-	?	-
Privatisation	+	?	?	+	-
Structural Reforms					
Employment increasing	++	+	?	++	?
Productivity increasing	+	?	?	++	?

Notes: Positive and negative effects are denoted by "+"and "-", uncertainty about the direction of the effect is denoted by "?". The number of "+" and "-" signs shows the strength of the effects.
1. All transfers or all tax rates changed by the same proportion in percentage points.
Source: OECD calculations.

StatLink ⬛ᵍ█ http://dx.doi.org/10.1787/888932348244

instruments, the trade-offs, particularly as regards equity concerns, may be less stark when considering a large package of different measures.

Spending cuts

Reducing the government wage bill and raising public sector efficiency

Cutting the government wage bill can deliver sizeable consolidation gains...

Given that employment costs account for a large part of government spending (Figure 4.4), reductions in government wage bills can improve budget positions relatively quickly, even if such measures could have sizeable negative effects on aggregate demand in the short run. Indeed, several recent consolidation plans, in particular in Germany, France, Italy, Spain, Ireland, Greece and the United Kingdom, foresee some savings on the government wage bill.

... and might as well contribute to improving cost competitiveness...

Reducing government consumption *via* wage cuts (or lower wage increases than would otherwise take place) may be more appropriate and politically easier to implement if government wages are relatively high. In particular, private sector wage restraint during the crisis might have

Table 4.9. **Fiscal effects of consolidation instruments**

Percent of GDP unless otherwise stated

	United States	Japan	Germany	France	Italy	United Kingdom	Canada
Expenditure							
Public sector wages							
Reduce share of GDP to OECD average[1]	0.3			3.4	1.3	1.7	2.1
Subsidies							
Reduce share of GDP to OECD average[1]			0.4	0.7	0.2		0.3
Social transfers							
Reduce share of GDP to OECD average[1]	0.1		5.2	5.4	5.1	0.7	
Education							
Reduce public expenditure on education as a share of GDP to OECD average[2]	0.0			0.4		0.0	
Improve efficiency[3]	1.0	0.2	0.6	0.3	0.6	0.7	
Health							
Reduce public expenditure on health as a share of GDP to OECD average[1]	0.5		1.4	2.0		0.3	0.5
Improve efficiency while maintaining increase in life expectancy[4]	2.7	0.8	1.3	1.3	1.1	3.7	2.5
Investment							
Reduce share of GDP to OECD average[1]	0.1	0.9		0.2			
Revenue							
Environmental							
Raise current taxes (fuel and motor vehicles) share of GDP to OECD average[5]	0.9						0.6
Cut GHG emissions to 20% below 1990 levels via ETS with full permit auctioning[6]	2.2	1.2	1.8	1.8	1.8	1.8	2.5
Indirect tax							
Raise share of GDP to OECD average[5]	3.0	1.9					
Property and wealth taxes							
Raise share of GDP to OECD average[5]				1.5	1.1		
Corporate taxes							
Raise share of GDP to OECD average[5]	0.6		2.2	0.6	0.2	0.1	
Personal Income Taxes							
Raise share of GDP to OECD average[5]		4.0		0.9			
Structural reforms							
Cut Nairu by 1% through labour market reform[7]	0.5	0.5	0.6	0.7	0.5	0.5	0.5

1. Data are shown for countries where moving expenditure to the OECD average would improve the fiscal balance. Based on 2007.
2. Data are shown for countries where moving expenditure to the OECD average would improve the fiscal balance. Based on 2006.
3. Shows potential savings from reducing teacher-student ratios while holding outputs constant. Implied input cuts were applied to all staff in primary, secondary and post-secondary non-tertiary education in 2002. For details, see Sutherland *et al.* (2007).
4. Shows potential reductions in health care costs in terms of 2017 GDP by lifting efficiency while maintaining the pace of the increase in life expectancy as over the previous decade.
5. Data are shown for countries where moving revenues to the OECD average would improve the fiscal balance. Based on 2007.
6. For EU and EFTA countries, only an average effect across the area is available as the countries are grouped this way for the ENV-Linkages model simulations.
7. See Figure 4.11 below.
Source: OECD Economic Outlook 87 database; OECD Health dataset for public health expenditures; OECD Education and Training Dataset for education expenditures in 2006; Property and Wealth Tax Revenue from *OECD Revenue Statistics*; Environmental tax revenue in 2008 and GHG scenario from de Serres, Murtin and Nicoletti (2010).

StatLink ᘛᘌᔈ http://dx.doi.org/10.1787/888932348263

raised relative wages in the government sector, in which case public sector wage adjustment would also involve a realignment. Moreover, government wage restraint can be particularly appropriate for countries in a currency union that need to improve cost competitiveness as it may lower input costs of government services for other sectors of the economy

Figure 4.4. **General government wage consumption**

Per cent of GDP, 2009

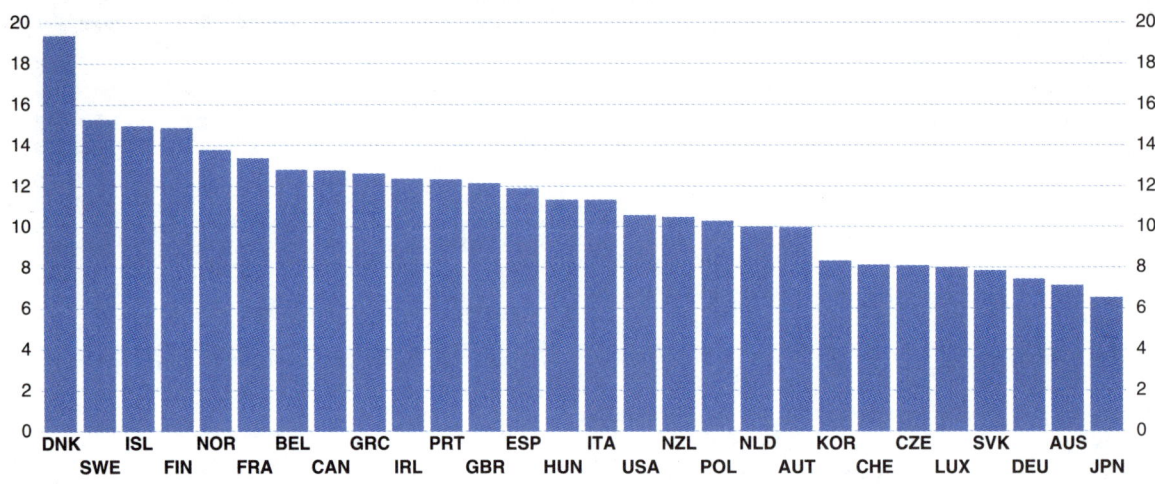

Source: OECD Economic Outlook 88 database.

StatLink http://dx.doi.org/10.1787/888932346439

and support wage moderation overall. However, pushing wage levels in the public sector below those for comparable jobs in the private sector would create problems for retaining and attracting qualified personnel, which might not be sustainable in the longer run as the quality of service delivery would suffer.

... provided growth-enhancing public sector services are left intact

Many governments also have an opportunity to use the coming wave of retirements in their public sectors to reduce government employment without lay-offs by replacing only a certain fraction of departures. To the extent that cuts in public sector employment are associated with reductions in public sector services, care should be taken that output and quality are not unduly affected in areas that are growth enhancing, such as education, research and development and health care. Moreover, such retrenchment, if associated with lower supply of services rather than with greater efficiency, may be more prejudicial to low-income groups and, hence, conflict with equity goals and raise political resistance. Short-term demand effects of employment cuts will depend on the extent to which private employment can expand to offset employment losses in the public sector which may affect the level of net short-term budgetary savings.

Scope to raise public sector efficiency should be fully exploited...

Exploiting the scope for increasing public sector efficiency would allow costs adjustments to generate budgetary saving without reductions in outputs, increasing economy-wide efficiency and avoiding adverse equity effects. OECD studies indicate that there is significant scope to improve efficiency in big ticket public spending items, such as education and health (see Table 4.9). Thus, the budgetary impact of moving to international – or even just national – best practice in key public services can be sizeable. For the health care sector, it has been estimated that on average across OECD countries potential efficiency gains from adopting international best practice could result in budget saving amounting to 2% of GDP (OECD 2010b). In primary and secondary education, moving to OECD highest efficiency could generate budgetary gains between one quarter and more than 1% of GDP (Sutherland *et al.*, 2007). However, higher public sector efficiency may have to be associated with wage increases for government employees, diminishing the consolidation effect.

... requiring a greater role
for cost-benefit analysis

More generally, cost-benefit analysis should become more of a guide for public sector spending programmes than is presently the case. This might include evaluating to what extent market mechanisms can be utilised for the provision of public services. In particular, it might be possible to realise efficiency gains if competition between private producers can be used to lower costs in the provision of public services.

Greater use of competitive tendering in government procurement

Competitive tendering in
government procurement
generates savings

In the same vein, various studies indicate that adopting open tendering procedures can be associated with substantial savings in government procurement.[11] While not all non-wage public-sector spending on goods and services is suitable for competitive tendering, and the degree of fiscal federalism within a country might play some role in determining the size of individual procurement lots, there seems to be considerable variation across countries in the extent to which governments subject their procurement to open tendering (Table 4.10). For example, among the EU member countries, the value of tenders relative to government spending appears relatively low in Germany, the Netherlands, Luxembourg and Italy, suggesting significant scope to generate budgetary savings by moving to competitive tendering procedures. However, vested interests might generate some political resistance to the adoption of more open procurement practices.

Reducing subsidies and tax expenditures

Subsidy reduction should
be considered...

The size of subsidies, as measured in national accounts terms, is relatively small in most OECD countries (Figure 4.5). While this indicates that budgetary and demand-restraining effects of cutting unwarranted subsidies might be relatively modest, it is important to note that the total level of subsidies is likely to be higher than national accounts suggest, both because some transfers that effectively subsidise certain sectors or activities might not be accounted for as subsidies in national accounts

11. See, for example, Ohashi (2009).

Table 4.10. **Value of open tenders and government spending in selected countries**

Per cent of GDP, 2008

	Value of tenders[1]	Expenditure on public works, goods and services[2]	Non-wage government consumption and investment[3]
Austria	2.4	19.4	10.6
Belgium	3.6	15.1	12.9
Czech Republic	5.3	25.1	17.8
Denmark	3.0	15.2	11.3
Finland	4.0	16.8	11.7
France	3.7	17.5	13.7
Germany	1.2	16.8	12.7
Greece	2.7	9.0	8.1
Hungary	5.2	19.6	
Ireland	2.4	15.8	12.5
Italy	2.3	14.1	12.4
Luxembourg	1.4	15.3	
Netherlands	1.9	25.5	19.9
Poland	7.2	18.9	
Portugal	2.6	17.4	10.2
Slovenia	5.1	15.5	
Slovak Republic	3.7	23.2	
Spain	3.6	14.9	12.6
Sweden	3.6	19.1	14.3
United Kingdom	4.4	18.8	13.2
EU27	3.1	17.2	

1. Value of tenders published in the EU Official Journal.
2. European Commission broad estimate of spending by total government sector and utilities on public works, good and services. It is an upper bound on the level of expenditure by the government sector (and relevant utilities) on goods, services and works in the economy. Utilities account for around 1/4 of the total estimate.
3. Non-wage consumption and investment by the general government sector.
Source: European Commission (2010) and OECD Economic Outlook 88 database.

StatLink 🔗 http://dx.doi.org/10.1787/888932348282

terms (notably capital investment grants) and because tax expenditures, unrecorded in the national accounts, add to subsidisation.[12]

... as many subsidies reduce economic efficiency...

In any case, subsidy reduction should rank high on the policy agenda as many subsidies may have surpassed their initial intended objective and may now have adverse economic effects. Cuts in subsidies can thus contribute to raising potential output, involving additional beneficial effects on public sector budgets in the medium term. Experience shows,

12. For example, in 2007, general government subsidies in Germany as reported in national accounts totalled €27.6 billion. By contrast, for the same year, the Subsidy Report of the federal government estimates that subsidies and tax expenditures at the level of the federal government, the states and the communities amounted to €49.7 billion. Likewise for 2007, the Kiel Institute for World Economics reported subsidies and tax expenditures by the federal government, the states and the communities of €133.6 billion. The discrepancies illustrate differences in the definition of subsidies and the coverage of tax expenditures. Moreover, there are methodological issues with respect to the computation and adding up of tax expenditures. See Bundesministerium der Finanzen (2010) and Boss and Rosenschon (2010).

Figure 4.5. **General government subsidies**
Per cent of GDP, 2009

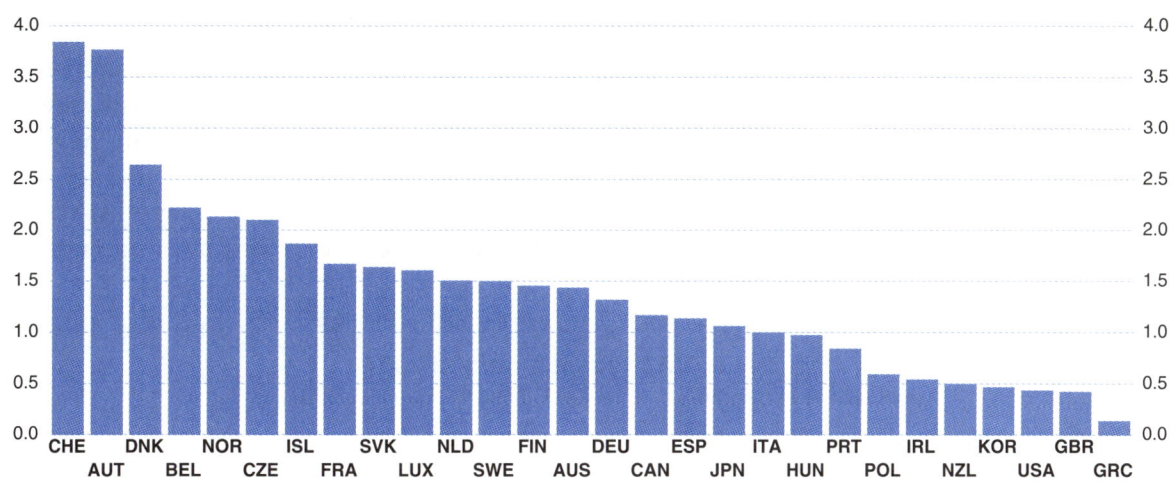

Source: OECD Economic Outlook 88 database.

StatLink ᐃᒥ᠊᠊ http://dx.doi.org/10.1787/888932346458

however, that such cuts are politically difficult to implement as they often conflict with vested interests and stranded investments. The crisis may nonetheless represent an opportunity to tackle issues of subsidisation that are difficult to address in normal times. It is important that governments resist replacing unwarranted subsidies and tax expenditures by regulatory measures designed to provide support to the sectors concerned (*e.g.* through price regulation or other competition-restraining measures).

... which also holds for a sizeable part of tax expenditures

Some tax expenditures (TEs), such as earned income tax credits and payroll tax rebates for low-wage workers, aim at improving social outcomes and are often assessed as quite effective in achieving their objectives, even if they are sometimes associated with adverse incentive effects. Other TEs for social purposes produce highly unequal outcomes or are costly in reaching social targets. For example, deductions in the taxable income of parents for their children's education disproportionately benefit families in high-income segments as they increase in value the higher the families' tax bracket is. Also, the effectiveness of tax reductions for pension saving plans to generate new, as opposed to reallocated, saving for retirement purposes remains highly uncertain, with impacts on national saving likely to be negative in many cases (Antolin, de Serres and de la Maisonneuve, 2004; Yoo and de Serres, 2004). While most of the latter TEs involve some kind of distortion, some can be efficiency enhancing, notably certain types of tax preferences for R&D.

Although assessing the overall volume of TEs raises issues of definition and methodology, it is clear that in some countries tax preferences are substantial (OECD, 2010e). Similarly, there are large differences within the OECD area with respect to the application of VAT across different types of consumption, as indicated by the "VAT revenue ratio" (Figure 4.6) reflecting for example, reduced VAT rates for restaurants, hotels, flowers, children clothes and newspapers which are difficult to justify on economic grounds.[13] While in some countries tax expenditures were reduced in the years prior to the crisis, several governments have reacted to the crisis by introducing new tax preferences. Overall, direct budgetary effects from reducing or eliminating distortionary TEs could be substantial, and associated efficiency improvements would contribute to raising potential output in the medium term.

Figure 4.6. **VAT revenue ratio in 2007**

Actual relative to theoretical VAT revenue, index increasing in efficiency

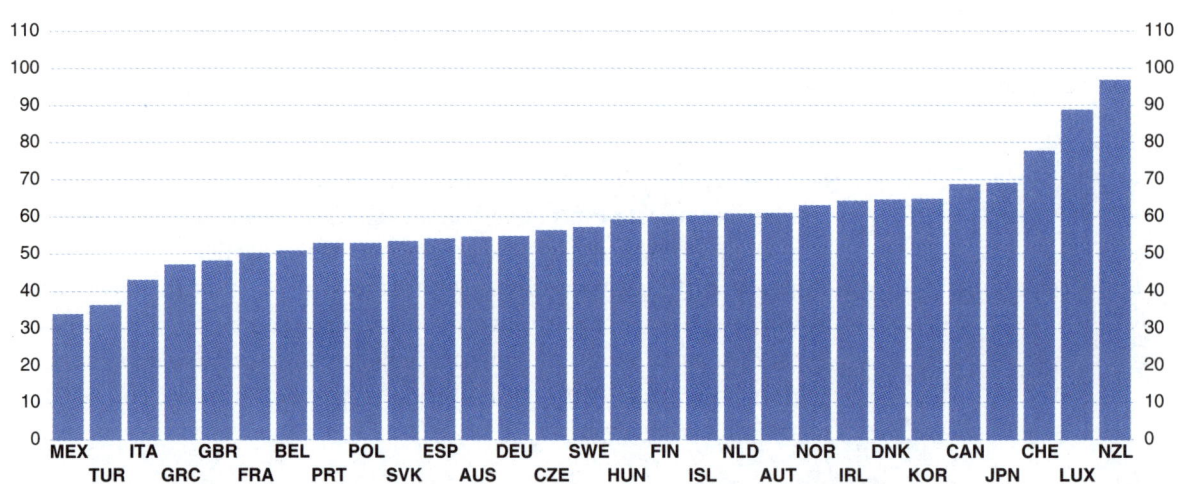

Note: The VAT revenue ratio is defined as the share of VAT revenues to consumption divided by the standard rate, expressed as a percentage ((VAT revenues/final consumption expenditure*100)/(Standard VAT rate))*100. This calculation takes the national accounts definition for final consumption expenditure (P3) which may include items not in the actual VAT base.

Source: OECD Revenue Statistics; and OECD calculations.

StatLink http://dx.doi.org/10.1787/888932346477

Revisiting current social transfers

Cuts in social transfers should avoid conflict with equity objectives...

On average, social transfers account for around 12% of GDP (in 2007), suggesting that they can potentially contribute to the consolidation effort. Indeed, in some countries (including Germany and the United Kingdom), sizable deficit cuts are to be achieved by freezing or reducing some social transfers. While cuts in this area may provide non-negligible savings, they may have adverse consequences for equity outcomes if social transfers go mainly to low-income individuals and families as they should. Another disadvantage is that income cuts for the poor are likely to be swiftly reflected in lower aggregate demand given the higher propensity to

13. Low values of the ratio indicate an erosion of the VAT tax base, either by exemption or reduced rates, poor compliance or poor tax administration.

consume at lower income levels. Means testing could ensure that cuts in social benefits are targeted on those that are better off, but this may in turn create adverse disincentives if marginal effective tax rates increase in the income range where benefits are phased out, from already high levels in many countries.

... while strengthening incentives for labour force participation and employment...

As part of the consolidation strategy, social and employment-related transfers should be revisited in terms of their effectiveness in reaching envisaged policy goals and the opportunity for reforms to increase efficiency. There is still considerable scope to better gear employment or unemployment-related benefit schemes, in combination with activation measures, to encourage work and labour force participation (OECD 2010a, 2010b).

... and contributing to activation strategies for the unemployed...

Unemployment-related income replacement paid by the general government sector accounts for some 0.8% of GDP across OECD countries (unweighted average for 2008),[14] with both duration and replacement rates differing significantly from country to country (Figure 4.7). High replacement rates and, in particular, long periods of unemployment insurance benefits until exhaustion have been found to reduce employment probabilities *ceteris paribus*, which suggests revisiting such

Figure 4.7. **Income support in OECD countries in 2007**
Average net replacement rates over a 5-year unemployment spell

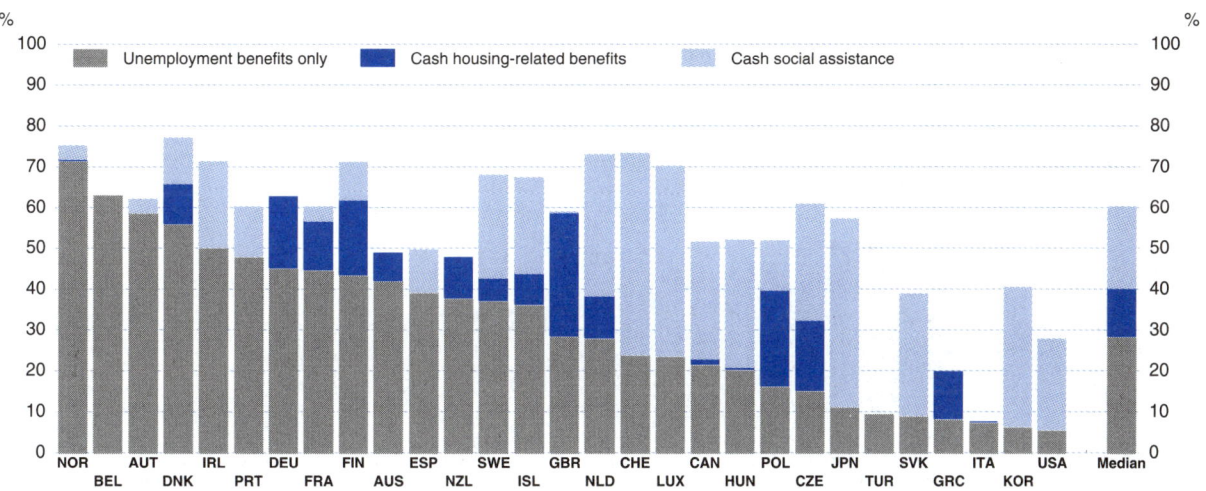

Note: The average of the replacement rate in the first five years of unemployment is shown. See OECD (2009d) for further details on how these averages are calculated. Housing-related benefits are those available to families living in rented accommodation with rent plus other housing costs (*e.g.* utility bills) assumed to equal 20 per cent of the average wage. In some countries, housing-related support is covered by social assistance payments instead. Social assistance in the United States also includes the value of a near-cash benefit (Food Stamps).Net replacement rates are evaluated for a prime-age worker (aged 40) with a 'long' and uninterrupted employment record. They are averages over four different stylised family types (single and one-earner couples, with and without children) and two earning levels (67% and 100% of average full-time wages).

Source: OECD (2009d); and OECD tax-benefit models (www.oecd.org/els/social/workincentives).

StatLink ⬛🇸🇵 *http://dx.doi.org/10.1787/888932346496*

14. Average without outlays for active labour market measures; source: OECD (2010c).

income support schemes. Crisis-induced extensions of benefit levels and duration should be unwound as the recovery strengthens and vacancies increase.[15] However, cuts in unemployment-related benefits run the risk of increasing inequalities and can be politically difficult to implement. Any review of income replacement schemes should therefore take into account interactions with other features of labour market policies, notably activation strategies. In particular, there might be scope to raise the effectiveness of core activation measures, such as job-search support and work-availability requirements. At the same time, ineffective activation programmes should be dropped or redesigned (see OECD, 2006b).

Tackling future age-related budget pressures

... and reforming disability schemes

The number of disability benefit receivers is very high in some countries, with the large dispersion across countries – from a rate of 12% in Hungary to less than 1% in Mexico – pointing to pronounced differences in eligibility conditions (Figure 4.8). Moreover, even during the past decade when economic growth was generally strong, more than half of OECD countries, including Sweden, Norway, the United States, France, Switzerland and New Zealand saw a significant increase in recipient rates. Reform of disability schemes, comprising stricter enforcement of health

Figure 4.8. **Disability benefit recipient rates**
Disability benefit recipients in per cent of the population aged 20-64 in 28 OECD countries

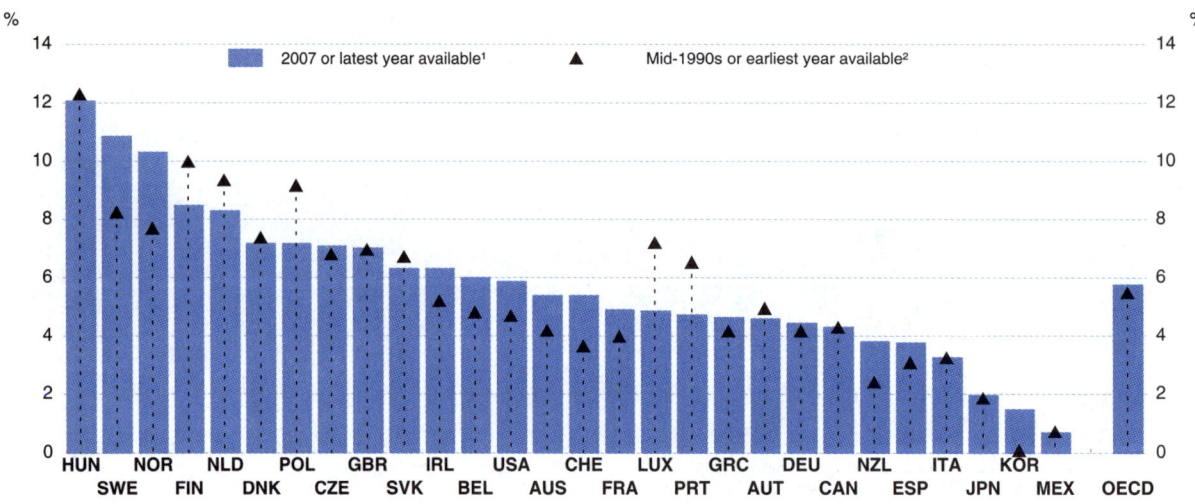

Note: OECD refers to the unweighted average of the 27 countries.
1. 2004 for France; 2005 for Luxembourg; 2006 for Denmark, Italy, Japan, the Slovak Republic and the United States.
2. 1996 for Belgium and Canada; 1999 for the Netherlands; 2000 for Hungary and Italy; 2001 for Ireland; 2003 for Japan and 2004 for Poland; 1995 for all other countries.
Source: OECD (2009c). Data provided by national authorities.

StatLink ᵃᵢˢᵖ *http://dx.doi.org/10.1787/888932346515*

15. By contrasts, extensions of coverage to groups not previously covered may in many cases have responded to a strong social need and any unwinding will need to be carefully considered.

criteria and a shift towards an appraisal of retained work capacity, including regular re-examination of residual work capacity, can likely raise labour force participation with beneficial effects for potential growth and aggregate demand. Reform along these lines would also be consistent with equity goals.

Pension, long-term care and health care reform need to be prepared now

Based on conservative estimates, age-related public spending could increase on average by 3 percentage points of GDP over the next 15 years in the OECD area, taking into account structural trends in health care spending that are not primarily driven by ageing (Table 4.5 above). Against this background, pension, long-term care and health care reform – already identified as being necessary well before the crisis – should play a prominent role in securing the sustainability of government finances and signalling the authorities' determination to do this. Preparation and implementation of legislation should start now as hurdles arise frequently in the legislative process in these areas and new legislation often has to be phased in only gradually and with considerable lags. This is particularly true for pension reform which is often associated with long grandfathering periods. To the extent pension reform is designed to raise the effective retirement age, there is a positive impact on potential output from higher labour force participation of older people. Such reform also fosters inter-generational equity as it eases the rise in the pensioners' dependency ratio and thus the increase in the fiscal burden with which the next generation will be confronted. Also, raising the retirement age may benefit aggregate demand in the near term, as people may to save less as they will face shorter retirement periods. This reinforces the case for swift legislative action. This positive demand effects would not happen if cuts in future pension outlays were based on reducing pension benefits, as households would seek to save more to make up for less retirement income in the future.

Revenue increases

Taxes

While there is some scope to increase revenues...

Announced consolidation plans generally include some revenue increases to supplement expenditure cuts. This is the case also in countries with already very high tax-to-GDP ratios (Figure 4.9), mostly the European countries, where the scope to add to the total tax burden may be more limited. The available room for tax increases would seem to be greater in the United States, Japan, the Czech Republic and the Slovak Republic, where tax-to-GDP ratios are well below the OECD average – though at least in the United States relatively low tax pressure should be seen in the context of widespread use of tax expenditures to pursue public policy goals.[16]

16. Comparison of tax and spending levels across countries is difficult. Adema and Ladaique (2009) attempt to correct measures of social spending for a wide range of institutional differences and find that cross-country differences in spending are much smaller when correcting for institutional differences.

Figure 4.9. **General government tax receipts**

Per cent of GDP, 2007

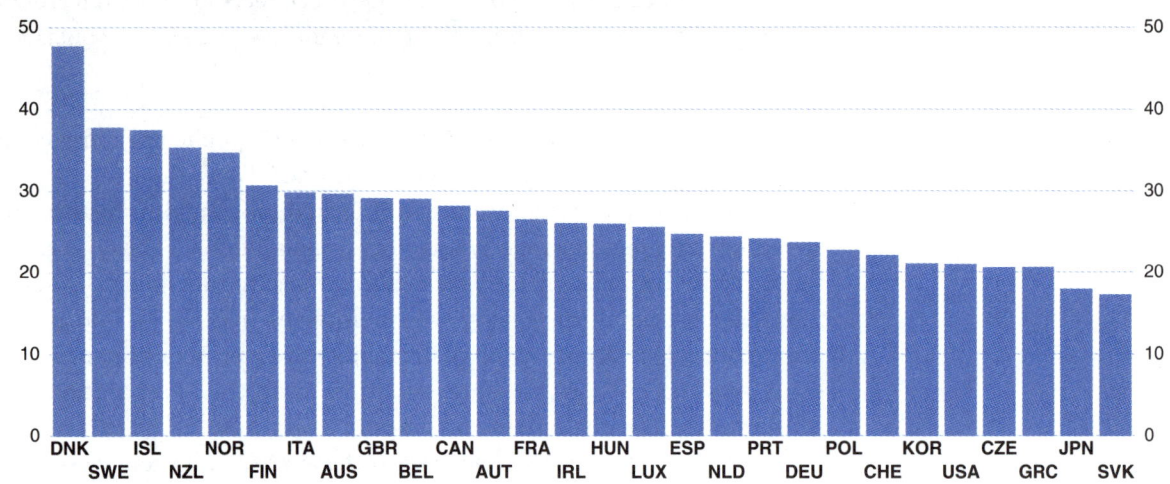

Note: Includes indirect and direct taxes.

Source: OECD Economic Outlook 88 database.

StatLink ⬛📈 *http://dx.doi.org/10.1787/888932346534*

... tax increases should be implemented in the least distortionary way

To the extent that tax increases are necessary they should be implemented in the least distortionary way. Evidence suggests that recurrent taxes on immovable property have the least negative impact on growth, followed by other property taxes and then consumption taxes, whereas taxes on labour and corporate income are most harmful for growth (Johansson *et al.*, 2008). Countries vary considerably in their reliance on property and indirect taxes, suggesting that for some countries, notably the United States and Japan, the scope to raise indirect taxes is particularly large while for others, including Mexico and the Slovak Republic, the scope to increase property taxes is important (Figure 4.10). However, these two tax categories have different equity consequences. As property taxes are inherently progressive, the distributional consequences of raising them appear consistent with equity goals.[17] On the other hand, increasing the weight of consumption taxes in total tax revenues, if conducted in isolation, would reduce the overall progressivity of the tax system, which could conflict with short-term demand objectives and equity considerations and might lead to political resistance. This could be the case, in particular, if lower VAT tax rates motivated by distributional aims were to be raised to the general level. This suggests that it may be more effective to consider a package of taxation measures and to implement it gradually.

17. Due to the weak state of real estate markets, policy makers might not want to increase property taxation soon, limiting their potential contribution to generating fast budgetary improvements. As well it is sometimes seen as an equity problem to raise property taxes on households with low current income, such as pensioners. Such concerns can to some extent be mitigated by allowing property taxes to be treated as a priority claim on the property in future sales.

Figure 4.10. **Property and indirect taxes in the OECD area**

Per cent of GDP, 2008

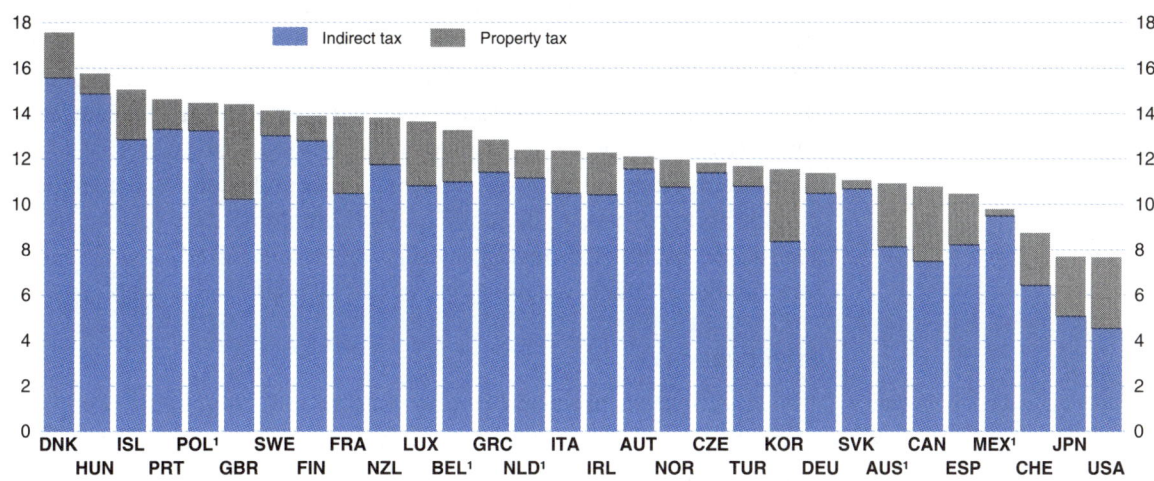

1. Data refer to 2007.

Source: OECD, Revenue Statistics database.

StatLink ᐧᐧᐧ http://dx.doi.org/10.1787/888932346553

Environmental taxes

Environmental taxes can be welfare enhancing

Environmental taxes and the auctioning of emission permits are potentially important revenue sources. For example, in the United States, raising current fuel taxes to the OECD average could generate additional revenues of close to 1% of GDP (disregarding reductions in fuel consumption in response to the tax increase) (Table 4.9). Also, it has been estimated that auctioning emission permits that target a reduction in greenhouse gas emissions by 20% relative to the level prevailing in 1990 would generate revenues of 2.3% of GDP on average in the OECD area by 2020 (de Serres, Murtin and Nicoletti, 2010). Indeed, environmental taxes and revenues have the advantages that the potential tax base is wide and that, as long as they do not exceed the cost of the environmental externality, they are welfare enhancing as they help to reduce environmental damage. There is some evidence that low-income groups spend a higher share of their income on energy products than others, so that they would be relatively more affected by energy taxes, although the difference is modest (O'Brien and Vourc'h, 2001). However, a more comprehensive analysis of the distributional implications would be necessary to take into account other effects as well. For example, low-income residential areas usually suffer relatively more from air pollution, so reductions in such pollutants may benefit those groups more than others.

Introducing or raising user fees

Raising user fees might require complementary policies to address equity concerns

User fees cover all individual payments to public service providers.[18] They are a potential revenue source, in particular at local levels of government, with beneficial effects on resource allocation, notably for infrastructure services. User fees can help contain excessive demand for public sector services, exclude free-riding and generate revenues for infrastructure investment. However, they can exclude low-income households from public sector services. Undesirable equity consequences would therefore need to be cushioned by complementary policies, such as fee reductions for low-income groups or means-tested income support, which would reduce budgetary gains and raise efficiency problems.

Privatisation

Privatisations require analysis of associated costs and benefits

Privatisation proceeds can be used to reduce general government gross debt levels. During the two decades or so prior to the crisis several countries engaged in significant privatisations. There is empirical evidence that divested firms often became more efficient and profitable and increased investment spending (Megginson and Netter, 2001). The evidence is mixed as to whether privatisations are associated with employment losses, although employment reductions seem to have been more frequent. On the other hand, cuts in employment appear to have been associated with efficiency improvements that supported the re-allocation of resources elsewhere. While privatisations can thus contribute to strengthening the growth potential of the economy, with associated beneficial effects on government budgets in the medium term, important reservations need to be made. First, enterprises in government ownership often operate in areas where there is market failure; privatising without addressing market failures by appropriate regulatory provisions would be counter-productive with respect to economic outcomes and might undermine acceptance by electorates. In this regard, sales justified merely by revenue needs that leave necessary regulatory changes unaddressed should be avoided. Second, with significant privatisations having already taken place, successful privatisations of public companies may be increasingly difficult to realise, though sales of governments' holdings of land and buildings could still yield substantial revenue. Third, the private sector may not yet be in a position to absorb large privatisations (including the sale of real estate) without significant discounts. These aspects reinforce the need for cost-benefit analyses of potential privatisations.

---

18. Government revenue from sales of goods and services vary by several percentage points across the OECD area. However, such data are only of limited value for international comparison of the extent to which user fees are employed since countries differ considerably in the degree to which certain services are provided within or outside the public sector.

Sale of assets acquired in response to the crisis can contribute to consolidation

Government assets acquired during the financial crisis through capital injections, purchase of assets and public lending can be sold to reduce gross debt. The value of assets acquired in such operations varies significantly across countries, from zero in Australia and Mexico to 5% of 2009 GDP or more in Germany, the United Kingdom and the United States (end of December 2009, see IMF, 2010a). Experience from past financial crises suggests that recovery rates for such assets tend to be around 50%, though estimated recovery rates on some recent operations are higher, such as some 70% for the US TARP (Congressional Budget Office, 2010b).

Structural reform

Structural reform can facilitate consolidation via various channels...

Structural reform in labour and product markets can raise potential output and facilitate consolidation *via* various channels on both the revenue and spending sides of general government budgets. More employment increases GDP and tax revenue and reduces unemployment benefits. Furthermore, to the extent the additional employment is in the private sector, the public-sector wage bill falls as a share of GDP. In addition, if non-wage public spending on things other than unemployment benefits does not increase with GDP, then the GDP share also falls. Assuming the higher employment increases GDP and tax revenue proportionally, stylised calculations using the OECD's regular elasticities for cyclical adjustments suggest that a 1 percentage point improvement in potential employment may improve government financial balances by between 0.3% and 0.8% of GDP, with the total effect largest in countries where the initial ratio of public to private sector employment and the initial proportion of primary public expenditure to GDP are highest (Figure 4.11).

... although budgetary effects could be limited by offsetting responses

Recent OECD research indicates that aligning anti-competitive product market regulation to OECD best practice might raise productivity levels by as much as 2.5% in the typical OECD country, net of potential additional effects arising from higher private R&D spending and increased employment levels (Boulhol, de Serres and Molnar, 2008). However, an increase in productivity might have only muted effects on public finances. This is because productivity gains are likely to be reflected in higher wages in general, including wages in the public sector, and public transfers are likely to follow suit, with the increase in public spending offsetting to some extent the extra tax revenues resulting from higher output. However, even if direct budgetary effects are limited, structural reform may ease adjustments to consolidation.

Institutional settings that foster fiscal consolidation

A fiscal framework can support sustained consolidation

Empirical evidence suggests that very high debt and deficits encourage governments to consolidate (Guichard *et al.*, 2007; Box 4.3). However, experience also shows that the resolve to consolidate can fade quickly. A mutually reinforcing framework of fiscal rules, independent

Figure 4.11. **Effect of 1% higher potential employment on the primary balance**
Percentage of GDP

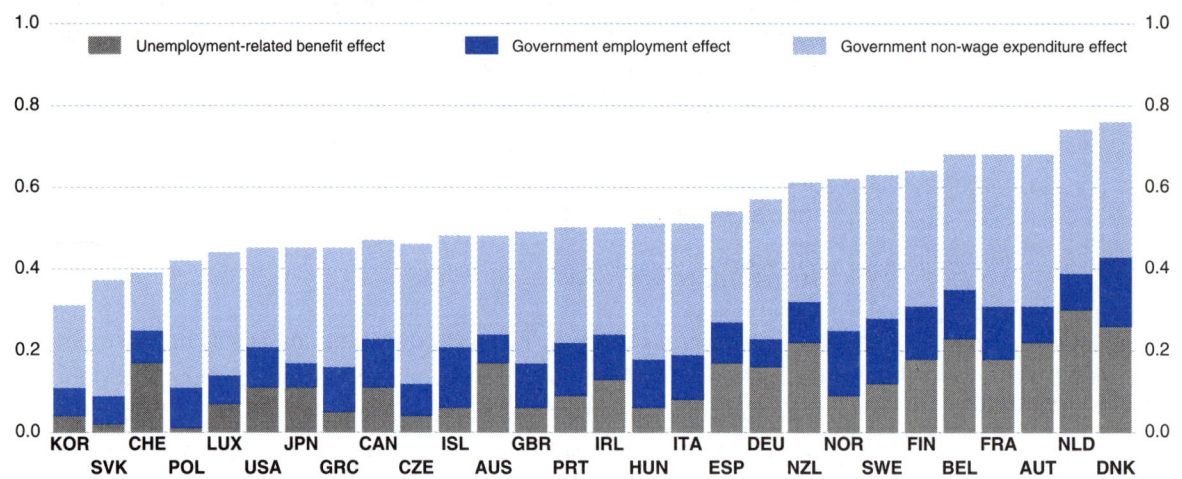

Note: The unemployment-related benefit effect arises as lower unemployment reduces benefit payments. The government employment effect and the government non-wage expenditure effect arise if the additional potential employment is entirely in the private sector and there is no multiplier effect on government employment and non-wage government expenditure, respectively.

Source: OECD Economic Outlook 88 database; and OECD calculations.

StatLink ⟲▦▶ http://dx.doi.org/10.1787/888932346572

fiscal agencies and budget procedures can contribute to returning public finances to sustainable positions and keeping them there.

Fiscal rules

Fiscal rules can take various forms

Fiscal rules can potentially help to keep consolidation efforts on track as the economy improves, revenue picks up and political enthusiasm for consolidation fades. At present, such rules must be tuned to current consolidation needs rather than to imposing fiscal discipline as would be appropriate in more "ordinary" times. As revenues start to improve in the current cyclical upturn, spending needs to be kept under control and tax reductions should be avoided. One option would therefore be to anchor consolidation efforts in a debt rule that specifies, first, a path leading to stabilisation of the debt-to-GDP ratio and, following stabilisation, a path of debt-to-GDP reductions.[19] This might be supplemented by budget rules that can help correct the tendency for slippages to occur and for pro-cyclicality which can lead to a ratchet effect in tax and spending. There are two broad categories of such rules: deficit rules that specify a limit for the annual budget deficit, and expenditure rules that limit discretionary increases or stipulate cuts in spending and in some cases limit revenue-losing changes in tax policy. Both types of rules have been used simultaneously, with positive effect as outlined in Box 4.3, implying an implicit rule for government revenues (Table 4.11).

19. Care needs to be exercised that manipulations on the asset side do not distort such a rule.

Table 4.11. **Fiscal rules applied in OECD countries**

		Characteristics of the set of rules			
		Budget target	Expenditure target	Rule to deal with revenue windfalls	Golden rule
Australia	Charter of Budget Honesty (1998)	yes	no	no	no
Austria	Stability and Growth Pact (1997) Domestic Stability Pact (2000)	yes	yes	no	no
Belgium	Stability and Growth Pact (1997) National budget rule (2000)	yes	yes	yes	no
Czech Republic	Stability and Growth Pact (2004) Law on budgetary rules (2004)	yes	yes	no	no
Denmark	Medium-term fiscal strategy (1998)	yes	yes	no	no
Finland	Stability and Growth Pact (1997) Multiyear spending limits (since 1991)	yes	yes	no	no
France	Stability and Growth Pact (1997) Central government expenditure ceiling (1998)	yes	yes	yes	no
Germany	Stability and Growth Pact (1997) Constitutional Rule (2009)	yes	yes	no	no
Greece	Stability and Growth Pact (1997)	yes	no	no	no
Hungary	Stability and Growth Pact (2004) Fiscal Responsibility law (2008)	yes	yes	no	no
Ireland	Stability and Growth Pact (1997)	yes	yes	no	no
Italy	Stability and Growth Pact (1997) Domestic Stability Pact (since 1999)	yes	no	no	no
Luxembourg	Stability and Growth Pact (1997) Coalition agreement on expenditure ceiling (since 1999)	yes	no	no	no
Mexico	Budget and fiscal responsibility law (2006)	yes	no	yes	no
Netherlands	Stability and Growth Pact (1997) Coalition agreement on multiyear expenditure targets (since 1994)	yes	yes	yes	no
New Zealand	Fiscal responsibility act (1994)	yes	yes	no	no
Norway	Fiscal Stability guidelines (2001)	yes	no	yes	no
Poland	Stability and Growth Pact (2004) Act on Public Finance (1999)	yes	no	no	no
Portugal	Stability and Growth Pact (1997)	yes	no	no	no
Slovak Republic	Stability and Growth Pact (2004)	yes	yes	yes	no
Spain	Stability and Growth Pact (1997) Fiscal Stability Law (since 2001)	yes	yes	no	no
Sweden	Fiscal Budget Act (since 1996)	yes	yes	no	no
Switzerland	Debt containment rule (2001, but in force since 2003)	yes	yes	yes	no
United Kingdom	Code for fiscal stability (1998); superseded by multi-year fiscal mandate	yes	no	no	no
United States	PAYGO rules (2010)	yes	no	no	no

Source: Based on Guichard *et al.* (2007), OECD.

StatLink 🔗 *http://dx.doi.org/10.1787/888932348301*

Targeting deficits is made more difficult by the cycle

Simple deficit limit rules have the advantage of being easy to communicate. However, as budget outcomes are closely related to the economic cycle, deficit targets may be met as cyclical conditions improve without changes in underlying balances. This might be addressed by focusing on the cyclically-adjusted balance or a balance "over the cycle", but only at the expense of introducing a further dimension of uncertainty into the budgeting process, as these concepts are unobservable and need to be estimated.[20] All in all, given the current difficulty to assess the output gap, which is likely to last for a number of years, and the importance of having a non-manipulative rule, a simple deficit rule is probably more suitable to the current situation, possibly including sufficient flexibility to deal with the difficulty of forecasting the exact future growth rate.

Expenditure rules are less sensitive to the cycle...

Expenditure rules are less affected by the economic cycle. When revenues rise in an upturn, they will automatically be saved under an appropriately designed expenditure rule, which is not the case with a deficit limit rule (Anderson and Minarik, 2006). Well-designed expenditure rules also have the advantage that violations are relatively transparent and spending ministers can be held directly accountable for their actions (Atkinson and van den Noord, 2001; Guichard *et al.*, 2007; Price, 2010). Expenditure rules can, however, be subject to manipulation, as the frontier between higher spending and lower revenues is sometimes blurred.

... but are not without problems

Spending rules have been criticised for lowering the quality of public spending. This has led to the adoption of golden rules that specifically exclude investment spending from the cap on the grounds that there is a natural myopic bias towards cutting investment over current expenditure. This type of rule is, however, more difficult to monitor and easier to circumvent (Fatás, 2005). In practice, the distinction between current and investment spending is less than clear cut. Both the United Kingdom and Germany have abandoned golden rules. Moreover, all rules encourage "gimmickry", including one-off measures and creative accounting, to circumvent them (Koen and van den Noord, 2005). This problem might be more serious with an ambitious expenditure rule that will "bite" more often than a deficit rule, giving a stronger incentive to circumvent it. Part of the solution is to ensure that the expenditure rule has a wide ambit to include total expenditure (Price, 2010), applies to different levels of government and includes monitoring of tax expenditures (Anderson and Minarik, 2006). Within this framework, decisions on individual spending

---

20. For example, it has been difficult for the Swedish Fiscal Policy Council to assess compliance with the government's target of a 1% surplus over the cycle (Calmfors, 2010). Disputes concerning when the cycle started and finished was also one of the most contentious aspects of the rule that operated in the United Kingdom until the end of 2008 (OECD, 2009b).

categories should be made in line with considerations for efficiency and other government objectives.

Independent fiscal councils and better budgetary procedures

Independent fiscal councils can bolster commitment

An independent fiscal council (IFC) can be an important ingredient to strengthen governments' compliance with announced fiscal targets by raising the political cost of deviating from them. An IFC with a remit to examine fiscal sustainability may also help strengthen political commitment to consolidation and possibly also broaden such commitment across the political spectrum with associated gains in credibility. By improving the credibility and predictability of fiscal consolidation efforts an IFC can also help coordination with monetary policy. To be effective, an IFC needs to have a central role in the budget process (Debrun, Hauner and Kumar, 2009). Over-optimistic macroeconomic forecasts have been a principal culprit in past episodes of fiscal indiscipline, a practice that can be avoided *e.g.* if short-term fiscal projections are based on average economic projections from a survey of private-sector forecasters. The key roles for an independent budget agency would be to provide independent short-term and long-term economies and fiscal projections that the government could take as a given in its budget process. Likewise, identifying underlying and more ephemeral elements of the budget position is crucial.

There is increasing evidence and support for IFCs

Cross-country evidence suggests that there is a strong relationship between *de jure* influence of IFCs and their perceived effect on fiscal performance (Debrun and Kumar, 2008). There is also evidence that IFCs which provide normative judgments on fiscal policy decisions are more effective (Debrun, Hauner and Kumar, 2009). The political cost of ignoring purely advisory bodies is smaller than ignoring normative assessments and recommendations because these provide a benchmark against which to judge the government's policies. There is also empirical evidence that independent agencies more generally can help to improve equity and efficiency in fiscal decision making and reduce distortions arising from political incentives (Khemati, 2007) and improve fiscal discipline (Eichenberger and Schelker, 2007). Interest in setting up this type of agency is growing. The Swedish Fiscal Policy Council was established in August 2007. In May 2010, the United Kingdom decided to set up an independent agency, the Office of Budget Responsibility, to *inter alia* provide independent economic forecast assumptions that feed into the Budget process. More recently the ECB proposed creating an independent EU fiscal agency (ECB, 2010). Among the lessons from recent experiences is the need for IFCs to be appropriately resourced and to be set up institutionally so as to be truly independent of the government. Another lesson specific to the euro area is that the institutional framework for economic governance needs to be strengthened to avoid the kind of turbulence related to fiscal sustainability seen in the spring of this year (see Box 1.5 in Chapter 1).

Transparency and a top-down determination of spending helps consolidation

More generally, there is empirical evidence that transparent budgetary processes increase the likelihood of success of fiscal consolidation episodes (European Commission, 2007). The increasingly common practice of operating top-down spending ceilings together with managerial discretion in spending within those limits, can help in implementing expenditure targets while still allowing scope for discretion to achieve efficiency gains. Research also suggests that a process that puts the finance minister in a position to discipline spending ministers contributes to fiscal discipline (Hallerberg and von Hagen, 1999; von Hagen, 2002).

Bibliography

Adema, W. and M. Ladaique (2009), "How Expensive is the Welfare State? Gross and Net Indicators in the OECD Social Expenditure Database (SOCX)", *OECD Social,Employment and Migration Working Papers*, No. 92.

Ahrend, R., P. Catte and R. Price (2006a), "Factors behind low long-term interest rates", *OECD Economics Department Working Papers*, No. 490.

Ahrend, R., P. Catte and R. Price (2006b), "Interactions between monetary and fiscal policy: How monetary conditions affect fiscal consolidation", *OECD Economics Department Working Papers*, No. 521.

Alesina, A. F. (2010), "Fiscal Adjustments: Lessons from Recent History," paper prepared for the ECOFIN meeting, Madrid, April 15, available at: *www.economics.harvard.edu/faculty/alesina/files/Fiscal%2BAdjustments_lessons.pdf*.

Alesina, A. F. and S. Ardagna (1998), "Tales of Fiscal Adjustment,"*Economic Policy*, Vol. 13, No. 27.

Alesina, A. F. and S. Ardagna (2009), "Large Changes in Fiscal Policy: Taxes *versus* Spending", *NBER Working Papers*, No. 15438, Cambridge, MA.

Alesina, A. F. and R. Perotti (1995), "Fiscal Expansions and Fiscal Adjustments in OECD Countries,"*Economic Policy*, Vol. 10, No. 21.

Alesina, A. F. and R. Perotti (1997), "Fiscal Adjustments in OECD Countries: Composition and Macroeconomic Effects,"*IMF Staff Papers*, Vol. 44.

Anderson, B and J. J. Minarik (2006), "Design Choices for Fiscal Policy Rules", *OECD Journal on Budgeting*, Vol. 5.

Antolin, P., A. de Serres and C. de La Maisonneuve, (2004), "Long-Term Budgetary Implications of Tax-Favoured Retirement Saving Plans", *OECD Economic Studies*, Vol. 39.

Ardagna, S., F. Caselli and T. Lane (2004), "Fiscal Discipline and the Cost of Public Debt Service: Some Estimates for OECD Countries", *The B.E. Journal of Macroeconomics*, Vol. 7.

Atkinson, P. and P. van den Noord (2001), "Managing Public Expenditure: Some Emerging Policy Issues and A Framework for Analysis", *OECD Economics Department Working Papers*, No. 285.

Baldacci, E., S. Gupta and A. Mati (2010), "Political and Fiscal Risk Determinants of Sovereign Spreads in Emerging Markets", *Review of Development Economics*, forthcoming.

Baldacci, E. and M. S. Kumar (2010), "Fiscal Deficits, Public Debt, and Sovereign Bond Yields", *IMF Working Paper*, No. 10/184, IMF.

Bayoumi, T., M. Goldstein and G. Woglom (1995), "Do Credit Markets Discipline Sovereign Borrowers? Evidence from US States", *Journal of Money, Credit and Banking*, Vol. 27.

Bernanke, B. (2005), "The Global Saving Glut and the US Current Account Deficit", Sandridge Lecture, Virginia Association of Economics, Richmond, Virginia, March.

Blanchard, O. J. (1990), "Comment", in O.J. Blanchard and S. Fischer (eds.), *NBER Macroeconomics Annual 1990, Volume 5*, MIT Press.

Boulhol, H., A. de Serres and M. Molnar (2008), "The Contribution of Economic Geography to GDP Per Capita", *OECD Economics Department Working Papers*, No. 602.

Boss, A. and A. Rosenschon (2010), "Subventionen in Deutschland: Der Kieler Subventionsbericht", *Kieler Diskussionsbeiträge* No. 479/480, June.

Bundesministerium der Finanzen (2010), *Bericht der Bundesregierung über die Entwicklung der Finanzhilfen des Bundes und der Steuervergünstigungen für die Jahre 2007-2010* (Zweiundzwanzigster Subventionsbericht), Berlin.

Caceres, C., V. Guzzo and M. Segoviano (2010), "Sovereign Spreads: Global Risk Aversion, Contagion or Fundamentals?", *IMF Working Paper*, No. 10/120, IFM, Washington, D.C.

Calmfors, L. (2010), "The Swedish Fiscal Policy Council – Experiences and Lessons", *Paper for Conference on Independent Fiscal Policy Institutions*, Budapest, 18-19 March 2010. Available at: *http://people.su.se/~calmf/sweFiscPolCoBudapestMars2010.pdf*.

Caner, M., T. Grennes and F. Koehler-Geib (2010), "Finding the Tipping Point – When Sovereign Debt Turns Bad", *World Bank Policy Research Working Paper*, No. 5391, The World Bank, Washington, D.C.

Caprio, G. Jr, and D. Klingebiel (1997), "Bank Insolvency: Bad Luck, Bad Policy, or Bad Banking?" in Michael Bruno and Boris Pleskovic (eds.), *Annual World Bank Conference on Development Economics*, The World Bank, Washington, D.C.

Checherita, C. and P. Rother (2010), "The Impact of High and Growing Government Debt on Economic Growth: An Empirical Investigation for the Euro Area", *ECB Working Paper*, No. 1237, ECB, Frankfurt.

Commonwealth of Australia (2010), "Australia to 2050: Future Challenges", January.

Congressional Budget Office (CBO) (2010a), "The Long-Term Budget Outlook", June.

Congressional Budget Office (2010b), "Report on the Troubled Asset Relief Program – March 2010". Available at: *www.cbo.gov/ftpdocs/112xx/doc11227/03-17-TARP.pdf*.

Conway, P. and A. Orr (2002) "The GIRM: A Global Interest Rate Model", *Westpac Institutional Bank Occasional Paper*, Westpac Institutional Bank, Wellington.

Corden, W. M. (2009), "The World Credit Crisis: Understanding It, and What to Do", *The World Economy*, Vol. 32.

Dang T-T, P. Antolín and H. Oxley (2001), "Fiscal Implications of Ageing: Projections of Age-Related Spending", *OECD Economics Department Working Papers*, No.305.

DeBrun, X., D. Hauner and M. S. Kumar (2009), "Independent Fiscal Agencies", *Journal of Economic Surveys*, Vol. 23.

Debrun, X. and M. S. Kumar (2008), "Fiscal Rules, Fiscal Councils and All That: Commitment Devices, Signalling Tools, or Smoke Screens?", *Proceedings of the 9th Banca d'ItaliaWorkshop on Public Finance*, Banca d'Italia, Rome.

De Serres, A., F. Murtin and G. Nicoletti (2010), "A Framework for Assessing Green Growth Policies", *OECD Economics Department Working Papers*, No. 774.

Dötz, N. and C. Fischer (2010), "What Can EMU Countries' Sovereign Bond Spreads Tell us about Market Perceptions of Default Probabilities During the Recent Financial Crisis?", *Discussion Paper*, Series 1: *Economic Studies* No. 11/2010, Deutsche Bundesbank, Frankfurt.

Duval, R. and C. de la Maisonneuve (2009), "Long-Run GDP Growth Framework and Scenarios for the World Economy", *OECD Economics Department Working Papers*, No. 663.

ECB (2010), *Reinforcing Economic Governance in the Euro Area*, 10 June 2010, available at: *www.ecb.int/pub/pdf/other/reinforcingeconomicgovernanceintheeuroareaen.pdf*

Égert. B. (2010), "Fiscal Policy Reaction to the Cycle in the OECD: Pro- or Counter-Cyclical?", *OECD Economics Department Working Papers*, No. 763.

Eichenberger, R. and M. Schelker (2007), "Independent and Competing Agencies: An Effective Way to Control Government", *Public Choice*, Vol. 130.

European Commission (2007), *European Economy*, No. 3/2007.

European Commission (2009), *Impact of Ageing Populations on Public Spending*, Brussels.

European Commission (2010), "Measurement of Indicators for the Economic Impact of Public Procurement Policy", *European Commission Working Document* available at: *http://ec.europa.eu/internal_market/publicprocurement/studies_en.htm*.

Faini, R. (2006), "Fiscal Policy and Interest Rates in Europe", *Economic Policy*, Vol. 21.

Fatás, A. (2005), "Is there a Case for Sophisticated Balanced-Budget Rules?", *OECD Economics DepartmentWorking Papers*, No. 466.

Fukawa, T. and I. Sato (2009), "Projection of Pension, Health and Long-Term Care Expenditures in Japan through Macro Simulation", *The Japanese Journal of Social Security Policy*, Vol. 8.

Furceri, D. and A. Zdzienicka (2010), "The Consequences of Banking Crises for Public Debt"*OECD Economics Department Working Papers*, No. 801.

Gianella, C., I. Koske, E. Rusticelli and O. Chatal (2008), "What Drives the NAIRU? Evidence from a Panel of OECD Countries", *OECD Economics Department Working Papers*, No. 649.

Giavazzi, F. and M. Pagano (1990), "Can Severe Fiscal Contractions Be Expansionary? Tales of Two Small European Countries", in O. J. Blanchard and S. Fischer (eds.), *NBER Macroeconomics Annual 1990, Volume 5*, MIT Press.

Giavazzi, F. and M. Pagano (1996), "Non-Keynesian Effects of Fiscal Policy Changes: International Evidence and the Swedish Experience", *Swedish Economic Policy Review*, Vol. 3.

Girouard, N. and C. André (2005), "Measuring Cyclically-Adjusted Budget Balances for OECD Countries", *OECD Economics Department Working Papers*, No. 434.

Guichard, S. and E. Rusticelli (2010), "Assessing the Impact of the Financial Crisis on Structural Unemployment in OECD Countries", *OECD Economics Department Working Papers*, No. 767.

Guichard, S., M. Kennedy, E. Wurzel and C. André (2007), "What Promotes Fiscal Consolidation: OECD Country Experiences", *OECD Economics Department Working Papers*, No. 553.

Hagen, J. von (2002), "Fiscal Rules, Fiscal Institutions and Fiscal Performance", *Economic and Social Review*, Vol. 33.

Hagen, J. von, L. Schuknecht and G. Wolswijk (2010), "Government Bond Risk Premiums in the EU Revisited: The Impact of the Financial Crisis", *European Journal of Political Economy*, forthcoming.

Hallerberg, M. and J. von Hagen (1999), "Electoral Institutions, Cabinet Negotiations, and Budget Deficits in the European Union" in James M. Poterba (ed.), *Fiscal Institutions and Fiscal Performance*, Chicago University Press.

Haugh, D., P. Ollivaud and D. Turner (2009), "What Drives Sovereign Risk Premiums? An Analysis of Recent Evidence from the Euro Area"*OECD Economics Department Working Papers*, No. 718.

Hauner, D. and M. S. Kumar (2006), "Fiscal Policy and Interest Rates: How Sustainable is the New Economy?"*IMF Working Paper*, No. 06/112, IMF, Washington, D.C.

Hellwig, M. and M. J. M. Neumann (1987), "Economic policy in Germany: Was there a turnaround?", *Economic Policy*, Vol. 2, No. 5 .

Hervé, K., N. Pain, P. Richardson, F. Sédillot and P.-O. Beffy (2010), "The OECD's New Global Model", *Economic Modelling*, Article in Press, available at: *http://doi:10.1016/j.econmod.2010.06.012*.

Honohan, P. and D. Klingebiel (2000), "Deposit Insurance Design and Implementation: Policy Lessons from Research and Practice", *Policy Research Working Paper Series*, No. 3969, World Bank, Washington, D.C.

IMF (2010a), Fiscal Monitor May 14, 2010. Available at: *www.imf.org/external/pubs/ft/fm/2010/fm1001.pdf*.

IMF (2010b), "Will it Hurt? Macroeconomic Effects of Fiscal Consolidation", *Chapter 3 of IMF World Economic Outlook*, October.

Johansson, Å., C. Heady, J. Arnold, B. Brys and L. Vartia (2008), "Taxation and Economic Growth", *OECD Economics Department Working Papers*, No. 620.

Joumard, I., C. André and C. Nicq (2010), "Health Care Systems: Efficiency and Institutions", *OECD Economics Department Working Papers*, No. 769.

Khemani, S. (2007), "Does delegation of Fiscal Policy to an Independent Agency Make a Difference? Evidence from Intergovernmental Transfers in India", *Journal of Development Economics*, Vol. 82.

Kinoshita, N. (2006), "Government Debt and Long-Term Interest Rate", *IMF Working Paper*, No. 06/63, IMF, Washington, D.C.

Koen, V. and P. van den Noord (2005), "Fiscal Gimmickry in Europe: One-off Measures and Creative Accounting", *OECD Economics Department Working Papers*, No. 417.

Kumar, M. S. and J. Woo (2010), "Public Debt and Growth", *IMF Working Paper*, No. 10/174, IMF, Washington, D.C.

Laeven, L. and F. Valencia (2008), "Systemic Banking Crises: a New Database", *IMF Working Papers*, No. 08/224.

Laubach, T. (2009), "New Evidence on the Interest Rate Effects of Budget Deficits and Debt", *Journal of the European Economic Association*, Vol. 7.

Megginson, W. and J. Netter (2001), "From State to Market: A Survey of Empirical Studies on Privatization", *Journal of Economic Literature*, Vol. 39.

New Zealand Treasury (2009), "Challenges and Choices, New Zealand's Long-Term Fiscal Statement", *Statements in the Long-Term Fiscal Position*, October.

O'Brien, P. and A. Vourc'h (2001), "Encouraging Environmentally Sustainable Growth: Experience in OECD Countries", *OECD Economics Department Working Papers*, No. 293.

O'Donovan, B., A. Orr and D. Rae (1996), "A World Interest Rate Model", *Financial Research Paper*, No. 7, National Bank of New Zealand Ltd.

OECD (2006a), Projecting OECD Health and Long-Term Care Expenditures: What are the Main Drivers? *OECD Economics Department Working Papers*, No. 477.

OECD (2006b), *OECD Employment Outlook 2006 – Boosting Jobs and Incomes: Policy Lessons from Reassessing the OECD Job Strategy*, Paris.

OECD (2009a), *OECD Economic Outlook*, Interim Report, Paris.

OECD (2009b), *OECD Economic Outlook*, No. 85, Paris.

OECD (2009c), *Sickness, Disability and Work, Keeping on Track in the Economic Downturn*, Paris.

OECD (2009d), *OECD Employment Outlook*, Paris.

OECD (2010a), *Economic Policy Reforms 2010: Going for Growth*, Paris.

OECD (2010b), *Health Care Systems: Efficiency and Policy Settings*, Paris.

OECD (2010c), *OECD Employment Outlook*, Paris.

OECD (2010d), *OECD Economic Outlook*, No. 87 (May), Paris.

OECD (2010e), "Choosing a Broad Base – Low Rate Approach to Taxation", *OECD Tax Policy Studies*, No. 19.

Office of the Parliamentary Budget Officer (2010), "Fiscal Sustainability Report", February.

Ohashi, H. (2009), "Effects of Transparency in Procurement Practices on Government Expenditure: A Case Study of Municipal Public Works", *Review of Industrial Organisation*, Vol. 34.

Price, R. (2010), "Political Economy of Fiscal Consolidation", *OECD Economics Department Working Papers*, No. 776.

Reinhart, C. M. and K. S. Rogoff (2008), "This Time is Different: A Panoramic View of Eight Centuries of Financial Crises", *NBER Working Papers*, No. 13882.

Reinhart, C. M. and K. S. Rogoff (2009), *This Time is Different: Eight Centuries of Financial Folly*, Princeton University Press.

Reinhart, C. M. and K. S Rogoff (2009), "The Aftermath of Financial Crises", *American Economic Review*, Vol. 99.

Reinhart, C. M. and K. S. Rogoff (2010), "Growth in a Time of Debt", *American Economic Review*, Vol. 100.

Röhn, O. (2010), "New Evidence on the Private Saving Offset and Ricardian Equivalence", *OECD Economics Department Working Papers*, No. 762.

Schuknecht, L., J. von Hagen and G. Wolswijk (2009), "Government Risk Premiums in the Bond Market: EMU and Canada", *European Journal of Political Economy*, No. 25.

Sgherri, S. and E. Zoli (2009), "Euro Area Sovereign Risk During the Crisis", *IMF Working Paper*, No. 09/222, IMF, Washington, D.C.

Sutherland, D., R. Price, I. Joumard and C. Nicq (2007), "Performance Indicators for Public Spending Efficiency in Primary and Secondary Education", *OECD Economics Department Working Papers*, No. 546.

Visco, I. (2005), "Ageing and Pension System Reform: Implications for Financial Markets and Economic Policies", *Financial Market Trends*, November 2005 Supplement, OECD, Paris.

Yoo, K. and A. de Serres (2004), "Tax Treatment of Private Pension Savings in OECD Countries and the Net Tax Cost per Unit of Contribution to Tax-Favoured Schemes"*OECD Economics Department Working Papers*, No. 406.

Special chapters in recent issues of OECD Economic Outlook

No. 87, June 2010

Prospects for growth and imbalances beyond the short term

Return to work after the crisis

Counter-cyclical economic policy

No. 86, November 2009

The automobile industry in and beyond the crisis

No. 85, June 2009

Beyond the crisis: medium-term challenges relating to potential output unemployment and fiscal positions

No. 84, December 2008

Responses to inflation shocks: Do G7 counties behave differently?

No. 83, June 2008

The implication of supply-side uncertainties for economic policy

No. 82, December 2007

Corporate saving and investment: recent trends and prospects

No. 81, June 2007

Making the most of globalisation

Fiscal consolidation: lessons from pas experiences

No. 80, December 2006

Has the rise in debt made households more vulnerable?

No. 79, June 2006

Future budget pressures arising from spending on health and long-term care

No. 78, December 2006

Recent house price developments: the role of fundamentals

No. 77, June 2005

Measuring and assessing underlying inflation

STATISTICAL ANNEX

This annex contains data on some main economic series which are intended to provide a background to the recent economic developments in the OECD area described in the main body of this report. Data for 2010 to 2012 are OECD estimates and projections. The data on some of the tables have been adjusted to internationally agreed concepts and definitions in order to make them more comparable as between countries, as well as consistent with historical data shown in other OECD publications. They are using weights that change each period, with the weights depending on the quantity considered. For details on aggregation see the OECD Economic Outlook Sources and Methods.

The OECD projection methods and underlying statistical concepts and sources are described in detail in documentation that can be downloaded from the OECD Internet site:

● *OECD Economic Outlook* Sources and Methods (*www.oecd.org/eco/sources-and-methods*).

● *OECD Economic Outlook* Database Inventory (*www.oecd.org/pdf/M00024000/M00024521.pdf*).

● "The construction of macroeconomic data series of the euro area" (*www.oecd.org/pdf/M00017000/M00017861.pdf*).

Corrigenda for the current and earlier issues, as applicable, can be found at *www.oecd.org/document/53/0,2340,en_2649_33733_37352309_1_1_1_1,00.html.*

The statistical data for Israel are supplied by and under the responsibility of the relevant Israeli authorities. The use of such data by the OECD is without prejudice to the status of the Golan Heights, East Jerusalem and Israeli settlements in the West Bank under the terms of international law.

NOTE ON NEW FORECASTING FREQUENCIES

OECD is making quarterly projections on a seasonal and working day-adjusted basis for selected key variables. This implies that differences between adjusted and unadjusted annual data may occur, though these in general are quite small. In some countries, official forecasts of annual figures do not include working-day adjustment. Even when official forecasts do adjust for working days, the size of the adjustment may in some cases differ from that used by the OECD. The cut-off date for information used in the compilation of the projections is 12 November 2010.

Country classification

OECD	
Euro area OECD countries	Euro area countries in December 2008 that are members of the OECD: Austria, Belgium, Finland, France, Germany, Greece, Ireland, Italy, Luxembourg, Netherlands, Portugal, Slovak Republic, Slovenia and Spain.

Non-OECD	
Other industrialised Asia:	Dynamic Asia (Chinese Taipei; Hong Kong, China; Malaysia; Philippines; Singapore; Thailand and Vietnam) plus Indonesia and India.
Other producers:	Azerbaijan, Kazakhstan, Turkmenistan, Brunei, Timor-Leste, Bahrain, Iran, Iraq, Kuwait, Libya, Oman, Qatar, Saudi Arabia, United Arab Emirates, Yemen, Ecuador, Trinidad and Tobago, Venezuela, Algeria, Angola, Chad, Rep of Congo, Equatorial Guinea, Gabon, Nigeria, Sudan.
Rest of the world	

Irrevocable euro conversion rates

National currency unit per euro

Austria	13.7603	Italy	1936.27
Belgium	40.3399	Luxembourg	40.3399
Finland	5.94573	Netherlands	2.20371
France	6.55957	Portugal	200.48200
Germany	1.95583	Spain	166.38600
Greece	340.750	Slovak Republic	30.126
Ireland	0.78756	Slovenia	239.64

Source: European Central Bank.

National accounts reporting systems, base years and latest data updates

In the present edition of the OECD Economic Outlook, *the status of national accounts in the OECD countries is as follows :*

	Expenditure accounts	Household accounts	Government accounts	Benchmark/ base year
Australia	SNA08 (1959q3-2010q2)	SNA08 (1959q3-2010q2)	SNA08 (1959q3-2010q2)	2007/2008
Austria	ESA95 (1988q1-2010q2)	ESA95 (1995-2009)	ESA95 (1976-2009)	2005
Belgium	ESA95 (1995q1-2010q3)	ESA95 (1995-2009)	ESA95 (1985-2009)	2008
Canada	SNA93 (1961q1-2010q2)	SNA93 (1961q1-2010q2)	SNA93 (1961q1-2010q2)	2002
Chile	SNA93 (1995q1-2010q2)	..	..	2003
Czech Republic	ESA95 (1995q1-2010q2)	ESA95 (1995-2009)	ESA95 (1995-2009)	2000
Denmark	ESA95 (1990q1-2010q2)	ESA95 (1990-2009)	ESA95 (1990-2009)	2000
Finland	ESA95 (1990q1-2010q2)	ESA95 (1975-2009)	ESA95 (1975-2009)	2000
France	ESA95 (1949q1-2010q2)	ESA95 (1978q1-2010q2)	ESA95 (1978-2009)	2000
Germany	ESA95 (1991q1-2010q2)	ESA95 (1991-2009)	ESA95 (1991-2009)	2000
Greece	ESA95 (2000-2009)	..	ESA95 (2000-2009)	2000
Hungary	ESA95 (1995q1-2010q2)	ESA95 (1995-2008)	ESA95 (1995-2009)	2000
Iceland	SNA93 (1997q1-2010q2)	..	SNA93 (1995-2009)	2000
Ireland	ESA95 (1997q1-2010q2)	ESA95 (2002-2009)	ESA95 (1990-2009)	2008
Israel	ESA95 (1997q1-2010q2)	..	ESA95 (1990-2009)	2005
Italy	ESA95 (1980q1-2010q2)	ESA95 (1990-2009)	ESA95 (1980-2009)	2000
Japan	SNA93 (1980q1-2009q4)	SNA93 (1980-2008)	SNA93 (1980-2008)	2000
Korea	SNA93 (2000q1-2010q3)	SNA93 (2000-2009)	SNA93 (2000-2008)	2005
Luxembourg	ESA95 (1995q1-2010q1)	..	ESA95 (1990-2009)	2000
Mexico	SNA93 (2000q1-2010q2)	..	..	2003
Netherlands	ESA95 (1987q1-2010q2)	ESA95 (1990-2009)	ESA95 (1969-2009)	2000
New Zealand	SNA93 (1987q2-2010q2)	..	SNA93 (1986-2008)	1995/1996
Norway	SNA93 (1978q1-2010q2)	SNA93 (1978-2009)	SNA93 (1991-2009)	2007
Poland	ESA95 (1995q1-2010q2)	ESA95 (1995-2008)	ESA95 (1995-2009)	2000
Portugal	ESA95 (1995q1-2010q2)	ESA95 (1995-2009)	ESA95 (1995-2009)	2006
Slovak Republic	ESA95 (1997q1-2010q2)	ESA95 (1995q1-2009q4)	ESA95 (1993-2009)	2000
Slovenia	ESA95 (1995q1-2009q4)	ESA95 (2000-2009)	ESA95 (1995-2009)	2000
Spain	ESA95 (1995q1-2010q2)	ESA95 (2000-2009)	ESA95 (1995-2009)	2000
Sweden	ESA95 (1980q1-2010q2)	ESA95 (1993q1-2010q2)	ESA95 (1993-2009)	2009
Switzerland	SNA93 (1981q1-2010q2)	SNA93 (1990-2008)	SNA93 (1990-2009)	2000
Turkey	SNA93 (1998q1-2010q2)	..	..	1998
United Kingdom	ESA95 (1955q1-2010q2)	ESA95 (1987q1-2010q2)	ESA95 (1987q1-2010q2)	2006
United States	NIPA (SNA93) (1947q1-2010q3)	NIPA (SNA93) (1947q1-2010q3)	NIPA (SNA93) (1947q1-2010q2)	2005

Note: SNA: System of National Accounts. ESA: European Standardised Accounts. NIPA: National Income and Product Accounts. GFS: Government Financial Statistics. The numbers in brackets indicate the starting year for the time series and the latest available historical data included in this Outlook database.
1. Data prior to 1991 refer to the new SNA93/ESA95 accounts for western Germany data.

Annex Tables

Interest Rates and Exchange Rates

External Trade and Payments

Other background Data

Annex Table 1. Real GDP
Percentage change from previous year

	Average 1986-96	1997	1998	1999	2000	2001	2002	2003	2004	2005	2006	2007	2008	2009	2010	2011	2012	Fourth quarter 2010	2011	2012
Australia	3.3	3.9	5.1	4.3	3.3	2.6	3.8	3.5	3.2	3.5	2.4	5.0	2.1	1.2	3.3	3.6	4.0	3.5	3.7	4.2
Austria	2.4	2.2	3.8	3.7	3.3	0.5	1.6	0.7	2.6	2.8	3.5	3.7	1.9	-3.8	2.0	2.0	2.0	2.7	1.3	2.3
Belgium	2.3	3.9	1.9	3.5	3.8	0.7	1.4	0.8	3.1	2.0	2.7	2.8	0.8	-2.7	2.1	1.8	1.8	2.1	1.6	1.9
Canada	2.2	4.2	4.1	5.5	5.2	1.8	2.9	1.9	3.1	3.0	2.8	2.2	0.5	-2.5	3.0	2.3	3.0	2.8	2.6	3.2
Chile	..	6.7	3.3	-0.8	4.6	3.4	2.1	3.8	5.9	5.6	4.8	4.7	3.4	-1.4	5.2	6.2	5.4	6.4	4.9	5.7
Czech Republic	..	-0.7	-0.7	1.2	3.9	2.4	1.8	3.6	4.3	6.4	7.0	6.1	2.3	-4.0	2.4	2.8	3.2	3.2	2.3	3.9
Denmark	1.7	3.2	2.2	2.6	3.5	0.7	0.5	0.4	2.3	2.4	3.4	1.7	-0.9	-4.7	2.2	1.6	2.1	2.8	1.6	2.2
Finland	1.4	6.1	5.1	4.0	5.3	2.2	1.7	2.1	4.1	3.0	4.4	5.3	1.0	-8.1	2.7	3.0	3.0	3.4	3.0	2.9
France	2.1	2.2	3.5	3.2	4.1	1.8	1.1	1.1	2.3	2.0	2.4	2.3	0.1	-2.5	1.6	1.6	2.0	1.7	1.7	2.1
Germany	2.6	1.8	1.8	1.9	3.5	1.4	0.0	-0.2	0.7	0.9	3.6	2.8	0.7	-4.7	3.5	2.5	2.2	4.1	2.1	2.3
Greece	1.4	3.6	3.4	3.4	4.5	4.2	3.4	5.9	4.4	2.3	4.5	4.3	1.3	-2.3	-3.9	-2.7	0.5	-4.3	-1.3	1.4
Hungary	..	3.9	4.8	4.1	4.9	3.8	4.1	4.0	4.5	3.2	3.6	0.8	0.8	-6.7	1.1	2.5	3.1	2.8	2.5	3.6
Iceland	1.6	4.9	6.3	4.1	4.3	3.9	0.1	2.4	7.7	7.5	4.6	6.0	1.0	-6.8	-3.6	1.5	2.6	0.6	0.4	3.5
Ireland	5.5	11.5	8.4	10.7	9.4	5.7	6.6	4.4	4.6	6.0	5.3	5.6	-3.6	-7.6	-0.3	1.5	2.5	2.3	1.9	2.7
Israel	..	3.5	4.1	3.3	9.2	0.0	-0.4	1.5	5.0	4.9	5.7	5.4	4.2	0.8	3.9	4.0	4.3	3.9	4.2	4.3
Italy	2.0	1.9	1.3	1.4	3.9	1.7	0.5	0.1	1.4	0.8	2.1	1.4	-1.3	-5.1	1.0	1.3	1.6	1.3	1.5	1.7
Japan	3.2	1.6	-2.0	-0.1	2.9	0.2	0.3	1.4	2.7	1.9	2.0	2.4	-1.2	-5.2	3.7	1.7	1.3	3.3	1.3	1.6
Korea	8.6	5.8	-5.7	10.7	8.8	4.0	7.2	2.8	4.6	4.0	5.2	5.1	2.3	0.2	6.2	4.3	4.8	5.3	4.7	4.9
Luxembourg	4.9	5.9	6.5	8.4	8.4	2.5	4.1	1.5	4.4	5.4	5.0	6.6	1.4	-3.7	3.3	3.3	3.2	2.3	3.4	3.4
Mexico	2.6	7.2	5.0	3.6	6.0	-0.9	0.1	1.4	4.0	3.2	4.9	3.3	1.5	-6.6	5.0	3.5	4.2	2.9	4.1	4.3
Netherlands	2.8	4.3	3.9	4.7	3.9	1.9	0.1	0.3	2.2	2.0	3.4	3.9	1.9	-3.9	1.7	1.7	1.8	1.8	1.8	1.9
New Zealand	2.2	2.9	0.7	4.6	3.8	2.4	4.6	4.4	4.0	3.1	2.3	3.1	-0.5	-0.4	2.2	2.7	2.5	1.6	3.4	2.2
Norway	2.8	5.4	2.7	2.0	3.3	2.0	1.5	1.0	3.9	2.7	2.3	2.7	0.8	-1.4	0.5	1.8	2.3	0.9	2.3	2.3
Poland	..	7.0	4.9	4.4	4.5	1.3	1.4	4.0	5.2	3.6	6.2	6.8	5.0	1.7	3.5	4.0	4.3	3.5	4.1	4.5
Portugal	3.6	4.4	5.0	4.1	3.9	2.0	0.7	-0.9	1.6	0.8	1.4	2.4	0.0	-2.5	1.5	-0.2	1.8	1.2	0.2	2.6
Slovak Republic	..	5.7	4.4	0.0	1.4	3.5	4.6	4.8	5.0	6.7	8.5	10.6	6.2	-4.7	4.1	3.5	4.4	2.8	4.4	4.5
Slovenia	..	4.9	3.6	5.4	4.4	2.8	4.0	2.8	4.3	4.5	5.9	6.9	3.7	-8.1	1.1	2.0	2.7	1.5	2.3	3.0
Spain	2.9	3.9	4.5	4.7	5.0	3.6	2.7	3.1	3.3	3.6	4.0	3.6	0.9	-3.7	-0.2	0.9	1.8	0.5	1.2	2.1
Sweden	1.5	2.9	4.1	4.4	4.6	1.4	2.5	2.5	3.7	3.1	4.6	3.4	-0.6	-5.1	4.4	3.3	3.4	5.1	3.0	3.5
Switzerland	1.4	2.1	2.6	1.3	3.6	1.2	0.4	-0.2	2.5	2.6	3.6	3.6	1.9	-1.9	2.7	2.2	2.5	2.5	2.5	2.3
Turkey	4.4	7.5	3.1	-3.3	6.8	-5.7	5.9	5.6	8.8	8.7	6.8	4.9	0.5	-4.8	8.2	5.3	5.4			
United Kingdom	2.4	3.3	3.6	3.5	3.9	2.5	2.1	2.8	3.0	2.2	2.8	2.7	-0.1	-5.0	1.8	1.7	2.0	2.9	1.3	2.3
United States	2.9	4.5	4.4	4.8	4.1	1.1	1.8	2.5	3.6	3.1	2.7	1.9	0.0	-2.6	2.7	2.2	3.1	2.3	2.6	3.4
Euro area	..	2.6	2.8	2.9	4.0	1.9	0.9	0.8	1.9	1.8	3.1	2.8	0.3	-4.1	1.7	1.7	2.0	2.1	1.7	2.1
Total OECD	2.9	3.7	2.7	3.4	4.2	1.2	1.7	2.0	3.2	2.8	3.1	2.7	0.3	-3.4	2.8	2.3	2.8	2.7	2.4	3.0

Note: The adoption of national accounts systems SNA93 or ESA95 has been proceeding at an uneven pace among OECD member countries, both with respect to variables and the time period covered. As a consequence, there are breaks in many national series. Moreover, most countries have shifted to chain-weighted price indices to calculate real GDP and expenditures components. For further information, see table "National Accounts Reporting Systems, base years and latest data updates" at the beginning of the Statistical Annex and *OECD Economic Outlook Sources and Methods* (*http://www.oecd.org/eco/sources-and-methods*). These numbers are working-day adjusted and hence may differ from the basis used for official projections.

Source: OECD Economic Outlook 88 database.

StatLink 🔗 *http://dx.doi.org/10.1787/888932348339*

Annex Table 2. Nominal GDP
Percentage change from previous year

	Average 1986-96	1997	1998	1999	2000	2001	2002	2003	2004	2005	2006	2007	2008	2009	2010	2011	2012	Fourth quarter 2010	2011	2012
Australia	7.2	5.3	5.3	5.4	7.8	6.5	7.1	5.9	7.5	8.1	7.8	9.2	8.6	1.6	9.3	7.2	6.7	10.9	6.0	7.0
Austria	5.2	2.0	4.0	3.8	4.7	2.5	3.1	1.9	4.0	4.6	5.7	5.7	3.5	-2.8	3.5	3.1	3.2	4.1	2.5	3.5
Belgium	4.9	4.8	3.8	3.8	5.8	2.8	3.4	2.8	5.3	4.4	5.0	5.2	2.8	-1.6	3.6	3.3	3.5	3.7	3.1	3.7
Canada	5.0	5.5	3.7	7.4	9.6	2.9	4.0	5.2	6.4	6.4	5.6	5.5	4.6	-4.5	5.8	3.9	4.6	4.8	4.3	4.9
Chile	..	11.2	5.3	1.7	9.3	7.3	6.5	10.0	14.0	13.5	17.6	10.3	4.0	2.6	15.3	13.2	9.9	16.4	10.0	10.0
Czech Republic	..	7.6	10.2	4.1	5.5	7.4	4.7	4.6	9.1	6.1	8.2	9.7	4.2	-1.5	2.4	5.1	4.7	4.4	3.9	5.4
Denmark	4.3	5.3	3.4	4.3	6.6	3.2	2.8	2.0	4.7	5.4	5.6	3.7	2.7	-4.3	5.2	2.6	4.2	4.6	3.4	4.5
Finland	4.9	8.0	8.8	4.9	7.9	5.4	3.0	1.5	4.7	3.4	5.5	8.3	2.8	-7.2	4.5	4.8	4.8	5.7	4.8	4.8
France	4.3	3.2	4.5	3.2	5.6	3.8	3.5	3.0	3.9	4.0	4.9	4.9	2.7	-2.0	2.0	2.6	3.1	2.7	2.7	3.3
Germany	5.2	2.1	2.4	2.2	2.8	2.6	1.4	0.9	1.7	1.6	4.0	4.7	1.7	-3.3	4.3	3.6	3.4	4.9	3.1	3.5
Greece	16.0	10.7	8.7	6.6	8.0	7.4	7.0	10.1	7.5	5.2	7.7	7.4	4.8	-1.0	-0.7	-0.3	1.5	-0.6	-1.0	2.9
Hungary	..	23.9	18.6	11.4	14.9	14.5	12.6	9.3	10.5	5.5	8.0	6.7	5.7	-2.6	2.7	4.5	6.3	3.6	5.2	7.0
Iceland	11.7	8.0	11.8	7.5	8.1	12.9	5.8	3.0	10.4	10.5	13.8	12.0	12.9	1.5	2.2	5.1	4.5	-1.6	5.4	4.0
Ireland	8.4	15.7	15.6	15.1	16.1	11.6	11.4	7.3	6.7	8.7	9.3	6.7	-4.9	-11.3	-1.9	2.2	3.7	2.6	4.3	3.4
Israel	..	11.5	11.5	9.8	10.9	1.7	3.5	1.0	5.2	6.0	8.1	5.9	5.2	5.9	4.7	5.5	6.7	5.3	6.2	6.8
Italy	7.7	4.6	3.9	3.2	5.9	4.8	3.7	3.2	4.0	2.9	4.0	4.0	1.4	-3.0	1.7	2.5	2.7	2.5	2.6	2.9
Japan	4.0	2.1	-2.1	-1.4	1.1	-1.0	-1.3	-0.2	1.6	0.7	1.1	1.6	-2.0	-6.1	1.8	0.9	0.5	2.2	0.4	0.9
Korea	16.5	9.8	-1.0	9.6	9.9	8.0	10.6	6.5	7.8	4.6	5.0	7.3	5.3	3.6	9.6	6.2	7.6	7.9	7.0	7.9
Luxembourg	8.0	4.0	6.1	14.2	10.6	2.6	6.3	7.7	6.3	10.3	12.0	10.5	5.7	-4.0	4.9	3.4	5.2	0.4	7.3	5.0
Mexico	40.1	26.0	20.2	21.5	17.4	4.4	2.7	10.9	13.5	7.9	12.2	7.9	8.2	-2.6	9.2	7.6	8.4	6.8	8.5	8.6
Netherlands	4.5	7.0	5.9	6.5	8.2	7.1	3.9	2.5	3.0	4.5	5.2	5.8	4.3	-4.1	3.3	3.1	3.2	4.3	3.1	3.4
New Zealand	6.2	3.5	1.5	5.0	6.4	6.7	5.9	6.1	8.1	5.5	4.7	7.4	3.1	1.2	5.2	7.1	4.7	7.2	6.8	3.9
Norway	6.1	8.3	1.9	8.8	19.4	3.8	-0.3	4.0	9.4	11.6	11.0	5.2	10.8	-5.4	4.7	4.6	4.6	5.8	4.8	4.6
Poland	..	21.9	16.5	10.7	12.1	5.1	3.7	4.3	9.3	6.6	7.8	11.1	8.3	5.3	5.5	7.1	7.7	6.1	7.1	8.0
Portugal	12.6	8.5	9.0	7.5	7.3	5.6	4.5	2.0	4.1	3.3	4.3	5.3	2.0	-2.3	2.6	1.1	3.0	2.2	1.1	3.6
Slovak Republic	..	10.9	9.7	7.4	10.9	8.7	8.6	10.9	11.2	9.2	11.7	11.8	9.2	-5.8	4.2	5.8	6.9	4.3	6.1	7.2
Slovenia	..	13.8	10.8	12.3	10.0	11.8	12.0	8.6	7.8	6.2	8.0	11.3	7.9	-5.1	1.6	3.0	4.6	1.8	3.7	5.1
Spain	8.7	6.3	7.1	7.5	8.7	8.0	7.1	7.4	7.4	8.1	8.3	7.0	3.3	-3.1	0.2	1.0	2.1	0.8	1.4	2.5
Sweden	6.3	4.3	4.8	5.6	5.9	3.7	4.1	4.1	4.6	4.1	6.3	6.2	2.8	-3.3	5.5	4.5	5.0	6.2	4.3	5.3
Switzerland	3.9	1.9	2.9	1.9	4.8	2.0	0.9	0.8	3.1	2.8	5.8	6.2	4.4	-1.6	2.8	2.9	3.2	2.9	3.2	3.2
Turkey	76.2	95.2	81.1	49.0	59.3	44.1	45.9	29.8	22.9	16.1	16.9	11.2	12.7	0.2	15.9	11.8	11.5	..	..	..
United Kingdom	7.2	6.2	5.9	5.6	5.1	4.6	5.3	6.0	5.5	4.2	5.9	5.8	2.9	-3.7	5.1	3.7	3.2	5.8	3.2	3.5
United States	5.8	6.3	5.5	6.4	6.4	3.4	3.5	4.7	6.5	6.5	6.0	4.9	2.2	-1.7	3.7	3.4	4.1	3.9	3.6	4.4
Euro area	..	4.1	4.4	3.9	5.5	4.4	4.2	3.0	3.8	3.8	5.1	5.3	2.4	-3.1	2.5	2.7	3.1	3.2	2.7	3.3
Total OECD	9.2	8.0	6.4	6.3	7.4	4.4	4.2	4.6	5.9	5.2	5.9	5.4	2.9	-2.4	4.3	3.7	4.1	4.5	3.8	4.4

StatLink http://dx.doi.org/10.1787/888932248358

Note: The adoption of national accounts systems SNA93 or ESA95 has been proceeding at an uneven pace among OECD member countries, both with respect to variables and the time period covered. As a consequence, there are breaks in many national series. For further information, see table "National Accounts Reporting Systems, base years and latest data updates" at the beginning of the Statistical Annex and *OECD Economic Outlook* Sources and Methods *(http://www.oecd.org/eco/sources-and-methods).* Working-day adjusted -- see note to Annex Table 1.

Source: OECD Economic Outlook 88 database.

Annex Table 3. Real private consumption expenditure
Percentage change from previous year

	Average 1986-96	1997	1998	1999	2000	2001	2002	2003	2004	2005	2006	2007	2008	2009	2010	2011	2012	Fourth quarter 2010	Fourth quarter 2011	Fourth quarter 2012
Australia	3.2	3.7	4.4	5.3	3.7	3.2	3.8	3.8	5.3	3.7	3.0	5.2	1.9	1.7	3.3	3.2	3.2	3.5	3.2	3.2
Austria	2.5	1.1	1.7	2.2	2.3	1.3	1.1	1.4	1.8	2.1	1.8	0.9	0.7	1.1	0.9	1.1	1.5	0.9	1.3	1.6
Belgium	2.0	2.1	2.6	2.0	2.8	1.3	0.5	0.7	1.4	1.3	1.8	1.7	1.4	-0.2	1.5	1.7	1.8	1.2	1.8	1.8
Canada	2.2	4.6	2.8	3.8	4.0	2.3	3.6	3.0	3.3	3.7	4.2	4.6	2.9	0.4	3.2	2.1	3.0	2.5	2.4	3.2
Chile	..	6.6	4.7	-1.0	3.7	2.9	2.4	4.2	7.2	7.4	7.1	7.0	4.6	0.9	9.4	6.3	5.2	8.7	5.3	5.1
Czech Republic	..	2.2	-0.8	2.6	1.5	2.2	2.1	5.9	2.9	2.5	5.3	5.0	3.5	-0.1	1.5	1.5	2.4	2.9	1.3	3.2
Denmark	1.1	3.0	2.3	-0.4	0.2	0.1	1.5	1.0	4.7	3.8	3.6	2.4	-0.2	-4.6	3.0	1.6	2.2	2.9	1.9	2.4
Finland	1.4	3.3	4.6	2.8	2.2	2.8	2.5	4.8	3.5	3.1	4.3	3.5	1.6	-1.9	2.2	2.5	2.7	1.9	2.4	2.8
France	1.8	0.4	3.9	3.5	3.7	2.5	2.3	2.1	2.4	2.5	2.6	2.5	0.5	0.6	1.5	1.6	2.2	1.1	1.9	2.4
Germany	2.7	0.9	1.4	2.9	2.5	1.9	-0.8	0.1	-0.2	0.4	1.5	-0.2	0.6	-0.1	-0.1	1.3	1.6	0.9	1.5	1.5
Greece	2.9	2.7	3.5	2.5	2.0	5.0	4.7	3.3	3.6	4.6	5.3	3.3	2.3	-1.8	-3.9	-4.3	-0.3	..	..	..
Hungary	..	1.6	4.1	6.3	4.3	6.5	10.8	8.6	3.1	3.3	1.9	0.2	0.4	-7.9	-3.9	2.0	3.0	-2.2	3.9	2.3
Iceland	0.9	6.3	10.2	7.9	4.2	-2.8	-1.5	6.1	7.0	12.7	3.6	5.6	-7.9	-16.0	-0.8	2.2	2.8	-0.7	2.2	2.8
Ireland	3.8	7.7	7.5	8.9	10.0	4.7	3.9	2.9	3.5	6.7	6.5	6.3	-1.8	-7.2	-1.2	-0.6	0.8	-1.0	-0.2	1.0
Israel	..	3.1	5.6	3.9	8.7	3.5	0.8	-0.1	5.3	3.0	4.3	6.4	3.0	1.7	5.2	3.9	4.2	3.6	3.9	4.2
Italy	1.9	3.2	3.5	2.6	2.3	0.7	0.2	1.0	0.8	1.2	1.3	1.1	-0.8	-1.7	0.4	0.6	1.0	0.2	0.8	1.1
Japan	3.1	0.7	-0.9	1.0	0.7	1.6	1.1	0.4	1.6	1.3	1.5	1.6	-0.7	-1.0	2.4	1.0	1.4	1.7	1.1	1.5
Korea	8.5	4.0	-12.5	11.9	9.2	5.7	8.9	-0.4	0.3	4.6	4.7	5.1	1.3	0.2	4.3	4.6	5.0	3.9	4.8	5.0
Luxembourg	3.4	3.8	5.7	3.6	5.0	3.4	5.8	-5.3	2.1	2.2	3.2	3.3	4.8	0.3	2.7	3.2	3.3	3.7	3.5	3.3
Mexico	2.2	6.5	5.5	4.3	8.2	2.5	1.6	2.3	5.6	4.8	5.6	4.0	1.9	-6.2	3.9	4.1	4.1	4.0	4.2	4.0
Netherlands	2.3	3.5	5.1	5.3	3.7	1.8	0.9	-0.2	1.0	1.0	-0.3	1.8	1.1	-2.5	0.2	1.0	1.4	0.8	1.1	1.6
New Zealand	2.2	2.4	2.6	3.5	1.8	2.0	4.4	5.8	5.4	4.7	2.2	3.9	-0.4	-0.6	1.7	2.0	2.2	0.3	3.3	1.6
Norway	1.7	3.1	2.8	3.7	4.2	2.1	3.1	2.8	5.6	4.0	4.8	5.4	1.6	0.2	2.5	2.8	3.5	1.1	3.5	3.4
Poland	..	7.6	5.1	5.2	2.8	2.6	3.1	2.5	4.3	2.5	5.0	4.8	5.3	2.6	2.5	3.0	3.5	2.7	3.5	3.5
Portugal	3.6	3.7	5.1	5.5	3.8	1.3	1.3	-0.2	2.7	1.7	1.8	2.5	1.8	-1.0	1.9	-0.7	0.6	0.9	-1.0	1.1
Slovak Republic	..	7.3	6.6	0.3	2.2	5.5	5.7	1.7	4.6	6.5	5.9	6.9	6.0	-0.7	-0.1	0.4	3.3	0.3	0.8	4.0
Slovenia	..	2.8	2.8	6.8	1.2	2.5	2.5	3.3	2.7	2.6	2.9	6.7	2.9	-0.8	-0.6	1.0	2.5	-0.8	2.0	2.7
Spain	2.8	3.2	4.8	5.3	5.0	3.4	2.8	2.9	4.2	4.2	3.8	3.7	-0.6	-4.2	1.5	1.7	2.3	2.2	2.2	2.4
Sweden	1.0	2.9	3.2	3.9	5.3	0.8	2.6	2.3	2.6	2.8	2.8	3.8	-0.2	-0.8	3.6	3.0	2.8	4.3	2.8	2.8
Switzerland	1.3	1.4	2.2	2.3	2.4	2.3	0.1	0.9	1.6	1.7	1.6	2.3	1.3	1.0	1.7	1.7	2.4	1.5	2.4	2.3
Turkey	3.4	8.4	0.6	0.1	5.9	-6.6	4.7	10.2	11.0	7.9	4.6	5.5	-0.3	-2.2	6.3	4.6	5.6	..	..	..
United Kingdom	2.8	3.8	4.3	5.2	4.7	3.1	3.5	3.0	3.1	2.2	1.7	2.2	0.4	-3.3	1.2	1.7	1.8	1.8	1.3	1.9
United States	2.9	3.7	5.2	5.5	5.1	2.7	2.7	2.8	3.5	3.4	2.9	2.4	-0.3	-1.2	1.7	2.4	2.7	2.3	2.3	3.1
Euro area	..	1.8	3.1	3.4	3.1	2.1	0.9	1.2	1.5	1.8	2.1	1.7	0.3	-1.1	0.6	1.0	1.7	0.7	1.4	1.7
Total OECD	2.8	3.1	3.2	4.2	4.2	2.3	2.4	2.3	3.0	2.9	2.8	2.6	0.3	-1.3	1.9	2.1	2.5	2.0	2.2	2.7

StatLink ⏬ http://dx.doi.org/10.1787/888932348377

Note: The adoption of national accounts systems SNA93 or ESA95 has been proceeding at an uneven pace among OECD member countries, both with respect to variables and the time period covered. As a consequence, there are breaks in many national series. Moreover, most countries have shifted to chain-weighted price indices to calculate real GDP and expenditures components. For further information, see table "National Accounts Reporting Systems, base years and latest data updates" at the beginning of the Statistical Annex and OECD Economic Outlook Sources and Methods (http://www.oecd.org/eco/sources-and-methods). Working-day adjusted -- see note to Annex Table 1.

Source: OECD Economic Outlook 88 database.

Annex Table 4. Real public consumption expenditure
Percentage change from previous year

	Average 1986-96	1997	1998	1999	2000	2001	2002	2003	2004	2005	2006	2007	2008	2009	2010	2011	2012	Fourth quarter 2010	2011	2012
Australia	2.9	2.8	3.5	3.1	3.8	2.3	2.6	3.9	3.9	2.2	3.6	3.3	3.3	2.8	5.2	2.1	1.7	3.9	1.8	1.7
Austria	2.1	3.7	2.6	3.7	0.3	-0.5	0.7	1.0	1.1	1.7	2.5	2.4	3.7	0.5	0.8	-0.2	-0.5	0.8	-0.7	-0.4
Belgium	1.2	1.1	1.6	2.7	3.1	1.6	3.2	1.4	1.8	1.2	0.6	2.1	2.5	0.4	1.1	1.3	0.4	1.5	1.2	0.0
Canada	1.3	-1.0	3.2	2.1	3.1	3.9	2.5	3.1	2.0	1.4	3.0	2.7	3.9	3.5	3.3	0.8	-0.3	1.8	0.1	-0.4
Chile	..	5.8	2.2	2.7	3.0	2.9	3.1	2.4	6.1	5.9	6.4	7.1	0.5	6.8	2.9	4.2	3.1	4.1	3.9	2.8
Czech Republic	..	3.0	-1.6	3.7	0.7	3.6	6.7	7.1	-3.5	2.9	1.2	0.7	1.0	4.2	1.1	0.6	1.1	0.6	-1.3	2.4
Denmark	1.5	0.7	3.5	2.4	2.3	2.2	2.1	0.7	1.8	1.3	2.8	1.3	1.6	3.4	2.0	-0.3	0.3	0.7	0.2	0.3
Finland	1.2	4.0	1.8	1.2	0.5	1.5	2.7	1.6	1.7	2.2	0.3	1.0	2.6	1.2	0.4	0.6	0.6	0.1	1.0	0.5
France	2.3	1.2	-0.6	1.4	2.0	1.1	1.9	2.0	2.2	1.3	1.3	1.5	1.6	2.8	1.6	0.6	0.0	1.0	0.2	-0.1
Germany	1.7	0.5	1.8	1.2	1.4	0.5	1.5	0.4	-0.7	0.4	1.0	1.6	2.3	2.9	2.6	0.7	0.6	2.3	0.8	0.6
Greece	0.4	3.0	1.7	2.1	14.8	0.7	7.2	-0.9	3.5	1.1	-0.1	8.4	0.6	9.6	-8.9	-6.9	-5.8	..	..	..
Hungary	..	0.0	-0.5	1.5	0.7	3.1	5.6	5.0	1.5	2.2	3.7	-7.3	1.0	-0.1	0.3	-4.3	0.0	-0.5	-6.5	4.8
Iceland	3.0	2.6	4.2	4.4	3.8	4.7	5.3	1.8	2.2	3.5	4.0	4.1	4.6	-1.7	-2.0	-2.5	-2.0	-1.3	-2.8	-1.4
Ireland	1.1	5.5	5.7	5.9	9.3	10.4	7.2	1.9	2.4	4.6	5.9	7.3	2.8	-4.2	-3.8	-2.7	-0.3	-3.7	-1.0	0.0
Israel	..	2.7	1.5	2.7	1.7	3.6	5.0	-2.8	-1.7	2.0	3.1	3.1	2.4	1.9	1.1	1.5	1.5	1.2	1.5	1.5
Italy	0.8	0.5	0.4	1.4	2.2	3.9	2.4	1.9	2.2	1.9	0.5	0.9	0.8	0.6	-0.3	0.1	0.0	-0.1	0.0	0.1
Japan	3.4	0.8	1.8	4.2	4.3	3.0	2.4	2.3	1.9	1.6	0.4	1.5	0.3	1.5	1.6	1.7	0.3	1.7	1.2	0.1
Korea	6.6	2.7	2.2	3.0	1.8	5.0	4.9	4.4	3.8	4.3	6.6	5.4	4.3	5.0	3.9	2.0	3.0	5.9	3.0	3.0
Luxembourg	5.3	3.2	1.6	8.3	4.7	6.1	4.6	4.1	4.5	3.3	1.6	2.8	2.7	4.5	1.0	0.3	0.9	2.4	-3.0	4.6
Mexico	1.3	2.6	2.5	4.5	2.6	-2.4	-0.2	1.0	-2.8	2.5	1.9	3.1	0.9	2.3	3.8	1.5	1.2	4.3	1.4	1.0
Netherlands	2.1	2.5	2.5	2.8	2.0	4.6	3.3	2.9	-0.1	0.5	9.5	3.5	2.5	3.7	1.9	0.2	-0.4	1.6	-0.6	-0.4
New Zealand	1.6	6.3	-0.3	6.8	-2.4	4.2	1.4	3.4	5.6	4.0	5.0	4.4	5.0	1.4	2.9	0.6	0.5	2.3	0.7	0.5
Norway	3.0	3.3	3.4	3.1	1.9	4.6	3.1	1.7	1.5	0.7	1.9	3.0	4.1	4.7	2.9	2.0	2.0	3.6	1.7	2.2
Poland	3.3	3.3	2.2	1.9	1.5	2.3	2.0	4.6	3.4	5.5	5.6	3.6	6.9	2.6	2.1	1.6	1.5	1.2	1.8	1.4
Portugal	3.9	2.6	6.2	3.8	4.2	3.8	1.6	0.4	2.4	3.3	-0.7	0.5	0.8	2.9	2.1	-6.0	-1.3	1.6	-6.5	-0.8
Slovak Republic	..	0.2	5.6	-7.3	4.6	5.4	3.0	4.3	-2.9	3.9	9.7	0.1	5.3	2.8	1.6	-3.7	1.0	0.0	-3.6	2.7
Slovenia	..	3.3	4.8	3.3	3.1	3.8	3.3	2.2	3.4	3.4	4.0	0.7	6.2	3.0	0.3	-0.8	-0.3	-0.5	-0.6	-0.2
Spain	4.3	2.5	3.5	4.0	5.3	3.9	4.5	4.8	6.3	5.5	4.6	5.5	5.8	3.2	0.3	-0.8	-1.3	0.8	-1.2	-1.3
Sweden	1.3	-0.6	3.6	1.5	-1.1	0.9	2.1	1.1	-0.9	0.2	2.0	0.8	1.0	1.8	1.6	1.2	1.0	1.6	1.0	0.9
Switzerland	2.5	0.4	-1.1	0.5	2.3	4.5	1.2	1.9	0.8	1.2	0.3	0.3	1.7	1.6	0.2	0.4	0.9	-1.3	1.4	0.6
Turkey	4.2	4.1	7.8	4.0	5.7	-1.1	5.8	-2.6	6.0	2.5	8.4	6.5	1.7	7.8	0.1	4.4	4.8	..	..	..
United Kingdom	0.9	-0.5	1.1	3.6	3.1	2.4	3.5	3.4	3.0	2.0	1.4	1.3	1.6	1.0	1.9	-1.1	-1.7	1.8	-2.1	-1.5
United States	1.1	1.7	1.8	2.8	1.8	3.7	4.5	2.2	1.4	0.6	1.0	1.3	2.5	1.9	1.1	1.0	0.6	1.5	0.6	0.7
Euro area	..	1.3	1.3	1.8	2.4	2.0	2.4	1.7	1.6	1.6	2.0	2.2	2.3	2.4	1.0	0.0	-0.1	0.9	-0.2	-0.1
Total OECD	1.8	1.3	1.8	2.7	2.5	2.8	3.2	2.2	1.7	1.5	1.8	2.0	2.3	2.3	1.5	0.7	0.4	1.4	0.3	0.5

Note: The adoption of national accounts systems SNA93 or ESA95 has been proceeding at an uneven pace among OECD member countries, both with respect to variables and the time period covered. As a consequence, there are breaks in many national series. Moreover, most countries have shifted to chain-weighted price indices to calculate real GDP and expenditures components. For further information, see table "National Accounts Reporting Systems, base years and latest data updates" at the beginning of the Statistical Annex and *OECD Economic Outlook* Sources and Methods *(http://www.oecd.org/eco/sources-and-methods)*. Working-day adjusted -- see note to Annex Table 1.

Source: OECD Economic Outlook 88 database.

StatLink ⬛ http://dx.doi.org/10.1787/888932348396

Annex Table 5. Real total gross fixed capital formation
Percentage change from previous year

	Average 1986-96	1997	1998	1999	2000	2001	2002	2003	2004	2005	2006	2007	2008	2009	2010	2011	2012	Fourth quarter 2010	2011	2012
Australia	3.5	9.3	6.4	4.6	2.0	-3.7	16.1	9.7	6.2	9.6	4.1	9.8	9.0	-1.1	7.0	6.6	8.5	4.7	7.5	8.7
Austria	3.8	0.2	3.0	1.7	4.8	-1.5	-4.0	3.3	1.6	2.4	0.9	3.5	2.8	-8.9	-2.4	2.5	3.2	0.1	2.3	3.6
Belgium	3.9	6.2	3.4	2.6	5.1	1.1	-4.5	0.1	7.6	7.5	2.0	6.3	2.4	-4.9	-1.7	2.8	3.7	-0.2	3.3	4.1
Canada	2.0	15.2	2.4	7.3	4.7	4.0	1.6	6.2	7.8	9.3	7.1	3.5	1.4	-11.7	6.6	4.8	2.6	7.2	4.0	2.1
Chile	..	10.5	1.9	-18.2	8.9	4.3	1.5	5.7	10.0	23.9	2.3	11.2	18.6	-15.3	24.2	14.2	10.5	30.2	11.5	10.0
Czech Republic	..	-5.7	-0.9	-3.3	5.1	6.6	5.1	0.4	3.9	1.8	6.0	10.8	-1.5	-9.2	-3.6	5.8	6.2	-2.1	6.1	6.2
Denmark	1.4	10.3	8.1	-0.1	7.6	-1.4	0.1	-0.2	3.9	4.7	14.3	2.8	-4.8	-13.0	-3.9	4.4	6.2	4.8	2.7	8.7
Finland	-0.7	10.5	11.4	3.8	6.0	3.0	-4.0	2.9	4.9	3.6	2.2	10.1	0.0	-14.5	1.1	5.3	4.5	6.4	4.2	4.5
France	2.0	0.4	7.2	8.1	7.5	2.3	-1.6	2.2	3.3	4.5	4.5	5.9	0.3	-7.0	-1.8	2.8	4.3	0.8	3.6	4.4
Germany	3.1	0.8	3.6	4.4	3.7	-3.4	-6.1	-0.3	-1.3	1.1	8.7	4.9	1.8	-10.0	4.9	2.7	1.2	7.6	1.0	1.6
Greece	1.3	6.8	10.6	11.0	8.0	4.8	9.5	11.8	1.4	-4.5	9.8	4.6	-7.4	-13.9	-18.2	-10.6	-2.2	..	..	..
Hungary	..	4.3	9.7	4.9	6.8	4.7	10.3	2.6	7.6	6.5	-3.5	3.7	3.2	-9.2	-4.3	3.2	4.3	-1.2	5.1	3.6
Iceland	1.4	9.3	34.4	-4.1	11.8	-4.3	-14.0	11.1	28.1	35.7	22.4	-11.1	-20.9	-50.9	-14.7	8.4	17.1	-23.6	9.8	18.5
Ireland	5.6	16.5	14.1	13.4	6.3	0.1	2.9	6.5	9.5	15.0	4.4	2.6	-14.4	-30.9	-17.9	2.8	1.8	-5.1	0.9	2.4
Israel	..	-0.9	-4.0	-0.3	3.2	-3.7	-6.5	-4.1	0.5	3.4	13.6	14.6	4.1	-6.5	6.1	6.2	6.5	9.5	6.2	6.6
Italy	1.7	1.9	3.6	3.7	7.1	2.4	3.7	-0.9	1.5	1.4	3.1	1.3	-4.0	-12.2	2.0	1.5	3.1	2.5	2.3	3.4
Japan	3.9	-0.3	-7.2	-0.8	1.2	-0.9	-4.9	-0.5	1.4	3.1	0.5	-1.2	-2.6	-14.0	-0.1	3.2	2.3	3.4	1.9	3.7
Korea	12.9	-1.5	-22.0	8.7	12.3	0.3	7.1	4.4	2.1	1.9	3.4	4.2	-1.9	-0.2	7.9	5.7	5.3	7.5	4.4	5.9
Luxembourg	5.9	10.4	6.1	22.0	-4.7	8.8	5.5	6.3	2.7	2.5	3.8	17.9	1.4	-19.2	3.5	3.6	2.6	5.7	2.6	2.7
Mexico	3.1	21.1	10.5	7.7	11.4	-5.6	-0.7	0.4	7.9	7.4	9.9	7.0	4.4	-10.1	1.3	5.2	7.9	2.5	6.7	8.0
Netherlands	3.0	8.5	6.8	8.7	0.6	0.2	-4.5	-1.5	-1.6	3.7	7.5	5.5	5.1	-12.7	-4.6	1.8	3.8	1.3	3.1	4.2
New Zealand	3.0	1.2	-3.4	6.8	8.4	-1.1	10.8	10.3	12.6	5.1	-1.1	5.5	-3.5	-12.0	4.1	11.6	7.0	8.5	12.2	5.4
Norway	0.1	15.8	13.6	-5.4	-3.5	-1.1	-1.1	0.2	10.2	13.3	11.7	12.5	2.0	-9.1	-5.4	4.6	3.8	-2.8	3.5	4.0
Poland	..	20.7	14.2	6.6	2.5	-9.7	-6.3	0.0	6.5	6.3	14.8	17.3	9.7	-0.7	-0.6	17.8	12.5	8.2	13.3	12.1
Portugal	5.9	14.2	11.8	6.0	3.9	0.6	-3.2	-7.1	0.0	-0.5	-1.3	2.6	-1.8	-11.9	-4.1	-3.5	2.3	-1.9	-1.9	3.9
Slovak Republic	..	14.0	9.4	-15.7	-9.6	13.0	0.2	-2.7	4.8	17.5	9.3	9.1	1.8	-10.5	-0.7	6.1	6.9	1.1	8.1	6.6
Slovenia	..	13.3	8.9	14.6	2.2	0.7	0.7	8.1	5.6	3.7	10.1	12.8	8.5	-21.6	-5.3	4.2	6.6	-3.0	6.1	6.8
Spain	4.3	5.0	11.3	10.4	6.6	4.8	3.4	5.9	5.1	7.0	7.2	4.5	-4.8	-16.0	-6.8	-1.8	2.0	-4.0	-0.4	3.2
Sweden	1.2	0.8	8.6	8.3	6.0	0.6	-1.3	1.8	5.0	8.0	9.7	9.1	1.3	-15.9	4.5	6.8	6.5	6.1	6.5	6.4
Switzerland	1.7	2.1	6.4	1.5	4.2	-3.5	-0.5	-1.2	4.5	3.8	4.7	5.1	0.5	-4.9	3.7	4.2	2.8	3.1	3.4	2.4
Turkey	9.2	14.8	-3.9	-16.2	17.5	-30.0	14.7	14.2	28.4	17.4	13.3	3.1	-6.2	-19.1	25.3	13.4	12.2	..	..	..
United Kingdom	3.0	6.8	13.7	3.0	2.7	2.6	3.6	1.1	5.1	2.4	6.4	7.8	-5.0	-15.1	2.0	2.3	4.3	5.1	2.7	5.1
United States	3.3	8.1	9.7	9.0	6.8	-1.0	-2.7	3.1	6.2	5.3	2.5	-1.2	-4.5	-14.8	3.4	7.2	6.8	7.1	6.6	7.1
Euro area	..	2.7	5.8	6.0	5.3	0.6	-1.5	1.3	1.9	3.4	5.6	4.6	-1.0	-11.3	-1.0	1.6	2.8	1.6	1.9	3.2
Total OECD	3.6	5.4	3.8	5.1	5.6	-1.0	-0.9	2.3	4.6	4.9	4.4	2.6	-1.8	-12.1	2.4	5.0	5.2	5.1	4.6	5.7

StatLink ⟐⟐⟐ http://dx.doi.org/10.1787/888932348415

Note: The adoption of national accounts systems SNA93 or ESA95 has been proceeding at an uneven pace among OECD member countries, both with respect to variables and the time period covered. As a consequence, there are breaks in many national series. Moreover, most countries have shifted to chain-weighted price indices to calculate real GDP and expenditures components. For further information, see table "National Accounts Reporting Systems, base years and latest data updates" at the beginning of the Statistical Annex and OECD Economic Outlook Sources and Methods (http://www.oecd.org/eco/sources-and-methods). Working-day adjusted -- see note to Annex Table 1.

Source: OECD Economic Outlook 88 database.

Annex Table 6. Real gross private non-residential fixed capital formation
Percentage change from previous year

	Average 1986-96	1997	1998	1999	2000	2001	2002	2003	2004	2005	2006	2007	2008	2009	2010	2011	2012	Fourth quarter 2010	2011	2012
Australia	4.5	7.6	3.9	4.3	0.5	-1.5	13.7	14.4	7.5	15.0	7.4	12.4	9.7	-0.7	1.2	9.0	11.9	1.0	11.0	12.0
Austria	4.5	6.7	6.4	3.8	10.0	2.0	-4.8	6.3	2.7	2.5	0.5	4.5	4.0	-10.5	-2.5	3.7	4.5	0.9	3.4	5.0
Belgium	4.3	6.1	7.3	0.4	7.7	4.2	-4.7	-1.2	8.3	5.2	2.0	7.9	3.4	-7.5	-1.0	2.9	4.5	0.9	3.1	5.6
Canada	3.1	22.6	5.3	7.2	4.7	0.2	-4.1	6.9	8.2	12.4	9.9	3.3	3.4	-19.9	2.7	9.5	6.3	11.0	7.7	5.4
Denmark	2.6	12.1	11.9	-1.5	6.7	-0.3	0.7	-3.0	-0.3	-0.2	16.3	3.4	-0.2	-14.2	-3.0	9.7	9.3	8.7	10.3	7.8
Finland	-0.9	6.0	15.0	2.7	8.8	9.5	-8.5	-2.2	1.6	6.5	2.6	17.2	5.8	-19.1	-12.7	3.9	7.6	-6.2	6.1	8.1
France	2.4	2.0	10.4	9.1	8.7	3.3	-3.0	1.2	3.6	3.2	5.6	6.9	2.6	-8.5	-1.8	4.1	6.3	1.4	5.3	6.6
Germany	2.5	2.8	6.0	5.8	7.9	-2.6	-7.0	0.7	0.7	4.3	10.3	8.5	3.0	-16.1	6.0	3.7	3.6	10.6	2.5	3.7
Greece	11.7	5.1	13.0	20.7	13.3	5.8	9.4	12.2	1.1	-2.8	-3.1	16.6	5.3	-13.3	-18.2	-10.2	-1.1	..	..	..
Iceland	0.8	17.6	46.2	-7.4	11.1	-11.3	-20.2	20.9	33.9	60.2	24.2	-22.1	-25.8	-55.0	-3.1	17.7	23.6	-30.7	20.4	22.7
Ireland	7.0	18.4	19.6	12.6	2.4	-9.0	0.2	6.0	14.1	17.5	4.6	10.0	-20.1	-34.1	-6.5	15.6	3.8	10.3	3.4	4.2
Italy	2.6	3.4	4.0	4.1	8.4	2.0	4.5	-3.4	1.1	-0.3	3.3	2.0	-5.8	-17.6	6.0	3.2	3.6	6.9	3.5	3.8
Japan	3.1	8.4	-6.5	-4.3	7.5	1.3	-5.2	4.4	5.6	9.2	2.3	2.6	0.1	-19.2	1.8	4.6	5.5	4.3	5.5	4.8
Korea	13.2	-2.5	-28.1	13.8	18.8	-3.3	8.1	2.3	1.9	2.0	7.6	7.0	-0.2	-2.8	15.0	8.1	6.1	15.4	4.6	6.9
Netherlands	3.0	13.5	8.3	11.3	-2.0	-3.0	-7.6	-1.0	-2.7	2.2	9.7	6.4	7.1	-18.2	-2.4	3.4	6.7	3.0	5.5	7.3
New Zealand	5.4	-5.9	-1.1	7.0	19.4	-3.0	-1.0	13.0	13.6	8.1	-1.0	10.9	5.5	-17.0	1.6	10.8	8.3	8.0	12.4	7.2
Norway	0.1	16.1	16.0	-8.3	-3.9	-4.3	-1.9	-2.9	10.3	17.3	14.5	16.3	5.7	-10.1	-5.5	5.7	4.2	3.3	4.7	4.1
Spain	5.4	6.5	11.4	11.7	7.9	3.2	1.2	5.3	6.8	7.7	7.8	3.9	-3.1	-18.5	-2.7	4.8	5.2	2.9	5.4	5.2
Sweden	2.9	5.4	9.8	8.5	7.9	-1.0	-5.7	2.4	4.0	8.3	9.0	10.6	4.3	-18.8	3.8	8.2	7.6	6.0	7.8	7.5
Switzerland	1.8	2.5	8.2	4.4	5.4	-2.3	-0.5	-4.4	4.7	6.4	7.6	8.1	1.5	-7.0	4.2	5.4	3.6	3.6	4.6	3.0
United Kingdom	4.5	10.0	19.3	4.1	4.4	1.5	1.2	-1.0	1.2	17.9	-7.1	12.5	-1.1	-18.8	2.3	6.1	7.0	12.3	6.4	7.4
United States	4.6	12.1	12.0	10.4	9.8	-2.8	-7.9	0.9	6.0	6.7	7.9	6.7	0.3	-17.1	5.9	10.1	9.0	11.5	9.0	9.1
Euro area	..	4.3	7.6	7.0	7.6	0.8	-2.5	0.9	2.6	3.6	6.3	6.2	0.3	-14.9	0.7	3.7	4.7	4.5	3.9	5.0
Total OECD	4.1	6.2	5.2	6.4	8.4	-0.8	-3.6	1.9	4.6	7.0	5.9	6.4	0.7	-15.4	3.7	6.9	6.9	8.0	6.5	7.0

Note: The adoption of national account systems SNA93 or ESA95 has been proceeding at an uneven pace among OECD member countries, both with respect to variables and the time period covered. As a consequence, there are breaks in many national series. Moreover, most countries have shifted to chain-weighted price indices to calculate real GDP and expenditures components. For further information, see table "National Account Reporting Systems, base years and latest data updates" at the beginning of the Statistical Annex. Some countries (e.g. United States, Canada and France) use hedonic price indices to deflate current-price values of investment in certain information and communication technology products such as computers. National account data do not always have a sectoral breakdown of investment expenditures, and for some countries data are estimated by the OECD. See also *OECD Economic Outlook Sources and Methods* (*http://www.oecd.org/eco/sources-and-methods*). Working-day adjusted -- see note to Annex Table 1.

Source: OECD Economic Outlook 88 database.

StatLink 🔗 *http://dx.doi.org/10.1787/888932348434*

Annex Table 7. Real gross residential fixed capital formation

Percentage change from previous year

	Average 1986-96	1997	1998	1999	2000	2001	2002	2003	2004	2005	2006	2007	2008	2009	2010	2011	2012	Fourth quarter 2010	Fourth quarter 2011	Fourth quarter 2012
Australia	2.2	16.3	12.0	5.7	1.3	-10.9	25.9	4.6	2.9	-3.5	-2.5	2.5	2.5	-4.5	5.0	5.9	5.8	3.9	5.4	5.9
Austria	4.3	-1.2	-3.0	-1.7	-5.0	-6.4	-5.0	-4.2	-0.5	1.5	2.5	1.8	-1.7	-4.4	-2.9	-1.6	-0.4	-2.9	-1.0	0.0
Belgium	5.6	7.5	-4.4	3.1	-1.1	-2.7	-5.5	3.4	8.1	10.9	6.4	3.4	-0.6	-3.0	-3.6	0.6	1.6	-1.6	1.0	2.0
Canada	-0.7	8.2	-3.6	3.6	5.2	10.5	14.1	5.4	7.5	3.3	2.2	2.9	-3.7	-8.1	10.3	0.4	3.2	3.0	3.0	2.7
Denmark	-2.1	9.7	1.9	4.3	10.3	-9.3	0.8	11.8	11.9	17.3	9.6	3.4	-14.2	-18.1	-13.9	-0.2	3.3	-7.9	2.7	3.5
Finland	-0.9	16.5	10.9	8.8	5.8	-9.4	-0.2	11.3	11.8	5.6	4.6	0.1	-9.7	-13.4	27.2	9.1	2.3	30.6	3.5	1.5
France	0.7	1.0	3.7	7.1	2.5	1.4	1.3	2.1	3.2	5.8	6.2	4.8	-2.3	-8.1	-2.5	1.3	2.4	0.1	1.9	2.5
Germany	6.0	0.2	0.2	1.6	-1.8	-5.9	-6.0	-0.9	-3.6	-3.7	6.2	-1.7	-1.8	-1.0	3.5	1.6	2.0	4.4	1.5	2.0
Greece	-4.1	6.6	8.8	3.8	-4.3	4.3	15.2	12.1	-0.9	-0.7	29.6	-8.6	-29.1	-21.7	-20.0	-15.5	-6.1	..	..	..
Iceland	1.8	-9.3	1.0	0.6	12.7	12.3	12.4	3.7	14.2	11.9	16.5	13.2	-21.9	-55.7	-26.3	3.2	5.0	25.1	3.5	5.3
Ireland	6.1	15.8	6.4	12.9	7.6	1.9	5.4	18.3	11.2	16.0	3.0	-10.6	-23.3	-42.1	-37.1	-14.6	1.3	-33.8	0.3	1.9
Italy	0.8	-2.4	-1.2	1.3	5.1	1.5	2.5	3.5	2.4	5.3	4.1	0.5	-3.1	-9.3	-3.4	0.5	1.8	-0.4	1.1	1.9
Japan	3.8	-12.1	-14.3	0.2	0.9	-5.3	-4.0	-1.0	1.9	-1.5	0.5	-9.6	-8.1	-14.2	-7.3	4.5	6.1	3.8	5.0	7.1
Korea	13.4	-4.8	-13.4	-5.5	-9.6	12.5	11.2	8.6	3.6	2.4	-2.4	-3.0	-7.8	-6.5	-9.7	-2.1	2.1	-10.9	1.6	2.3
Netherlands	2.6	5.6	3.0	2.8	1.6	3.2	-6.5	-3.7	4.1	5.0	5.8	4.7	0.9	-13.6	-9.8	0.7	3.2	-3.2	2.0	4.0
New Zealand	4.1	6.8	-12.8	7.5	0.5	-11.7	21.3	19.8	4.6	-4.4	-2.5	5.0	-19.1	-19.3	12.8	8.3	9.7	9.9	11.5	9.6
Norway	-2.9	12.1	7.7	3.0	5.6	8.1	-0.7	1.9	16.3	10.8	4.1	2.9	-12.1	-18.9	-5.8	2.8	4.0	0.7	3.6	4.2
Spain	3.4	2.2	10.9	11.4	10.3	7.5	7.0	9.3	5.9	6.1	6.2	2.5	-10.7	-24.5	-16.6	-3.6	-0.3	-9.9	-1.5	-0.1
Sweden	-8.3	-8.1	5.4	13.3	14.8	7.4	11.3	4.3	12.4	11.9	15.5	8.0	-9.5	-23.4	17.1	7.8	7.0	17.6	6.9	7.0
Switzerland	1.2	-0.1	2.8	-5.5	-2.7	-4.1	-3.7	14.4	7.0	1.1	-1.6	-3.0	-4.2	-1.2	1.8	1.6	1.0	..	..	..
United Kingdom	1.2	7.4	5.6	2.1	1.1	0.4	6.0	0.5	11.5	-3.6	9.0	0.2	-23.4	-27.0	7.9	8.6	3.3	12.6	3.3	3.4
United States	1.3	1.9	7.7	6.3	1.0	0.6	5.3	8.2	9.8	6.2	-7.3	-18.7	-24.0	-22.9	-2.6	2.8	6.4	-2.6	5.0	7.5
Euro area	..	1.2	1.8	3.7	1.4	-1.1	-1.0	2.7	1.9	3.4	6.3	0.8	-5.3	-10.7	-3.6	0.4	1.7	-0.4	1.0	1.9
Total OECD	2.3	0.0	1.3	4.0	1.2	-0.3	3.3	4.9	6.1	3.7	-0.5	-7.7	-13.1	-15.1	-2.3	2.1	3.8	-0.4	3.0	4.2

Note: The adoption of national account systems SNA93 or ESA95 has been proceeding at an uneven pace among OECD member countries, both with respect to variables and the time period covered. As a consequence, there are breaks in many national series. Moreover, most countries have shifted to chain-weighted price indices to calculate real GDP and expenditures components. For further information, see table "National Account Reporting Systems, base years and latest data updates" at the beginning of the Statistical Annex and OECD Economic Outlook Sources and Methods (http://www.oecd.org/eco/sources-and-methods). Working-day adjusted -- see note to Annex Table 1.

Source: OECD Economic Outlook 88 database.

StatLink http://dx.doi.org/10.1787/888932348453

Annex Table 8. Real total domestic demand
Percentage change from previous year

	Average 1986-96	1997	1998	1999	2000	2001	2002	2003	2004	2005	2006	2007	2008	2009	2010	2011	2012	Fourth quarter 2010	2011	2012
Australia	3.3	3.3	6.3	4.8	2.5	1.5	5.8	6.2	4.9	5.0	2.8	7.0	3.7	0.5	5.1	4.0	4.5	3.8	4.2	4.6
Austria	2.5	0.9	2.5	3.0	2.0	0.1	-0.1	1.7	2.1	2.3	2.1	2.3	1.1	-1.5	0.3	1.1	1.5	0.9	1.1	1.6
Belgium	2.8	2.9	2.2	2.2	3.9	-0.1	0.1	0.6	2.9	2.8	2.4	2.8	1.9	-2.1	1.5	1.9	1.8	2.0	1.9	1.8
Canada	2.0	6.1	2.5	4.2	4.7	1.3	3.2	4.5	4.1	4.9	4.4	3.9	2.5	-2.6	4.8	2.5	2.2	4.1	2.3	2.2
Chile	..	7.2	3.7	-6.2	6.1	2.3	2.3	4.8	7.3	10.5	7.0	7.6	7.4	-5.8	16.8	8.3	6.3	16.6	6.6	6.1
Czech Republic	..	-1.0	-1.3	1.0	4.0	3.7	3.7	4.2	2.9	1.8	5.6	5.2	1.1	-3.6	1.6	2.2	2.9	3.1	1.7	3.7
Denmark	1.2	4.7	3.7	-0.6	3.2	0.0	1.7	0.2	4.3	3.4	5.2	1.9	-0.5	-6.2	2.2	1.5	2.3	2.7	1.5	2.9
Finland	0.8	5.5	5.8	1.7	3.7	2.0	1.3	3.7	3.5	4.3	2.2	4.6	0.6	-5.5	1.9	2.9	2.6	3.6	2.4	2.6
France	1.9	0.9	4.1	3.7	4.5	1.7	1.1	1.7	3.0	2.7	2.7	3.2	0.4	-2.3	1.5	2.0	2.1	1.9	1.8	2.2
Germany	2.6	0.9	2.2	2.6	2.4	-0.4	-2.0	0.6	-0.5	0.1	2.5	1.3	1.0	-1.9	2.3	1.5	1.3	3.9	1.2	1.3
Greece	2.0	3.4	4.4	3.7	5.4	4.1	4.4	5.7	2.5	1.4	5.8	5.0	1.0	-2.5	-5.9	-5.8	-1.4	..	..	..
Hungary	..	4.9	8.5	5.1	4.2	2.2	6.5	6.3	4.4	1.0	1.7	-1.2	0.7	-11.5	-0.6	0.9	2.6	-0.2	1.6	3.1
Iceland	1.6	5.5	13.8	4.2	5.9	-2.1	-2.3	5.7	9.9	15.7	9.5	-0.1	-8.8	-20.9	-3.7	1.5	3.5	-3.0	1.8	4.0
Ireland	4.8	10.6	10.1	8.3	9.7	3.9	4.3	4.2	4.2	8.9	6.4	5.2	-5.5	-13.8	-4.0	-0.3	0.7	0.0	-0.2	1.0
Israel	..	2.2	2.6	4.1	5.6	2.1	-0.1	-1.7	2.8	4.4	4.6	6.4	2.6	-0.4	3.6	3.7	4.0	4.7	3.8	4.1
Italy	1.7	2.6	2.8	2.7	3.2	1.5	1.3	0.8	1.3	1.0	2.0	1.2	-1.4	-3.8	0.7	0.6	1.2	0.3	0.9	1.3
Japan	3.4	0.5	-2.4	0.0	2.4	1.0	-0.4	0.8	1.9	1.7	1.2	1.3	-1.3	-4.0	1.7	1.6	1.4	2.4	1.3	1.7
Korea	9.6	1.4	-16.9	14.6	9.5	3.7	7.9	1.5	1.5	3.8	4.9	4.7	1.4	-3.8	7.9	4.4	4.8	6.5	4.4	5.0
Luxembourg	4.3	6.0	6.3	8.0	4.5	4.5	2.6	0.5	3.3	5.0	1.9	5.9	3.1	-5.9	5.0	1.6	2.6	2.9	1.7	3.4
Mexico	2.6	9.2	5.8	3.9	7.2	-0.4	0.1	0.8	3.9	3.7	5.5	3.8	2.3	-8.0	4.4	4.3	4.6	3.0	4.4	4.5
Netherlands	2.4	4.5	5.1	4.9	2.7	2.3	-0.4	0.4	0.5	1.3	4.1	3.2	2.2	-4.0	1.0	0.3	1.3	1.4	1.0	1.5
New Zealand	2.4	2.5	0.5	5.8	1.9	1.7	5.6	6.1	7.2	4.6	1.1	4.7	0.4	-5.1	2.9	3.6	2.9	1.3	4.6	2.2
Norway	1.3	6.8	5.8	0.4	2.9	0.6	2.3	1.7	6.7	5.5	5.6	5.0	1.9	-3.7	3.8	3.2	3.1	4.7	3.0	3.2
Poland	..	9.6	6.5	4.8	2.7	-1.1	0.8	3.0	6.1	2.8	7.1	8.6	5.3	-0.6	4.0	5.3	5.1	5.0	5.2	5.0
Portugal	4.2	5.5	7.4	5.8	3.3	1.7	-0.2	-1.9	2.9	1.4	0.8	2.0	1.2	-3.0	0.9	-2.0	0.5	0.5	-2.2	1.2
Slovak Republic	..	6.1	4.7	-6.2	1.2	8.2	4.0	-0.7	5.8	8.6	6.6	6.4	6.0	-5.8	2.6	1.3	3.7	3.8	1.6	4.3
Slovenia	..	5.1	4.7	8.4	1.9	1.1	3.0	4.8	4.8	2.3	5.6	8.9	4.2	-9.8	0.6	2.4	2.8	2.9	2.4	3.0
Spain	3.4	3.4	6.2	6.4	5.3	3.8	3.2	3.8	4.8	5.1	5.2	4.1	-0.6	-6.0	-0.7	0.4	1.5	0.5	0.9	1.8
Sweden	1.1	1.6	4.6	3.5	4.0	0.4	1.5	2.1	1.8	3.0	4.1	4.7	0.0	-5.0	5.7	3.4	3.0	6.4	3.0	3.0
Switzerland	1.5	0.6	3.7	0.2	2.2	2.0	0.1	0.5	1.9	1.8	1.4	1.4	0.2	0.6	0.7	2.6	2.3	2.7	2.5	2.2
Turkey	5.3	8.9	0.9	-1.9	7.8	-11.5	8.7	8.6	11.5	9.2	6.7	5.7	-1.0	-6.4	9.2	6.6	6.8	..	..	..
United Kingdom	2.4	3.5	5.1	4.6	3.9	2.9	3.2	3.0	3.5	2.1	2.4	3.1	-0.7	-5.5	2.7	1.3	1.4	3.4	0.8	1.7
United States	2.7	4.7	5.5	5.7	4.8	1.2	2.4	2.8	4.0	3.2	2.6	1.3	-1.1	-3.6	3.4	2.7	3.0	3.8	2.5	3.3
Euro area	..	2.0	3.5	3.4	3.5	1.3	0.4	1.4	1.7	2.0	3.0	2.6	0.3	-3.4	0.9	1.0	1.5	1.7	1.1	1.6
Total OECD	2.8	3.5	3.1	4.0	4.3	1.1	1.9	2.3	3.3	2.9	3.0	2.5	-0.1	-3.8	3.0	2.4	2.7	3.2	2.3	2.9

StatLink ⟜⟊ http://dx.doi.org/10.1787/888932348472

Note: The adoption of national accounts systems SNA93 or ESA95 has been proceeding at an uneven pace among OECD member countries, both with respect to variables and the time period covered. As a consequence, there are breaks in many national series. Moreover, most countries have shifted to chain-weighted price indices to calculate real GDP and expenditures components. For further information, see table "National Accounts Reporting Systems, base years and latest data updates" at the beginning of the Statistical Annex and *OECD Economic Outlook Sources and Methods* (*http://www.oecd.org/eco/sources-and-methods*). Working-day adjusted -- see note to Annex Table 1.

Source: OECD Economic Outlook 88 database.

Annex Table 9. Foreign balance contributions to changes in real GDP
Percentage points

	Average 1986-96	1997	1998	1999	2000	2001	2002	2003	2004	2005	2006	2007	2008	2009	2010	2011	2012	Fourth quarter[1] 2010	2011	2012
Australia	0.4	1.0	-0.9	-0.2	1.1	1.2	-1.5	-2.0	-1.6	-1.0	-0.7	-1.7	-1.7	2.0	-1.8	-0.6	-0.6	-0.8	-0.7	-0.6
Austria	-0.2	1.3	1.3	0.6	1.3	0.6	1.5	-0.9	0.5	0.7	1.5	1.4	0.7	-1.8	1.6	0.9	0.6	1.2	0.3	0.8
Belgium	-0.1	1.0	-0.4	1.3	0.3	0.8	1.4	0.0	0.3	-0.7	0.5	0.1	-1.0	-0.5	1.0	0.0	0.0	0.3	-0.3	0.2
Canada	0.2	-1.7	1.7	1.4	0.6	0.7	-0.1	-2.5	-0.9	-1.7	-1.5	-1.5	-2.0	-0.3	-1.9	-0.2	0.8	-0.2	0.5	1.0
Chile	0.2	-0.8	-0.5	4.7	-1.2	1.1	-0.2	-0.9	-1.1	-3.7	-1.4	-1.0	-2.6	3.3	-8.8	-0.6	0.2	-0.3	0.0	0.8
Czech Republic	-3.5	0.4	0.6	0.2	-0.1	-1.4	-2.0	-0.6	1.4	4.6	1.5	1.1	1.3	-0.6	0.9	0.7	0.5	0.3	0.4	0.3
Denmark	0.6	-1.3	-1.4	3.2	0.5	0.7	-1.1	0.2	-1.8	-0.8	-1.5	-0.1	-0.4	1.3	-0.1	-0.2	-0.1	-0.4	0.3	-0.8
Finland	0.4	1.6	0.9	2.9	1.8	0.3	0.3	-1.8	0.8	-1.0	2.1	0.9	0.3	-1.9	0.5	0.5	0.5	-2.8	0.6	0.6
France	0.2	1.3	-0.5	-0.4	-0.3	0.0	0.0	-0.6	-0.7	-0.7	-0.3	-0.9	-0.3	-0.2	0.1	-0.5	-0.1	-0.2	-0.1	-0.2
Germany	0.1	0.9	-0.3	-0.6	1.1	1.8	2.0	-0.8	1.2	0.8	1.2	1.5	-0.2	-2.9	1.4	1.1	1.0	0.6	1.0	1.0
Greece	-0.8	-0.4	-1.7	-1.1	-2.0	-0.4	-1.5	-0.4	1.8	0.7	-1.8	-1.2	0.9	0.7	3.0	3.7	1.9	..	..	..
Hungary	2.3	-0.5	-3.2	-0.9	0.7	1.7	-2.1	-2.1	-0.1	2.4	2.2	2.1	0.0	4.0	2.0	1.6	0.7	1.5	0.7	0.7
Iceland	-0.2	-0.8	-7.5	-0.3	-1.9	6.2	2.5	-3.2	-2.5	-9.1	-6.0	6.1	10.7	14.7	-0.2	0.1	-0.5	-2.3	-1.0	0.3
Ireland	2.2	2.7	0.1	4.2	1.7	2.5	3.0	1.7	0.5	-1.7	-0.5	1.0	1.4	3.8	3.2	1.8	1.9	2.5	1.8	2.0
Israel	-1.0	1.1	1.4	-0.8	3.5	-2.0	-0.3	3.3	2.1	0.4	1.1	-1.1	1.5	1.1	1.0	0.4	0.4	-0.5	0.3	0.3
Italy	0.3	-0.6	-1.4	-1.2	0.8	0.2	-0.8	-0.8	0.1	-0.2	0.1	0.1	0.1	-1.2	0.3	0.8	0.4	0.6	0.4	0.4
Japan	-0.2	1.0	0.4	-0.1	0.5	-0.8	0.7	0.7	0.8	0.3	0.8	1.1	0.1	-1.3	1.9	0.1	0.0	-0.1	-0.1	-0.1
Korea	-0.7	4.2	11.2	-2.1	-0.2	0.4	-0.5	1.3	3.1	0.4	0.3	0.5	1.0	4.0	-1.3	0.0	0.1	-0.8	0.1	-0.1
Luxembourg	1.3	1.2	1.3	1.7	4.8	-1.1	2.0	1.1	1.9	1.6	3.6	2.5	-0.6	0.3	1.2	2.3	1.4	2.2	1.7	1.0
Mexico	-0.1	-1.7	-0.8	-0.3	-1.3	-0.5	0.0	0.5	0.0	-0.6	-0.7	-0.6	-0.8	1.7	0.5	-0.8	-0.4	-2.0	-0.5	-0.4
Netherlands	0.5	0.0	-0.9	0.1	1.3	-0.2	0.5	-0.1	1.7	0.8	-0.3	1.0	-0.2	-0.2	0.6	1.5	0.7	1.1	0.8	0.7
New Zealand	-0.3	0.5	0.1	-1.2	2.2	0.5	-0.8	-1.9	-2.7	-1.7	1.2	-1.6	-1.0	5.0	-1.0	-0.9	-0.3	-0.8	-0.3	0.0
Norway	1.7	-0.8	-2.6	1.6	0.6	1.5	-0.4	-0.5	-2.0	-2.0	-2.4	-1.4	-0.8	1.4	-2.7	-0.9	-0.4	-0.4	-0.3	-0.5
Poland	-0.7	-2.5	-1.7	-1.0	1.2	2.3	0.5	0.9	-0.8	0.5	-1.5	-2.1	-0.3	3.4	-0.1	-1.1	-0.9	-1.7	-1.2	-0.4
Portugal	-0.8	-1.4	-2.5	-2.1	0.2	0.1	0.9	1.1	-1.5	-0.8	0.6	0.2	-1.2	0.7	0.5	2.0	1.3	-3.8	1.2	1.3
Slovak Republic	-0.9	-1.2	-0.8	6.9	0.1	-4.9	0.3	5.5	-0.9	-2.1	1.6	3.9	0.1	1.3	1.7	2.4	0.8	-0.9	0.9	0.2
Slovenia	-3.0	-0.2	-1.1	-3.3	2.5	1.7	1.0	-1.9	-0.5	2.2	0.2	-2.0	-0.4	2.0	0.7	-0.1	-0.1	0.0	-0.1	0.2
Spain	-0.7	0.5	-1.7	-1.7	-0.4	-0.2	-0.6	-0.8	-1.7	-1.7	-1.4	-0.8	1.5	2.7	0.5	0.4	0.3	0.8	0.2	0.3
Sweden	0.5	1.3	-0.1	1.2	0.7	1.0	1.1	0.5	2.3	0.4	0.7	-1.0	-0.5	-0.6	-0.4	0.2	0.5	0.0	0.4	0.8
Switzerland	-0.1	1.6	-0.8	1.1	1.5	-0.7	0.4	-0.7	0.8	1.0	2.3	2.4	1.7	-2.5	2.1	-0.1	0.4	-0.1	0.4	0.5
Turkey	-0.1	-0.9	2.1	-1.5	-1.1	6.5	-3.0	-3.8	-2.4	-1.3	-0.3	-1.3	1.7	2.8	-1.8	-1.7	-1.7	..	..	..
United Kingdom	0.0	-0.2	-1.4	-1.0	-0.1	-0.5	-1.1	-0.4	-0.7	0.0	0.2	-0.5	0.7	0.7	-1.0	0.4	0.5	0.6	0.5	0.6
United States	0.1	-0.3	-1.2	-1.0	-0.8	-0.2	-0.7	-0.4	-0.6	-0.3	-0.1	0.6	1.1	1.2	-0.7	-0.6	0.0	-0.3	0.0	0.0
Euro area	0.3	0.5	-0.6	-0.5	0.5	0.6	0.5	-0.6	0.2	-0.1	0.2	0.3	0.1	-0.8	0.8	0.7	0.6	0.5	0.6	0.6
Total OECD	0.0	0.2	-0.3	-0.6	-0.1	0.2	-0.2	-0.4	-0.1	-0.2	0.0	0.2	0.1	0.6	-0.1	-0.1	0.1	-0.1	0.1	0.1

Note: The adoption of national accounts systems SNA93 or ESA95 has been proceeding at an uneven pace among OECD member countries, both with respect to variables and the time period covered. As a consequence, there are breaks in many national series. Moreover, most countries have shifted to chain-weighted price indices to calculate real GDP and expenditures components. For further information, see table "National Accounts Reporting Systems, base years and latest data updates" at the beginning of the Statistical Annex and *OECD Economic Outlook* Sources and Methods (*http://www.oecd.org/eco/sources-and-methods*). Working-day adjusted -- see note to Annex Table 1.

1. Contributions to per cent change from the previous period, seasonnaly adjusted at annual rates.

Source: OECD Economic Outlook 88 database.

StatLink ⟲ http://dx.doi.org/10.1787/888932348491

Annex Table 10. Output gaps
Deviations of actual GDP from potential GDP as a per cent of potential GDP

	1993	1994	1995	1996	1997	1998	1999	2000	2001	2002	2003	2004	2005	2006	2007	2008	2009	2010	2011	2012
Australia	-2.0	-0.6	-0.6	-0.6	-0.6	0.7	1.1	0.6	-0.2	0.2	0.4	0.5	0.8	0.0	1.6	-0.1	-2.4	-2.6	-2.3	-1.6
Austria	-1.1	-1.7	-1.2	-0.9	-0.9	0.5	1.7	2.4	0.2	-0.7	-2.3	-1.9	-1.1	0.5	2.4	2.4	-3.0	-2.7	-2.4	-2.1
Belgium	-2.5	-1.3	-1.0	-1.9	-0.4	-0.9	0.1	1.3	-0.4	-1.2	-2.2	-0.9	-1.0	-0.5	-0.2	-1.5	-6.0	-5.9	-5.9	-5.8
Canada	-4.2	-1.8	-1.5	-2.7	-1.8	-1.1	0.8	2.4	0.8	0.9	0.2	0.7	0.9	0.9	0.7	-0.9	-5.1	-3.9	-3.4	-2.5
Chile	..	..	..	-1.0	2.0	1.8	-2.3	-1.2	-1.2	-2.6	-2.5	-0.7	0.9	1.6	2.1	1.6	-3.3	-0.9	1.4	2.1
Czech Republic	..	-1.4	1.8	3.9	1.2	-1.2	-1.9	-0.4	-0.5	-1.7	-1.9	-1.9	-0.1	2.2	3.4	2.9	-3.2	-3.3	-3.0	-2.6
Denmark	-3.8	-0.6	-0.1	0.2	0.9	0.5	0.8	2.1	0.9	-0.4	-1.4	-0.6	-0.1	1.5	1.8	-0.6	-6.6	-5.6	-5.3	-4.7
Finland	-8.7	-6.1	-4.3	-3.6	-1.0	0.1	0.2	1.6	0.0	-1.6	-2.7	-1.7	-1.6	-0.2	2.0	0.2	-8.8	-7.4	-5.8	-4.4
France	-1.7	-1.1	-0.7	-1.4	-1.2	0.1	0.7	1.9	1.0	-0.1	-0.9	-0.4	-0.2	0.4	1.0	-0.4	-3.8	-3.6	-3.4	-2.9
Germany	-1.0	-0.3	-0.2	-0.9	-0.7	-0.6	-0.5	1.2	0.8	-0.5	-1.8	-2.0	-2.0	0.3	1.6	0.6	-5.2	-3.0	-1.9	-1.2
Greece	-3.1	-2.9	-2.7	-2.6	-1.9	-1.5	-1.9	-1.7	-1.7	-2.3	-0.5	-0.3	-1.6	0.1	1.7	1.0	-2.1	-6.1	-8.5	-8.3
Hungary	..	..	0.4	-1.6	-1.0	-0.1	-0.3	0.2	-0.1	0.0	0.3	1.3	1.1	1.7	-0.1	-1.1	-8.3	-8.1	-6.8	-5.1
Iceland	-4.7	-2.6	-4.3	-2.0	-0.5	1.6	1.6	1.5	1.4	-1.8	-2.6	1.1	4.8	3.6	5.0	1.6	-5.2	-8.1	-6.4	-4.7
Ireland	-4.3	-4.5	-2.2	-1.6	1.5	1.1	3.1	4.1	2.4	2.4	1.6	1.4	2.4	3.0	4.4	-1.7	-9.1	-9.0	-7.9	-6.7
Israel	..	..	..	..	..	..	-0.1	4.8	1.2	-2.5	-4.0	-2.5	-1.2	0.6	2.1	2.4	0.0	0.0	0.1	0.5
Italy	-3.3	-2.3	-0.8	-1.3	-0.9	-1.1	-1.3	0.8	0.9	0.0	-1.0	-0.5	-0.3	1.0	1.5	-0.4	-5.5	-4.7	-3.9	-3.0
Japan	0.1	-0.6	-0.3	1.0	1.3	-1.8	-2.9	-1.1	-2.1	-2.8	-2.6	-1.2	-0.3	0.8	2.4	0.4	-5.3	-2.3	-1.5	-0.7
Luxembourg	2.1	1.2	-2.1	-5.1	-4.0	-2.7	0.5	3.8	1.7	1.7	-0.7	-0.5	0.9	1.8	4.6	2.2	-5.2	-5.1	-4.4	-3.9
Mexico	0.6	2.7	-6.3	-4.0	-0.2	1.5	1.9	4.8	1.0	-1.6	-2.7	-1.3	-0.5	2.0	3.0	2.6	-5.9	-3.1	-1.8	-0.9
Netherlands	-1.2	-1.0	-0.6	-0.1	0.9	1.4	2.5	3.0	2.0	-0.5	-2.2	-1.8	-1.4	0.2	2.2	2.0	-3.6	-3.2	-2.4	-1.5
New Zealand	-1.9	0.7	1.3	1.7	0.6	-2.1	-0.6	0.1	-0.3	1.3	1.8	2.7	2.7	0.7	1.1	-1.2	-4.3	-3.6	-2.3	-1.9
Norway[1]	-1.6	-0.7	-0.1	1.0	2.5	2.8	1.8	2.0	1.5	0.6	-0.6	1.1	1.8	1.8	2.0	-0.5	-3.8	-3.9	-2.7	-1.1
Poland	..	..	-2.2	-1.0	0.9	0.6	0.5	0.9	-1.5	-3.1	-2.3	-0.6	-0.7	0.9	2.2	1.8	-1.4	-1.6	-0.7	0.3
Portugal	-1.2	-3.0	-1.7	-1.1	0.0	1.6	2.2	3.0	2.4	1.0	-1.4	-1.2	-1.7	-1.2	0.2	-0.6	-3.4	-2.4	-3.1	-2.1
Slovak Republic	..	-2.0	-0.8	1.7	3.3	3.9	0.3	-2.0	-2.3	-1.9	-2.0	-2.6	-2.1	0.1	4.3	5.9	-3.1	-2.8	-2.7	-1.7
Spain	-3.5	-3.4	-3.3	-3.6	-2.5	-1.0	0.3	1.6	1.5	0.5	-0.2	-0.4	-0.2	0.3	0.5	-1.0	-5.5	-5.6	-5.0	-3.7
Sweden	-5.8	-3.8	-1.9	-2.4	-1.8	-0.5	0.8	2.0	0.3	0.1	0.3	1.7	2.2	3.7	4.1	0.4	-6.8	-4.5	-3.4	-2.5
Switzerland	-1.4	-1.1	-1.8	-2.1	-1.1	0.1	-0.3	1.4	0.5	-1.0	-2.9	-2.2	-1.3	0.5	2.0	1.6	-2.3	-1.5	-1.1	-0.4
United Kingdom	-2.9	-0.9	-0.4	-0.3	0.1	0.4	0.4	0.9	0.3	-0.2	0.2	1.0	1.0	1.8	2.6	1.0	-5.0	-4.4	-4.0	-3.4
United States	-1.8	-0.6	-1.2	-0.8	0.1	0.7	1.6	2.0	-0.2	-0.9	-0.6	0.7	1.4	1.7	1.3	-0.7	-4.6	-3.4	-3.0	-2.0
Euro area	-2.0	-1.4	-0.9	-1.4	-0.9	-0.4	0.1	1.5	0.9	-0.2	-1.3	-1.0	-0.9	0.4	1.4	0.1	-4.9	-4.1	-3.5	-2.7
Total OECD	-1.7	-0.9	-1.1	-0.9	-0.1	0.0	0.4	1.4	0.0	-0.9	-1.1	-0.1	0.4	1.2	1.7	0.0	-4.7	-3.5	-2.9	-2.1

StatLink ᴍᴪ http://dx.doi.org/10.1787/888932248510

Note: Potential output for countries where data availability permits follows the methodology outlined in Beffy, P.O., P. Olivaud, P. Richardson and F. Sedillot (2006), "New OECD Methods for Supply-Side and Medium-Term Assessments: A Capital Services Approach", OECD Economics Department Working Papers, No. 482. Revisions to this method are discussed in Chapter 4 of OECD Economic Outlook no. 85 "Beyond the crisis: medium-term challenges relating to potential output, employment and fiscal positions". In countries where extensive data are not available, more simplified methodologies are used.

1. Mainland Norway.

Source: OECD Economic Outlook 88 database.

Annex Table 11. **Compensation per employee in the private sector**

Percentage change from previous period

	Average 1983-1993	1994	1995	1996	1997	1998	1999	2000	2001	2002	2003	2004	2005	2006	2007	2008	2009	2010	2011	2012
Australia	5.8	3.1	3.4	5.6	4.6	2.8	3.7	3.4	4.9	3.3	4.1	6.3	5.0	6.1	5.7	4.5	1.1	3.4	4.8	5.0
Austria	4.9	3.5	1.6	1.2	1.1	2.7	1.7	2.4	1.9	2.1	2.3	0.6	2.2	3.0	3.1	3.5	1.2	0.7	1.9	2.1
Belgium	5.2	3.9	0.0	1.4	2.9	1.1	3.6	1.9	3.8	3.4	1.5	2.0	1.3	3.5	3.5	3.2	1.7	0.9	2.5	2.6
Canada	4.5	0.3	1.8	2.9	5.9	2.6	3.2	5.3	2.2	0.8	1.8	5.1	5.0	4.5	3.9	3.1	1.6	2.0	2.6	3.9
Czech Republic	..	..	..	16.5	9.2	9.7	7.9	7.4	7.2	7.0	8.7	6.1	4.8	6.2	6.4	6.8	-0.3	2.3	3.1	4.0
Denmark	5.1	1.7	2.2	4.0	3.8	4.0	3.7	3.1	4.1	3.7	3.5	3.2	4.5	3.4	4.2	2.7	1.6	2.1	1.7	3.2
Finland	7.2	4.4	5.2	2.3	2.0	4.6	2.6	4.3	4.7	1.2	2.5	3.7	3.3	3.1	3.4	4.6	1.6	1.2	2.2	1.7
France	4.7	1.1	1.4	1.4	1.4	1.4	1.9	2.3	2.4	3.4	3.0	3.9	3.0	3.7	2.4	2.5	1.2	2.8	2.2	2.5
Germany	4.1	2.9	3.4	1.0	0.6	0.8	1.0	2.0	1.6	1.3	1.6	0.1	-0.1	1.3	1.1	2.1	-0.3	2.0	2.6	2.3
Greece	..	..	..	..	..	5.5	6.4	6.3	3.0	12.0	6.7	2.2	3.9	5.0	7.0	4.4	4.1	1.8	0.9	0.9
Hungary	20.6	..	..	22.4	21.7	12.7	4.0	20.4	9.2	10.8	7.5	13.1	7.1	5.2	7.3	5.8	-1.4	0.4	2.2	4.4
Iceland	5.6	3.7	4.9	5.1	3.8	9.4	8.5	9.8	5.8	7.6	0.7	12.2	10.0	13.1	8.4	1.6	-6.1	6.2	5.9	5.2
Ireland	..	1.5	3.4	4.3	4.2	5.0	3.8	8.4	6.4	3.5	5.3	4.5	4.7	4.6	5.1	2.6	-0.3	-2.1	-1.0	-0.5
Israel	..	..	..	..	..	8.0	7.0	6.9	2.4	0.7	-1.5	0.1	3.2	8.1	2.4	2.6	1.1	4.6	2.9	3.7
Italy	7.8	4.4	5.4	4.2	3.6	-1.0	1.9	1.9	2.4	1.8	1.8	3.2	2.7	1.8	2.9	2.5	0.2	0.8	2.8	2.0
Japan	3.0	1.4	1.0	-0.1	1.2	-1.2	-1.6	0.1	-1.2	-2.1	-1.2	-0.9	0.0	0.4	-1.8	0.1	-3.2	1.4	1.2	1.3
Korea	11.9	12.0	14.9	12.3	4.4	4.1	3.3	4.2	7.5	6.1	7.2	4.8	5.3	3.5	4.4	4.1	1.4	4.3	6.4	7.3
Luxembourg	5.1	4.1	0.4	1.0	2.0	1.4	4.7	6.0	3.4	2.4	0.5	3.1	4.6	2.5	3.8	2.1	1.0	1.0	3.3	2.9
Mexico	..	9.3	8.1	19.1	23.4	16.1	17.8	11.6	9.2	3.9	3.6	3.2	5.1	2.6	5.5	3.5	4.1	4.1	4.9	4.9
Netherlands	1.1	1.9	0.3	1.9	2.5	4.3	3.5	4.8	4.8	4.4	3.2	3.4	0.9	2.6	3.1	3.4	1.9	1.4	2.6	2.2
Norway	6.3	3.1	3.2	2.5	2.5	7.5	6.1	4.5	7.0	3.9	2.5	4.4	5.5	8.2	6.3	5.1	4.6	3.1	3.9	4.6
Poland	..	..	..	29.0	20.5	14.7	12.6	10.2	9.5	0.6	0.3	1.3	0.6	1.0	4.3	8.5	4.9	6.5	6.0	6.6
Portugal	..	..	..	5.1	4.6	3.6	3.6	5.1	3.4	2.4	5.7	2.4	4.5	3.0	5.4	3.2	3.3	2.5	0.8	1.6
Slovak Republic	..	..	..	11.8	18.6	9.6	7.1	15.7	4.6	7.8	8.5	10.0	12.0	6.6	10.0	4.4	4.8	2.6	3.7	4.7
Slovenia	..	..	..	13.5	13.2	8.8	8.2	10.5	11.0	8.9	7.9	8.5	6.4	5.7	7.1	6.0	0.9	5.4	3.7	3.4
Spain	9.0	4.0	3.5	5.2	3.6	1.3	1.9	2.9	4.1	3.5	2.7	1.8	2.8	2.4	3.9	5.6	3.4	1.1	0.8	0.7
Sweden	7.8	6.9	2.3	7.1	5.5	2.7	1.3	6.8	4.0	2.6	2.5	4.6	3.2	2.0	5.2	0.4	0.9	1.0	2.6	2.8
Switzerland	4.3	2.5	2.6	0.6	2.9	0.3	1.6	2.7	3.8	1.4	-0.5	-0.9	3.3	2.4	3.5	2.2	2.1	0.1	1.1	1.2
United Kingdom	6.8	3.4	2.6	2.2	4.0	7.2	4.6	5.8	4.8	2.9	4.6	3.3	3.0	4.1	5.4	0.8	1.6	3.8	2.4	3.3
United States	4.2	1.9	2.3	3.0	4.0	5.4	4.2	7.0	3.2	3.0	4.0	4.1	3.3	4.0	4.0	2.9	0.5	2.2	2.5	2.6
Euro area	5.1	2.9	3.0	2.6	2.3	1.5	2.1	3.0	2.8	2.8	2.7	2.3	2.1	2.5	2.9	3.1	1.2	1.7	2.1	2.0
Total OECD	5.1	3.3	3.4	5.2	5.5	4.5	4.1	5.1	3.6	2.4	2.9	2.9	2.9	3.0	3.3	2.8	0.8	2.4	2.8	3.0

Note: The private sector in the OECD terminology is defined as total economy less the public sector. Hence private sector employees are defined as total employees less public sector employees. For further information, see also *OECD Economic Outlook* Sources and Methods (*http://www.oecd.org/eco/sources-and-methods*).

Source: OECD Economic Outlook 88 database.

StatLink ᕯᕤ http://dx.doi.org/10.1787/888932348529

Annex Table 12. Labour productivity in the total economy
Percentage change from previous period

	Average 1983-1993	1994	1995	1996	1997	1998	1999	2000	2001	2002	2003	2004	2005	2006	2007	2008	2009	2010	2011	2012
Australia	1.4	1.6	-0.2	2.6	2.9	3.2	2.6	0.8	1.5	1.7	1.2	1.3	0.0	-0.2	1.8	-0.7	0.5	1.0	1.5	1.9
Austria	1.7	.8	2.5	2.0	1.5	2.8	2.2	2.3	-0.2	1.7	0.7	1.2	1.3	2.0	1.8	0.2	-2.9	1.3	1.2	1.2
Belgium	1.6	3.7	1.7	0.8	3.2	0.2	2.1	1.7	-0.7	1.5	0.8	2.1	0.6	1.5	1.2	-0.9	-2.3	1.6	1.3	1.2
Canada	1.1	2.7	1.0	0.7	2.1	1.5	2.9	2.7	0.6	0.5	-0.5	1.3	1.6	0.9	-0.1	-1.0	-0.9	1.3	0.7	1.5
Chile	..	..	..	..	4.7	1.1	0.7	2.7	2.4	0.2	-0.1	3.1	1.8	3.1	1.8	0.5	-1.4	-1.5	1.9	2.1
Czech Republic	..	.3	5.2	3.2	-0.9	0.8	4.8	4.1	2.0	1.3	5.0	4.0	5.3	5.0	3.4	1.1	-2.9	3.7	2.0	2.5
Denmark	1.6	3.8	2.3	1.9	1.8	0.7	1.7	3.0	-0.2	0.4	1.5	2.9	1.4	1.3	-1.2	-2.7	-1.4	4.0	1.0	0.9
Finland	2.9	5.1	2.2	2.1	2.6	3.2	1.5	3.2	0.9	0.8	2.0	3.7	1.6	2.5	3.0	-0.6	-5.4	3.0	2.5	2.4
France	1.9	2.0	1.4	0.7	1.8	2.0	1.1	1.4	0.0	0.4	0.9	2.1	1.4	1.4	0.9	-0.5	-1.3	1.6	0.9	1.3
Germany	1.8	2.8	1.7	1.3	1.9	0.6	0.5	1.6	0.9	0.6	0.7	0.3	1.0	2.9	1.1	-0.7	-4.7	3.3	2.1	2.2
Greece	0.8	0.1	1.2	1.1	4.0	-1.0	3.1	3.0	4.3	1.2	3.5	3.4	1.0	2.5	2.9	0.2	-1.2	-1.5	-0.3	0.8
Hungary	..	..	..	0.5	4.0	3.0	1.4	3.9	4.2	4.3	3.9	6.0	3.4	3.0	1.1	2.1	-4.0	1.4	2.6	1.8
Iceland	1.2	2.8	-2.9	4.8	4.9	2.1	0.4	2.3	2.2	1.6	2.3	8.2	4.1	-0.5	1.4	0.2	-0.8	-2.9	3.0	1.9
Ireland	3.4	2.4	4.5	4.3	5.6	0.0	3.9	4.7	2.5	4.9	2.5	1.2	1.0	1.0	1.9	-2.5	0.6	3.6	2.2	0.7
Israel	..	..	..	1.2	0.5	0.5	-0.1	5.4	-1.5	-0.8	0.7	3.2	1.4	2.7	0.9	0.2	0.3	0.3	1.0	1.7
Italy	1.9	4.0	3.1	0.4	1.6	0.3	0.3	1.9	-0.3	-1.2	-1.4	0.9	0.2	0.1	0.1	-1.6	-3.5	1.4	0.8	0.8
Japan	2.8	0.8	1.8	2.2	0.5	-1.4	0.7	3.1	0.7	1.5	1.6	2.5	1.5	1.6	1.9	-0.8	-3.7	4.1	1.7	1.6
Korea	6.1	5.4	5.9	4.9	4.0	0.3	8.9	4.3	2.0	4.3	2.9	2.7	2.6	3.8	3.8	1.7	0.5	4.9	3.3	3.9
Luxembourg	3.4	1.2	-1.6	-1.0	2.8	1.9	3.3	2.7	-2.9	0.8	-0.3	2.1	2.5	1.3	2.1	-3.2	-4.6	2.0	1.6	2.3
Mexico	..	1.2	-5.4	1.3	1.4	2.3	2.4	3.7	-1.2	-2.2	0.5	0.6	2.6	2.0	1.6	0.4	-7.0	3.2	1.2	2.1
Netherlands	0.1	2.3	0.8	1.1	1.1	1.3	2.1	1.7	-0.1	-0.4	0.8	3.1	1.5	1.7	1.3	0.4	-2.8	2.4	1.8	1.5
New Zealand	1.4	1.4	-0.2	0.8	1.5	0.6	2.7	1.8	0.0	1.6	1.5	0.8	0.2	-1.4	0.9	-0.8	-0.6	1.2	1.0	0.5
Norway	2.6	3.5	1.9	2.5	2.4	0.2	1.6	2.8	1.6	1.1	1.8	3.6	2.1	-0.9	-0.7	-2.4	-0.8	0.4	1.0	0.8
Poland	..	7.0	6.0	5.1	5.5	3.7	8.7	6.1	3.6	4.6	5.2	3.9	1.2	2.7	2.3	1.3	1.2	2.5	2.5	2.9
Portugal	2.1	1.1	4.9	2.0	1.7	2.2	2.7	1.8	0.1	0.1	-0.3	1.6	1.1	0.9	2.4	-0.4	0.0	2.7	0.8	1.4
Slovak Republic	..	..	4.0	4.8	6.8	4.9	2.6	3.4	2.9	4.5	3.7	5.3	5.2	6.1	8.3	3.3	-2.4	5.8	3.1	3.4
Slovenia	..	..	..	5.7	6.9	3.8	3.9	3.1	2.4	2.4	3.2	4.0	4.7	4.3	3.8	0.9	-6.4	3.4	2.9	2.4
Spain	1.8	2.9	0.9	0.7	0.3	0.0	0.2	0.0	0.5	0.3	0.0	-0.3	-0.5	0.1	0.5	1.3	3.1	1.8	0.6	0.5
Sweden	1.9	4.9	2.5	2.5	4.3	2.4	2.2	2.1	-0.7	2.4	3.1	4.4	2.9	2.8	0.9	-1.5	-3.1	3.2	1.8	2.1
Switzerland	0.3	1.9	0.4	0.7	2.0	1.2	0.5	2.5	-0.5	-0.1	0.2	2.2	1.9	1.2	-0.1	-1.0	-2.5	2.1	0.8	1.0
Turkey	4.0	-12.4	4.2	4.0	7.5	0.4	-4.5	9.0	-5.7	6.3	6.5	6.8	6.4	5.0	3.4	-1.6	-5.2	2.2	3.3	2.8
United Kingdom	1.7	3.5	1.8	1.9	1.5	2.6	2.1	2.7	1.6	1.3	1.8	1.9	1.1	1.9	2.0	-0.8	-3.5	1.7	1.4	1.5
United States	1.4	1.0	0.2	1.8	2.1	2.1	2.8	2.4	1.2	3.0	2.5	2.5	1.4	0.9	1.1	0.7	1.6	3.3	1.3	1.4
Euro area	1.7	2.7	2.0	1.1	1.9	1.0	1.0	1.6	0.5	0.4	0.5	1.3	0.9	1.6	1.1	-0.4	-2.2	2.2	1.3	1.4
Total OECD	2.0	1.6	1.3	2.0	2.2	1.2	2.1	2.9	0.6	1.7	1.8	2.2	1.7	1.7	1.5	0.0	-1.6	2.8	1.6	1.7

Note: Labour productivity measured as GDP per person employed. For further information, see *OECD Economic Outlook Sources and Methods* (*http://www.oecd.org/eco/sources-and-methods*).
Source: OECD Economic Outlook 88 database.

StatLink 🔗 http://dx.doi.org/10.1787/888932348548

Annex Table 13. Unemployment rates: commonly used definitions
Per cent of labour force

	2007 Unemployment thousands	1997	1998	1999	2000	2001	2002	2003	2004	2005	2006	2007	2008	2009	2010	2011	2012	Fourth quarter 2010	Fourth quarter 2011	Fourth quarter 2012
Australia	484	8.2	7.7	6.9	6.2	6.7	6.3	5.9	5.4	5.0	4.8	4.4	4.2	5.6	5.2	4.9	4.7	5.1	4.8	4.6
Austria	185	4.3	4.3	3.7	3.5	3.6	3.9	4.3	4.9	5.2	4.7	4.4	3.8	4.8	4.5	4.4	4.3	4.5	4.4	4.3
Belgium	359	9.2	9.3	8.5	6.9	6.6	7.6	8.2	8.4	8.5	8.3	7.5	7.0	7.9	8.6	8.8	8.7	8.7	8.8	8.5
Canada	1 083	9.1	8.3	7.6	6.8	7.3	7.6	7.6	7.2	6.8	6.3	6.0	6.2	8.3	8.1	7.8	7.4	8.0	7.7	7.2
Chile	497	6.1	6.4	10.1	9.7	9.9	9.8	9.5	10.0	9.2	7.8	7.2	7.8	10.8	8.1	7.3	7.2	7.7	7.1	7.4
Czech Republic	276	4.8	6.5	8.8	8.9	8.2	7.3	7.8	8.3	7.9	7.2	5.3	4.4	6.7	7.5	7.1	6.8	7.5	6.9	6.7
Denmark	110	5.2	4.8	5.0	4.3	4.4	4.5	5.3	5.5	4.8	3.9	3.6	3.2	5.9	7.2	7.2	6.5	7.4	6.9	6.2
Finland	183	12.8	11.4	10.3	9.8	9.1	9.1	9.0	8.8	8.4	7.7	6.9	6.4	8.3	8.6	8.2	8.0	8.3	8.1	7.9
France	2 222	10.8	10.3	10.0	8.6	7.8	7.9	8.5	8.8	8.9	8.8	8.0	7.4	9.1	9.3	9.1	8.8	9.3	9.0	8.8
Germany	3 608	9.3	8.9	8.2	7.4	7.5	8.3	9.2	9.7	10.5	9.8	8.3	7.3	7.4	6.9	6.3	6.2	6.6	6.2	6.2
Greece	407	10.6	11.2	12.1	11.4	10.8	10.3	9.7	10.5	9.8	8.9	8.3	7.7	9.5	12.2	14.5	15.2	..	..	..
Hungary	312	8.9	7.9	7.1	6.5	5.8	5.9	5.9	6.2	7.3	7.5	7.4	7.9	10.1	11.3	11.7	11.0	11.3	11.9	10.2
Iceland	4	3.9	2.7	2.0	2.3	2.3	3.3	3.4	3.0	2.6	2.9	2.3	3.0	7.3	7.5	8.1	7.5	7.7	8.1	7.0
Ireland	101	10.7	7.6	5.6	4.3	3.9	4.4	4.7	4.5	4.3	4.4	4.6	6.0	11.7	13.6	13.6	12.6	14.0	13.1	12.3
Israel	212	..	..	8.8	8.7	9.4	10.3	10.7	10.3	9.0	8.4	7.3	6.1	7.6	6.4	6.1	5.9	6.1	6.1	5.9
Italy	1 525	11.3	11.3	11.0	10.1	9.1	8.6	8.4	8.0	7.7	6.8	6.2	6.7	7.8	8.6	8.5	8.3	8.7	8.4	8.2
Japan	2 566	3.4	4.1	4.7	4.7	5.0	5.4	5.3	4.7	4.4	4.1	3.8	4.0	5.1	5.1	4.9	4.5	5.0	4.8	4.3
Korea	783	2.6	7.0	6.6	4.4	4.0	3.3	3.6	3.7	3.7	3.5	3.2	3.2	3.6	3.7	3.4	3.3	3.4	3.3	3.2
Luxembourg	10	3.6	3.1	2.9	2.6	2.5	2.9	3.7	4.2	4.7	4.4	4.4	4.4	5.7	6.0	5.9	5.8	6.0	5.8	5.8
Mexico[1]	1 643	6.7	3.6	2.6	2.6	4.0	2.9	3.0	3.7	3.6	3.6	3.7	4.0	5.5	5.2	4.6	4.1	5.0	4.3	4.0
Netherlands	278	4.7	3.7	3.1	2.8	2.2	2.7	3.6	4.5	4.7	3.8	3.1	2.7	3.4	4.1	4.4	4.3	4.2	4.4	4.2
New Zealand	83	6.9	7.7	7.0	6.1	5.5	5.3	4.8	4.0	3.8	3.8	3.7	4.2	6.2	6.5	5.9	5.3	6.5	5.5	5.1
Norway	63	4.0	3.2	3.2	3.4	3.5	3.9	4.5	4.5	4.6	3.4	2.5	2.6	3.2	3.6	3.9	3.5	3.6	4.0	3.2
Poland	1 619	11.2	10.6	14.0	16.1	18.2	19.9	19.6	19.0	17.7	13.8	9.6	7.1	8.2	9.6	8.9	7.8	9.3	8.6	7.4
Portugal	449	6.7	5.0	4.4	4.0	4.0	5.0	6.3	6.7	7.7	7.7	8.0	7.6	9.5	10.7	11.4	11.1	10.8	11.5	10.8
Slovak Republic	296	11.9	12.6	16.4	18.8	19.3	18.7	17.5	18.2	16.2	13.4	11.1	9.5	12.1	14.1	13.4	12.5	13.7	13.3	11.9
Slovenia	50	..	..	7.4	6.7	6.2	6.3	6.7	6.3	6.5	6.0	4.8	4.4	5.9	7.2	7.6	7.4	7.6	7.5	7.3
Spain	1 834	16.3	14.6	12.2	10.8	10.1	11.0	11.0	10.5	9.2	8.5	8.3	11.3	18.0	19.8	19.1	17.4	19.9	18.5	16.6
Sweden	298	11.8	9.9	8.3	6.9	5.9	6.1	6.8	7.7	7.7	7.1	6.1	6.2	8.3	8.4	8.0	7.5	8.3	7.8	7.3
Switzerland	158	4.2	3.5	3.0	2.6	2.6	3.2	4.3	4.4	4.4	4.0	3.6	3.5	4.4	4.4	4.3	4.1	4.4	4.1	4.1
Turkey	2 376	7.3	7.3	8.1	6.9	8.7	10.7	10.8	10.6	10.4	10.0	10.1	10.7	13.7	12.0	11.7	11.0	..	..	7.6
United Kingdom	1 653	7.0	6.3	6.0	5.5	5.1	5.2	5.0	4.8	4.8	5.4	5.4	5.7	7.6	7.9	7.8	7.6	7.9	7.8	7.6
United States	7 079	4.9	4.5	4.2	4.0	4.8	5.8	6.0	5.5	5.1	4.6	4.6	5.8	9.3	9.7	9.5	8.7	9.7	9.2	8.3
Euro area	11 506	10.4	9.9	9.2	8.3	7.9	8.2	8.7	8.9	8.9	8.2	7.4	7.4	9.3	9.9	9.6	9.2	9.8	9.5	9.0
Total OECD	32 804	6.7	6.6	6.5	6.0	6.3	6.8	7.0	6.8	6.6	6.1	5.7	6.0	8.1	8.3	8.1	7.5	8.3	7.9	7.3

Note: Labour market data are subject to differences in definitions across countries and to many breaks in series, though the latter are often of a minor nature. For information about definitions, sources, data coverage, breaks in series and rebasings, see *OECD Economic Outlook Sources and Methods (http://www.oecd.org/eco/sources-and-methods).*

1. Based on National Employment Survey.

Source: OECD Economic Outlook 88 database.

StatLink ⟲ http://dx.doi.org/10.1787/888932348567

Annex Table 14. Harmonised unemployment rates
Per cent of civilian labour force

	1991	1992	1993	1994	1995	1996	1997	1998	1999	2000	2001	2002	2003	2004	2005	2006	2007	2008	2009
Australia	9.3	10.5	10.6	9.5	8.2	8.2	8.3	7.7	6.9	6.3	6.8	6.4	5.9	5.4	5.0	4.8	4.4	4.2	5.6
Austria	..	..	4.0	3.8	3.9	4.3	4.4	4.5	3.9	3.6	3.6	4.2	4.3	4.9	5.2	4.8	4.4	3.8	4.8
Belgium	6.4	7.1	8.6	9.8	9.7	9.6	9.2	9.3	8.5	6.9	6.6	7.6	8.2	8.4	8.5	8.3	7.5	7.0	7.9
Canada	10.3	11.2	11.4	10.4	9.5	9.6	9.1	8.3	7.6	6.8	7.2	7.7	7.6	7.2	6.8	6.3	6.0	6.1	8.3
Chile	8.2	6.7	6.5	7.8	7.3	6.3	6.1	6.4	10.1	9.7	9.9	9.8	9.5	10.0	9.2	7.8	7.1	7.8	10.8
Czech Republic	4.4	2.3	4.4	4.3	4.1	3.9	4.8	6.4	8.6	8.7	8.0	7.3	7.8	8.3	7.9	7.2	5.3	4.4	6.7
Denmark	7.9	8.6	9.5	7.7	6.8	6.3	5.2	4.9	5.1	4.3	4.5	4.6	5.4	5.5	4.8	3.9	3.8	3.3	6.0
Finland	6.7	11.6	16.2	16.7	15.1	14.9	12.7	11.4	10.3	9.6	9.1	9.1	9.1	8.8	8.3	7.7	6.9	6.4	8.2
France	8.9	9.8	11.0	11.6	11.0	11.5	11.4	11.0	10.4	9.0	8.3	8.6	9.0	9.2	9.3	9.3	8.4	7.8	9.5
Germany	4.2	6.3	7.6	8.2	8.0	8.7	9.4	9.1	8.3	7.5	7.6	8.4	9.3	9.8	10.6	9.8	8.4	7.3	7.5
Greece	6.9	7.8	8.6	8.9	9.1	9.7	9.6	11.0	12.0	11.2	10.7	10.3	9.7	10.5	9.9	8.9	8.3	7.7	9.5
Hungary	..	9.9	12.1	11.0	10.4	9.6	9.0	8.4	6.9	6.4	5.7	5.8	5.9	6.1	7.2	7.5	7.4	7.8	10.0
Iceland	2.5	4.3	5.3	5.3	4.9	3.7	3.9	2.7	2.0	2.3	2.3	3.3	3.4	3.1	2.6	2.9	2.3	3.0	7.2
Ireland	14.7	15.4	15.6	14.4	12.3	11.7	9.9	7.6	5.7	4.2	4.0	4.5	4.6	4.5	4.4	4.5	4.6	6.4	11.9
Israel	..	..	..	..	..	..	..	..	..	..	9.3	10.3	10.7	10.4	9.0	8.4	7.3	6.1	7.6
Italy	8.5	8.8	9.8	10.6	11.2	11.2	11.2	11.3	10.9	10.1	9.1	8.6	8.5	8.0	7.7	6.8	6.2	6.8	7.8
Japan	2.1	2.2	2.5	2.9	3.1	3.4	3.4	4.1	4.7	4.7	5.0	5.4	5.3	4.7	4.4	4.1	3.9	4.0	5.1
Korea	2.4	2.5	2.9	2.5	2.1	2.0	2.6	7.0	6.6	4.4	4.0	3.3	3.6	3.7	3.7	3.5	3.2	3.2	3.6
Luxembourg	1.6	2.1	2.6	3.2	2.9	2.9	2.7	2.7	2.4	2.2	1.9	2.6	3.8	5.0	4.6	4.6	4.2	4.9	5.2
Mexico	2.6	2.8	3.4	3.7	6.2	5.5	3.7	3.2	2.5	2.5	2.8	3.0	3.4	3.9	3.6	3.6	3.7	4.0	5.5
Netherlands	4.8	4.9	5.6	6.2	7.0	6.4	5.4	4.3	3.6	3.0	2.6	3.1	4.1	5.1	5.3	4.3	3.6	3.1	3.7
New Zealand	10.6	10.7	9.8	8.4	6.5	6.3	6.8	7.7	7.1	6.2	5.5	5.3	4.8	4.1	3.8	3.9	3.7	4.2	6.1
Norway	6.0	6.5	6.6	6.0	5.5	4.8	3.9	3.1	3.0	3.2	3.4	3.7	4.2	4.3	4.5	3.4	2.5	2.5	3.2
Poland	..	..	14.0	14.4	13.3	12.4	10.9	10.2	13.4	16.2	18.3	20.0	19.7	19.0	17.8	13.9	9.6	7.2	8.2
Portugal	4.2	4.1	5.5	6.8	7.2	7.2	6.7	5.0	4.5	4.0	4.1	5.1	6.4	6.8	7.7	7.8	8.1	7.7	9.6
Slovak Republic	..	..	..	13.7	13.1	11.3	11.8	12.6	16.4	18.8	19.3	18.7	17.6	18.2	16.3	13.4	11.1	9.5	12.0
Slovenia	..	..	..	..	..	6.9	6.9	7.4	7.4	6.7	6.2	6.3	6.7	6.3	6.5	6.0	4.9	4.4	5.9
Spain	13.0	14.7	18.4	19.5	18.4	17.8	16.7	15.0	12.5	11.1	10.4	11.1	11.1	10.6	9.2	8.5	8.3	11.4	18.0
Sweden	3.1	5.6	9.0	9.3	8.8	9.5	9.9	8.2	6.7	5.6	5.9	6.0	6.6	7.4	7.7	7.1	6.1	6.2	8.3
Switzerland	1.9	3.1	4.0	3.8	3.5	3.9	4.2	3.5	3.0	2.6	2.6	3.2	4.3	4.4	4.4	4.0	3.6	3.5	4.4
Turkey	..	..	..	..	..	..	..	..	..	..	..	..	..	..	9.2	8.7	8.9	9.7	12.6
United Kingdom	8.6	9.8	10.2	9.3	8.5	7.9	6.8	6.1	5.9	5.4	5.0	5.1	5.0	4.7	4.8	5.4	5.3	5.6	7.6
United States	6.8	7.5	6.9	6.1	5.6	5.4	4.9	4.5	4.2	4.0	4.7	5.8	6.0	5.5	5.1	4.6	4.6	5.8	9.3
Euro area	7.8	8.5	10.0	10.7	10.4	10.6	10.6	10.1	9.3	8.5	8.0	8.4	8.8	9.0	9.0	8.4	7.5	7.6	9.4
Total OECD	6.8	7.4	7.8	7.7	7.3	7.2	6.9	6.9	6.7	6.2	6.5	7.1	7.3	7.1	6.8	6.3	5.8	6.1	8.3

StatLink http://dx.doi.org/10.1787/888932348586

Note: In so far as possible, the data have been adjusted to ensure comparability over time and to conform to the guidelines of the International Labour Office. Annual figures are calculated by averaging the monthly and/or quarterly estimates (for both unemployed and the labour force). Further information is available from OECD.stat (http://stats.oecd.org/index.aspx), see the metadata relating to the harmonised unemployment rate.

Source: OCDE, Main Economic Indicators.

Annex Table 15. Labour force, employment and unemployment

Millions

	1994	1995	1996	1997	1998	1999	2000	2001	2002	2003	2004	2005	2006	2007	2008	2009	2010	2011	2012
Labour force																			
Major seven countries	329.3	331.2	334.1	337.9	340.4	343.1	347.5	349.6	351.4	353.7	355.5	358.7	361.8	364.5	366.8	366.9	366.9	368.9	369.9
Total of smaller countries	177.2	179.8	182.2	185.2	187.6	192.9	195.1	197.4	200.7	202.4	206.4	209.4	212.7	215.9	219.4	222.4	225.6	227.6	229.6
Euro area	135.6	136.4	137.5	138.4	140.0	142.4	144.4	146.0	147.7	149.1	150.7	152.5	153.8	155.3	156.9	157.3	157.4	157.5	157.6
Total OECD	506.5	511.0	516.3	523.1	528.0	536.0	542.7	547.0	552.0	556.1	561.9	568.0	574.5	580.4	586.2	589.3	592.5	596.5	599.5
Employment																			
Major seven countries	306.8	309.5	312.0	316.3	319.3	322.5	328.2	329.2	328.9	330.4	333.1	336.6	340.9	344.8	345.4	337.5	336.9	339.5	342.3
Total of smaller countries	162.4	164.5	168.1	171.7	173.9	178.8	181.8	183.6	185.7	186.9	190.4	193.9	198.5	202.8	205.8	203.7	206.2	208.9	212.1
Euro area	121.4	122.4	123.2	124.0	126.2	129.4	132.5	134.5	135.5	136.2	137.3	138.9	141.2	143.7	145.2	142.6	141.9	142.3	143.1
Total OECD	469.1	474.0	480.1	488.0	493.1	501.3	510.0	512.8	514.5	517.3	523.5	530.5	539.5	547.6	551.1	541.3	543.1	548.3	554.4
Unemployment																			
Major seven countries	22.6	21.7	22.0	21.6	21.1	20.6	19.4	20.3	22.5	23.3	22.5	22.0	20.9	19.7	21.4	29.3	30.0	29.4	27.6
Total of smaller countries	14.8	15.3	14.3	13.6	13.8	14.1	13.3	13.9	15.0	15.4	16.0	15.5	14.2	13.1	13.7	18.7	19.4	18.7	17.6
Euro area	14.2	14.1	14.3	14.4	13.9	13.1	12.0	11.5	12.2	12.9	13.4	13.5	12.7	11.5	11.7	14.7	15.5	15.2	14.5
Total OECD	37.3	37.0	36.3	35.1	34.9	34.7	32.7	34.2	37.5	38.8	38.4	37.5	35.0	32.8	35.1	48.0	49.4	48.1	45.2

Source: OECD Economic Outlook 88 database.

StatLink ⟐ http://dx.doi.org/10.1787/888932348605

Annex Table 16. GDP deflators
Percentage change from previous year

	Average 1986-96	1997	1998	1999	2000	2001	2002	2003	2004	2005	2006	2007	2008	2009	2010	2011	2012	Fourth quarter 2010	2011	2012
Australia	3.8	1.3	0.1	1.1	4.3	3.8	3.2	2.3	4.2	4.4	5.2	4.0	6.4	0.3	5.9	3.5	2.5	7.2	2.3	2.7
Austria	2.7	-0.2	0.1	0.1	1.3	2.0	1.5	1.2	1.4	1.8	2.1	2.0	1.5	1.0	1.5	1.1	1.2	1.3	1.2	1.2
Belgium	2.5	0.3	1.9	0.3	1.9	2.1	2.0	2.0	2.2	2.4	2.3	2.3	1.9	1.1	1.5	1.5	1.7	1.5	1.5	1.7
Canada	2.7	1.2	-0.4	1.7	4.1	1.1	1.1	3.3	3.2	3.3	2.7	3.2	4.0	-2.1	2.8	1.6	1.6	1.9	1.6	1.6
Chile	..	4.3	2.0	2.6	4.5	3.8	4.3	6.0	7.6	7.5	12.2	5.4	0.5	4.1	9.6	6.6	4.3	9.4	4.9	4.1
Czech Republic	..	8.4	11.1	2.9	1.5	4.9	2.8	0.9	4.5	-0.3	1.1	3.4	1.8	2.6	0.0	2.2	1.4	1.2	1.5	1.5
Denmark	2.6	2.0	1.2	1.7	3.0	2.5	2.3	1.6	2.3	2.9	2.1	1.9	3.6	0.4	2.9	1.0	2.0	1.7	1.7	2.2
Finland	3.4	1.8	3.6	0.9	2.5	3.1	1.2	-0.6	0.5	0.4	1.1	2.9	1.8	1.0	1.8	1.7	1.7	2.2	1.7	1.8
France	2.2	1.0	0.9	0.1	1.4	2.0	2.4	1.9	1.6	2.0	2.4	2.5	2.6	0.5	0.4	1.0	1.1	1.0	1.0	1.2
Germany	2.6	0.3	0.6	0.3	-0.7	1.2	1.4	1.2	1.0	0.7	0.4	1.8	1.0	1.4	0.8	1.0	1.2	0.8	1.0	1.2
Greece	14.4	6.8	5.2	3.0	3.4	3.1	3.4	3.9	3.0	2.8	3.1	3.0	3.5	1.3	3.3	2.4	1.0	3.9	0.4	1.4
Hungary	..	19.3	13.2	6.9	9.5	10.3	8.1	5.1	5.7	2.3	4.2	5.9	4.8	4.4	1.6	1.9	3.1	0.8	2.6	3.3
Iceland	10.0	2.9	5.1	3.3	3.6	8.6	5.6	0.6	2.5	2.8	8.8	5.7	11.9	8.9	6.0	3.5	1.8	-2.2	5.0	0.5
Ireland	2.7	3.8	6.6	4.1	6.1	5.5	4.5	2.8	2.0	2.5	3.8	1.1	-1.4	-4.0	-1.7	0.7	1.2	0.3	2.4	0.6
Israel	..	7.8	7.1	6.3	1.6	1.7	4.0	-0.5	0.2	1.1	2.3	0.5	0.9	5.0	0.7	1.5	2.3	1.4	1.9	2.4
Italy	5.6	2.6	2.6	1.8	1.9	3.0	3.3	3.1	2.6	2.1	1.8	2.6	2.8	2.1	0.7	1.2	1.1	1.2	1.1	1.2
Japan	0.8	0.5	0.0	-1.3	-1.7	-1.2	-1.5	-1.6	-1.1	-1.2	-0.9	-0.7	-0.8	-0.9	-1.8	-0.8	-0.8	-1.1	-0.9	-0.7
Korea	7.2	3.9	5.0	-1.0	1.0	3.9	3.2	3.6	3.0	0.7	-0.1	2.1	2.9	3.4	3.2	1.8	2.6	2.5	2.3	2.8
Luxembourg	3.0	-1.9	-0.4	5.3	2.0	0.1	2.1	6.0	1.8	4.6	6.7	3.7	4.2	-0.4	1.5	0.1	1.9	-1.8	3.8	1.6
Mexico	36.6	17.5	14.5	17.4	10.7	5.4	2.6	9.4	9.1	4.5	6.9	4.5	6.6	4.3	4.0	3.9	4.0	3.8	4.2	4.2
Netherlands	1.6	2.6	1.9	1.8	4.1	5.1	3.8	2.2	0.7	2.4	1.8	1.8	2.4	-0.2	1.6	1.4	1.4	2.4	1.3	1.4
New Zealand	4.0	0.6	0.8	0.4	2.5	4.2	1.2	1.7	3.9	2.3	2.4	4.1	3.6	1.6	3.0	4.3	2.1	5.5	3.2	1.7
Norway	3.2	2.8	-0.8	6.6	15.7	1.7	-1.8	3.0	5.3	8.7	8.5	2.4	10.0	-4.0	4.2	2.7	2.3	4.9	2.4	2.2
Poland	..	14.0	11.0	6.0	7.3	3.8	2.2	0.3	3.8	2.9	1.5	4.0	3.1	3.6	2.0	3.0	3.2	2.5	2.9	3.3
Portugal	8.6	3.5	3.8	3.3	3.2	3.6	3.7	3.0	2.5	2.5	2.8	2.8	2.0	0.2	1.1	1.3	1.1	1.0	0.9	1.0
Slovak Republic	..	4.5	5.1	7.4	9.4	5.0	3.9	5.3	5.9	2.4	2.9	1.1	2.9	-1.2	0.1	2.2	2.3	1.4	1.6	2.6
Slovenia	..	8.5	7.0	6.6	5.3	8.7	7.7	5.6	3.4	1.6	2.0	4.2	4.0	3.2	0.5	1.0	1.9	0.3	1.4	2.0
Spain	5.6	2.4	2.5	2.6	3.5	4.2	4.3	4.1	4.0	4.3	4.1	3.3	2.4	0.6	0.4	0.2	0.3	0.3	0.2	0.3
Sweden	4.8	1.3	0.6	1.2	1.3	2.2	1.5	1.6	0.8	0.9	1.7	2.6	3.4	1.9	1.1	1.2	1.5	1.0	1.3	1.7
Switzerland	2.5	-0.1	0.3	0.6	1.1	0.8	0.5	1.0	0.6	0.1	2.1	2.5	2.5	0.3	0.1	0.7	0.7	0.4	0.6	0.8
Turkey	68.9	81.5	75.7	54.1	49.2	52.9	37.7	22.8	12.9	6.8	9.4	5.9	12.1	5.3	7.1	6.2	5.7	..	..	..
United Kingdom	4.7	2.8	2.2	2.1	1.2	2.1	3.1	3.1	2.5	2.0	3.1	3.0	3.0	1.4	3.3	2.0	1.3	2.8	1.9	1.2
United States	2.8	1.8	1.1	1.5	2.2	2.3	1.6	2.2	2.8	3.3	3.3	2.9	2.2	0.9	1.0	1.2	0.9	1.6	1.0	0.9
Euro area	..	1.4	1.6	1.0	1.4	2.5	2.6	2.2	1.9	1.9	1.9	2.4	2.0	1.0	0.8	1.0	1.1	1.1	1.0	1.2
Total OECD	6.1	4.1	3.6	2.9	3.0	3.2	2.5	2.5	2.6	2.4	2.6	2.6	2.5	1.1	1.4	1.4	1.3	1.7	1.3	1.4

StatLink http://dx.doi.org/10.1787/888932348624

Note: The adoption of national accounts systems SNA93 or ESA95 has been proceeding at an uneven pace among OECD member countries, both with respect to variables and the time period covered. As a consequence, there are breaks in many national series. For further information, see table "National Accounts Reporting Systems, base years and latest data updates" at the beginning of the Statistical Annex and *OECD Economic Outlook* Sources and Methods (http://www.oecd.org/eco/sources-and-methods).

Source: OECD Economic Outlook 88 database.

Annex Table 17. Private consumption deflators
Percentage change from previous year

	Average 1986-96	1997	1998	1999	2000	2001	2002	2003	2004	2005	2006	2007	2008	2009	2010	2011	2012	Fourth quarter 2010	2011	2012
Australia	4.1	1.4	1.2	0.9	3.1	3.6	3.1	1.9	1.3	1.9	3.4	3.2	3.7	3.1	2.6	2.7	2.9	2.6	2.8	2.9
Austria	2.4	1.5	0.5	0.5	2.5	1.8	0.7	1.6	2.0	2.6	2.1	2.7	2.5	-0.7	1.8	1.8	1.9	1.8	2.0	1.8
Belgium	2.5	1.6	1.0	0.4	3.4	1.9	1.2	1.5	2.4	2.7	3.0	2.9	3.2	-0.5	2.3	1.7	1.8	2.9	1.7	1.9
Canada	2.9	1.6	1.2	1.7	2.2	1.8	2.0	1.6	1.5	1.7	1.4	1.6	1.6	0.5	1.2	1.5	1.3	1.0	1.4	1.3
Chile	..	4.5	3.4	2.3	4.7	4.6	3.2	3.2	0.5	3.7	2.5	3.6	7.7	2.9	1.2	3.7	3.1	3.6	3.6	3.0
Czech Republic	..	9.0	8.9	1.9	3.1	3.9	1.2	-0.4	3.3	0.8	1.4	2.9	4.9	0.3	0.8	1.8	1.7	1.1	2.0	1.6
Denmark	2.6	2.0	1.4	1.9	2.7	2.3	1.7	1.3	1.3	1.5	1.9	2.0	3.2	1.4	2.4	1.4	1.5	2.4	1.4	1.6
Finland	3.4	1.9	2.1	1.4	4.4	2.4	2.2	-0.5	0.3	0.8	1.4	2.2	3.5	0.6	1.4	2.3	2.0	2.1	2.1	2.0
France	2.4	0.9	0.2	-0.5	2.3	1.7	1.0	1.9	1.9	1.8	2.1	2.1	2.9	-0.4	1.1	0.9	1.0	1.2	1.0	1.1
Germany	2.4	1.4	0.5	0.3	0.9	1.8	1.2	1.5	1.3	1.4	1.1	1.8	1.7	0.0	1.9	1.4	1.4	1.7	1.3	1.5
Greece	14.3	5.6	4.5	2.3	3.3	2.7	2.6	3.4	2.9	3.3	3.4	3.0	4.1	1.3	4.0	2.5	0.7	..	..	..
Hungary	..	18.4	14.7	9.5	9.8	7.9	3.6	3.8	4.5	3.8	3.6	6.3	5.4	4.1	4.5	2.7	2.9	3.6	2.6	3.0
Iceland	10.3	0.8	1.5	2.8	5.0	7.8	4.8	1.3	3.0	1.9	7.7	4.6	14.0	15.3	5.7	2.3	1.6	4.0	2.1	1.4
Ireland	2.8	2.6	3.7	2.6	7.2	4.4	5.4	4.1	1.8	1.8	2.3	3.4	2.8	-4.1	-2.1	1.0	1.2	-0.6	1.2	1.2
Israel	5.6	5.6	6.3	5.9	2.1	1.0	4.3	0.3	0.5	1.9	2.7	1.8	4.8	2.4	3.0	2.2	2.7	2.6	2.1	2.8
Italy	5.7	2.2	1.8	1.8	3.4	2.6	2.9	2.8	2.6	2.3	2.7	2.3	3.2	-0.1	1.6	1.5	1.4	1.8	1.3	1.5
Japan	1.1	1.2	0.1	-0.5	-1.1	-1.1	-1.4	-0.9	-0.7	-0.8	-0.2	-0.6	0.4	-2.2	-1.7	-0.7	-0.8	-0.9	-1.0	-0.6
Korea	7.3	6.2	6.2	2.8	4.4	4.3	3.1	3.2	3.2	2.3	1.5	2.0	4.5	2.6	2.4	3.1	3.4	2.6	3.3	3.5
Luxembourg	2.7	1.4	1.7	2.5	4.0	2.0	0.5	2.2	2.6	3.2	2.4	2.2	2.0	0.8	1.1	1.9	2.2	1.0	2.0	2.2
Mexico	37.1	16.6	20.4	14.0	10.3	7.1	5.3	7.1	6.5	3.3	3.5	4.8	5.1	8.4	3.4	4.0	3.5	4.3	3.6	3.8
Netherlands	2.0	2.3	2.0	1.9	3.8	4.5	3.0	2.4	1.0	2.1	2.2	1.8	1.4	-0.6	1.3	1.4	1.4	1.2	1.5	1.4
New Zealand	4.1	1.8	1.9	0.7	2.2	2.2	2.0	0.8	1.5	2.2	3.1	1.5	3.6	2.5	2.0	3.9	1.8	4.6	2.0	1.7
Norway	3.6	2.4	2.5	2.0	2.9	2.2	1.4	3.0	0.7	1.1	1.9	1.2	3.6	2.5	2.0	1.9	2.5	2.4	2.3	2.5
Poland	..	14.1	10.5	6.7	10.1	3.4	3.5	0.2	3.3	1.8	1.3	2.6	4.5	2.0	2.5	2.5	3.0	2.4	2.6	3.2
Portugal	8.6	3.0	2.4	2.3	3.5	3.5	2.8	3.0	2.5	2.7	3.0	3.0	2.7	-2.3	1.5	2.3	1.3	2.5	1.9	1.1
Slovak Republic	..	4.8	5.7	9.9	8.3	5.6	2.9	6.5	7.3	2.6	4.9	2.6	4.5	1.0	0.4	3.3	2.9	1.1	3.7	2.9
Slovenia	..	8.6	6.9	6.4	7.2	7.6	7.8	5.3	3.0	2.1	2.2	4.1	5.4	0.0	2.4	1.7	2.1	2.0	2.0	2.2
Spain	5.5	2.7	1.9	2.3	3.7	3.4	2.8	3.1	3.6	3.4	3.6	3.3	3.5	0.1	2.3	1.0	0.3	2.4	0.4	0.3
Sweden	5.3	1.3	0.5	1.5	0.8	2.1	1.5	1.6	1.0	1.1	1.1	1.3	2.9	1.9	0.8	0.9	1.7	-0.2	1.4	1.9
Switzerland	2.6	0.8	-0.1	0.4	0.8	0.7	0.9	0.4	0.8	0.5	1.3	1.3	2.6	-0.4	0.5	0.7	0.8	0.7	0.7	0.8
Turkey	70.4	82.1	83.0	53.4	54.9	49.7	38.5	23.4	10.8	8.3	9.8	6.6	10.8	5.0	8.5	6.7	6.4	..	..	..
United Kingdom	4.7	2.5	2.4	1.2	1.1	2.0	1.5	1.9	1.8	2.4	2.8	2.9	3.1	1.3	4.4	3.0	1.8	4.1	2.8	1.7
United States	3.2	1.9	0.9	1.6	2.5	1.9	1.4	2.0	2.6	3.0	2.7	2.7	3.3	0.2	1.7	0.9	0.9	1.0	0.9	0.8
Euro area	..	1.8	1.1	0.9	2.5	2.4	1.9	2.1	2.0	2.1	2.2	2.3	2.7	-0.2	1.7	1.4	1.2	1.8	1.2	1.3
Total OECD	6.5	4.4	3.9	3.0	3.7	3.2	2.3	2.4	2.4	2.3	2.4	2.4	3.2	0.6	1.8	1.5	1.4	1.7	1.4	1.4

StatLink ⟋ http://dx.doi.org/10.1787/888932348643

Note: The adoption of national accounts systems SNA93 or ESA95 has been proceeding at an uneven pace among OECD member countries, both with respect to variables and the time period covered. As a consequence, there are breaks in many national series. For further information, see table "National Accounts Reporting Systems, base years and latest data updates" at the beginning of the Statistical Annex and *OECD Economic Outlook* Sources and Methods (*http://www.oecd.org/eco/sources-and-methods*).

Source: OECD Economic Outlook 88 database.

Annex Table 18. Consumer price indices
Percentage change from previous year

	Average 1986-96	1997	1998	1999	2000	2001	2002	2003	2004	2005	2006	2007	2008	2009	2010	2011	2012	Fourth quarter 2010	2011	2012
Australia	4.5	0.3	0.9	1.5	4.5	4.4	3.0	2.8	2.3	2.7	3.5	2.3	4.4	1.8	2.9	2.8	2.9	3.0	2.8	2.9
Austria	..	1.2	0.8	0.5	2.0	2.3	1.7	1.3	2.0	2.1	1.7	2.2	3.2	0.4	1.6	1.8	1.9	1.5	2.0	1.8
Belgium	..	1.5	0.9	1.1	2.7	2.4	1.6	1.5	1.9	2.5	2.3	1.8	4.5	0.0	2.1	1.6	1.8	2.3	1.7	1.9
Canada	..	1.6	1.0	1.7	2.7	2.5	2.3	2.7	1.8	2.2	2.0	2.1	2.4	0.3	1.6	1.7	1.5	1.4	1.7	1.5
Chile	15.3	6.1	5.1	3.3	3.8	3.6	2.5	2.8	1.1	3.1	3.4	4.4	8.7	0.4	1.6	3.8	3.1	3.1	3.6	3.0
Czech Republic	..	8.5	10.7	2.1	3.9	4.7	1.8	0.1	2.8	1.9	2.6	3.0	6.3	1.0	1.6	1.9	1.7	2.7	2.0	1.6
Denmark	2.8	2.2	1.8	2.5	2.9	2.3	2.4	2.1	1.2	1.8	1.9	1.7	3.4	1.3	2.3	1.4	1.5	2.6	1.4	1.6
Finland	..	1.2	1.3	1.3	2.9	2.7	2.0	1.3	0.1	0.8	1.3	1.6	3.9	1.6	1.4	1.8	2.0	1.3	2.1	2.0
France	..	1.3	0.7	0.6	1.8	1.8	1.9	2.2	2.3	1.9	1.9	1.6	3.2	0.1	1.6	1.1	1.1	1.4	1.1	1.2
Germany	..	1.5	0.6	0.6	1.4	1.9	1.4	1.0	1.8	1.9	1.8	2.3	2.8	0.2	1.0	1.2	1.4	1.2	1.3	1.5
Greece	..	5.4	4.5	2.1	2.9	3.7	3.9	3.4	3.0	3.5	3.3	3.0	4.2	1.3	4.7	2.5	0.7	5.2	1.3	0.4
Hungary	..	18.3	14.2	10.0	9.8	9.1	5.3	4.7	6.7	3.6	3.9	8.0	6.0	4.2	4.9	2.9	3.1	4.5	3.1	3.1
Iceland[1]	9.7	1.8	1.7	3.2	5.1	6.4	5.2	2.1	3.2	4.0	6.7	5.1	12.7	12.0	5.3	1.8	1.6	2.3	2.1	1.4
Ireland	..	1.3	2.1	2.5	5.3	4.0	4.7	4.0	2.3	2.2	2.7	2.9	3.1	-1.7	-1.6	0.9	1.2	-0.5	1.2	1.2
Israel	14.8	9.0	5.4	5.2	1.1	1.1	5.7	0.7	-0.4	1.3	2.1	0.5	4.6	3.3	2.6	2.5	2.7	2.2	2.1	2.8
Italy	..	1.9	2.0	1.7	2.6	2.3	2.6	2.8	2.3	2.2	2.2	2.0	3.5	0.8	1.5	1.4	1.4	1.5	1.3	1.5
Japan	1.3	1.7	0.7	-0.3	-0.5	-0.8	-0.9	-0.2	0.0	-0.6	0.2	0.1	1.4	-1.4	-0.9	-0.8	-0.5	-0.6	-0.7	-0.4
Korea	6.0	4.4	7.5	0.8	2.3	4.1	2.7	3.6	3.6	2.8	2.2	2.5	4.7	2.8	2.8	3.2	3.4	2.8	3.3	3.5
Luxembourg	..	1.4	1.0	1.0	3.8	2.4	2.1	2.5	3.2	3.8	3.0	2.7	4.1	0.0	2.6	1.8	2.2	2.0	2.0	2.2
Mexico	36.7	20.6	15.9	16.6	9.5	6.4	5.0	4.5	4.7	4.0	3.6	4.0	5.1	5.3	4.1	3.8	3.5	4.1	3.6	3.8
Netherlands	..	1.9	1.8	2.0	2.3	5.1	3.9	2.2	1.4	1.5	1.7	1.6	2.2	1.0	0.8	1.4	1.4	1.1	1.5	1.4
New Zealand	4.6	1.2	1.3	-0.1	2.6	2.6	2.7	1.8	2.3	3.0	3.4	2.4	4.0	2.1	2.4	4.3	2.3	4.4	2.5	2.2
Norway	3.7	2.6	2.3	2.3	3.1	3.0	1.3	2.5	0.5	1.5	2.3	0.7	3.8	2.2	2.4	1.5	2.5	2.1	2.1	2.5
Poland	..	14.9	11.6	7.2	9.9	5.4	1.9	0.7	3.4	2.2	1.3	2.4	4.2	3.8	2.4	2.5	3.1	2.3	2.7	3.3
Portugal	..	1.9	2.2	2.2	2.8	4.4	3.7	3.3	2.5	2.1	3.0	2.4	2.7	-0.9	1.4	2.3	1.3	2.3	1.9	1.1
Slovak Republic	..	6.0	6.7	10.4	12.2	7.2	3.5	8.4	7.5	2.8	4.3	1.9	3.9	0.9	0.8	3.4	2.9	1.5	3.7	2.9
Slovenia	..	8.3	7.9	6.1	8.9	8.6	7.5	5.7	3.7	2.5	2.5	3.8	5.5	0.9	2.1	1.9	2.2	2.0	2.1	2.3
Spain	..	1.9	1.8	2.2	3.5	2.8	3.6	3.1	3.1	3.4	3.6	2.8	4.1	-0.2	1.5	0.9	0.3	1.5	0.4	0.3
Sweden[2]	4.8	0.7	-0.3	0.5	0.9	2.4	2.2	1.9	0.4	0.5	1.4	2.2	3.4	-0.3	1.1	1.5	2.3	1.1	1.9	2.4
Switzerland	2.8	0.5	0.0	0.8	1.6	1.0	0.6	0.6	0.8	1.2	1.1	0.7	2.4	-0.5	0.5	0.1	1.1	-0.3	0.7	1.2
Turkey	70.0	85.7	84.6	64.9	54.9	54.4	45.0	21.6	8.6	8.2	9.6	8.8	10.4	6.3	8.5	6.9	6.4	..	..	..
United Kingdom[3]	..	1.8	1.6	1.3	0.8	1.2	1.3	1.4	1.3	2.0	2.3	2.3	3.6	2.2	3.1	2.6	1.6	2.7	2.6	1.5
United States[4]	3.6	2.3	1.5	2.2	3.4	2.8	1.6	2.3	2.7	3.4	3.2	2.9	3.8	-0.3	1.6	1.1	1.1	0.8	1.1	1.0
Euro area	..	1.7	1.2	1.2	2.3	2.4	2.3	2.1	2.2	2.2	2.2	2.1	3.3	0.3	1.5	1.3	1.2	1.5	1.2	1.3

StatLink http://dx.doi.org/10.1787/888932348662

Note: For the euro area countries, the euro area aggregate and the United Kingdom: harmonised index of consumer prices (HICP).
1. Excluding rent, but including imputed rent.
2. The consumer price index includes mortgage interest costs.
3. Known as the CPI in the United Kingdom.
4. The methodology for calculating the Consumer Price Index has changed considerably over the past years, lowering measured inflation substantially.
Source: OECD Economic Outlook 88 database.

Annex Table 19. Oil and other primary commodity markets

	1995	1996	1997	1998	1999	2000	2001	2002	2003	2004	2005	2006	2007	2008	2009	2010	2011	2012
Oil market conditions[1]																		
Demand							Million barrels per day											
OECD	44.9	46.0	46.8	47.0	47.9	48.0	48.1	48.0	48.7	49.5	49.9	49.6	49.3	47.6	45.5	45.8	45.5	..
of which: North America	21.6	22.2	22.7	23.1	23.8	24.1	24.1	24.2	24.6	25.5	25.6	25.4	25.5	24.2	23.3	23.8	23.7	..
Europe	14.7	15.0	15.1	15.4	15.4	15.2	15.4	15.3	15.5	15.5	15.7	15.7	15.5	15.4	14.5	14.3	14.2	..
Pacific	8.6	8.8	8.9	8.4	8.7	8.7	8.6	8.5	8.6	8.5	8.6	8.5	8.4	8.0	7.7	7.7	7.5	..
Non-OECD	25.2	26.0	27.2	27.5	28.3	29.0	29.6	30.3	31.1	33.4	34.2	35.6	37.2	38.4	39.3	41.2	42.7	..
Total	70.1	72.1	73.9	74.5	76.2	77.0	77.6	78.3	79.9	82.9	84.1	85.1	86.5	86.0	84.8	86.9	88.2	..
Supply																		
OECD	21.0	21.7	22.0	21.8	21.4	21.9	21.7	21.8	21.5	21.0	20.1	19.8	19.5	18.7	18.8	18.8	18.5	..
OPEC total	27.4	28.1	29.7	30.6	29.2	30.8	30.3	28.9	30.8	33.3	34.7	35.0	34.6	35.6	33.4	..	..	..
Former USSR	7.1	7.1	7.2	7.3	7.4	8.0	8.6	9.5	10.5	11.4	11.8	12.3	12.8	12.8	13.3	13.6	13.8	..
Other non-OECD	15.1	15.7	16.0	16.3	16.6	16.8	16.9	17.2	17.4	17.7	18.0	18.4	18.6	19.4	19.6	-32.4	..	..
Total	70.7	72.6	74.9	76.0	74.6	77.4	77.6	77.4	80.2	83.5	84.7	85.5	85.5	86.6	85.0	..	..	..
Trade																		
OECD net imports	23.6	24.4	25.1	25.5	25.8	26.3	26.6	26.0	27.5	28.7	30.0	30.0	29.7	29.2	26.7	27.3	27.0	..
Former USSR net exports	2.8	3.2	3.4	3.5	3.7	4.2	4.8	5.7	6.6	7.6	7.9	8.3	8.7	8.6	9.3	9.4	9.5	..
Other non-OECD net exports	20.7	21.2	21.7	22.0	22.1	22.1	21.8	20.3	20.9	21.1	22.1	21.8	21.0	20.6	17.4	17.9	17.5	..
Prices[2]							cif, $ per bl											
Brent crude oil price	17.0	20.7	19.1	12.7	17.9	28.4	24.5	25.0	28.8	38.2	54.4	65.1	72.5	97.0	61.5	77.8	80.0	80.0
Prices of other primary commodities[2]							$ indices											
Food and tropical beverages	120	126	126	106	86	80	75	84	91	101	100	111	140	188	162	174	191	191
Agricultural raw materials	122	102	98	84	82	87	74	74	90	99	100	112	135	130	108	146	152	152
Minerals, ores and metals	74	64	66	55	53	60	54	53	60	82	100	148	167	174	123	179	196	196
Total[3]	112	116	112	93	80	80	74	80	90	103	100	116	147	184	148	168	184	184

1. Based on data published in various issues of International Energy Agency, *Oil Market Report*.
2. Indices through 2009 are based on data compiled by the International Energy Agency for oil and by the Hamburg Institute of International Economics for the prices of other primary commodities; OECD estimates and projections for 2010 to 2012.
3. OECD calculations. The total price index for non-energy primary commodities is a weighted average of the individual HWWI non-oil commodities indices with the weights based on the commodities' share in total non-energy commodities world trade.

Source: OECD Economic Outlook 88 database.

StatLink http://dx.doi.org/10.1787/888932348681

Annex Table 20. Employment rates, participation rates and labour force

	Employment rates						Labour force participation rates						Labour force					
	Per cent						Per cent						Percentage change					
	Average 1989-98	Average 1999-08	2009	2010	2011	2012	Average 1989-98	Average 1999-08	2009	2010	2011	2012	Average 1989-98	Average 1999-08	2009	2010	2011	2012
Australia	68.3	72.2	74.1	74.5	75.0	75.6	74.5	76.4	78.5	78.6	78.9	79.2	1.4	2.1	2.2	1.9	1.7	1.8
Austria	67.7	69.3	72.2	72.0	72.2	72.6	70.4	72.3	75.8	75.4	75.4	75.4	1.2	1.2	0.7	-0.3	0.4	0.3
Belgium	58.9	62.7	63.4	63.2	63.1	63.0	64.3	67.9	68.9	69.2	69.1	69.0	0.6	1.0	0.6	1.3	0.7	0.4
Canada	69.2	73.4	73.5	73.8	74.2	74.6	76.5	78.8	80.1	80.3	80.5	80.5	1.0	1.8	0.7	1.4	1.3	1.0
Chile	54.6	55.4	57.3	60.4	62.1	63.3	58.8	60.9	64.3	65.7	67.0	68.3	2.2	2.2	3.4	3.6	3.3	3.0
Czech Republic	69.0	65.7	66.3	65.2	65.8	66.7	72.4	71.0	71.0	70.5	70.8	71.5	..	0.1	1.1	-0.7	0.1	0.3
Denmark	75.2	78.3	79.0	77.7	78.4	79.5	81.0	82.0	83.9	83.7	84.4	84.9	0.0	0.6	-0.7	-0.3	0.6	0.4
Finland	64.8	68.4	69.0	68.9	69.6	70.3	73.7	74.8	75.2	75.4	75.8	76.4	-0.3	0.6	-0.9	0.0	0.3	0.4
France	61.2	63.1	63.2	63.0	63.2	63.4	67.7	68.9	69.5	69.5	69.5	69.5	0.4	0.7	1.0	0.5	0.5	0.5
Germany	68.0	70.8	74.6	75.1	75.5	75.7	73.3	77.5	80.5	80.6	80.6	80.7	0.7	0.4	0.2	-0.3	-0.2	0.0
Greece	55.1	60.1	62.4	60.8	59.3	59.2	60.9	66.7	69.0	69.3	69.4	69.7	1.4	0.8	0.9	0.6	0.3	0.4
Hungary	51.9	55.4	54.5	54.6	54.5	55.3	57.8	59.4	60.6	61.6	61.7	62.1	..	0.4	0.0	1.3	0.2	0.5
Iceland	82.1	83.6	78.0	78.2	77.9	78.6	85.3	85.9	84.1	84.5	84.8	84.9	0.9	1.8	-1.7	-0.5	-0.8	0.0
Ireland	56.0	67.9	63.3	61.7	61.7	62.6	64.4	71.3	71.7	71.4	71.4	71.6	2.3	3.0	-2.9	-1.0	-0.4	0.6
Israel	..	58.0	60.4	61.4	61.9	62.3	..	63.7	65.4	65.6	65.9	66.2	..	2.6	1.9	2.2	2.2	2.0
Italy	53.4	57.3	58.5	58.0	58.2	58.6	59.4	62.4	63.4	63.4	63.7	63.9	0.0	0.8	-0.3	0.2	0.5	0.5
Japan	73.9	75.2	77.1	77.4	77.8	78.4	76.0	78.8	81.2	81.6	81.8	82.0	0.9	-0.2	-0.5	-0.4	-0.2	-0.8
Korea	62.4	64.9	66.4	66.8	67.1	67.5	64.2	67.6	69.0	69.4	69.5	69.7	1.9	1.3	0.2	1.3	0.7	0.8
Luxembourg	60.7	64.2	64.9	65.0	65.2	64.9	62.2	66.7	68.8	69.2	69.3	68.9	1.2	2.4	2.7	2.0	1.0	0.4
Mexico	61.2	62.3	61.6	..	..	..	63.9	64.4	65.1	..	..	..	..	1.9	2.0	1.5	1.7	1.5
Netherlands	67.3	75.9	77.6	76.9	76.9	77.4	71.1	78.5	80.3	80.2	80.4	80.9	1.7	1.0	-0.4	0.1	0.1	0.3
New Zealand	68.6	74.3	75.4	..	..	..	74.7	78.0	80.3	..	..	80.9	1.5	2.1	1.0	0.9	0.9	1.4
Norway	74.3	77.4	78.4	77.7	77.9	78.6	78.2	80.3	80.9	80.7	81.0	81.4	0.8	1.2	-0.1	0.5	1.1	1.1
Poland	58.3	54.3	58.4	58.8	59.5	60.2	66.8	64.3	63.5	65.0	65.3	65.3	..	-0.1	1.6	2.5	0.6	0.2
Portugal	68.8	72.1	70.3	69.4	68.7	68.8	73.0	76.8	77.8	77.7	77.5	77.5	0.9	1.0	-0.7	0.1	-0.2	0.1
Slovak Republic	60.5	58.0	60.3	59.0	59.4	60.1	69.1	69.0	68.6	68.7	68.6	68.6	..	0.6	0.1	0.4	-0.1	-0.1
Slovenia	..	66.5	69.3	68.2	67.3	67.5	..	70.9	73.7	73.5	72.9	72.9	..	1.0	0.0	0.2	-0.8	0.1
Spain	50.3	62.1	61.1	59.9	60.2	61.2	59.4	69.3	74.5	74.7	74.4	74.1	1.3	3.4	0.8	-0.1	-0.7	-0.8
Sweden	75.7	74.6	73.9	..	..	..	82.3	80.2	80.7	..	..	..	-0.3	0.8	0.2	1.1	1.2	0.7
Switzerland	81.0	81.0	81.9	81.4	81.6	82.1	83.4	84.0	85.6	85.1	85.2	85.6	0.9	1.1	1.5	0.5	1.0	1.2
Turkey	51.5	46.3	45.1	46.9	47.0	47.4	56.2	51.3	52.2	53.3	53.2	53.2	1.8	1.0	3.9	3.8	1.5	1.7
United Kingdom	69.7	72.0	70.9	70.5	70.3	70.3	76.0	76.0	76.7	76.5	76.3	76.1	-0.1	0.9	0.5	0.3	0.3	0.3
United States	71.6	71.9	68.1	..	..	..	76.1	75.7	75.0	..	..	..	1.2	1.1	-0.1	-0.1	1.0	0.6
Euro area	60.6	65.0	66.2	65.8	66.0	66.3	66.7	70.9	73.0	73.0	73.0	73.1	0.8	1.1	0.3	0.1	0.1	0.1
Total OECD	64.5	66.9	66.5	66.5	66.7	67.1	69.2	71.5	72.4	72.4	72.5	72.6	1.2	1.0	0.5	0.5	0.7	0.5

StatLink ⟶ http://dx.doi.org/10.1787/888932348700

Note: Employment rates are calculated as the ratio of total employment to the population of working age. The working age population concept used here and for the labour force participation rate is defined as all persons of the age 15 to 64 years (16 to 64 years for Spain). This definition does not correspond to the commonly-used working age population concepts for Mexico (15 years and above), the United States and New Zealand (16 years and above) and Sweden (15-74). Hence for these countries no projections are available. For information about sources and definitions, see *OECD Economic Outlook* Sources and Methods (*http://www.oecd.org/eco/sources-and-methods*).

Source: OECD Economic Outlook 88 database.

Annex Table 21. Potential GDP, employment and capital stock

Percentage change from previous period

	Potential GDP						Employment						Capital stock[1]					
	Average 1989-98	Average 1999-08	2009	2010	2011	2012	Average 1989-98	Average 1999-08	2009	2010	2011	2012	Average 1989-98	Average 1999-08	2009	2010	2011	2012
Australia	3.3	3.4	3.7	3.4	3.2	3.3	1.2	2.4	0.7	2.3	2.0	2.1	3.1	5.5	7.0	7.0	7.0	7.2
Austria	2.4	2.2	1.6	1.6	1.7	1.7	1.1	1.1	-0.3	0.0	0.6	0.8	2.9	2.4	0.8	0.6	0.8	1.0
Belgium	2.2	2.2	2.0	2.0	1.8	1.7	0.4	1.1	-0.3	0.5	0.5	0.6	3.3	2.5	2.4	2.2	2.3	2.4
Canada	2.6	2.8	1.8	1.7	1.9	2.0	0.9	1.9	-1.6	1.7	1.6	1.5	4.5	4.8	2.9	2.3	2.9	3.2
Chile	..	3.8	3.6	2.6	3.9	4.6	2.4	2.5	0.0	6.8	4.2	3.2	..	..	..	..	..	..
Czech Republic	..	3.6	2.0	2.5	2.5	2.8	..	0.6	-1.3	-1.6	0.6	0.6	..	..	..	..	..	..
Denmark	2.2	1.7	1.3	1.2	1.3	1.4	0.3	0.9	-3.4	-1.7	0.6	1.2	3.6	4.0	3.7	3.5	3.7	3.9
Finland	2.0	3.2	1.0	1.2	1.3	1.5	-1.2	1.1	-2.9	-0.3	0.7	0.6	2.2	2.1	-1.5	-1.5	-0.8	-0.4
France	1.9	2.0	1.0	1.4	1.4	1.5	0.1	1.1	-0.9	0.3	0.7	0.7	2.8	3.3	2.7	2.4	2.5	2.6
Germany	2.3	1.3	1.2	1.2	1.4	1.4	0.5	0.5	0.0	0.2	0.4	0.1	3.0	1.9	1.2	1.5	1.6	1.5
Greece	2.1	3.5	0.8	0.1	-0.1	0.3	1.0	1.4	-1.1	-2.4	-2.4	-0.3	2.9	4.9	2.7	1.5	1.0	1.0
Hungary	..	3.4	0.7	0.8	1.1	1.4	..	0.3	-2.3	-0.1	-0.3	1.3	3.7	5.2	1.0	0.5	0.8	1.2
Iceland	2.0	4.1	-0.1	-0.5	-0.4	0.8	0.9	1.7	-6.0	-0.7	-1.4	0.7	..	..	..	..	..	..
Ireland	6.5	5.4	-0.1	-0.3	0.3	1.2	3.3	3.0	-8.8	-3.1	-0.4	1.8	3.5	6.5	1.9	1.2	1.5	1.5
Israel	..	3.6	3.2	3.9	3.9	3.9	..	2.9	0.3	3.6	2.5	2.2	..	..	..	..	..	..
Italy	1.8	1.0	0.0	0.3	0.4	0.7	-0.1	1.3	-1.5	-0.6	0.6	0.8	3.0	3.0	1.1	1.2	1.3	1.4
Japan	2.1	1.0	0.5	0.5	0.9	0.5	0.7	-0.1	-1.6	-0.4	0.1	-0.3	4.2	1.5	0.0	0.1	0.2	0.7
Korea	5.1	4.2	3.8	3.2	2.6	..	1.4	1.7	-0.3	1.2	1.0	0.9	..	..	..	..	..	..
Luxembourg	..	2.5	1.8	2.0	2.2	2.6	1.0	2.2	1.3	1.7	1.2	0.5	..	..	..	..	..	..
Mexico	..	2.2	1.7	1.2	0.9	3.3	..	1.7	0.5	1.7	2.3	2.1	..	..	..	..	..	..
Netherlands	3.0	3.0	1.5	1.1	0.9	0.9	2.0	1.1	-1.1	-0.7	-0.1	0.4	3.4	2.9	2.8	2.5	2.5	2.6
New Zealand	2.4	3.0	1.5	1.1	1.2	2.1	1.5	2.4	-1.1	0.5	1.6	2.0	3.1	5.1	2.4	0.6	3.3	3.5
Norway	2.5	3.5	2.0	1.5	1.3	1.7	1.0	1.2	-0.6	0.0	0.8	1.5	1.4	2.1	-1.9	-2.6	-1.5	-0.8
Poland	..	4.1	4.9	3.6	3.1	3.3	..	0.8	0.4	0.9	1.4	1.4	..	..	..	..	..	..
Portugal	3.2	1.6	0.3	0.4	0.5	0.8	0.9	0.6	-2.7	-1.1	-1.0	0.4	4.4	2.8	-0.4	-0.7	-1.0	-0.7
Slovak Republic	..	5.0	4.1	3.8	3.4	3.4	..	1.5	-2.7	-2.0	0.6	1.0	..	..	..	..	..	..
Slovenia	..	3.7	1.1	1.8	1.2	1.4	..	1.3	-1.5	-1.2	-1.2	0.3	..	..	..	..	..	..
Spain	2.8	3.5	0.9	-0.1	0.2	0.4	1.1	3.6	-6.8	-2.3	0.2	1.3	5.0	6.0	4.0	3.5	3.1	3.2
Sweden	1.9	2.8	2.3	1.8	2.2	2.3	-1.2	1.1	-2.0	1.0	1.6	1.3	3.6	4.1	1.0	1.1	1.7	2.0
Switzerland	1.4	1.9	2.0	1.8	1.8	1.8	0.6	1.1	0.6	0.4	1.1	1.4	3.7	2.9	2.5	2.5	2.6	2.6
Turkey	..	..	..	..	..	..	2.0	0.7	0.4	5.9	1.9	2.5	..	..	..	..	..	..
United Kingdom	2.5	2.4	1.0	1.1	1.3	1.4	0.0	0.9	-1.6	0.0	0.3	0.5	4.5	4.2	1.2	1.1	1.1	1.3
United States	3.1	2.6	1.4	1.4	1.8	2.1	1.3	1.0	-3.8	-0.5	1.2	1.6	4.5	4.3	1.9	2.1	2.7	3.3
Euro area	2.2	2.0	1.0	0.9	1.0	1.2	0.5	1.3	-1.8	-0.5	0.3	0.6	3.2	3.1	2.0	1.8	1.8	1.9
Total OECD	2.6	2.3	1.3	1.3	1.5	1.6	1.4	1.1	-1.8	0.3	1.0	1.1	4.0	3.7	1.8	1.8	2.1	2.5

Note: Estimates of potential output are based on a production function approach outlined in Beffy *et al.* (2006), "New OECD methods for supply-side and medium-term assessments: a new capital services approach", *OECD Economics Department Working Papers*, No. 482. Revisions to this method are discussed in Chapter 4 of *OECD Economic Outlook* No. 85, "Beyond the crisis: medium-term challenges relating to potential output, employment and fiscal positions".

1. Total economy less housing.

Source: OECD Economic Outlook 88 database.

StatLink ⇒ http://dx.doi.org/10.1787/888932348719

Annex Table 22. Structural unemployment and unit labor costs

| | Structural unemployment rate | | | | | | | | | Unit labour costs[1] | | | | | | | | |
| | Per cent | | | | | | | | | Percentage change | | | | | | | | |
	Average 1986-95	Average 1996-05	2006	2007	2008	2009	2010	2011	2012	Average 1986-95	Average 1996-05	2006	2007	2008	2009	2010	2011	2012
Australia	7.7	6.4	5.2	5.1	5.1	5.1	5.2	5.2	5.2	3.5	2.3	5.8	4.0	5.5	0.7	2.4	3.4	3.1
Austria	3.6	4.0	4.3	4.3	4.3	4.3	4.3	4.3	4.3	3.1	0.3	1.2	1.4	3.3	4.8	-0.3	0.5	0.8
Belgium	8.0	8.1	8.0	7.9	8.0	8.1	8.2	8.3	8.5	2.5	1.5	2.0	2.3	4.6	4.2	-0.4	0.9	1.2
Canada	8.6	7.5	6.6	6.5	6.5	6.6	6.6	6.6	6.6	2.5	1.9	4.0	3.3	3.8	2.6	0.9	1.6	2.0
Czech Republic	..	..	..	..	..	..	..	..	..	11.7	3.8	0.9	3.1	5.3	2.6	-2.1	0.3	0.8
Denmark	6.6	5.2	4.5	4.4	4.4	4.8	4.8	4.9	5.0	2.6	2.4	2.3	5.2	6.6	4.3	-1.3	0.3	1.7
Finland	8.0	9.6	7.8	7.5	7.4	7.6	7.8	7.8	7.8	2.9	1.3	0.3	0.7	5.4	7.2	-1.0	-0.1	-0.6
France	8.9	9.1	8.5	8.3	8.3	8.6	8.7	8.8	8.8	2.1	1.5	1.8	1.6	3.0	2.7	0.8	0.9	0.7
Germany	6.9	8.1	8.6	8.4	8.2	8.1	8.1	8.1	8.1	2.4	0.0	-1.8	-0.1	2.8	5.2	-1.5	0.3	-0.1
Greece	7.2	9.4	9.1	8.9	8.9	9.1	9.8	10.6	10.9	15.0	5.0	1.5	4.2	4.6	6.3	-0.5	-0.2	-0.2
Hungary	2.5	3.2	2.8	2.8	2.8	3.0	3.2	3.4	3.5	11.6	9.4	2.9	6.2	4.6	1.8	0.4	0.0	2.4
Iceland	14.3	7.0	4.7	4.7	5.1	6.8	8.0	8.7	8.9	1.4	5.2	12.0	7.9	4.4	-1.8	8.4	1.8	2.3
Ireland	..	9.3	8.3	7.9	7.6	7.7	7.3	6.9	6.5	..	3.2	4.5	2.5	5.2	-0.9	-5.0	-2.8	-1.1
Israel	9.1	8.6	6.6	6.3	6.4	6.8	7.1	7.2	7.3	4.7	2.3	3.3	1.6	2.5	0.2	3.8	2.3	2.1
Japan	2.8	4.0	4.1	4.1	4.1	4.1	4.1	4.1	4.2	1.3	-1.5	0.0	-2.9	1.9	1.3	-2.2	-0.6	-0.6
Korea	..	..	..	..	..	..	..	..	..	9.4	2.1	0.7	1.7	3.3	3.0	0.9	2.8	3.0
Luxembourg	..	..	..	..	..	..	..	..	..	3.0	1.9	1.5	1.9	5.6	6.8	0.0	0.6	-0.4
Mexico	..	..	..	..	..	..	..	..	..	37.1	11.1	3.2	3.9	5.2	10.1	-0.2	2.3	1.8
Netherlands	6.6	4.3	3.6	3.6	3.5	3.5	3.7	3.8	3.8	1.2	2.5	0.7	1.8	3.2	5.3	-0.7	0.7	0.5
New Zealand	7.0	5.7	4.1	4.0	4.0	4.1	4.2	4.3	4.3	1.5	2.4	4.8	2.7	4.2	3.8	0.9	1.7	2.2
Norway	4.2	4.0	3.6	3.3	3.3	3.3	3.4	3.4	3.5	2.4	3.2	6.7	7.8	8.5	4.6	3.0	2.5	2.7
Poland	13.0	14.8	16.9	14.7	12.4	10.5	9.8	9.8	9.8	28.8	4.0	0.9	3.9	8.3	4.6	2.9	2.7	2.5
Portugal	6.4	6.1	6.8	6.9	7.0	7.7	8.1	8.4	8.6	9.4	3.7	1.5	1.6	3.7	4.4	0.7	-1.2	-0.4
Slovak Republic	..	..	..	..	..	..	..	..	..	..	4.2	1.5	-0.1	1.8	5.2	-3.1	-1.1	1.1
Slovenia	..	6.4	5.9	5.9	6.0	6.0	6.2	6.5	6.7	..	5.3	1.1	2.7	6.0	8.3	1.5	3.1	2.0
Spain	14.1	12.0	9.1	8.9	9.5	11.1	12.6	13.2	13.3	6.6	3.2	3.7	4.4	4.9	1.0	-1.2	-1.0	-0.7
Sweden	5.7	7.6	7.2	7.2	7.1	7.0	7.0	7.0	7.0	4.3	1.2	-0.8	4.1	3.2	4.5	-1.8	0.7	0.7
Switzerland	2.0	3.4	3.7	3.7	3.7	3.7	3.8	3.9	3.9	3.2	0.6	0.6	1.6	3.5	5.0	-1.1	0.7	0.7
United Kingdom	9.0	6.2	5.3	5.3	5.4	5.6	5.8	5.9	5.9	4.5	2.8	2.3	2.8	2.3	5.5	1.0	0.8	1.4
United States	6.1	5.3	5.0	4.9	5.0	5.2	5.3	5.5	5.6	2.7	2.1	3.1	3.2	2.6	-0.6	-0.9	1.3	1.3
Euro area	8.8	8.5	7.8	7.6	7.6	8.0	8.4	8.6	8.6	3.8	1.7	1.1	1.8	3.8	4.0	-0.7	0.3	0.2
Total OECD	6.7	6.7	6.3	6.2	6.1	6.3	6.4	6.5	6.6	4.1	2.4	2.0	2.1	3.5	2.9	-0.5	1.0	1.0

Note: The structural unemployment rate corresponds to "NAIRU" and is estimated on the basis of the methods outlined in Richardson *et al.* (2000), "The concept, policy use and measurement of structural unemployment", *OECD Economics Department Working Papers*, No 250. The most recent updates of the OECD's estimates are described in Gianella *et al.* (2008) "What drives the NAIRU? Evidence from a panel of OECD countries", *OECD Economics Department Working Papers*, No. 649. Details on the methods used to project the NAIRUs can be found in the technical note "Adjustments to the OECD method of projecting the NAIRU" (*http://www.oecd.org/dataoecd/56/9/43098869.pdf*). For more information about sources and definitions, see *OECD Economic Outlook Sources and Methods (http://www.oecd.org/eco/sources-and-methods)*.

1. Total economy.

Source: OECD Economic Outlook 88 database.

StatLink ⇒ http://dx.doi.org/10.1787/888932348738

Annex Table 23. Household saving rates
Per cent of disposable household income

	1993	1994	1995	1996	1997	1998	1999	2000	2001	2002	2003	2004	2005	2006	2007	2008	2009	2010	2011	2012
Net saving																				
Australia	6.0	7.2	6.1	7.1	6.6	4.1	3.0	2.6	3.5	0.3	-0.4	-0.5	-0.2	1.2	1.4	1.9	5.1	2.2	2.5	2.9
Austria	11.3	11.5	11.8	9.3	7.7	8.5	9.8	9.2	8.0	8.0	9.1	9.3	9.7	10.4	11.6	11.8	11.1	10.0	9.7	9.5
Belgium	15.1	14.8	16.3	14.3	13.2	12.7	13.1	12.3	13.7	12.9	12.2	10.7	10.2	11.0	11.3	11.9	13.4	12.2	12.0	11.6
Canada	11.9	9.5	9.2	7.0	4.9	4.9	4.0	4.7	5.2	3.5	2.6	3.2	2.1	3.5	2.8	3.6	4.6	4.6	4.0	3.9
Czech Republic	6.4	1.2	10.0	6.1	6.0	4.1	3.4	3.3	2.2	3.0	2.4	0.5	3.2	4.8	6.3	5.7	4.5	1.3	0.6	1.0
Denmark	1.3	-2.7	0.2	-0.2	-2.8	-1.2	-5.6	-4.0	2.1	2.1	2.4	-1.3	-4.2	-2.3	-3.2	-2.8	0.1	-1.2	-2.3	-2.5
Finland	7.2	1.4	4.2	0.7	2.5	0.6	2.4	0.5	0.4	0.5	1.4	2.7	0.9	-1.1	-0.9	-0.2	4.0	4.0	3.0	1.7
Germany	12.1	11.4	11.0	10.5	10.1	10.1	9.5	9.2	9.4	9.9	10.3	10.4	10.5	10.6	10.8	11.7	11.1	11.5	11.6	11.4
Hungary	..	..	14.4	15.6	14.2	13.5	9.9	8.9	8.5	6.4	4.3	6.8	6.1	7.5	4.6	3.0	3.4	5.0	5.2	3.9
Ireland	..	..	..	..	..	..	..	..	..	4.1	3.8	7.0	5.2	3.7	1.2	4.0	10.7	11.1	9.8	9.3
Italy	19.5	18.1	17.0	17.9	15.1	11.4	10.2	8.4	10.5	11.2	10.3	10.2	9.9	9.1	8.4	8.2	7.1	5.1	5.8	5.9
Japan	14.2	13.3	12.6	10.5	10.3	11.4	10.0	8.7	5.1	5.0	3.9	3.6	3.9	3.8	2.4	2.3	2.2	2.7	2.8	3.1
Korea	23.1	21.8	18.5	18.1	16.1	23.2	16.1	9.3	5.2	0.4	5.2	9.2	7.2	5.2	2.9	2.9	3.6	2.8	2.9	2.8
Netherlands	14.1	14.4	14.3	12.7	13.3	12.2	9.0	6.9	9.7	8.7	7.6	7.4	6.4	6.1	6.9	5.7	6.8	8.1	7.6	7.4
Norway	6.4	5.4	4.8	2.6	3.0	5.7	4.7	4.3	3.1	8.2	8.9	7.2	10.1	0.1	1.5	3.7	7.3	6.3	6.9	6.9
Poland	..	..	14.6	11.7	11.7	12.1	10.5	10.0	11.9	8.3	7.7	7.0	7.3	7.5	6.1	0.8	3.3	5.5	5.0	3.9
Slovak Republic	..	..	5.5	8.5	8.9	7.6	6.9	6.8	4.3	3.9	1.6	0.4	1.5	1.2	3.2	1.9	1.4	4.3	3.9	2.9
Sweden	9.4	8.1	8.3	6.3	3.4	2.8	2.8	4.3	8.4	8.2	7.2	6.1	5.5	6.6	8.8	11.2	12.9	10.3	10.1	8.6
Switzerland	13.0	12.4	12.7	10.9	10.7	10.7	10.8	11.7	11.9	10.7	9.4	9.0	10.1	11.4	12.6	11.8	11.1	10.7	10.6	10.1
United States	5.8	5.2	5.2	4.9	4.6	5.3	3.1	2.9	2.7	3.5	3.5	3.4	1.4	2.4	2.1	4.1	5.9	5.7	6.0	6.1
Gross saving																				
France	15.5	14.8	15.9	15.0	16.0	15.5	15.2	15.0	15.7	16.9	15.7	15.8	15.0	15.0	15.5	15.4	16.2	15.9	15.5	14.9
Portugal	..	..	12.6	11.7	10.9	10.3	10.7	10.6	10.6	10.3	10.7	10.0	10.0	8.0	7.0	7.8	11.0	10.8	8.4	8.1
Spain	15.5	13.1	17.5	17.4	16.0	14.4	12.7	11.1	11.1	11.4	12.0	11.3	11.3	11.1	10.7	13.4	18.0	16.9	15.9	15.3
United Kingdom	10.8	9.3	10.3	9.4	9.6	7.4	5.2	4.7	6.0	4.8	5.1	3.7	3.9	3.4	2.6	2.0	6.3	4.4	3.5	3.4

Note: The adoption of new national accounst systems SNA93 or ESA95 has been proceeding at an uneven pace among OECD member countries, both with respect to variables and the time period covered. As a consequence, there are breaks in many national series. See table "National Accounts Reporting Systems and Base-years and latest data updates" at the beginning of the Statistical Annex and *OECD Economic Outlook* Sources and Methods (*http://www.oecd.org/eco/sources-and-methods*). Countries differ in the way household disposable income is reported (in particular whether private pension benefits less pension contributions are included in disposable income or not), but the calculation of household saving is adjusted for this difference. Most countries report household saving on a net basis (i.e. excluding consumption of fixed capital by households and unincorporated businesses). In most countries household saving includes saving by non-profit institutions (in some cases referred to as personal saving). Other countries (Czech Republic, Finland, France and Japan) report saving of households only.

Source: OECD Economic Outlook 88 database.

StatLink ⇒ http://dx.doi.org/10.1787/888932348757

Annex Table 24. Gross national saving
Per cent of nominal GDP

	1990	1991	1992	1993	1994	1995	1996	1997	1998	1999	2000	2001	2002	2003	2004	2005	2006	2007	2008	2009
Australia	19.8	17.5	19.4	21.2	20.3	20.3	21.2	21.3	20.6	21.3	20.7	21.5	21.0	21.6	21.0	22.5	22.8	23.3	23.7	..
Austria	23.8	23.5	22.7	21.9	21.8	22.2	22.1	22.7	23.3	23.1	23.6	23.0	24.8	24.5	25.0	24.7	25.6	27.2	26.9	23.8
Belgium	23.6	22.8	23.2	24.3	25.5	25.4	24.4	25.7	25.6	26.3	26.7	25.4	25.0	24.9	25.3	25.1	25.8	26.7	25.1	22.2
Canada	17.3	14.7	13.4	14.0	16.2	18.3	18.8	19.6	19.1	20.7	23.6	22.2	21.2	21.4	23.0	23.9	24.5	23.7	23.5	17.7
Chile	..	..	..	..	..	..	22.3	22.2	21.1	20.4	20.0	19.9	20.0	20.0	22.2	23.4	24.9	25.1	23.2	..
Czech Republic	..	..	28.6	28.7	28.4	29.0	27.0	24.4	26.3	24.6	24.8	24.2	22.4	20.7	22.0	23.9	24.7	24.4	24.5	20.5
Denmark	20.3	19.5	20.0	19.1	19.3	20.4	20.5	21.4	20.7	21.7	22.6	23.5	22.9	23.1	23.4	25.2	25.7	24.5	24.0	21.4
Finland	23.7	16.3	13.7	14.8	18.1	21.7	20.7	23.8	24.8	26.4	28.5	28.9	27.7	24.5	26.3	25.3	25.9	27.1	25.2	18.8
France	20.8	20.2	19.6	18.3	18.7	19.1	18.7	19.9	21.0	21.8	21.6	21.3	19.8	19.1	19.0	18.5	19.3	20.0	19.3	16.1
Germany	25.3	22.6	22.3	21.2	20.9	21.0	20.5	20.7	20.9	20.3	20.2	19.5	19.4	19.5	22.0	22.1	24.2	26.0	25.2	21.5
Greece	10.7	10.7	10.9	10.9	11.0	11.3	11.4	11.2	11.3	11.3	11.3	11.8	9.6	12.2	12.0	9.0	8.0	6.3	4.4	2.5
Iceland	16.9	16.0	15.7	17.6	17.9	17.1	17.2	17.9	17.4	15.0	13.1	17.0	19.7	15.0	13.6	12.3	11.4	12.6	2.4	11.6
Ireland	17.7	17.4	15.4	17.5	17.8	20.4	21.7	23.4	24.8	23.7	23.7	21.7	20.5	22.9	23.3	23.6	24.8	21.7	16.4	11.5
Israel	18.5	23.2	24.4	21.8	19.9	19.9	19.6	20.3	20.7	20.0	18.6	18.3	17.0	17.8	19.7	22.0	24.0	22.9	19.5	20.3
Italy	20.8	20.0	19.1	19.7	19.9	22.0	22.2	22.2	21.6	21.1	20.6	20.9	20.8	19.8	20.3	19.5	19.6	20.1	18.0	15.8
Japan	33.4	34.3	33.6	32.2	30.5	29.5	29.7	29.7	28.8	27.2	27.5	25.8	25.2	25.4	25.8	26.8	26.9	27.3	25.0	..
Korea	37.9	37.9	37.0	37.0	36.4	36.1	34.6	34.4	36.4	34.3	32.9	31.0	30.4	31.8	34.0	32.0	30.8	30.8	30.7	30.1
Mexico	23.9	21.7	18.8	16.7	16.2	21.3	26.0	28.5	23.5	23.8	24.1	20.3	21.1	21.9	24.1	23.6	25.5	24.8	25.4	..
Netherlands	26.0	25.6	24.8	25.0	26.1	27.2	26.7	28.1	25.2	27.1	28.4	26.7	25.8	25.4	27.6	26.5	29.0	28.8	25.7	21.8
New Zealand	16.7	13.6	14.4	17.0	17.8	17.7	16.7	16.3	15.9	15.7	17.0	19.0	18.6	18.6	17.8	15.7	15.2	16.2	14.9	..
Norway	25.2	24.0	23.1	23.3	24.2	25.9	27.9	29.6	26.3	28.5	35.4	35.1	31.5	30.5	32.7	37.4	39.2	37.7	39.9	33.3
Poland	..	4.0	4.0	4.2	5.6	6.0	5.7	6.4	7.7	6.6	6.1	4.8	2.9	3.3	2.8	5.2	5.3	7.3	..	..
Portugal	25.8	22.9	21.8	19.3	18.5	20.6	19.8	20.1	20.6	19.9	17.8	17.2	17.3	16.9	15.8	13.3	12.4	12.7	10.6	9.4
Slovak Republic	..	..	..	23.8	26.4	26.8	24.6	25.1	24.2	23.8	23.5	22.5	21.7	18.3	19.8	20.4	19.8	22.7	21.3	17.0
Slovenia	..	..	..	..	..	23.0	23.2	24.2	24.6	24.1	24.1	24.4	24.7	24.3	24.8	25.5	26.5	27.2	25.2	21.7
Spain	22.2	21.6	20.0	20.0	19.5	21.7	21.5	22.2	22.4	22.4	22.3	22.0	22.9	23.4	22.4	22.0	22.0	21.0	19.4	18.9
Sweden	24.8	20.7	16.9	14.4	18.0	21.0	20.6	21.0	21.8	22.3	23.3	23.2	22.5	24.0	23.7	24.8	26.6	28.9	29.3	23.9
Switzerland	33.1	31.1	28.6	29.7	29.3	29.6	28.8	30.8	32.0	32.9	34.7	31.4	29.0	33.1	32.9	36.0	35.5	31.0	23.6	..
United Kingdom	16.4	15.4	14.3	14.0	15.7	15.9	16.1	17.1	18.0	15.7	15.0	15.4	15.3	15.1	15.0	14.4	14.1	15.6	15.0	12.4
United States	14.9	15.0	13.9	13.7	14.9	16.0	16.7	18.0	18.5	17.9	17.8	16.2	14.3	13.5	14.1	14.6	15.8	13.9	11.9	10.3

Note: Based on SNA93 or ESA95.
Source: National accounts of OECD countries database.

StatLink http://dx.doi.org/10.1787/888932348776

Annex Table 25. **General government total outlays**

Per cent of nominal GDP

	1993	1994	1995	1996	1997	1998	1999	2000	2001	2002	2003	2004	2005	2006	2007	2008	2009	2010	2011	2012
Australia	37.0	37.1	37.0	36.1	35.1	34.4	34.4	34.8	35.3	34.7	34.1	34.6	34.0	33.5	33.3	33.9	32.3	35.0	34.5	33.9
Austria	56.4	56.2	56.5	56.0	53.6	53.9	53.6	52.2	51.6	50.9	51.5	54.1	50.3	49.4	48.5	49.1	52.5	52.9	52.8	52.6
Belgium	54.9	52.6	52.1	52.6	51.2	50.4	50.2	49.1	49.2	49.9	51.1	49.5	52.2	48.6	48.5	50.3	54.3	53.9	53.6	53.1
Canada	52.2	49.7	48.5	46.6	44.3	44.8	42.7	41.1	42.0	41.2	41.2	39.9	39.3	39.4	39.4	39.8	44.1	43.5	42.5	41.0
Czech Republic	..	..	54.5	42.6	43.2	43.2	42.3	41.8	44.3	46.3	47.3	45.2	45.0	43.7	42.4	42.9	45.9	46.1	45.1	44.3
Denmark	60.2	60.2	59.3	58.9	56.7	56.3	55.5	53.7	54.2	54.6	55.1	54.6	52.8	51.6	50.9	51.8	58.5	58.9	58.2	57.1
Finland	64.8	63.7	61.4	60.0	56.6	52.9	51.7	48.3	47.8	48.9	50.2	50.0	50.2	49.0	47.3	49.3	56.0	56.3	55.4	54.4
France	55.0	54.2	54.4	54.5	54.1	52.7	52.6	51.6	51.6	52.6	53.2	53.3	53.4	52.7	52.3	52.8	56.0	56.2	55.4	54.6
Germany	48.3	47.9	54.8	49.3	48.3	48.1	48.2	45.1	47.5	48.0	48.4	47.2	46.9	45.3	43.5	43.8	47.5	46.8	45.4	44.3
Greece	46.5	44.7	45.7	44.1	44.9	44.3	44.4	46.7	45.3	45.1	44.7	45.5	43.9	43.3	45.2	47.4	51.2	48.3	48.8	48.1
Hungary	..	..	55.3	50.3	49.4	50.4	48.6	46.8	47.2	51.2	49.4	48.7	50.2	52.0	50.0	48.8	50.5	49.6	48.1	47.1
Iceland	40.4	39.9	42.7	42.2	40.7	41.3	42.0	41.9	42.6	44.3	45.6	44.1	42.2	41.6	42.3	57.8	50.9	48.8	46.3	44.7
Ireland	44.6	43.9	41.1	39.1	36.7	34.5	34.1	31.3	33.1	33.4	33.2	33.6	34.0	34.4	36.8	42.7	48.7	66.1	44.5	43.4
Israel	..	..	52.6	53.0	52.4	54.9	53.6	51.5	53.7	55.4	54.1	50.8	49.0	46.9	46.0	45.1	44.8	45.0	45.0	44.7
Italy	56.4	53.5	52.5	52.5	50.2	49.3	48.2	46.1	48.0	47.4	48.3	47.8	48.1	48.7	47.9	48.9	51.9	51.4	50.8	50.3
Japan	34.5	35.0	36.0	36.7	35.7	42.5	38.6	39.0	38.6	38.8	38.4	37.0	38.4	36.2	35.9	37.1	41.4	40.6	40.6	40.2
Korea	21.2	20.6	20.4	21.2	21.8	24.1	23.2	22.4	23.9	23.6	28.9	26.1	26.6	27.7	28.7	30.4	31.9	28.1	28.0	27.3
Luxembourg	39.8	38.9	39.7	41.1	40.7	41.1	39.2	37.6	38.1	41.5	41.8	42.6	41.5	38.6	36.2	36.9	42.2	42.7	42.6	41.5
Netherlands	55.7	53.5	56.4	49.4	47.5	46.7	46.0	44.2	45.4	46.2	47.1	46.1	44.8	45.5	45.3	46.0	51.4	51.2	49.8	49.1
New Zealand	45.1	42.7	41.7	40.6	41.2	41.0	40.7	38.8	38.3	37.3	37.8	37.5	38.5	39.9	40.1	42.2	43.9	44.2	43.8	43.2
Norway	54.7	53.6	50.9	48.5	46.9	49.2	47.7	42.3	44.2	47.1	48.3	45.6	42.3	40.6	41.2	40.7	46.5	46.6	46.9	46.9
Poland	..	..	47.7	51.1	46.6	44.5	42.9	41.2	43.7	44.2	44.6	42.7	43.5	43.9	42.2	43.3	44.5	45.3	45.0	44.1
Portugal	43.9	42.4	41.5	42.1	41.1	40.8	41.0	41.1	42.5	42.3	43.8	44.7	45.8	44.5	43.8	43.6	48.1	47.8	45.6	44.7
Slovak Republic	..	..	48.6	53.8	49.0	45.8	48.1	52.2	44.5	45.1	40.2	37.7	38.0	36.6	34.3	34.9	41.3	40.9	38.4	37.0
Slovenia	..	..	52.6	44.5	44.8	45.7	46.5	46.7	47.6	46.3	46.4	45.8	45.2	44.5	42.4	44.1	49.0	50.0	48.9	47.4
Spain	49.0	46.7	44.4	43.2	41.6	41.1	39.9	39.1	38.6	38.9	38.4	38.9	38.4	38.4	39.2	41.3	45.8	45.1	43.3	41.4
Sweden	71.7	69.6	64.9	62.9	60.7	58.8	58.1	55.1	54.5	55.6	55.7	54.2	53.9	52.7	51.0	51.5	54.9	54.5	53.8	53.0
Switzerland	35.1	35.2	35.0	35.3	35.5	35.8	34.3	35.1	34.8	36.2	36.4	35.9	35.3	33.5	32.3	32.2	33.7	33.6	33.1	32.3
United Kingdom	45.3	44.6	44.1	42.2	40.6	39.5	38.8	36.6	39.9	40.9	42.4	43.1	44.0	44.3	44.1	47.4	51.4	51.0	49.9	48.8
United States[1]	38.1	37.1	37.1	36.6	35.4	34.6	34.2	33.9	35.0	35.9	36.3	36.0	36.2	36.0	36.8	39.0	42.2	42.2	41.1	40.0
Euro area	52.2	50.9	53.1	50.6	49.3	48.5	48.1	46.2	47.2	47.6	48.0	47.6	47.4	46.6	45.9	46.9	50.8	50.7	49.3	48.3
Total OECD	42.9	42.0	42.7	41.7	40.4	40.8	39.8	38.9	39.9	40.4	40.9	40.2	40.4	39.9	39.9	41.5	44.9	44.6	43.6	42.6

StatLink ᴎᴵᴸ http://dx.doi.org/10.1787/888932348795

Note: Data refer to the general government sector, which is a consolidation of accounts for the central, state and local governments plus social security. Total outlays are defined as current outlays plus capital outlays. For more details, see *OECD Economic Outlook* Sources and Methods (*http://www.oecd.org/eco/sources-and-methods*).

1. These data include outlays net of operating surpluses of public enterprises.

Source: OECD Economic Outlook 88 database.

Annex Table 26. General government total tax and non-tax receipts
Per cent of nominal GDP

	1993	1994	1995	1996	1997	1998	1999	2000	2001	2002	2003	2004	2005	2006	2007	2008	2009	2010	2011	2012
Australia	32.7	32.9	33.6	34.1	34.6	35.7	35.9	35.3	34.9	35.5	35.5	35.7	35.4	35.0	35.0	34.3	28.3	31.7	32.7	33.5
Austria	52.0	51.3	50.6	51.8	51.7	51.5	51.2	50.3	51.4	50.0	49.9	49.6	48.5	47.8	48.0	48.6	49.0	48.6	49.4	49.7
Belgium	47.4	47.4	47.6	48.5	49.0	49.5	49.6	49.0	49.5	49.7	51.0	49.1	49.3	48.7	48.1	48.9	48.2	48.9	49.1	49.4
Canada	43.5	43.0	43.2	43.8	44.5	44.9	44.3	44.1	42.6	41.1	40.7	40.7	40.8	41.1	41.8	39.8	38.5	38.6	39.0	38.9
Czech Republic	..	..	41.0	39.3	39.4	38.2	38.6	38.1	38.7	39.5	40.7	42.2	41.4	41.1	41.8	40.2	40.1	40.9	40.9	40.9
Denmark	56.3	56.8	56.4	56.9	56.1	56.2	56.8	55.8	55.4	54.8	55.0	56.4	57.8	56.6	55.7	55.3	55.7	54.3	54.3	54.3
Finland	56.5	57.0	55.3	56.5	55.2	54.4	53.2	55.2	52.8	52.9	52.5	52.1	52.7	52.8	52.4	53.5	53.2	53.0	53.7	53.7
France	48.5	48.8	48.9	50.4	50.8	50.0	50.8	50.1	50.0	49.4	49.1	49.6	50.5	50.3	49.6	49.5	48.4	48.9	49.3	49.7
Germany	45.3	45.6	45.1	45.9	45.7	45.9	46.7	46.4	44.7	44.4	44.4	43.5	43.6	43.7	43.8	43.9	44.5	42.8	42.5	42.2
Greece	34.6	36.5	36.7	37.4	39.0	40.5	41.3	43.0	40.9	40.3	39.0	38.1	38.6	39.4	39.8	39.6	37.4	40.0	41.2	41.6
Hungary	..	..	46.6	45.8	43.3	42.5	43.2	43.7	43.1	42.2	42.2	42.3	42.3	42.6	45.0	45.1	46.1	45.3	45.0	44.2
Iceland	35.9	35.3	39.8	40.6	40.7	40.9	43.2	43.6	41.9	41.7	42.8	44.1	47.1	48.0	47.7	44.2	40.9	42.6	43.6	45.3
Ireland	41.9	41.9	39.1	39.0	38.1	36.8	36.7	36.1	34.1	33.1	33.6	35.0	35.6	37.4	36.8	35.4	34.5	33.8	35.0	36.0
Israel	..	..	48.5	47.1	47.8	46.9	47.3	47.4	47.2	47.4	45.9	44.7	44.3	44.9	44.5	42.1	39.0	40.2	41.3	41.9
Italy	46.3	44.4	45.1	45.5	47.6	46.2	46.5	45.3	44.9	44.4	44.7	44.2	43.8	45.3	46.4	46.2	46.6	46.4	46.9	47.2
Japan	32.0	31.2	31.2	31.6	31.7	31.3	31.2	31.4	32.2	30.8	30.5	30.9	31.7	34.5	33.5	35.0	34.3	32.9	33.1	32.8
Korea	23.0	22.9	23.9	24.4	24.8	25.5	25.5	27.9	28.3	28.7	29.4	28.8	30.0	31.7	33.3	33.4	31.9	29.7	30.1	30.3
Luxembourg	41.2	41.4	42.1	42.3	44.3	44.4	42.6	43.6	44.2	43.6	42.2	41.5	41.5	39.9	39.9	39.9	41.5	40.5	41.4	41.2
Netherlands	52.9	50.0	47.2	47.5	46.3	45.8	46.4	46.1	45.1	44.1	43.9	44.3	44.5	46.1	45.4	46.6	46.0	45.3	45.8	46.0
New Zealand	44.8	45.5	44.4	43.3	42.6	41.4	40.7	40.7	40.0	40.9	41.6	41.4	43.0	45.0	44.1	42.6	40.2	38.9	39.3	39.7
Norway	53.3	53.8	54.2	54.8	54.5	52.5	53.7	57.7	57.5	56.3	55.5	56.7	57.3	59.1	58.9	59.9	56.3	56.1	55.7	55.7
Poland	..	35.3	43.3	46.3	41.9	40.2	40.6	38.1	38.5	39.2	38.4	37.3	39.4	40.3	40.3	39.6	37.7	37.5	38.2	39.2
Portugal	36.4	..	36.5	37.5	37.8	37.3	38.3	38.2	38.2	39.4	40.7	41.3	39.9	40.5	40.9	40.6	38.8	40.5	40.6	40.4
Slovak Republic	..	..	45.2	43.9	42.6	40.5	40.7	39.9	38.0	36.9	37.4	35.3	35.2	33.5	32.5	32.8	33.4	32.9	33.2	33.1
Slovenia	..	..	44.3	43.3	42.5	43.3	43.4	43.0	43.6	43.9	43.7	43.6	43.8	43.2	42.4	42.3	43.2	44.3	44.2	43.4
Spain	41.7	40.0	38.0	38.4	38.2	37.8	38.4	38.1	38.0	38.4	38.2	38.5	39.4	40.4	41.1	37.1	34.7	36.0	36.9	36.9
Sweden	60.5	60.5	57.6	59.6	59.0	59.7	58.9	58.7	56.1	54.1	54.4	54.6	55.8	54.9	54.5	53.7	53.7	53.3	53.2	53.6
Switzerland	31.6	32.4	33.0	33.5	32.7	33.8	33.8	35.2	34.7	35.0	34.6	34.2	34.6	34.3	34.0	34.5	34.9	32.9	32.6	32.2
United Kingdom	37.3	37.8	38.2	38.0	38.4	39.4	39.8	40.3	40.6	39.0	38.7	39.6	40.8	41.5	41.2	42.6	40.4	41.4	41.7	42.2
United States[1]	33.0	33.4	33.8	34.3	34.6	34.9	34.9	35.4	34.4	31.9	31.3	31.6	33.0	33.8	33.9	32.6	30.9	31.6	32.3	33.3
Euro area	46.4	45.9	45.6	46.4	46.6	46.2	46.7	46.2	45.4	44.9	44.9	44.6	44.8	45.3	45.3	44.9	44.5	44.3	44.7	44.8
Total OECD	37.8	37.6	37.9	38.4	38.6	38.7	38.8	38.9	38.4	37.1	36.8	36.8	37.6	38.6	38.6	38.2	36.9	37.0	37.4	37.8

StatLink ⬛⬛⬛ http://dx.doi.org/10.1787/888932348814

Note: Data refer to the general government sector, which is a consolidation of accounts for central, state and local governments (including dividends and other transfers from public enterprises), fees, charges, sales, fines, capital tranfers received by the general government, etc. For more details, see OECD Economic Outlook Sources and Methods (http://www.oecd.org/eco/sources-and-methods).
1. Excludes the operating surpluses of public enterprises.
Source: OECD Economic Outlook 88 database.

Annex Table 27. **General government financial balances**
Surplus (+) or deficit (-) as a per cent of nominal GDP

	1993	1994	1995	1996	1997	1998	1999	2000	2001	2002	2003	2004	2005	2006	2007	2008	2009	2010	2011	2012
Australia	-4.2	-4.2	-3.4	-2.0	-0.5	1.3	1.5	0.5	-0.5	0.7	1.4	1.1	1.4	1.5	1.7	0.4	-4.0	-3.3	-1.7	-0.4
Austria	-4.4	-4.9	-5.9	-4.1	-2.0	-2.5	-2.4	-1.9	-0.2	-0.9	-1.6	-4.5	-1.8	-1.6	-0.6	-0.5	-3.5	-4.4	-3.4	-3.0
Belgium	-7.5	-5.2	-4.5	-4.0	-2.3	-1.0	-0.7	-0.1	0.4	-0.2	-0.2	-0.4	-2.9	0.1	-0.4	-1.4	-6.1	-4.9	-4.5	-3.6
Canada	-8.7	-6.7	-5.3	-2.8	0.2	0.1	1.6	2.9	0.7	-0.1	-0.1	0.9	1.5	1.6	1.4	0.0	-5.5	-4.9	-3.4	-2.1
Czech Republic	..	..	-13.4	-3.3	-3.8	-5.0	-3.7	-3.7	-5.6	-6.8	-6.6	-2.9	-3.6	-2.6	-0.7	-2.7	-5.8	-5.2	-4.2	-3.4
Denmark	-3.9	-3.4	-2.9	-2.0	-0.6	-0.1	1.3	2.2	1.2	0.3	-0.1	1.9	5.0	5.0	4.8	3.4	-2.8	-4.6	-3.9	-2.8
Finland	-8.3	-6.7	-6.2	-3.5	-1.4	1.5	1.6	6.8	5.0	4.0	2.3	2.1	2.5	3.9	5.2	4.2	-2.7	-3.3	-1.7	-0.7
France	-6.4	-5.5	-5.5	-4.0	-3.3	-2.6	-1.8	-1.5	-1.6	-3.2	-4.1	-3.6	-3.0	-2.3	-2.7	-3.3	-7.6	-7.4	-6.1	-4.8
Germany	-3.0	-2.3	-9.7	-3.3	-2.6	-2.2	-1.5	1.3	-2.8	-3.6	-4.0	-3.8	-3.3	-1.6	0.3	0.1	-3.0	-4.0	-2.9	-2.1
Greece	-11.9	-8.3	-9.1	-6.6	-5.9	-3.8	-3.1	-3.7	-4.4	-4.8	-5.7	-7.4	-5.3	-3.9	-5.4	-7.8	-13.7	-8.3	-7.6	-6.5
Hungary	..	..	-8.7	-4.6	-6.1	-7.9	-5.4	-3.0	-4.1	-8.9	-7.2	-6.4	-7.9	-9.4	-5.0	-3.7	-4.4	-4.2	-3.1	-2.9
Iceland	-4.5	-4.7	-3.0	-1.6	0.0	-0.4	1.1	1.7	-0.7	-2.6	-2.8	0.0	4.9	6.3	5.4	-13.5	-9.9	-6.3	-2.7	0.6
Ireland	-2.7	-2.0	-2.1	-0.1	1.4	2.3	2.6	4.8	1.0	-0.3	0.4	1.4	1.7	2.9	0.0	-7.3	-14.2	-32.3	-9.5	-7.4
Israel	..	..	-4.2	-5.9	-4.6	-8.0	-6.3	-4.1	-6.5	-7.9	-8.2	-6.1	-4.7	-2.0	-1.5	-3.1	-5.8	-4.8	-3.8	-2.7
Italy	-10.1	-9.1	-7.4	-7.0	-2.7	-3.1	-1.8	-0.9	-3.1	-3.0	-3.5	-3.6	-4.4	-3.3	-1.5	-2.7	-5.2	-5.0	-3.9	-3.1
Japan	-2.5	-3.8	-4.7	-5.1	-4.0	-11.2	-7.4	-7.6	-6.3	-8.0	-7.9	-6.2	-6.7	-1.6	-2.4	-2.1	-7.1	-7.7	-7.5	-7.3
Korea	1.7	2.3	3.5	3.2	3.0	1.3	2.4	5.4	4.3	5.1	0.5	2.7	3.4	3.9	4.7	3.0	0.0	1.6	2.1	3.0
Luxembourg	1.5	2.5	2.4	1.2	3.7	3.4	3.4	6.0	6.1	2.1	0.5	-1.1	0.0	1.4	3.7	3.0	-0.7	-2.2	-1.2	-0.3
Netherlands	-2.8	-3.5	-9.2	-1.9	-1.2	-0.9	0.4	2.0	-0.3	-2.1	-3.2	-1.8	-0.3	0.5	0.2	0.5	-5.4	-5.8	-4.0	-3.1
New Zealand	-0.3	2.9	2.7	2.7	1.4	0.3	0.0	1.9	1.7	3.6	3.8	3.9	4.5	5.1	4.0	0.4	-3.7	-5.3	-4.5	-3.4
Norway	-1.4	0.3	3.2	6.3	7.6	3.3	6.0	15.4	13.3	9.2	7.3	11.1	15.1	18.5	17.7	19.3	9.9	9.5	8.7	8.8
Poland	..	..	-4.4	-4.9	-4.6	-4.3	-2.3	-3.0	-5.3	-5.0	-6.2	-5.4	-4.1	-3.6	-1.9	-3.7	-6.8	-7.9	-6.7	-4.8
Portugal	-7.5	-7.1	-5.0	-4.5	-3.4	-3.5	-2.7	-2.9	-4.3	-2.9	-3.1	-3.4	-5.9	-4.1	-2.8	-3.0	-9.4	-7.3	-5.0	-4.4
Slovak Republic	..	..	-3.4	-9.9	-6.3	-5.3	-7.4	-12.3	-6.5	-8.2	-2.8	-2.4	-2.8	-3.2	-1.8	-2.1	-7.9	-8.0	-5.2	-4.0
Slovenia	..	..	-8.4	-1.1	-2.4	-2.4	-3.0	-3.7	-4.0	-2.5	-2.7	-2.2	-1.4	-1.3	0.0	-1.8	-5.8	-5.7	-4.7	-3.9
Spain	-7.3	-6.8	-6.5	-4.9	-3.4	-3.2	-1.4	-1.0	-0.7	-0.5	-0.2	-0.4	1.0	2.0	1.9	-4.2	-11.1	-9.2	-6.3	-4.4
Sweden	-11.2	-9.1	-7.3	-3.3	-1.6	0.9	0.8	3.6	1.6	-1.5	-1.3	0.4	1.9	2.2	3.5	2.2	-1.2	-1.2	-0.6	0.6
Switzerland	-3.5	-2.8	-2.0	-1.8	-2.8	-1.9	-0.5	0.1	-0.1	-1.2	-1.7	-1.8	-0.7	0.8	1.7	2.3	1.2	-0.7	-0.4	0.0
United Kingdom	-8.0	-6.8	-5.8	-4.2	-2.2	-0.1	0.9	3.7	0.6	-2.0	-3.7	-3.6	-3.3	-2.7	-2.8	-4.8	-11.0	-9.6	-8.1	-6.5
United States	-5.1	-3.7	-3.3	-2.3	-0.9	0.3	0.7	1.5	-0.6	-4.0	-5.0	-4.4	-3.3	-2.2	-2.9	-6.3	-11.3	-10.5	-8.8	-6.8
Euro area	-5.8	-5.0	-7.5	-4.3	-2.7	-2.3	-1.4	-0.1	-1.9	-2.6	-3.1	-3.0	-2.6	-1.3	-0.6	-2.0	-6.2	-6.3	-4.6	-3.5
Total OECD	-5.1	-4.3	-4.8	-3.2	-1.8	-2.1	-1.0	0.1	-1.4	-3.3	-4.1	-3.4	-2.7	-1.2	-1.3	-3.3	-7.9	-7.6	-6.1	-4.7
Memorandum items																				
General government financial balances excluding social security																				
United States	-5.8	-4.5	-4.1	-3.2	-1.9	-0.9	-0.7	-0.1	-2.2	-5.5	-6.3	-5.8	-4.6	-3.6	-4.3	-7.6	-12.1	-11.1	-9.6	-7.6
Japan	-4.8	-5.8	-6.7	-6.9	-5.8	-12.5	-8.5	-8.2	-6.5	-7.9	-8.0	-6.6	-7.0	-1.7	-2.2	-1.7	-6.5	-6.9	-6.6	-6.5

Note: Financial balances include one-off factors, such as those resulting from the sale of the mobile telephone licenses, but exclude most financial transactions. As data are on a national accounts basis (SNA93/ESA95), the government financial balances may differ from the numbers reported to the European Commission under the Excessive Deficit Procedure for some EU countries. For more details, see footnotes to Annex Tables 25 and 26 and *OECD Economic Outlook Sources and Methods (http://www.oecd.org/eco/sources-and-methods).*

Source: OECD Economic Outlook 88 database.

StatLink ᴬᵉˢᵖ http://dx.doi.org/10.1787/888932348833

Annex Table 28. General government cyclically-adjusted balances

Surplus (+) or deficit (−) as a per cent of potential GDP

	1993	1994	1995	1996	1997	1998	1999	2000	2001	2002	2003	2004	2005	2006	2007	2008	2009	2010	2011	2012
Australia	-3.3	-3.8	-3.1	-1.7	-0.2	1.2	1.2	0.1	-0.5	0.8	1.3	0.9	1.1	1.3	1.1	0.1	-3.3	-2.5	-1.0	0.1
Austria	-4.0	-4.2	-5.2	-3.6	-1.4	-2.4	-3.1	-3.4	-0.7	-0.8	-0.7	-3.4	-1.0	-1.5	-1.3	-1.7	-2.7	-3.0	-2.3	-1.9
Belgium	-6.1	-4.2	-3.8	-2.8	-1.9	-0.3	-0.6	-1.0	0.0	0.3	0.9	0.1	-2.3	0.4	-0.4	-0.9	-3.1	-1.9	-1.5	-0.7
Canada	-6.5	-5.6	-4.6	-1.7	1.0	0.6	1.4	2.2	0.3	-0.4	-0.2	0.7	1.3	1.3	1.1	0.2	-3.7	-3.2	-2.1	-1.1
Czech Republic	..	..	..	..	..	..	-3.0	-3.5	-5.4	-6.1	-5.8	-2.2	-3.5	-3.4	-1.9	-3.8	-4.5	-3.8	-3.0	-2.4
Denmark	-1.7	-2.3	-2.7	-2.0	-1.1	-0.6	0.9	1.1	0.2	0.1	0.6	2.5	5.2	4.4	3.7	2.9	0.0	-1.0	-0.5	0.0
Finland	-3.5	-3.2	-3.6	-1.4	-0.8	1.6	1.5	6.3	4.9	4.6	3.4	2.9	3.2	4.0	4.5	3.8	0.7	-0.1	0.7	1.0
France	-5.7	-4.7	-5.0	-3.3	-2.6	-2.4	-1.9	-2.3	-2.4	-3.4	-3.8	-3.3	-2.8	-2.4	-3.2	-3.5	-6.0	-5.4	-4.4	-3.4
Germany	-2.6	-2.0	-9.5	-2.8	-2.1	-1.8	-1.2	-1.7	-3.3	-3.5	-3.2	-2.8	-2.2	-1.4	-0.3	-0.4	-1.2	-3.0	-2.4	-2.0
Greece	-10.6	-7.1	-7.9	-5.6	-5.1	-3.1	-2.2	-3.0	-4.1	-3.8	-5.5	-7.3	-4.7	-3.9	-6.2	-8.3	-12.7	-5.4	-3.5	-2.6
Hungary	..	..	..	-4.0	-5.6	-7.8	-5.3	-3.1	-4.1	-9.0	-7.4	-6.9	-8.4	-10.1	-5.1	-3.2	-1.1	-0.5	0.0	-0.5
Iceland	-2.6	-3.5	-1.5	-0.7	0.3	-0.8	0.5	1.1	-1.2	-2.2	-1.9	0.0	3.6	4.9	3.7	-14.7	-8.2	-3.1	0.1	2.7
Ireland	-1.0	0.1	-1.0	0.6	1.2	1.8	1.5	3.3	-0.2	-1.4	-0.2	0.9	0.8	1.9	-1.5	-6.8	-9.9	-26.1	-5.7	-4.3
Italy	-8.3	-7.6	-6.7	-6.2	-2.1	-2.4	-1.0	-2.1	-3.5	-3.1	-3.1	-3.2	-4.1	-3.7	-2.2	-2.7	-2.7	-2.1	-1.5	-1.2
Japan	-2.7	-3.7	-4.6	-5.4	-4.5	-10.6	-6.4	-7.1	-5.6	-7.0	-6.9	-5.7	-6.5	-1.8	-3.1	-2.3	-5.4	-6.7	-6.8	-7.0
Luxembourg	0.5	1.9	2.9	3.1	5.7	4.7	3.6	4.8	5.1	1.3	0.5	-0.8	-0.2	0.7	2.3	1.9	0.9	0.3	1.0	1.6
Netherlands	-2.7	-2.9	-8.8	-1.7	-1.5	-1.7	-0.8	-0.2	-1.9	-2.7	-2.6	-0.7	0.6	0.8	-0.5	-0.6	-4.9	-4.1	-2.6	-2.1
New Zealand	0.6	2.7	2.2	2.1	1.2	1.2	0.3	1.9	1.7	3.2	3.2	2.9	3.6	4.8	3.5	0.8	-1.7	-3.5	-3.3	-2.6
Norway[1]	-6.8	-5.5	-2.2	-2.0	-1.4	-2.4	-0.8	1.2	0.1	-2.4	-4.4	-2.6	-1.4	1.1	3.5	2.6	-0.7	-1.2	-2.1	-2.1
Poland	..	..	..	-4.4	-5.0	-4.5	-2.5	-3.3	-4.7	-3.9	-5.3	-5.2	-3.8	-4.0	-2.7	-4.4	-6.4	-7.3	-6.5	-4.9
Portugal	-7.1	-5.9	-4.3	-4.0	-3.3	-4.2	-3.7	-4.6	-5.5	-3.5	-2.6	-2.9	-5.1	-3.5	-2.8	-2.7	-7.7	-6.1	-3.5	-3.3
Spain	-5.8	-4.8	-4.6	-3.0	-2.0	-2.5	-1.5	-2.0	-1.5	-0.8	-0.2	-0.2	1.0	1.8	1.6	-3.6	-8.3	-5.9	-3.4	-2.3
Sweden	-7.4	-6.5	-6.0	-1.7	-0.4	1.3	0.5	2.6	1.2	-1.7	-1.5	-0.3	1.0	0.5	1.7	1.9	2.1	1.1	1.1	1.8
Switzerland	-2.8	-2.2	-1.3	-1.0	-2.3	-1.9	-0.4	-0.5	-0.5	-1.0	-0.7	-0.9	-0.1	0.8	1.1	1.8	1.9	-0.1	0.0	0.1
United Kingdom	-6.6	-6.2	-5.6	-4.0	-2.2	-0.3	0.7	1.0	0.4	-2.0	-3.8	-3.9	-3.8	-3.4	-3.9	-5.4	-8.9	-7.2	-6.0	-4.7
United States	-4.4	-3.4	-3.0	-2.0	-0.9	0.1	0.1	0.8	-0.8	-3.7	-4.7	-4.5	-3.7	-2.7	-3.4	-6.2	-9.5	-8.8	-7.4	-5.7
Euro area	-5.0	-4.1	-6.9	-3.5	-2.1	-2.0	-1.3	-1.7	-2.5	-2.7	-2.6	-2.4	-2.0	-1.3	-1.2	-2.2	-4.2	-4.2	-2.8	-2.1
Total OECD	-4.6	-4.0	-4.7	-3.1	-1.9	-2.1	-1.1	-1.1	-1.9	-3.4	-3.9	-3.6	-3.1	-1.9	-2.2	-3.7	-6.5	-6.3	-5.2	-4.1

Note: Cyclically-adjusted balances exclude one-off revenues from the sale of mobile telephone licenses. For more details on the methodology used for estimating the cyclical component of government balances, see *OECD Economic Outlook* Sources and Methods (*http://www.oecd.org/eco/sources-and-methods*).

1. As a percentage of mainland potential GDP. The financial balances shown are adjusted to exclude net revenues from petroleum activities.

Source: OECD Economic Outlook 88 database.

StatLink ᘛᘈᗝ http://dx.doi.org/10.1787/888932348852

Annex Table 29. General government underlying balances
Surplus (+) or deficit (-) as a per cent of potential GDP

	1993	1994	1995	1996	1997	1998	1999	2000	2001	2002	2003	2004	2005	2006	2007	2008	2009	2010	2011	2012
Australia	-3.4	-3.9	-3.1	-1.7	-0.3	1.0	1.0	0.0	-0.1	1.0	1.1	1.0	1.2	1.4	1.2	0.2	-2.9	-2.5	-1.2	-0.1
Austria	-4.1	-4.4	-5.7	-3.8	-1.6	-2.2	-3.2	-3.4	-0.6	-1.0	-1.1	-0.3	-1.1	-1.6	-1.4	-1.9	-3.0	-3.3	-2.4	-2.1
Belgium	-5.9	-4.1	-3.8	-2.7	-1.6	0.0	-0.5	-0.8	-0.1	0.1	-0.5	-0.4	-0.3	0.0	-0.5	-1.2	-2.9	-1.8	-1.4	-0.7
Canada	-6.7	-5.7	-4.6	-1.8	0.7	0.4	1.1	2.1	0.2	-0.4	-0.2	0.8	1.4	1.5	1.2	0.1	-3.6	-3.2	-2.1	-1.1
Czech Republic	..	..	..	..	..	..	-4.3	-5.2	-4.2	-4.2	-4.9	-2.1	-2.9	-3.3	-2.0	-3.5	-5.0	-4.0	-2.9	-2.0
Denmark	-1.5	-2.0	-2.5	-1.8	-0.9	-0.3	1.0	1.3	0.3	0.0	0.6	2.2	5.0	4.1	3.6	3.3	0.1	-0.6	-0.5	-0.1
Finland	-2.9	-2.3	-1.7	-0.8	-1.3	1.1	1.5	5.9	4.7	4.4	3.1	2.7	3.1	3.8	4.4	3.7	0.9	0.0	0.9	1.2
France	-5.3	-4.5	-4.5	-3.4	-2.9	-2.3	-1.7	-2.4	-2.4	-3.5	-4.1	-3.5	-3.4	-2.5	-3.1	-3.4	-5.8	-5.3	-4.2	-3.3
Germany	-3.3	-2.8	-3.7	-3.6	-2.8	-2.2	-1.6	-1.8	-3.1	-3.3	-2.9	-2.6	-2.0	-1.4	-0.3	-0.2	-1.0	-2.9	-2.3	-1.9
Greece	-8.9	-7.8	-8.4	-6.9	-5.1	-3.2	-1.4	-3.8	-3.6	-3.6	-5.6	-6.7	-4.9	-5.3	-6.3	-8.3	-12.7	-5.3	-3.4	-2.6
Hungary	..	..	..	-5.4	-6.3	-6.6	-6.4	-3.6	-4.2	-7.6	-7.5	-7.5	-8.7	-9.8	-4.2	-2.4	-0.6	-1.6	-0.6	-0.5
Iceland	-3.1	-3.2	-1.9	-0.8	0.1	-1.4	-0.1	0.5	-1.7	-3.0	-2.5	-0.8	2.6	3.7	2.4	-2.8	-9.4	-4.4	-1.2	1.3
Ireland	-1.2	0.7	-0.7	0.6	1.0	1.6	3.0	3.2	0.0	-1.2	-0.2	1.0	0.9	1.8	-1.9	-6.7	-9.9	-10.5	-5.7	-4.2
Italy	-8.6	-7.6	-6.1	-6.1	-2.7	-2.6	-0.9	-2.1	-3.2	-2.6	-3.9	-3.6	-3.9	-2.5	-2.0	-2.6	-3.2	-2.1	-1.6	-1.1
Japan	-2.9	-4.1	-4.9	-5.5	-4.9	-5.4	-6.7	-6.8	-6.1	-7.1	-6.7	-6.8	-5.3	-3.8	-3.6	-3.5	-5.7	-6.7	-6.4	-6.3
Luxembourg	0.5	2.2	3.0	3.1	5.6	4.5	3.4	4.8	3.5	1.4	0.6	-0.5	0.0	1.2	2.2	1.6	0.8	0.4	1.2	1.8
Netherlands	-3.4	-3.6	-4.1	-2.8	-2.1	-2.2	-1.2	-0.4	-1.7	-2.7	-2.4	-0.9	0.3	0.3	-0.8	-0.7	-4.2	-3.4	-2.6	-2.3
New Zealand	-0.2	2.1	2.0	2.2	1.3	1.2	0.4	2.0	1.8	3.4	3.3	3.0	3.6	4.8	3.6	0.9	-1.5	-3.4	-3.3	-2.6
Norway[1]	-6.8	-5.5	-2.4	-2.4	-1.7	-2.7	-1.0	1.7	0.0	-2.4	-4.5	-2.8	-1.5	1.0	3.5	2.7	-0.7	-1.2	-2.0	-2.1
Poland	..	..	..	-4.0	-5.0	-4.3	-2.8	-3.4	-4.7	-3.9	-4.9	-5.2	-3.9	-4.0	-2.9	-4.4	-6.3	-7.3	-6.4	-4.9
Portugal	-7.1	-6.0	-4.4	-4.1	-3.4	-3.4	-3.2	-4.1	-5.2	-4.7	-4.8	-4.4	-4.6	-3.0	-2.4	-2.9	-6.7	-7.1	-3.4	-2.9
Spain	-4.8	-4.5	-4.8	-3.6	-2.3	-2.4	-1.6	-1.6	-1.4	-0.8	-0.4	0.0	0.7	1.6	1.6	-2.8	-7.8	-6.3	-4.0	-3.0
Sweden	-5.7	-6.3	-6.1	-2.2	-0.3	0.2	0.4	2.3	1.1	-1.8	-1.5	-0.4	1.1	0.6	1.7	1.8	2.1	1.2	1.3	1.9
Switzerland	-2.9	-2.4	-1.6	-1.4	-2.7	-1.7	-0.9	0.8	-0.1	-0.4	-0.8	-1.0	-0.3	0.6	1.1	2.1	1.8	-0.3	-0.1	0.0
United Kingdom	-6.3	-6.1	-5.2	-3.8	-2.2	-0.3	0.5	0.7	0.4	-2.1	-3.8	-4.1	-4.1	-3.5	-4.2	-5.4	-8.6	-7.0	-5.7	-4.6
United States	-4.4	-3.4	-3.0	-2.1	-1.0	-0.1	0.1	0.6	-1.0	-3.8	-4.6	-4.6	-3.6	-3.0	-3.5	-5.9	-8.8	-8.6	-7.6	-6.0
Euro area	-5.0	-4.4	-4.4	-3.8	-2.6	-2.1	-1.4	-1.7	-2.3	-2.6	-2.8	-2.4	-2.0	-1.3	-1.2	-2.1	-4.1	-3.9	-2.8	-2.2
Total OECD	-4.6	-4.1	-4.0	-3.3	-2.2	-1.6	-1.3	-1.1	-2.0	-3.4	-3.9	-3.7	-3.0	-2.2	-2.3	-3.7	-6.2	-6.1	-5.2	-4.2

Note: The underlying balances are adjusted for the cycle and for one-offs. For more details, see *OECD Economic Outlook* Sources and Methods (*http://www.oecd.org/eco/sources-and-methods*).
1. As a percentage of mainland potential GDP. The financial balances shown are adjusted to exclude net revenues from petroleum activities.
Source: OECD Economic Outlook 88 database.

StatLink ⟨⟨⟨ http://dx.doi.org/10.1787/888932348871

Annex Table 30. General government underlying primary balances
Surplus (+) or deficit (-) as a per cent of potential GDP

	1993	1994	1995	1996	1997	1998	1999	2000	2001	2002	2003	2004	2005	2006	2007	2008	2009	2010	2011	2012
Australia	-0.9	-0.6	0.4	1.1	2.1	3.0	2.8	1.7	1.3	2.4	2.4	2.2	2.2	2.2	1.9	0.7	-2.1	-1.6	-0.1	1.2
Austria	-1.0	-1.5	-2.4	-0.4	1.5	0.9	-0.3	-0.5	2.1	1.5	1.2	1.9	1.1	0.5	0.7	0.1	-1.0	-1.2	-0.1	0.3
Belgium	4.1	4.6	4.5	5.1	5.7	6.9	6.0	5.6	6.0	5.5	4.4	4.2	3.8	3.8	3.1	2.3	0.4	1.3	1.8	2.7
Canada	-1.5	-0.6	1.0	3.4	5.4	5.2	5.4	5.2	3.1	2.2	1.7	2.4	2.5	2.2	1.8	0.1	-2.7	-2.8	-1.9	-1.0
Czech Republic	..	..	..	..	..	..	-3.8	-5.0	-3.8	-3.9	-4.4	-1.5	-2.2	-2.6	-1.3	-2.7	-3.9	-2.9	-1.7	-0.7
Denmark	2.2	1.5	1.0	1.4	2.1	2.3	3.5	3.4	2.2	1.7	2.1	3.4	5.9	4.8	3.9	3.3	0.5	-0.1	-0.1	0.3
Finland	-3.3	-1.3	-0.9	0.5	0.4	2.6	2.9	6.9	5.2	4.4	3.0	2.6	2.9	3.4	3.7	2.8	0.3	-0.6	0.2	0.6
France	-2.6	-1.6	-1.5	-0.2	0.2	0.8	1.1	0.3	0.4	-0.8	-1.5	-0.9	-0.9	-0.1	-0.6	-0.8	-3.7	-3.2	-2.2	-1.1
Germany	-0.7	-0.3	-0.8	-0.7	0.1	0.8	1.2	0.9	-0.5	-0.8	-0.4	-0.2	0.4	1.0	2.1	2.1	1.1	-0.7	-0.2	0.4
Greece	1.6	3.7	2.0	2.8	2.9	4.2	5.1	2.8	2.2	1.5	-0.9	-2.1	-0.6	-1.1	-2.0	-3.9	-8.0	-0.3	1.7	2.6
Hungary	..	..	..	2.0	0.8	-0.6	-0.4	1.1	-0.3	-4.0	-3.8	-3.5	-4.8	-6.1	-0.4	1.2	3.1	2.4	3.5	3.7
Iceland	-1.7	-1.8	-0.5	0.6	1.2	-0.3	0.8	1.2	-1.1	-2.6	-1.9	-0.5	2.2	3.0	1.4	-3.3	-6.6	-1.2	1.8	4.4
Ireland	4.6	6.0	4.1	4.7	4.4	4.7	5.2	5.0	1.1	-0.1	0.9	2.0	1.9	2.6	-0.9	-5.5	-8.3	-5.5	-1.1	1.1
Italy	3.1	2.8	4.5	4.6	6.0	5.1	5.4	4.1	2.9	2.8	1.0	1.0	0.6	2.0	2.8	2.2	0.9	2.0	2.9	3.7
Japan	-1.7	-2.9	-3.6	-4.1	-3.6	-3.9	-5.2	-5.3	-4.7	-5.8	-5.4	-5.6	-4.5	-3.1	-3.0	-2.6	-4.7	-5.5	-5.3	-4.7
Luxembourg	-1.5	0.6	1.7	2.0	4.6	3.5	2.5	3.5	2.2	0.3	-0.2	-1.2	-0.7	0.4	1.1	0.4	0.3	0.6	1.3	2.1
Netherlands	0.9	0.6	0.3	1.6	2.1	1.9	2.5	2.5	0.8	-0.5	-0.5	0.9	2.1	2.0	0.9	1.0	-2.8	-2.0	-1.1	-0.5
New Zealand	2.1	3.4	3.4	2.8	2.2	1.9	0.6	2.4	1.9	3.5	3.4	2.8	3.2	3.3	2.5	0.1	-2.3	-4.0	-3.8	-2.8
Norway[1]	-9.7	-7.7	-4.3	-4.4	-3.5	-4.0	-2.7	-0.6	-2.6	-5.1	-6.8	-5.3	-4.2	-2.1	-0.4	-1.7	-3.7	-4.1	-5.1	-5.1
Poland	..	..	1.1	0.1	-1.2	-0.5	-0.4	-0.9	-2.1	-1.9	-2.5	-2.8	-1.8	-1.9	-1.2	-2.8	-4.4	-5.3	-4.1	-2.4
Portugal	-0.3	-0.3	1.1	0.7	0.3	-0.3	-0.3	-1.1	-2.2	-1.9	-2.2	-1.9	-2.2	-0.4	0.5	0.1	-4.0	-4.3	0.2	0.9
Spain	-0.5	-0.3	-0.3	1.0	1.9	1.4	1.7	1.4	1.3	1.6	1.7	1.8	2.3	3.0	2.8	-1.7	-6.5	-4.7	-2.3	-1.3
Sweden	-3.6	-3.4	-3.7	0.5	2.7	2.8	2.9	4.5	2.8	0.3	-0.2	0.5	2.1	1.4	2.4	2.3	2.4	1.9	2.2	3.0
Switzerland	-2.2	-1.6	-0.8	-0.6	-1.9	-0.8	0.2	1.8	0.8	0.6	0.1	0.0	0.6	1.3	1.6	2.6	2.1	0.0	0.1	0.3
United Kingdom	-4.0	-3.5	-2.2	-0.8	1.0	2.7	3.0	3.1	2.4	-0.4	-2.0	-2.4	-2.3	-1.7	-2.3	-3.5	-7.0	-5.0	-3.3	-1.9
United States	-1.0	0.0	0.5	1.3	2.2	3.0	2.8	3.1	1.2	-1.8	-2.8	-2.8	-1.8	-1.1	-1.5	-4.2	-7.4	-7.0	-5.8	-3.9
Euro area	-0.1	0.3	0.3	1.0	1.8	2.0	2.3	1.8	1.0	0.5	0.1	0.4	0.6	1.3	1.5	0.6	-1.7	-1.4	-0.3	0.5
Total OECD	-1.0	-0.6	-0.4	0.3	1.2	1.7	1.6	1.5	0.5	-1.2	-1.9	-1.8	-1.1	-0.4	-0.5	-2.0	-4.7	-4.4	-3.3	-2.1

Note: Adjusted for the cycle and for one-offs, and excludes the impact of net interest payments. For more details, see *OECD Economic Outlook Sources and Methods* (*http://www.oecd.org/eco/sources-and-methods*).
1. As a percentage of mainland potential GDP. The financial balances shown are adjusted to exclude net revenues from petroleum activities.
Source: OECD Economic Outlook 88 database.

StatLink http://dx.doi.org/10.1787/888932348890

Annex Table 31. General government net debt interest payments

Per cent of nominal GDP

	1993	1994	1995	1996	1997	1998	1999	2000	2001	2002	2003	2004	2005	2006	2007	2008	2009	2010	2011	2012
Australia	2.5	3.4	3.5	2.9	2.4	2.0	1.8	1.7	1.4	1.4	1.3	1.2	1.0	0.8	0.6	0.5	0.8	1.0	1.1	1.3
Austria	3.1	2.9	3.3	3.4	3.2	3.1	2.9	2.8	2.7	2.5	2.4	2.2	2.2	2.2	2.0	2.0	2.1	2.2	2.4	2.4
Belgium	10.3	8.8	8.4	8.0	7.3	7.0	6.5	6.3	6.1	5.4	5.0	4.6	4.1	3.8	3.7	3.6	3.4	3.3	3.4	3.6
Canada	5.3	5.2	5.7	5.3	4.8	4.8	4.3	3.1	2.9	2.6	1.8	1.6	1.0	0.7	0.6	0.0	0.9	0.4	0.2	0.1
Czech Republic	..	..	0.3	0.5	0.4	0.5	0.5	0.2	0.4	0.3	0.5	0.7	0.7	0.7	0.7	0.8	1.1	1.2	1.3	1.3
Denmark	3.9	3.6	3.5	3.2	2.9	2.7	2.5	2.1	1.8	1.7	1.5	1.3	0.9	0.6	0.4	0.0	0.4	0.5	0.5	0.5
Finland	-0.5	1.0	0.8	1.4	1.8	1.6	1.4	0.9	0.5	0.0	-0.1	-0.1	-0.2	-0.4	-0.6	-1.0	-0.6	-0.7	-0.7	-0.6
France	2.8	2.9	3.0	3.2	3.1	3.0	2.8	2.7	2.7	2.7	2.6	2.6	2.5	2.4	2.5	2.7	2.2	2.1	2.1	2.3
Germany	2.6	2.6	2.9	2.9	2.9	3.0	2.7	2.7	2.6	2.5	2.6	2.5	2.4	2.4	2.4	2.3	2.3	2.2	2.2	2.3
Greece	10.8	11.9	10.7	10.0	8.1	7.5	6.6	6.7	6.0	5.2	4.7	4.6	4.4	4.2	4.2	4.4	4.8	5.3	5.6	5.6
Hungary	..	..	8.1	7.5	7.2	6.1	6.0	4.7	4.0	3.6	3.7	4.0	3.9	3.7	3.8	3.6	4.1	4.3	4.4	4.5
Iceland	1.4	1.5	1.5	1.4	1.1	1.0	0.9	0.7	0.5	0.3	0.6	0.3	-0.4	-0.7	-0.9	-0.5	3.0	3.4	3.2	3.2
Ireland	6.1	5.6	4.9	4.1	3.4	3.1	2.1	1.7	1.1	1.0	1.1	1.0	0.9	0.8	0.9	1.2	1.8	5.5	4.9	5.7
Israel	..	..	5.3	4.9	5.3	5.1	4.6	4.6	4.5	4.1	5.0	4.9	4.2	4.0	4.0	3.1	3.1	3.2	3.3	3.3
Italy	12.1	10.6	10.7	10.8	8.8	7.8	6.4	6.1	6.0	5.4	5.0	4.7	4.5	4.4	4.7	4.9	4.4	4.3	4.6	4.9
Japan	1.2	1.2	1.3	1.3	1.3	1.5	1.5	1.5	1.4	1.4	1.3	1.2	0.8	0.6	0.6	0.9	1.1	1.2	1.2	1.6
Korea	-0.5	-0.4	-0.6	-0.7	-0.9	-1.2	-1.0	-1.2	-0.9	-0.9	-0.8	-1.0	-1.0	-1.2	-1.5	-1.3	-0.9	-0.7	-0.7	-0.7
Luxembourg	-1.9	-1.6	-1.4	-1.1	-1.0	-1.0	-0.9	-1.2	-1.4	-1.1	-0.9	-0.8	-0.7	-0.7	-1.0	-1.2	-0.5	0.2	0.2	0.3
Netherlands	4.4	4.2	4.4	4.4	4.2	4.0	3.6	2.9	2.4	2.2	2.0	1.9	1.8	1.6	1.6	1.6	1.5	1.4	1.5	1.8
New Zealand	2.3	1.2	1.4	0.7	0.8	0.7	0.2	0.4	0.1	0.1	0.0	-0.3	-0.4	-1.5	-1.0	-0.9	-0.9	-0.6	-0.6	-0.3
Norway	-2.5	-1.9	-1.6	-1.6	-1.4	-1.1	-1.5	-1.7	-1.9	-2.1	-1.9	-2.0	-2.0	-2.2	-2.9	-3.2	-2.5	-2.3	-2.4	-2.4
Poland	..	5.9	5.1	4.2	3.8	3.7	2.4	2.5	2.7	2.1	2.4	2.5	2.2	2.1	1.7	1.6	1.9	2.0	2.4	2.5
Portugal	6.9	..	5.6	4.8	3.7	3.1	2.9	2.9	2.9	2.8	2.7	2.6	2.4	2.7	2.9	3.0	2.8	2.9	3.7	3.9
Slovak Republic	..	..	1.3	1.6	1.8	2.1	2.9	3.1	3.1	3.0	1.7	1.4	1.1	0.5	0.7	0.6	1.0	1.4	1.5	1.6
Slovenia	..	..	1.6	1.7	2.0	1.8	1.9	1.8	1.8	1.8	1.5	1.4	1.3	1.2	1.1	0.7	1.1	1.4	1.4	1.6
Spain	4.5	4.4	4.7	4.7	4.2	3.8	3.3	2.9	2.6	2.4	2.1	1.8	1.6	1.3	1.1	1.1	1.4	1.6	1.8	1.8
Sweden	2.3	3.0	2.4	2.8	3.0	2.6	2.5	2.1	1.7	2.1	1.3	0.9	1.0	0.8	0.7	0.5	0.2	0.7	0.9	1.1
Switzerland	0.7	0.8	0.8	0.8	0.9	0.9	1.1	1.0	0.9	1.0	1.0	1.0	0.9	0.7	0.6	0.5	0.4	0.3	0.3	0.2
United Kingdom	2.4	2.6	3.1	3.1	3.2	3.0	2.5	2.4	2.0	1.7	1.7	1.7	1.8	1.8	1.9	1.9	1.7	2.1	2.5	2.7
United States	3.4	3.4	3.5	3.4	3.2	3.1	2.7	2.5	2.2	2.0	1.8	1.8	1.8	1.8	1.9	1.8	1.4	1.7	1.9	2.1
Euro area	5.0	4.7	4.8	4.9	4.4	4.2	3.7	3.5	3.3	3.1	3.0	2.8	2.7	2.6	2.6	2.6	2.5	2.5	2.6	2.8
Total OECD	3.5	3.4	3.6	3.5	3.2	3.1	2.7	2.5	2.3	2.1	2.0	1.9	1.8	1.7	1.7	1.7	1.6	1.7	1.8	2.0

Note: In the case of New Zealand where data on net interest payments are not available, net property income paid is used as a proxy. For Denmark, net interest payments include dividends received. For further information, see OECD Economic Outlook Sources and Methods (http://www.oecd.org/eco/sources-and-methods).

Source: OECD Economic Outlook 88 database.

StatLink 🖳 http://dx.doi.org/10.1787/888932348909

Annex Table 32. General government gross financial liabilities
Per cent of nominal GDP

	1993	1994	1995	1996	1997	1998	1999	2000	2001	2002	2003	2004	2005	2006	2007	2008	2009	2010	2011	2012
Australia	30.3	39.6	41.3	38.6	37.0	32.0	27.6	24.7	21.8	19.8	18.3	16.6	16.1	15.3	14.3	13.6	19.2	23.6	25.9	26.8
Austria	62.1	65.5	69.8	70.2	66.7	68.4	71.2	71.1	72.0	73.0	71.2	70.8	70.9	66.6	63.1	67.5	72.7	75.9	78.0	79.7
Belgium[1]	140.7	137.8	135.4	133.4	128.0	123.2	119.7	113.7	112.0	108.4	103.4	98.4	95.9	91.6	88.0	93.4	100.4	102.5	104.3	105.2
Canada	96.3	98.0	101.6	101.7	96.3	95.2	91.4	82.1	82.7	80.6	76.6	72.6	71.6	70.3	66.5	71.3	83.4	84.4	85.5	87.0
Czech Republic	..	..	..	..	..	..	..	32.8	..	32.8	34.7	34.5	34.3	33.9	33.6	36.3	42.4	49.0	52.3	55.0
Denmark	85.0	78.9	81.7	79.1	74.8	72.4	67.1	60.4	58.4	58.2	56.6	54.0	45.9	41.2	34.1	42.3	51.8	53.7	55.2	58.0
Finland	57.8	60.9	65.3	66.2	64.8	61.2	54.9	52.5	50.0	49.6	51.5	51.5	48.4	45.5	41.4	40.6	52.6	58.4	62.7	65.8
France	51.0	60.2	62.7	66	68.8	70.3	66.8	65.6	64.3	67.3	71.4	73.9	75.7	70.9	70.0	75.9	87.1	92.4	97.1	100.2
Germany[2]	46.2	46.5	55.7	58.8	60.3	62.2	61.5	60.4	59.8	62.2	65.4	68.8	71.2	69.3	65.3	69.4	76.5	79.9	81.3	82.0
Greece	..	..	101.1	103.1	100.0	97.7	101.1	114.9	117.7	117.2	112.0	114.4	114.0	108.5	104.6	105.6	120.2	129.2	136.8	142.2
Hungary	92.3	92.1	88.8	75.8	66.5	64.5	66.6	60.9	59.7	60.7	61.7	65.0	68.9	72.3	72.5	76.4	85.2	89.0	90.2	90.1
Iceland	..	..	..	..	..	77.3	73.6	72.9	75.0	72.0	71.0	64.5	52.6	57.4	53.3	102.4	119.5	124.9	116.9	111.3
Ireland	..	..	..	..	..	62.2	51.3	40.1	37.3	35.3	34.1	32.9	33.2	29.4	28.9	49.4	72.7	104.9	112.7	115.6
Israel	..	..	102.2	100.2	99.3	100.9	94.8	84.4	88.9	96.6	99.2	97.4	93.5	84.1	77.5	76.7	79.2	79.4	78.1	75.0
Italy	116.3	120.9	122.5	128.9	130.3	132.6	126.4	121.6	120.8	119.4	116.8	117.3	119.9	117.2	112.7	115.1	127.7	131.3	132.7	133.0
Japan[3]	73.9	79.0	86.2	93.8	100.5	113.2	127.1	135.4	143.7	152.3	158.0	165.5	175.3	172.2	167.1	173.9	192.8	198.4	204.2	210.2
Korea[4]	..	..	..	..	..	..	..	..	..	19.2	19.3	22.6	24.6	27.7	27.9	29.6	32.6	33.2	32.8	32.6
Luxembourg	..	..	9.5	10.1	10.2	11.2	10.0	9.2	8.2	8.4	7.9	8.6	7.6	11.5	11.8	16.5	18.0	21.0	26.0	28.1
Netherlands	96.5	86.7	89.6	88.1	82.2	80.8	71.6	63.9	59.4	60.3	61.9	62.2	61.1	54.9	52.0	66.0	69.4	74.6	77.6	79.5
New Zealand	..	56.8	50.7	44.4	41.8	41.7	39.1	37.0	35.0	33.1	31.0	28.3	27.0	26.7	25.8	29.1	34.5	38.8	43.5	46.6
Norway	40.8	37.3	40.9	36.6	32.1	30.3	31.0	34.2	33.0	40.6	50.2	52.7	49.1	60.5	58.6	56.7	49.5	51.8	53.6	51.8
Poland	..	..	51.6	51.5	48.4	44.0	46.8	45.4	43.7	55.0	55.3	54.8	54.8	55.2	51.8	54.5	58.5	63.9	66.7	67.4
Portugal	..	..	66.8	66.5	65.3	63.0	59.9	59.7	61.0	64.3	65.9	68.3	71.8	70.9	68.8	74.1	86.3	92.9	98.7	100.6
Slovak Republic	..	..	38.2	37.7	39.0	41.2	53.5	57.6	57.1	50.3	48.3	47.6	39.2	34.1	32.8	31.7	39.8	47.1	51.1	53.3
Slovenia	..	..	..	..	..	..	..	..	33.7	34.8	34.2	35.0	33.9	33.8	30.0	29.7	44.1	49.9	54.8	58.5
Spain	65.5	64.3	69.3	76.0	75.0	75.3	69.4	66.5	61.9	60.3	55.3	53.4	50.7	46.2	42.3	47.4	62.4	72.2	78.2	79.6
Sweden	78.2	82.5	81.1	84.4	83.0	82.0	73.2	64.3	62.7	60.2	59.3	59.2	59.9	52.8	47.4	46.7	51.9	51.3	48.8	45.2
Switzerland	42.9	45.5	47.7	50.1	52.1	54.8	51.9	52.4	51.2	57.2	57.0	57.9	56.4	50.3	46.5	44.3	42.2	42.1	41.1	40.5
United Kingdom	48.7	46.8	51.6	51.2	52.0	52.5	47.4	45.1	40.4	40.8	41.5	43.8	46.4	46.1	47.2	57.0	72.4	81.3	88.6	94.5
United States	71.9	71.1	70.7	69.9	67.4	64.2	60.5	54.5	54.4	56.8	60.2	61.2	61.4	60.9	62.0	71.1	84.4	92.8	98.5	101.4
Euro area	69.0	71.3	75.5	79.9	80.8	81.6	78.2	75.9	74.4	75.3	75.9	77.2	78.0	74.3	70.9	76.0	86.3	91.6	94.8	96.3
Total OECD	68.7	69.8	72.3	73.8	73.5	74.2	72.6	69.8	69.7	71.6	73.5	75.0	76.3	74.5	72.9	79.1	90.6	96.9	100.7	102.8

Note: Gross debt data are not always comparable across countries due to different definitions or treatment of debt components. Notably, they include the funded portion of government employee pension liabilities for some OECD countries, including Australia and the United States. The debt position of these countries is thus overstated relative to countries that have large unfunded liabilities for such pensions which according to ESA95/SNA93 are not counted in the debt figures, but rather as a memorandum item to the debt. Maastricht debt for European Union countries is shown in Annex Table 62. For more details, see *OECD Economic Outlook* Sources and Methods (*http://www.oecd.org/eco/sources-and-methods*).

1. Includes the debt of the Belgium National Railways Company (SNCB) from 2005 onwards.
2. Includes the debt of the Inherited Debt Fund from 1995 onwards.
3. Includes the debt of the Japan Railway Settlement Corporation and the National Forest Special Account from 1998 onwards.
4. Data are on a non-consolidated basis (SNA93).

Source: OECD Economic Outlook 88 database.

StatLink ⟲ *http://dx.doi.org/10.1787/888932348928*

Annex Table 33. General government net financial liabilities
Per cent of nominal GDP

	1993	1994	1995	1996	1997	1998	1999	2000	2001	2002	2003	2004	2005	2006	2007	2008	2009	2010	2011	2012
Australia	20.8	25.0	25.6	20.4	20.6	15.7	14.5	8.6	6.2	4.4	2.3	0.2	-1.4	-4.7	-7.3	-7.6	-3.8	0.4	2.7	3.6
Austria	33.3	35.2	38.8	40.3	36.5	36.7	35.8	34.8	35.6	37.0	36.1	37.9	38.0	33.8	30.8	33.7	38.7	41.7	43.9	45.5
Belgium[1]	115.1	114.5	114.6	115.5	110.9	107.8	103.1	97.6	95.1	93.3	90.4	84.0	82.0	77.2	73.3	74.0	80.2	82.4	84.2	85.0
Canada	64.2	67.9	70.7	70.0	64.7	60.8	55.8	46.2	44.3	42.6	38.7	35.2	31.0	26.3	22.9	22.4	28.4	31.4	33.7	34.3
Czech Republic	..	..	..	..	..	..	..	..	..	..	-16.2	-9.7	-11.4	-11.7	-14.4	-6.4	-1.7	3.5	7.5	10.6
Denmark	31.1	31.5	33.4	33.3	32.3	35.1	28.4	22.5	20.1	19.1	18.0	14.8	10.5	1.9	-3.8	-6.7	-4.5	0.3	4.2	6.8
Finland[2]	-16.0	-16.3	-7.3	-6.7	-7.5	-14.6	-50.3	-31.1	-31.7	-31.4	-38.5	-46.7	-58.6	-69.4	-72.6	-52.4	-62.6	-56.6	-52.3	-49.2
France	26.8	29.7	37.5	41.8	42.3	40.5	33.5	35.1	36.7	41.8	44.2	45.3	43.2	37.2	33.8	43.4	50.8	57.1	61.8	64.7
Germany[3]	18.3	19.1	29.7	32.7	32.4	36.2	34.7	34.0	36.3	40.4	43.2	47.2	49.5	47.5	42.2	44.0	48.5	50.5	51.6	52.0
Greece	..	..	81.0	81.4	76.8	72.6	70.2	88.7	92.9	94.7	87.2	88.0	85.0	78.3	72.5	78.7	88.3	97.3	105.1	110.1
Hungary	-19.4	3.3	24.4	25.1	24.9	31.6	33.8	32.3	32.0	36.7	37.6	41.5	46.3	51.6	52.8	51.5	58.9	61.6	62.1	61.3
Iceland	..	..	..	..	..	42.6	35.9	37.5	29.2	28.5	30.7	27.7	13.6	7.9	-1.0	26.1	39.8	45.2	45.7	43.1
Ireland	..	..	..	..	..	42.2	27.3	16.4	13.0	14.0	11.5	8.7	6.5	1.4	-0.3	11.3	28.6	61.5	69.7	74.6
Italy	100.5	104.5	99.0	104.5	104.6	107.0	101.1	95.6	96.3	95.7	92.7	92.5	93.7	90.5	87.0	89.7	100.0	103.3	104.7	105.0
Japan[4]	17.1	19.6	23.8	29.2	34.8	46.2	53.8	60.4	66.3	72.6	76.5	82.7	84.6	84.3	81.5	94.9	108.2	114.0	120.4	127.1
Korea[5]	..	..	..	..	..	..	..	..	..	-32.3	-30.9	-31.4	-35.6	-37.0	-40.4	-37.9	-38.5	-36.6	-36.6	-37.1
Luxembourg	..	..	-37.7	-41.0	-41.6	-46.8	-47.8	-50.7	-58.2	-55.5	-56.7	-52.2	-48.6	-44.7	-44.2	-44.7	-45.9	-41.6	-39.0	-36.8
Netherlands	45.5	44.6	54.1	52.8	49.7	48.2	36.7	34.9	33.0	34.9	36.2	37.6	35.0	31.6	27.9	26.8	29.9	34.7	37.7	39.6
New Zealand	..	43.9	37.6	32.4	29.8	27.8	25.5	23.5	21.1	16.9	11.0	4.8	-1.5	-8.1	-13.1	-12.7	-8.9	-4.4	0.4	3.8
Norway	-32.0	-30.6	-36.1	-41.1	-48.5	-52.1	-57.5	-67.4	-85.1	-80.6	-95.0	-104.4	-122.4	-136.3	-142.5	-126.1	-154.4	-157.0	-158.9	-160.6
Poland	..	..	-15.0	-5.7	0.3	6.4	13.5	15.5	18.5	22.1	22.7	20.8	23.5	22.4	17.0	17.3	22.3	29.0	33.8	36.2
Portugal	..	..	24.3	26.5	31.2	32.2	29.8	27.4	29.2	33.3	35.9	40.7	43.5	42.7	42.7	47.1	57.4	63.2	67.6	70.0
Slovak Republic	..	..	-30.7	-18.2	-12.1	-3.7	1.2	12.5	10.9	1.7	1.8	7.6	4.9	6.5	7.3	8.9	17.1	24.5	28.4	30.5
Slovenia	..	..	..	..	..	..	..	..	-15.7	-14.2	-9.5	-9.7	-8.5	-9.9	-17.6	-5.5	-0.4	5.4	9.9	13.4
Spain	43.5	46.4	51.6	55.5	54.2	53.7	47.7	44.2	41.5	40.3	36.8	34.6	29.9	23.5	18.5	22.9	34.3	43.4	49.3	52.8
Sweden	10.5	20.7	25.6	26.6	24.6	22.0	12.4	5.5	-2.5	3.9	0.0	-3.6	-8.7	-20.0	-24.7	-18.3	-23.5	-21.1	-19.6	-19.3
Switzerland	..	..	..	..	..	..	12.5	11.4	10.9	15.7	15.9	17.7	16.7	13.5	8.9	6.2	5.1	5.7	6.0	5.8
United Kingdom	17.4	19.7	26.3	27.9	30.6	32.6	29.0	26.8	23.2	23.7	23.9	25.9	27.1	27.5	28.5	33.0	43.8	51.3	57.6	62.3
United States	54.9	54.4	53.8	51.9	48.8	44.9	40.2	35.3	34.6	37.2	40.5	42.1	42.5	41.7	42.4	48.3	59.7	67.8	74.3	78.2
Euro area	42.8	44.3	49.0	53.4	53.4	54.0	48.6	47.6	48.2	50.5	50.6	51.5	50.7	46.4	42.1	46.4	53.7	58.7	61.7	63.3
Total OECD	40.5	41.7	43.3	44.2	43.5	44.0	40.6	38.3	37.9	40.1	41.5	42.6	42.2	40.0	38.0	43.3	51.9	57.9	62.3	64.9

StatLink ᴍⱽ http://dx.doi.org/10.1787/888932348947

Note: Net debt measures are not always comparable across countries due to different definitions or treatment of debt (and asset) components. First, the treatment of government liabilities with respect to their employee pension plans may be different (see note to Annex Table 32). Second, the range of items included as general government assets differs across countries. For example, equity holdings are excluded from government assets in some countries whereas foreign exchange, gold and SDR holdings are considered as assets in the United States and the United Kingdom. For details, see *OECD Economic Outlook* Sources and Methods (http://www.oecd.org/eco/sources-and-methods).
1. Includes the debt of the Belgium National Railways Company (SNCB) from 2005 onwards.
2. From 1995 onwards housing corporation shares are no longer classified as financial assets.
3. Includes the debt of the Inherited Debt Fund from 1995 onwards.
4. Includes the debt of the Japan Railway Settlement Corporation and the National Forest Special Account from 1998 onwards.
5. Data are on a non-consolidated basis (SNA93).
Source: OECD Economic Outlook 88 database.

Annex Table 34. Short-term interest rates
Per cent, per annum

	1996	1997	1998	1999	2000	2001	2002	2003	2004	2005	2006	2007	2008	2009	2010	2011	2012	Fourth quarter 2010	2011	2012
Australia	7.2	5.4	5.0	5.0	6.2	4.9	4.7	4.9	5.5	5.6	6.0	6.7	7.0	3.4	4.7	5.4	5.8	5.0	5.5	5.8
Austria	3.4	3.5	3.6	3.0																
Belgium	3.2	3.4	3.6	3.0																
Canada	4.5	3.6	5.1	4.9	5.7	4.0	2.6	3.0	2.4	2.8	4.1	4.6	3.5	0.8	0.8	1.6	2.8	1.1	2.1	3.4
Chile	..	..	16.4	11.0	10.8	7.2	3.9	2.8	1.8	3.5	4.8	5.2	7.3	1.7	1.9	5.4	7.0	3.7	6.2	7.2
Czech Republic	12.0	16.0	14.3	6.9	5.4	5.2	3.5	2.3	2.4	2.0	2.3	3.1	4.0	2.2	1.3	1.5	2.5	1.2	1.5	2.6
Denmark	3.9	3.7	4.1	3.3	4.9	4.6	3.5	2.4	2.1	2.2	3.1	4.3	4.9	1.8	0.7	1.1	1.8	0.8	1.2	2.1
Finland	3.6	3.2	3.6	3.0																
France	3.9	3.5	3.6	3.0																
Germany	3.3	3.3	3.5	3.0																
Greece	12.8	10.4	11.6	8.9	6.1															
Hungary	24.0	20.1	18.0	14.7	11.0	10.8	8.9	8.2	11.3	7.0	6.9	7.6	8.9	8.5	5.4	5.4	5.5	5.4	5.4	5.7
Iceland	7.0	7.1	7.5	9.3	11.2	12.0	9.0	5.3	6.3	9.4	12.4	14.3	15.8	11.3	7.1	5.4	5.0	6.2	5.0	5.0
Ireland	5.4	6.1	5.4	3.0																
Israel	15.7	13.8	11.9	12.0	9.0	6.5	7.2	6.6	4.3	3.9	5.5	4.3	3.6	0.6	1.6	3.0	4.0	2.0	3.5	4.5
Italy	8.8	6.9	5.0	3.0																
Japan	0.6	0.6	0.7	0.2	0.2	0.1	0.1	0.0	0.0	0.0	0.2	0.7	0.7	0.3	0.2	0.2	0.2	0.3	0.2	0.2
Korea	12.6	13.4	15.2	6.8	7.1	5.3	4.8	4.3	3.8	3.6	4.5	5.2	5.5	2.6	2.7	4.0	4.9	3.0	4.5	5.0
Luxembourg	3.2	3.4	3.6	3.0																
Mexico	32.9	21.3	26.2	22.4	16.2	12.2	7.4	6.5	7.1	9.3	7.3	7.4	7.9	5.5	4.6	4.9	5.9	4.6	5.2	6.3
Netherlands	3.0	3.3	3.5	3.0																
New Zealand	9.3	7.7	7.3	4.8	6.5	5.7	5.7	5.4	6.1	7.1	7.5	8.3	8.0	3.0	3.0	3.5	4.4	3.3	3.8	5.0
Norway	4.9	3.7	5.8	6.5	6.7	7.2	6.9	4.1	2.0	2.2	3.1	5.0	6.2	2.5	2.6	2.9	3.7	2.8	3.0	4.0
Poland	21.3	23.1	19.9	14.7	18.9	15.7	8.8	5.7	6.2	5.2	4.2	4.8	6.3	4.3	4.1	5.6	6.4	4.5	6.4	6.4
Portugal	7.4	5.7	4.3	3.0																
Slovak Republic	12.0	22.4	21.1	15.7	8.6	7.8	7.8	6.2	4.7	2.9	4.3	4.3	4.2							
Slovenia							8.0	6.8	4.7	4.0	3.6	4.3								
Spain	7.5	5.4	4.2	3.0																
Sweden	5.8	4.1	4.2	3.1	4.0	4.0	4.1	3.0	2.1	1.7	2.3	3.6	3.9	0.4	0.5	1.7	2.6	1.0	2.0	2.9
Switzerland	2.0	1.6	1.5	1.4	3.2	2.9	1.1	0.3	0.5	0.8	1.6	2.6	2.5	0.4	0.2	0.5	1.4	0.2	0.9	1.8
Turkey	..	..	..	..	38.9	92.4	59.5	38.5	23.8	15.6	17.9	18.3	18.9	11.0	7.6	9.2	9.8	7.7	9.7	9.9
United Kingdom	6.0	6.8	7.3	5.4	6.1	5.0	4.0	3.7	4.6	4.7	4.8	6.0	5.5	1.2	0.7	0.9	1.8	0.7	1.1	2.5
United States	5.4	5.7	5.5	5.4	6.5	3.7	1.8	1.2	1.6	3.5	5.2	5.3	3.2	0.9	0.5	0.7	1.8	0.3	1.1	2.5
Euro area	5.0	4.5	4.1	3.1	4.4	4.3	3.4	2.4	2.1	2.2	3.1	4.3	4.6	1.2	0.8	1.1	1.8	1.0	1.2	2.1

StatLink ⇒ http://dx.doi.org/10.1787/888932348966

Note: Three-month money market rates where available, or rates on similar financial instruments. For further information, see OECD Economic Outlook Sources and Methods (http://www.oecd.org/eco/sources-and-methods). Individual euro area countries are not shown after 1998 (2000 for Greece, 2007 for Slovenia and 2008 for the Slovak Republic) since their short-term interest rates are equal to the euro area rate.

Source: OECD Economic Outlook 88 database.

Annex Table 35. Long-term interest rates
Per cent, per annum

	1996	1997	1998	1999	2000	2001	2002	2003	2004	2005	2006	2007	2008	2009	2010	2011	2012	Fourth quarter 2010	2011	2012
Australia	8.2	7.0	5.5	6.0	6.3	5.6	5.8	5.4	5.6	5.3	5.6	6.0	5.8	5.0	5.3	5.5	6.5	5.0	5.8	6.8
Austria	6.3	5.7	4.7	4.7	5.6	5.1	5.0	4.2	4.2	3.4	3.8	4.3	4.4	3.9	3.2	3.4	4.2	2.8	3.7	4.6
Belgium	6.3	5.6	4.7	4.7	5.6	5.1	4.9	4.1	4.1	3.4	3.8	4.3	4.4	3.8	3.3	3.6	4.1	3.2	3.8	4.4
Canada	7.2	6.1	5.3	5.5	5.9	5.5	5.3	4.8	4.6	4.1	4.2	4.3	3.6	3.2	3.2	3.3	4.0	2.8	3.6	4.3
Chile	..	..	..	..	..	..	..	..	..	6.0	6.1	6.1	7.0	5.7	6.8	7.8	8.6	7.5	8.0	9.0
Czech Republic	..	..	..	..	..	6.3	4.9	4.1	4.8	3.5	3.8	4.3	4.6	4.8	3.9	4.0	4.4	3.7	4.0	4.6
Denmark	7.2	6.3	5.0	4.9	5.7	5.1	5.1	4.3	4.3	3.4	3.8	4.3	4.3	3.6	2.9	3.0	3.8	2.5	3.3	4.2
Finland	7.1	6.0	4.8	4.7	5.5	5.0	5.0	4.1	4.1	3.4	3.8	4.3	4.3	3.7	3.0	3.1	4.0	2.6	3.4	4.3
France	6.3	5.6	4.6	4.6	5.4	4.9	4.9	4.1	4.1	3.4	3.8	4.3	4.2	3.6	3.0	3.3	4.1	2.7	3.6	4.5
Germany	6.2	5.7	4.6	4.5	5.3	4.8	4.8	4.1	4.0	3.4	3.8	4.2	4.0	3.2	2.7	3.0	3.8	2.4	3.3	4.2
Greece	..	9.8	8.5	6.3	6.1	5.3	5.1	4.3	4.3	3.6	4.1	4.5	4.8	5.2	9.1	10.4	7.5	10.8	10.2	5.9
Hungary	..	..	..	..	8.6	7.9	7.1	6.8	8.3	6.6	7.1	6.7	8.2	9.1	7.2	7.5	7.0	7.2	7.4	7.0
Iceland	9.2	8.7	7.7	8.5	11.2	10.4	8.0	6.7	7.5	7.7	9.3	9.8	11.1	8.0	5.1	4.7	5.6	4.2	5.0	5.9
Ireland	7.2	6.3	4.7	4.8	5.5	5.0	5.0	4.1	4.1	3.3	3.8	4.3	4.6	5.2	5.5	6.0	6.2	6.3	6.0	6.3
Israel	..	4.1	4.9	5.2	5.5	4.8	5.3	4.7	7.6	6.4	6.3	5.6	5.9	5.1	4.7	4.6	5.0	4.4	4.7	5.1
Italy	9.4	6.9	4.9	4.7	5.6	5.2	5.0	4.3	4.3	3.6	4.0	4.5	4.7	4.3	3.8	3.7	4.5	3.2	4.0	4.9
Japan	3.1	2.4	1.5	1.7	1.7	1.3	1.3	1.0	1.5	1.4	1.7	1.7	1.5	1.3	1.1	1.2	1.7	0.9	1.4	1.8
Korea	10.9	11.7	12.8	..	8.5	6.9	6.6	5.0	4.7	5.0	5.2	5.4	5.6	5.2	4.9	5.9	6.2	4.9	6.2	6.2
Luxembourg	6.3	5.6	4.7	4.7	5.5	4.9	4.7	3.3	2.8	2.4	3.3	4.4	4.7	3.8	3.1	3.3	4.2	2.8	3.6	4.5
Mexico	34.4	22.4	24.8	24.1	16.9	13.8	8.5	7.4	7.7	9.3	7.5	7.6	8.1	5.8	5.0	5.3	6.4	5.0	5.7	6.8
Netherlands	6.2	5.6	4.6	4.6	5.4	5.0	4.9	4.1	4.1	3.4	3.8	4.3	4.2	3.7	2.9	3.1	4.0	2.6	3.5	4.3
New Zealand	7.9	7.2	6.3	6.4	6.9	6.4	6.5	5.9	6.1	5.9	5.8	6.3	6.1	5.5	5.5	4.9	5.4	5.1	4.8	6.0
Norway	6.8	5.9	5.4	5.5	6.2	6.2	6.4	5.0	4.4	3.7	4.1	4.8	4.5	4.0	3.5	3.5	4.2	3.3	3.6	4.5
Portugal	8.6	6.4	4.9	4.8	5.6	5.2	5.0	4.2	4.1	3.4	3.9	4.4	4.5	4.2	5.2	5.2	5.0	5.5	5.1	5.0
Slovak Republic	9.7	9.4	21.7	16.2	9.8	8.0	6.9	5.0	5.0	3.5	4.4	4.5	4.7	4.7	3.8	3.9	4.6	3.6	4.1	5.0
Slovenia	..	..	..	..	..	..	..	6.4	4.7	3.8	3.9	4.5	4.6	4.4	3.7	4.1	5.0	3.6	4.4	5.3
Spain	8.7	6.4	4.8	4.7	5.5	5.1	5.0	4.1	4.1	3.4	3.8	4.3	4.4	4.0	4.1	4.0	4.2	3.9	4.0	4.5
Sweden	8.1	6.7	5.0	5.0	5.4	5.1	5.3	4.6	4.4	3.4	3.7	4.2	3.9	3.2	2.9	3.5	4.2	3.0	3.8	4.4
Switzerland	4.0	3.4	3.0	3.0	3.9	3.4	3.2	2.7	2.7	2.1	2.5	2.9	2.9	2.2	1.6	1.9	2.8	1.4	2.2	3.1
Turkey	..	..	..	..	37.7	99.6	63.5	44.1	24.9	16.2	18.0	18.3	19.2	11.7	8.9	9.8	10.4	9.0	10.3	10.5
United Kingdom	7.8	7.1	5.6	5.1	5.3	4.9	4.9	4.5	4.9	4.4	4.5	5.0	4.6	3.6	3.5	3.6	4.5	3.1	3.9	4.8
United States	6.4	6.4	5.3	5.6	6.0	5.0	4.6	4.0	4.3	4.3	4.8	4.6	3.7	3.3	3.1	3.3	4.5	2.6	3.7	4.9
Euro area	7.1	6.0	4.8	4.7	5.4	5.0	4.9	4.2	4.1	3.4	3.8	4.3	4.3	3.8	3.4	3.6	4.3	3.2	3.9	4.5

Note: 10-year benchmark government bond yields where available or yield on similar financial instruments (for Korea a 5-year bond is used). For further information, see also OECD Economic Outlook Sources and Methods (http://www.oecd.org/eco/sources-and-methods).
Source: OECD Economic Outlook 88 database.

StatLink http://dx.doi.org/10.1787/888932348985

Annex Table 36. Nominal exchange rates (*vis-à-vis* the US dollar)
Average of daily rates

	Monetary unit	1999	2000	2001	2002	2003	2004	2005	2006	2007	2008	2009	Estimates and assumptions[1] 2010	2011	2012
Australia	Dollar	1.550	1.727	1.935	1.841	1.542	1.359	1.313	1.328	1.195	1.198	1.282	1.091	1.015	1.015
Austria	Schilling	12.91													
Belgium	Franc	37.86													
Canada	Dollar	1.486	1.485	1.548	1.570	1.400	1.301	1.212	1.134	1.074	1.068	1.141	1.033	1.024	1.024
Chile	Peso	508.8	539.5	634.9	688.9	691.4	609.5	559.8	530.3	522.5	523.5	558.9	512.2	491.3	491.3
Czech Republic	Koruny	34.59	38.64	38.02	32.73	28.13	25.69	23.95	22.59	20.29	17.08	19.05	18.95	17.77	17.767
Denmark	Krone	6.980	8.088	8.321	7.884	6.577	5.988	5.996	5.943	5.443	5.099	5.359	5.593	5.380	5.380
Finland	Markka	5.580													
France	Franc	6.156													
Germany	Deutschemark	1.836													
Greece	Drachma	305.7	365.5												
Hungary	Forint	237.1	282.3	286.5	257.9	224.3	202.6	199.5	210.4	183.6	172.5	202.1	206.4	197.9	197.9
Iceland	Krona	72.43	78.84	97.67	91.59	76.69	70.19	62.88	69.90	64.07	88.00	123.66	121.85	111.76	111.76
Ireland	Pound	0.739													
Israel	Sheqel	4.14	4.08	4.21	4.74	4.55	4.48	4.49	4.46	4.11	3.58	3.93	3.73	3.63	3.63
Italy	Lira	1 817													
Japan	Yen	113.9	107.8	121.5	125.3	115.9	108.1	110.1	116.4	117.8	103.4	93.6	87.5	81.4	81.4
Korea	Won	1 186.7	1 130.6	1 290.4	1 251.0	1 191.0	1 145.2	1 024.2	954.7	929.5	1 100.9	1 274.9	1 152.8	1 122.0	1 122.0
Luxembourg	Franc	37.86													
Mexico	Peso	9.553	9.453	9.344	9.660	10.790	11.281	10.890	10.903	10.929	11.153	13.504	12.639	12.405	12.405
Netherlands	Guilder	2.068													
New Zealand	Dollar	1.892	2.205	2.382	2.163	1.724	1.509	1.421	1.542	1.361	1.425	1.600	1.391	1.333	1.333
Norway	Krone	7.797	8.797	8.993	7.986	7.078	6.739	6.441	6.415	5.858	5.648	6.290	6.025	5.854	5.854
Poland	Zloty	3.964	4.346	4.097	4.082	3.888	3.651	3.234	3.103	2.765	2.410	3.119	2.993	2.834	2.834
Portugal	Escudo	188.2													
Slovak Republic	Koruna	41.36	46.23	48.35	45.30	36.76	32.23	31.04	29.65	24.68					
Slovenia	Tolar	181.7	222.7	242.8	240.3	207.1	192.3	192.8	191.0						
Spain	Peseta	156.2													
Sweden	Krona	8.262	9.161	10.338	9.721	8.078	7.346	7.472	7.373	6.758	6.597	7.653	7.181	6.714	6.714
Switzerland	Franc	1.503	1.688	1.687	1.557	1.345	1.243	1.246	1.253	1.200	1.084	1.086	1.044	0.984	0.984
Turkey	Lira	0.419	0.624	1.228	1.512	1.503	1.426	1.341	1.430	1.300	1.299	1.547	1.489	1.413	1.413
United Kingdom	Pound	0.618	0.661	0.694	0.667	0.612	0.546	0.550	0.543	0.500	0.546	0.641	0.647	0.631	0.631
United States	Dollar	1.000	1.000	1.000	1.000	1.000	1.000	1.000	1.000	1.000	1.000	1.000	1.000	1.000	1.000
Euro area	Euro	0.938	1.084	1.118	1.060	0.885	0.806	0.805	0.797	0.730	0.681	0.718	0.750	0.722	0.722

1. On the technical assumption that exchange rates remain at their levels of 26 October 2010.
Source: OECD Economic Outlook 88 database.

StatLink http://dx.doi.org/10.1787/888932349004

Annex Table 37. Effective exchange rates
Indices 2005 = 100, average of daily rates

	1997	1998	1999	2000	2001	2002	2003	2004	2005	2006	2007	2008	2009	Estimates and assumptions[1] 2010	2011	2012
Australia	96.0	89.0	89.4	83.0	77.7	80.8	90.3	97.5	100.0	98.6	104.8	102.6	98.0	111.1	115.6	115.6
Austria	95.0	96.9	97.2	95.0	95.4	96.2	99.6	100.7	100.0	100.1	100.8	101.3	102.3	99.9	100.1	100.1
Belgium	92.4	94.7	94.4	90.6	91.7	93.6	98.6	100.4	100.0	100.2	101.6	103.7	104.6	101.6	102.1	102.1
Canada	87.1	82.9	82.7	83.5	81.0	79.7	88.1	93.5	100.0	106.6	111.3	110.7	104.8	114.8	114.7	114.7
Chile	119.5	115.6	107.8	105.0	94.0	92.0	86.8	94.5	100.0	103.6	100.6	98.2	95.3	102.1	104.0	104.0
Czech Republic	78.5	79.7	79.2	80.1	84.2	93.9	93.8	94.1	100.0	105.0	107.4	119.7	114.9	117.6	120.6	120.6
Denmark	94.1	96.5	95.8	91.8	93.4	94.9	99.5	100.9	100.0	99.9	101.2	103.2	105.7	101.7	101.8	101.8
Finland	88.6	91.4	93.9	89.6	91.5	93.5	98.9	100.8	100.0	99.9	101.6	103.7	106.0	101.1	101.4	101.4
France	93.7	96.1	95.4	91.8	92.7	94.3	99.0	100.5	100.0	100.1	101.5	103.2	103.9	101.2	101.7	101.7
Germany	91.2	94.5	94.4	90.2	91.3	93.2	99.0	101.1	100.0	100.1	101.6	103.0	104.6	100.8	101.1	101.1
Greece	101.4	98.1	98.3	91.6	92.5	94.4	99.2	100.9	100.0	100.0	101.3	103.2	104.2	101.3	101.6	101.6
Hungary	108.8	98.4	94.7	89.7	91.4	97.8	97.4	99.5	100.0	93.7	99.2	99.6	90.6	89.7	89.9	89.9
Iceland	91.8	94.2	95.5	96.3	82.1	84.8	89.0	89.9	100.0	89.7	90.7	65.8	47.7	48.9	51.3	51.3
Ireland	98.6	96.0	93.3	86.8	87.9	90.1	97.9	100.2	100.0	100.2	102.6	107.9	110.1	106.2	107.3	107.3
Israel	126.3	120.3	113.3	122.9	124.3	109.1	104.9	101.1	100.0	100.3	103.7	115.6	109.9	114.8	115.0	115.0
Italy	92.9	94.9	94.6	91.0	92.3	94.3	99.1	100.8	100.0	100.1	101.4	102.9	104.1	100.9	101.2	101.2
Japan	83.9	86.4	99.4	108.0	99.5	95.6	98.9	103.1	100.0	92.6	87.5	97.5	111.2	116.2	121.9	121.9
Korea	106.6	76.7	88.3	94.5	87.3	90.3	89.8	89.8	100.0	107.4	106.8	86.0	73.4	78.9	78.4	78.4
Luxembourg	97.0	97.7	97.5	94.7	95.1	96.2	99.5	100.6	100.0	100.2	101.6	102.8	102.4	100.7	101.0	101.0
Mexico	136.9	121.6	116.1	118.6	122.0	118.5	103.4	97.2	100.0	99.3	97.3	94.6	78.7	83.2	83.9	83.9
Netherlands	90.4	93.6	93.3	88.3	89.6	91.8	98.2	100.7	100.0	100.1	102.0	104.0	104.6	100.8	101.3	101.3
New Zealand	93.8	83.8	81.1	73.4	72.3	78.4	89.3	95.5	100.0	92.4	98.8	92.4	84.8	91.2	91.3	91.3
Norway	95.5	92.6	92.3	90.2	93.2	101.2	99.1	95.8	100.0	99.5	101.0	100.9	97.8	101.9	100.7	100.7
Poland	102.3	100.3	93.4	96.1	105.9	101.5	91.4	89.5	100.0	103.1	106.8	116.3	95.5	101.2	102.7	102.7
Portugal	98.1	98.0	97.5	95.1	96.0	97.1	99.8	100.5	100.0	100.0	100.8	101.9	102.5	100.4	100.6	100.6
Slovak Republic	97.0	96.3	89.2	90.6	88.5	88.9	94.0	98.1	100.0	103.1	113.6	122.6	131.3	127.1	126.8	126.8
Slovenia	117.0	118.5	117.4	107.6	102.3	100.1	101.7	101.3	100.0	99.8	101.0	102.2	104.5	101.2	101.6	101.6
Spain	94.6	96.1	95.6	92.5	93.6	95.4	99.3	100.5	100.0	100.2	101.3	102.9	104.0	101.4	101.7	101.7
Sweden	101.1	101.0	100.7	100.9	92.7	95.1	100.7	102.5	100.0	100.4	101.6	99.6	91.4	98.7	102.0	102.0
Switzerland	86.9	91.2	91.9	90.1	93.8	98.7	100.4	100.8	100.0	98.6	96.1	101.6	107.2	113.1	115.9	115.9
Turkey	910.1	548.7	361.9	263.0	148.1	110.3	97.4	95.0	100.0	93.2	95.3	91.4	81.4	85.0	86.7	86.7
United Kingdom	91.3	97.2	97.7	100.0	99.1	100.6	96.9	101.5	100.0	100.6	102.4	89.5	79.5	79.2	78.5	78.5
United States	95.9	105.5	105.2	107.7	113.3	113.9	107.3	102.6	100.0	98.3	94.0	90.6	95.7	92.1	89.5	89.5
Euro area	85.8	90.7	89.8	81.6	83.5	87.0	97.7	101.6	100.0	100.2	103.4	107.1	109.6	102.4	103.2	103.2

Note: For details on the method of calculation, see the section on exchange rates and competitiveness indicators in *OECD Economic Outlook Sources and Methods* (*http://www.oecd.org/eco/sources-and-methods*).

1. On the technical assumption that exchange rates remain at their levels of 26 October 2010.

Source: OECD Economic Outlook 88 database.

StatLink ⬛⬛⬛ http://dx.doi.org/10.1787/888932349023

Annex Table 38. Export volumes of goods and services
National accounts basis, percentage changes from previous year

	1993	1994	1995	1996	1997	1998	1999	2000	2001	2002	2003	2004	2005	2006	2007	2008	2009	2010	2011	2012
Australia	8.3	9.0	5.0	10.5	11.6	-0.1	4.7	10.7	2.2	0.4	-2.2	4.0	2.4	3.4	3.3	3.1	1.0	4.7	6.1	6.5
Austria	-1.8	6.0	7.2	2.4	12.0	8.4	6.4	13.1	6.5	3.4	1.8	9.8	7.9	7.9	8.5	-0.4	-13.9	8.1	7.6	5.8
Belgium	-0.4	8.3	5.0	3.3	10.3	4.8	4.3	12.0	1.0	2.7	0.8	6.3	5.0	5.0	4.3	1.4	-11.4	10.1	5.2	4.8
Canada	10.8	12.7	8.5	5.6	8.3	9.1	10.7	8.9	-3.0	1.2	-2.3	5.0	1.9	0.6	1.2	-4.6	-14.2	6.8	5.3	9.4
Chile	..	..	..	11.8	11.2	5.2	7.3	5.1	7.2	1.6	6.5	13.3	4.3	5.1	7.6	3.1	-5.6	-0.5	9.9	8.5
Czech Republic	..	0.2	16.7	5.7	8.4	10.4	5.0	17.3	11.2	2.0	7.2	20.3	11.8	16.2	15.0	5.7	-10.5	11.4	7.7	6.0
Denmark	1.0	8.4	3.1	4.2	4.9	4.1	11.6	12.7	3.1	4.1	-1.0	2.8	8.0	9.0	2.2	2.4	-10.2	3.7	4.5	5.1
Finland	16.3	13.4	8.7	5.8	14.0	9.4	10.9	17.3	1.7	3.3	-1.8	8.1	7.0	12.2	8.2	6.4	-20.5	4.6	9.0	5.7
France[1]	0.5	8.2	8.5	3.3	13.1	8.4	4.2	13.0	2.5	1.4	-1.2	3.5	3.5	5.0	2.5	-0.8	-12.2	9.9	6.4	6.3
Germany	-4.8	8.1	6.7	6.2	11.8	7.4	5.6	14.2	6.8	4.3	2.4	9.2	8.0	13.5	7.9	2.0	-14.3	15.2	9.0	5.6
Greece	-2.6	7.4	3.0	3.5	20.0	5.3	18.1	14.1	0.0	-8.4	2.9	17.4	2.4	5.3	5.8	4.0	-18.1	-3.5	3.9	8.2
Hungary	..	..	..	11.1	21.0	16.5	11.1	19.7	8.0	3.8	6.2	15.0	11.3	18.6	16.2	5.7	-9.6	13.3	8.1	8.4
Iceland	6.5	9.3	-2.3	9.9	5.6	2.5	4.0	4.2	7.4	3.8	1.6	8.4	7.5	-4.6	17.7	7.1	7.4	-0.1	1.6	2.0
Ireland	9.7	15.1	20.0	12.5	17.6	23.1	15.6	20.2	8.7	5.2	0.5	7.5	4.7	4.9	8.2	-0.8	-4.2	9.8	6.7	5.8
Israel	..	..	..	5.9	9.1	6.8	14.2	22.9	-10.5	-2.0	8.1	17.6	4.2	5.9	9.3	5.9	-11.7	16.3	8.9	8.8
Italy	8.7	10.6	12.7	0.6	5.7	1.7	-0.6	13.0	2.2	-2.8	-1.5	3.6	2.0	6.5	3.9	-3.9	-19.1	7.9	6.7	5.3
Japan	0.4	3.9	4.2	5.9	11.1	-2.7	1.9	12.7	-6.9	7.5	9.2	13.9	7.0	9.7	8.4	1.6	-23.9	25.4	6.7	5.8
Korea	7.9	16.4	24.7	11.6	19.8	12.9	14.4	18.1	-3.4	12.1	14.5	19.7	7.8	11.4	12.6	6.6	-0.8	14.3	12.8	13.5
Luxembourg	4.8	7.7	4.6	2.3	11.4	11.2	14.2	12.6	4.5	2.1	6.8	11.1	4.6	13.0	9.1	6.6	-8.2	8.8	4.8	3.4
Mexico	8.1	17.7	30.2	18.2	10.6	12.3	12.3	16.3	-3.5	1.4	2.7	11.5	6.7	11.0	5.7	0.7	-15.1	24.2	7.2	8.3
Netherlands	4.0	8.7	9.2	4.4	10.9	6.8	8.7	13.5	1.9	0.9	1.5	7.9	6.0	7.3	6.4	2.8	-7.9	10.4	6.0	6.0
New Zealand	4.8	9.9	3.8	3.8	3.9	1.5	7.9	7.0	3.3	6.4	2.3	6.2	-0.5	1.7	3.9	-1.1	0.4	3.4	4.0	6.0
Norway	3.1	8.4	5.0	10.0	7.8	0.7	2.8	3.2	4.3	-0.3	-0.2	1.1	1.1	0.0	2.3	1.0	-4.0	-0.4	1.8	2.8
Poland	..	13.1	22.9	10.9	13.3	14.3	-2.6	22.3	4.2	4.8	13.9	12.7	9.3	14.9	9.1	5.8	-6.0	11.6	5.8	6.7
Portugal	-3.3	8.4	8.8	7.2	7.2	8.2	3.8	8.8	1.8	2.8	3.6	4.1	0.2	11.6	7.6	-0.3	-11.8	8.4	6.3	7.6
Slovak Republic	..	14.8	4.5	-1.4	10.0	21.0	12.2	8.9	6.9	5.2	15.9	7.4	10.0	21.0	14.3	3.2	-16.5	14.1	9.9	6.9
Slovenia	..	..	..	..	11.1	7.5	1.6	13.1	6.4	6.8	3.1	12.4	10.6	12.5	13.7	3.3	-17.7	8.7	6.4	6.6
Spain	7.8	16.7	9.4	10.3	15.0	8.0	7.5	10.2	4.2	2.0	3.7	4.2	2.5	6.7	6.7	-1.1	-11.6	9.2	8.1	10.4
Sweden	8.3	13.3	11.7	4.5	14.1	8.8	6.7	11.9	0.8	1.3	4.4	10.0	6.6	9.4	5.9	1.0	-12.3	10.6	8.0	6.6
Switzerland	1.4	1.9	0.6	3.7	11.2	4.3	6.5	12.5	0.5	-0.1	-0.5	7.9	7.8	10.3	9.6	3.3	-8.7	10.6	4.8	5.5
Turkey	7.7	15.2	8.0	22.0	19.1	12.0	-10.7	16.0	3.9	6.9	6.9	11.2	7.9	6.6	7.3	2.7	-5.3	7.1	5.8	8.2
United Kingdom	4.5	9.2	9.4	8.8	8.1	3.1	3.7	9.1	3.0	1.0	1.8	5.0	7.9	11.1	-2.6	1.0	-11.1	4.4	5.0	6.4
United States[1]	3.3	8.7	10.1	8.3	11.9	2.3	4.4	8.6	-5.6	-2.0	1.6	9.5	6.7	9.0	9.3	6.0	-9.5	11.4	8.1	9.9
Total OECD	2.8	9.0	9.0	6.6	11.3	5.3	5.5	12.1	0.0	1.9	2.5	8.4	6.0	8.8	6.4	2.0	-11.8	11.3	7.2	7.2

StatLink http://dx.doi.org/10.1787/888932349042

Note: Regional aggregates are calculated inclusive of intra-regional trade as the sum of volumes expressed in 2005 $.
1. Volume data use hedonic price deflators for certain components.
Source: OECD Economic Outlook 88 database.

Annex Table 39. Import volumes of goods and services
National accounts basis, percentage changes from previous year

	1993	1994	1995	1996	1997	1998	1999	2000	2001	2002	2003	2004	2005	2006	2007	2008	2009	2010	2011	2012
Australia	4.7	14.1	8.3	8.0	10.4	6.7	8.4	7.4	-4.6	11.2	10.6	15.1	8.6	7.2	12.2	11.1	-8.3	13.3	8.1	8.4
Austria	-3.6	8.7	6.5	4.1	7.8	5.1	5.1	10.3	5.3	0.3	4.0	9.4	7.1	5.5	6.5	-1.7	-11.9	5.5	6.6	5.3
Belgium	-0.4	7.3	4.7	3.8	9.1	5.6	2.6	12.4	0.0	0.9	0.8	6.3	6.4	4.6	4.4	2.8	-10.9	9.1	5.3	5.0
Canada	7.4	8.1	5.7	5.1	14.2	5.1	7.8	8.1	-5.1	1.7	4.1	8.0	7.1	4.9	5.9	1.2	-13.9	12.7	5.7	6.6
Chile	..	..	..	11.8	13.2	6.7	-9.5	10.1	4.1	2.3	9.7	18.4	17.2	10.6	14.5	12.2	-14.3	28.3	13.2	9.4
Czech Republic	..	7.8	21.2	12.2	6.9	8.4	4.6	17.1	12.7	4.9	8.0	17.5	5.2	14.7	14.2	4.3	-10.4	11.0	7.2	5.8
Denmark	-1.1	12.8	7.2	3.3	9.5	8.5	3.5	13.0	1.9	7.5	-1.6	7.7	11.1	13.4	2.6	3.3	-13.2	4.1	5.5	6.0
Finland	1.3	13.0	8.2	7.2	11.9	8.7	4.2	16.7	1.3	3.2	3.2	7.4	11.4	7.9	7.0	6.5	-18.1	3.5	8.4	4.8
France[1]	-3.2	8.8	7.3	2.0	8.1	11.6	6.4	15.4	2.4	1.6	1.2	6.4	6.3	5.9	5.7	0.3	-10.6	8.8	7.5	6.2
Germany	-4.6	8.3	6.8	3.7	8.3	9.0	8.2	10.7	1.5	-1.4	5.3	6.5	6.9	12.3	5.2	2.9	-9.4	13.6	7.4	4.1
Greece	0.6	1.5	8.9	7.0	14.2	9.2	15.0	15.1	1.2	-1.3	3.0	5.2	-0.3	9.1	7.1	0.2	-14.1	-11.7	-10.0	-0.5
Hungary	-7.5	3.8	..	9.0	22.2	22.9	12.3	18.0	5.4	6.7	9.3	14.3	7.1	14.8	13.3	5.8	-14.6	11.5	6.6	8.1
Iceland	..	..	3.6	16.5	8.0	23.4	4.4	8.6	-9.1	-2.6	10.7	14.5	29.3	10.4	-0.7	-18.2	-24.1	0.4	1.7	3.5
Ireland	7.5	15.5	16.4	12.9	16.6	27.5	12.4	21.7	7.1	2.7	-1.6	8.5	8.3	6.5	7.9	-2.9	-9.8	7.5	6.2	5.0
Israel	..	..	..	7.3	4.0	1.8	15.6	11.8	-5.1	-1.1	-1.3	11.7	3.3	3.2	11.9	2.3	-14.1	14.3	8.4	8.3
Italy	-11.6	8.7	9.7	-1.2	9.8	8.6	4.7	10.7	1.4	0.2	1.6	3.3	2.7	6.2	3.3	-4.3	-14.6	6.6	3.7	3.9
Japan	-1.3	8.2	14.2	13.4	0.5	-6.8	3.6	9.2	0.6	0.9	3.9	8.1	5.8	4.2	1.6	1.2	-16.7	10.5	6.6	6.5
Korea	4.9	22.8	22.5	14.7	4.2	-22.0	26.4	22.6	-4.9	14.4	11.1	11.7	7.6	11.3	11.7	4.4	-8.2	18.3	13.3	13.5
Luxembourg	5.2	6.7	4.2	5.4	12.6	11.8	14.8	10.5	6.0	0.8	6.9	11.8	4.2	12.8	9.3	8.5	-10.3	10.0	4.3	3.2
Mexico	1.9	21.2	-15.1	22.7	22.7	16.8	13.9	21.6	-1.5	1.4	0.7	10.7	8.4	12.7	7.0	3.1	-18.5	20.8	9.2	9.0
Netherlands	0.4	9.0	10.2	5.3	11.9	9.0	9.3	12.2	2.5	0.3	1.8	5.7	5.4	8.8	5.6	3.4	-8.5	10.5	4.6	5.9
New Zealand	5.4	13.1	8.7	7.6	2.1	1.3	12.0	-0.4	2.0	9.6	8.4	15.9	5.4	-2.5	8.9	2.3	-14.8	7.2	7.7	7.4
Norway	4.8	5.8	5.8	8.8	12.5	8.8	-1.6	2.0	1.7	1.0	1.4	8.8	8.7	8.4	8.6	4.3	-11.4	9.0	6.1	5.4
Poland	..	11.3	24.2	26.2	23.1	18.5	1.2	13.7	-3.6	2.6	9.6	14.2	7.6	18.8	13.7	6.2	-13.2	11.7	8.4	8.4
Portugal	-3.3	8.8	7.4	5.8	10.6	14.6	9.0	5.6	1.0	-0.5	-0.5	7.6	2.3	7.2	5.5	2.8	-10.9	5.1	0.0	3.2
Slovak Republic	..	-4.7	11.6	17.3	10.2	19.1	0.4	8.2	13.5	4.4	7.4	8.3	12.4	17.8	9.2	3.1	-17.6	11.6	7.0	6.1
Slovenia	..	..	..	..	11.3	9.6	7.8	7.1	3.1	4.9	6.7	13.3	6.7	12.2	16.7	3.8	-19.7	7.6	6.6	6.6
Spain	-5.2	11.4	11.1	8.8	13.3	14.8	13.7	10.8	4.5	3.7	6.2	9.6	7.7	10.2	8.0	-5.3	-17.8	6.4	5.8	8.7
Sweden	-2.1	12.6	7.6	3.5	12.9	11.1	4.6	12.0	-1.5	-1.2	4.0	5.6	6.9	9.6	9.3	2.4	-12.9	13.3	8.7	6.2
Switzerland	-0.1	7.7	4.0	4.0	8.1	7.4	4.1	10.3	2.3	-1.1	1.3	7.3	6.6	6.5	6.1	0.3	-5.4	8.3	6.4	6.2
Turkey	35.8	-21.9	29.6	20.5	22.4	2.3	-3.7	21.8	-24.8	20.9	23.5	20.8	12.2	6.9	10.7	-4.1	-14.3	14.1	11.5	12.9
United Kingdom	3.3	5.9	5.5	9.7	9.7	9.3	7.9	8.9	4.8	4.9	2.2	6.9	7.1	9.1	-0.8	-1.2	-12.3	7.5	3.1	4.0
United States[1]	8.6	11.9	8.0	8.7	13.5	11.7	11.5	13.0	-2.8	3.4	4.4	11.0	6.1	6.1	2.7	-2.6	-13.8	14.3	9.9	7.7
Total OECD	0.9	9.6	8.3	7.3	10.2	7.6	8.4	12.2	-0.1	2.5	3.9	8.7	6.6	8.0	5.1	0.5	-12.6	11.2	7.3	6.6

Note: Regional aggregates are calculated inclusive of intra-regional trade as the sum of volumes expressed in 2005 $.
1. Volume data use hedonic price deflators for certain components.
Source: OECD Economic Outlook 88 database.

StatLink http://dx.doi.org/10.1787/888932349061

Annex Table 40. Export prices of goods and services

National accounts basis, percentage changes from previous year, national currency terms

	1993	1994	1995	1996	1997	1998	1999	2000	2001	2002	2003	2004	2005	2006	2007	2008	2009	2010	2011	2012
Australia	1.0	-3.8	6.0	-2.3	0.0	2.3	-4.8	12.9	6.7	-2.0	-5.0	4.5	12.4	12.1	0.8	23.4	-10.5	10.7	3.0	-0.6
Austria	0.2	1.3	1.6	0.5	0.9	0.1	0.6	1.4	0.6	0.3	-0.4	1.1	1.7	2.6	1.8	2.8	-1.1	2.1	1.0	1.1
Belgium	-1.3	1.3	1.6	-1.5	1.2	-1.0	-0.1	5.5	1.4	-0.7	-1.3	2.0	4.1	2.7	2.2	4.1	-5.3	4.2	1.5	1.3
Canada	4.4	5.9	6.4	0.6	0.2	-0.3	1.1	6.2	1.3	-1.9	-1.3	2.2	2.8	0.3	0.8	10.5	-9.4	2.5	1.7	1.5
Chile	..	..	..	-8.1	-0.7	-2.9	6.6	11.0	5.5	7.1	11.2	12.3	10.3	23.9	5.9	-4.4	-7.4	17.7	7.4	3.1
Czech Republic	..	5.2	6.4	4.7	5.6	3.9	1.1	3.2	-0.3	-5.5	0.1	2.7	-2.2	-1.3	-0.1	-5.2	-1.2	-0.6	1.0	0.6
Denmark	-1.7	-0.3	1.0	1.5	2.7	-2.1	-0.5	8.2	1.6	-1.3	-1.1	1.9	5.4	3.0	2.1	5.3	-8.5	8.4	3.0	2.0
Finland	6.6	1.5	4.8	-0.5	-1.0	-1.0	-5.1	3.5	-1.3	-2.6	-1.4	-0.4	1.2	2.2	0.9	-0.9	-7.4	4.4	2.7	2.5
France[1]	-2.2	-0.4	-0.5	0.9	1.3	-1.5	-1.6	2.4	-0.3	-1.7	-1.8	0.6	2.1	2.5	1.5	3.9	-3.5	2.3	2.4	1.2
Germany	0.1	0.8	1.2	-0.5	0.9	-0.9	-0.9	2.5	0.4	-0.2	-1.7	0.0	0.7	1.3	0.4	0.6	-3.0	2.0	0.8	0.6
Greece	9.1	8.6	8.7	5.6	3.6	4.1	1.9	8.0	3.9	2.4	1.6	2.3	2.9	3.3	2.3	3.8	-1.7	11.2	-0.6	0.1
Hungary	..	18.5	45.5	19.3	15.8	13.2	4.8	10.3	3.0	-4.1	0.1	-1.1	-0.4	6.5	-4.0	1.0	2.2	-1.1	2.2	1.8
Iceland	4.8	6.2	4.8	-0.2	2.1	4.5	0.0	3.8	21.5	-1.7	-7.1	1.3	-4.5	21.3	2.2	35.5	12.5	10.2	4.7	3.0
Ireland	6.8	0.2	1.9	-0.3	1.2	2.8	2.3	6.2	4.6	-0.4	-5.0	-0.6	1.0	1.3	0.1	-0.7	0.6	1.0	1.4	0.8
Israel	..	..	..	7.8	6.3	6.7	9.7	-1.9	0.9	11.9	-2.0	0.8	5.0	2.2	-3.7	-6.3	3.7	-0.7	-1.0	1.7
Italy	10.4	3.4	8.2	0.3	1.3	1.4	0.7	4.4	2.3	1.4	0.4	2.6	4.0	4.6	4.1	5.1	-0.4	4.4	2.1	1.6
Japan	-7.1	-3.4	-1.9	3.5	1.8	0.9	-8.8	-4.1	2.2	-1.2	-3.4	-1.2	1.4	3.7	2.5	-4.1	-11.7	-1.3	-2.5	-0.7
Korea	1.5	1.8	1.8	-2.0	5.0	22.7	-19.6	-3.6	3.6	-8.5	-0.7	4.1	-6.7	-4.7	0.7	24.9	-1.7	1.8	-3.6	-2.1
Luxembourg	5.7	3.1	1.5	6.8	1.6	0.6	5.3	9.8	-4.0	-0.1	-1.8	6.3	7.8	8.1	4.9	0.6	-1.8	6.3	0.5	1.2
Mexico	3.3	5.9	79.5	23.0	7.2	9.3	6.6	3.4	-2.3	3.3	11.2	6.7	3.0	4.3	3.0	7.4	13.4	-3.9	3.5	4.0
Netherlands	-2.5	0.6	0.7	0.8	2.5	-2.0	-1.2	6.0	0.9	-1.8	-0.8	0.6	3.4	2.6	1.3	4.7	-5.8	5.6	1.6	1.1
New Zealand	2.1	-2.6	-0.5	-2.5	-2.4	4.9	-0.1	14.3	7.2	-7.2	-7.3	-0.1	1.2	6.9	1.2	15.2	-7.3	5.1	3.2	1.2
Norway	2.1	-2.8	1.8	6.9	2.0	-7.9	10.7	36.7	-2.2	-10.2	2.1	12.9	17.3	15.4	1.4	16.6	-14.1	4.0	1.8	1.2
Poland	..	31.7	19.6	8.5	12.7	11.8	7.1	1.8	1.0	4.5	7.6	8.8	-3.5	1.9	3.2	0.0	10.6	-1.6	3.7	2.8
Portugal	4.9	6.4	5.6	-0.8	3.2	1.5	0.4	5.4	0.7	0.0	-1.4	1.5	1.7	4.4	1.9	2.8	-4.8	3.5	1.7	1.2
Slovak Republic	..	10.7	8.4	4.3	6.5	-4.8	-1.1	17.3	4.9	1.0	1.5	1.8	1.6	2.2	0.5	1.4	-4.7	2.6	2.1	1.0
Slovenia	30.4	17.3	9.6	13.0	5.4	2.6	2.1	10.3	8.1	4.4	2.9	3.0	2.9	2.8	2.3	1.2	-0.5	2.4	1.3	0.6
Spain	5.0	4.6	5.9	1.4	3.0	0.5	0.0	7.3	1.8	0.7	-0.2	1.6	4.3	4.1	2.5	2.8	-3.3	2.2	1.0	0.5
Sweden	8.7	3.8	6.2	-4.7	-0.3	-1.4	-1.0	2.2	2.3	-1.6	-2.1	0.4	2.9	2.5	1.7	4.5	0.4	-0.2	0.9	1.1
Switzerland	2.0	-0.4	-0.3	-1.1	0.7	-0.3	-0.8	2.9	0.3	-2.4	0.5	0.5	0.8	2.7	3.8	1.6	-1.5	-0.8	0.3	0.6
Turkey	59.9	164.8	73.0	69.0	87.0	60.1	52.0	42.0	89.4	25.4	10.7	13.3	-0.2	13.7	2.1	17.5	2.8	1.7	7.9	5.7
United Kingdom	9.1	1.2	3.3	1.6	-4.1	-4.7	0.3	1.9	-0.4	0.3	1.7	-0.5	0.9	2.9	1.5	11.9	2.7	4.2	1.0	1.3
United States[1]	0.0	1.1	2.3	-1.3	-1.7	-2.3	-0.6	1.8	-0.4	-0.4	2.2	3.5	3.6	3.4	3.3	4.7	-5.4	3.8	1.7	1.5
Total OECD	2.7	4.3	6.8	2.7	2.8	2.1	-0.1	4.1	2.5	-0.2	0.4	2.2	2.1	3.1	1.9	5.0	-2.9	2.6	1.2	1.1

Note: Regional aggregates are calculated inclusive of intra-regional trade. They are calculated as the geometric averages of prices weighted by 2005 GDP volumes expressed in $.
1. Certain components are estimated on a hedonic basis.
Source: OECD Economic Outlook 88 database.

StatLink http://dx.doi.org/10.1787/888932349080

Annex Table 41. Import prices of goods and services
National accounts basis, percentage changes from previous year, national currency terms

	1993	1994	1995	1996	1997	1998	1999	2000	2001	2002	2003	2004	2005	2006	2007	2008	2009	2010	2011	2012
Australia	5.6	-4.4	3.2	-6.5	-1.5	6.5	-4.3	7.4	5.9	-4.2	-8.5	-4.8	0.6	4.2	-3.7	7.8	-2.4	-6.6	-0.2	1.0
Austria	0.8	1.2	1.4	2.2	1.8	0.3	0.5	2.9	0.5	-1.1	-0.6	1.3	2.6	3.1	2.3	4.5	-2.0	3.7	1.2	0.8
Belgium	-2.8	1.8	1.7	-0.6	1.5	-1.8	1.1	7.7	1.3	-1.8	-1.2	3.0	4.2	3.6	2.0	6.6	-8.5	5.7	1.6	1.3
Canada	6.4	6.6	3.4	-1.1	0.8	3.7	-0.2	2.1	3.0	0.6	-6.5	-2.2	-0.7	-0.7	-2.2	5.5	0.2	-3.5	1.5	1.6
Chile	..	..	..	5.4	-1.0	-0.2	3.9	8.0	10.2	3.6	2.9	-6.2	0.7	-0.5	4.3	14.0	-11.1	-1.0	3.9	3.1
Czech Republic	..	2.6	5.8	1.7	5.2	-1.7	1.6	6.1	-2.6	-8.4	-0.4	1.3	-0.5	-0.1	-1.2	-3.7	-3.6	1.0	0.6	0.7
Denmark	-1.3	0.5	0.5	-0.1	2.4	-2.1	-0.5	7.2	1.5	-2.5	-2.0	0.7	3.3	3.3	3.2	4.1	-7.9	4.9	2.2	0.7
Finland	8.1	-0.5	0.1	0.3	0.5	-2.8	-2.0	7.4	-3.0	-2.7	0.0	1.9	4.8	5.7	1.1	1.8	-7.9	4.8	2.6	2.8
France[1]	-2.2	-0.5	-0.5	0.8	0.6	-2.8	-1.7	5.4	-0.9	-4.2	-1.6	1.3	3.2	3.2	0.7	3.9	-5.2	4.6	1.5	1.2
Germany	-1.8	-0.1	-0.3	0.2	3.1	-2.4	-1.4	7.7	0.5	-2.2	-2.6	0.2	2.2	2.7	0.0	1.8	-6.8	4.4	1.4	0.4
Greece	7.4	5.6	7.5	5.0	2.8	3.8	1.7	9.3	3.0	0.8	-0.3	2.0	3.6	3.8	2.4	4.3	-1.4	3.9	-1.1	..
Hungary	..	15.6	41.1	20.8	13.7	12.0	5.6	12.7	2.4	-5.3	0.4	-1.0	1.3	8.0	-4.3	1.7	1.5	2.0	3.6	1.5
Iceland	8.7	5.9	3.7	3.1	0.0	-0.7	0.6	6.3	21.1	-2.3	-3.1	2.6	-5.4	17.3	2.1	44.4	24.8	7.5	2.7	3.0
Ireland	4.5	2.4	3.8	-0.5	0.8	2.6	2.6	7.5	3.9	-1.4	-4.0	0.1	1.8	2.3	1.6	1.9	-0.3	0.2	1.0	0.6
Israel	..	..	..	5.0	3.0	4.4	7.4	0.6	1.5	12.2	0.8	3.8	6.8	3.0	-1.9	-2.4	-4.4	2.1	0.7	2.7
Italy	15.4	4.8	11.4	-2.6	1.7	-1.6	0.7	11.2	1.4	-0.3	-1.3	2.7	6.3	7.7	2.6	6.8	-6.1	7.5	2.5	1.6
Japan	-8.4	-4.7	-2.5	8.4	6.5	-2.7	-8.5	1.5	2.4	-0.9	-0.8	2.9	8.3	11.4	7.3	5.5	-20.6	5.3	-2.4	0.1
Korea	0.2	1.0	4.3	3.0	11.4	26.8	-17.0	4.0	6.4	-8.6	0.2	7.0	-3.2	-1.2	1.4	35.2	-4.3	2.1	-2.1	-2.5
Luxembourg	3.2	2.1	1.3	5.9	5.2	1.7	3.0	12.3	-3.2	-1.0	-5.8	7.6	7.7	6.0	4.4	-1.0	-1.3	8.3	1.6	1.2
Mexico	3.7	5.1	95.1	21.4	3.6	12.0	3.7	0.1	-2.8	2.0	12.5	8.4	0.2	1.8	2.9	7.2	14.9	0.5	3.5	3.9
Netherlands	-2.4	0.3	0.3	0.7	1.5	-2.4	-0.9	5.8	-0.4	-2.9	-0.9	1.4	2.7	3.0	1.5	4.5	-5.0	5.5	1.6	1.1
New Zealand	-1.6	-3.8	-1.8	-3.7	-0.4	5.7	0.7	15.4	2.2	-5.9	-11.4	-4.3	1.0	10.0	-4.7	13.1	-1.6	-2.0	2.1	1.3
Norway	1.6	0.7	0.6	0.8	0.3	1.2	-1.1	7.5	-0.1	-5.0	1.1	4.8	1.5	3.1	3.9	3.0	-0.2	-1.9	1.1	1.6
Poland	..	27.0	18.0	11.4	15.1	11.7	7.0	7.5	0.3	5.1	7.5	6.3	-6.8	1.7	1.1	2.8	10.2	-1.9	3.7	2.8
Portugal	4.4	4.3	3.9	1.7	2.5	-1.4	-0.8	8.5	0.4	-1.6	-1.7	2.2	3.0	3.9	1.3	4.6	-8.5	4.8	1.4	1.1
Slovak Republic	..	12.3	7.3	9.6	3.6	-2.4	0.3	14.1	6.0	1.0	1.9	2.1	1.7	3.6	1.6	3.0	-5.7	3.8	2.6	1.1
Slovenia	23.1	14.4	6.9	11.6	5.0	1.9	1.9	13.9	6.3	2.5	2.1	4.1	5.0	3.3	1.4	2.7	-4.6	5.3	3.0	1.1
Spain	6.1	5.8	4.4	0.4	3.4	-1.5	0.3	10.6	-0.2	-2.0	-1.5	2.2	3.7	3.8	1.9	4.5	-6.7	6.2	1.6	0.4
Sweden	14.0	3.3	4.2	-3.9	0.0	-0.8	1.6	3.8	3.7	0.1	-2.3	1.9	4.6	2.8	0.3	4.9	-0.4	0.3	1.1	1.8
Switzerland	-1.4	-4.5	-2.6	-0.4	3.8	-1.6	-0.1	5.8	0.5	-5.9	-1.4	1.2	3.3	3.9	4.1	2.2	-6.1	-0.7	-0.6	0.2
Turkey	48.9	163.3	85.0	80.4	74.1	62.5	47.9	56.7	93.4	22.1	7.1	10.8	0.2	19.0	0.1	21.3	0.7	7.7	6.0	3.4
United Kingdom	8.6	3.0	5.9	0.1	-7.0	-5.7	-1.1	3.1	-0.2	-2.2	0.4	-0.7	3.8	2.9	0.2	11.9	3.7	3.5	2.2	2.1
United States[1]	-0.8	0.9	2.7	-1.7	-3.5	-5.4	0.6	4.3	-2.4	-1.1	3.5	4.8	6.2	4.1	3.3	10.4	-10.7	5.4	0.1	2.0
Total OECD	2.5	4.6	7.9	2.8	2.6	1.3	0.2	6.5	2.2	-1.3	0.3	2.6	3.2	4.0	1.7	7.8	-5.2	3.6	1.1	1.3

Note: Regional aggregates are calculated inclusive of intra-regional trade. They are calculated as the geometric averages of prices weighted by 2005 GDP volumes expressed in $.
1. Certain components are estimated on a hedonic basis.
Source: OECD Economic Outlook 88 database.

StatLink http://dx.doi.org/10.1787/888932349099

Annex Table 42. Competitive positions: relative consumer prices
Indices, 2005 = 100

	1993	1994	1995	1996	1997	1998	1999	2000	2001	2002	2003	2004	2005	2006	2007	2008	2009	2010
Australia	79.3	83.2	81.9	89.6	88.5	80.8	81.5	77.7	74.7	79.1	89.5	97.0	100.0	99.9	105.9	103.8	100.6	114.5
Austria	102.4	102.6	105.5	103.1	99.3	99.6	98.4	95.9	96.1	96.6	99.5	100.5	100.0	99.4	99.8	100.0	100.6	98.2
Belgium	98.0	99.6	103.0	100.5	95.3	96.1	94.8	91.1	92.0	93.5	98.0	99.8	100.0	99.7	100.5	103.3	103.4	100.6
Canada	99.4	91.3	89.3	89.4	88.7	83.7	83.1	83.6	81.1	80.4	89.4	94.2	100.0	105.6	109.6	107.3	101.9	111.6
Chile	..	..	..	..	113.1	111.8	105.5	104.1	95.7	94.7	88.6	94.7	100.0	104.0	102.1	103.6	100.0	106.6
Czech Republic	62.2	65.3	67.6	72.0	73.1	80.1	78.9	80.4	85.9	95.5	93.5	94.3	100.0	105.5	108.3	123.9	118.9	121.7
Denmark	94.2	94.0	97.3	95.9	93.4	95.5	95.6	92.2	93.5	95.4	100.3	101.0	100.0	99.7	100.2	101.8	104.9	101.3
Finland	97.8	101.5	109.0	102.7	98.9	100.6	100.3	96.0	97.3	98.5	102.7	102.6	100.0	99.0	100.3	102.1	103.0	97.2
France	102.0	101.9	104.1	103.4	99.0	99.8	97.8	93.3	93.2	94.7	99.4	101.0	100.0	99.6	99.9	100.7	100.8	97.7
Germany	107.4	108.1	112.2	107.7	102.2	103.3	100.9	94.8	94.8	95.8	100.5	101.9	100.0	99.4	100.5	100.4	101.2	96.4
Greece	88.5	89.2	92.1	94.7	95.4	93.9	94.3	88.2	89.2	91.8	97.4	99.6	100.0	100.9	102.6	104.8	106.1	105.0
Hungary	72.1	70.4	66.9	67.5	71.7	72.1	74.2	75.1	81.3	89.7	91.9	98.0	100.0	95.4	106.3	109.0	102.4	104.5
Iceland	83.9	78.6	77.5	77.0	78.6	80.6	82.7	85.9	76.3	81.6	85.8	88.1	100.0	93.7	97.5	76.4	62.0	65.9
Ireland	86.9	86.8	87.8	89.3	88.4	86.4	83.7	80.6	83.7	88.4	97.6	100.0	100.0	101.8	106.9	112.7	108.8	101.1
Israel	..	..	..	..	128.7	125.5	120.9	128.6	127.6	115.6	109.4	102.5	100.0	99.7	100.6	112.5	109.5	114.7
Italy	93.7	91.1	84.6	93.6	93.8	95.2	94.3	90.6	91.9	94.0	99.4	101.0	100.0	99.7	100.5	101.3	102.4	98.6
Japan	118.8	128.3	130.5	109.1	102.7	103.3	116.1	122.8	110.0	103.2	104.5	106.1	100.0	90.5	83.0	89.7	100.4	101.3
Korea	93.1	94.2	95.3	98.7	92.6	70.2	80.2	86.3	81.7	86.1	87.5	89.0	100.0	107.8	107.1	86.7	76.0	82.8
Luxembourg	98.7	99.9	102.3	99.9	96.2	96.2	95.5	93.5	94.1	95.4	98.9	100.2	100.0	100.9	102.3	103.2	102.9	101.6
Mexico	104.6	100.0	67.8	75.7	87.5	88.3	96.7	105.1	112.1	112.5	100.4	96.4	100.0	100.0	99.1	97.4	85.4	91.7
Netherlands	94.2	94.3	97.9	95.2	89.9	92.5	91.9	86.9	89.5	93.0	99.7	101.3	100.0	99.0	99.8	100.2	101.2	96.5
New Zealand	76.4	80.5	86.3	91.5	92.9	82.7	78.9	71.6	70.7	77.5	88.3	94.6	100.0	93.2	99.7	93.1	86.7	93.4
Norway	94.3	91.9	94.1	93.0	94.0	91.6	92.1	91.0	94.5	102.0	100.5	96.0	100.0	99.9	99.7	99.7	98.0	102.7
Poland	69.0	69.7	74.5	79.9	82.6	88.0	85.4	94.0	106.2	101.5	90.2	89.4	100.0	102.2	105.7	115.4	97.6	103.7
Portugal	92.2	90.8	94.1	94.0	92.7	93.5	93.6	91.7	94.0	96.2	99.9	100.7	100.0	100.6	101.2	101.1	100.3	103.7
Slovak Republic	66.0	65.3	66.7	66.6	70.2	70.7	69.7	76.9	77.9	78.9	89.1	97.6	100.0	105.4	116.1	125.8	135.2	129.7
Slovenia	..	..	..	..	91.4	96.5	97.3	94.1	93.9	96.3	100.9	101.4	100.0	99.8	101.6	104.2	106.0	102.5
Spain	94.9	90.7	92.0	93.5	89.2	90.2	90.1	88.1	90.1	92.5	97.2	99.3	100.0	101.5	103.0	105.1	105.1	102.0
Sweden	110.8	109.2	108.4	116.7	110.8	107.8	105.7	104.2	95.6	98.2	104.0	104.2	100.0	99.6	100.5	98.1	89.0	95.0
Switzerland	99.6	104.1	110.4	106.4	98.0	100.2	99.1	96.2	98.5	102.3	102.7	101.8	100.0	97.4	93.2	97.1	101.1	105.4
Turkey	83.3	61.2	66.4	67.1	71.5	78.8	82.8	92.5	75.5	82.4	86.9	89.9	100.0	99.7	108.1	109.7	102.6	112.9
United Kingdom	88.2	88.1	84.3	85.7	98.6	104.1	103.7	104.4	101.8	102.3	97.9	101.6	100.0	100.6	102.1	89.0	80.3	81.2
United States	89.8	90.0	88.7	91.5	95.9	103.3	102.3	105.6	111.6	112.0	105.7	101.4	100.0	99.3	95.1	91.4	95.3	91.2
Euro area	100.2	99.7	103.5	102.0	92.8	95.3	91.9	82.8	84.3	87.8	98.5	102.0	100.0	99.6	101.9	103.9	105.0	96.8

StatLink ⟳ http://dx.doi.org/10.1787/888932349118

Note Competitiveness-weighted relative consumer prices in dollar terms. Competitiveness weights take into account the structure of competition in both export and import markets of the manufacturing sector of 42 countries. An increase in the index indicates a real effective appreciation and a corresponding deterioration of the competitive position. For details on the method of calculation see Durand, M., C. Madaschi and F. Terrible (1998), "Trends in OECD Countries' International Competitiveness: The Influence of Emerging Market Economies", *OECD Economics Department Working Papers*, No. 195. See also *OECD Economic Outlook Sources and Methods (http://www.oecd.org/eco/sources-and-methods)*.

Source: OECD Economic Outlook 88 database.

Annex Table 43. Competitive positions: relative unit labour costs

Indices, 2005 = 100

	1993	1994	1995	1996	1997	1998	1999	2000	2001	2002	2003	2004	2005	2006	2007	2008	2009	2010
Australia	64.5	68.2	71.3	79.4	80.5	73.3	77.5	73.2	67.0	71.4	81.6	92.1	100.0	100.3	109.4	106.6	105.6	116.6
Austria	111.2	111.6	109.1	103.6	100.5	101.7	100.4	94.8	93.9	95.1	98.8	100.5	100.0	97.5	96.7	93.9	95.6	96.1
Belgium	99.8	103.4	105.2	100.9	93.3	94.0	95.3	90.3	92.4	94.4	99.7	100.5	100.0	102.5	103.3	103.1	104.2	99.7
Canada	72.0	67.2	69.0	71.7	71.5	68.1	68.5	65.7	66.0	69.1	79.7	92.1	100.0	109.4	117.9	115.5	109.5	115.7
Czech Republic	65.5	63.8	63.2	68.8	69.3	78.5	74.9	75.1	85.7	96.9	102.4	99.2	100.0	100.5	102.1	109.3	108.8	102.8
Denmark	82.3	80.2	83.9	85.1	82.5	85.7	86.5	83.6	85.5	89.4	95.8	98.7	100.0	100.7	104.4	105.9	108.1	104.2
Finland	103.7	109.2	126.6	119.7	112.6	112.3	112.6	101.6	100.1	97.9	100.5	101.7	100.0	93.7	88.0	87.0	89.4	84.5
France	109.8	110.9	112.7	111.9	105.1	102.5	99.8	95.0	93.8	95.7	98.5	101.2	100.0	101.2	103.4	104.1	106.7	101.4
Germany	104.8	105.0	114.6	112.6	103.6	106.1	105.9	99.3	98.0	100.3	104.7	104.8	100.0	96.0	95.2	97.3	100.3	97.0
Greece	83.2	85.2	89.3	91.5	97.9	94.0	91.1	86.2	86.1	103.2	105.8	105.5	100.0	103.0	104.0	96.2	102.5	96.4
Hungary	100.4	89.7	81.3	76.7	78.0	75.9	75.4	81.1	85.8	92.7	90.6	97.0	100.0	92.1	97.7	99.6	94.1	88.2
Iceland	61.7	60.4	61.0	60.8	64.2	69.9	77.6	84.2	73.5	78.2	82.5	85.6	100.0	97.4	104.3	77.0	52.8	60.1
Ireland	129.7	128.2	119.7	118.8	113.2	102.3	94.8	88.8	87.0	81.6	90.2	94.3	100.0	99.6	95.9	100.6	92.7	81.7
Israel	..	..	..	..	114.4	114.3	114.3	124.4	127.2	113.1	104.5	100.9	100.0	102.2	107.0	117.0	107.8	112.2
Italy	80.5	76.6	69.6	79.0	81.7	82.3	83.3	79.1	80.6	84.6	94.1	98.6	100.0	101.0	103.9	107.8	109.9	106.1
Japan	134.2	152.9	151.3	123.6	117.9	122.0	138.9	143.2	131.2	122.2	114.6	111.7	100.0	88.6	79.1	84.8	91.3	86.3
Korea	102.6	106.5	117.9	127.3	112.7	77.8	80.5	85.0	79.3	84.2	84.3	87.5	100.0	103.9	101.3	76.8	62.9	65.1
Luxembourg	90.0	90.4	98.2	96.8	92.0	88.5	84.7	83.3	88.4	89.5	92.7	95.6	100.0	106.1	99.9	103.9	118.1	112.2
Mexico	93.4	90.4	56.2	59.1	70.3	72.0	82.2	96.5	106.1	110.1	99.3	97.2	100.0	101.7	100.3	94.0	78.0	83.3
Netherlands	97.3	95.1	97.6	94.4	91.6	94.9	94.6	87.9	89.5	93.4	101.4	103.4	100.0	98.1	97.7	100.0	98.5	94.2
New Zealand	64.4	69.7	73.9	80.2	83.4	74.6	72.0	64.6	64.4	70.9	83.0	92.6	100.0	95.4	103.4	95.5	86.7	94.1
Norway	68.9	71.7	76.1	75.8	80.2	82.9	87.2	88.4	90.8	101.4	96.8	93.8	100.0	108.4	115.1	115.8	111.2	119.0
Poland	99.6	105.7	111.5	118.0	121.7	128.9	122.7	125.7	129.4	114.2	93.8	88.7	100.0	98.0	98.5	105.1	82.9	83.5
Portugal	93.0	93.0	95.6	92.1	90.7	93.6	95.3	93.2	93.6	95.1	96.8	98.5	100.0	101.1	99.7	100.0	98.4	97.2
Slovak Republic	73.9	89.0	96.5	100.5	120.8	109.6	100.0	116.6	103.6	104.1	104.7	100.6	100.0	104.7	108.5	110.1	109.5	99.7
Slovenia	..	..	..	..	81.7	85.6	87.8	87.1	88.2	89.8	95.3	99.5	100.0	101.1	103.7	105.2	111.3	110.8
Spain	90.6	86.7	87.0	89.0	87.0	87.2	85.6	84.7	85.7	88.2	93.9	97.7	100.0	102.6	106.5	108.7	107.7	105.8
Sweden	144.2	134.9	129.3	145.9	135.4	126.8	117.9	118.1	113.0	108.6	110.8	106.3	100.0	95.2	99.1	97.2	94.1	96.4
Turkey	117.9	82.2	70.0	68.4	77.0	83.9	108.2	116.5	88.2	89.8	87.5	90.7	100.0	96.7	101.9	102.4	88.4	92.4
United Kingdom	71.5	70.8	68.9	69.8	83.3	94.6	96.3	98.6	95.9	99.6	96.5	101.2	100.0	102.4	105.7	91.6	87.4	93.0
United States	126.7	124.8	118.5	119.9	124.1	131.7	128.7	135.0	138.0	128.9	119.8	105.3	100.0	96.8	88.6	85.0	89.9	84.7
Euro area	99.5	98.7	103.8	104.5	94.0	94.9	93.5	82.9	82.4	87.2	98.5	103.0	100.0	98.8	100.5	104.0	107.3	99.2

Note: Competitiveness-weighted relative unit labour costs in the manufacturing sector in dollar terms. Competitiveness weights take into account the structure of competition in both export and import markets of the manufacturing sector of 42 countries. An increase in the index indicates a real effective appreciation and a corresponding deterioration of the competitive position. For details on the method of calculation see Durand, M., C. Madaschi and F. Terribile (1998), "Trends in OECD Countries' International Competitiveness: The Influence of Emerging Market Economies", *OECD Economics Department Working Papers*, No. 195. See also *OECD Economic Outlook Sources and Methods (http://www.oecd.org/eco/sources-and-methods)*.

Source: OECD Economic Outlook 88 database.

StatLink ⌦ http://dx.doi.org/10.1787/888932349137

Annex Table 44. **Export performance for total goods and services**

Percentage changes from previous year

	1995	1996	1997	1998	1999	2000	2001	2002	2003	2004	2005	2006	2007	2008	2009	2010	2011	2012
Australia	-7.0	0.7	4.4	1.2	-0.1	-1.9	2.1	-5.2	-9.7	-8.3	-6.6	-5.1	-4.1	-1.9	12.3	-7.7	-3.4	-3.1
Austria	-1.2	-2.8	2.1	0.2	0.2	1.5	4.2	1.7	-3.2	0.9	0.4	-2.5	1.0	-3.2	-2.6	-2.3	0.3	-0.3
Belgium	-3.0	-2.1	0.2	-3.5	-2.0	-0.1	-0.9	1.0	-3.0	-1.9	-2.0	-3.8	-1.8	-0.6	-0.1	-0.3	-1.6	-1.3
Canada	0.4	-3.0	-3.8	-0.9	0.2	-3.6	-1.0	-2.3	-6.7	-5.5	-4.5	-5.8	-2.4	-3.4	-1.2	-6.2	-3.9	1.4
Chile	..	1.8	1.0	2.2	1.7	-6.6	6.8	-1.2	-0.3	1.6	-3.9	-4.1	-0.8	-0.8	5.4	-12.7	0.5	-1.0
Czech Republic	7.5	-0.6	-1.5	0.8	-0.6	5.5	8.1	0.6	2.0	11.0	3.7	4.4	7.1	2.8	2.0	0.8	0.6	0.2
Denmark	-4.9	-2.1	-5.1	-3.8	5.5	1.2	2.0	2.3	-5.3	-5.4	0.3	-0.4	-4.5	0.0	1.9	-6.5	-2.8	-1.3
Finland	-0.3	-0.2	3.6	3.6	7.0	4.0	-0.7	-0.2	-7.5	-2.3	-2.3	1.0	-1.8	1.6	-7.7	-5.9	0.4	-1.7
France	0.1	-2.7	2.5	1.0	-1.7	1.6	0.7	-1.1	-5.6	-5.1	-4.0	-3.8	-4.3	-3.1	-0.7	0.4	-0.6	-0.4
Germany	-2.1	-0.4	1.2	-0.1	0.0	1.6	4.8	1.2	-2.2	-0.5	0.3	4.1	0.4	-0.2	-2.4	5.0	1.6	-1.5
Greece	-4.9	-2.3	8.8	-1.8	12.9	3.7	-1.7	-11.3	-2.3	7.0	-5.7	-3.5	-2.4	0.0	-6.9	-9.6	-3.2	1.2
Hungary	25.0	5.1	10.4	7.8	5.2	7.9	5.2	2.1	1.1	5.8	3.4	7.5	7.9	2.8	2.8	3.9	1.0	2.3
Iceland	-9.6	3.2	-4.0	-5.7	-3.0	-6.2	5.0	1.3	-1.9	0.2	0.1	-12.9	11.5	5.4	21.9	-8.6	-4.5	-3.8
Ireland	11.4	5.6	7.0	14.2	7.8	7.7	7.4	2.5	-3.2	-0.8	-2.0	-3.2	3.4	-1.7	8.5	-0.8	-0.1	-0.4
Israel	..	-1.6	-1.8	0.6	7.7	8.7	-9.7	-5.3	2.5	5.8	-3.0	-1.9	3.2	4.5	0.3	2.9	0.2	0.6
Italy	4.2	-5.6	-4.1	-5.5	-6.1	1.1	0.2	-5.4	-6.2	-5.6	-5.8	-2.7	-3.9	-6.9	-8.4	-1.2	-0.6	-1.5
Japan	-6.8	-2.8	1.2	-3.9	-6.3	-1.9	-5.9	0.2	-0.3	-0.1	-2.2	-0.3	0.1	-2.4	-16.6	8.5	-3.5	-4.0
Korea	11.8	1.5	9.6	10.6	7.3	3.6	-4.1	4.7	3.7	4.7	-2.2	0.8	3.4	1.9	7.9	-0.2	2.1	2.8
Luxembourg	-2.8	-2.3	1.8	2.7	7.6	0.8	2.7	0.8	3.3	3.5	-2.1	4.0	3.3	5.2	3.7	-1.1	-1.7	-2.1
Mexico	20.6	8.9	-2.2	1.4	1.8	3.4	-1.3	-1.7	-1.9	0.5	0.1	4.2	1.9	2.2	-2.0	9.5	-2.1	0.5
Netherlands	1.3	-1.0	1.1	-1.1	2.5	1.4	0.2	-1.0	-2.5	-0.5	-1.4	-1.9	-0.1	0.5	4.3	0.2	-0.9	0.0
New Zealand	-5.8	-4.5	-4.5	-1.4	1.0	-4.0	4.3	0.4	-4.8	-5.5	-8.8	-6.5	-3.8	-6.5	11.8	-8.0	-4.5	-2.5
Norway	-2.6	3.5	-2.3	-7.1	-3.8	-7.6	2.7	-2.8	-3.6	-6.5	-5.8	-8.3	-2.5	-0.5	9.1	-9.8	-4.5	-3.1
Poland	13.2	5.6	3.5	5.9	-7.5	9.8	1.1	2.9	8.4	3.6	1.4	3.6	1.1	2.3	7.4	1.7	-1.3	0.8
Portugal	0.6	1.0	-3.1	-1.1	-3.4	-2.5	-0.8	0.2	-0.6	-4.3	-7.0	2.3	0.5	-1.1	0.8	-0.5	-0.4	0.7
Slovak Republic	-5.3	-7.4	-0.1	10.9	5.9	-3.0	3.4	3.2	9.8	-2.5	2.9	8.7	5.2	0.2	-5.3	3.7	2.7	0.9
Slovenia	-7.5	-1.7	1.5	-0.4	-2.9	2.0	2.9	4.8	-1.7	3.5	2.8	2.1	4.9	0.0	-5.9	1.0	-0.4	0.6
Spain	1.9	4.5	4.4	-0.8	1.5	-0.9	2.2	0.2	0.3	-3.7	-4.3	-1.9	0.4	-3.4	-0.2	0.1	1.6	4.1
Sweden	3.4	-2.3	3.2	1.1	2.0	0.7	-0.7	-1.6	0.4	0.5	-1.9	0.0	-0.9	-2.2	-0.1	0.9	0.6	-0.2
Switzerland	-7.3	-2.1	1.3	-2.8	0.1	0.7	-1.0	-2.2	-5.1	-1.1	0.2	1.0	2.6	0.9	3.0	0.0	-2.5	-1.2
Turkey	0.2	15.8	3.3	4.5	-14.9	4.8	0.4	3.7	2.3	1.7	-1.2	-2.6	-2.1	-2.0	6.9	0.3	-1.0	1.5
United Kingdom	0.3	2.1	-2.2	-4.4	-2.4	-3.1	1.9	-1.7	-2.4	-4.4	-0.2	2.4	-9.4	-1.3	0.3	-5.5	-2.6	-0.8
United States	3.1	-0.5	0.9	-1.6	-1.9	-3.5	-5.2	-4.9	-3.3	-1.1	-1.7	0.1	1.3	2.0	2.6	-1.6	0.0	1.5
Total OECD	0.4	-0.6	0.8	-1.1	-0.9	-0.2	-0.8	-1.3	-2.6	-1.6	-1.9	-0.3	-0.8	-0.7	-0.4	-0.1	-0.8	-0.3
Memorandum items																		
China	-3.0	9.2	13.0	3.3	6.0	13.5	6.5	21.4	19.7	11.5	14.5	14.4	12.3	4.9	2.7	15.8	3.9	3.6
Other industrialised Asia[1]	1.1	-1.7	-0.7	-0.8	-0.9	3.2	-2.7	1.8	0.7	2.1	1.5	1.4	0.1	-0.1	-0.6	3.2	-0.8	-0.2
Russia	..	-3.0	-10.3	-5.1	6.0	-1.7	2.3	6.6	6.3	1.7	-1.7	-2.2	-2.2	-2.9	6.5	-2.9	-3.1	-2.0
Brazil	..	..	-2.0	-1.0	2.6	2.0	10.5	8.4	2.5	1.8	-0.9	-4.5	-3.5	-5.9	1.8	-4.9	-5.4	-0.5
Other oil producers	-4.0	-4.4	0.0	-0.8	-7.9	-3.4	0.8	-3.8	4.1	-4.0	0.7	-4.2	-2.2	-0.5	2.8	-7.8	-0.8	-0.9
Rest of the world	-0.6	-0.9	-3.0	-1.8	-0.9	-3.5	2.9	-0.3	0.0	-0.4	-2.3	-3.1	-2.4	0.3	4.2	-5.7	-0.5	-0.6

Note: Regional aggregates are calculated inclusive of intra-regional trade. Export performance is the ratio between export volumes and export markets for total goods and services. The calculation of export markets is based on a weighted average of import volumes in each exporting country's markets, with weights based on trade flows in 2005.

1. Chinese Taipei; Hong Kong, China; Malaysia; Philippines; Singapore; Vietnam; Thailand; India and Indonesia.

Source: OECD Economic Outlook 88 database.

StatLink ⟶ http://dx.doi.org/10.1787/888932349156

Annex Table 45. Shares in world exports and imports
Percentage, values for goods and services, national accounts basis

	1996	1997	1998	1999	2000	2001	2002	2003	2004	2005	2006	2007	2008	2009	2010	2011	2012
A. Exports																	
Canada	3.5	3.6	3.7	4.0	4.2	4.1	3.8	3.5	3.4	3.3	3.1	2.9	2.7	2.5	2.5	2.4	2.4
France	5.4	5.3	5.7	5.4	4.8	4.9	4.9	5.0	4.7	4.3	4.1	4.0	3.9	3.9	3.5	3.6	3.5
Germany	9.1	8.6	9.2	8.8	8.0	8.7	9.0	9.4	9.3	8.9	9.0	9.1	8.7	8.7	8.2	8.3	8.1
Italy	4.7	4.4	4.5	4.1	3.8	4.0	3.9	4.0	3.9	3.6	3.5	3.6	3.4	3.2	2.9	2.9	2.9
Japan	6.8	6.7	6.2	6.4	6.5	5.7	5.6	5.5	5.4	5.1	4.7	4.5	4.3	4.1	4.5	4.5	4.3
United Kingdom	5.3	5.6	5.7	5.5	5.2	5.2	5.2	5.1	4.9	4.7	4.7	4.3	4.0	3.8	3.5	3.4	3.3
United States	13.0	13.8	14.0	14.0	13.9	13.4	12.5	11.2	10.5	10.2	9.9	9.6	9.3	10.1	9.8	9.6	9.7
Other OECD countries	26.4	26.0	27.2	27.2	26.5	27.1	27.4	27.9	28.0	27.4	27.0	27.4	27.3	27.8	26.8	26.9	26.7
Total OECD	74.3	73.9	76.0	75.4	72.8	73.1	72.4	71.5	70.1	67.4	66.0	65.4	63.6	64.0	61.8	61.5	60.9
China	2.6	3.0	3.0	3.1	3.5	3.9	4.5	5.2	5.8	6.5	7.2	7.8	8.0	8.5	9.5	9.9	10.4
Other industrialised Asia	12.4	12.4	11.4	11.6	12.4	11.8	11.9	11.5	11.6	11.6	11.7	11.5	11.2	11.9	12.9	12.8	13.0
Brazil	0.8	0.9	0.9	0.8	0.8	0.9	0.9	0.9	1.0	1.0	1.1	1.1	1.1	1.1	1.3	1.4	1.4
Russia	1.5	1.4	1.3	1.2	1.5	1.5	1.5	1.6	1.8	2.1	2.3	2.3	2.6	2.2	2.4	2.3	2.2
Other oil producers	3.9	3.8	2.9	3.5	4.7	4.3	4.3	4.6	5.1	6.5	6.9	7.0	8.1	6.6	7.2	7.0	7.0
Rest of the world	4.5	4.6	4.6	4.4	4.3	4.5	4.5	4.6	4.7	4.8	4.9	5.0	5.3	5.6	5.1	5.1	5.1
Total of non-OECD countries	25.7	26.1	24.0	24.6	27.2	26.9	27.6	28.5	29.9	32.6	34.0	34.6	36.4	36.0	38.2	38.5	39.1
B. Imports																	
Canada	3.2	3.5	3.6	3.7	3.7	3.5	3.4	3.2	3.0	3.0	3.0	2.8	2.6	2.7	2.7	2.6	2.6
France	5.2	4.8	5.2	5.0	4.7	4.7	4.7	4.8	4.7	4.5	4.4	4.4	4.3	4.3	4.0	4.0	3.9
Germany	8.9	8.4	8.8	8.7	8.0	8.1	7.9	8.4	8.1	7.8	8.0	7.9	7.7	7.8	7.5	7.5	7.2
Italy	3.9	3.8	4.0	3.8	3.7	3.8	3.8	3.9	3.8	3.6	3.7	3.7	3.5	3.4	3.1	3.1	3.0
Japan	6.6	6.1	5.2	5.4	5.6	5.3	4.9	4.7	4.7	4.6	4.4	4.1	4.4	4.0	4.3	4.2	4.1
United Kingdom	5.4	5.6	5.9	5.9	5.5	5.7	5.8	5.6	5.5	5.3	5.3	5.0	4.4	4.3	4.0	3.8	3.7
United States	14.7	15.6	16.6	17.8	18.7	18.3	17.9	16.7	16.1	15.9	15.4	14.1	13.2	12.8	13.1	12.8	12.8
Other OECD countries	26.1	25.7	26.4	26.5	25.8	25.9	26.3	26.9	27.1	26.7	26.7	27.4	27.3	26.8	26.1	26.2	26.0
Total OECD	74.1	73.5	75.7	76.8	75.7	75.3	74.8	74.3	73.0	71.6	70.8	69.3	67.3	66.0	64.8	64.3	63.3
China	2.4	2.4	2.4	2.7	3.2	3.5	4.1	4.8	5.4	5.6	5.9	6.1	6.4	7.2	8.4	8.8	9.3
Other industrialised Asia	12.8	12.8	10.8	10.9	11.6	10.9	10.9	10.6	10.9	11.1	11.1	10.9	11.2	11.6	12.8	12.9	13.2
Brazil	1.1	1.2	1.1	0.9	1.0	1.0	0.8	0.7	0.7	0.8	0.9	1.0	1.2	1.2	1.4	1.6	1.8
Russia	1.3	1.3	1.1	0.7	0.8	1.0	1.1	1.1	1.2	1.3	1.4	1.7	1.9	1.6	1.7	1.8	1.8
Other oil producers	3.1	3.2	3.1	2.9	2.9	3.2	3.4	3.4	3.5	4.1	4.2	4.8	5.3	5.7	5.2	5.1	5.1
Rest of the world	5.3	5.6	5.8	5.2	4.9	5.2	5.0	5.1	5.3	5.5	5.8	6.2	6.8	6.6	5.6	5.6	5.6
Total of non-OECD countries	25.9	26.5	24.3	23.2	24.3	24.7	25.2	25.7	27.0	28.4	29.2	30.7	32.7	34.0	35.2	35.7	36.7

Note: Regional aggregates are calculated inclusive of intra-regional trade.
Source: OECD Economic Outlook 88 database.

StatLink ⟋⟍ http://dx.doi.org/10.1787/888932349175

Annex Table 46. **Geographical structure of world trade growth**
Average of export and import volumes

	1996	1997	1998	1999	2000	2001	2002	2003	2004	2005	2006	2007	2008	2009	2010	2011	2012
A. Trade growth																	
						Percentage changes from previous year											
OECD America[1]	8.8	12.7	7.8	8.8	11.3	-3.7	1.2	2.7	9.8	6.2	6.9	5.2	0.7	-12.8	13.5	8.5	8.5
OECD Europe	5.4	10.6	8.2	5.9	12.3	2.9	1.7	2.5	7.2	6.3	9.2	5.6	1.0	-11.8	9.5	6.4	5.8
OECD Asia & Pacific[2]	10.4	7.1	-4.1	7.1	12.6	-2.9	6.6	7.7	12.1	6.5	7.9	7.7	3.4	-13.0	16.0	8.9	9.0
Total OECD	7.0	10.7	6.5	6.9	12.1	0.3	2.1	3.2	8.5	6.3	8.4	5.8	1.2	-12.2	11.4	7.3	7.0
China	23.0	17.4	1.7	17.5	25.3	6.9	25.7	28.2	23.8	18.9	20.2	17.1	6.5	-4.0	25.8	13.5	13.3
Other industrialised Asia	6.5	7.7	-2.7	3.9	17.5	-4.1	7.8	9.9	16.8	11.4	10.9	7.6	6.9	-10.3	17.9	10.2	10.1
Brazil	..	13.3	2.2	-6.7	11.6	5.8	-2.9	4.8	14.4	9.0	10.8	12.5	8.4	-11.0	21.3	8.0	12.0
Russia	2.8	-0.2	-5.0	2.4	15.3	8.4	11.7	14.2	15.7	10.1	12.6	14.4	7.0	-17.1	8.9	8.3	7.0
Other oil producers	4.7	9.7	1.2	-2.2	9.2	4.1	3.7	9.0	9.5	13.8	5.9	12.0	8.1	-6.4	3.0	8.1	8.4
Rest of the world	6.1	9.0	5.1	0.5	5.3	4.8	1.2	6.8	10.9	8.9	9.0	10.3	7.4	-10.7	0.5	7.3	7.4
Total Non-OECD	7.1	8.9	0.3	2.2	13.8	1.6	7.9	12.0	15.4	12.6	11.7	11.4	7.1	-8.8	14.1	10.1	10.2
World	7.0	10.2	4.9	5.7	12.5	0.7	3.6	5.5	10.5	8.1	9.4	7.5	3.1	-11.1	12.3	8.3	8.1
B. Contribution to World Trade growth																	
						Percentage points											
OECD America[1]	1.7	2.5	1.6	1.8	2.4	-0.8	0.2	0.5	1.9	1.2	1.3	0.9	0.1	-2.2	2.3	1.5	1.5
OECD Europe	2.4	4.6	3.6	2.7	5.5	1.3	0.8	1.1	3.2	2.7	3.9	2.3	0.4	-4.8	3.8	2.5	2.2
OECD Asia & Pacific[2]	1.0	0.7	-0.4	0.6	1.1	-0.3	0.5	0.7	1.1	0.6	0.7	0.7	0.3	-1.1	1.4	0.8	0.8
Total OECD	5.1	7.8	4.8	5.1	9.1	0.3	1.6	2.3	6.1	4.4	5.8	4.0	0.8	-8.1	7.5	4.7	4.5
China	0.5	0.4	0.0	0.4	0.7	0.2	0.9	1.1	1.2	1.0	1.2	1.1	0.5	-0.3	2.1	1.2	1.3
Other industrialised Asia	0.7	0.8	-0.2	0.2	1.7	-0.4	0.7	1.0	1.8	1.3	1.2	0.9	0.8	-1.2	2.2	1.3	1.3
Brazil	..	0.1	0.0	-0.1	0.1	0.1	0.0	0.0	0.1	0.1	0.1	0.1	0.1	-0.1	0.2	0.1	0.1
Russia	0.0	0.0	0.0	0.0	0.2	0.1	0.2	0.2	0.2	0.2	0.2	0.3	0.1	-0.3	0.2	0.1	0.1
Other oil producers	0.3	0.5	0.1	-0.1	0.4	0.2	0.2	0.4	0.5	0.7	0.3	0.6	0.4	-0.4	0.2	0.4	0.5
Rest of the world	0.3	0.5	0.3	0.0	0.3	0.2	0.1	0.3	0.6	0.5	0.5	0.5	0.4	-0.6	0.0	0.4	0.4
Total Non-OECD	2.0	2.4	0.1	0.6	3.4	0.4	2.0	3.2	4.3	3.7	3.6	3.5	2.3	-2.9	4.8	3.5	3.6
World	7.0	10.2	4.9	5.7	12.5	0.7	3.6	5.5	10.5	8.1	9.4	7.5	3.1	-11.1	12.3	8.3	8.1

Note: Regional aggregates are calculated inclusive of intra-regional trade as the sum of volumes expressed in 2005 $.
1. Canada, Chile, Mexico and United States.
2. Australia, Japan, Korea and New Zealand.
Source: OECD Economic Outlook 88 database.

StatLink http://dx.doi.org/10.1787/888932349194

Annex Table 47. **Trade balances for goods and services**
$ billion, national accounts basis

	1993	1994	1995	1996	1997	1998	1999	2000	2001	2002	2003	2004	2005	2006	2007	2008	2009	2010	2011	2012
Australia	-1.7	-4.6	-5.4	-0.6	1.7	-6.7	-10.2	-4.2	2.3	-4.4	-13.8	-18.0	-13.5	-9.2	-18.1	-9.3	-6.2	17.4	23.8	14.7
Austria	0.0	-1.7	-1.3	-4.2	-1.7	0.8	1.9	2.9	4.1	8.7	8.3	10.3	11.1	15.3	21.3	22.7	15.7	18.2	22.0	25.4
Belgium	7.2	8.9	11.1	8.7	9.4	9.8	10.6	6.7	8.5	14.4	17.0	17.8	15.4	15.3	17.6	4.6	13.2	12.3	12.8	12.8
Canada	0.0	6.7	18.9	24.7	12.6	12.3	24.2	41.6	41.2	32.4	32.5	42.7	42.5	32.0	27.1	24.8	-23.1	-24.4	-26.9	-15.6
Chile	..	..	1.5	-1.3	-1.7	-2.6	1.6	1.4	1.0	1.6	3.1	8.8	10.2	22.1	22.9	7.5	13.0	11.0	13.7	14.5
Czech Republic	0.0	-1.0	-2.4	-3.6	-3.0	-0.7	-0.7	-1.7	-1.6	-1.6	-2.1	0.1	4.0	4.9	8.8	10.0	10.8	10.2	13.1	14.0
Denmark	9.4	8.1	7.4	9.1	6.3	3.7	8.8	9.6	10.7	10.2	13.3	11.9	12.7	8.7	7.6	9.3	11.0	15.9	17.5	19.6
Finland	4.0	5.6	9.7	8.9	9.0	10.5	11.8	11.1	11.6	12.5	11.2	12.3	8.0	9.8	12.5	11.2	5.9	6.5	8.2	9.4
France	12.3	12.2	18.1	23.2	40.9	38.0	30.7	12.8	15.0	25.1	17.7	2.3	-18.2	-29.5	-50.3	-64.6	-51.7	-63.8	-73.3	-77.9
Germany	-0.9	2.7	11.8	22.1	27.0	29.6	18.0	7.0	38.4	93.4	98.2	137.7	147.0	168.1	239.4	234.4	165.4	172.5	211.5	252.6
Greece	-10.7	-9.3	-12.4	-14.1	-13.1	-14.7	-15.7	-17.2	-17.2	-20.1	-23.9	-22.7	-22.3	-28.0	-34.5	-36.0	-32.1	-19.0	-8.0	-1.9
Hungary	..	..	0.0	0.3	0.6	-0.6	-1.2	-1.6	-0.5	-1.3	-3.2	-3.7	-2.4	-1.2	1.6	0.8	6.9	5.9	6.9	8.4
Iceland	0.2	0.3	0.3	0.0	0.0	-0.4	-0.4	-0.6	-0.1	0.1	-0.3	-0.7	-2.0	-3.0	-2.2	-0.7	1.1	1.3	1.6	1.6
Ireland	5.5	5.7	7.9	8.9	10.6	10.4	13.5	12.9	16.3	21.3	25.5	27.8	23.9	21.7	23.4	23.8	34.1	41.5	48.3	53.3
Israel	..	..	-7.8	-7.9	-5.4	-3.0	-3.1	-0.4	-3.0	-3.4	-0.9	0.1	-0.3	0.7	-2.2	-3.0	4.8	4.9	4.5	4.6
Italy	31.4	36.1	43.2	58.5	46.3	37.1	22.1	10.5	15.3	11.6	9.0	11.4	-0.9	-14.9	-5.2	-13.4	-8.3	-18.8	-6.0	2.7
Japan	96.9	96.5	74.8	23.4	47.4	72.4	69.4	68.0	26.2	51.2	69.3	89.0	63.3	54.5	73.3	6.1	15.7	69.3	76.6	67.1
Korea	3.1	-1.5	-2.8	-15.8	-3.6	43.2	29.8	15.3	11.4	8.4	14.7	29.9	22.8	13.2	15.8	-12.3	33.1	22.9	13.7	17.9
Luxembourg	2.8	3.6	4.4	4.2	3.2	3.2	4.1	4.3	3.6	4.4	7.0	8.3	9.6	13.1	16.6	18.9	17.5	16.9	18.0	19.0
Mexico	-15.8	-20.1	7.8	7.2	0.0	-8.5	-7.6	-11.3	-13.7	-11.4	-10.1	-13.2	-12.2	-11.7	-16.3	-23.7	-12.4	-21.8	-31.7	-37.9
Netherlands	17.7	19.8	23.8	22.1	21.9	18.9	17.4	21.3	23.2	28.8	33.9	45.1	54.5	52.5	64.5	71.4	57.7	64.3	80.1	86.6
New Zealand	1.2	1.1	0.7	0.3	0.3	0.2	-0.6	0.4	1.5	0.8	0.7	-0.4	-2.2	-1.7	-1.5	-2.4	1.5	3.2	2.6	2.1
Norway	7.6	7.6	9.2	14.3	13.0	2.8	11.6	28.7	28.9	25.8	29.2	35.1	49.6	60.7	59.8	87.0	56.3	57.1	56.6	54.9
Poland	1.0	2.3	3.3	-1.7	-6.1	-9.2	-10.3	-10.7	-6.9	-6.6	-5.3	-5.8	-1.0	-5.7	-11.0	-20.8	-1.5	-1.4	-6.9	-11.8
Portugal	-6.9	-7.2	-7.9	-8.7	-9.4	-11.4	-13.0	-13.0	-12.3	-11.0	-11.0	-15.5	-18.1	-17.5	-18.6	-25.4	-17.9	-17.5	-13.7	-10.7
Slovak Republic	-0.6	0.9	0.4	-2.3	-2.1	-2.4	-0.9	-0.5	-1.7	-1.8	-0.6	-1.1	-2.2	-2.2	-0.8	-2.2	-0.1	0.5	2.4	3.1
Slovenia	..	..	-0.4	-0.2	-0.2	-0.3	-0.9	-0.7	-0.2	0.3	-0.1	-0.4	-0.1	-0.2	-0.8	-1.7	0.6	0.1	-0.5	-0.7
Spain	-3.2	0.1	0.0	3.3	5.0	-1.4	-11.3	-18.2	-15.4	-14.7	-21.1	-41.8	-59.5	-79.0	-97.3	-92.9	-31.1	-39.1	-37.6	-33.1
Sweden	7.5	9.7	17.3	18.3	18.9	17.0	16.8	15.7	15.2	17.0	21.6	29.6	29.0	32.4	34.6	33.7	28.0	27.2	29.6	30.9
Switzerland	14.4	14.6	16.1	14.7	14.1	13.1	14.9	14.6	12.6	18.4	21.4	25.1	25.0	32.4	44.7	57.4	54.3	66.2	72.2	76.0
Turkey	-4.8	6.1	-0.1	-3.1	-1.1	2.7	0.8	-8.0	7.7	3.7	-3.1	-10.4	-16.9	-26.1	-33.9	-33.6	-7.6	-30.0	-44.3	-56.4
United Kingdom	-7.4	-4.5	-1.4	1.0	7.3	-11.3	-21.9	-27.2	-34.6	-42.2	-42.7	-59.5	-77.7	-76.7	-86.1	-71.3	-51.7	-71.4	-72.3	-65.6
United States	-64.4	-92.7	-90.7	-96.3	-101.4	-161.8	-262.1	-382.1	-371.0	-427.2	-504.1	-618.7	-722.7	-769.3	-714.0	-710.5	-386.4	-538.9	-597.3	-621.6
Euro area	58.6	77.3	108.5	130.3	146.8	128.0	88.1	39.7	89.1	172.7	171.1	191.5	148.1	124.4	187.8	150.9	168.9	174.5	264.1	340.5
Total OECD	105.9	105.9	155.2	113.3	146.5	90.5	-52.0	-212.9	-183.4	-155.7	-208.7	-266.6	-443.8	-518.5	-401.2	-500.2	-83.6	-200.8	-183.0	-142.0

Source: OECD Economic Outlook 88 database.

StatLink ᴬˢ⁴ http://dx.doi.org/10.1787/888932349213

Annex Table 48. Investment income, net
$ billion

	1993	1994	1995	1996	1997	1998	1999	2000	2001	2002	2003	2004	2005	2006	2007	2008	2009	2010	2011	2012
Australia	-7.9	-11.4	-13.4	-14.2	-13.8	-11.3	-11.9	-11.0	-10.2	-11.5	-15.0	-21.9	-27.6	-31.8	-40.9	-39.6	-38.2	-45.2	-50.0	-53.4
Austria	-1.5	-1.7	-2.1	-0.6	-1.3	-1.8	-2.8	-2.3	-3.0	-1.5	-1.1	-1.2	-2.0	-1.8	-2.2	-2.5	-1.3	-0.8	-1.4	-1.4
Belgium[1]	6.9	7.4	7.3	6.8	6.3	6.9	6.6	6.4	4.6	4.5	6.5	5.7	5.0	5.2	7.5	12.6	7.1	8.7	8.7	9.4
Canada	-20.8	-18.9	-22.7	-21.5	-20.9	-20.0	-22.6	-22.3	-25.4	-19.3	-21.3	-18.6	-18.9	-11.9	-12.6	-15.2	-12.6	-14.9	-15.7	-16.5
Chile	..	..	..	-2.5	-2.6	-1.9	-2.9	-2.9	-2.5	-2.8	-4.5	-7.8	-10.5	-18.4	-18.6	-13.4	-10.3	-17.1	-18.5	-19.2
Czech Republic	-0.1	0.0	-0.1	-0.7	-0.8	-1.1	-1.4	-1.4	-2.2	-3.5	-4.3	-6.1	-6.0	-7.4	-12.7	-10.4	-12.1	-13.1	-14.2	-14.9
Denmark	-3.8	-3.8	-3.8	-3.7	-3.4	-2.8	-2.6	-3.6	-3.6	-2.7	-2.6	-2.2	1.6	2.8	1.8	3.5	3.9	2.4	1.4	1.7
Finland	-4.9	-4.4	-4.4	-3.7	-2.4	-3.1	-2.0	-1.7	-1.0	-0.6	-2.6	0.2	-0.3	0.8	-0.7	-1.5	2.4	-0.1	-0.8	-0.9
France	-7.0	-6.2	-8.4	-1.9	7.1	8.7	22.9	19.4	19.6	8.7	14.9	22.5	29.5	37.1	42.8	42.6	32.3	36.9	39.8	39.8
Germany	11.5	1.4	-2.9	0.8	-2.7	-10.8	-12.4	-8.9	-10.0	-17.4	-17.4	24.7	29.9	55.7	60.0	63.6	48.7	42.9	47.4	53.7
Greece	-1.6	-1.4	-1.8	-2.1	-1.7	-1.6	-0.7	-0.9	-1.8	-2.0	-4.5	-5.4	-7.0	-9.1	-12.7	-15.6	-13.6	-15.4	-17.9	-19.0
Hungary	..	..	-1.7	-2.0	-2.7	-3.0	-2.9	-2.6	-2.9	-3.6	-4.2	-5.4	-6.2	-6.6	-10.0	-11.2	-7.8	-8.4	-9.6	-11.5
Iceland	-0.1	-0.2	-0.2	-0.2	-0.2	-0.2	-0.2	-0.2	-0.3	0.0	-0.2	-0.6	-0.6	-1.0	-1.2	-3.4	-1.3	-1.0	-0.9	-0.8
Ireland	-5.2	-5.4	-7.3	-8.2	-9.7	-10.5	-13.7	-13.5	-16.4	-22.4	-24.8	-28.0	-31.0	-30.2	-38.1	-37.1	-38.8	-40.0	-43.4	-43.4
Israel	..	..	-2.6	-3.4	-4.0	-4.0	-5.1	-8.3	-5.5	-4.6	-4.7	-4.0	-1.4	-0.8	-0.2	-4.1	-4.5	-5.9	-6.1	-6.5
Italy	-17.4	-16.9	-15.9	-15.2	-10.3	-11.2	-11.1	-11.9	-10.5	-14.5	-20.3	-18.2	-17.6	-17.1	-27.7	-42.2	-37.0	-28.9	-34.5	-34.5
Japan	40.7	40.6	44.2	53.3	58.1	54.8	58.0	60.6	69.3	66.0	71.8	86.2	103.4	118.2	139.0	153.4	131.8	128.4	153.8	165.8
Korea	-0.4	-0.5	-1.3	-1.8	-2.5	-5.6	-5.2	-2.4	-1.2	0.4	0.3	1.1	-1.6	0.5	1.0	5.9	4.6	3.0	3.2	3.8
Luxembourg	..	..	1.6	1.3	0.5	0.2	-0.5	-1.3	-1.6	-3.4	-4.0	-4.3	-6.5	-11.0	-15.3	-17.2	-15.9	-16.7	-19.1	-19.6
Mexico	-11.4	-13.0	-13.3	-13.9	-12.8	-13.3	-12.9	-15.1	-13.9	-12.7	-12.4	-10.6	-14.7	-18.8	-18.7	-17.3	-14.6	-19.0	-18.0	-18.5
Netherlands	0.9	3.6	7.3	3.5	7.0	-2.7	3.5	-2.3	-0.2	0.1	1.3	11.3	3.8	16.7	-0.7	-19.6	-11.8	-7.1	-10.0	-10.3
New Zealand	-2.9	-3.4	-4.0	-4.7	-4.9	-2.6	-3.1	-3.2	-2.8	-3.0	-3.9	-5.3	-6.8	-7.6	-9.5	-10.0	-5.0	-8.3	-11.9	-12.8
Norway	-3.3	-2.2	-1.9	-1.9	-1.7	-1.2	-1.3	-2.3	0.2	0.6	1.4	0.5	2.1	-0.3	-1.3	-2.8	-2.5	6.4	10.2	13.3
Poland	..	-2.6	-2.0	-1.1	-1.1	-1.2	-1.0	-0.7	-0.6	-1.1	-2.4	-8.2	-6.7	-9.7	-16.4	-12.8	-16.6	-17.8	-19.5	-21.0
Portugal	0.3	-0.5	0.2	-0.9	-1.3	-1.5	-1.6	-2.4	-3.5	-3.0	-2.6	-3.7	-4.8	-7.9	-9.6	-11.4	-10.9	-10.3	-12.1	-13.4
Slovak Republic	0.0	-0.1	0.0	0.0	-0.1	-0.2	-0.3	-0.3	-0.3	-0.5	-1.9	-2.2	-1.9	-2.4	-3.1	-3.2	-2.1	-3.4	-3.4	-3.5
Slovenia	..	..	..	0.2	0.1	0.1	0.1	0.0	0.0	-0.2	-0.3	-0.4	-0.4	-0.6	-1.1	-1.5	-1.1	-0.8	-0.9	-1.0
Spain	-3.6	-7.8	-5.4	-7.5	-7.4	-8.6	-9.5	-6.9	-11.3	-11.6	-11.7	-15.1	-21.3	-26.2	-41.4	-52.7	-42.1	-37.6	-44.3	-45.0
Sweden	-8.7	-5.9	-5.5	-6.3	-4.9	-3.2	-2.0	-1.4	-1.4	-1.8	3.9	0.0	2.7	5.5	10.8	16.6	7.0	9.0	10.2	12.9
Switzerland	7.4	6.0	9.8	10.7	14.2	15.2	17.8	19.2	11.8	9.3	24.2	25.2	33.5	32.8	3.1	-38.7	16.7	13.7	1.6	-1.8
Turkey	-2.7	-3.3	-3.2	-2.9	-3.0	-3.0	-3.5	-4.0	-5.0	-4.6	-5.6	-5.6	-5.8	-6.7	-7.1	-8.2	-7.7	-6.5	-6.0	-6.1
United Kingdom	-3.8	2.0	-1.4	-3.8	0.5	19.6	-1.7	3.0	13.6	27.6	28.7	32.8	40.0	15.5	40.5	54.6	47.5	47.5	60.2	61.1
United States	25.3	17.1	20.9	22.3	12.6	4.3	13.9	21.1	31.7	27.4	45.3	67.2	72.4	48.1	99.6	152.0	121.4	162.2	155.7	147.7
Euro area	-21.7	-31.9	-31.9	-27.6	-16.2	-36.1	-21.6	-26.6	-35.3	-63.7	-68.5	-14.2	-24.6	9.2	-42.4	-85.7	-84.2	-72.6	-91.7	-89.1
Total OECD	-14.4	-31.3	-34.0	-25.9	-9.9	-16.6	-11.4	-4.1	13.7	-3.7	26.0	102.5	124.2	111.6	104.1	113.2	115.5	142.9	134.3	134.1

Note: The classification of non-factor services and investment income is affected by the change in reporting system to the International Monetary Fund, Fifth Balance of Payments Manual.
1. Including Luxembourg until 1994.
Source: OECD Economic Outlook 88 database.

StatLink ⟨⟩ http://dx.doi.org/10.1787/888932349232

Annex Table 49. Total transfers, net
$ billion

	1993	1994	1995	1996	1997	1998	1999	2000	2001	2002	2003	2004	2005	2006	2007	2008	2009	2010	2011	2012
Australia	0.3	0.2	0.3	0.5	0.4	0.2	0.4	0.1	0.3	0.4	0.3	0.1	-0.3	-0.5	-0.1	-0.3	-0.7	-0.9	-1.0	-1.0
Austria	-1.0	-1.1	-1.7	-2.0	-2.0	-1.9	-2.1	-1.7	-1.7	-1.5	-1.8	-1.7	-1.8	-1.6	-1.7	-2.5	-2.4	-2.6	-3.1	-3.1
Belgium[1]	-2.6	-3.3	-4.2	-4.1	-3.7	-4.3	-4.6	-3.9	-4.1	-4.4	-6.4	-6.5	-6.4	-6.5	-6.4	-9.5	-8.9	-8.2	-6.9	-6.9
Canada	-0.6	-0.3	-0.1	0.5	0.5	0.6	0.5	0.8	1.0	0.0	-0.2	-0.5	-1.2	-1.3	-1.8	-0.6	-1.9	-1.7	-2.7	-3.1
Chile	..	..	..	0.5	0.5	0.6	0.6	0.6	0.4	0.6	0.6	1.1	1.8	3.4	3.1	2.9	1.6	4.7	3.5	3.5
Czech Republic	0.1	..	0.6	0.4	0.4	0.5	0.6	0.4	0.5	0.9	0.6	0.2	0.3	-0.9	-1.4	-1.0	-0.8	-0.8	-0.8	-0.8
Denmark	-1.7	-2.0	-2.4	-2.6	-1.8	-2.3	-2.9	-3.0	-2.6	-2.6	-3.7	-4.6	-4.2	-4.8	-5.3	-5.5	-5.2	-5.5	-5.2	-5.5
Finland	-0.4	-0.5	-0.4	-0.9	-0.7	-1.0	-1.0	-0.7	-0.8	-0.8	-1.1	-1.1	-1.5	-1.7	-1.9	-2.3	-2.3	-2.6	-2.8	-2.8
France	-8.1	-10.6	-5.9	-7.4	-13.1	-12.3	-13.2	-14.0	-14.8	-14.2	-19.2	-21.8	-27.3	-27.5	-32.1	-35.4	-37.4	-34.8	-37.5	-37.5
Germany	-33.0	-36.2	-38.8	-34.0	-30.5	-30.2	-26.6	-25.9	-24.1	-26.0	-32.1	-34.7	-36.1	-34.3	-44.4	-50.1	-47.2	-45.2	-45.7	-45.7
Greece[2]	6.5	6.9	8.0	8.0	8.3	7.9	4.1	3.4	3.5	3.6	4.3	4.5	3.8	4.3	2.2	4.1	1.7	1.6	1.8	1.8
Hungary	..	..	0.2	0.0	0.2	0.2	0.4	0.4	0.4	0.5	0.6	-0.2	-0.4	-0.4	-0.7	-1.0	0.5	0.4	-0.6	-0.6
Iceland	0.0	0.0	0.0	0.0	0.0	0.0	0.0	0.0	0.0	0.5	0.0	0.0	0.0	0.0	-0.1	-0.1	-0.1	-0.4	-0.4	-0.4
Ireland	1.9	1.7	1.8	2.2	2.0	1.5	1.3	0.9	0.3	0.7	0.5	0.5	0.3	-0.6	-1.4	-1.7	-1.2	-1.5	-2.1	-1.3
Israel	..	..	5.5	6.1	6.1	6.1	6.3	6.6	6.7	6.9	6.5	6.3	6.1	7.5	7.3	8.4	7.4	8.2	8.9	9.5
Italy	-7.3	-7.2	-4.2	-6.6	-4.2	-7.4	-5.4	-4.3	-5.8	-5.5	-8.1	-10.3	-12.3	-16.7	-19.7	-22.6	-18.2	-18.3	-19.4	-19.4
Japan	-5.3	-6.1	-7.8	-9.3	-8.8	-8.8	-10.8	-9.8	-8.1	-5.6	-7.7	-8.0	-7.3	-10.6	-11.6	-13.2	-12.3	-13.2	-14.7	-14.7
Korea	1.2	1.3	0.2	0.0	0.7	3.4	1.9	0.6	-0.4	-1.6	-2.9	-2.4	-2.5	-4.1	-3.5	-0.7	-0.8	-1.5	-2.0	-3.0
Luxembourg	..	..	-0.6	-0.6	-0.5	-0.4	-0.6	-0.5	-0.5	-0.3	-0.6	-1.1	-1.1	-1.2	-2.0	-2.6	-1.3	-1.1	-1.3	-1.3
Mexico	3.6	3.8	4.0	4.5	5.2	6.0	6.3	7.0	9.3	10.3	15.5	18.8	22.1	25.9	26.4	25.5	21.5	22.7	24.4	25.4
Netherlands	-4.5	-5.2	-6.4	-6.8	-6.1	-7.2	-6.4	-6.2	-6.7	-6.5	-6.8	-9.6	-10.8	-10.4	-16.2	-17.3	-10.3	-19.7	-21.8	-21.8
New Zealand	0.2	0.3	0.3	0.6	0.3	0.3	0.2	0.2	0.2	0.1	0.2	0.1	0.2	0.4	0.4	0.7	0.3	0.6	0.9	0.8
Norway	0.3	-1.7	-2.1	-1.5	-1.4	-1.5	-1.4	-1.3	-1.6	-2.2	-2.9	-2.6	-2.7	-2.3	-3.5	-3.7	-4.3	-4.4	-4.6	-4.6
Poland	..	1.3	1.0	1.7	2.0	2.9	2.2	1.3	1.5	2.0	2.4	3.7	4.9	6.5	8.4	8.2	6.5	8.2	9.5	11.1
Portugal[2]	6.8	5.4	7.3	4.4	3.8	4.0	3.8	3.4	3.4	2.8	3.3	3.5	2.8	3.2	3.6	3.6	3.0	3.2	3.1	3.0
Slovak Republic	0.0	0.1	0.1	0.2	0.2	0.4	0.2	0.1	0.2	0.2	0.4	0.1	-0.1	-0.1	-0.6	-1.2	-0.6	-0.1	-0.1	-0.1
Slovenia																				
Spain	1.3	1.2	4.8	3.2	3.0	3.2	3.0	1.6	1.3	2.4	-0.6	-0.1	-4.2	-8.2	-9.8	-13.7	-11.2	-9.5	-7.3	-7.6
Sweden	-1.2	-1.2	-2.6	-1.9	-2.4	-2.5	-2.7	-2.5	-2.5	-2.9	-2.2	-4.7	-4.6	-5.0	-4.7	-6.3	-4.8	-4.8	-4.9	-4.9
Switzerland	-3.0	-3.5	-4.4	-4.3	-4.0	-4.6	-5.3	-4.5	-5.5	-5.9	-5.6	-6.5	-11.0	-9.3	-9.4	-12.7	-12.2	-12.9	-11.0	-11.0
Turkey	3.7	3.0	4.4	4.1	4.5	5.5	4.9	4.8	3.0	2.4	1.0	1.1	1.5	1.9	2.2	2.1	2.3	1.2	1.6	2.0
United Kingdom	-7.6	-7.9	-11.6	-7.1	-9.4	-13.6	-11.8	-14.7	-9.4	-13.3	-16.1	-18.8	-21.5	-21.9	-27.2	-26.3	-22.9	-25.4	-26.0	-26.0
United States	-39.8	-40.3	-38.1	-43.0	-45.1	-53.2	-50.4	-58.6	-51.3	-64.9	-71.8	-88.4	-105.8	-91.5	-115.6	-122.0	-124.9	-134.1	-129.7	-125.7
Euro area	-40.3	-48.6	-40.2	-44.3	-43.4	-47.6	-47.2	-47.7	-49.8	-49.5	-68.2	-78.3	-94.7	-101.7	-130.8	-151.6	-136.5	-139.0	-143.4	-143.0
Total OECD	-90.2	-101.8	-92.9	-95.2	-95.5	-107.9	-108.3	-119.6	-107.8	-124.6	-153.5	-183.8	-219.2	-208.4	-267.7	-297.3	-287.6	-298.7	-298.3	-292.1

1. Including Luxembourg until 1994.
2. Breaks between 1998 and 1999 for Greece and between 1995 and 1996 for Portugal, reflecting change in methodology to the International Monetary Fund, Fifth Balance of Payments Manual (capital transfers from European Union are excluded from the current account).

Source: OECD Economic Outlook 88 database.

StatLink ◉ http://dx.doi.org/10.1787/888932349251

Annex Table 50. Current account balances
$ billion

	1993	1994	1995	1996	1997	1998	1999	2000	2001	2002	2003	2004	2005	2006	2007	2008	2009	2010	2011	2012
Australia	-9.3	-15.8	-18.4	-14.3	-11.7	-17.7	-21.7	-15.2	-7.6	-15.5	-28.5	-39.7	-41.4	-41.5	-59.1	-49.0	-45.5	-28.7	-27.2	-39.7
Austria	-1.4	-3.3	-6.9	-6.7	-5.2	-3.5	-3.6	-1.4	-1.6	5.6	4.3	6.4	6.6	9.2	13.2	13.7	10.4	9.9	12.5	15.8
Belgium[1]	12.2	13.5	15.4	13.8	13.8	13.3	12.9	9.4	7.9	11.6	12.9	12.6	9.5	8.4	7.7	-8.6	4.1	4.1	5.3	5.9
Canada	-21.7	-13.0	-4.4	3.4	-8.2	-7.7	1.7	19.7	16.3	12.6	10.6	22.9	21.6	18.0	11.8	8.0	-38.6	-42.1	-46.3	-36.2
Chile	0.5	..	..	-3.1	-3.7	-3.9	0.1	-0.9	-1.1	-0.6	-5.8	2.1	1.4	7.2	7.5	-2.5	4.2	-2.7	-3.1	-3.0
Czech Republic	..	-0.8	-1.4	-4.1	-3.6	-1.3	-1.5	-2.7	-3.3	-4.2	-5.8	-5.7	-1.7	-3.4	-5.6	-1.3	-1.8	-3.7	-1.8	-1.6
Denmark	3.9	2.3	1.2	2.7	0.7	-1.5	3.4	2.5	4.2	5.0	7.3	5.7	11.1	8.2	4.4	9.0	11.1	13.9	14.8	16.8
Finland	-1.1	1.0	5.4	5.1	6.8	7.3	8.1	9.9	10.8	12.0	8.5	12.5	7.1	9.5	10.5	7.9	6.7	3.5	4.4	5.5
France	9.4	8.2	11.0	20.8	37.2	38.9	45.8	19.3	23.5	17.5	13.6	10.7	-10.1	-12.4	-26.1	-55.5	-51.6	-55.9	-64.1	-68.6
Germany	-19.4	-30.3	-29.4	-13.6	-10.0	-17.0	-28.3	-34.1	0.1	40.8	47.5	125.6	141.0	187.6	256.0	247.5	166.4	170.4	213.2	260.6
Greece[2]	-1.9	-1.4	-4.5	-6.4	-5.3	-3.8	-7.7	-9.9	-9.5	-10.1	-12.8	-13.3	-18.3	-29.8	-44.8	-51.2	-37.1	-32.7	-24.1	-19.1
Hungary	..	..	-1.6	-1.7	-2.0	-3.4	-3.7	-4.2	-3.3	-4.7	-6.7	-8.2	-8.0	-8.1	-9.1	-10.9	0.7	-0.4	-1.6	-2.0
Iceland	0.0	0.1	0.1	-0.1	-0.1	-0.6	-0.6	-0.9	-0.4	0.1	-0.5	-1.3	-2.6	-4.0	-3.3	-4.2	-0.3	-0.1	0.3	0.4
Ireland	1.8	1.5	1.7	2.0	1.9	0.7	0.3	-0.3	-0.7	-1.2	0.0	-1.1	-7.0	-7.9	-13.9	-15.2	-6.6	-0.5	1.5	7.3
Israel	..	..	-5.0	-5.3	-3.4	-1.0	-1.7	-4.0	-1.8	-1.2	0.9	2.1	4.4	7.6	4.3	1.9	7.6	6.3	6.0	6.3
Italy	7.5	12.7	24.8	39.7	33.3	22.8	8.0	-5.9	-0.8	-9.8	-19.8	-16.3	-29.8	-48.1	-51.7	-81.2	-67.8	-66.9	-60.8	-52.1
Japan	130.0	130.6	114.3	65.8	96.6	119.7	115.7	118.1	89.0	112.6	136.2	171.6	166.0	171.5	212.8	157.4	142.2	190.8	218.8	221.2
Korea	0.8	-4.0	-8.7	-23.1	-8.3	40.4	24.5	12.3	8.0	5.4	11.9	28.2	15.0	5.4	5.9	-5.8	42.7	29.7	25.0	28.8
Luxembourg	..	..	2.5	2.3	1.9	1.8	1.8	2.7	1.8	2.3	2.4	4.1	4.4	4.4	5.2	3.2	3.5	4.1	2.9	3.4
Mexico	-23.4	-29.7	-1.6	-2.5	-7.7	-16.0	-14.0	-18.7	-17.7	-14.2	-7.3	-5.2	-4.9	-4.8	-8.7	-16.2	-5.8	-9.0	-15.8	-21.4
Netherlands	13.2	17.3	25.8	21.5	25.0	13.0	15.7	7.3	9.8	11.1	30.3	46.8	47.3	63.3	52.7	37.9	36.9	42.0	52.0	58.3
New Zealand	-1.7	-2.0	-3.0	-3.9	-4.3	-2.0	-3.4	-2.4	-1.2	-2.2	-3.1	-5.7	-8.8	-8.9	-10.6	-11.6	-3.4	-4.5	-8.3	-9.9
Norway	3.8	3.8	5.2	10.9	10.0	0.0	8.9	25.1	27.5	24.2	27.7	33.0	49.1	58.4	55.0	80.5	49.4	57.1	59.5	61.0
Poland	..	1.0	0.9	-3.3	-5.7	-6.9	-12.5	-10.3	-5.9	-5.5	-5.5	-10.1	-3.7	-9.4	-20.3	-25.6	-9.6	-11.4	-17.1	-21.8
Portugal[2]	0.3	-2.3	-0.2	-4.9	-6.8	-8.8	-11.0	-12.2	-12.4	-10.9	-10.5	-15.5	-19.8	-21.5	-23.5	-31.9	-24.0	-23.6	-21.3	-19.8
Slovak Republic	-0.5	0.8	0.5	-2.0	-1.8	-2.0	-1.0	-0.7	-1.7	-1.9	-1.9	-3.3	-4.0	-4.4	-4.0	-6.3	-2.8	-2.7	-0.9	-0.3
Slovenia	..	..	..	0.1	0.1	-0.2	-0.9	-0.6	0.0	0.2	-0.2	-0.9	-0.6	-1.0	-2.3	-3.7	-0.7	-1.3	-2.0	-2.4
Spain	-5.6	-6.5	-1.7	-1.5	-0.6	-7.2	-17.9	-23.0	-24.0	-22.5	-31.1	-54.9	-83.1	-111.1	-144.7	-156.4	-80.6	-76.7	-76.7	-73.2
Sweden	-2.6	2.5	8.4	9.8	10.3	9.7	10.7	9.4	8.5	9.8	22.4	24.0	25.3	31.3	38.2	45.9	30.0	31.1	34.8	38.9
Switzerland	18.8	16.9	20.8	21.1	24.6	25.2	29.0	30.1	21.0	24.8	43.4	48.4	51.9	59.3	39.7	7.2	59.7	66.5	62.5	62.9
Turkey	-6.4	2.6	-2.3	-2.4	-2.6	2.0	-0.9	-9.9	3.8	-0.6	-7.5	-14.4	-22.1	-32.1	-38.2	-41.9	-14.0	-37.8	-49.9	-61.7
United Kingdom	-18.7	-10.4	-14.3	-9.8	-1.6	-5.3	-35.4	-38.9	-30.4	-27.9	-30.0	-45.6	-59.2	-83.1	-72.8	-43.1	-27.1	-49.4	-38.1	-30.5
United States	-84.8	-121.6	-113.6	-124.8	-140.7	-215.1	-301.6	-417.4	-384.7	-458.1	-520.7	-630.5	-747.6	-802.6	-718.1	-668.9	-378.4	-495.7	-558.5	-586.8
Euro area	14.4	11.2	44.3	70.2	90.4	55.3	22.2	-39.6	3.2	44.7	43.2	113.2	43.0	46.2	34.3	-99.7	-43.2	-26.3	41.9	121.2
Total OECD	3.6	-26.3	20.9	-14.7	28.9	-30.1	-180.8	-348.0	-275.8	-295.4	-312.6	-315.2	-511.1	-584.9	-531.9	-670.6	-220.2	-316.4	-303.9	-257.0

Note: The balance-of-payments data in this table are based on the concepts and definition of the International Monetary Fund, Fifth Balance of Payments Manual.
1. Including Luxembourg until 1994.
2. Breaks between 1998 and 1999 for Greece and between 1995 and 1996 for Portugal, reflecting change in methodology to the International Monetary Fund, Fifth Balance of Payments Manual (capital transfers from European Union are excluded from the current account).
Source: OECD Economic Outlook 88 database.

StatLink ᴙᴪᴘ http://dx.doi.org/10.1787/888932349270

Annex Table 51. Current account balances as a percentage of GDP

	1993	1994	1995	1996	1997	1998	1999	2000	2001	2002	2003	2004	2005	2006	2007	2008	2009	2010	2011	2012
Australia	-3.0	-4.4	-4.8	-3.3	-2.8	-4.7	-5.3	-3.7	-2.0	-3.6	-5.2	-6.0	-5.6	-5.3	-6.2	-4.5	-4.4	-2.3	-1.9	-2.6
Austria	-0.8	-1.6	-2.9	-2.9	-2.5	-1.6	-1.7	-0.7	-0.8	2.7	1.7	2.2	2.2	2.8	3.5	3.3	2.7	2.6	3.1	3.8
Belgium[1]	5.5	5.6	5.4	5.0	5.5	5.2	5.1	4.0	3.4	4.6	4.1	3.5	2.6	1.9	1.6	-1.9	0.8	1.0	1.0	1.1
Canada	-3.9	-2.3	-0.8	0.5	-1.3	-1.2	0.3	2.7	2.3	1.7	1.2	2.3	1.9	1.4	0.8	0.4	-2.8	-2.7	-2.8	-2.1
Chile	..	..	..	-4.1	-4.4	-4.9	0.2	-1.2	-1.5	-0.9	-1.1	2.2	1.2	4.9	4.6	-1.8	2.5	-1.3	-1.3	-1.1
Czech Republic	1.2	-1.8	-2.5	-6.6	-6.2	-2.0	-2.4	-4.8	-5.3	-5.5	-6.2	-5.2	-1.3	-2.4	-3.2	-0.6	-1.0	-1.9	-0.8	-0.7
Denmark	2.8	1.5	0.7	1.4	0.4	-0.9	1.9	1.6	2.6	2.9	3.4	2.3	4.3	3.0	1.4	2.7	3.6	4.4	4.4	4.8
Finland	-1.3	1.1	4.1	4.0	5.6	5.6	6.2	8.1	8.6	8.9	5.2	6.6	3.6	4.6	4.3	2.9	2.7	1.5	1.7	2.0
France	0.7	0.6	0.7	1.3	2.6	2.6	3.1	1.4	1.8	1.2	0.7	0.5	-0.5	-0.5	-1.0	-1.9	-1.9	-2.2	-2.3	-2.4
Germany	-1.0	-1.4	-1.2	-0.6	-0.4	-0.8	-1.3	-1.8	0.0	2.0	1.9	4.6	5.1	6.4	7.7	6.7	4.9	5.1	5.9	7.0
Greece[2]	-1.9	-1.2	-3.4	-4.6	-3.9	-2.8	-5.6	-7.8	-7.3	-6.8	-6.5	-5.8	-7.6	-11.3	-14.5	-14.7	-11.4	-10.5	-7.5	-5.9
Hungary	..	..	-3.3	-3.8	-4.3	-6.9	-7.5	-8.8	-6.1	-6.9	-8.0	-8.0	-7.3	-7.2	-6.6	-7.0	0.3	-0.3	-1.1	-1.3
Iceland	0.7	1.9	0.7	-1.8	-1.8	-6.8	-6.8	-10.2	-4.3	1.5	-4.8	-9.8	-16.1	-23.8	-16.3	-22.1	-2.2	-0.9	2.2	2.4
Ireland	3.6	2.7	2.6	2.7	2.4	0.8	0.3	-0.4	-0.6	-1.0	0.0	-0.6	-3.5	-3.6	-5.3	-5.6	-3.0	-0.3	0.7	3.2
Israel	..	..	-5.2	-5.0	-3.1	-0.9	-1.5	-3.2	-1.5	-1.1	0.8	1.6	3.3	5.2	2.6	1.0	3.9	3.0	2.6	2.5
Italy	0.8	1.2	2.2	3.1	2.8	1.9	0.7	-0.6	-0.1	-0.8	-1.3	-0.9	-1.7	-2.6	-2.4	-3.6	-3.2	-3.3	-2.8	-2.3
Japan	3.0	2.7	2.2	1.4	2.3	3.1	2.6	2.5	2.2	2.9	3.2	3.7	3.6	3.9	4.9	3.3	2.8	3.4	3.7	3.7
Korea	0.2	-0.9	-1.6	-4.1	-1.3	11.4	5.3	2.3	1.6	0.9	1.8	3.9	1.8	0.6	0.6	-0.5	5.2	3.0	2.3	2.4
Luxembourg	..	..	12.1	11.2	10.4	9.2	8.4	13.2	8.8	10.5	8.1	11.9	11.5	10.4	10.1	5.3	6.7	7.8	5.1	5.7
Mexico	-4.8	-5.8	-0.4	-0.7	-1.6	-3.3	-2.5	-2.8	-2.5	-2.0	-1.0	-0.7	-0.6	-0.5	-0.8	-1.5	-0.7	-0.9	-1.4	-1.8
Netherlands	4.0	4.9	6.2	5.1	6.5	3.2	3.8	1.9	2.4	2.5	5.6	7.6	7.4	9.3	6.7	4.3	4.6	5.3	6.2	6.7
New Zealand	-3.9	-3.8	-5.0	-5.7	-6.3	-3.5	-5.9	-4.5	-2.3	-3.6	-3.9	-5.7	-7.9	-8.3	-8.1	-8.8	-2.9	-3.2	-5.3	-6.0
Norway	3.2	3.0	3.5	6.8	6.3	0.0	5.6	15.0	16.1	12.6	12.3	12.7	16.3	17.3	14.1	17.7	13.0	13.8	13.4	13.1
Poland	..	0.9	0.6	-2.1	-3.7	-4.0	-7.5	-6.0	-3.1	-2.8	-2.5	-4.0	-1.2	-2.7	-4.7	-4.8	-2.2	-2.4	-3.2	-3.8
Portugal[2]	0.4	-2.2	-0.1	-4.1	-5.9	-7.1	-8.7	-10.4	-10.3	-8.3	-6.5	-8.4	-10.4	-10.7	-10.1	-12.6	-10.3	-10.3	-8.8	-8.0
Slovak Republic	-3.9	4.9	2.6	-9.3	-8.5	-8.9	-4.8	-3.5	-8.3	-7.9	-5.9	-7.8	-8.5	-7.8	-5.3	-6.5	-3.2	-3.1	-0.9	-0.3
Slovenia	..	..	..	0.3	0.3	-0.7	-4.0	-3.2	0.2	1.1	-0.8	-2.7	-1.7	-2.5	-4.8	-6.7	-1.5	-2.8	-3.9	-4.5
Spain	-1.1	-1.2	-0.3	-0.2	-0.1	-1.2	-2.9	-4.0	-3.9	-3.3	-3.5	-5.3	-7.4	-9.0	-10.0	-9.7	-5.5	-5.5	-5.2	-4.9
Sweden	-1.3	1.1	3.3	3.5	4.1	3.8	4.1	3.8	3.7	4.0	7.1	6.6	6.8	7.8	8.2	9.3	7.4	6.8	6.8	7.3
Switzerland	7.7	6.2	6.6	6.9	9.3	9.3	10.8	12.0	8.2	8.8	13.3	13.3	13.9	15.2	9.2	1.5	12.0	12.6	10.9	10.6
Turkey	-2.7	2.0	-1.2	-1.0	-1.0	0.9	-0.6	-3.7	2.0	-0.3	-2.5	-3.7	-4.6	-6.1	-5.9	-5.6	-2.2	-5.1	-5.7	-6.3
United Kingdom	-1.9	-1.0	-1.2	-0.8	-0.1	-0.4	-2.4	-2.6	-2.1	-1.7	-1.6	-2.1	-2.6	-3.4	-2.6	-1.6	-1.3	-2.2	-1.6	-1.2
United States	-1.3	-1.7	-1.5	-1.6	-1.7	-2.4	-3.2	-4.2	-3.7	-4.3	-4.7	-5.3	-5.9	-6.0	-5.1	-4.7	-2.7	-3.4	-3.7	-3.7
Euro area	0.3	0.2	0.6	1.0	1.4	0.8	0.3	-0.6	0.0	0.6	0.5	1.2	0.4	0.4	0.3	-0.8	-0.4	-0.2	0.3	0.9
Total OECD	0.0	-0.1	0.1	-0.1	0.1	-0.1	-0.7	-1.3	-1.1	-1.1	-1.0	-0.9	-1.4	-1.5	-1.3	-1.5	-0.5	-0.7	-0.7	-0.5

1. Including Luxembourg until 1994.
2. Breaks between 1998 and 1999 for Greece and between 1995 and 1996 for Portugal, reflecting change in methodology to the International Monetary Fund, Fifth Balance of Payments Manual (capital transfers from European Union are excluded from the current account).

Source: OECD Economic Outlook 88 database.

StatLink ⇒ http://dx.doi.org/10.1787/888932349289

Annex Table 52. **Structure of current account balances of major world regions**

$ billion

	1995	1996	1997	1998	1999	2000	2001	2002	2003	2004	2005	2006	2007	2008	2009	2010	2011
Goods and services trade balance[1]																	
OECD	155	113	147	91	-52	-213	-183	-156	-209	-267	-444	-519	-401	-500	-84	-201	-183
China	12	18	43	44	31	29	28	37	36	49	125	209	307	349	220	250	297
Other industrialised Asia[2]	-22	-7	-7	51	62	67	66	84	95	86	86	118	139	42	93	81	50
Russia	10	16	9	12	33	52	39	37	49	72	105	126	113	155	92	133	111
Brazil	-12	-15	-19	-17	-8	-11	-8	6	16	26	32	32	20	3	-2	-22	-38
Other oil producers	28	59	50	-12	46	143	85	75	119	180	321	416	409	575	160	394	447
Rest of the world	-48	-49	-62	-75	-55	-49	-49	-37	-44	-63	-91	-122	-185	-259	-150	-63	-65
World[3]	124	135	160	93	56	17	-21	47	62	83	133	260	402	365	330	571	618
Investment income, net																	
OECD	-34	-26	-10	-17	-11	-4	14	-4	26	103	124	112	104	113	116	143	134
China	-12	-12	-11	-17	-14	-15	-19	-15	-8	-4	11	15	26	41	43	51	57
Other industrialised Asia[2]	-6	-9	-8	-9	-15	-18	-12	-17	-13	-23	-34	-29	-28	-18	-22	-41	-46
Russia	-3	-5	-9	-12	-8	-7	-4	-7	-13	-13	-19	-29	-31	-49	-40	-46	-48
Brazil	-11	-12	-15	-18	-19	-18	-20	-18	-19	-21	-26	-27	-29	-41	-34	-41	-47
Other oil producers	0	-2	0	1	-5	-11	-11	-19	-24	-30	-38	-23	-30	-55	-46	-51	-56
Rest of the world	-19	-24	-25	-24	-26	-28	-29	-31	-37	-42	-44	-47	-61	-67	-61	-68	-78
World[3]	-85	-90	-77	-94	-98	-100	-82	-110	-88	-30	-26	-29	-49	-75	-44	-52	-85
Net transfers, net																	
OECD	-93	-95	-95	-108	-108	-120	-108	-125	-153	-184	-219	-208	-268	-297	-288	-299	-298
China	1	2	5	4	5	6	8	13	18	23	25	29	39	46	34	40	42
Other industrialised Asia[2]	7	10	11	7	15	16	17	20	27	24	34	42	54	67	67	70	77
Russia	0	0	0	0	1	0	-1	-1	0	-1	-1	-2	-4	-3	-3	-6	-6
Brazil	4	2	2	1	2	2	2	2	3	3	4	4	4	4	3	3	3
Other oil producers	-22	-19	-18	-18	-18	-19	-20	-20	-19	-19	-12	-8	-16	-24	-26	-31	-34
Rest of the world	32	33	35	39	40	46	52	58	68	79	90	105	121	138	133	135	149
World[3]	-70	-67	-61	-74	-64	-69	-50	-53	-58	-74	-79	-37	-69	-68	-79	-88	-67
Current balance																	
OECD	21	-15	29	-30	-181	-348	-276	-295	-313	-315	-511	-585	-532	-671	-220	-316	-304
China	2	7	37	31	21	21	17	35	46	69	161	253	372	436	297	340	396
Other industrialised Asia[2]	-28	-18	-9	46	59	46	59	77	103	76	70	119	156	95	135	69	65
Russia	7	11	0	0	25	47	34	29	35	60	85	95	77	102	49	84	59
Brazil	-18	-24	-30	-33	-25	-24	-23	-8	4	12	14	14	2	-28	-24	-53	-76
Other oil producers	1	30	23	-35	16	107	50	31	72	129	270	386	363	497	92	313	358
Rest of the world	-37	-42	-55	-62	-42	-34	-27	-9	-14	-29	-49	-70	-131	-194	-85	-3	-1
World[3]	-53	-50	-6	-82	-127	-186	-165	-139	-65	1	40	212	307	237	244	434	497

StatLink ᎂ᎒ https://dx.doi.org/10.1787/888932349308

Note: Historical data for the OECD area are aggregates of reported balance-of-payments data of each individual country. Because of various statistical problems as well as a large number of non-reporters among non-OECD countries, trade and current account balances estimated on the basis of these countries' own balance-of-payments records may differ from corresponding estimates shown in this table.
1. National-accounts basis for OECD countries and balance-of-payments basis for the non-OECD regions.
2. Dynamic Asian Economies (Chinese Taipei; Hong Kong, China; Malaysia; Philippines; Singapore; Vietnam and Thailand), India and Indonesia.
3. Reflects statistical errors and asymmetries. Given the very large gross flows of world balance-of-payments transactions, statistical errors and asymmetries easily give rise to world totals (balances) that are significantly different from zero.
Source: OECD Economic Outlook 83 database.

Annex Table 53. Export market growth in goods and services
Percentage changes from previous year

	1993	1994	1995	1996	1997	1998	1999	2000	2001	2002	2003	2004	2005	2006	2007	2008	2009	2010	2011	2012
Australia	3.8	10.2	12.9	9.8	6.9	-1.3	4.8	12.8	0.1	5.9	8.3	13.3	9.7	8.9	7.7	5.1	-10.1	13.4	9.9	9.9
Austria	-1.1	7.2	8.4	5.3	9.7	8.2	6.2	11.5	2.2	1.6	5.2	8.8	7.4	10.6	7.4	2.9	-11.6	10.6	7.3	6.1
Belgium	-0.6	7.9	8.3	5.5	10.0	8.6	6.5	12.2	1.9	1.7	3.9	8.4	7.1	9.1	6.2	2.0	-11.3	10.4	6.9	6.2
Canada	7.1	11.2	8.0	8.9	12.6	10.1	10.5	13.0	-2.0	3.5	4.7	11.0	6.7	6.8	3.7	-1.2	-13.1	13.8	9.6	7.9
Chile	3.2	8.8	8.8	9.8	10.1	3.0	5.5	12.4	0.4	2.8	6.8	11.5	8.5	9.6	8.4	4.0	-10.5	13.9	9.3	9.6
Czech Republic	..	6.7	8.5	6.3	10.1	9.6	5.7	11.2	2.8	1.4	5.1	8.4	7.8	11.3	7.3	2.8	-12.2	10.5	7.1	5.8
Denmark	0.3	8.4	8.3	6.5	10.5	8.2	5.8	11.3	1.1	1.8	4.5	8.7	7.7	9.4	7.0	2.4	-11.9	10.9	7.5	6.5
Finland	0.6	6.1	9.0	6.0	10.5	5.6	3.6	12.8	2.5	3.5	6.1	10.7	9.6	11.1	10.1	4.8	-13.9	11.1	8.6	7.5
France	0.0	6.7	8.3	6.2	10.3	7.4	6.0	11.2	1.8	2.6	4.7	9.1	7.8	9.2	7.1	2.4	-11.6	9.5	7.0	6.8
Germany	0.8	7.4	9.0	6.6	10.4	7.5	5.6	12.4	1.9	3.1	4.6	9.8	7.7	9.0	7.6	2.2	-12.1	9.8	7.4	7.2
Greece	3.8	4.4	8.3	5.9	10.4	7.2	4.6	10.1	1.7	3.3	5.4	9.7	8.6	9.1	8.4	4.0	-12.0	6.7	7.4	6.9
Hungary	..	6.4	8.4	5.7	9.6	8.1	5.6	11.0	2.7	1.7	5.0	8.7	7.7	10.4	7.7	2.9	-12.0	9.1	7.1	6.0
Iceland	-0.1	8.0	8.1	6.5	10.0	8.7	7.2	11.0	2.3	2.5	3.6	8.2	7.4	9.5	5.6	1.6	-11.9	9.3	6.3	6.0
Ireland	0.6	8.3	7.7	6.5	9.9	7.7	7.2	11.6	1.2	2.6	3.8	8.5	6.9	8.3	4.6	0.9	-11.6	10.7	6.8	6.3
Israel	1.3	6.2	8.2	6.6	10.2	7.6	5.8	11.8	2.0	2.7	5.0	9.8	8.2	9.5	8.1	3.2	-11.7	9.2	7.4	7.0
Japan	5.9	11.0	11.9	8.9	9.8	1.3	8.7	14.8	-1.1	7.3	9.5	14.0	9.4	10.0	8.3	4.0	-8.7	15.6	10.5	10.2
Korea	5.4	8.7	11.6	10.0	9.2	2.1	6.6	13.9	0.7	7.1	10.4	14.4	10.1	10.5	9.0	4.6	-8.1	14.5	10.4	10.4
Luxembourg	-2.3	7.9	7.6	4.7	9.4	8.3	6.2	11.7	1.7	1.2	3.4	7.4	6.8	8.6	5.6	1.3	-11.5	10.0	6.6	5.7
Mexico	7.7	10.9	7.9	8.5	13.1	10.7	10.3	12.5	-2.2	3.1	4.7	11.0	6.6	6.6	3.7	-1.4	-13.4	13.5	9.5	7.7
Netherlands	-0.9	7.4	7.9	5.5	9.7	7.9	6.0	11.8	1.7	2.0	4.1	8.4	7.5	9.4	6.5	2.3	-11.7	10.1	7.0	6.0
New Zealand	3.8	9.5	10.2	8.7	8.8	3.0	6.7	11.6	-0.9	6.0	7.4	12.3	9.1	8.7	8.1	5.8	-10.2	12.4	8.9	8.7
Norway	0.8	8.5	7.8	6.3	10.3	8.3	6.9	11.7	1.6	2.6	3.5	8.1	7.3	9.1	4.9	1.5	-12.0	10.4	6.7	6.1
Poland	..	6.7	8.5	5.0	9.4	8.0	5.3	11.4	3.0	1.8	5.0	8.8	7.8	10.8	8.0	3.4	-12.5	9.7	7.2	5.9
Portugal	-1.4	7.5	8.2	6.1	10.7	9.5	7.5	11.6	2.6	2.6	4.3	8.7	7.8	9.1	7.0	0.8	-12.5	9.0	6.7	6.8
Slovak Republic	..	7.6	10.4	6.4	10.1	9.1	6.0	12.3	3.5	2.0	5.6	10.1	6.8	11.3	8.7	3.0	-11.8	10.1	7.1	5.9
Slovenia	-0.9	6.3	8.6	4.4	9.5	7.9	4.7	10.9	3.4	1.8	4.9	8.6	7.5	10.2	8.4	3.4	-12.6	7.6	6.9	5.9
Spain	-0.5	7.0	7.4	5.5	10.1	8.9	5.9	11.2	1.9	1.8	3.3	8.2	7.1	8.7	6.3	2.4	-11.4	9.1	6.4	6.1
Sweden	1.5	7.5	8.1	6.9	10.6	7.5	4.6	11.2	1.5	3.0	4.0	9.5	8.7	9.5	7.0	3.3	-12.2	9.6	7.4	6.8
Switzerland	-0.5	7.5	8.5	5.9	9.8	7.3	6.3	11.8	1.5	2.2	4.9	9.1	7.5	9.3	6.9	2.3	-11.4	10.5	7.5	6.8
Turkey	-0.3	3.5	7.8	5.3	9.0	7.1	4.9	10.6	3.5	3.1	4.4	9.3	9.2	9.5	9.6	4.8	-11.4	6.8	6.9	6.6
United Kingdom	1.1	7.8	9.2	6.6	10.6	7.9	6.3	12.7	1.1	2.8	4.3	9.8	8.1	8.4	7.5	2.4	-11.3	10.5	7.8	7.2
United States	3.1	8.6	6.8	8.8	10.9	4.0	6.4	12.5	-0.5	3.1	5.1	10.7	8.6	8.9	7.9	3.9	-11.8	13.3	8.1	8.3
Total OECD	1.8	8.1	8.6	7.2	10.4	6.5	6.5	12.3	0.9	3.2	5.3	10.2	8.0	9.1	7.2	2.7	-11.4	11.5	8.0	7.6
Memorandum items																				
China	3.5	9.1	10.6	8.1	9.1	2.8	6.5	12.6	-0.8	3.9	5.7	11.3	8.2	8.2	6.7	3.4	-12.5	12.4	8.9	8.2
Other industrialised Asia[1]	5.0	10.8	12.7	9.1	8.5	0.8	6.7	14.1	-0.5	6.7	9.4	14.0	10.0	10.1	8.0	5.3	-8.8	14.6	10.3	10.1
Russia	2.6	5.2	9.7	6.9	11.0	7.4	4.9	11.4	1.9	3.4	6.0	9.9	8.3	9.7	8.7	3.6	-10.5	8.2	7.4	7.5
Brazil	4.7	8.3	6.0	9.1	12.8	6.2	3.1	10.5	-0.2	-1.2	7.9	13.4	10.4	10.0	10.1	5.5	-11.9	12.7	9.0	8.5
Other oil producers	2.8	8.3	11.4	8.6	8.6	1.7	6.3	12.7	0.1	4.7	6.8	11.4	8.5	8.7	7.7	3.5	-10.9	12.1	9.0	9.1
Rest of the world	2.3	5.2	8.8	6.9	10.5	5.7	3.5	11.7	2.0	3.4	5.7	11.0	9.3	9.7	9.6	4.8	-12.2	9.9	8.3	8.0

StatLink http://dx.doi.org/10.1787/888932349327

Note: Regional aggregates are calculated inclusive of intra-regional trade. The calculation of export markets is based on a weighted average of import volumes in each exporting country's market, with weights based on goods and services trade flows in 2005.

1. Chinese Taipei; Hong Kong, China; Malaysia; Philippines; Singapore; Vietnam; Thailand; India and Indonesia.
Source: OECD Economic Outlook 88 database.

Annex Table 54. Import penetration

Goods and services import volume as a percentage of total final expenditure, constant prices

	1993	1994	1995	1996	1997	1998	1999	2000	2001	2002	2003	2004	2005	2006	2007	2008	2009	2010	2011	2012
Australia	9.8	10.6	11.0	11.3	11.9	12.1	12.5	13.0	12.2	12.9	13.6	15.0	15.6	16.2	17.1	18.4	16.8	18.1	18.7	19.4
Austria	24.5	25.7	26.3	26.9	27.8	28.1	28.4	29.8	30.7	30.5	31.1	32.6	33.6	33.9	34.5	33.8	31.9	32.6	33.6	34.3
Belgium	37.5	38.3	38.5	39.1	40.3	41.2	41.0	43.0	42.8	42.6	42.7	43.5	44.5	45.0	45.4	45.9	43.7	45.3	46.2	47.0
Canada	24.0	24.6	25.1	25.8	27.6	27.8	28.2	28.8	27.3	27.1	27.5	28.5	29.4	29.8	30.6	30.8	28.1	30.1	30.8	31.6
Chile	..	..	..	22.4	23.5	24.1	22.4	23.3	23.5	23.5	24.5	26.6	28.7	29.8	31.7	33.5	30.5	34.8	36.3	37.2
Czech Republic	27.5	28.6	31.3	32.8	34.4	36.3	37.1	39.9	42.3	43.0	44.1	47.3	47.0	48.9	51.0	51.6	49.6	52.0	53.3	54.1
Denmark	22.6	23.8	24.5	24.6	25.7	26.9	27.0	28.8	29.1	30.5	30.1	31.2	33.0	35.2	35.4	36.4	34.2	34.5	35.5	36.4
Finland	20.1	21.4	21.8	22.5	23.3	23.7	23.7	25.6	25.5	25.8	26.1	26.7	28.4	29.1	29.4	30.5	27.9	28.1	29.2	29.5
France	15.9	16.7	17.4	17.5	18.3	19.5	19.9	21.7	21.8	21.8	21.9	22.6	23.3	24.0	24.6	24.6	23.0	24.3	25.4	26.1
Germany	18.3	19.1	19.9	20.3	21.3	22.5	23.6	24.8	24.9	24.6	25.6	26.7	27.9	29.6	30.1	30.5	29.4	31.5	32.5	32.9
Greece	19.3	19.2	20.2	21.0	22.7	23.7	25.8	27.7	27.1	26.2	25.7	25.8	25.3	26.1	26.6	26.2	23.8	22.2	20.9	20.8
Hungary	25.6	26.8	29.7	31.3	34.9	38.6	40.4	43.3	43.7	44.3	45.7	48.2	49.2	52.3	55.7	57.2	54.4	57.6	58.8	60.3
Iceland	22.3	22.3	22.9	24.8	25.3	28.1	28.2	29.0	26.3	25.8	27.3	28.6	32.5	33.7	32.3	27.8	24.1	24.7	24.7	24.8
Ireland	31.8	33.5	34.5	35.4	36.2	39.8	39.9	42.2	42.5	41.6	40.1	41.1	41.7	42.0	42.5	42.6	42.4	44.1	45.2	45.8
Israel	31.8	33.5	34.5	35.4	36.2	39.8	39.9	42.2	42.5	41.6	40.1	41.1	41.7	42.0	42.5	42.6	42.4	44.1	45.2	45.8
Italy	15.6	16.5	17.4	17.1	18.1	19.2	19.7	20.8	20.7	20.7	20.9	21.2	21.6	22.2	22.6	22.0	20.3	21.2	21.5	21.9
Japan	6.5	6.9	7.7	8.4	8.3	8.0	8.2	8.7	8.7	8.8	9.0	9.4	9.7	9.9	9.8	10.1	9.0	9.6	10.0	10.4
Korea	18.3	20.1	22.0	23.1	22.9	19.8	21.8	23.9	22.4	23.5	24.9	26.1	26.8	27.9	29.1	29.6	27.9	30.0	31.6	33.3
Luxembourg	..	..	50.4	51.5	53.1	54.4	55.8	56.3	57.2	56.3	57.7	59.5	59.2	61.0	61.7	63.4	61.5	62.9	63.1	63.1
Mexico	12.1	13.7	12.5	14.3	16.0	17.5	18.9	21.1	21.0	21.2	21.1	22.2	23.1	24.3	25.0	25.3	22.8	25.4	26.4	27.3
Netherlands	30.8	32.0	33.4	33.8	35.3	36.4	37.4	39.2	39.3	39.4	39.8	40.6	41.4	42.8	43.2	43.6	42.3	44.5	45.3	46.3
New Zealand	20.0	21.0	21.7	22.4	22.2	22.4	23.6	22.9	22.9	23.7	24.3	26.4	26.9	25.9	27.0	27.7	24.2	25.3	26.2	27.1
Norway	17.9	18.0	18.2	18.7	19.6	20.5	20.0	19.8	19.7	19.7	19.7	20.4	21.4	22.4	23.3	24.0	22.0	23.5	24.2	24.8
Poland	14.2	15.0	16.9	19.4	21.7	23.8	23.3	24.9	24.0	24.3	25.3	26.8	27.6	30.0	31.3	31.6	28.0	29.4	30.2	31.1
Portugal	20.3	21.5	22.1	22.5	23.5	25.1	25.9	26.2	26.0	25.8	25.9	27.0	27.3	28.4	29.1	29.6	27.8	28.5	28.6	28.8
Slovak Republic	35.4	33.1	34.3	36.5	37.5	40.5	40.6	42.2	44.5	44.4	45.0	45.8	47.2	49.3	49.0	48.2	44.4	46.2	47.0	47.4
Slovenia	..	..	..	32.8	34.1	35.3	35.9	36.5	36.5	36.7	37.6	39.7	40.2	41.6	43.8	43.9	40.4	42.1	43.2	44.2
Spain	15.7	16.9	18.0	19.0	20.3	21.9	23.3	24.3	24.5	24.7	25.3	26.4	27.2	28.5	29.4	28.0	24.8	26.1	27.1	28.5
Sweden	21.7	23.1	23.7	24.0	25.7	27.0	27.0	28.4	27.8	27.1	27.4	27.7	28.4	29.4	30.6	31.2	29.4	31.0	32.1	32.7
Switzerland	22.7	23.8	24.5	25.1	26.2	27.1	27.6	28.9	29.1	28.8	29.1	30.1	30.9	31.5	32.1	31.7	30.9	32.1	33.0	33.9
Turkey	13.8	11.8	13.9	15.2	16.9	16.8	16.7	18.7	15.4	17.2	19.7	21.3	21.9	22.0	23.0	22.1	20.2	21.1	22.1	23.4
United Kingdom	16.1	16.3	16.7	17.6	18.5	19.3	20.0	20.8	21.1	21.6	21.4	22.1	22.9	24.0	23.4	23.2	21.8	22.7	23.0	23.3
United States	8.4	9.0	9.4	9.8	10.6	11.2	11.9	12.7	12.3	12.5	12.7	13.5	13.8	14.2	14.3	14.0	12.6	13.8	14.7	15.2
Total OECD	13.4	14.1	14.8	15.3	16.2	16.8	17.5	18.6	18.4	18.5	18.8	19.6	20.2	21.0	21.4	21.5	19.9	21.2	22.0	22.7

Note: The OECD aggregate is calculated inclusive of intra-regional trade as the sum of import volumes expressed in 2005 $ divided by the sum of total final expenditure expressed in 2005 $.

Source: OECD Economic Outlook 88 database.

StatLink http://dx.doi.org/10.1787/888932349346

Annex Table 55. **Quarterly demand and output projections**
Percentage changes from previous period, seasonally adjusted at annual rates, volume

	2010	2011	2012	2010 Q4	2011 Q1	2011 Q2	2011 Q3	2011 Q4	2012 Q1	2012 Q2	2012 Q3	2012 Q4	2010 Q4/Q4	2011 Q4/Q4	2012 Q4/Q4
Private consumption															
Canada	3.2	2.1	3.0	1.7	2.0	2.4	2.6	2.8	3.0	3.2	3.2	3.4	2.5	2.4	3.2
France	1.5	1.6	2.2	0.7	1.4	1.8	2.0	2.2	2.2	2.4	2.4	2.5	1.1	1.9	2.4
Germany	-0.1	1.3	1.6	0.9	1.1	1.6	1.6	1.6	1.6	1.6	1.4	1.3	0.9	1.5	1.5
Italy	0.4	0.6	1.0	0.5	0.6	0.8	1.0	1.0	1.0	1.1	1.1	1.1	0.2	0.8	1.1
Japan	2.4	1.0	1.4	-1.0	0.8	0.9	1.1	1.3	1.3	1.5	1.5	1.7	1.7	1.1	1.5
United Kingdom	1.2	1.7	1.8	3.0	0.7	1.7	1.4	1.6	1.8	1.9	2.0	2.1	1.8	1.3	1.9
United States	1.7	2.4	2.7	2.4	2.3	2.3	2.3	2.4	2.7	3.0	3.2	3.4	2.3	2.3	3.1
Euro area	0.6	1.0	1.7	0.7	1.0	1.3	1.5	1.6	1.7	1.8	1.8	1.8	0.7	1.4	1.7
Total OECD	1.9	2.1	2.5	1.8	2.0	2.2	2.3	2.4	2.6	2.7	2.8	2.9	2.0	2.2	2.7
Public consumption															
Canada	3.3	0.8	-0.3	1.0	0.8	0.2	-0.2	-0.2	-0.3	-0.3	-0.5	-0.5	1.8	0.1	-0.4
France	1.6	0.6	0.0	1.0	0.2	0.2	0.2	0.1	0.0	0.0	-0.2	-0.4	1.0	0.2	-0.1
Germany	2.6	0.7	0.6	0.0	1.4	1.0	0.4	0.4	0.9	0.8	0.4	0.4	2.3	0.8	0.6
Italy	-0.3	0.1	0.0	0.2	0.0	0.0	0.0	0.0	0.1	0.1	0.1	0.1	-0.1	0.0	0.1
Japan	1.6	1.7	0.3	3.4	3.0	0.4	0.8	0.7	0.3	-0.7	0.5	0.4	1.7	1.2	0.1
United Kingdom	1.9	-1.1	-1.7	-1.5	-2.4	-2.0	-2.0	-2.0	-1.8	-1.4	-1.4	-1.4	1.8	-2.1	-1.5
United States	1.1	1.0	0.6	0.8	0.5	0.5	0.6	0.6	0.7	0.7	0.7	0.7	1.5	0.6	0.7
Euro area	1.0	0.0	-0.1	0.2	-0.4	-0.2	-0.2	-0.2	0.0	0.0	-0.1	-0.2	0.9	-0.2	-0.1
Total OECD	1.5	0.7	0.4	0.9	0.4	0.3	0.3	0.3	0.5	0.4	0.5	0.5	1.4	0.3	0.5
Business investment															
Canada	2.7	9.5	6.3	11.0	8.0	8.0	8.0	7.0	6.0	5.5	5.0	5.0	11.0	7.7	5.4
France	-1.8	4.1	6.3	2.4	4.1	4.9	5.7	6.6	6.6	6.6	6.6	6.6	1.4	5.3	6.6
Germany	6.0	3.7	3.6	4.7	0.4	3.0	2.8	3.8	3.8	3.8	3.6	3.5	10.6	2.5	3.7
Italy	6.0	3.2	3.6	1.4	2.7	3.5	4.0	3.6	3.1	3.7	3.8	4.5	6.9	3.5	3.8
Japan	1.8	4.6	5.5	2.5	4.0	6.0	6.0	6.0	6.0	5.0	4.2	4.2	4.3	5.5	4.8
United Kingdom	2.3	6.1	7.0	5.7	5.9	6.3	6.5	6.8	7.2	7.2	7.4	7.6	12.3	6.4	7.4
United States	5.9	10.1	9.0	11.3	9.9	8.5	8.8	8.8	9.1	9.1	9.1	9.2	11.5	9.0	9.1
Euro area	0.7	3.7	4.7	3.3	2.8	4.0	4.2	4.6	4.7	4.9	5.0	5.2	4.5	3.9	5.0
Total OECD	3.7	6.9	6.9	6.9	6.3	6.4	6.6	6.8	7.0	7.0	6.9	7.0	8.0	6.5	7.0
Total investment															
Canada	6.6	4.8	2.6	5.2	5.3	3.7	3.7	3.3	2.2	2.1	1.7	2.5	7.2	4.0	2.1
France	-1.8	2.8	4.3	1.7	2.7	3.3	3.9	4.4	4.4	4.3	4.4	4.4	0.8	3.6	4.4
Germany	4.9	2.7	1.2	3.0	0.6	1.3	1.1	1.0	1.0	0.5	2.2	2.8	7.6	1.0	1.6
Italy	2.0	1.5	3.1	-0.2	1.2	2.1	2.9	2.9	2.9	3.3	3.4	3.9	2.5	2.3	3.4
Japan	-0.1	3.2	2.3	5.7	8.0	-1.2	-0.7	1.8	2.8	3.9	3.9	4.0	3.4	1.9	3.7
United Kingdom	2.0	2.3	4.3	0.1	2.1	2.3	2.7	3.7	4.7	5.0	5.2	5.5	5.1	2.7	5.1
United States	3.4	7.2	6.8	9.3	7.1	6.2	6.4	6.5	7.0	7.1	7.3	7.3	7.1	6.6	7.1
Euro area	-1.0	1.6	2.8	0.9	0.9	1.7	2.2	2.5	2.8	2.9	3.5	3.8	1.6	1.9	3.2
Total OECD	2.4	5.0	5.2	5.5	5.0	4.0	4.5	5.1	5.4	5.5	5.8	6.0	5.1	4.6	5.7

Note: The adoption of national accounts systems SNA93 or ESA95 has been proceeding at an uneven pace among OECD member countries, both with respect to variables and the time period covered. As a consequence, there are breaks in many national series. Moreover, most countries have shifted to chain-weighted price indices to calculate real GDP and expenditures components. For further information, see table "National Account Reporting Systems, base years and latest data updates" at the beginning of the Statistical Annex and *OECD Economic Outlook* Sources and Methods *(http://www.oecd.org/eco/sources-and-methods).*

Source: OECD Economic Outlook 88 database.

StatLink http://dx.doi.org/10.1787/888932349365

Annex Table 55. **Quarterly demand and output projections** *(cont'd)*
Percentage changes from previous period, seasonally adjusted at annual rates, volume

	2010	2011	2012	2010 Q4	2011 Q1	Q2	Q3	Q4	2012 Q1	Q2	Q3	Q4	2010 Q4/Q4	2011 Q4/Q4	2012 Q4/Q4
Total domestic demand															
Canada	4.8	2.5	2.2	2.3	2.4	2.2	2.2	2.3	2.1	2.2	2.1	2.4	4.1	2.3	2.2
France	1.5	2.0	2.1	1.6	1.4	1.7	2.0	2.2	2.1	2.2	2.2	2.2	1.9	1.8	2.2
Germany	2.3	1.5	1.3	1.1	1.1	1.4	1.3	1.2	1.4	1.2	1.3	1.4	3.9	1.2	1.3
Italy	0.7	0.6	1.2	0.4	0.6	0.9	1.1	1.2	1.2	1.3	1.3	1.4	0.3	0.9	1.3
Japan	1.7	1.6	1.4	1.1	2.7	0.4	0.7	1.3	1.4	1.6	1.8	1.9	2.4	1.3	1.7
United Kingdom	2.7	1.3	1.4	1.2	0.2	1.0	0.9	1.1	1.4	1.6	1.7	1.8	3.4	0.8	1.7
United States	3.4	2.7	3.0	2.1	2.1	2.6	2.6	2.7	3.0	3.2	3.4	3.6	3.8	2.5	3.3
Euro area	0.9	1.0	1.5	0.8	0.6	1.1	1.3	1.4	1.5	1.6	1.7	1.7	1.7	1.1	1.6
Total OECD	3.0	2.4	2.7	1.8	2.1	2.3	2.4	2.5	2.7	2.8	2.9	3.0	3.2	2.3	2.9
Export of goods and services															
Canada	6.8	5.3	9.4	3.6	5.0	6.5	8.0	8.5	9.0	10.0	12.0	12.0	5.6	7.0	10.7
France	9.9	6.4	6.3	5.7	4.9	5.3	5.5	6.1	6.6	6.6	6.8	6.8	11.7	5.5	6.7
Germany	15.2	9.0	5.6	7.4	7.0	6.8	6.0	5.5	5.5	5.5	5.5	5.5	16.9	6.3	5.5
Italy	7.9	6.7	5.3	6.1	6.1	6.0	5.3	5.3	5.3	5.3	5.3	5.3	10.2	5.7	5.3
Japan	25.4	6.7	5.8	4.0	4.4	6.0	6.0	5.5	5.5	5.9	6.0	6.3	17.0	5.5	5.9
United Kingdom	4.4	5.0	6.4	4.2	4.9	5.2	6.0	6.3	6.5	6.6	6.6	6.7	3.2	5.6	6.6
United States	11.4	8.1	9.9	8.0	8.0	8.0	10.0	10.0	10.0	10.0	10.0	10.0	8.3	9.0	10.0
Total OECD[1]	11.6	7.4	7.6	6.2	6.7	7.0	7.4	7.4	7.5	7.7	7.8	7.9	10.4	7.1	7.7
Import of goods and services															
Canada	12.7	5.7	6.6	4.0	5.0	5.0	6.0	6.4	6.5	6.5	7.5	8.5	9.7	5.6	7.2
France	8.8	7.5	6.2	5.7	4.9	5.5	5.7	5.9	6.3	6.3	6.6	6.8	11.8	5.5	6.5
Germany	13.6	7.4	4.1	6.8	5.7	5.4	4.5	3.9	3.9	3.9	3.9	3.9	18.6	4.9	3.9
Italy	6.6	3.7	3.9	3.6	3.5	3.3	3.7	3.9	4.0	4.1	4.1	4.1	5.7	3.6	4.1
Japan	10.5	6.6	6.5	5.4	5.0	4.9	5.3	6.6	6.5	6.7	7.4	7.4	11.7	5.4	7.0
United Kingdom	7.5	3.1	4.0	1.6	2.7	3.6	3.9	3.9	3.9	4.0	4.1	4.3	5.1	3.5	4.1
United States	14.3	9.9	7.7	8.0	7.0	7.0	7.5	7.5	7.5	8.0	8.0	8.0	17.1	7.2	7.9
Total OECD[1]	11.8	7.5	6.9	6.5	6.2	6.5	6.8	6.8	6.8	7.0	7.1	7.2	12.4	6.6	7.1
GDP															
Canada	3.0	2.3	3.0	2.1	2.4	2.6	2.8	2.8	2.8	3.2	3.4	3.4	2.8	2.6	3.2
France	1.6	1.6	2.0	1.5	1.2	1.6	1.8	2.1	2.1	2.2	2.2	2.1	1.7	1.7	2.1
Germany	3.5	2.5	2.2	1.7	1.8	2.3	2.2	2.2	2.3	2.2	2.3	2.3	4.1	2.1	2.3
Italy	1.0	1.3	1.6	1.0	1.3	1.6	1.5	1.5	1.5	1.7	1.7	1.8	1.3	1.5	1.7
Japan	3.7	1.7	1.3	1.0	2.7	0.6	0.8	1.2	1.3	1.5	1.7	1.8	3.3	1.3	1.6
United Kingdom	1.8	1.7	2.0	1.8	0.7	1.3	1.3	1.7	2.1	2.3	2.4	2.5	2.9	1.3	2.3
United States	2.7	2.2	3.1	1.9	2.1	2.5	2.8	2.9	3.2	3.3	3.5	3.7	2.3	2.6	3.4
Euro area	1.7	1.7	2.0	1.3	1.3	1.7	1.8	1.9	2.0	2.1	2.2	2.2	2.1	1.7	2.1
Total OECD	2.8	2.3	2.8	1.7	2.2	2.4	2.5	2.6	2.8	2.9	3.1	3.2	2.7	2.4	3.0

Note: The adoption of national accounts systems SNA93 or ESA95 has been proceeding at an uneven pace among OECD member countries, both with respect to variables and the time period covered. As a consequence, there are breaks in many national series. Moreover, most countries have shifted to chain-weighted price indices to calculate real GDP and expenditures components. For further information, see table "National Account Reporting Systems, base years and latest data updates" at the beginning of the Statistical Annex and *OECD Economic Outlook* Sources and Methods *(http://www.oecd.org/eco/sources-and-methods)*.

1. Includes intra-regional trade.
Source: OECD Economic Outlook 88 database.

StatLink http://dx.doi.org/10.1787/888932349365

Annex Table 56. **Quarterly price, cost and unemployment projections**

Percentage changes from previous period, seasonally adjusted at annual rates, volume

	2010	2011	2012	2010 Q4	2011 Q1	2011 Q2	2011 Q3	2012 Q4	2012 Q1	2012 Q2	2012 Q3	2012 Q4	2010 Q4/Q4	2011 Q4/Q4	2012 Q4/Q4
Consumer price index[1]															
Canada	1.6	1.7	1.5	1.9	1.9	1.7	1.5	1.5	1.5	1.5	1.5	1.5	1.4	1.7	1.5
France	1.6	1.1	1.1	1.0	1.2	1.2	0.9	1.1	1.1	1.2	1.3	1.3	1.4	1.1	1.2
Germany	1.0	1.2	1.4	1.3	1.3	1.3	1.2	1.2	1.4	1.4	1.5	1.6	1.2	1.3	1.5
Italy	1.5	1.4	1.4	1.2	1.5	1.2	1.2	1.4	1.4	1.4	1.5	1.6	1.5	1.3	1.5
Japan	-0.9	-0.8	-0.5	-0.6	-0.8	-0.7	-0.6	-0.6	-0.5	-0.4	-0.3	-0.2	-0.6	-0.7	-0.4
United Kingdom	3.1	2.6	1.6	1.9	4.6	2.5	1.8	1.5	1.4	1.4	1.5	1.5	2.7	2.6	1.5
United States	1.6	1.1	1.1	1.1	1.1	1.1	1.1	1.0	1.0	1.0	1.0	0.9	0.8	1.1	1.0
Euro area	1.5	1.3	1.2	1.3	1.4	1.3	1.1	1.2	1.2	1.2	1.3	1.3	1.5	1.2	1.3
GDP deflator															
Canada	2.8	1.6	1.6	1.6	1.7	1.6	1.5	1.6	1.6	1.6	1.6	1.6	1.9	1.6	1.6
France	0.4	1.0	1.1	1.0	1.1	1.1	0.8	1.0	1.1	1.2	1.2	1.2	1.0	1.0	1.2
Germany	0.8	1.0	1.2	0.8	1.0	0.9	1.0	1.1	1.2	1.2	1.4	1.2	0.8	1.0	1.2
Italy	0.7	1.2	1.1	1.3	1.2	1.0	1.0	1.1	1.1	1.1	1.2	1.3	1.2	1.1	1.2
Japan	-1.8	-0.8	-0.8	0.7	-0.9	-0.9	-0.9	-0.8	-0.8	-0.7	-0.6	-0.5	-1.1	-0.9	-0.7
United Kingdom	3.3	2.0	1.3	1.6	3.2	1.8	1.4	1.2	1.1	1.3	1.3	1.2	2.8	1.9	1.2
United States	1.0	1.2	0.9	1.0	1.0	1.0	1.0	0.9	0.9	0.9	0.9	0.9	1.6	1.0	0.9
Euro area	0.8	1.0	1.1	0.9	1.0	1.0	1.0	1.0	1.1	1.1	1.2	1.2	1.1	1.0	1.2
Total OECD	1.4	1.4	1.3	1.5	1.5	1.0	1.3	1.4	1.4	1.0	1.5	1.5	1.7	1.3	1.4
Unit labour cost (total economy)															
Canada	0.9	1.6	2.0	1.0	1.3	1.7	1.8	1.9	2.2	1.9	2.0	1.9	1.3	1.7	2.0
France	0.8	0.9	0.7	0.3	1.6	1.2	1.0	0.7	0.5	0.6	0.9	1.1	0.8	1.1	0.8
Germany	-1.5	0.3	-0.1	0.1	2.4	1.8	1.0	0.6	-0.5	-0.7	-1.1	-1.2	-1.8	1.4	-0.9
Italy	-0.4	1.3	0.5	1.8	1.3	0.8	0.2	0.1	0.7	0.6	0.6	0.6	1.1	0.6	0.6
Japan	-2.2	-0.6	-0.6	0.1	-1.3	0.4	0.2	-0.9	-0.6	-0.8	-0.9	-0.9	-0.4	-0.4	-0.8
United Kingdom	1.0	0.8	1.4	0.2	1.9	1.5	1.8	1.4	1.3	1.1	1.3	1.2	-0.2	1.6	1.2
United States	-0.9	1.3	1.3	0.9	1.7	1.5	1.4	1.3	1.3	1.3	1.1	1.1	0.1	1.5	1.2
Euro area	-0.7	0.3	0.2	0.3	0.9	0.6	0.3	0.3	0.1	0.0	-0.1	-0.1	-0.4	0.5	0.0
Total OECD	-0.5	1.0	1.0	1.2	1.1	1.3	1.1	1.0	0.9	1.0	0.9	0.9	0.5	1.1	0.9
Unemployment				Per cent of labour force											
Canada	8.1	7.8	7.4	8.0	7.9	7.9	7.8	7.7	7.6	7.5	7.3	7.2			
France	9.3	9.1	8.8	9.3	9.2	9.1	9.1	9.0	8.9	8.9	8.8	8.8			
Germany	6.9	6.3	6.2	6.6	6.5	6.3	6.2	6.2	6.2	6.2	6.2	6.2			
Italy	8.6	8.5	8.3	8.7	8.6	8.6	8.5	8.4	8.4	8.3	8.2	8.2			
Japan	5.1	4.9	4.5	5.0	4.9	4.9	4.8	4.8	4.6	4.5	4.4	4.3			
United Kingdom	7.9	7.8	7.6	7.9	7.9	7.9	7.8	7.8	7.7	7.7	7.6	7.6			
United States	9.7	9.5	8.7	9.7	9.7	9.6	9.4	9.2	9.0	8.8	8.5	8.3			
Euro area	9.9	9.6	9.2	9.8	9.8	9.7	9.6	9.5	9.4	9.3	9.2	9.0			
Total OECD	8.3	8.1	7.5	8.3	8.2	8.1	8.0	7.9	7.7	7.6	7.5	7.3			

Note: The adoption of national accounts systems SNA93 or ESA95 has been proceeding at an uneven pace among OECD member countries, both with respect to variables and the time period covered. As a consequence, there are breaks in many national series. Moreover, most countries have shifted to chain-weighted price indices to calculate real GDP and expenditures components. For further information, see table "National Account Reporting Systems, base years and latest data updates" at the beginning of the Statistical Annex and *OECD Economic Outlook* Sources and Methods (http://www.oecd.org/eco/sources-and-methods).

1. For the United Kingdom, the euro area countries and the euro area aggregate, the Harmonised Index of Consumer Prices (HICP) is used.

Source: OECD Economic Outlook 88 database.

StatLink http://dx.doi.org/10.1787/888932349384

Annex Table 57. **Contributions to changes in real GDP in OECD countries**

	2009	2010	2011	2012		2009	2010	2011	2012
Australia					**Germany**				
Final domestic demand	1.1	4.8	4.2	4.7	Final domestic demand	-1.4	1.3	1.4	1.2
Stockbuilding	-0.5	0.4	0.0	0.0	Stockbuilding	-0.3	0.8	0.0	0.0
Net exports	2.0	-1.8	-0.6	-0.6	Net exports	-2.9	1.4	1.1	1.0
GDP	1.2	3.3	3.6	4.0	GDP	-4.7	3.5	2.5	2.2
Austria					**Greece**				
Final domestic demand	-1.3	0.2	1.1	1.4	Final domestic demand	-2.7	-7.9	-6.1	-1.5
Stockbuilding	-0.9	0.5	0.0	0.0	Stockbuilding	-0.1	1.3	-0.3	0.0
Net exports	-1.8	1.6	0.9	0.6	Net exports	0.7	3.0	3.7	1.9
GDP	-3.8	2.0	2.0	2.0	GDP	-2.3	-3.9	-2.7	0.5
Belgium					**Hungary**				
Final domestic demand	-1.1	0.7	1.8	1.8	Final domestic demand	-6.6	-3.1	0.7	2.5
Stockbuilding	-1.0	0.8	0.1	0.0	Stockbuilding	-4.4	1.9	0.4	0.0
Net exports	-0.5	1.0	0.0	0.0	Net exports	4.0	2.0	1.6	0.7
GDP	-2.7	2.1	1.8	1.8	GDP	-6.7	1.1	2.5	3.1
Canada					**Iceland**				
Final domestic demand	-1.9	4.1	2.6	2.4	Final domestic demand	-20.7	-2.8	1.4	2.9
Stockbuilding	-0.7	0.9	0.1	0.0	Stockbuilding	-0.1	-0.1	0.0	0.1
Net exports	-0.3	-1.9	-0.2	0.8	Net exports	14.7	-0.2	0.1	-0.5
GDP	-2.5	3.0	2.3	3.0	GDP	-6.8	-3.6	1.5	2.6
Chile					**Ireland**				
Final domestic demand	-3.0	13.0	9.3	7.5	Final domestic demand	-11.2	-4.2	-0.4	0.6
Stockbuilding	-3.4	4.8	0.4	0.0	Stockbuilding	-1.4	0.7	0.2	0.0
Net exports	3.3	-8.8	-0.6	0.2	Net exports	3.8	3.2	1.8	1.9
GDP	-1.4	5.2	6.2	5.4	GDP	-7.6	-0.3	1.5	2.5
Czech Republic					**Israel**				
Final domestic demand	-1.4	0.2	2.2	2.8	Final domestic demand	0.3	4.2	3.6	3.8
Stockbuilding	-2.0	1.3	0.0	0.0	Stockbuilding	-0.6	-0.7	0.0	0.0
Net exports	-0.6	0.9	0.7	0.5	Net exports	1.1	1.0	0.4	0.4
GDP	-4.0	2.4	2.8	3.2	GDP	0.8	3.9	4.0	4.3
Denmark					**Italy**				
Final domestic demand	-4.1	1.4	1.5	2.3	Final domestic demand	-3.4	0.6	0.7	1.2
Stockbuilding	-2.0	1.2	0.0	0.0	Stockbuilding	-0.4	0.2	-0.1	0.0
Net exports	1.3	-0.1	-0.2	-0.1	Net exports	-1.2	0.3	0.8	0.4
GDP	-4.7	2.2	1.6	2.1	GDP	-5.1	1.0	1.3	1.6
Finland					**Japan**				
Final domestic demand	-3.6	1.4	2.3	2.3	Final domestic demand	-3.4	1.6	1.5	1.3
Stockbuilding	-1.4	0.3	0.3	0.0	Stockbuilding	-0.4	0.0	0.0	0.0
Net exports	-1.9	0.5	0.5	0.5	Net exports	-1.3	1.9	0.1	0.0
GDP	-8.1	2.7	3.0	3.0	GDP	-5.2	3.7	1.7	1.3
France					**Korea**				
Final domestic demand	-0.5	0.9	1.7	2.2	Final domestic demand	0.8	5.0	4.2	4.5
Stockbuilding	-1.8	0.6	0.4	0.0	Stockbuilding	-4.6	2.3	-0.1	0.0
Net exports	-0.2	0.1	-0.5	-0.1	Net exports	4.0	-1.3	0.0	0.1
GDP	-2.5	1.6	1.6	2.0	GDP	0.2	6.2	4.3	4.8

Note: The adoption of national accounts systems SNA93 or ESA95 has been proceeding at an uneven pace among OECD member countries, both with respect to variables and the time period covered. As a consequence, there are breaks in many national series. Moreover, most countries have shifted to chain-weighted price indices to calculate real GDP and expenditures components. For further information, see table "National Account Reporting Systems, base years and latest data updates" at the beginning of the Statistical Annex and *OECD Economic Outlook* Sources and Methods (http://www.oecd.org/eco/sources-and-methods).

Source: OECD Economic Outlook 88 database.

StatLink ⬚⬚⬚ http://dx.doi.org/10.1787/888932349403

Annex Table 57. **Contributions to changes in real GDP in OECD countries** *(cont'd)*

	2009	2010	2011	2012		2009	2010	2011	2012
Luxembourg					**Spain**				
Final domestic demand	-3.5	1.9	1.9	1.9	Final domestic demand	-6.5	-0.7	0.5	1.6
Stockbuilding	-0.8	1.6	-0.7	0.0	Stockbuilding	0.0	0.0	0.0	0.0
Net exports	0.3	1.2	2.3	1.4	Net exports	2.7	0.5	0.4	0.3
GDP	-3.7	3.3	3.3	3.2	GDP	-3.7	-0.2	0.9	1.8
Mexico					**Sweden**				
Final domestic demand	-6.4	3.5	4.1	4.7	Final domestic demand	-3.1	3.0	3.0	2.8
Stockbuilding	-1.9	1.0	0.3	0.0	Stockbuilding	-1.5	2.4	0.3	0.0
Net exports	1.7	0.5	-0.8	-0.4	Net exports	-0.6	-0.4	0.2	0.5
GDP	-6.6	5.0	3.5	4.2	GDP	-5.1	4.4	3.3	3.4
Netherlands					**Switzerland**				
Final domestic demand	-2.8	-0.3	0.8	1.2	Final domestic demand	-0.3	1.8	2.1	2.1
Stockbuilding	-0.9	1.2	-0.5	0.0	Stockbuilding	0.9	-1.2	0.2	0.0
Net exports	-0.2	0.6	1.5	0.7	Net exports	-2.5	2.1	-0.1	0.4
GDP	-3.9	1.7	1.7	1.8	GDP	-1.9	2.7	2.2	2.5
New Zealand					**Turkey**				
Final domestic demand	-2.9	2.5	3.7	3.0	Final domestic demand	-4.3	8.8	6.4	7.0
Stockbuilding	-0.6	0.2	0.2	0.0	Stockbuilding	-2.3	0.5	0.4	0.0
Net exports	5.0	-1.0	-0.9	-0.3	Net exports	2.8	-1.8	-1.7	-1.7
GDP	-0.4	2.2	2.7	2.5	GDP	-4.8	8.2	5.3	5.4
Norway					**United Kingdom**				
Final domestic demand	-1.0	0.6	2.6	2.7	Final domestic demand	-4.5	1.5	1.2	1.4
Stockbuilding	-2.0	2.6	0.2	0.0	Stockbuilding	-1.1	1.2	0.1	0.0
Net exports	1.4	-2.7	-0.9	-0.4	Net exports	0.7	-1.0	0.4	0.5
GDP	-1.4	0.5	1.8	2.3	GDP	-5.0	1.8	1.7	2.0
Poland					**United States**				
Final domestic demand	1.9	1.8	5.8	5.3	Final domestic demand	-3.2	1.9	2.9	3.1
Stockbuilding	-2.5	2.2	-0.3	0.0	Stockbuilding	-0.6	1.6	-0.1	0.0
Net exports	3.4	-0.1	-1.1	-0.9	Net exports	1.2	-0.7	-0.6	0.0
GDP	1.7	3.5	4.0	4.3	GDP	-2.6	2.7	2.2	3.1
Portugal					**Euro area**				
Final domestic demand	-2.7	0.9	-2.4	0.6	Final domestic demand	-2.5	0.3	0.9	1.4
Stockbuilding	-0.6	0.0	0.2	0.0	Stockbuilding	-0.7	0.6	0.1	0.0
Net exports	0.7	0.5	2.0	1.3	Net exports	-0.8	0.8	0.7	0.6
GDP	-2.5	1.5	-0.2	1.8	GDP	-4.1	1.7	1.7	2.0
Slovak Republic					**Total OECD**				
Final domestic demand	-2.4	0.1	0.8	3.4	Final domestic demand	-2.9	1.9	2.4	2.7
Stockbuilding	-3.4	2.4	0.5	0.0	Stockbuilding	-1.1	1.0	0.0	0.0
Net exports	1.3	1.7	2.4	0.8	Net exports	0.6	-0.1	-0.1	0.1
GDP	-4.7	4.1	3.5	4.4	GDP	-3.4	2.8	2.3	2.8
Slovenia									
Final domestic demand	-6.1	-1.5	1.4	2.9					
Stockbuilding	-4.0	1.7	0.7	0.0					
Net exports	2.0	0.7	-0.1	-0.1					
GDP	-8.1	1.1	2.0	2.7					

Note: The adoption of national accounts systems SNA93 or ESA95 has been proceeding at an uneven pace among OECD member countries, both with respect to variables and the time period covered. As a consequence, there are breaks in many national series. Moreover, most countries have shifted to chain-weighted price indices to calculate real GDP and expenditures components. For further information, see table "National Account Reporting Systems, base years and latest data updates" at the beginning of the Statistical Annex and *OECD Economic Outlook* Sources and Methods (http://www.oecd.org/eco/sources-and-methods).

Source: OECD Economic Outlook 88 database.

StatLink ⌖ http://dx.doi.org/10.1787/888932349403

Annex Table 58. **Household wealth and indebtedness**

	1998	1999	2000	2001	2002	2003	2004	2005	2006	2007	2008	2009
Canada												
Net wealth	498.4	507.0	502.2	503.2	512.7	516.1	518.1	534.5	545.5	548.5	547.4	549.2
Net financial wealth	233.7	239.1	240.1	235.5	231.4	224.0	214.6	216.5	217.9	210.6	211.7	211.0
Non-financial assets	264.7	267.9	262.0	267.7	281.3	292.1	303.5	318.0	327.7	337.9	335.6	338.2
Financial assets	345.6	353.2	352.7	349.6	348.5	344.7	338.9	345.9	349.6	347.9	353.4	359.4
of which: Equities	79.5	81.1	84.3	84.2	83.6	81.0	79.4	79.4	85.2	85.2	96.3	92.3
Liabilities	112.0	114.1	112.6	114.1	117.1	120.6	124.3	129.4	131.8	137.3	141.7	148.4
of which: Mortgages	71.8	71.8	69.6	69.6	71.2	73.2	75.9	79.1	80.7	84.7	87.9	92.3
France												
Net wealth	494.9	545.8	552.5	552.3	571.3	621.2	682.1	748.2	792.6	806.3	753.2	746.3
Net financial wealth	185.5	211.8	205.7	188.4	183.1	189.6	194.9	200.5	210.4	213.6	185.8	201.7
Non-financial assets	309.4	334.1	346.8	363.9	388.2	431.6	487.2	547.7	582.2	592.7	567.4	544.6
Financial assets	258.1	287.2	282.5	266.4	258.7	269.3	278.6	291.5	306.9	313.9	288.1	308.3
of which: Equities	67.3	86.6	83.5	69.8	63.1	69.7	72.4	77.5	87.1	92.2	66.2	73.6
Liabilities	72.5	75.4	76.8	78.0	75.6	79.7	83.7	91.0	96.5	100.3	102.3	106.6
of which: Long-term loans	51.5	53.8	53.4	53.6	54.6	57.1	60.2	65.3	69.5	73.2	76.6	..
Germany												
Net wealth	527.6	539.1	536.5	531.2	533.7	547.8	561.1	581.4	605.7	627.6	614.6	..
Net financial wealth	143.4	153.8	151.4	150.7	145.9	158.2	167.2	180.2	189.4	198.2	184.9	202.0
Non-financial assets	384.1	385.3	385.2	380.5	387.8	389.6	394.0	401.2	416.3	429.4	429.7	..
Financial assets	252.8	267.9	265.9	262.4	257.9	269.1	276.8	287.3	294.2	299.9	282.4	300.6
of which: Equities	61.1	74.5	75.2	71.3	57.4	63.3	63.9	71.3	72.0	72.7	54.2	59.2
Liabilities	109.4	114.2	114.5	111.8	112.1	110.9	109.6	107.1	104.8	101.7	97.5	98.6
of which: Mortgages	67.1	71.0	71.7	71.2	72.3	72.2	71.8	71.0	70.8	68.9	66.1	67.1
Italy												
Net wealth	718.5	744.6	758.3	737.7	746.2	770.0	793.9	823.5	845.8	855.0	820.8	..
Net financial wealth	293.5	324.8	330.0	306.9	293.0	290.7	297.6	304.8	304.0	293.1	254.5	..
Non-financial assets	424.9	419.9	428.3	430.8	453.2	479.3	496.3	518.7	541.8	561.8	566.3	..
Financial assets	339.0	373.5	382.8	359.2	351.3	353.0	364.3	376.7	379.7	372.3	334.3	..
of which: Equities	63.0	94.0	98.0	82.0	75.1	70.8	74.3	84.2	86.1	79.6	47.9	..
Liabilities	45.5	48.8	52.8	52.3	58.3	62.3	66.7	71.9	75.7	79.2	79.8	..
of which: Medium and long-term loans	24.6	27.3	28.5	28.3	33.6	36.3	39.9	43.7	46.2	48.6	48.6	..
Japan												
Net wealth	722.5	746.2	743.9	740.5	719.4	728.1	720.1	739.2	744.7	735.3	697.0	..
Net financial wealth	296.3	327.3	335.6	341.6	340.7	361.1	369.4	397.1	401.4	386.3	356.5	..
Non-financial assets	426.2	418.9	408.3	398.9	378.7	367.0	350.7	342.1	343.3	349.0	340.6	..
Financial assets	428.8	460.7	470.2	477.5	474.4	494.7	500.8	529.0	531.8	513.7	483.6	..
of which: Equities	27.0	45.6	41.5	31.8	29.8	42.1	48.9	75.5	75.8	50.3	29.7	..
Liabilities	132.5	133.4	134.5	135.9	133.6	133.6	131.4	131.8	130.4	127.4	127.2	..
of which: Mortgages[1]	56.0	58.9	61.0	63.1	62.8	63.9	63.4	64.1	65.2	64.9	64.7	..
United Kingdom												
Net wealth	686.4	769.1	768.1	714.3	715.6	748.0	797.2	827.0	866.7	900.8	752.7	810.5
Net financial wealth	359.6	410.3	380.3	323.5	260.8	265.9	270.0	304.3	310.7	307.6	243.3	295.3
Non-financial assets	326.8	358.8	387.8	390.8	454.9	482.2	527.2	522.7	556.0	593.2	509.3	515.2
Financial assets	469.0	524.0	497.4	445.0	394.7	410.9	430.0	466.6	486.7	491.3	420.9	466.0
of which: Equities	97.1	121.4	113.6	85.9	61.4	67.3	71.4	76.0	77.2	72.9	46.6	64.2
Liabilities	109.4	113.7	117.1	121.4	134.0	145.0	160.0	162.3	176.0	183.6	177.6	170.6
of which: Mortgages	79.4	82.7	85.4	88.5	97.1	106.8	119.0	121.2	130.1	138.2	135.6	132.8
United States												
Net wealth	577.7	626.2	583.5	556.1	515.4	563.2	593.8	640.7	646.5	616.3	469.5	486.1
Net financial wealth	366.8	407.2	354.5	316.4	267.6	304.0	317.1	335.5	349.4	348.2	248.0	273.6
Non-financial assets	210.8	219.0	229.0	239.7	247.8	259.2	276.7	305.2	297.1	268.1	221.5	212.5
Financial assets	462.3	506.8	455.2	421.1	377.5	421.8	441.2	466.8	485.0	486.0	378.3	401.1
of which: Equities	151.8	186.2	148.1	123.5	92.2	115.8	122.7	126.8	139.5	136.4	83.1	103.5
Liabilities	95.4	99.6	100.7	104.7	109.9	117.8	124.1	131.3	135.6	137.8	130.3	127.5
of which: Mortgages	63.8	66.6	67.2	71.3	77.2	84.2	90.2	97.7	101.7	103.4	98.1	95.9

Note: Assets and liabilities are amounts outstanding at the end of the period, in per cent of nominal disposable income.

Households include non-profit institutions serving households, except for Italy. Net wealth is defined as non-financial and financial assets minus liabilities; net financial wealth is financial assets minus liabilities. Non-financial assets consist mainly of dwellings and land. For a more detailed description of the variables, see *OECD Economic Outlook* Sources and Methods *(http://www.oecd.org/eco/sources-and-methods).*

1. Fiscal year data.

Sources: Canada: Statistics Canada; France: INSEE; Germany: Deutsche Bundesbank, Federal Statistical Office (Destatis); Italy: Banca d'Italia; Japan: Economic Planning Agency; United Kingdom: Office for National Statistics; United States: Federal Reserve.

StatLink ⟱ *http://dx.doi.org/10.1787/888932349422*

Annex Table 59. **House prices**
Percentage change from previous year

	1993	1994	1995	1996	1997	1998	1999	2000	2001	2002	2003	2004	2005	2006	2007	2008	2009
Nominal																	
United States	2.1	2.3	3.0	3.6	3.6	5.1	4.8	6.5	7.7	6.5	6.3	9.5	11.4	7.2	1.7	-3.1	-4.0
Japan	-4.3	-2.4	-1.6	-1.9	-1.4	-1.6	-3.2	-3.8	-4.2	-4.6	-5.4	-6.1	-4.8	-3.0	-1.0	-1.6	-3.8
Germany			1.0	-0.9	-1.8	-1.9	1.9	0.0	0.0	-2.8	-1.0	-1.9	-2.0	0.0	1.0	1.0	-1.0
France				-1.7	0.1	1.9	7.1	8.8	7.9	8.3	11.7	15.2	15.3	12.1	6.6	1.2	-7.1
Italy	0.2	-2.8	0.8	-3.3	-4.6	2.1	5.6	8.3	8.2	9.6	10.3	9.9	7.5	6.4	5.2	1.7	-3.7
United Kingdom	-1.7	2.6	0.7	3.7	8.8	11.5	10.9	14.9	8.1	16.1	15.7	11.9	5.5	6.3	10.9	-0.9	-7.8
Canada	2.0	3.3	-4.6	0.1	2.9	-1.4	3.8	3.7	4.6	9.8	9.5	9.4	9.9	11.4	10.8	-1.3	4.6
Australia	2.6	3.6	1.2	0.8	4.0	7.3	7.2	8.3	11.2	18.8	18.2	6.5	1.5	7.8	11.3	4.4	3.4
Belgium	5.3	6.4	4.5	2.2	2.4	6.4	7.1	5.4	4.8	6.4	6.9	8.7	12.7	11.8	9.3	4.8	-0.3
Denmark	-1.0	12.2	7.6	10.7	11.5	9.0	6.7	6.5	5.8	3.6	3.2	8.9	17.6	21.6	4.6	-4.5	-12.0
Finland								3.9	-1.4	6.0	6.3	8.2	8.1	6.4	5.5	0.6	-0.3
Ireland	2.0	4.7	6.3	8.6	14.7	24.1	21.5	20.6	12.4	7.0	14.2	11.2	7.4	13.5	-0.5	-9.1	-13.7
Korea	-3.5	-1.6	-0.1	1.0	2.7	-9.2	-1.3	1.8	4.0	16.6	9.1	1.1	0.8	6.1	9.0	4.0	0.2
Netherlands	8.2	12.3	6.9	10.8	12.0	10.9	16.3	18.2	11.1	6.5	3.6	4.3	3.8	4.6	4.2	2.9	-3.3
Norway	1.0	13.2	7.2	9.2	11.8	11.1	11.2	15.7	7.0	4.9	1.7	10.1	8.2	13.7	12.6	-1.1	2.0
New Zealand	4.1	13.7	9.3	10.3	6.1	-1.7	2.1	-0.4	1.8	9.5	19.4	17.8	14.5	10.5	10.9	-4.4	-1.6
Spain	-0.3	1.5	3.5	2.6	4.2	4.9	7.0	7.5	9.5	16.9	20.0	18.3	14.6	10.0	5.5	0.2	-7.6
Sweden	-11.0	4.6	0.3	0.8	6.6	9.5	9.4	11.2	7.9	6.3	6.6	9.3	9.0	12.2	10.4	3.3	1.6
Switzerland	-5.2	-0.1	-3.9	-5.3	-3.5	-0.9	-0.1	0.9	1.9	4.6	3.0	2.4	1.1	2.5	2.1	2.6	5.1
Real[1]																	
United States	-0.1	0.3	0.7	1.4	1.7	4.1	3.2	3.9	5.7	5.0	4.2	6.7	8.1	4.4	-1.0	-6.2	-4.1
Japan	-5.3	-2.9	-1.3	-1.8	-2.6	-1.7	-2.6	-2.7	-3.1	-3.2	-4.6	-5.5	-4.1	-2.8	-0.4	-2.0	-1.7
Germany			-0.3	-1.8	-3.1	-2.3	1.6	-0.9	-1.7	-3.9	-2.5	-3.2	-3.3	-1.1	-0.8	-0.7	-1.0
France				-3.3	-0.8	1.7	7.7	6.4	6.0	7.3	9.7	13.1	13.3	9.8	4.4	-1.6	-6.7
Italy	-4.9	-7.6	-5.0	-7.1	-6.7	0.3	3.7	4.7	5.4	6.5	7.3	7.2	5.2	3.7	2.8	-1.4	-3.5
United Kingdom	-5.1	0.6	-2.5	0.2	6.2	8.9	9.5	13.7	6.1	14.4	13.6	9.9	3.0	3.4	7.8	-3.9	-9.0
Canada	-0.3	2.2	-5.8	-1.5	1.3	-2.6	2.1	1.5	2.7	7.7	7.8	7.8	8.1	9.8	9.1	-2.8	4.0
Australia	0.7	2.1	-1.5	-1.3	2.5	6.1	6.3	5.1	7.3	15.2	16.0	5.1	-0.4	4.2	7.9	0.7	0.3
Belgium	2.0	3.6	2.4	1.5	0.8	5.4	6.7	1.9	2.9	5.1	5.3	6.2	9.7	8.6	6.3	1.6	0.1
Denmark	-2.1	9.3	5.6	9.0	9.4	7.5	4.8	3.7	3.4	1.9	1.9	7.6	15.8	19.3	2.5	-7.4	-13.2
Finland								-0.4	-3.7	3.7	6.9	7.8	7.2	4.9	3.3	-2.8	-0.8
Ireland	-0.1	2.1	3.8	5.7	11.7	19.1	18.5	12.6	7.8	1.5	9.7	9.2	5.5	11.0	-3.7	-11.6	-10.0
Korea	-9.5	-10.3	-6.2	-5.5	-3.3	-14.6	-3.9	-2.5	-0.4	13.2	5.7	-2.0	-1.4	4.5	6.9	-0.5	-2.3
Netherlands	5.9	9.5	4.7	8.6	9.4	8.7	14.1	13.8	6.4	3.4	1.2	3.3	1.7	2.3	2.3	1.5	-2.7
Norway	-1.4	12.1	4.7	7.9	9.2	8.4	9.0	12.4	4.8	3.5	-1.2	9.3	7.1	11.6	11.3	-4.5	-0.6
New Zealand	3.0	12.1	6.8	7.5	4.2	-3.6	1.4	-2.6	-0.4	7.3	18.4	16.0	12.1	7.2	9.2	-7.7	-4.0
Spain	-5.3	-3.2	-1.3	-0.6	1.5	2.9	4.6	3.6	5.8	13.7	16.3	14.2	10.8	6.2	2.1	-3.2	-7.7
Sweden	-16.8	1.8	-2.5	-0.1	5.2	9.0	7.7	10.3	5.7	4.7	4.9	8.2	7.9	11.0	9.0	0.4	-0.3
Switzerland	-7.7	-0.4	-5.2	-6.5	-4.3	-0.8	-0.5	0.1	1.3	3.7	2.6	1.5	0.6	1.1	0.7	0.0	5.5

1. Nominal house prices deflated by the private consumption deflator.
Source: Various national sources and Nomisma, see table A.1 in Girouard, N., M. Kennedy, P. van den Noord and C. André, "Recent house price developments: the role of fundamentals", *OECD Economics Department Working Papers,* No. 475, 2006.

StatLink http://dx.doi.org/10.1787/888932349441

Annex Table 60. **House price ratios**
Long-term average = 100

	1993	1994	1995	1996	1997	1998	1999	2000	2001	2002	2003	2004	2005	2006	2007	2008	2009
Price-to-rent ratio																	
United States	90.4	89.8	89.6	89.9	90.4	91.9	93.7	96.6	100.3	102.9	106.8	113.9	123.6	128.1	125.7	118.8	112.9
Japan	118.4	113.1	109.1	105.5	102.6	100.3	97.2	93.4	89.3	85.3	80.7	76.0	72.3	70.2	69.6	68.4	65.9
Germany			99.0	95.2	91.4	88.6	89.5	88.5	87.6	84.0	82.3	80.1	77.8	76.8	76.6	76.3	74.6
France				76.1	75.1	75.1	79.0	86.0	92.4	97.6	106.1	118.9	132.3	143.4	148.2	146.8	133.6
Italy	114.1	103.2	97.9	88.1	78.8	76.4	78.1	82.5	87.3	93.5	100.4	107.3	112.9	117.2	120.6	119.7	111.5
United Kingdom	75.2	73.6	70.6	69.9	73.2	78.9	84.9	94.6	99.1	112.0	127.5	139.4	142.7	147.7	158.2	151.1	135.8
Canada	93.4	96.6	90.9	91.1	94.0	92.3	94.8	96.3	98.3	106.0	113.2	121.1	129.9	139.8	148.8	141.6	146.4
Australia	83.6	86.0	85.6	83.7	84.6	88.1	92.1	96.7	104.2	120.9	140.2	145.8	144.7	151.0	159.4	154.6	149.7
Belgium	85.9	87.5	88.9	88.6	89.3	93.8	99.1	103.0	105.9	110.0	115.0	122.7	135.6	146.5	157.3	161.9	158.2
Denmark	66.0	72.1	76.0	83.0	90.1	96.3	100.1	103.9	107.1	108.1	108.7	115.1	132.1	157.4	161.3	150.3	128.5
Finland								104.6	99.5	106.0	113.3	121.5	127.7	130.1	129.4	124.9	129.1
Ireland	58.6	66.4	66.2	72.6	78.4	94.1	137.7	148.5	138.0	151.1	183.2	198.3	196.1	181.9	137.8	111.4	144.3
Korea	103.3	97.3	93.1	90.6	90.1	80.0	82.0	83.6	83.6	92.8	97.6	96.5	97.1	102.2	109.2	110.5	108.7
Netherlands	72.3	77.3	78.6	83.7	90.3	96.7	109.2	125.6	135.6	140.3	141.0	142.6	144.4	147.5	150.3	152.0	144.0
Norway	63.1	70.6	74.1	79.6	86.8	94.2	101.3	112.7	115.9	116.5	114.1	122.8	129.9	144.4	158.0	151.5	150.5
New Zealand	70.9	75.4	77.4	81.4	83.8	80.5	83.1	82.5	92.8	99.7	115.5	131.9	147.4	159.3	171.8	159.3	154.4
Spain	97.7	94.0	92.2	88.0	86.4	86.4	89.3	92.5	97.1	108.8	125.2	142.3	156.4	164.9	166.6	160.3	143.7
Sweden	67.2	67.7	65.8	64.0	66.2	71.9	78.6	87.0	92.3	96.1	99.9	105.9	112.7	125.4	136.2	137.3	135.0
Switzerland	97.1	96.4	91.7	85.7	82.3	81.5	80.8	80.4	79.7	82.5	84.7	85.7	85.4	85.8	85.7	85.8	88.0
Price-to-income ratio																	
United States	94.2	92.6	91.7	91.1	90.5	90.0	91.1	91.1	95.0	97.5	100.0	104.1	112.1	113.5	111.0	103.3	99.3
Japan	109.2	104.8	102.9	101.2	98.2	96.7	94.7	93.0	92.3	88.2	84.9	79.1	74.7	71.6	71.0	70.0	66.4
Germany			103.5	100.8	97.5	94.1	93.5	91.1	87.8	84.8	82.3	79.5	76.5	74.8	74.1	72.4	72.8
France				81.4	79.8	78.9	82.7	85.6	88.5	92.1	101.1	112.3	126.3	136.2	138.9	137.3	126.8
Italy	106.0	98.6	93.6	85.6	80.0	81.2	83.5	87.3	89.6	94.6	101.4	108.1	114.3	118.3	121.4	121.7	121.8
United Kingdom	78.7	78.3	74.6	72.7	74.4	79.6	85.3	93.5	95.4	107.6	119.0	130.8	132.8	136.6	147.9	140.2	124.8
Canada	101.9	105.0	97.8	97.4	97.8	93.3	93.2	90.9	91.9	98.3	104.6	109.6	116.4	121.9	129.3	122.7	127.7
Australia	92.6	91.6	88.5	85.0	85.5	90.1	93.1	96.0	100.1	116.2	132.2	133.8	129.8	131.4	136.9	137.6	134.1
Belgium	88.7	90.9	88.4	90.5	90.9	94.0	98.2	98.5	98.7	104.5	110.9	118.4	130.1	138.3	145.2	145.9	144.6
Denmark	71.0	77.1	76.7	82.9	91.2	95.8	104.6	108.3	108.4	108.6	108.3	113.7	129.2	152.0	155.9	145.5	128.6
Finland								96.8	90.5	92.1	93.1	96.0	102.1	104.8	104.8	100.2	97.5
Ireland	74.5	76.1	73.7	74.0	78.1	87.5	101.1	111.0	111.2	122.9	133.8	139.1	143.8	156.2	148.5	130.3	116.3
Korea	114.5	97.0	87.1	78.1	75.0	67.2	63.2	62.0	61.6	67.8	68.7	64.5	62.3	63.6	66.5	65.5	63.6
Netherlands	75.5	81.0	83.2	88.3	93.3	98.6	111.0	124.5	126.4	132.3	138.0	142.1	145.4	148.2	148.1	151.1	147.4
Norway	68.6	76.1	77.8	81.3	86.1	88.8	95.0	103.6	109.1	105.1	100.0	106.2	106.4	128.0	135.3	126.4	121.8
New Zealand	79.9	88.7	90.6	94.8	97.0	92.2	88.3	89.3	85.4	93.8	105.8	118.5	134.7	144.5	150.3	144.1	147.9
Spain	96.9	95.9	88.7	86.6	87.0	87.4	89.4	90.7	94.2	105.4	120.8	136.0	147.1	153.7	155.8	149.5	136.5
Sweden	76.9	79.2	77.2	77.8	82.3	88.2	92.4	97.0	96.5	98.3	102.4	110.1	116.8	125.5	130.6	128.3	127.4
Switzerland	100.9	100.3	94.0	89.5	84.8	82.1	79.9	77.6	76.9	81.4	84.7	84.8	83.7	82.8	81.2	82.5	86.9

Source: Various national sources and Nomisma, see table A.1 in Girouard, N., M. Kennedy, P. van den Noord and C. André, "Recent house price developments: the role of fundamentals", *OECD Economics Department Working Papers,* No. 475, 2006 and OECD estimates.

StatLink ⟪⟫ http://dx.doi.org/10.1787/888932349460

Annex Table 61. **Central government financial balances**
Surplus (+) or deficit (-) as a percentage of nominal GDP

	1995	1996	1997	1998	1999	2000	2001	2002	2003	2004	2005	2006	2007	2008	2009
Canada	-3.9	-2.0	0.7	0.8	0.9	1.9	1.1	0.8	0.3	0.8	0.1	0.9	1.0	-0.1	-2.6
France	-4.5	-3.6	-3.1	-2.8	-2.4	-2.1	-2.1	-3.1	-3.6	-2.6	-2.6	-2.1	-2.3	-2.8	-6.0
Germany[1]	-7.9	-1.9	-1.6	-1.8	-1.5	1.4	-1.3	-1.7	-1.8	-2.4	-2.1	-1.5	-0.8	-0.6	-1.6
Italy	-7.5	-6.8	-2.6	-2.5	-1.5	-1.2	-3.1	-3.1	-3.0	-3.0	-4.0	-2.8	-2.0	-2.6	-4.8
Japan[2]	-4.1	-4.1	-3.5	-10.6	-7.3	-6.4	-5.9	-6.7	-6.7	-5.2	-6.2	-1.0	-2.6	-2.6	-5.8
United Kingdom[3]	-5.5	-4.1	-2.0	0.2	1.1	3.9	0.8	-1.9	-3.4	-3.1	-3.0	-2.7	-2.6	-4.6	-10.9
United States	-2.8	-2.0	-0.6	0.5	1.0	1.9	0.3	-2.6	-3.8	-3.6	-2.8	-1.8	-2.2	-5.3	-10.5
less social security	-3.6	-2.9	-1.7	-0.7	-0.4	0.3	-1.3	-4.2	-5.2	-4.9	-4.1	-3.3	-3.6	-6.5	-11.3
Total of above countries	-4.3	-2.9	-1.6	-2.0	-1.0	0.2	-1.2	-3.0	-3.8	-3.4	-3.2	-1.7	-2.0	-3.8	-7.9

Note: Central government financial balances include one-off revenues from the sale of mobile telephone licenses.
1. In 1995, this includes the central government's assumption of the debt of the Inherited Debt Fund.
2. Data for central government financial balances are only available for fiscal years beginning April 1 of the year shown. The 1998 deficit includes the central government's assumption of the debt of the Japan Railway Settlement Corporation and the National Forest Special Account which represent some 5.3 percentage points of GDP.
3. The data for 2000 and onwards reflect Eurostat's decision concerning the recording of one-off revenues from the sale of the mobile telephone licenses.
Source: OECD Economic Outlook 88 database.   *StatLink* http://dx.doi.org/10.1787/888932349479

Annex Table 62. **Maastricht definition of general government gross public debt**
As a percentage of nominal GDP

	1998	1999	2000	2001	2002	2003	2004	2005	2006	2007	2008	2009	2010	2011	2012
Austria	64.8	67.1	66.6	67.1	66.3	65.5	64.9	64.1	62.1	59.4	62.9	67.7	71.0	73.0	74.7
Belgium[1]	117.4	113.8	107.9	106.6	103.5	98.5	94.3	92.0	88.0	84.2	89.8	96.3	98.4	100.2	101.0
Czech Republic	15.0	16.4	18.5	24.8	28.2	29.8	30.2	29.7	29.4	28.9	30.0	35.3	41.7	45.1	47.7
Denmark	61.4	58.1	52.4	49.6	49.5	47.2	45.1	37.8	32.1	27.4	34.2	41.4	43.3	44.8	47.6
Finland	48.4	45.7	43.9	42.5	41.6	44.6	44.4	41.7	39.6	35.2	34.1	43.8	49.5	53.8	56.9
France	59.4	58.9	57.3	56.9	58.8	62.9	65.0	66.4	63.6	63.8	67.6	78.1	83.2	88.0	91.0
Germany	60.4	61.0	59.7	58.7	60.3	63.9	66.0	68.1	67.5	64.8	66.3	73.5	76.9	78.3	79.0
Greece	94.5	94.0	103.4	103.7	101.7	97.4	98.8	100.2	98.0	96.1	100.4	116.9	125.9	133.5	138.9
Hungary	59.9	59.8	54.9	52.0	55.6	58.3	59.1	61.8	65.7	66.1	72.3	78.4	82.1	83.3	83.1
Ireland	53.6	48.5	37.8	35.5	32.1	30.9	29.6	27.4	24.8	25.0	44.3	65.5	97.4	105.0	108.0
Italy	115.0	113.9	109.1	108.8	105.7	104.3	103.9	105.8	106.5	103.6	106.3	116.0	119.5	120.9	121.2
Luxembourg	7.1	6.4	6.2	6.3	6.3	6.1	6.3	6.1	6.7	6.7	13.6	14.5	17.7	22.5	24.7
Netherlands	65.7	61.1	53.8	50.7	50.5	52.0	52.4	51.8	47.4	45.3	58.2	60.8	65.9	68.9	70.9
Poland	39.0	39.7	36.9	37.5	42.1	47.0	45.8	47.1	47.8	45.0	47.2	51.0	54.8	57.9	58.7
Portugal	50.4	49.6	48.5	51.2	53.8	55.9	57.6	62.8	63.9	62.7	65.3	76.1	82.7	88.5	90.3
Slovak Republic	34.5	47.9	50.3	48.9	43.4	42.4	41.5	34.2	30.5	29.6	27.7	35.3	42.6	46.6	48.8
Slovenia	..	..	..	26.8	28.0	27.5	27.2	27.0	26.7	23.4	22.5	35.4	38.0	39.8	40.8
Spain	64.1	62.3	59.3	55.5	52.5	48.7	46.2	43.0	39.6	36.1	39.8	53.2	62.9	68.9	70.3
Sweden	68.6	64.4	53.2	53.9	52.1	51.7	50.4	50.2	45.0	40.0	38.2	41.9	41.2	38.8	35.1
United Kingdom	46.7	43.7	41.0	37.7	37.5	39.0	40.9	42.5	43.4	44.5	52.1	68.2	77.1	84.3	90.3
Euro area	72.7	71.9	69.3	68.2	67.9	69.0	69.6	70.1	68.3	65.9	69.6	79.0	84.3	87.4	88.9

Note: For the period before 2010, gross debt figures are provided by Eurostat, the Statistical Office of the European Communities, unless more recent data are available, while GDP figures are provided by national authorities. This explains why these ratios can differ significantly from the ones published by Eurostat. The 2010 to 2012 debt ratios are in line with the OECD projections for general government gross financial liabilities and GDP. For further information, see *OECD Economic Outlook* Sources and Methods (http://www.oecd.org/eco/sources-and-methods).
1. Includes the debt of the Belgium National Railways Company (SNCB) from 2005 onwards.   *StatLink* http://dx.doi.org/10.1787/888932349498
Source: OECD Economic Outlook 88 database.

Annex Table 63. **Monetary and credit aggregates: recent trends**

Annualised percentage change, seasonally adjusted

		Annual change (to 4th quarter)					Latest twelve months	
		2005	2006	2007	2008	2009		
Canada	M2	5.6	8.9	6.4	12.5	10.9	5.5	(Sep 2010)
	BL[1]	8.6	7.5	9.9	7.3	3.8	4.9	(Aug 2010)
Japan	M2	1.9	0.6	2.0	1.9	3.3	2.8	(Sep 2010)
	BL[1]	1.0	-0.2	-0.9	3.4	3.5	3.5	(Aug 2010)
United Kingdom	M2	9.0	8.1	7.6	5.1	5.7	4.2	(Sep 2010)
	M4	11.8	13.3	12.5	15.9	6.6	8.4	(Sep 2010)
	BL[1]	8.8	12.6	12.5	14.3	11.5	5.4	(Sep 2010)
United States	M2	4.1	5.7	6.3	8.6	5.1	3.0	(Sep 2010)
	BL[1]	12.1	12.1	11.2	8.1	-7.8	1.7	(Oct 2010)
Euro area	M2	9.0	8.8	11.3	9.7	2.1	1.9	(Sep 2010)
	M3	8.3	9.0	12.2	9.0	-0.2	1.0	(Sep 2010)
	BL[1]	9.1	7.9	11.5	9.1	3.1	3.0	(Sep 2010)

1. Commercial bank credit.

Source: OECD Main Economic Indicators; US Federal Reserve Board; Bank of Japan; European Central Bank; Bank of England; Statistics Canada.

StatLink http://dx.doi.org/10.1787/888932349517

Annex Table 64. **Macroeconomic indicators for selected non-member economies**

Calendar year basis

	1998	1998	1999	2000	2001	2002	2003	2004	2005	2006	2007	2008	2009	2010	2011	2012
Real GDP growth																
China	9.3	7.8	7.6	8.4	8.3	9.1	10.0	10.1	11.3	12.7	14.2	9.6	9.1	10.5	9.7	9.7
Brazil	3.4	0.0	0.2	4.3	1.3	2.6	1.2	5.7	3.1	3.9	6.1	5.1	-0.2	7.5	4.3	5.0
India	4.4	5.9	7.0	5.5	4.0	4.5	7.0	7.9	9.0	9.6	9.9	6.3	5.8	9.9	8.0	8.5
Indonesia	4.7	-13.1	0.8	5.3	3.6	4.5	4.8	5.0	5.7	5.5	6.3	6.1	4.6	6.1	6.3	6.0
Russian Federation	1.4	-5.3	6.4	10.0	5.1	4.7	7.3	7.2	6.4	8.2	8.5	5.2	-7.9	3.7	4.2	4.5
South Africa	2.6	0.5	2.4	4.2	2.7	3.7	2.9	4.6	5.3	5.6	5.5	3.7	-1.8	3.0	4.2	4.5
Inflation[1]																
China	2.8	-0.8	-1.4	0.3	0.7	-0.7	1.1	3.8	1.8	1.7	4.8	5.9	-0.7	3.1	3.3	3.0
Brazil	5.2	1.7	8.9	6.0	7.7	12.5	9.3	7.6	5.7	3.1	4.5	5.9	4.3	5.6	5.3	5.1
India	7.4	13.2	4.7	3.9	3.7	4.5	3.7	3.9	4.0	6.3	6.4	8.3	10.9	11.5	5.8	5.2
Indonesia	6.2	58.4	20.5	3.7	11.5	11.9	6.8	6.1	10.5	13.1	6.4	10.2	4.4	5.1	6.4	5.3
Russian Federation	14.7	27.8	85.7	20.8	21.5	15.8	13.7	10.9	12.7	9.7	9.0	14.1	11.7	6.8	7.7	6.0
South Africa	..	..	..	..	5.7	9.2	5.9	1.4	3.4	4.6	7.1	11.0	7.1	4.2	4.5	4.8
Fiscal balance[2]																
China	-0.4	-0.9	-1.6	-2.0	-1.6	-1.6	-1.2	-0.4	-0.2	0.5	1.9	0.9	-1.2	-1.9	-2.2	-2.1
Brazil	..	..	-5.3	-3.4	-3.3	-4.4	-5.1	-2.8	-3.4	-3.5	-2.7	-1.9	-3.3	-0.9	-0.5	-0.4
India	-6.4	-8.8	-9.4	-8.6	-10.0	-9.1	-9.1	-7.2	-6.9	-5.4	-4.3	-7.0	-10.2	-8.3	-7.6	-6.8
Indonesia	..	..	..	..	..	..	..	..	..	-1.0	-1.2	-0.1	-1.6	-1.4	-1.3	-1.3
Russian Federation	..	..	..	..	..	-0.5	1.9	6.2	6.2	7.9	7.1	5.7	-5.3	-2.7	-2.0	-0.9
South Africa	..	..	..	..	..	..	..	..	0.3	1.3	1.7	-1.1	-7.6	-5.0	-3.9	-2.0
Current account balance[2]																
China	3.9	3.1	1.9	1.7	1.3	2.4	2.8	3.6	7.1	9.3	10.6	9.6	6.0	5.8	5.9	5.5
Brazil	-3.5	-4.0	-4.3	-3.8	-4.1	-1.2	0.7	1.8	1.6	1.3	0.1	-1.7	-1.5	-2.6	-3.2	-4.0
India	-0.8	-1.5	-0.6	-1.0	0.3	1.4	1.6	0.2	-1.1	-1.1	-0.8	-2.7	-2.0	-3.5	-3.0	-2.9
Indonesia	-1.9	4.1	3.7	4.9	4.3	4.0	3.5	0.7	0.1	3.0	2.4	0.0	1.9	0.4	0.0	-0.4
Russian Federation	0.0	2.4	12.8	18.1	11.1	8.5	8.2	10.1	11.1	9.6	5.9	6.1	3.9	5.7	3.6	2.7
South Africa	-1.5	-1.8	-0.5	-0.1	0.3	0.8	-1.0	-3.0	-3.5	-5.3	-7.2	-7.1	-4.0	-3.4	-4.9	-5.8

1. Percentage change from previous period in Consumer Price Index (CPI).
2. Percentage of GDP. Fiscal balances are not comparable across countries due to different definitions.
Source: OECD Economic Outlook 88 database.

StatLink http://dx.doi.org/10.1787/888932366826

OECD ECONOMICS DEPARTMENT

A wide range of news and information about recent Economics Department studies and publications on a variety of topics is now regularly available via Internet on the OECD website at the following address: *www.oecd.org/eco*. This includes links to the *Economics Department Working Papers* series (*www.oecd.org/eco/Working_Papers*), which can be downloaded free of charge, as well as summaries of recent editions in the *OECD Economic Surveys* (*www.oecd.org/eco/surveys*) series, the Department's *Economic Policy Reforms: Going for Growth* (*www.oecd.org/growth/GoingForGrowth2007*) and the *OECD Economic Outlook* (*www.oecd.org/OECDEconomicOutlook*).

OECD ECONOMIC OUTLOOK

The *OECD Economic Outlook* Flashfile, containing a summary of the *Economic Outlook* forecasts is available on Internet at the time of its preliminary publication (a month to six weeks before the final publication date) at *www.oecd.org/OECDEconomicOutlook* under extracts. This includes key macroeconomic variables for all OECD countries and regions in Excel format, which can be input directly into most statistical and analytical software. The *Economic Outlook* Flashfile is available free of charge.

Subscribers to the *OECD Economic Outlook,* in addition to the two print editions, also have access to an online (PDF) edition, published on internet six to eight weeks prior to the release of the print edition :

www.SourceOECD.org/periodical/OECDEconomicOutlook

The full set of historical time series data and projections underlying the *OECD Economic Outlook* is available online as a **statistical database** via SourceOECD and on CD-ROM. It contains approximately 4 000 macroeconomic time series for OECD countries and non-OECD zones, beginning in 1960 and extending to the end of the published forecast horizon. Subscriptions to the database editions can be combined in sets with the subscriptions to the Print and PDF editions and can be made at any time of the year.

For more information, visit the OECD bookshop at *www.OECDbookshop.org,* or contact your nearest OECD supplier : *www.oecd.org/publishing/distributors* .

ORGANISATION FOR ECONOMIC CO-OPERATION AND DEVELOPMENT

The OECD is a unique forum where governments work together to address the economic, social and environmental challenges of globalisation. The OECD is also at the forefront of efforts to understand and to help governments respond to new developments and concerns, such as corporate governance, the information economy and the challenges of an ageing population. The Organisation provides a setting where governments can compare policy experiences, seek answers to common problems, identify good practice and work to co-ordinate domestic and international policies.

The OECD member countries are: Australia, Austria, Belgium, Canada, Chile, the Czech Republic, Denmark, Finland, France, Germany, Greece, Hungary, Iceland, Ireland, Israel, Italy, Japan, Korea, Luxembourg, Mexico, the Netherlands, New Zealand, Norway, Poland, Portugal, the Slovak Republic, Slovenia, Spain, Sweden, Switzerland, Turkey, the United Kingdom and the United States. The European Commission takes part in the work of the OECD.

OECD Publishing disseminates widely the results of the Organisation's statistics gathering and research on economic, social and environmental issues, as well as the conventions, guidelines and standards agreed by its members.

OECD PUBLISHING, 2, rue André-Pascal, 75775 PARIS CEDEX 16
(12 2010 02 1 P) ISBN 978-92-64-08524-4 – No. 57757 2010